Oracle Press™

Oracle Fusion Developer Guide

Building Rich Internet Applications with Oracle ADF Business Components and Oracle ADF Faces

Frank Nimphius
Lynn Munsinger

New York   Chicago   San Francisco
Lisbon   London   Madrid   Mexico City   Milan
New Delhi   San Juan   Seoul   Singapore   Sydney   Toronto

The McGraw·Hill Companies

Cataloging-in-Publication Data is on file with the Library of Congress

McGraw-Hill books are available at special quantity discounts to use as premiums and sales promotions, or for use in corporate training programs. To contact a representative, please e-mail us at bulksales@mcgraw-hill.com.

Oracle Fusion Developer Guide: Building Rich Internet Applications with Oracle ADF Business Components and Oracle ADF Faces

1234567890 DOC DOC 019

ISBN 978-0-07-162254-7
MHID   0-07-162254-3

Sponsoring Editor
Lisa McClain

Editorial Supervisor
Jody McKenzie

Project Editor
Rachel Gunn

Acquisitions Coordinator
Meghan Riley

Copy Editor
Lisa Theobald

Technical Editors
Matt Cooper, Susan Duncan, Jeff Falk, Yuan Gao, David Giammona, Maria Kaval, Chris Lewis, Glenn Maslen, Duncan Mills, Steve Muench, Katia Obradovic-Sarkic, Grant Ronald, Dana Singleterry, Pavitra Subramaniam, Henry van den Broek, Matthias Wessendorf, Hugh Zhang

Proofreader
Nancy Bell

Indexer
Jack Lewis

Production Supervisor
George Anderson

Composition
Apollo Publishing Service

Illustration
Apollo Publishing Service

Art Director, Cover
Jeff Weeks

Cover Designer
Pattie Lee

To old dogs learning new tricks.

About the Authors

Frank Nimphius has been a principal product manager for Application Development Tools at Oracle Corporation since 1999. Prior to this he worked for Oracle Germany for more than three years in the Oracle Sales Consulting Organization with a focus on Oracle Forms. As a product manager, Frank actively contributes to the development of Oracle JDeveloper and the Oracle Application Development Framework (ADF). Frank runs the ADF Code Corner website at www.oracle.com/technology/products/jdev/tips/fnimphius/index.html and helps users at the Oracle JDeveloper forum at http://forums.oracle.com/forums/forum.jspa?forumID=83.

Lynn Munsinger is a principal product manager for the Application Development Tools group at Oracle, specializing in JDeveloper and ADF. Her career at Oracle began in 1998, and she has been responsible for the support, education, and technical evangelism of Oracle's application development tools ever since. Lynn is the primary developer of the Fusion Order Demo sample application for Fusion Middleware, and she is a frequent presenter at user group and industry conferences.

Contents

Forewords

Over the past 18 months the adoption of Oracle's JDeveloper and Application Development Framework (ADF) has skyrocketed. With our 11*g* release, I think we crossed the tipping point with regards to depth of functionality and ease of use. We spent over three years building and improving JDeveloper and ADF and the result, and corresponding customer response, has been impressive. Now more than ever the tool and framework help users build enterprise applications faster and easier, while protecting them against the constant change of the underlying technologies.

Since the first 11*g* release in late 2008, we have been working nonstop helping customers design, implement, and deploy their applications with JDeveloper and ADF 11*g*. When a customer situation arises where the challenges of their architecture go beyond the normal documentation and training found in the product and on OTN, we send in Lynn or Frank. Between the two of them, they have seen first-hand some of the most advanced and challenging implementations of enterprise software outside of Oracle's own packaged applications. There are very few people at Oracle who know the ADF framework and how to apply it in a wide variety of situations better than Lynn and Frank.

In an effort to help distribute their knowledge, Lynn and Frank have been able to carve out some time over the past year to write this book. While the JDeveloper 11*g* Handbook will teach you the fundamentals of JDeveloper and ADF, along with good design and implementation practices, this book will take you to the next level of detail and depth on the different components and technologies. Once you get the hang of the fundamentals and start to dig in, this reference will be an invaluable tool to have at your side. I would strongly recommend this book to any person or organization using JDeveloper and ADF 11*g* to build their enterprise applications.

Ted Farrell
Chief Architect and Senior Vice President, Tools and Middleware
Oracle Corporation

For 20 years at Oracle, I've helped developers make the most of our declarative development tools. Over that time, while the user interfaces of enterprise applications have evolved from terminals, to workstations, to web and mobile devices, their basic business functionality has changed very little. Regardless of the problem domain, an application's core capabilities continue to be efficiently finding, creating, modifying, validating, and saving data, as well as presenting it in an attractive and user-friendly way. Both inside Oracle and out, tens of thousands of developers trust Oracle's tools to provide the foundation for these fundamental features, so they are free to focus on the bits that make their application unique.

From Java's earliest days, Larry Ellison and others at Oracle saw its long-term promise as an object-oriented language for server-side business application development. However, they also realized it was too low-level to gain wide adoption in corporate IT departments or our own internal Oracle Applications division. So, in the summer of 1996, six months after Sun shipped Java 1.0, our team got the mission to bring the declarative, rapid application development productivity of our traditional tools to an emerging audience of Java programmers. This was the genesis of the Oracle JDeveloper IDE and its standards-based, end-to-end application-building productivity layer, Oracle Application Development Framework.

Since its first public release in 1999 under a different name, Oracle ADF has powered all of the self-service web applications in the Oracle E-Business Suite in releases 11 and 12. In addition, Oracle's next-generation Fusion Applications suite has the latest Oracle ADF 11*g* release at the heart of its service-oriented technology stack. As the largest and most demanding user of its own tools and frameworks, Oracle literally bets its business on the productivity they provide and has invested heavily to steadily improve them. Since JDeveloper and ADF are available for free download, thousands of external customers, software partners, and value-added resellers have also benefitted from our ongoing investment for their own applications, which contrary to popular belief, can work with any SQL92 database, can run on all popular Java application servers, and can be debugged and extended using the framework source code Oracle makes available. After teams using Oracle ADF won the Java RAD Race competition two years in a row, the framework has steadily opened the eyes of more and more Java experts around the world.

When you use Oracle ADF, you stand on the shoulders of the same road-tested, reusable Java components that implement practical solutions to common challenges our own application development teams have encountered over many years. Key framework layers and components enable declarative development for transactional business services with complex relationships, validation, and queries, search forms, lists of values, data binding, sophisticated, multipage, transaction-aware page flows, application security, and a rich library of interactive AJAX components for a thoroughly modern web and mobile user interface. When you use them in concert with an integrated development environment like Oracle JDeveloper that supports framework-based development, you leverage not only our prebuilt components but also a prescriptive approach for applying them to your business domain. Besides saving you from designing and implementing these solutions yourself, a well-architected framework like Oracle ADF ensures your application is cleanly layered, well-organized, and easier to maintain. While its components typically support the bulk of your requirements, it also gives you extension points at all layers where you can write code to react to common events to tailor the default behavior to your specific needs.

As with any framework, getting the maximum out of Oracle ADF's functionality requires familiarizing yourself with its core features, and then learning how to extend the built-in functionality to tackle advanced requirements as needed. While Oracle's *Fusion Developer's Guide for Oracle ADF* that I coauthored explains the product's capabilities, it is not a step-by-step tutorial guide. Oracle Press' *Oracle JDeveloper 11g Handbook: A Guide to Oracle Fusion Web Development* fills that need, and I recommend starting with it to gain a good, practical knowledge of Oracle ADF through its example-driven approach. However, once you've mastered the basics, in order to take your knowledge to the next level you need to understand what's going on under the hood to go beyond what's possible with drag and drop, declarative development. The book in your hands, *Oracle Fusion Developer Guide: Building Rich Internet Applications with Oracle ADF Business Components and ADF Faces*, is the perfect companion volume when you are ready to dive deeper into these more advanced scenarios. Frank and Lynn have packed this book with tips, tricks, and techniques you can apply in your own applications across major functional areas like

- mastering taskflows, regions, and reusable components

- exploiting sophisticated data display, data entry, and data visualization components

- customizing the look and feel using skins

- implementing drag and drop and leveraging JavaScript in the client

- internationalizing and securing your application, among other topics.

As one of the book's technical reviewers, I've been impressed with the authors' depth and breadth of knowledge and straightforward way they explain things. Many gems await you in these pages.

Steve Muench
Oracle ADF Development Team
Oracle Corporation

Acknowledgments

So it is done. But though it is done, it is not over until we can give credit to those who helped us over the last year and a half that we worked on this project. It is unbelievable how many people it takes to write a book, but see for yourself.

From Frank Nimphius: You don't write technical books for your family, but you can't do it without their support. A very special thank you goes to my family, my wife Nicole who I love and my two little boys—Niklas and Erik—who didn't see their father over the last year as often as they would have liked. A hearty thank you also must go to my parents for their lifetime achievement in making me who I am and for taking the kids so I could do even more writing on the weekends.

From Lynn Munsinger: Thank you to my parents and to my friends—without your encouragement, I never would have had the confidence to even start a project like this. And to Craig, thank you for your unwavering patience and understanding throughout this endeavor. I am fortunate to have such an inspirational and loving partner. It's finally our time now!

From both the authors: Though we put in a lot of our personal time, heart blood, and know-how into writing this book, we could not have done this without the technical and organizational support of others.

In alphabetical order, we would like to thank our technical reviewers for ensuring this book stands technically correct and for all the useful comments they provided. Our thanks go to Matt Cooper, Jeff Falk, Yuan Gao, David Giammona, Maria Kaval, Chris Lewis, Katia Obradovic-Sarkic, Grant Ronald, Dana Singleterry, Pavitra Subramaniam, Henry van den Broek, Matthias Wessendorf, and Hugh Zhang.

A very special thank you to Susan Duncan, Duncan Mills, and Steve Muench, who each reviewed each chapter of this book, providing valuable feedback on the technical content and the overall flow as well.

Glenn Maslen coordinated the review schedule of this book and dispatched between us, the reviewers, and the publisher to get this book done on time. Thank you, Glenn, you really deserve applause.

We'd like to thank the Oracle JDeveloper and ADF development team for fixing bugs at our request and for taking time out of their very busy schedules to answer our questions.

Our fellow JDeveloper product managers deserve our thanks for picking up the slack when we were engrossed in writing and couldn't take on our usual share of the work. If you ever plan to write a book, let us know and we will happily stand in for you during that time.

Duncan Mills, our boss, mentor, and most importantly, our dear friend, deserves extra praise. Thank you for believing in us and in this book, for all the book-writing advice you have given us, and for all the little tasks that we know you diverted without our asking. We couldn't ask for a more supportive, understanding manager and we are indebted to you further yet.

A book is only a book when it is published. We'd like to thank the team at McGraw-Hill who guided us well along this book project, helping us to meet our writing, copy editing, and final review milestones.

We, Lynn and Frank, need to give each other a pat on the back for what we achieved as a team. For us, writing this book was a great experience, to put into words what usually we put into Java and metadata.

Last but not least, thank you for purchasing this book.

Introduction

ich Internet Applications (RIA), or to put it into its broader scope, the Rich Enterprise Application (REA) paradigm, has become reality and new business applications are primarily built for web and mobile clients and less for the desktop. Through the adoption of Service Oriented Architecture (SOA) in business application development and interactive web user interfaces, the development of traditional web applications in which the application represents the complete business solution has come to an end. The modern web application is a component-based user interface that accesses remote and local services for the business logic. But still, business application users measure web applications by the interactivity and responsiveness of desktop applications. Developers are therefore tasked with creating REA applications that have all the benefits of reusability that come with an SOA application, while still creating a user interface experience that matches that of desktop applications. This challenge, coupled with the vast array of technologies available to build dynamic and rich web user interfaces, makes it difficult for developers to easily choose the tool and technology that meets their requirement and that makes them productive immediately.

The Java and Java EE Dilemma

The first decision application developers have to make before testing the waters of rich Internet application development is the platform. Though rich Internet applications can be developed with Java, Microsoft .NET, PLSQL, scripting, and more, the base decision is for the platform, which in enterprise application development usually means Java EE or Microsoft .NET. Obviously, a book about Java EE application development cannot provide an unbiased view of which platform is better than the other. However, given that you are reading this book, we assume your decision has been made in favor of the performance, elegance, and most importantly, the standard of the Java EE platform. So we congratulate you and continue with the problem statement that will lead us to the Oracle Application Development Framework as the solution.

The complexity and diversity of the Java EE platform is typically the largest hurdle to overcome in the adoption of the platform by business application developers who come from different programming backgrounds. But it is incorrect to blame the platform alone for this. Most of the complexity that leaves developers stunned as to which technology to learn and where to start is caused by technology changes and the frequency in which new themes and trends, like the REA paradigm, enter the market. Often Java is only the implementation language and not the solution itself. An example of this statement is Ajax. Ajax is the unofficial industry slang for interactive web applications built with the combination of HTML, JavaScript, XML, and CSS. Ajax is not dependent on Java and Java EE. However, Java and Java EE are a choice for developers to build Ajax applications.

Still, there is a problem with Java and Java EE that needs to be addressed. Since the early Java days in the late 1990s, the Java enterprise platform has grown massively and today is used by a large community of developers. However, the developer community is not homogenous and includes developers who are not expert Java programmers but are instead business developers who have core competencies in the industries they build applications for. This means that even as the Java EE platform and community is growing, the average programmer skill level is declining. It is hard to imagine that there is a single developer who understands all aspects of the Java EE platform in depth. Even if there is one, would he or she know about Service Oriented Architecture and Ajax too? Very unlikely! So the problem to address in Java EE is to provide a technology abstraction that empowers developers to build cutting edge web and SOA applications without limiting them in their agility. The best way to address this problem is through frameworks.

The Role of Frameworks in Java EE

Java frameworks are blankets pulled over areas of complexity that expose simpler controls for developers to work with. Or, more technically, frameworks in Java EE are sets of Java classes and configuration files that provide an abstraction of the underlying platform to simplify application development in Java while enforcing the use of best practices and design patterns. Frameworks exist on all layers within a Model-View-Controller architecture and handle tasks like CRUD database interaction, business logic, business rules, page flow and UI logic, validation, security, and transaction management. Examples of Java EE frameworks include Enterprise JavaBeans, the Java Persistence Architecture (JPA), Eclipse Link, ADF Business Components, JavaServer Faces, Struts, the Google Web Toolkit (GWT), Spring, and many more in open source and vendor-owned frameworks. Using frameworks, developers no longer work with the Java core APIs but instead interact with interfaces and services exposed by the framework. This enables developers to build business applications much more easily and efficiently. However, many frameworks solve a single problem and don't provide an end-to-end solution, which puts developers into the role of integrators to align different frameworks to a single application development and deployment platform (which they also need to find the right tooling for). What seems to be a small problem for experienced developers is another hurdle for business developers who are new to Java and Java EE development. If you don't know the technology yet, how would you be able to choose a framework and integrate it with others? This and the fact that modern web application development spans beyond Java EE by integrating SOA services and Ajax technologies bears the risk of the Java EE platform losing the big and attractive community of business application developers. This type of developer may turn to single development environments that promise the integration of all aspects of application development in a single technology choice. For example, you often see developers coming from a 4GL desktop development background being attracted by PLSQL, Microsoft .NET, or Adobe Flash. As an experienced Java developer you may see this as a big mistake, but how would those developers know, unless Java too provides a single solution for them to try? The solution for this dilemma is end-to-end application development frameworks that pull another blanket over the technologies, one that combines different frameworks and technologies into a single product that exposes visual and declarative development gestures as its predominant programming methodology. The most comprehensive solution of such a framework today is the Oracle Application Development Framework (ADF).

Oracle Application Development Framework (ADF)

Oracle ADF is a Java EE design-time and runtime framework that simplifies application development with Java, Java EE, and SOA to attract a broad audience of business domain and technology experts who need to work together building future-proof enterprise software solutions. The metadata layer in Oracle ADF simplifies the binding of business logic to the view layer and controller layer, enabling business application developers to work with a single set of APIs that is independent of the technology used on the business service level. The Oracle ADF binding is an integration layer that combines different Java EE frameworks and technologies, as well as the elements of SOA, into a single development and runtime platform. In combination with Oracle JDeveloper, Oracle ADF provides a development environment that reaches a broad audience of users, including business developers and technology experts.

Oracle has a long tradition of building enterprise development tools and frameworks that are used by internal and external customers. Oracle Forms is one of the most successful products in Oracle application development tools history, and, with almost 30 years on the market, still proves to be the tool of choice for many companies when building custom business applications. Oracle Applications, the organization within Oracle that builds standard business software solutions for Oracle customers, used Oracle Forms, which shows the great confidence Oracle had in this product. Over the years however, markets have changed and technology has evolved. The way businesses worked yesterday no longer proves successful today. This is demonstrated by an increasing demand for web and mobile-based solutions as the user interfaces for distributed business services. The challenge that Oracle faced, as a standard business software vendor, was to find a development platform that combined cutting edge user interfaces with the agility achieved in standards-based technologies, and that provided shortened time to market development cycles. These requirements, as well as the need for scalability, security, and portability, lead to a new development platform that is Oracle ADF and the Oracle Fusion development platform. The Oracle Fusion architecture, which Oracle ADF is a part of, is SOA-based and therefore provides the infrastructure for large-scale enterprise application development and deployments through Oracle Fusion Middleware. With Oracle JDeveloper and the Oracle Application Development Framework, business developers of all programming backgrounds work productively within an integrated development environment that provides the same functionality and maturity that Oracle Forms did in the past.

Oracle ADF is designed as a visual and declarative development environment for building future-proof Java EE and SOA applications, which provides developers with a choice of development styles and technologies that are well integrated within the Oracle JDeveloper IDE. Applications developed with Oracle ADF are accessible from even web, mobile, and desktop clients like Microsoft Excel. Using the Oracle Fusion stack, application developers build Rich Internet Applications that automatically leverage framework features such as:

- **Meta Data Services (MDS)** for out-of-the-box end user personalization and customization

- **Declarative reusable components** to save development time by reusing existing developments and by modularizing the application development process

- **Page templates** that, in combination with skinning, allow developers to build sophisticated layouts that are customizable without changes required in the code

- **Rich ADF Controller** for providing navigation to views and functionality within pages or between pages

- **Application client and server events** that are available on the view layer to dynamically communicate between independent areas on a page and on the server to push message notifications to the clients

- **Rich Java ServerFaces user interface components** that implement Ajax functionality, thus shielding developers from the fine-grained details of RIA interface development

These functionalities and more are declaratively and visually exposed in Oracle JDeveloper, the Oracle integrated Java, Java FE, SOA, and PLSQL development environments.

About This Book

Everyone in application development, so we believe, eagerly absorbs the knowledge, experience, and ideas of others who are willing to share their expertise with the developer community. This book is the medium we have chosen to share the expertise we gained from working with Oracle JDeveloper and Oracle Application Development Framework (ADF) as product managers from the early days of ADF until today.

The idea for this book was born in 2007 at Oracle headquarters in an office with a great view toward San Francisco International Airport. Watching the planes coming in to San Francisco and between several cups of coffee, we came up with the outline of an advanced Oracle ADF developer guide, which would cover topics and scenarios that are frequently asked on the Oracle JDeveloper forums and internal mailing lists. The idea for this book was to provide help to Oracle Fusion developers who have little time to learn, but who are experienced enough in Java and Java EE to go on a fast track to learning Oracle ADF.

While the dominant development gesture in Oracle ADF is visual and declarative, it only abstracts the fact that business application development is about building software with software, which requires a specific skill set to be available on the developer side. A common perception is that a good framework should solve all programming tasks with a click or two, and in many ways this is true in Oracle ADF. However, where there is an "easy" way, there must be an "advanced" way worth discovering.

In this book, we intentionally go beyond drag and drop, the dominant development gesture in Oracle ADF, to showcase the power and benefit the Oracle Fusion development platform brings to Java and Java EE developers. This book is a fast track to Rich Enterprise Application (REA) development with Oracle JDeveloper 11*g* and the Oracle Application Development Framework, written for web application developers who have a background in Java and Java EE development and who are looking for the more advanced features in Oracle ADF. If you are new to Oracle JDeveloper and ADF, or if you have limited knowledge in Java and Java EE application development, then this book is still for you. In this case, however, it may be the second ADF book on your reading list.

The technology focus in this book is set to Oracle ADF Business Components (ADF BC), the Oracle ADF data control and data binding layer, ADF Faces JavaServer Faces UI component framework, Oracle Data Visualization Tools (DVT), and the graph and map components in ADF Faces.

The chapters in this book are organized such that readers can start with what they are most interested in. Where required, we provide pointers to other chapters and the Oracle product documentation so that you are able to get all the information you need for a particular topic.

CHAPTER
1

The Quick Learner's Guide to Oracle Fusion Web Application Development

A data control is an implementation of the contract that exists in Oracle ADF between the proprietary APIs of a business service and the consistent set of APIs that are exposed through the ADF model to the web application developer working with the ADF binding layer. It enables any business service to leverage the ADF declarative, two-way data binding features, of the ADF model.

 his chapter briefly introduces the technologies of the Oracle Fusion development stack that are used in examples and content throughout the book. Our intention is to provide you with a crash course in Oracle Fusion development that gets you, as a quick learner, started immediately. In detail, this chapter covers the following:

- An overview of Oracle Fusion application development in Oracle JDeveloper 11*g*

- An architecture overview of the Oracle Application Development Framework (ADF)

- A quick learner overview of ADF Business Components

- A quick learner introduction to JavaServer Faces (JSF)

- A quick learner introduction of the ADF Faces Rich Client UI framework

More Books About Oracle ADF

For an entry-level introduction to Oracle Fusion application development, we recommend *Oracle JDeveloper 11g Handbook: A Guide to Fusion Web Development*, by Duncan Mills, Peter Koletzke, and Avrom Roy-Faderman, published in 2009 by McGraw-Hill. This tutorial-driven developer guide requires no reader prerequisites. Both *Oracle JDeveloper 11g Handbook* and the book you hold in your hands were written at the same time, and the authors made sure that only a reasonable overlap between the two existed.

Another book to recommend for Oracle WebCenter customers is *Oracle WebCenter 11g Handbook: Build Rich, Customizable Enterprise 2.0 Applications*, by Desbiens, Moskovits, and Weckerle (McGraw Hill). Oracle WebCenter 11*g* is a powerful Web 2.0 portal framework within Oracle Fusion Middleware that is build on top of Oracle ADF.

The Oracle product documentation for ADF and the ADF Faces Rich Client component framework ship as two books, which are available online in HTML and for download in a PDF format. The books are referenced in the "Developer Guide" section of the Oracle JDeveloper documentation website available on the Oracle Technology Network (OTN), which you access from pointing your browser to http://otn.oracle.com. On the OTN homepage, choose Documentation | JDeveloper from the page menu.

- Oracle Fusion Middleware Web User Interface Developer's Guide for Oracle Application Development Framework 11*g* Release 1

- Oracle Fusion Middleware Fusion Developer's Guide for Oracle Application Development Framework 11*g* Release 1

Building Oracle Fusion Applications

The Oracle Fusion development stack is the technology choice that Oracle Applications, the group within Oracle that creates Oracle standard business software based on Java Enterprise Edition (Java EE) and Service Oriented Architecture (SOA) standards, uses to build their next generation of Rich Enterprise Application (REA) software. The Fusion development stack has been chosen with service orientation in mind and includes technologies such as ADF Business Components, ADF Faces Rich Client, Data Visualization Components (DVT), Web Services, Business Process Execution Language (BPEL), Enterprise Service Bus (ESB), and Extensible Markup Language (XML).

Oracle ADF

Oracle ADF is grown out of a series of Java EE frameworks that are integrated through the ADF model layer. The ADF core binding layer is proposed for standardization in JSR-227 "A Standard Data Binding & Data Access Facility for J2EE", which formalizes the value and method binding of UI components to functionality exposed on business services. While JSR-227 is the core of Oracle ADF, the term "ADF" has become a synonym for declarative Java and Java EE development in Oracle JDeveloper.

Oracle ADF consists of the following components:

- **ADFv**   The view layer bindings that exist for ADF include JavaServer Pages (JSP) with Struts, JSF, ADF Faces Rich Client, and Apache MyFaces Trinidad. Using the mobile development support in JavaServer Faces, ADF applications also display on devices such as iPhones and PDAs. "ADFv" refers to the ADF Faces Rich Client framework used in this book.

- **ADFc**   The controller component in ADF is an extension of the JSF navigation model and promotes modularization and reuse. In addition, ADFc provides declarative transaction handling and clearly defined process boundaries.

- **ADFm**   The binding layer and model are represented by data controls and the binding container object. ADFm is built on JSR-227 and abstracts the view layer model access from the implementation details of the underlying business service.

- **ADFbc**   ADF Business Components has a special role within the list of supported business services in that it incorporates the ADF APIs in its Application module. Furthermore, ADF Business Components is the most functional and declarative option, which is why it is the preferred business service within the Oracle Fusion development stack.

- **ADFdi**   Desktop integration with Microsoft Office 2007 allows developers to access the server-side ADF binding layer from Excel workbooks.

Figure 1-1 shows the ADF architecture for the Oracle Fusion developer stack. The view layer is based on JSF 1.2 and includes ADF Faces Rich Client components (ADF Faces RC), Data Visualization Components (DVT), JSF mobile support, and the desktop integration client, which provides MS Excel access to the ADF binding layer. The controller used with ADF Faces RC and DVT is ADF Task Flow, an enhanced navigation handler built on top of the JSF navigation model. Oracle mobile support is based on the Apache Trinidad open source JSF components and uses the JSF navigation handler as its controller. The controller handles page and activity navigation and maintains the application state.

The ADF binding layer exposes a consistent API to the UI layer, hiding the implementation details of the business service the application accesses to read and write data from data services such as RDBMS or XML. The binding layer accesses attributes and business methods that are exposed on the business services through ADF data controls. Data controls are business service implementation–dependent and map service–specific APIs to those understood by ADF. A variety of built-in data controls exist in ADF that can be used with ADF Business Components, EJB 3.0/ JPA services, Web Services, Plain Old Java Object (POJO) services, and many more. Those relevant to ADF Fusion developers are shown in Figure 1-1.

Building a Fusion Application Workspace in Oracle JDeveloper

Oracle JDeveloper 11*g* is the Oracle SOA and Java EE integrated development environment (IDE). To build a web application, with the Oracle Fusion stack, start the new application project with the Fusion Web Application (ADF) application template. Assuming a fresh install of Oracle JDeveloper 11*g*, click the New Application entry in the Application Navigator, or choose File | New and select the Fusion Web Application (ADF) template from the list of available templates in the dialog, as shown in Figure 1-2.

The template creates the following projects and folders:

■ **Model** A project that is preconfigured for building the ADF Business Components business service. Model is the default name and may be changed in the template wizard.

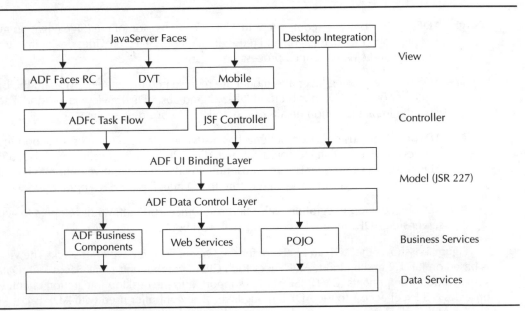

FIGURE 1-1 *ADF Fusion architecture*

- **ViewController** A project that is preconfigured for using ADF Faces RC and the ADF Controller. ViewController is the default name and may be changed in the template wizard.

- **.adf\META-INF** A folder created on the file system for the application that contains ADF-specific configuration files such as adf-config.xml. The file content of this directory is accessible in JDeveloper from the Descriptors | ADF META-INF folder in the Application Navigator's Application Resources accordion panel.

- **src\META-INF** A folder created on the file system for the application that contains deployment descriptor files. The file content of this directory is accessible in JDeveloper from the Descriptors | META-INF folder in the Application Navigator's Application Resources accordion panel.

Additional projects, if needed, are created by choosing File | New, which opens the New Gallery dialog. Select the General | Projects node to choose from a list of preconfigured project types.

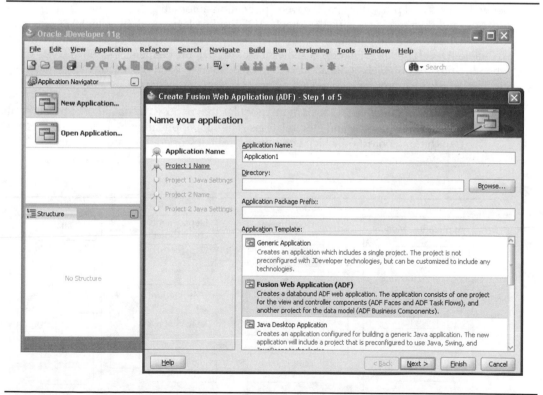

FIGURE 1-2 *Building a new application in Oracle JDeveloper based on the Fusion Web Application template*

ADF Business Components for Quick Learners

Oracle ADF Business Components is the business services layer of choice in Oracle Fusion application development. Compared to other persistence layers, ADF Business Components provides exceptional built-in business application functionality and maximally declarative experience that makes it a perfect match for those who seek an end-to-end fourth generation language (4GL) Java EE development architecture.

ADF Business Components provides a foundation of lightweight Java classes and XML metadata configuration files for building database-centric business models that include business logic, validation, queries, transaction handling, and data access. XML files are created for each of the ADF BC components, such as view object, entity object, and application module. The name of the configuration file matches the name of the component. For example, the configuration for an `EmployeesView` view object is stored in a file called EmployeesView.xml. If custom business logic is required, additional Java classes can be created that extend the component base framework class.

The ADF Business Components framework does not create user interfaces and focuses purely on the backend application logic and data management. It provides options for developers to define UI hints and properties that the web application automatically leverages to display labels, tool tips, and data formats. Using the Oracle ADF binding layer, ADF BC client APIs are exposed on the ADF data control palette, a hierarchical view of the data model objects and functionality in Oracle JDeveloper 11g. Figure 1-3 shows the core ADF BC elements that developers work with when building Fusion web applications and their relation to each other.

These core elements include the following:

- **Application module**   One or more modules that expose the data model based on the defined view objects and their relations. The root application module represents the transaction context on which commit and rollback operations are executed.

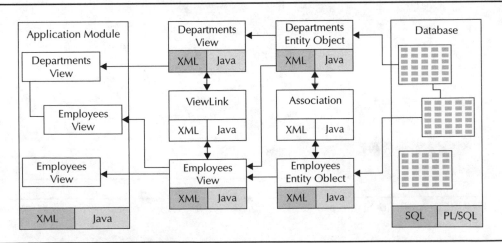

FIGURE 1-3   *ADF Business Components component architecture*

- **View object** A query definition that provides data based on SQL queries, programmatic Java, and stored procedure access and static lists. SQL query-based view objects that reference one or many entity objects make the query result updateable, allowing Data Manipulation Language (DML) operations. A set of one or more view objects used in an application module define the business service access layer.

- **Entity object** Java object that represents a row in a database table. It automatically handles data validation, storage and persistence.

- **Association** Entity object associations define the relationships between two entity objects. The association can be read from defined database constraints or manually defined. Associations allow programmatic navigation between related objects to implement complex business rules as well as simplify building join queries over sets of related business data.

- **ViewLink** Relations that are based on entity associations or defined manually, providing master-detail coordination between view objects.

NOTE

In depth coverage of ADF Business Components is the subject of Oracle JDeveloper 11g Handbook: A Guide to Fusion Web Development, published by McGraw Hill, and the "Oracle Fusion Middleware Fusion Developer's Guide for Oracle Application Development Framework 11g Release 1," available online at http://otn.oracle.com.

Maturity Through History

Oracle ADF Business Components is a road tested Java EE business application logic and persistence framework that has existed within Oracle JDeveloper since 1999. Originally code named Oracle Java Business Objects (JBO), and still showing this legacy in the oracle.jbo package naming, Oracle ADF Business Components has been used by Oracle internal and external customers for a long time. The Oracle ADF Business Components framework gained importance with its adoption in the Oracle Applications developer stack, where it is used as the model layer for Java-based commercial, self-service applications. Today, when building Oracle Fusion applications, Oracle Applications uses the same version of Oracle ADF Business Components that ships with Oracle JDeveloper and the Oracle Fusion Middleware, which demonstrates Oracle's confidence in the quality of the stack and improved productivity features. Basing big parts of its own business on the ADF Business Components technology, Oracle adds even more road testing to this software layer, eating more of its own dog food than probably any other vendor or open-source project.

Framework Classes

Default ADF Business Components implementation base classes exist in the oracle.jbo.server package for the entity object and all the component interfaces in the oracle.jbo package. The base classes are referenced in the metadata that is generated for the created ADF BC objects in an application. Application developers can extend the default framework classes to expose additional helper methods or to customize the default framework behavior. Extended framework classes are configured in Oracle JDeveloper either on the project level, in which case only new objects created in this single project will be based on the custom classes, or on the IDE level, in which case any ADF Business Components project uses the custom classes.

Project-level Configuration

To configure custom framework classes for a project, select the project root folder in the Oracle JDeveloper Application Navigator view and choose Project Properties from the context menu. In the project Properties editor, expand the Business Components entry and select the Base Classes entry. Use this dialog to replace the listed base classes with the custom subclasses.

IDE-level Configuration

To configure custom framework classes for all ADF Business Components projects that are created in an IDE, choose Tools | Preferences and expand the Business Components node. Select the Base Classes entry and replace the listed base classes with the custom subclasses.

It is worthwhile to explore the various options that exist in the tool preferences to refine the ADF Business Components settings. For example, the "Packages" entry should be used to locate the different class types in their own subpackage folders for better readability.

Creating a Business Components Model

Starting from a model project created by the Fusion Web Application (ADF) template, choose the New option from the context menu to open the Oracle JDeveloper New Gallery. Expand the Business Tier node and select the Business Components entry. As shown in Figure 1-4, Oracle JDeveloper 11*g* provides various options to create business component objects. Selecting one of the options expands the item area, displaying the item description.

Select the Business Components From Tables entry and click OK. In the first dialog, create a database connection to the RDBM instance and schema that holds the application database tables, views, and synonyms. The database connection is referenced in the ADF Business Components application module and defined for the application. To change the database connection properties, you can open the Application Resources accordion panel in the Application Navigator and expand the Database node. Right click and choose Properties to edit the connect information.

NOTE
The database connection used by the ADF Business Components project is also accessible from the model project. Open the project properties by selecting Project Properties from the context menu and choose the Business Components entry. Click the green plus icon to create a new database connection, or click the pencil icon to edit the existing database connection.

Creating Entities

In the first wizard page, query the table, views, and synonyms for which you want to build entity object representations. By default, the entity object name is the same as the selected database object, but this can be changed by typing the new name into the Entity Name field. Entity associations are automatically created for database objects that have a foreign-key relationship defined. The database object name is transformed in a Java-friendly format, which is to use camel case letters. For example, a table named PERSON_DETAIL creates an entity named PersonDetail.

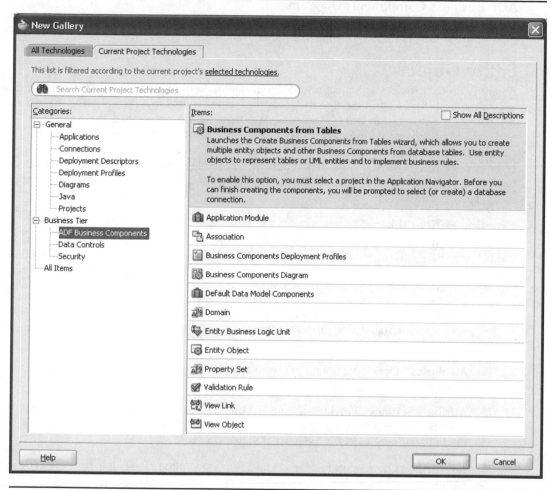

FIGURE 1-4 *ADF Business Components creation options in the Oracle JDeveloper New Gallery*

Creating View Objects

The second page in the wizard shows the list of created entity objects for which default view objects will be built. The names of the view objects can be changed in the Object Name field. View links are automatically created for view objects that are based on entities with defined associations.

Step 3 of the Business Components wizard creates read-only view objects that are not based on an entity object.

Creating an Application Module Instance

The fourth wizard page allows application developers to associate the created view objects with an existing or new application module instance that exposes the view objects as a part of its data model.

ADF Business Components Diagram

The last, optional, step of the creation wizard allows developers to create a diagram for further ADF Business Components modeling that includes the created objects.

Entity Objects

An entity object provides an object-oriented representation of a row in a table or view. It exposes access methods for its attributes that correspond to table or view row columns and maps the database SQL types to standard Java types or ADF Business Components domain types. In addition, it holds domain business logic for consistent validation of business policies and rules. An entity object holds a copy of the data object queried from the database, as well as a local copy to work with. The ADF Business Components base class that implements the default entity behavior is `EntityImpl` and is referenced in the generated entity metadata of an application entity, such as Employees.

Creating Entity Objects

Entity objects are created in a "bulk" operation with the Create Business Components from Tables wizard or individually after you select the Entity Object entry in the Business Tier | ADF Business Components New Gallery section. The Create Entity Object wizard steps the developer through the creation and configuration of the new entity:

- **Name**   Developer option to specify the name and Java package for the new entity, the base entity if any, shared property sets to use, and the data source as a database schema or ADF Business Components service interface.

- **Attributes**   Developer option to create additional entity attributes or remove existing attributes from the entity.

- **Attribute Settings**   Provides options to configure each attribute with query, update, and refresh flags, and to change the attribute data type—for example, to use `DBSequence` if the field value is added by a database trigger on insert.

- **Java**   Allows developers to generate Java implementation classes that extend the default framework classes. If there is no immediate need for such a Java class—for example, to override the default entity methods, such as the `beforeCommit` and `beforeRollback` methods—then the class creation can be deferred to later.

- **Generate**   Allows developers to create a default view object and configure the view object with an application module.

Editing Entity Objects

Existing entity objects are edited in Oracle JDeveloper entity editors and the Property Inspector (CTRL-SHIFT-I). Open the editor by double-clicking the entity entry in the Application Navigator, or right-click and choose Open <*Entity*> from the context menu. The editor shows a categorized view of the entity object configuration options. You use the icons on top of the editor dialog to create, remove, or edit configuration options. In addition, for each selected configuration options, the Property Inspector shows other options. The editor window and the Property Inspector window are synchronized when both are open.

<Entity>Impl

Business Service developers can build a custom implementation class for an entity that extends the configured base framework class and is referenced from the entity metadata. The entity implementation class allows developers to expose typed attribute setter and getter methods, create attribute validation methods, access child collections in a master-detail relation, retrieve the entity object key, or modify the entity create and DML behavior. All changes to the default framework behavior applied in an <Entity>Impl class apply only to the entity for which the class is built.

To create a custom entity implementation class, select the entity object in the Application Navigator view of the ADF Business Components project and choose Open <Entity> from the context menu. In the entity editor, select the Java menu option and click the pencil icon on top. This opens the Java Options dialog where you can create entity-related Java classes, including an option to create the implementation class. For a list of public and protected methods that can be overridden, choose Source | Override Methods from the opened Java class in the Oracle JDeveloper code view.

The following custom entity classes can be created through the Java Options dialog:

- **<Entity>DefImpl**   The entity definition object that describes the structure of the entity at runtime and that manages the instances of the entity object it describes. The DefImpl class is a singleton and changes applied at runtime to this object are reflected by all instance. The class exposes methods to create new entity instances, find existing instances by their primary key, and access entity properties.

- **<Entity>CollImpl**   Extends the EntityCache object that caches queried rows for a particular entity type. The entity cache is referenced from View Object queries and improves performance for cases in which multiple views access the same entity object.

Associations

An association describes the relationship that exists between two entities. When creating an association between two entity objects, you establish an active link between them. The active link is accessible from your Java code to work with the dependent entity. An association can be created from a foreign key constraint in the database or manually at design time. It is defined in XML metadata that is referenced by an instance of the EntityAssociation class at runtime and maps attributes of two entities in a where clause. To edit an existing association, double-click the association in the JDeveloper Application Navigator to open the editor view.

Creating Associations

Associations are automatically created for dependent entity objects when running the Create Business Components from Tables wizard. To create associations manually, right-click anywhere in the project package structure and choose New Association from the context menu. Alternatively, press CTRL-N to open the Oracle JDeveloper New Gallery and expand the Business Tier node to select the Business Components entry. Then choose the Association entry. In the Association wizard, select the two entity attributes you want to link together and click the Add button. In the next step, define the accessor names to be added to the source and target entity for programmatic access.

Compositions

A composition is an attribute of the association and describes a relationship in that the parent entity doesn't reference the child entity but contains it. For example, using compositions, creating or updating a child entity always ensures that a parent entity exists and that it is updated before its children. The relationship between an order and an order item is a good example for a composition. An order item cannot exist without a valid order, and deleting an order must cascade delete the contained order items. If the parent entity is created at the same time as the detail item, no primary key may exist yet for the detail to reference. If the primary key becomes available after commit of the parent, then all foreign key references of the order items entity are updated with this key.

View Objects

The hierarchy of view objects represents the business service data structure and the business logic that is contained in the entity objects to the application client. It exposes a business service client interface for the web application developer to bind UI components to. In general terms, a view object manages the client data for display and update operations. View objects that are based on entities provide DML access to the application client, whereas a nonentity view object is read-only. Other data access options for a view object are *programmatic*, in which Java is used to read in the data, and *static*, in which the view object shows a static list of values such as those imported from a character-delimited file.

A view object can be linked with another view object to describe a master-detail relationship that at runtime is synchronized by the ADF Business Components framework.

View objects use SQL to query the data from the database. Developers can modify the default view object query by adding a where clause or a group by clause, or by adding bind variables that allow a query by example.

Creating a View Object

To create a view object, you use the Create Business Components from Tables wizard or one of the following options:

- **Create View Object for an entity**   Select an entity object in the Oracle JDeveloper Application Navigator, right-click it, and choose New Default View Object from the context menu.

- **Create a View Object from the New Gallery**   Choose File | New or press CTRL-N to open the New Gallery dialog in Oracle JDeveloper. Select the View Object entry in the Business Tier | ADF Business Components node.

- **Create a View Object anywhere in the project**   Select a package node in the project, right-click it, and choose New View Object from the context menu.

The Create View Object wizard steps the developer through the creation and configuration of the new entity:

- **Name**   The Name category allows developers to define the view object name and package location where the XML definition files and optional generated Java classes are located. In addition, developers choose the type of View Object as SQL based, programmatic, or static.

■   **Entity Objects**   SQL query type view object can be based on one or many entity objects. If a view object is based on many entities, a link is created based on existing entity associations, using inner or outer joins to display the data.

■   **Attributes**   Displays the available list of attributes exposed by the view object entity or entities from which the developer can choose. In addition, the developer may create transient attributes that don't have an equivalent in the entity object. Such attributes are used, for example, to display calculated fields.

■   **Attribute Settings**   Each exposed attribute can be configured for its update and refresh behavior, if it is queryable, and its default value. The default value may be chosen as a static literal or a Groovy expression. Groovy is an open source Java based scripting language.

■   **Query**   The SQL query that is used to retrieve the result set. Possible SQL modes are Normal for queries that are created by the framework based on the selected entities and objects, Expert for queries that are fully hand-edited by the application developer, and Declarative for queries that are defined by the framework and that are further filtered through the use of declarative query builders.

■   **Bind variables**   To filter the returned result set dynamically, developers can use named bind variables to pass the condition for the query clause. Bind variables are exposed in the `ExecuteWithParams` operation of the view object but can also be set using the view object API. Note that the difference between a named bind variable in ADF Business Components and a standard bind variable in SQL is by the reference in a query. Named bind variables are referenced by a leading colon and the variable name, whereas SQL bind variables are referenced by a question mark (?) in the query. Bind variables in ADF Business Components must be created in the View Object prior to using them.

■   **Java**   Like entity objects, view objects are defined in XML that is mapped to a framework class at runtime. Custom implementations of the runtime classes can be created for the view object and for the view object rows to expose typed user interfaces for the contained attributes, to change the default framework behavior, and to provide default values in Java.

■   **Application module**   View objects are exposed on an application module that developers can create or reference in the last wizard dialog.

<View Object>Impl

Developers can build a custom implementation class for a view object that extends the framework `ViewObjectImpl` base class. A custom view object implementation class allows developers to override or hook into the default framework functionality.

To create a custom view object implementation class, right-click the view object in the Application Navigator view of the ADF Business Components project and choose Open <*View Object*> from the context menu. In the View Object editor dialog, select the Java menu option and click the pencil icon on top. This opens the Java Options dialog, where you can create an application-specific view object implementation class. For a list of public methods to override in the `ViewObjectImpl` class, choose Source | Override Methods from the opened Java class in the Oracle JDeveloper code view.

Other custom entity classes that can be created through the Java Options dialog are as follows:

- **<ViewObject>DefImpl**   A custom runtime object that describes the view object structure based on the XML metadata defined at design time. All custom implementations extend the `ViewDefImpl` base class.

- **<ViewObject>RowImpl**   An object that provides access to a view object row and that extends the `ViewRowImpl` framework class. ADF Business Components instantiates one object of this class for each record that is returned by a view object query. The `RowImpl` class allows developers to access row data and their child collections.

Named View Criteria

Named view criteria are predefined and reusable where-clause definitions that are dynamically applied to a ViewObject query and that are exposed for declarative use in the ADF data control. Developers use named view criteria to build search forms, to expose filtered view object instances on the application module, and to apply them programmatically at runtime to restrict the returned result set.

To create a named view criteria, in the Oracle JDeveloper Application Navigator, select the view object to own the criteria and open it in the editor. Choose the Query criteria and click the green plus icon to open the Create View Criteria dialog. A view criteria can exist of several groups, which are criteria rows that are AND'ed or OR'ed together. To create a new criteria within a group, press Add Item. Select a view object attribute and an operator, as well as whether the where clause should be based on a literal value or a bind variable. If the bind variable doesn't exist, it can be created within the same dialog. After the view criteria is created, it shows in the ADF Data Control palette under the view object node's Named Criteria entry.

Operations

View objects expose a set of operations to the client application to navigate within the exposed collection, to execute the query, to create and delete rows, and to search within the rowset. All operations are also exposed on the ADF binding layer for developers to bind UI components to declaratively. The following list describes some of the commonly used operations:

- **Create/CreateInsert**   Create a new row in the view object. The `CreateInsert` operation also adds the new row to the RowSet, after which it is initialized. Using the `Create` operation only creates the row but doesn't add it to the transaction.

- **Create with Parameters**   Create a new row with default values declaratively set for some of the view object attributes. Adding this operation from the ADF Data Control palette to a page creates an operation binding entry in the ADF binding definition of the web page to which developers can add `NamedData` items that reference a `ViewObject` attribute name and a source for the value. A use case for this operation is to create a copy of a selected row.

- **Delete**   Removes the current selected row from the collection.

- **Find**   Calling this operation sets the view object into query mode, also known as Find mode. All view object attributes take search criteria values so that after a call to Execute, the result set is filtered. The Find operation has been used in previous versions of ADF to build search forms but lost its importance in Oracle JDeveloper 11*g* with the introduction of the ADF Faces RC `af:query` component and the recommended use of named view criteria.

- **SetCurrentRowWithKey**   Makes the row current that is defined by its string serialized row key.

- **RemoveRowWithKey**   Removes the row that is identified by its serialized row key.

Client Methods

It is best practices when working with ADF Business Components not to type cast to a business service implementation class on the client layer. So instead of type casting the handle to a view object to its `ViewObjectImpl` class, you should generate and use the client interface with the public methods defined. For example, let's assume that a public method `printHelloWorld(String s)` exists in the `DepartmentsViewImpl` class of the `DepartmentsView` object. To create the client interface class and expose the method for the application client to use, right-click the view object in the Application Navigator and choose Open DepartmentsView from the context menu. In the opened editor view, select the Java category and click the pencil icon next to the Client Interface section. In the opened Edit Client Interface dialog, select the `printHelloWorld` method entry and move it into the selection list. This creates the client interface and exposes the method on it. The type casting on the user interface to execute the method now is to `DepartmentsView` and is no longer the implementation class.

Bind Variables

Bind variables are used in view criteria and the where clause of a view object query. They are named value holders that developers can access from the client to provide the filter criteria. Bind variables can be created when creating the view criteria and view object, but they can also be created later using the view object overview editor launched by double-clicking the view object entry in the Application Navigator.

View Links

View links, like associations, define the relationship between two View objects. They are created through manual mapping of a view object attribute to the equivalent attribute of a dependent View object or based on an existing entity association.

Creating View Links

View links are automatically created for dependent view objects when running the Create Business Components from Tables wizard. To create a view link manually, right-click anywhere in the project package structure and choose New View Link from the context menu. Alternatively, press CTRL-N to open the Oracle JDeveloper New Gallery and expand the Business Tier node to select the Business Components entry. Choose the View Link entry. In the View Link wizard, select the two entity attributes to link together and press the Add button, or use existing entity associations. In the following dialogs, optionally define accessors methods to be generated in the view object implementation classes, modify the generated query, and configure the view link to display in an application module.

Application Modules

An application module is a container for view objects, view links, and other application module instances. It is defined in XML metadata at design time and encapsulates the Business Components data model and methods. As shown on the right-hand side of Figure 1-5, the root application module is the root of the data model and provides the transaction context for all the objects contained in it. View objects are added as instances to the data model with a hierarchical structure built based on existing view links. Shown on the left hand side of Figure 1-5, Application modules are exposed as data controls in the Data Controls panel of the Oracle JDeveloper Application Navigator. View Object instance hierarchies of the data model are displayed as collection hierarchies in the Data Controls panel.

\<Application Module\>Impl

Developers build a custom implementation class for an application module to easier access view object instances and to expose public client methods. The application module implementation

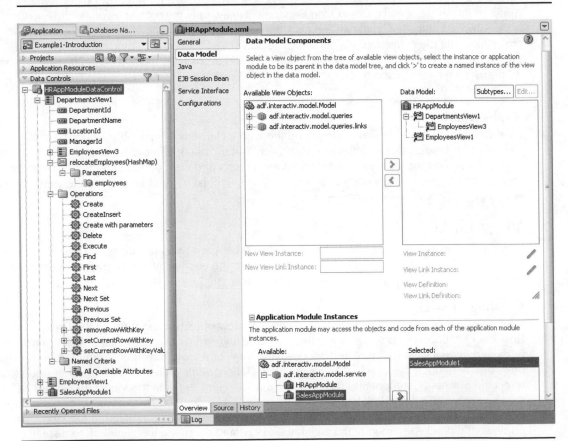

FIGURE 1-5 *ADF Business Components data model and its exposure in the ADF Data Control palette*

extends the `ApplicationModuleImpl` framework class and is referenced from the application module XML metadata.

To create a custom application module implementation class, right-click the application module in the Application Navigator view of the ADF Business Components project and choose Open <Application Module> from the context menu. In the Entity Editor dialog, select the Java menu option and click the pencil icon on top. This opens the Java Options dialog, where you can create application module–specific Java classes, including an option to create the implementation class. For a list of public methods that can be overridden, choose Source | Override Methods from the opened Java class in the Oracle JDeveloper code view.

Another custom class that can be created through the Java Options dialog is <Application Module> DefImpl, a custom object that stores the runtime metadata for the application modules. The object is needed to load an application module and the components it contains from XML metadata. If a custom DefImpl class is created, then the class name contains the name of the custom application module. If no custom object is created, the framework uses the `ApplicationModuleDefImpl` base implementation class.

Defining the Data Model

Open the application module by double-clicking its entry in the Application Navigator. Select the data model category to build the data model from the list of Available View Objects. Selecting a view object from the list of available view objects and adding it to the data model creates a new instance of the view object, with a number added to the view object name. Selecting the view object instance and clicking the Edit button allows you to assign a named view criteria to the instance, assuming a view criteria is defined for this view object. Figure 1-6, which is shown in "The Role of the ADF Binding Layer" section later in this chapter, shows the view object instance hierarchy of the data model displays in the Data Controls palette with all the view object operations and client methods defined for the view object.

Root application modules may have nested application modules configured that share the parent module transaction context.

Building Client Interface Methods

Similar to client interfaces that can be exposed on view objects, application modules can also expose public methods to the client. To write and expose a public method, you first create the application module implementation class. Open the application module in the editor and select the Java category. Click the pencil icon to open the Select Java Options dialog. Check the option that creates the application module implementation class and close the dialog. Open the application module implementation class and add the public method to expose to the client. In the Application Module editor, click the pencil icon next to the Client Interface section. In the Edit Client Interface dialog, move the public method entry to the selected list to create the interface.

Testing

ADF Business Components services can be tested using the integrated generic Java client. To launch the tester, right-click the application module in the JDeveloper Application Navigator and choose Run from the context menu.

Oracle ADF for Quick Learners

The ADF model exists of two layers: data controls and bindings. Data controls abstract the implementation of a business service and map the service attributes and methods to consistent access patterns in ADF. Data controls are not used directly from the application view layer or controller and are instead accessed by Oracle JDeveloper at design time and the ADF binding layer at runtime. The ADF binding layer is also referred to as the "data binding" layer and exposes methods, attributes, and query result sets that exist on the business services layer and that are published through the data control interface to the view layer. The binding layer shapes the data control access to the functionality needed on the current displayed page.

Maturity Through History

A common safe harbor thesis in software development is to wait for a second version of a Java EE or open source framework before adopting it. Before Oracle ADF, Oracle provided a Swing and JSP binding for Oracle ADF BC so applications developers had it easy when building desktop and web applications in Java and Java EE. In early 2004, Oracle released Oracle ADF as a generic binding layer to link UIX, Swing, and JSP interfaces to their Java EE models, which included Enterprise JavaBeans (EJB), Plain Old Java Objects (POJO), and Web Services. The Oracle JDeveloper version for this initial release was Oracle JDeveloper 9.0.5. Since then, a new version of the ADF binding has been released with each version of Oracle JDeveloper. Therefore, Oracle ADF in Oracle JDeveloper 11*g* is the fourth version of this technology.

Since 2004, the Oracle ADF developer community has constantly grown, a proof point for the value add and maturity of this technology. The support for business service models and view layer technologies has also grown and now includes JSF, mobile, and MS Excel.

Introduction to Data Controls

A data control is an implementation of the contract that exists in Oracle ADF between the proprietary APIs of a business service and the consistent set of APIs that are exposed through the ADF model to the web application developer working with the ADF binding layer (Figure 1-6). It enables any business service to leverage the ADF declarative, two-way data binding features, of the ADF model. As a web application developer, you don't need to know about the classes that make up a data control because you are exposed to the ADF binding layer only. Knowledge about the data control internals is important for data control developers and to some degree for business service developers that expose a service as a data control.

The `oracle.adf.model.binding.DCDataControl` class is the abstract base class in ADF that infrastructure developers extend to build specific business service data controls for the Oracle ADF model. Implementations of the `DCDataControl` class manage connections to data providers, handle exceptions raised by the business service, and manage the iterator binding to RowIterators in the data provider.

ADF Data Control functionality

Depending on the business service to which the ADF binding layer is mapped, the ADF model provides the following functionality:

■ **Iterator service**   ADF provides an implementation of the iterator pattern that can be used with any business collection. Data controls optionally can use built-in operations

for the implementation, such as first, next, previous, and last in ADF BC to navigate the iterator.

- **Find**   The ADF model provides functionality to set a business service into a query by example (QBE) mode.

- **Business object properties access**   The ADF model allows access to properties of the business object through JavaBeans setter and getter methods.

- **Method invocation service**   Business service operations and methods are exposed through the data control for the UI developer to invoke through the binding layer. An iterator may reference the result set of such a method invocation to display the returned data in a collection model used, for example, with tables and trees. Methods referenced by an iterator are implicitly invoked by the ADF model.

- **Transaction services**   ADF does not handle transactions but notifies the business service about logical transaction events such as commits and rollbacks. Custom data controls may respond to the default commit and rollback operations that are exposed on the data control palette by calling the equivalent built-in functionality on the business service. Not all data controls support this functionality.

- **Collection manipulation**   The ADF model provides default operations to work with the collection exposed by an iterator. Application developers can use these operations to add, modify, and remove objects from a collection. The data control's responsibility is to notify the business service about these changes if an equivalent operation is available.

- **Lifecycle notification**   Data controls receive lifecycle event notification from ADF for the developer to passivate or activate business service user state.

This functionality, and more, is exposed through the Oracle ADF model for declarative use. The data control developer and the business service technology that are used determine the completeness of the mapping of the standard ADF services to functionality of the business service.

ADF Business Components Data Control

The ADF Business Components data control extends `DCDataControl` and is implemented by the `oracle.adf.model.bc4j.DCJboDataControl` class. It exposes ADF Business Components root application modules as data controls in the ADF Data Control palette. Nested application modules, view object instances, view object attributes, and operations are exposed in a hierarchical structure to the business application developer.

Oracle Fusion developers use ADF Business Components as the business service and don't need to bother with exposing the service as a data control because application modules automatically show in the Oracle JDeveloper 11*g* data control panel. ADF BC business service developers control the functionality that is exposed by the data control through configuration in the ADF Business Components Data Model panel of the application module. At runtime, the ADF Business Components data control, `DCJboDataControl`, provides an application module instance for each application request. From an application module perspective, the data control serves as the client that interacts with the business service. All exceptions raised by the ADF Business Components framework that aren't handled in the business service itself are passed on to the data control, which forwards them to the ADF error handler.

To work with the ADF Business Components data control in a view layer project, you should ensure that a project dependency to the model project exists in the view project properties. Double-click the view project node and select the Dependencies option. If the model project doesn't show in the list of dependencies, click the pencil icon to build it. If the ADF Business Components data control doesn't show in the Data Controls panel of the Application Navigator, right-click to view the context menu and refresh the panel.

Creating Data Controls for non–ADF BC Services

For business services such as EJB, Web Services, or POJO, application developers need to create the data control metadata definition files explicitly to be used with the default data control implementation classes in ADF. To do so, they right-click the EJB session bean, the Web Service, or the POJO in the Oracle JDeveloper Application Navigator and choose Create Data Control from the context menu.

An alternative option exists for Web Services: choose File | New from the Oracle JDeveloper menu and then choose All Technologies | Business Tier | Web Services to launch the Web Service Data Control wizard to provide the online or local reference to the service's Web Services Description Language (WSDL) file.

The data control definition is stored as XML in the DataControls.dcx file that maps the generic data control implementation class to the session facade or service endpoint. Default data control implementations exist in ADF for the standard business services mentioned earlier. The generated data control metadata describe the entities, attributes, and methods of the referenced service instance with which ADF should work.

NOTE
The web service data control allows any Web service of Simple Object Access Protocol (SOAP) runtime or Web Services Invocation Framework (WSIF) to be invoked. The web service can be invoked purely from the data described in the metadata file at design time.

The Oracle JDeveloper Data Control Palette

The Data Control palette in Oracle JDeveloper 11*g* exposes the ADF Business Components data model to the application developer for declarative use.

As shown in Figure 1-5 (earlier in the chapter), the following information is exposed to the application developer:

- **View objects** Collections of row objects that developers work with to build input forms, tables, trees, tree tables, and navigation controls. A view object that has a view link defined to a child collection shows the detail view object in its expanded view hierarchy. The DepartmentsView1 collection instance in Figure 1-5 shows that a detail view object instance EmployeesView3 is defined. Dragging both collections to an ADF Faces page, say as a form and a table, creates a master-detail behavior in which the table is refreshed with the change of the row currency in the form.

- **View object attributes** Exposed in the expanded view object hierarchy and can be dragged onto a page as input components, output components, and select choice components. A common use case for dragging an attribute to a page is to replace a form text input field, which you've deleted from the form, with a select list component.

- **Operations**   Built-in methods available on the application module and the view object. Operations are added as command actions to a page. Operations such as `setCurrentRowWithKey` that require an input argument display a dialog in which the developer can provide values or value references.

- **Methods**   Exposed on the ADF Business Components client interface of a view object or application module and dragged as command components or input forms. The method arguments are exposed as attributes that can be dragged as UI input components to a page if the argument type is a simple object. If the argument type is a complex object, a managed bean property is required that returns the complex object.

- **View criteria**   Named query predicates for the View Object they are exposed under. Dragging a View Criteria on a page allows you to declaratively build search forms.

- **Application modules**   Show as root nodes in the Data Control palette or nested controls for application module instances that are nested in a parent instance from which they inherit the transaction context. Figure 1-5 shows an instance of SalesAppModule as a nested application module.

Dragging and Dropping Content from the Data Control Palette

Dragging an entry of the Oracle JDeveloper data control palette to an ADF Faces page leads to the following:

- A context menu option appears for the application developer to select a UI component to which the selected entry should be data bound.

- If this is the first ADF element that is added to the view project, the web.xml configuration file is updated with filter references to the `ADFBindingFilter` and Oracle DVT filters that are used to visualize data on a page graphically. In addition, the DataBindings.cpx registry file is created.

- If this is the first ADF bounded component added to the JavaServer Faces page, a metadata file is created to hold the ADF binding information for this page. The metadata filename is defined as the name of the JavaServer Faces page followed by PageDef.xml.

- The ADF metadata file is updated with a reference to the collection, attribute, or operation added to the page.

- Expression language references are created to link the ADF metadata in the page-specific ADF binding file to the UI component.

NOTE
The PageDef metadata file is also called ADF binding definition and page definition.

The Role of the ADF Binding Layer

Oracle ADF data controls expose the business services' attributes and functionality to which the web application developer binds UI components. These components, however, don't bind directly to the data control, but, as shown in Figure 1-6, to the ADF binding layer. The ADF binding layer consists of metadata that is generated for each ADF-enabled page and a set of generic framework classes. The binding layer exposes the configured data controls' information in the binding context. It exposes a consistent API that is independent of the technology used to build the business service.

Oracle ADF is designed for declarative and visual application development. Fusion web applications that use ADF Faces Rich Client and Oracle DVT components for rendering the UI bind the component properties to the ADF binding through Expression Language, a scripting notation.

Figure 1-6 shows the ADF binding entries for a master detail page that renders the master view as a form and the detail as a table. As shown in the image, UI components such as tables or select lists are linked to entries in the binding page definition. Each entry in the bindings category holds a reference to an entry in the executables category.

NOTE
The exception are method bindings, like relocateEmployees, that invoke methods on the data control or the collection directly.

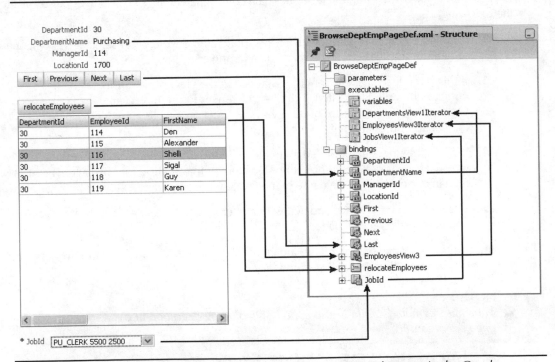

FIGURE 1-6 *ADF binding metadata linked to UI components on the page in the Oracle JDeveloper Structure window*

An iterator in the executables category is a reference to a `RowIterator` exposed on the data control. The relocateEmployees button is bound to the relocateEmployees method binding through Expression Language that invokes the method on the binding layer when the button is clicked:

```
#{bindings.relocateEmployees.execute}
```

In addition to the default functionality that is configured when an entry is dragged from the data control palette to the page, developers may need to access the binding definitions from Java, covered next.

ADF Binding Classes

All binding metadata that you work with at design time is used to configure a framework object instance at runtime. Figure 1-7 shows the hierarchy of the core ADF binding classes from the perspective of the ADF Faces Rich Client view layer. ADF Faces RC components access the ADF binding layer through specialist binding classes that work as an abstraction between the UI component model APIs and the generic ADF binding classes they extend. As shown in Figure 1-7, ADF Faces–specific binding classes have a *FacesCtrl* naming prefix and extend from the generic binding layer classes, which are the classes with which developers work when accessing the ADF binding from Java. The role of the ADF Faces–specific binding classes is to map the ADF binding API to the interface expected by the UI component model and to expose functionality contained in the binding to Expression Language access.

NOTE
Fusion application developers who work declaratively with ADF and ADF Faces are not directly exposed to these framework classes but use them implicitly in the Expression Language references that are created in Oracle JDeveloper. Knowing about the binding classes and how to use them is important only for developers who want to access the binding layer from Java. Sooner or later, however, this includes all of us.

When programming against the ADF binding layer with Java, you work with the generic binding classes that start with *JUCtrl* prefix. Chapter 2 contains examples for the most common used classes.

JavaServer Faces for Quick Learners

JSF 1.2 was chosen as the view layer of choice in Fusion web application development of Oracle JDeveloper 11*g*. JSF is a Java EE standard since 2004 and in its current version 1.2 is part of the Java EE 5 platform. JSF is designed to simplify web application development and changes the programming model for building web pages from HTML markup development to the assembly of reusable UI components that are declaratively linked to their data model and server-side event handlers.

Architecture Overview

As shown in Figure 1-8, a JSF web application request is always dispatched by the front controller, which is an instance of `FacesServlet` that is configured in the web.xml descriptor file. The

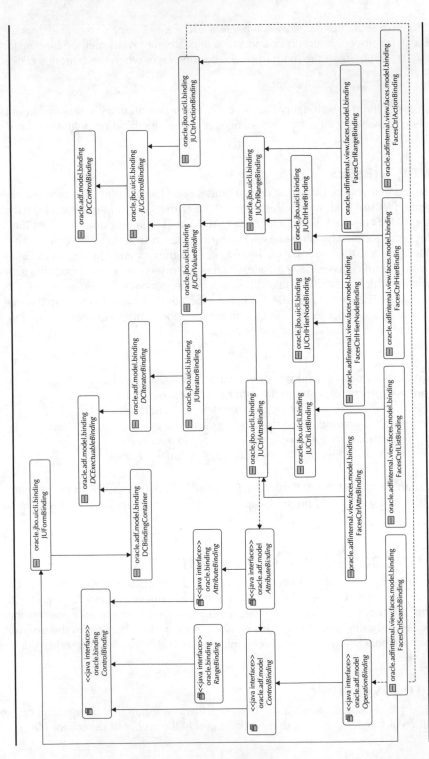

FIGURE 1-7 *ADF binding class diagram*

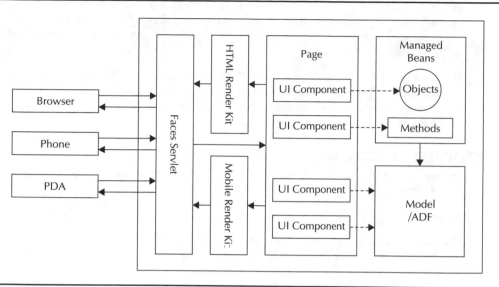

FIGURE 1-8 *JavaServer Faces architecture diagram*

request is routed to the page that is identified by the `viewId` in the request. Components on a page are represented on the server as memory object within a virtual component tree. A component may reference a managed bean to execute client logic, like a method that is invoked by clicking a button. The visual presentation of a JSF page that is downloaded to the client in response to a request is handled by render kits. A render kit is a specialized set of Java classes that produce the display code for a specific device.

Building Blocks

JSF application developers work with the following core building blocks:

- **UI component** A reusable component, such as a button or an input text field, that exposes its attributes as properties to the developer. Attributes are either set declaratively using the Oracle JDeveloper Property Inspector or, in Java, using a reference to the component instance and call the setter and getter methods for the attribute to set or read. UI components can display on many different devices and not just browsers.

- **Managed bean** A POJO with no argument constructor that is configured to be managed by the JSF framework. Configuring a managed bean with JSF makes its public methods and properties available to the Expression Language for use on the UI component attributes. The instantiation and dismissal of a managed bean is handled by JSF so that there is no need for developers to maintain a bean's lifetime.

- **Expression Language** A scripting notation that accesses public methods and properties on JavaBeans. Used to bind UI components to the data model, which can be a managed bean or the Oracle ADF binding.

■ **Navigation**   JSF provides an integrated controller that lets developers specify page navigation declaratively by defining named navigation cases. Navigation cases describe the page from which navigation starts, its destination, and the action or method that invokes this navigation.

■ **Lifecycle**   The lifecycle of markup-driven technologies such as JSP is request, compile, and render. Developers are not provided an option to interact with the lifecycle. In JSF, incoming requests are processed in six steps. Chapter 3 details the JSF lifecycle in the context of an ADF Fusion application.

Expression Language

Expression Language accesses *memory objects*, or objects exposed by the JSF configuration, using the following syntax:

```
#{<bean>.<method>}
```

The <bean> reference could be to a managed bean or the standard servlet scopes: request, session, and application. In Oracle ADF, additional scopes exist with `PageFlow`, `view`, and `backingBean`, which also are Expression Language accessible. The <method> referenced accesses either a pair of getter and setter methods if the access is from a component attribute that is not a listener, or a method if the reference is from a command component or a listener attribute to execute an action. Table 1-1 shows Expression Language examples for referencing values stored in the mentioned objects.

The context in which Expression Language is used allows developers to assume whether the accessed resource is a property or a method. The following access is to a property since the reference is from a component `value` attribute:

```
<af:inputText label="First Name" value="#{mybean.firstname}"/>
```

The access in the following is to an action listener, a method in a managed bean, since it is referenced from a listener attribute:

```
<af:inputText label="Label 1" id="it1" [...]
valueChangeListener="#{mybean.onValueChange}"/>
```

Expression Language expressions cannot take arguments, which sometimes is limiting to the developer and forces him or her to implement a work-around that may require coding.

Building Expressions in Oracle JDeveloper 11*g*

Oracle JDeveloper 11*g* provides an Expression Builder that helps you declaratively define expressions for JSF component attributes and ADF binding attributes. To open the Expression Builder, select a JSF component in the JDeveloper visual editor or the Structure window and open the property inspector. In the JDeveloper property inspector, click the arrow icon next to the property field—for example the *value* property—and choose Expression Builder or Method Builder. In the Expression Builder dialog, you can browse and select the object to which the attribute will be bound.

Expression	Accesses
`#{applicationScope.firstname}`	Accesses an attribute with the name "firstname" in the application scope. If the attribute doesn't exist on a first write attempt, it gets created. Because the scope is shared across application instances, it should not be used for attributes specific to a user instance.
`#{sessionScope.firstname}`	Accesses an attribute with the name "firstname" in the session scope. If the attribute doesn't exist on a first write attempt, it gets created. Because the scope lasts for the duration of the user session, it should not be used for page scoped attributes.
`#{requestScope.firstname}`	Accesses an attribute with the name "firstname" in the request scope. If the attribute doesn't exist on a first write attempt, it gets created.
`#{firstname}`	Searches the memory scopes for an attribute with the name "firstname" starting from the smallest scope. Since this expression is ambiguous, because there is no guarantee in which scope the attribute is found, we discourage its use.
`#{cookie.lastVisited.value}`	Searches the browser cookies for a cookie named lastVisited. Other cookie attributes that can be accessed from the Expression Language include domain, maxAge, path, and secure.
`#{param.firstname}`	The expression accesses a parameter on the request URL with the name "firstname".
`#{mybean.firstname}`	Accesses a bean property "firstname" that is exposed from a managed bean through its setter and getter methods. Managed beans have unique names within the JSF configuration so that their scope needn't be used within the expression for the standard request, session, and application servlet scopes.

TABLE 1-1 *Expression Language examples for accessing values in memory objects, managed beans, requests, and the Servlet context*

The Expression Builder in Oracle JDeveloper 11*g* exposes the following categories, as shown in Figure 1-9:

■ **ADF bindings** Contains references to the ADF binding layer of the current page and the ADF binding context, which exposes all configured binding definitions. Referencing the ADF binding layer in Expression Language is the key to simplicity in Fusion web application development.

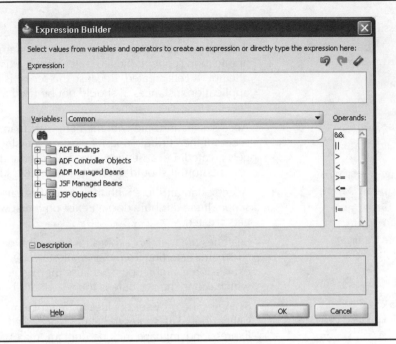

FIGURE 21-1   *Expression Builder in Oracle JDeveloper 11g*

- **ADF controller objects**   ADF task flows extend the JSF navigation model and expose a `ControllerContext` object for Expression Language access that allows developers to access information about the current displayed view, exceptions, the task flow URL for remote access, the train model, and much more. (ADF task flows are covered in detail in Chapters 4, 5, and 6.)

- **ADF managed beans**   ADF managed beans are configured in the task flow configuration, not in the standard JSF faces-config.xml file. The node contains subnodes that represent the available scopes, making it easy to prefix the bean reference with the name of the scope in which it is defined.

- **JSF managed beans**   Shows the managed beans that are defined in the faces-config.xml file, also categorized by the scopes in which they are defined.

- **JSP objects**   Allows access to the objects exposed by the JSF and servlet APIs. It exposes the `FacesContext` object and gives developers access to the servlet request header, cookies, servlet initialization parameters, and request parameters.

> **The Difference Between $ and # in Expression Language**
> Expression Language isn't new in Java EE and is used as well in JSP and the Java Standard Tag Library (JSTL). Though JSP 2.1 and JSF 1.2 use a unified Expression Language, the two uses are different. The most obvious difference between Expression Language used in JSP and JSF is that the Expression Language expression in JSP 2.1 starts with a $ character whereas Expression Language in JSF starts with a #. In addition to this visual difference, a behavior difference exists.
>
> Expression Language that uses the $ syntax executes the expressions *eagerly*, which means that the result is returned immediately when the page renders. Using the # syntax defers the expression evaluation to a point defined by the implementing technology. In general, JSF uses deferred Expression Language evaluation because of its multiple lifecycle phases in which events are handled. To ensure the model is prepared before the values are accessed by Expression Language, it must defer Expression Language evaluation until the appropriate point in the lifecycle.

Context and Application Objects

The JSF framework classes used most often by application developers are `FacesContext`, `ExternalContext`, and `Application`. These objects provide developers with access to the JSF framework, such as the access to the current displayed view and the Java EE environment—HTTP session, request, and response objects, plus many more.

- **FacesContext**   This static class provides the request context information for the application instance and grants developers access to application-wide settings, messages to be displayed to the end user, lifecycle methods, and the displayed view root. The following methods are most commonly used with the `FacesContext`:

    - `getCurrentInstance` returns a handle to the `FacesContext` instance.

    - `addMessage` is used to add a `FacesMessage` whose content is displayed to the user.

    - `getELContext` is one way of programmatically creating an Expression Language reference, which is accessible from the FacesContext.

    - `getViewRoot` returns `UIViewRoot`, the parent component of the page that allows developers to programmatically register lifecycle listeners, retrieve view root information, and traverse the page component structure.

    - `renderResponse` is used to short-circuit the request lifecycle to render the page response immediately. This method is used whenever developers don't want the model to be updated or all components on a page to be validated. (See Chapter 3 for more details.)

- **ExternalContext**   Wraps some of the external servlet functionality and information, such as the servlet context, cookie maps, the remote user, the request locale, page redirect, and much more. If developers don't find what they are looking for within the set of methods exposed on the `ExternalContext`, they can use a call to `getResponse` or to `getRequest` to return instances of `HttpServletResponse` and `HttpServletRequest` objects. The `ExternalContext` object is accessible from `FacesContext`.

■ **Application** Also exposed from the `FacesContext` instance and grants developers access to application-wide settings such as the `NavigationHandler` instance to invoke navigation from listeners and components that are not command components, the default locale setting, the list of supported locales, configured message bundles, and much more.

Configuration Files

JSF is configured through the faces-config.xml file and the web.xml file, which are both located in the WEB-INF directory of the web project.

faces-config.xml

The faces-config.xml file is the only configuration file available for all framework and application-specific configurations in JSF. Although multiple copies of faces-config.xml can be created in an application or added from the META-INF directory of an attached library, only one instance of the configuration exists at runtime with its content accessible from the `Application` instance exposed on the `FacesContext`. The faces-config.xml file is visually configured in Oracle JDeveloper 11*g*. To open the visual dialog, double-click the faces-config.xml file reference in the Application Navigator and choose the Overview or Diagram tab.

web.xml

The web.xml file contains the configuration of the `FacesServlet` class that is mapped to the /faces/ context path to serve all requests that include this path with the request. If a project uses multiple faces configuration files, the additional files are configured through the `javax.faces.CONFIG_FILES` context parameter.

Managed Beans and Backing Beans

Want to confuse a developer? Interview him or her about the difference between managed beans and backing beans in JSF. In short, backing beans are special uses of managed beans.

Managed Beans

A managed bean is a JavaBean that is configured in the faces-config.xml file and that is managed by the JSF framework. Managed beans are optional elements that can be used to hold presentation logic, navigation logic, and state; to execute Java methods; or to define event handlers. JSF instantiates managed beans when they are referenced from Expression Language. JavaBeans that should be configured as managed beans must have a no argument constructor. If a bean needs initialization parameters, these are configured through managed bean properties.

The following configuration example defines a managed bean `BrowseBean` with a managed property `bindingContainer` that makes the ADF binding layer available to the bean at runtime:

```
<managed-bean>
  <managed-bean-name>BrowseBean</managed-bean-name>
```

```
<managed-bean-class>
  adf.interactiv.view.BrowseBean
</managed-bean-class>
<managed-bean-scope>request</managed-bean-scope>
<managed-property>
  <property-name>bindingContainer</property-name>
  <property-class>
    oracle.binding.BindingContainer
  </property-class>
  <value>#{bindings}</value>
</managed-property>
</managed-bean>
```

The `BindingContainer` instance is referenced from the request scope bindings object using Expression Language. The `BrowseBean` JavaBean contains a property `bindingContainer` with its associated setter and getter methods.

```
import oracle.binding.BindingContainer;
...
BindingContainer bindingContainer = null;
public void setBindingContainer(BindingContainer bindingContainer) {
  this.bindingContainer = bindingContainer;
}
public BindingContainer getBindingContainer() {
  return bindingContainer;
}
```

As soon as the managed bean is instantiated by the JSF framework, the binding container becomes available to work with within the JavaBean.

Backing Beans

A backing bean is a special case of managed bean that has a one-to-one relationship to a single JSF page. Backing beans expose setter and getter methods for the component contained on the page. By default, Oracle JDeveloper does not create a backing bean when creating a new JSF page, because in many cases it is sufficient to work with a managed bean that is not strictly associated with a single page. Backing beans are good to use with pages, such as a login screen, for which you need to have Java access to the contained components. They produce unnecessary overhead if used with large and complex pages, unless you manually delete all the component references that are not used in your Java client programming.

To create backing beans for each new page in Oracle JDeveloper, you need to enable the Automatically Expose New UI Components in a New Managed Bean option that displays after expanding the Page Implementation header in the JSF page creation dialog.

To create backing beans for existing JSPs, open the JSF page in the visual editor and choose Tool | Design | Page Properties. Check the Auto Bind option and create or select an existing managed bean in which to store the UI component references and click OK.

While backing beans appear attractive to use, they do have a downside. The generated setter and getter entries in a backing bean are created for all components on a page, adding unnecessary weight to the size of the managed beans.

Backing Bean and Managed Bean Analogy

Here's a good analogy to help you remember the difference between backing and managed beans. A managed bean is like a backpack you use to carry your stuff when you go for a hike. You know how much your stuff weighs, so you carefully decide which items you want to put in the backpack and leave heavier items that you don't really need at home. A backing bean that gets generated by JDeveloper is like a backpack packed by your partner. Because he or she doesn't know what exactly you need for the trip—but he or she wants to make sure you have everything you need—everything goes into that backpack. You then must carry all that weight as you hike over the hills. Because generating a backing bean creates setter and getter methods for all components on a page, including those you don't use in your Java programming, the backing bean backpack grows big and heavy. If you use managed beans instead, you are packing the bean backpack yourself with better control over its weight.

Managed Bean Scopes

Managed beans have a scope, which is the lifetime between their instantiation by the JSF framework and their dismissal for garbage collection. As a rule of thumb, always use the smallest managed bean scope possible. The standard scopes are as follows:

- **None**   The managed bean does not store any state and is released immediately. Use beans in no scope for helper classes that don't need to keep any memory.

- **Request**   The managed bean lives for the duration of a request and stores its internal state until the request completes. This is the only scope available for backing beans.

- **Session**   The managed bean lives until the user session is invalidated or expires. This scope should be used carefully only for beans that carry information of use anywhere in the application. For example, a bean holding user information would be a good candidate for the session scope.

- **Application**   The managed bean is available to all instances of an application. This scope could be used to define static lists of data used by all instances.

Managed beans can reference other managed beans using managed properties with the ADF binding reference example. The limitation for this reference is that a managed bean cannot have a managed bean property referencing a bean of a smaller scope. This means that a bean in request scope can reference a bean in session scope, but a bean in session scope cannot reference a bean in request scope. The exceptions to this rule are beans with no scope, which can be accessed from all beans scopes.

Creating Managed Beans in Oracle JDeveloper

In Oracle JDeveloper, you can create and configure managed beans in the faces-config.xml file or an ADF task flow configuration file in one of the following ways:

- Double-click a command component such as a button or link within the visual page editor. This opens the dialog where you can create and configure a managed bean.

■ Select the Edit option in the context menu of an action or listener property, such as `ValueChangeListener` or `ActionListener`, in the JDeveloper Property Inspector. This also opens a dialog where you can configure the managed bean.

■ Create a JavaBean by choosing File | New to open the new gallery. Open the faces-config.xml file or ADF task flow configuration to register the bean class manually as a managed bean.

■ Select the faces-config.xml file or the task flow configuration XML file, for example adfc-config.xml, in the Oracle JDeveloper Application Navigator and open the Structure window (CTRL-SHIFT-S). Select the root node and choose FacesConfig | managed-bean | Insert or Task Flow | ADF Task Flow | Managed Bean | Insert based on the selected configuration file.

■ For Oracle task flows only, open the visual Task Flow diagrammer and drag and drop the managed-bean entry from the Source Elements category of the JDeveloper Component palette (CTRL-SHIFT-P) into it.

Recommended best practice for working with managed beans is to implement `java.io.Serializable` when creating the bean classes. Another good practice to follow is to extend a managed bean class from a base class, which allows you to add common methods easily.

Managed Beans That Are Not Beans

Instances of `java.util.HashMap` can be configured as a managed bean to provide a static list of values to a managed bean instance:

```
<managed-bean>
   <managed-bean-name>bookmarks</managed-bean-name>
   <managed-bean-class>java.util.HashMap</managed-bean-class>
   <managed-bean-scope>application</managed-bean-scope>
   <map-entries>
     <map-entry>
       <key>JDeveloperForum</key>
       <value>http://forums.oracle.com/forums/forum.jspa?forumID=83</value>
     </map-entry>
     <map-entry>
       <key>JDeveloperHome</key>
        <value>http://otn.oracle.com/products/jdev</value>
     </map-entry>
   </map-entries>
</managed-bean>
```

This creates a managed bean as an instance of `HashMap` that can be accessed from Java and Expression Language.

```
#{bookmarks['JDeveloperForum']};
```

But didn't we say that Expression Language cannot have arguments? Yes, we did. But here's an exception to the rule, which is for managed beans that are instances of `HashMap` and for resource bundles. In the `HashMap` example shown above, the expression resolves to `bookmarks.get("JDeveloperForum")` at runtime.

NOTE
Developers sometimes create subclasses of HashMap *and override the* get() *method to do something different from* HashMap*'s default behavior. This works around the existing limitation in Expression Language to not allow arguments.*

Events

The JSF event model is based on JavaBeans events, where events are represented by specific classes that pass information about the event to interested listener components. Two types of events are used in JSF: component events and lifecycle events.

Component Events

Component events are sent to the server to notify interested listeners about a user interaction such as a button click or value change. Input components, for example, expose a valueChangeListener attribute for developers to register a Java listener to handle the event:

```
<h:inputText id="lastname"
    valueChangeListener="#{EmployeesBacking.onLastNameValueChange}"/>
```

The input text component references a managed bean method from its valueChangeListener attribute. This registers the managed bean method as an event listener that is notified whenever the submitted component value differs from the previously displayed value. The managed bean method has the following signature:

```
public void onLastNameValueChange(ValueChangeEvent valueChangeEvent) {
    // Add event code here...
}
```

The method receives an instance of the ValueChangeEvent object that contains information about the new value, the old value, and the UI component instance that raised the event. The method code can now handle the event or queue the event for processing later during the request lifecycle. If the immediate attribute of the input text component is set to true, then the event is raised early in the request lifecycle, allowing developers to handle it and, if needed, prevent further processing of the request by a call to renderResponse on the FacesContext.

Another option to add a value change listener is to write a custom Java class that implements the javax.faces.event.ValueChangeListener interface and to reference it by its absolute package and class name from the type attribute in an f:valueChangeListener tag. To use the ValueChangeListener tag, add it as a child component to the input component about which value change the class should receive a notification. The ValueChangeListener interface defines a single method processValueChange that takes the ValueChangeEvent object as an input argument.

Navigation

Navigation in JSF is defined in the form of navigation rules stored in the faces-config.xml file. As shown in Figure 1-10, page navigation rules in Oracle JDeveloper are composed declaratively by linking together two page references with a JSF navigation-case component from the Component palette. Any edits that are performed in the visual diagrammer, the Property Inspector, or the structure window are written as metadata in the faces-config.xml file.

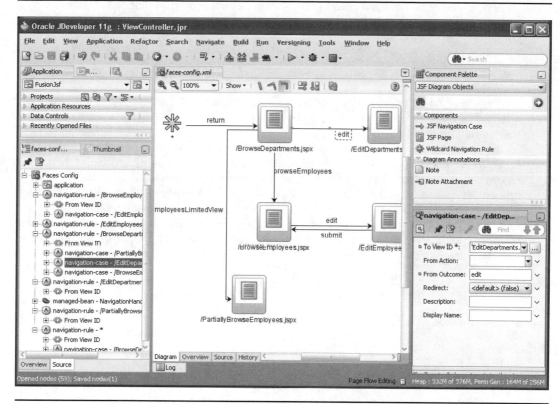

FIGURE 1-10   *Visual editing support for JSF navigation rules in JDeveloper 11g*

This navigation rule is defined for the BrowseDepartments.jspx page and contains two navigation cases:

```
<navigation-rule>
  <from-view-id>/BrowseDepartments.jspx</from-view-id>
    <navigation-case>
     <from-outcome>employeesLimitedView</from-outcome>
     <to-view-id>/PartiallyBrowseEmployees.jspx</to-view-id>
  </navigation-case>
  <navigation-case>
    <from-action>
      #{NavigationHandlerBean.accessBrowseEmployees}
    </from-action>
    <from-outcome>browseEmployees</from-outcome>
      <to-view-id>/BrowseEmployees.jspx</to-view-id>
  </navigation-case>
</navigation-rule>
```

If the outcome of a command component, such as a button or link click, matches the `browseEmployees` or `employeesLimitedView` outcome, JSF routes the request to the configured destination page:

```
<af:commandButton text="BrowseEmployees"
                  action=" employeesLimitedView"/>
```

Instead of hard-coding the action string, The `af:commandButton` action attribute may also reference a managed bean method that dynamically returns a valid outcome strings to perform routing decisions in Java.

Navigation case may use the "from-action" element in addition to or instead of the "from-outcome" element to configure navigation, as shown in the preceding example. If the from-action element is used without a from-outcome element, then any action string returned from the referenced managed bean method performs navigation to the defined destination. If the from-outcome element is included in addition, as shown in the preceding example, navigation is performed only if the returned method outcome is `browseEmployees`. Using the from-action element allows developers to define multiple navigation cases with the same outcome name. The use of the "from-action" element is not a common pattern in Fusion application development.

```
<af:commandButton text="BrowseEmployees"
                  action="#{EmployeesBean.accessBrowseEmployees}"/>
```

The method signature of the referenced bean looks like this:

```
public String accessBrowseEmployees(){
    if (…){
      return "employeesLimitedView";
    }
    else{
      return "browseEmployees";
    }
}
```

The lookup order in which JSF performs navigation based on the existence of the from-action and from-outcome elements is as follows:

1. Elements specifying both from-action and from-outcome
2. Elements specifying only from-outcome
3. Elements specifying only from-action

If no navigation case outcome matches the action string defined on a command component or returned by a managed bean method, the navigation is returned to the same page.

A special navigation case is the use of wildcards that can be accessed from any page that matches to the defined wildcard pattern. Wildcards are useful for navigation that needs to be defined on many pages, such as a logout or home command that navigates the request to a logout page or the home page. Here's an example:

```
<navigation-rule>
   <from-view-id>*</from-view-id>
     <navigation-case>
```

```
      <from-outcome>return</from-outcome>
      <to-view-id>/BrowseDepartments.jspx</to-view-id>
    </navigation-case>
  </navigation-rule>
```

NOTE
ADF task flows that you use when building ADF Fusion web applications do not use the faces-config.xml file to define the navigation but use adfc-config.xml instead. Chapters 4 and 5 discuss ADF task flows and how to work with them.

ADF Faces Rich Client for Quick Learners

Oracle ADF Faces RC is the chosen JSF-based view layer technology for Oracle Fusion. It provides more than 150 high-end Ajax-enabled UI components and an infrastructure that allows application developers to build future-safe rich internet applications. ADF Faces RC shields developers from the complexity that exists in Ajax for the orchestration of JavaScript, Cascading Style Sheets (CSS), Dynamic HyperText Markup Language (DHTML), and XML to render cross-browser functional, highly interactive and dynamic web user interfaces. Oracle fusion developers work with a single API, which is the JSF programming interface.

In addition to more than 150 Ajax-enabled JSF UI and graphical data visualization components and operations, ADF Faces also contains a client-side programming model and lifecycle that is similar to the JSF model but executes independently of the server. For example, field validation configured on a component is executed on the client first, and if it doesn't pass this validation, not request is sent to the server.

Using the public JavaScript API in ADF Faces, developers can search and manipulate components displayed on the client without needing to program to the browser Document Object Model (DOM), which is less error-prone and also simplifies cross-platform application development. Using the ADF Faces client framework, application developers call getter and setter methods on client objects to read and write component properties from JavaScript. Events can be received and queued on the client, with the ability to call server side managed bean methods directly from JavaScript. Any state change that is applied to a component on the client is automatically synchronized back to the server to ensure a consistent client and server state.

A list of the non UI functionality provided by the ADF Faces RC framework that simplify the work of a Rich Internet Application developer includes the following:

- **Drag-and-drop framework**   Tag library elements and listeners that declaratively implement drag-and-drop functionality for ADF Faces web applications (see Chapter 14).

- **Dialog and popup framework**   JSF components that render child components in lightweight dialogs with client- and server-side listeners to send notification about the launch and close event. These dialogs are also used to display context menus on tables and other components (see Chapter 10).

- **Partial page rendering (PPR)**   UI components are refreshed without page reload. PPR is the integrated behavior of components such as tree, table, accordion, panel splitter, and many more. Beside of the integrated component behavior, all components can be declaratively configured to become a partial event source and target, which means they can trigger other components to refresh or are refreshed in response to published events of other components. Using PPR in combination with the ADF binding layer automatically refreshes all dependent components based on data changes in the underlying iterator binding.

- **Active Data Service (ADS)**   Push mechanism that refreshes ADF Faces components based on server-side events (see Chapter 20).

- **JavaScript client API**   The ADF Faces RC architecture has a server side and a client side. The client-side framework consists of internal and public JavaScript objects and interfaces that developers optionally use to program client-side functionality (see Chapter 19).

- **Skinning**   Look and feel customization framework that exposes specific CSS selectors on the ADF Faces component renderers for developers to change the default look and feel at runtime without any code changes required in the application (see Chapter 16).

- **ADF binding**   ADF Faces uses a specific set of binding classes to enable ADF binding as the component model and to expose its functionality through Expression Language. For example, the ADF Faces tree component ADF uses the `FacesCtrlHierBinding` class that extends the ADF `JUCtrlHierBinding` base binding class. It exposes an additional `getTreeModel` method that returns an instance of Apache Trinidad `TreeModel` class as the tree component model. Similar, operation and method bindings are exposed through the `FacesCtrlActionBinding` class.

Maturity Through History

The Oracle ADF Faces RC components have their origin in Oracle User Interface XML (UIX). Oracle first released UIX in 2002 for its external and internal customers to build web applications that by this time already made use of partial page rendering, a behavior that today is described as an Ajax behavior pattern. Shortly after JSF became a Java EE standard in 2004, Oracle released more than 100 JSF components under the ADF Faces branding. After donating the ADF Faces components to the Apache open source community, where they have been further developed as part of the MyFaces Trinidad project, Oracle started a new Ajax JSF component project called ADF Faces Rich Client. The base component technology of ADF Faces RC is Apache Trinidad, which from an Oracle perspective is a great return of open source investment.

Two More Context Classes

Oracle ADF Faces provides two context objects in addition to the default JSF context objects.

The `RequestContext` object is defined by the Apache Trinidad component framework that is the basis of ADF Faces RC components. The context object is accessible from Expression Language, using `#{requestContext.<method>}`, and Java, using `RequestContext.getCurrentInstance()`. The `RequestContext` allows developers to do the following:

- Launch pages in external browser window dialogs

- Detect partial page requests

- Get information about the client, such as browser name, and type of device, such as browser, mobile, or phone

- Programmatically register components as partial targets, which is useful when the component needs to be refreshed at the end of a managed bean method execution

- Programmatically add partial listeners to a component and notify interested listeners about events

- Get a handle to the help provider that is configured for providing context-sensitive help

- Determine whether a request is an initial page request or a postback request

- Access the page flow scope, which is a scope with a length between request scope and session scope that is available for pages launched in dialogs and bounded task flows, a concept that is introduced in Chapter 4

The `AdfFacesContext` object mirrors the `RequestContext` object, but adds ADF Faces specific APIs, such as access to the ADF Faces view scope. All public methods of the `RequestContext` are accessible through the `AdfFacesContext` object as well. The `AdfFacesContext` object is accessible from Expression Language, using `#{adfFacesContext.<method>}`, and from Java, using a call to `AdfFacesContext.getCurrentInstance()`.

Configuration

ADF Faces is configured automatically when you choose the ADF Faces Technology Scope in the Oracle JDeveloper project properties, or when you are building a new application based on the Fusion Web Application (ADF) template.

The three configuration files of interest are web.xml, trinidad-config.xml, and trinidad-skins.xml.

web.xml

The web.xml file contains the configuration of the Trinidad servlet and resource filter mapping to the JSF `FacesServlet`. The Trinidad servlet filter initializes ADF Faces RC for each incoming request and sets the `RequestContext` object. Additional context parameters are available for the application developer to set and configure. Context parameters are added to the web.xml file as a child of the "web-app" element.

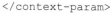

```
<context-param>
    <param-name>parameter<param-name>
    <param-value>value</param-value>
</context-param>
```

NOTE
A list and description of all context parameters is printed in Appendix A of the Oracle documentation "Oracle Fusion Middleware Web User Interface Developer's Guide for Oracle Application Development Framework 11g Release 1."

trinidad-config.xml

The trinidad-config.xml file is the main ADF Faces configuration file and exists in the WEB-INF directory of the ADF Faces view project. By default, the only configuration that exists in this file is the skin family string that determines the application look and feel.

NOTE
The default Oracle look and feel defined for ADF Faces RC applications is "fusion." An additional look and feel that is packaged with ADF Faces RC is "blafplus-rich." The screenshots of the examples in this book use the blafplus-rich look and feel.

NOTE
A list and description of parameters is printed in Appendix A of the Oracle documentation "Oracle Fusion Middleware Web User Interface Developer's Guide for Oracle Application Development Framework 11g Release 1."

All configurations in the trinidad-config.xml file are exposed to Expression Language and Java through the `AdfFacesContext` and the `RequestContext` object.

trinidad-skins.xml

ADF Faces allows developers to define the application look and feel in external CSS files. The trinidad-skins.xml file acts as the registration of custom skin definitions, including the CSS file reference, skin family name definitions, and skin inheritance references. Chapter 16 covers skinning and the settings of the trinidad-skins.xml file in great depth.

components

ADF Faces Components are Java EE– and JSF-compliant and are not dependent on Oracle Fusion Middleware or Oracle JDeveloper 11*g*.

Working with ADF Faces Components

Fusion web application developers add ADF Faces components declaratively at design time using the ADF Faces JSP tag library, or programmatically at runtime, by creating and adding a Java object instance of the component.

Declarative Development   Dragging-and-dropping an ADF Faces component from the Oracle JDeveloper Component palette to a JSP configures the `af` XML namespace as an attribute of the `jsp:root` element:

```
xmlns:af=http://xmlns.oracle.com/adf/faces/rich
```

With this namespace definition, all component markup elements that start with *af:* are handled by the ADF Faces RC tag library. For example, an ADF Faces `InputText` component is added as af: inputText to the JSF page source, whereas a `command button` shows as af:`commandButton`. Developers working with the WYSIWYG visual editing environment aren't exposed to the tag elements and instead see the rendered component output.

ADF Faces components are organized in three categories:

■ **Common component**   Contains all ADF Faces components that have a visual representation for the user to read and input data, invoke actions and navigation, or display dialogs and menus.

■ **Layout**   Layout development in JSF is through the nesting of panel components that each has a specific behavior regarding how child components are arranged on a page and where child components can be added. The layout category shows a list of all ADF Faces layout components.

■ **Operations**   Contains all operational, nonvisual components that can be used as a child of a visual component. Components include validators, converters, and action listeners.

Programming   At runtime, every ADF Faces component on a page has a JavaBean instance representation that is created by the ADF Faces JSP tag library. To add and bind components, this instance can be created dynamically in Java. All ADF Faces RC component classes start with `Rich`, so that an `InputText` component has a class of `RichInputText` and a `Table` has a component class of `RichTable`.

In JSF, components can be added as the direct child of a parent component or added to the facet of a component. To create a command button at runtime, you use the following code:

```
RichCommandButton button = new RichCommandButton();
button.setText("Delete");
[...]
panelGroup.getChildren().add(button);
```

ADF Faces Rich Client Tag Documentation   The full Oracle ADF Faces tag documentation is available online and contains a complete description of component attributes, facets, and useful information about how to work with the component. To access the tag documentation, go to http://otn.oracle.com and choose Documentation | JDeveloper. Click the "Oracle Fusion Middleware API References" link to navigate to the API reference documents site, which contains a reference to "Oracle ADF Faces Tag Reference."

ADF Component Binding

ADF Faces components are ADF binding–aware, in that the ADF Faces UI framework provides specific binding classes that allow UI components to bind directly to ADF. ADF Faces component expressions that bind to ADF have the following form:

```
#{bindings.<binding entry>.<property>}
```

The `<binding entry>` corresponds to a binding entry in the ADF page binding, the *<page>*PageDef.xml file. The type of the `<binding entry>` can be list, action, attribute, tree, or others and correspond to a specific Faces binding class. The `<property>` can be a method or a property exposed on the ADF Faces binding class.

As shown in Figure 1-7, all ADF Faces binding classes are contained in a private package, which means that though they are public classes, developers are not supposed to use them directly but use the generic ADF binding classes instead. Developers that need to access ADF Faces binding-specific methods from Java can do this using Expression Language, and we provide code examples in Chapter 9 when we discuss UI development with the ADF Faces Tree, Table, and TreeTable components. The following table associates the Faces control binding class with the generic ADF binding class and where it is used.

Faces Binding Class	Extended ADF Class	Usage
FacesCtrlAttrsBinding	JUCtrlAttrsBinding	Accesses attribute bindings in the pageDef file
FacesCtrlCalendarBinding	JUCtrlHierBinding	Represents the binding instance for ADF Calendar component. It provides CalendarModel and CalendarActivity instances for the Calendar component
FacesCtrlHierBinding	JUCtrlHierBinding	Implements the ADF Faces Component tree model interface to bind the tree component to the ADF tree binding
FacesCtrlHierNodeBinding	JUCtrlHierNodeBinding	Tree node binding object that adds functionality to the base binding class
FacesCtrlActionBinding	JUCtrlActionBinding	FacesCtrlActionBinding binds ADF Faces action components to ADF actions and methods that are invoked from Expression Language through an exposed "execute" method
FacesCtrlListBinding	JUCtrlListBinding	Provides access to the ADF list binding for SelectChoice Faces components
FacesCtrlLOVBinding	JUCtrlListBinding	Provides the model implementation for LOV components
FacesCtrlSearchBinding	JUFormBinding	Used to build the model for the af:query component

NOTE
Working with the ADF binding classes from Java is an advanced topic that developers who start with ADF do not need to know. In general, we recommend the use of declarative solutions over code-centric solutions because they are easier to maintain and upgrade.

Partial Page Rendering

Partial page rendering (PPR), or partial refresh, is a mechanism in ADF Faces to notify components about data change events or other triggering events so they can refresh their display without redrawing the full page. Two main Ajax patterns are implemented with PPR: single-component refresh and cross-component refresh.

Single-component refresh functionality is available on many ADF Faces components, such as the ADF Faces table component. The table component provides built-in partial refresh functionality that allows users to scroll over displayed rows, to sort the table by a click on the column headers, to change the table column order, and to mark a row or several rows as selected.

Cross-component refresh is implemented declaratively or programmatically in that an ADF Faces RC component is registered as a partial listener of another component. The following component attributes are used to initiate a cross-component partial page event to be triggered by a component:

- **autoSubmit**   When the `autoSubmit` attribute is set on an input component such as `af:inputText` or `af:selectManyListbox`, the component automatically submits the enclosing form in response to an event such as `ValueChangeEvent`. The submit is issued as a partial submit and doesn't lead to a page reload.

- **partialSubmit**   When the `partialSubmit` attribute of a command component is set to true, the page partially submits the form when the button or link is clicked. A partial submits sends an `ActionEvent` to the server without reloading the page.

To implement partial component refresh, your choices range from declarative, to automatic and programmatic.

Declarative PPR

ADF Faces components on a page can be declaratively configured to receive partial refresh notification when an action is performed on another component. For example, selecting a value in a select box should refresh a dependent list box to show a changed list of data. To configure a UI component on a page declaratively to refresh in response to a change of another, open the Property Inspector on the component that should receive the event notification and navigate to the `PartialTriggers` property. Choose Edit from the menu option that displays when you click the arrow button to the right to select the UI component that should send the change notification.

Automatic PPR Initiated by the ADF Binding Layer

In Oracle JDeveloper 11g, the change event policy feature can be used to refresh UI components automatically that are bound to an ADF binding when data has changed in the model layer. To use this feature, you set the `ChangeEventPolicy` property of the ADF iterator binding and the attribute bindings to ppr, which also is the default setting.

With the ADF Faces page open in Oracle JDeveloper, select the Bindings tab at the bottom of the visual editor or the source editor. In the Executables section, select the iterator that should refresh its bound UI components when changed. Open the Property Inspector if not open and navigate to the `ChangeEventPolicy property` in the advanced section and set its value to ppr.

In Oracle JDeveloper 11g R1, the automatic PPR functionality is implemented on the following ADF Faces binding objects:

- `FacesCtrlAttrsBinding`

- `FacesCtrlLOVBinding`

- `FacesCtrlListBinding`

- `FacesCtrlHierBinding`

Programmatic PPR

In ADF Faces, UI components can be refreshed programmatically through Java. For example, a managed bean method can be set up to listen and respond to events, such as `ValueChangeEvent`, on the component that should trigger the partial refresh on another component. To partially refresh a referenced component based on an action in the source component, the managed bean executes code like this:

```
AdfFacesContext adfFacesContext = AdfFacesContext.getCurrentInstance();
adfFacesContext.addPartialTargets(<target component instance>);
```

Summary

The Oracle ADF has become a cornerstone of Oracle Fusion Middleware. ADF is built on Java EE and SOA standards and designed to simplify web application development in Java EE. The Oracle Fusion development platform is a technology choice within ADF used to build Oracle's next generation of standard business software. It includes the ADF binding, ADF Business Components, and ADF Faces Rich Client frameworks, which are in the focus of this book. When working with Oracle ADF, we recommend you use declarative programming over code-centric programming when possible. We believe, however, that good developers need to understand both declarative and code-centric programming so they can identify the best solution to a problem.

If you ask us for a single recommendation of best practices to apply in all of your ADF development projects, it is to *keep the layers separated*! This means that at any time, the business service layer should not have dependencies on the view or binding layer and the view layer should not be dependent on business services classes other than domain types. Use the view layer for UI logic and the business service for your business logic.

CHAPTER
2

Oracle Application Development Framework (ADF)

ADF binding page definition (PageDef) files are binding containers at runtime.

he ADF model architecture defines the physical connection that a UI component has to its underlying business service. For example, if a page of an application should provide input text fields that are used to insert a new value in a row of the database, as shown in Figure 2-1, and there is a clean separation of business and view logic, the following artifacts should be created:

1. A *data model*, which is also referred to as the business service, should be built on top of the database to handle the mapping from database columns and rows to Java objects and attributes, as well as the transactional control for create, read, update, and delete (CRUD) operations. In Fusion applications, this data model layer is built using ADF Business Components, but you might also use Java classes, Web Services, or Enterprise JavaBeans (EJB) for the data model.

2. *UI components* should allow the user to enter data in a web application. In a Fusion application (and indeed the remainder of this book), ADF Faces Rich Client components are used.

3. A *binding mechanism* should be in place to bind the UI components in number 2 to the data model in number 1. This can be done using JavaBeans. Using JavaBeans, however, requires that you build a data access layer from scratch; the transactional elements (such as the Create and Commit buttons shown in Figure 2-1) must be coded so that they access from the data model, and accessors for the attributes of the input form (such as DepartmentId and DepartmentName) must be coded to accept the new values and pass these values on to the data model for further processing. Additionally, an accessor for the row (Departments) must be coded to set the row currency appropriately so that the application can present a new row to the user for insertion.

As it turns out, the functions discussed in number 3 are typical of all Model-View-Controller (MVC)–based applications, where the data model is defined separately from the view layer. As a result of years of experience in creating data-bound MVC applications, Oracle developers created the ADF model (ADFm) framework to facilitate an easier way of defining these common functions.

In Fusion applications, the ADFm framework is used to bind UI components to the underlying data model, because it enables the bindings to be created declaratively, thereby greatly reducing the amount of Java code necessary to create an application. The ADFm framework also encourages reuse, because JavaBeans are not created haphazardly each time a developer needs access to a row or attribute. Best practices are built into the framework so that web application developers are set up for success the moment they start using ADF, rather than attempting to implement best practices as the need for new accessor classes arises.

---

* DepartmentId	[ ]
* DepartmentName	[ ]
ManagerId	[ ]
LocationId	[ ]
	[Create] [Commit]

FIGURE 2-1   *A web application input form for inserting a row into a database*

As outlined in Chapter 1, ADFm is an implementation of JSR-227 and provides a layer of abstraction to connect any UI technology to any backend data service. In Fusion applications, the UI technology is ADF Faces and the backend data services are largely ADF Business Components (ADF BC), but developers can mix and match technologies on either side of the ADF model layer to build applications declaratively.

The ADF Model Framework

The ADF model consists of two key artifacts: data controls and data bindings. Both artifacts are metadata driven and are created and maintained by JDeveloper as XML files. The metadata contained in these files works together at runtime to access the underlying data model and to bind the attribute, row, and transactional controls from a business service to corresponding UI components. Application developers typically interact with these files via declarative means, such as using the Property Inspector or drag-and-drop facilities within the integrated development environment (IDE). ADF BC application modules are automatically exposed as data controls and are rarely modified by UI developers. Data binding files, however, are unique to the type of data being displayed and the types of controls that are displaying the data (such as an input text field, a drop-down list, or a button), and they are frequently modified to augment functionality according to a particular page's needs.

ADF Data Controls

As described in Chapter 1, the Data Control palette in JDeveloper is populated from an ADF BC application module (among other types of business services). This includes the attributes, collections, client methods, and built-in operations of collections, as well as client methods and built-in operations of the application module. The Data Control palette is synchronized with the application module so that if a view object or client method is exposed to the client via that application module, the Data Control palette will reflect the change upon refreshing the Data Control palette in JDeveloper. For other business service types, a separate file (.dcx) is used to store the service description, so when the service is created or updated, the Create Data Control option from the context menu of a Java class, web service, or EJB session bean must be used to create and modify the .dcx file. The .dcx file that is generated contains a unique entry for each service type, which describes the factory for the service access as well as object types included in the service methods and collections.

ADF data controls consist of an XML definition that describes the control. For ADF BC, this is the application module XML file. For non-ADF business services, an XML definition file is created for the service when the Create Data Control option is selected from the context menu. For example, in the case of an EJB session bean backed by Java Persistence API (JPA) entities, an XML definition file would be created for each entity class. Note that the remainder of this chapter (and most of the rest of this book) focuses on ADF BC data controls, since the Fusion development stack promotes the use of ADF Business Components.

Creating ADF Bindings

ADF bindings are the glue between the data controls; they provide an abstraction to the implementation internals of business services and the UI component model. ADF bindings can be created in several ways. The most direct way uses drag-and-drop, where a UI developer inspects the Data Control palette for the data control that is required (such as DepartmentId) and drags the control from the Data Control palette onto the visual editor or Structure window in the appropriate location on the page. Bindings may also be created manually, as discussed later in this section.

Drag-and-Drop Data Bindings

When you drag an object from the Data Control palette onto a page, several factors determine what happens at design time. The first factor depends on the type of page the object is dropped onto. Next, in the case of a .jsp or .jspx page, the JavaServer Pages (JSP) libraries included in the project are introspected. If the project includes the JSP libraries but not the ADF Faces component libraries, only JSP components will be available in the Create menu that appears when dropping components onto a page. For applications created using the Fusion application template, ADF Faces libraries will be included in the UI project, so the Create menu will display the common ADF Faces components that are appropriate for the type of control, as shown in Figure 2-2.

NOTE
To include JSF components in the Create menu, as well as ADF Faces components, modify the ADF View Settings in the project properties to enable Include JSF HTML Widgets. In most cases, however, only the ADF Faces components are required.

Finally, templates can be created to determine how certain types of components are added to a page. Use the _creator_configuration.xml file in the /adfdt/lib/adf-faces-databinding-dt-core.jar JAR file to customize the code that is added to a page upon drag-and-drop from the Data Control Palette.

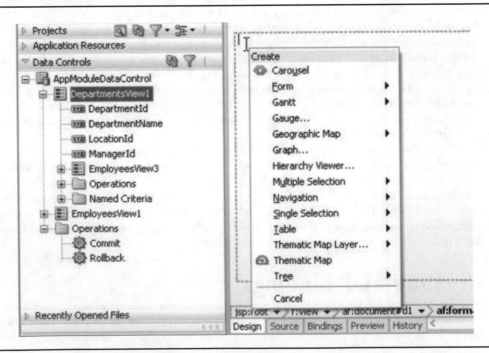

FIGURE 2-2 *Create menu for ADF*

As shown in Figure 2-2, the drag-and-drop operation is performed by dragging an attribute, collection, operation, or method from the Data Control palette and dropping it onto the page, typically onto the visual editor. The Create menu is unique for each type of component, because JDeveloper introspects the XML definition for the object that is being dropped to determine what type of element it is (collection, attribute, or method).

Selecting a value from the Create menu performs two separate actions. First, the bindings template is used to generate the correct tags to add to the page. If the binding is a simple type, such as an output text field for an attribute, the `af:outputText` tag is added to the page without further input from the developer. If the binding is more complex, a dialog specific to the type of binding appears so that the developer can define the types of components used for the attributes. For example, selecting an ADF Form in the Create menu launches an Edit Form Fields dialog that allows the developer to define which types of input components are used for each attribute in the dialog, their order of appearance, and whether or not navigation controls and/or a submit button should be created along with the form binding, as shown in Figure 2-3.

Once the bindings are defined, the tags representing the UI components are added to the page and the bindings for the components are created. Thus, dragging a view object collection from the Data Control palette and dropping it onto the page editor as an ADF input form brings three parts of the ADF technology stack together: ADF BC represented by the view object, ADF Faces represented by the `af:` components that are created on the page, and ADF data controls and bindings that are used to bind the ADF Faces components to the underlying service via Expression Language. This is best demonstrated in the following code that is generated by

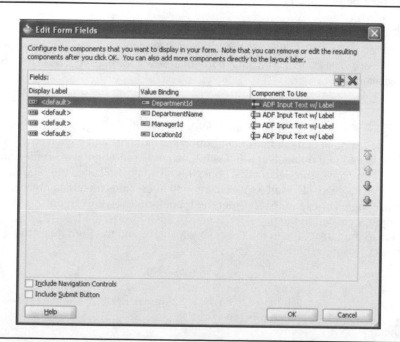

FIGURE 2-3 *Defining components in the Edit Form Fields dialog*

JDeveloper when the `DepartmentId` attribute from the `DepartmentsView` data collection is dropped onto the visual editor and `ADF Input Text` is selected from the Create menu:

```
<af:inputText value="#{bindings.DepartmentId.inputValue}"
  label="#{bindings.DepartmentId.hints.label}"
  required="#{bindings.DepartmentId.hints.mandatory}"
  columns="#{bindings.DepartmentId.hints.displayWidth}"
  maximumLength="#{bindings.DepartmentId.hints.precision}"
  shortDesc="#{bindings.DepartmentId.hints.tooltip}" id="it4">
  <f:validator binding="#{bindings.DepartmentId.validator}"/>
  <af:convertNumber groupingUsed="false"
    pattern="#{bindings.DepartmentId.format}"/>
</af:inputText>
```

It is important to point out a few aspects of this code listing. First, three UI components are created for a simple input field: `af:inputText`, `f:validator`, and `af:convertNumber`. Each of these components is discussed throughout the rest of this book, but what this demonstrates here is that the ADF framework is especially good at determining all the ancillary components that should accompany a particular component, and it includes these components when a component is dropped onto the page. Secondly, by using the ADF Model framework, a great deal of coding was saved to implement just this one input text field. At this point in development, the framework has created all the necessary infrastructure to access the current row of the `DepartmentsView` data model object, display the current value of the `DepartmentId` attribute, and ensure that any new value submitted to the data model adheres to the business logic defined in the Departments entity object. Lastly, most of the attributes of the components are set using Expression Language that points to the `bindings` object, which is the subject of the remainder of this chapter.

The Page Definition File

The following Expression Language binds the ADF Faces component to an attribute value in the current row of a data collection from a particular data control. The `bindings` object refers to the binding container:

```
<af:inputText value="#{bindings.DepartmentId.inputValue}" />
```

A binding container is created for a page's binding definition file. Thus, each page, page fragment, or template that contains data-bound components will have its own binding container definition, stored in the PageDef file. Essentially, ADF binding PageDef files are binding containers at runtime. Throughout this book, this file might be called the *bindings* file, or simply, the *PageDef*. The PageDef file is an XML document that contains metadata regarding the bindings for a particular page. For example, consider the input form shown in Figure 2-1. When the code in the example is created in the page, three entries are added to the `DataBindings.cpx` file. The first two map the `.JSPX` file to the PageDef via an `id`, and the third maps the data control usages for a project, as shown here:

```
<?xml version="1.0" encoding="UTF-8" ?>
<Application xmlns=http://xmlns.oracle.com/adfm/application
  version="11.1.1…" id="DataBindings" SeparateXMLFiles="false"
  Package="view" ClientType="Generic">
  <pageMap>
    <page path="/mypage.jspx" usageId="view_mypagePageDef"/>
```

```
    </pageMap>
    <pageDefinitionUsages>
      <page id="view_mypagePageDef" path="view.pageDefs.mypagePageDef"/>
    </pageDefinitionUsages>
    <dataControlUsages>
      <BC4JDataControl id="AppModuleDataControl" Package="model"
      FactoryClass="oracle.adf.model.bc4j.DataControlFactoryImpl"
      SupportsTransactions="true" SupportsFindMode="true"
      SupportsRangesize="true" SupportsResetState="true"
      SupportsSortCollection="true" Configuration="AppModuleLocal"
      syncMode="Immediate"
      xmlns="http://xmlns.oracle.com/adfm/datacontrol"/>
    </dataControlUsages>
</Application>
```

Note that the `BC4JDataControl` element is added only the first time that a data control object (attribute, collection, operation, or method) is dropped onto a page in the project. Additionally, the `pageMap` and `pageDefinitionUsages` elements are created only the first time a data control object is dropped onto a particular page.

The `DataBindings.cpx` file is maintained automatically by the framework and is generally not modified by developers. However, it is important that you understand the contents of this file for debugging purposes, or if a PageDef file is reused so that multiple `JSPX` pages refer to a single PageDef `usageId`.

The PageDef file, on the other hand, is frequently modified by developers, albeit via declarative means. The PageDef in this example (`mypagePageDef.xml`) contains the following XML:

```
<?xml version="1.0" encoding="UTF-8" ?>
<pageDefinition xmlns=http://xmlns.oracle.com/adfm/uimodel
   version="11.1.1…" id="mypagePageDef" Package="view.pageDefs">
   <parameters/>
   <executables>
     <variableIterator id="variables"/>
     <iterator Binds="DepartmentsView1" RangeSize="25"
       DataControl="AppModuleDataControl" id="DepartmentsView1Iterator"/>
   </executables>
   <bindings>
     <attributeValues IterBinding="DepartmentsView1Iterator"
       id="DepartmentId">
       <AttrNames>
         <Item Value="DepartmentId"/>
       </AttrNames>
     </attributeValues>
     <attributeValues IterBinding="DepartmentsView1Iterator"
       id="DepartmentName">
       <AttrNames>
         <Item Value="DepartmentName"/>
       </AttrNames>
     </attributeValues>
     <attributeValues IterBinding="DepartmentsView1Iterator"
       id="ManagerId">
       <AttrNames>
         <Item Value="ManagerId"/>
```

```
    </AttrNames>
  </attributeValues>
  <attributeValues IterBinding="DepartmentsView1Iterator"
    id="LocationId">
    <AttrNames>
      <Item Value="LocationId"/>
    </AttrNames>
  </attributeValues>
  <action IterBinding="DepartmentsView1Iterator" id="Create"
    RequiresUpdateModel="true" Action="createRow"/>
  <action id="Commit" RequiresUpdateModel="true"
    Action="commitTransaction" DataControl="AppModuleDataControl"/>
  </bindings>
</pageDefinition>
```

PageDef files are created automatically when dragging and dropping data controls onto a page. They can also be created manually for a page that doesn't yet contain bindings by right-clicking in the visual editor or Structure window and choosing Go To Page Definition. Typically, however, PageDef files are created automatically for JSPX pages via drag-and-drop operations initially, and then edited via the Bindings tab in the page editor (as shown below) or by opening the file directly from the Application Navigator.

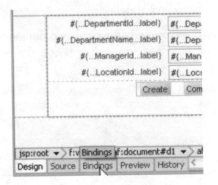

NOTE
PageDef files can also be created for non–ADF Faces pages, as is commonly done when configuring ADF Security, which is covered in Chapter 21. PageDef files can also be created for non-JSP artifacts, such as for use with non-page elements of task flows such as methods and routers, covered in Chapter 5.

NOTE
At runtime, the PageDef location for a page will be determined in the DataBindings.cpx file as explained. The adfmsrc/META-INF/adfm .xml file specifies the location of the DataBindings.cpx file for an application.

Clicking the Bindings tab of the page editor is the easiest way to access the bindings for a page. A link to the file is located in the top of the bindings editor in case you need to access the source (to view comments or make manual changes). To access the file directly, right-click within the visual editor and choose Go To Page Definition. The default location of this file is in the

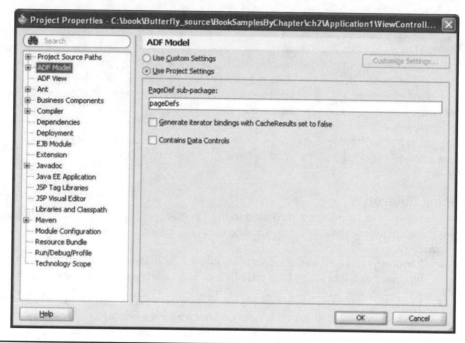

FIGURE 2-4   *ADF Model settings*

`pagedefs` subpackage of the UI project's package. This can be modified in the ADF Model settings of the Project Properties, as shown in Figure 2-4.

When working with large projects, it can sometimes be difficult to recognize which ADF component (such as an input text field) is bound to which data control (such as a view object attribute). To locate the view object related to a particular component, you can select the component in the visual editor or Structure window. Then, in the bindings editor, the binding for that component should be selected (click it if it is not selected). This will highlight the executable to which the binding belongs. Click the executable binding to select it and highlight the data control to which the executable belongs. Right-click the control and choose Edit Definition to navigate to the view object editor. Figure 2-5 demonstrates this procedure.

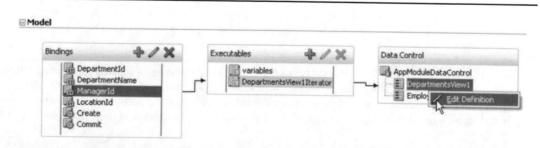

FIGURE 2-5   *The page definition editor*

Keeping Binding Files Clean
While you're developing pages (and thus binding files), remember that bindings may be defined in a PageDef but not used within the page. JDeveloper will attempt to delete bindings (and executables, if the deleted bindings are the only bindings that refer to the executable) when bound components are deleted from the visual editor or Structure window. However, if bound components are deleted from the source, the PageDef may become out of sync with the page, and the bindings will not be deleted. For maintenance purposes, it is important to keep the bindings file clean, meaning that each binding included in the PageDef is bound to at least one component in the page. Additionally, any unused executables should be deleted from the PageDef.

Binding Categories

Several categories of bindings are created in the PageDef, depending on the type of object created in the page, including parameters, variables, executables, and generic bindings.

- **Parameters**   Used to pass external context information into a binding within the page's binding container using URL parameters, such as request parameters.

- **Variables**   Used as value holders for items that have no persistence in the data model. For example, variables are created for forms bound to a view object's `ExecuteWithParams` operation to retrieve the data input of the user and pass it to the operation as an argument.

- **Executables**   Used to iterate over a collection, as discussed in the next section.

- **Generic bindings**   Collections of bindings used to relate UI components to attributes, methods, and collections; discussed in detail in the section "Generic Binding Types" later in this chapter.

Executables   Executables may be search, region, or iterator bindings. Iterator bindings are typically used to link other bindings to a data control, via attributes and collections that contain the `IterBinding` property. The following iterator is defined in a PageDef to refer to the collection represented by the `DepartmentsView` view object (the default name of the first instance is `DepartmentsView1`):

```
<executables>
  <iterator Binds="DepartmentsView1" RangeSize="25"
    DataControl="AppModuleDataControl" id="DepartmentsView1Iterator"/>
</executables>
```

Iterators are available in several types. In most cases, the type of iterator is defined when the drag-and-drop operation is performed to bind ADF Faces components to ADF data controls. The preceding code shows the iterator type of executable, which is by far the most common iterator used as an executable. The following describes additional iterators and their purpose:

- **Method iterator**   Provides a reference to the results of a method call.

- **Accessor iterator**   Provides a reference to detail collections for nested objects. This type of iterator is not used when the data model is based on ADF BC.

- **Variable iterator**   Provides access to local variables defined in the PageDef file (typically used as arguments to a method call). The variable iterator is not linked to a data control.

The following code is generated when an `ExecuteWithParams` operation is dropped as an ADF Parameter Form onto the visual editor from the `DepartmentsView` data control (where the `DepartmentsView` view object defines a bind variable in the where clause of the query):

```xml
<?xml version="1.0" encoding="UTF-8" ?>
<pageDefinition xmlns=http://xmlns.oracle.com/adfm/uimodel
  version="11.1.1…" id="mypagePageDef" Package="view.pageDefs">
  <parameters/>
  <executables>
    <variableIterator id="variables">
    <variableUsage DataControl="AppModuleDataControl"
      Binds="DepartmentsView1.variablesMap.bind_deptId"
      Name="ExecuteWithParams_bind_deptId" IsQueriable="false"/>
    </variableIterator>
    <iterator Binds="DepartmentsView1" RangeSize="25"
      DataControl="AppModuleDataControl" id="DepartmentsView1Iterator"/>
  </executables>
  <bindings>
    <action IterBinding="DepartmentsView1Iterator" id="ExecuteWithParams"
      RequiresUpdateModel="true" Action="executeWithParams">
      <NamedData NDName="bind_deptId" NDType="oracle.jbo.domain.Number"
        NDValue="${bindings.ExecuteWithParams_bind_deptId}"/>
    </action>
    <attributeValues IterBinding="variables" id="bind_deptId">
      <AttrNames>
        <Item Value="ExecuteWithParams_bind_deptId"/>
      </AttrNames>
    </attributeValues>
  </bindings>
</pageDefinition>
```

This code shows the use of two executables working together: a `variableIterator` that defines the value holder for the `bind_deptId` argument, and an `iterator` that provides access to the `DepartmentsView1` actions and rowsets. A generic binding (action binding) is used to call the `ExecuteWithParams` method, passing in the `bind_deptId` argument from the `variableIterator` definition.

Additionally, an action that calls another executable is available as an executable in the PageDef file. The `invokeAction` executable can be used to call a method action when a page is loaded, or as a result of the `refresh` and `refreshCondition` properties. The next chapter covers the ADF page lifecycle and these properties in detail, but generally, the `invokeAction` method is discouraged as a matter of best practice, because it discourages page reuse, as it may define that a particular iterator is executed each time a page is rendered. Additionally, the `invokeAction` method is not visually displayed within the page in the visual editor (meaning that developers would need to access the Bindings tab to see that the page "forces" a method action). To encourage page reuse and ease application maintenance in this case, you should define a method call in an ADF Controller task flow that calls the method or executable before a page is loaded. A method call can contain a condition so that it is executed only when a certain condition is met, so no functionality is lost by using this practice.

Furthermore, iterators themselves can contain refresh properties that define when an iterator should be refreshed, and iterators that should execute when the page is prepared for rendering should be defined in an ADF Controller task flow as a method call. This is covered in detail in Chapter 4.

Generic Binding Types   The following list of generic bindings are automatically defined in a PageDef file by the framework, according to the type of component selected in either the Create menu or in the component palette. However, application developers will frequently need to modify existing UI components so that they are bound to different types of bindings, and it is therefore important that you understand what each type of binding is used for. The following list may seem lengthy, but the interaction with each type of binding is explained thoroughly throughout this book, according to the UIs component for which the binding is used:

- **Attribute bindings**   Used to define the binding for a single attribute in the current row of a collection, as in the `DepartmentId` example provided earlier.

- **List bindings**   Used to define the contents of data-bound list components, such as radio groups and drop-down lists.

- **NavigationList bindings**   Used to navigate to a specific row in a data collection by choosing a value representing it from a list.

- **ListOfValues bindings**   A special type of binding used for displaying input text fields with a built-in pop-up dialog that allows users to search and filter values defined in a data model List Of Values object.

- **Tree bindings**   Used to bind to collections of data used to populate multiple, related collections, such as trees, treetables, or the hierarchy viewer components. In the case of single-level collections, the tree binding is also used to populate tables.

- **Table bindings**   Used to bind to a simple collection of data, such as lists. However, JDeveloper 11*g* uses tree bindings to populate tables.

- **Action bindings**   Used to define the binding of ADF BC built-in operations such as create, commit, first, last, and so on.

- **Method bindings**   Similar to action bindings, but are used to bind to methods defined in an ADF BC application module, view object, or view row client interfaces.
- **Boolean bindings**   Used to bind to checkbox components.

Accessing the Binding Layer

In Fusion application development, creating the data model (even when using the declarative features of ADF BC) consumes the largest amount of time in the development lifecycle, because this is where the business rules for an application are created. The second-most time consuming activity is augmenting the binding layer and the pages and task flows that use it. This is where application and UI logic are created, and it defines the functionality of the application as a whole. The binding layer can be accessed via Expression Language (covered in Chapter 1) or via Java by way of managed beans.

Accessing the Binding Layer from Expression Language

Bindings are created as Java objects at runtime and have properties other than just a value. All of these properties are accessible via Expression Language. In a previous example, the value of the `DepartmentId` was referenced by the expression `#{bindings.DepartmentId .inputValue}`. Additionally, the label and format mask attributes were referenced by using `#{bindings.DepartmentId.hints.label}` and `#{bindings.DepartmentId .format}`, respectively.

This same basic syntax (`#{bindings.<name_of_binding>.<property_of_ binding>}`) is useful for retrieving a value of a binding to perform conditional processing, creating component listeners that refresh when a property is true or false, and for binding command components such as buttons and links to call operations.

Accessing the Binding Layer from Java

Throughout this book, bindings are accessed via Java code. This should be done only as appropriate, when attribute or executable binding properties are not able to declaratively meet the needs of the application. In addition, it is important to remember to separate data model logic and view layer logic cleanly. If you find yourself coding business logic in a managed bean, then you've probably violated this tenet. However, accessing executable and attribute bindings via code is not a direct violation and is sometimes necessary, as you will see throughout the examples in this book. The framework classes introduced next are the most commonly used classes when accessing the ADF binding layer from Java.

DCControlBinding

The `oracle.adf.model.binding.DCControlBinding` class is the base class that is extended by all component binding classes. It defines access to the current `RowIterator`, the `BindingContainer`, and the `DataProvider` instance. A control binding can be an attribute binding, such as `DepartmentName` in Figure 2-6, or a tree binding, such as `EmployeesView3`.

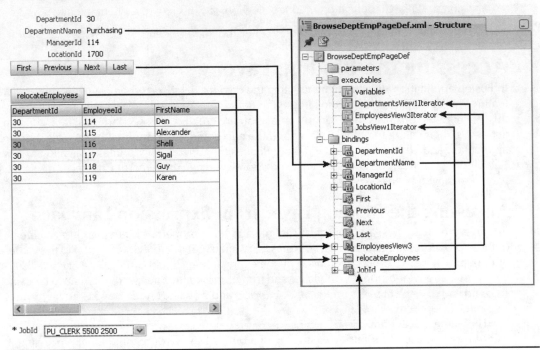

FIGURE 2-6 *ADF binding metadata linked to UI components*

BindingContainer and DCBindingContainer

In Figure 2-6, the `BrowseDeptEmpPageDef` root container is exposed by the bindings object at runtime. Different options exist to access the bindings object at runtime, and we consider the following option a best practice due to its reusability and readability:

```
import oracle.adf.model.BindingContext;
import oracle.binding.BindingContainer;
...
BindingContext bindingctx = BindingContext.getCurrent();
BindingContainer bindings = null;
bindings = bindingctx.getCurrentBindingsEntry();
```

The `BindingContext` class is an interface that exposes generic methods to access the binding layer. Application developers who prefer working with type-safe methods can cast the bindings instance to `DCBindingContainer`:

```
import oracle.adf.model.binding.DCBindingContainer;
...
DCBindingContainer bindingsImpl = (DCBindingContainer) bindings;
```

As with many implementation classes in Java, the `DCBindingContainer` class exposes more methods than are defined by the `BindingContainer` interface.

DCIteratorBinding

In Fusion applications, the abstract `DCIteratorBinding` class is used to access the rowset iterator of a view object. The `DCIteratorBinding` class handles the events generated from the associated `RowIterator` and sends the current `Row` to individual control bindings to display current data. To access the current `Row` of an iterator from Java, you use this:

```
import oracle.adf.model.binding.DCIteratorBinding;
import oracle.jbo.Row;
...
DCIteratorBinding dciter = null;
//access the iterator by its ID value in the PageDef file.
dciter  = bindingsImpl.findIteratorBinding("DepartmentsView1Iterator");
Row currentRow = dciter.getCurrentRow();
```

The iterator ID in the binding definition is `DepartmentsView1Iterator`, as shown in Figure 2-6, and is looked up in the `DCBindingContainer` instance.

OperationBinding

Method bindings such as `relocateEmployees`, or action bindings such as Next or Previous, exposed on a view object are instance of `JUCtrlActionBinding` that can be cast to the `OperationBinding` interface when accessed from Java. The following code is used to invoke the Next operation shown in Figure 2-6:

```
import oracle.binding.OperationBinding;
...
OperationBinding nextOperation = null;
nextOperation = bindingsImpl.getOperationBinding("Next");
Object result = nextOperation.execute();
```

The return value of the execute method operation is the result returned by the custom method, or null if there is no return value.

Other operations, such as `ExecuteWithParams` or `CreateWithParameters`, that are exposed on the data control palette for a view object require input arguments to be passed to it. The arguments may be added through Expression Language expressions in the operation binding in the PageDef, or they may be provided in Java before invoking the method execution. The `relocateEmployees` method in Figure 2-6 expects a single argument of type `Map<Number,Number>`, which is provided as follows:

```
import oracle.binding.OperationBinding;
import oracle.jbo.domain.Number;
...
OperationBinding relocateEmployees = null;
relocateEmployees = bindingsImpl.getOperationBinding("relocateEmployees");
HashMap<Number,Number> emps = new HashMap<Number,Number>();
emps.put(new Number(103),new Number(90));
emps.put(new Number(104),new Number(90));
emps.put(new Number(105),new Number(100));
relocateEmployees.getParamsMap().put("employees",emps);
relocateEmployees.execute();
```

> **Automatically Generating Bindings Code**
> For operation bindings, the code to access the `OperationBinding` can be automatically generated in a managed bean at design time. For example, to access a binding when the user clicks a command component such as a button or link at runtime, double-click the ADF bound command component in the visual editor and in the resulting dialog, choose the managed bean class and method to access the ADF binding, and then choose Generate ADF Binding Code.

The method arguments are provided in a map that is accessed from a call to `getParamsMap` on the `OperationBinding` reference. The argument name is the same name defined in the method signature, which can be seen in the Data Control palette that exposes the method and the PageDef file that contains the method binding.

AttributeBinding

Attribute definitions in the ADF binding definition, such as `DepartmentName` in Figure 2-6, are instances of `JUCtrlAttrsBinding` that can be cast to the `AttributeBinding` interface when accessed from Java. Attribute bindings are referenced from components such as `InputText` and `OutputText`:

```
import oracle.binding.AttributeBinding;
...
AttributeBinding departmentName =
        (AttributeBinding) bindings.get("DepartmentName");
String oldValue = (String)departmentName.getInputValue();
String newValue = oldValue+"_new";
departmentName.setInputValue(newValue);
```

JUCtrlListBinding

The list binding is used by select components and binds a single row attribute of an iterator to a secondary rowset that provides the list of valid choices. In Figure 2-6, the `JobId` list is bound to the `JobsView1Iterator`. A selection from the list updates the `JobId` attribute of the `EmployeesView3Iterator`. To access the list binding from Java, you use the `JUCtrlListBinding` class, as shown next:

```
import oracle.jbo.uicli.binding.JUCtrlListBinding;
import oracle.jbo.domain.Number;
...
JUCtrlListBinding listBinding = null;
listBinding = (JUCtrlListBinding) bindings.get("JobId");
ViewRowImpl selectedListRow = null;
selectedListRow = (ViewRowImpl) listBinding.getSelectedValue();
String jobIdValue = (String) selectedListRow.getAttribute("JobId");
Number maxSalary = (Number) selectedListRow.getAttribute("MaxSalary");
```

The list binding value, when accessed from Java, is the row in the secondary rowset that the user selected to update the bound attribute. Compared to plain HTML, in which lists cannot represent objects but only indexes and string values, this is a huge advantage of the ADF binding framework.

JUCtrlHierBinding

The `JUCtrlHierBinding` class is used to bind tree, treetable, and table components to the ADF model. Depending on the component you work with, the tree binding works with a single node or multiple node hierarchy. Chapter 9 covers the work with collections to populate trees, treetables, and tables. To access a tree binding such as `EmployeesView3` in the example shown in Figure 2-6, you use the following Java code:

```
JUCtrlHierBinding hierBinding = null;
hierBinding = (JUCtrlHierBinding)bindings.get("EmployeesView3");
```

Summary

Understanding how the ADF framework functions and how the various XML files that are created by the framework work together is an important part of Fusion application development. As you will see throughout the remainder of this book, the ADFm framework is a powerful feature for creating applications, and it unleashes the flexibility and functionality of the ADF Faces components. Development teams may use any part of the ADF stack on its own; ADF BC data controls can be bound to JSF components instead of ADF rich-client components, and ADF Faces components can be bound directly to managed beans that do not utilize the ADF model layer. However, these technologies are like wine and chocolate: they are good on their own, but they are better together!

CHAPTER
3

The Oracle ADF and ADF Faces Rich Client Lifecycle

From the perspective of an Oracle Fusion developer, the ADF page Lifecycle is where the rubber meets the road. The ADF page lifecycle is invoked by the JavaServer Faces lifecycle and synchronizes the ADF model and its underlying business service with data changes applied by the web request.

he lifecycle is a sequence of steps performed while a request is being handled. Usually users don't accomplish a task with only a single request. In traditional web applications, a request usually causes page changes to occur. In Oracle Fusion web applications that implement the patterns of the rich Internet, some requests are hidden from the application user and processed asynchronously in the background, with no page flicker.

This chapter introduces the Oracle Fusion application request lifecycle from the bottom up in incremental steps that cover the following:

- **JavaServer Faces lifecycle**   The request lifecycle of the JavaServer Faces (JSF) architecture is the foundation of all client-to-server interactions. You'll learn about the six lifecycle phases and their uses.

- **ADF Faces lifecycle**   The ADF Faces component framework adds improvements to the standard JSF lifecycle that helps to avoid a full page refresh when a single component refresh is all that is needed. You'll learn about partial page requests, triggers, and partial event roots that allow you to define the scope of a form submit.

- **ADF lifecycle**   Using Oracle ADF with ADF Faces components adds another lifecycle, the ADF lifecycle. The ADF lifecycle prepares the ADF model for the request and populates the binding container with the content of the ADF page definition file. This topic follows up on the preceding discussion. It shows you when ADF phases, such as `prepareModel` and `initContext`, are called and how to customize the application lifecycle.

- **Fusion application lifecycle**   The Oracle Fusion development stack uses ADF Business Components as the business service. All model actions, such as validations and updates, are passed to the ADF Business Component Data Control and from here to the ADF Business Component framework. This section completes the lifecycle by adding the persistence layer to the overall picture.

JavaServer Faces Lifecycle

The JSF lifecycle is managed by the JSF servlet, which is configured in the web.xml file and consists of six phases in which a page request is processed, request parameters are read and converted, new input values are validated, the model is updated with new values, and possible navigation cases are executed. The following six JSF request phases make up the lifecycle:

1. *Restore View.* The first phase receives the page request from the JSF servlet and attempts to find and restore the server-side component state, a set of in-memory objects that build the server-side hierarchical page structure. If the view cannot be found as identified by

the requested view ID, a new view is created on the server. The current page's view is stored in the `FacesContext` static object and is accessible through a call to the `getViewRoot` method. Restoring a view prepares the page by adding UI component instances and linking them to event handlers and validators.

2. *Apply Request Values.* The request values are read and converted to the data type expected by the underlying model attribute. The values are accessed from the UI component's submitted value and passed to the local value. When an input component has its `immediate` attribute set to `true`, its component validation is performed and configured component listeners are executed within this phase. This phase is one of two phases in which page navigation can occur.

3. *Process Validations.* The components are validated for missing data or data that doesn't conform to the expected component format. The process validation is done on the component local value, prior to that data being released to the JSF model. At the end of this phase, value change events are raised.

4. *Update Model Values.* During this phase, the JSF model is updated with the validated value of the UI component local value. The local value on the component is discarded afterward. The JSF model can be a managed bean or, in the Oracle ADF case, the binding container that is associated with the current page. It is the responsibility of the JSF model to ensure that the update is passed on to the Java Enterprise Edition (EE) persistence layer, which in Oracle Fusion development is ADF Business Components, or in a wide sense of interpretation, possibly a web service.

5. *Invoke Application.* During this phase, all application level events, such as form submits, are executed. This phase also executes the view layer logic that is stored in action listeners. If a navigation case is associated with a command action return value, page navigation is performed at this stage. This is the second phase of two phases in which page navigation can occur.

6. *Render Response.* The last phase prepares the page view for display on the user client—the web browser in most cases. If a view is called the first time, then the Restore View phase (phase 1) directly passes control to this phase.

Each phase shown in Figure 3-1 includes a before and after phase event to which a custom `PhaseListener` implementation can monitor and respond. If a phase listener needs to short-circuit the lifecycle in that it immediately renders the request response, this can be done by a call to `renderResponse`, a method exposed on the `FacesContext` object.

A development use case to short-circuit the lifecycle from a managed bean action is an undo button that does not need the request to be validated or the model to be updated. Setting the `immediate` attribute on a button to `true` executes its action and action listener methods during the Apply Request Values phase. The methods perform the work needed to undo a specific user interaction before the lifecycle continues with the Render Response phase. To change a component value within the action method of a button that has its `immediate` attribute set to `true`, you call the component's `setSubmittedValue()` method and provide the new value as the argument. This sets the new value on the component but does not update the model because the "update model values" phase is skipped for this use case.

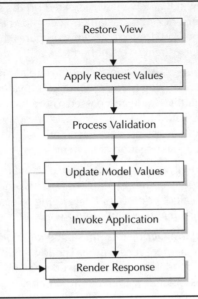

FIGURE 3-1 *JSF request lifecycle phases*

Phase Listener

A *phase listener* is a Java class that is configured in the faces-config.xml configuration file to monitor the JSF request lifecycle. By using a custom phase listener, application developers can respond to specific phases of the application request handling—for example, to handle image resources different from form requests, manipulate request attributes, or write and read cookies. Phase listeners are similar to servlet filters but differ in that they execute after the JSF servlet has created the faces context. This way, phase listeners have access to the JSF application, its configuration, and the UI component instances. Phase listeners can be implemented globally for the whole application or for a single page. The latter approach is useful if the executed phase listener code is required on a single page only.

Global PhaseListener

A global phase listener implements the `PhaseListener` interface and is configured in the faces-config.xml file located in the application view layer project's WEB-INF directory or the META-INF directory of a Java library file (JAR). An example of a custom phase listener skeleton is shown here:

```
import javax.faces.event.PhaseEvent;
import javax.faces.event.PhaseId;
import javax.faces.event.PhaseListener;

public class AdfInteractivePhaseListener implements PhaseListener{
  public AdfInteractivePhaseListener() {}
  public void afterPhase(PhaseEvent phaseEvent) {}
  public void beforePhase(PhaseEvent phaseEvent) {}
  public PhaseId getPhaseId() {
```

```
      return PhaseId.ANY_PHASE;
   }
}
```

The phase listener `getPhaseId` method outcome determines the phase or phases that the custom listener monitors. The static `PhaseId` class allows developers to configure the phase listener for any specific lifecycle phase. The `PhaseEvent` instance that is passed as an argument to the `afterPhase` and `beforePhase` methods allows developers to access the `FacesContext` object and to gain information about the current `PhaseId` performed. The custom phase listener configuration in the faces-config.xml file looks like this:

```
<?xml version="1.0" encoding="windows-1252"?>
<faces-config version="1.2" xmlns="http://java.sun.com/xml/ns/javaee">
  […]
  <lifecycle>
    <phase-listener>
      adf.sample.AdfInteractivePhaseListener
    </phase-listener>
  </lifecycle>
</faces-config>
```

The Oracle JDeveloper integrated development environment (IDE) can be used to create the listener class and configure it in the faces-config.xml file. To configure the listener class, double-click the faces-config.xml file entry in the Web Content | WEB-INF directory of the view layer project in the Application Navigator. As shown in Figure 3-2, select the Life Cycle category in the Overview tab panel of the opened editor window and click the green plus icon. Either type in the package and filename string of the phase listener class to register, or open the Oracle JDeveloper Property Inspector (CTRL-SHIFT-I) and type the listener class name so JDeveloper can look up its classpath.

NOTE
It is recommended that Oracle Fusion developers use the ADF Controller instead of the JSF. Chapter 4 discusses the benefits developers gain by using the ADF Controller.

Local Phase Listener

A local phase listener is a Java method that takes a `PhaseEvent` argument and that is referenced from the `f:view` root element of the JSF page. The listening method receives page phase notifications for all lifecycle phases except Restore View. To create a local phase listener method, select the `f:view` tag in the Oracle JDeveloper Structure window for the current page and open the Property Inspector. Click the icon next to the BeforePhase or AfterPhase property field and choose Edit to create the phase listener method in an existing or new managed bean. The name of the phase listener methods can be freely chosen. The generated method stubs look like this:

```
public void beforePhaseListener(PhaseEvent phaseEvent) {}
public void afterPhaseListener(PhaseEvent phaseEvent) {}
```

Calling `getPhaseId` on the `phaseEvent` argument allows developers to detect the current lifecycle phase for the page to respond to the phase in which they are interested.

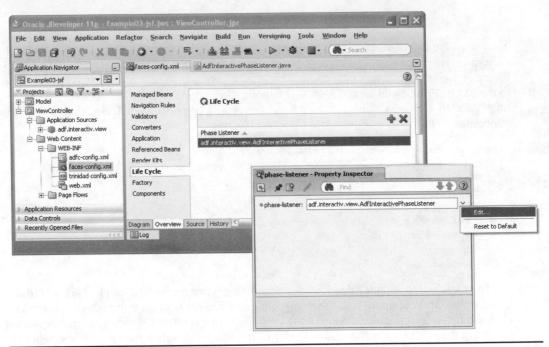

FIGURE 3-2 *JSF phase listener configuration in Oracle JDeveloper 11g*

A use case for a local phase listener configuration is to compare form field values and to raise an error message if a specific condition, such as if a start date that always must be lower than the end date, is not met. To implement this use case, you create a JSF component binding for the input date components to the same managed bean that has the `beforePhaseListener` method defined. In the phase listener method, wait for the Update Model Values phase:

```
if (phaseEvent.getPhaseId() == PhaseId.UPDATE_MODEL_VALUES){
  //compare component values
}
```

Before entering the Update Model Values phase, the user input has been validated during the Process Validations phase and written to the component value property. In the case of an error, to cancel the JSF model update and proceed with the Render Response phase, add a `FacesMessage` to the `FacesContext` that has its severity set to `FacesMessage.SEVERITY_ERROR`.

A Close Look at the immediate Attribute

The JSF UI component `immediate` attribute has its value set to `false` by default. Some assume that setting the `immediate` attribute to `true` on an input or action component skips the JSF lifecycle as a whole. This assumption is incorrect, however; instead, only the component event handling and validation is moved up to the Apply Request Values phase so it executes before anything else happens on components that don't have the `immediate` attribute set to `true`. If no error occurs, and if the developer does not explicitly call `renderResponse`, the request lifecycle continues as normal. The following table explains the effect that setting the `immediate` attribute to `true` has by example of a command button and an input text field.

Button	Input Field	Behavior
immediate = true	immediate = true	The field value is updated and available for the button event processing. If the input text field requires a value but the user has not provided one, an error is raised. In case of an error, the lifecycle continues with the Render Response phase. The JSF lifecycle does not handle the component first that initiates the request. This means that the button action cannot suppress the validation failure on the input text field. The lifecycle continues with the Render Response phase after the button action completes and if no navigation is performed.
immediate = true	immediate = false	The action and action listener event of the button are executed at the end of the Apply Request Values phase before anything happens with the input text field. If the button action returns a navigation outcome, navigation is performed and the form is abandoned. If the button action returns `null`, the lifecycle continues with the Render Response phase, skipping the Process Validations, Update Model Values, and Invoke Application phases.
immediate = false	immediate = true	Clicking the button handles the events, validation, and value conversion on the input text component. The value change listener, if set for the component, executes before the Update Model Values phase, so if it needs to access the value of another input field, this can't be done through the model but must be through direct access of the field, calling its `getSubmittedValue` method.
immediate = false	immediate = false	Follows the "normal" lifecycle.

Performing Model Updates

Using the `immediate` attribute for use cases other than cancel—for example, to update model attributes in a component listener—requires special developer attention. In the JSF lifecycle, the model update is performed during the Update Model Values phase. If a developer updates the JSF model during the Apply Request Values phase, the value is likely overridden during the Update Model Values phase if an input form field references the updated model attribute. A working solution for requests that are expected to pass the Update Model Values phase is to set the value on the input component directly by calling the component `setSubmittedValue` method.

Accessing Component Values During the "Apply Request Values" Phase

If the submitted value of a component is accessed in a component listener that executes during the Apply Request Values phase, the format of the returned value is `java.lang.String` for components that have their `immediate` attribute not set or set to `false`. Components that have their `immediate` attribute set to `true` return the value in the converted format. This differentiation is important to handle in Java code that accesses JSF components to read their submitted values for updating other attributes or to process them further. This distinction is best explained in the following code snippet:

```
if (phaseId.equals(PhaseId.APPLY_REQUEST_VALUES)
    && inputField.isImmediate()){
  //getSubmittedValue returns converted object format
}
else if(phaseId.equals(PhaseId.APPLY_REQUEST_VALUES)
        && !inputField.isImmediate()){
  //getSubmittedValue returns String format
}
```

To get access to the current `PhaseId` in a managed bean, you use a local phase listener method configured on the `f:view` element:

```
private PhaseId phaseId = null;
[...]
public void beforePhaseListener(PhaseEvent phaseEvent) {
  phaseId = phaseEvent.getPhaseId();
}
```

Phase Listeners vs. Component Listeners

Component listeners are event listeners that respond to some user interaction performed on a component. A user changing the value of an input text field raises a JSF `ValueChangeEvent` during the next submit request. A component listener references a Java class or method that the developer set up to receive an event notification. In this event notification, developers can analyze the data change—for example, to prepare the data of a dependent list field.

Phase listeners work on a request level and not on an individual component level. They are called when the lifecycle reaches a specific phase in which the application developer is interested. For example, receiving an event notification about when the Render Response phase is processed allows developers to set a browser cookie to the client.

Converter

Web developer wisdom says that page layouts are made of nested boxes and user input is provided as strings. One responsibility of the JSF lifecycle is to ensure that user input is transformed into the native objects expected by the model layer. A converter in JSF is a class that performs string to object and object to string conversion. Default converters are provided by the JSF and the ADF Faces RC component set.

During the JSF lifecycle, input data type conversion is handled during the Apply Request Values phase. Components that have their `immediate` attribute set to true are converted before the other components, which means that up to this time, the input value format of the other components still is `java.lang.String`. If the conversion of incoming data fails, the request is routed to the Render Response phase with an error message added to the Faces message stack for display. Validation of input data is performed on converted data only.

The second phase in which an applied converter is called is during the Render Response phase, in which native object formats, such as `java.util.Date`, or more specific for Oracle Fusion Developer, `oracle.jbo.domain.Number` or `oracle.jbo.domain.Date`, are converted to a string for the UI rendering.

ADF Faces Rich Client Lifecycle

The ADF Faces RC framework is built on top of the standard JSF specification and leverages the JSF Reference Implementation runtime. Therefore, the lifecycle phases of an ADF Faces RC application are the same as those of JSF. Oracle ADF Faces RC lifecycle optimizes the default JSF lifecycle and adds the following:

- Partial page rendering (PPR)

- Optimized lifecycle

- A client-side value lifecycle

- Additional memory scopes

- A new subform component

In addition to these optimizations, ADF Faces RC applications follow the JSF lifecycle, which means that within Oracle Fusion web applications, which use ADF Faces as the view layer framework, the lifecycle phases are the same six we've already covered.

Partial Page Rendering

PPR is the mechanism for partial page content updates and partial requests that have made Ajax so successful. Two types of PPR exist:

- **Partial submit** Components such as command buttons have a `partialSubmit` attribute that, if set to true, submits a form without a page refresh occurring. Other components such as `af:selectOneChoice` implement this behavior when their autosubmit attribute is set to true. Partial submits may also be triggered by components such as af:dialog that refresh only their children when submitted. Any component that should refresh itself in response to this submit must have its partialTrigger attribute set to the id attribute value of the component issuing the submit.

■ **Partial refresh** ADF Faces components have a partialTriggers attribute that developers use to reference other components by their id attribute value. Any change on a referenced component triggers the referencing component to refresh itself. A component can listen to multiple components to receive change notifications. For this to work, the application developer references a set of component IDs delimited by a blank character each.

In the following example, the af:selectBooleanCheckbox component is registered to listen to when the button cb3, located in the dialog, is clicked. The partial page rendering functionality is not limited to action events only, but is fired for any server-side event that is queued for the triggering component.

```
<af:form id="f1" >
  <af:panelFormLayout id="pfl1">
    <af:panelLabelAndMessage id="plm1">
      <af:spacer id="spc1" width="110" height="10"/>
      <af:selectBooleanCheckbox id="sbc1" readOnly="true"
      partialTriggers="cb3" value="#{PersonInput.isAddressProvided}"/>
    [...]
  </af:panelFormLayout>
  <af:popup id="p1">
    <af:dialog id="dlg" title="Address" type="none">
      <af:panelFormLayout id="pfl2">
        <f:facet name="footer">
         <af:commandButton text="Submit" partialSubmit="true" id="cb3"/>
        </f:facet>
        ...
      </af:panelFormLayout>
    </af:dialog>
  </af:popup>
</af:form>
```

If the component that triggers the partial refresh is located in a naming container, such as af:subform, the naming container ID needs to be added as a prefix to the component ID in the partialTriggers attribute. The format needs to be <naming container ID>:<component ID>. Oracle JDeveloper 11*g* provides declarative configuration help for the partialTriggers value reference. To use the declarative help, select the component in the Oracle JDeveloper 11*g* visual editor, or in the Structure window, and open the Property Inspector. Navigate to the PartialTriggers property, click the arrow icon at its right, and choose Edit. In the dialog that opens, browse to the component that triggers the refresh on the current component, and shuttle it to the Selected box.

Queuing a PPR Event in Java

Some use cases require a partial component refresh to be initiated from Java code in a managed bean. An API for this exists on the `AdfFacesContext` that takes the component instance as an argument:

```
AdfFacesContext.getCurrentInstance().addPartialTarget(<component>);
```

The `<component>` reference is obtained from the bean property that is created when developers build an Expression Language reference from the component `binding` attribute to the managed bean, or from calling `getSource` on an event object such as `ValueChangeEvent`.

Partial Page Refresh Through the Oracle ADF Binding

Prior to Oracle JDeveloper 11*g*, using the component `partialTriggers` attribute was the only option available to declaratively enforce a component refresh in response to an event on another component. Oracle ADF in Oracle JDeveloper 11*g* provides a new auto-PPR feature that triggers the component refresh from the binding layer. For auto-PPR to work, attribute and iterator bindings need to have the `ChangeEventPolicy` attribute set to ppr. A value change on a binding then triggers a UI refresh on the ADF Faces RC components bound to it. To disable auto PPR, set its value to none. Using auto PPR does not require a component to reference a triggering component to refresh.

NOTE
The auto-PPR features is part of the Active Data Services (ADS) framework in ADF Faces RC. Chapter 20 is about ADS and describes the auto-PPR functionality in detail.

Identifying PPR Requests in Java

Use cases exist in which server-side Java code needs to know whether a request is partial or a full page refresh. For this, the `AdfFacesContext` object exposes the `isPartialRequest` method that returns `true` if the request is a partial request.

Limitations

The PPR feature cannot be used to change the `rendered` attribute of a component. If you need to change the `rendered` property, the partial refresh must be performed on the parent component of the component that should have its `rendered` attribute changed. This parent container could be `af:form`, `af:panelFormLayout`, `af:panelGroupLayout`, or similar. This limitation exists because PPR looks for component instances within the Document Object Model (DOM). A component that has its `rendered` attribute set to `false` does not have an entry in the page DOM tree and therefore cannot be refreshed.

Optimized Lifecycle

In standard JSF, no partial submit exists and instead the form as a whole is submitted to the server. If a JSF form contains dependent lists, then selecting a value in the parent list requires a form submit for server-side code to determine the dependent list values of the child list. To avoid the evaluation and update of all form fields during the JSF lifecycle, developers set the `immediate` attribute on the parent list component to `true`. In a value change listener that is attached to the parent list, the `renderResponse` method is called on the `FacesContext`, after the dependent list values are updated.

In ADF Faces RC, these extra programming steps are not needed and instead the optimized lifecycle handles the partial submit. Technically, the optimized lifecycle uses defined event roots to determine the scope of an update. An event root describes the outermost boundaries in which fields are validated on the client and for which the server-side lifecycle is executed. An exception to this occurs when a component outside of the event root has its `partialTrigger` property set so that it is refreshed by a component change within the event boundaries. The optimized lifecycle is implemented by the components, which means that developers must do nothing to enable the functionality.

Component-based Event Roots

The `af:dialog` component is an example of an event root that is implicitly set to the component root. Any form submits performed within the dialog affects only the child components of the dialog, but not the components on the page that launches the dialog.

The example in Figure 3-3 shows an input form that uses a Plain Old Java Object (POJO) model that is configured as a managed bean. The input form contains a command link that, when clicked, launches a dialog for the user to provide additional address information. The `immediate` attribute of the command link is set to `true` so that no error is thrown by the Mail input field, which is configured to require a value. Setting `immediate` to `true` skips the client and server validation and proceeds with the invoke action defined for the pop-up dialog. All input fields on the page, except those located in the dialog, are submitted when the Submit button on the page is clicked. A submit that is performed in the dialog is limited to the components contained in the dialog.

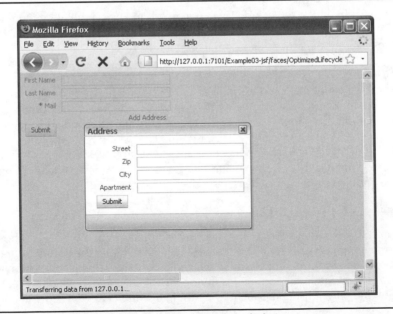

FIGURE 3-3   *Input form with detail items launched in a dialog*

The simplified page source of the example in Figure 3-3 is shown next:

```
<af:form id="f1">
  <af:panelFormLayout id="pfl1">
    <f:facet name="footer">
      <af:commandButton text="Submit" id="cb1"/>
    </f:facet>
    <af:inputText id="fld1" label="First Name value= … />
    <af:inputText id="fld2" label="Last Name" value = …/>
    <af:inputText id="fld3" label="Mail" value= … required="true"/>
    <af:panelLabelAndMessage id="plm1">
      <af:spacer id="sp1" width="110" height="10"/>
      <af:commandLink id="cln1" text="Add Address"
          immediate="true" partialSubmit="true">
        <af:showPopupBehavior popupId="p1" triggerType="action"/>
      </af:commandLink>
    </af:panelLabelAndMessage>
  </af:panelFormLayout>
  <af:popup id="p1">
    <af:dialog id="dlg1" title="Address" type="none">
      <af:panelFormLayout id="pfl2">
        <f:facet name="footer">
          <af:commandButton text="Submit" id="cb3"/>
        </f:facet>
        …
      </af:panelFormLayout>
    </af:dialog>
  </af:popup>
</af:form>
```

NOTE
If you need to submit the form fields of an `af:popup` *dialog when the user presses the* ENTER *key, instead of using a submit button, use an* `af:subform` *component as introduced later in this chapter.*

The `af:showPopupBehavior` tag is a declarative way to show an `af:popup` component in response to client-side events such as a mouse click or a keyboard action. The work with `af:popup` and `af:dialog` in ADF Faces RC components is explained in Chapter 10.

NOTE
The command button in the dialog does not issue a `partialSubmit`, *which leads to a full-page refresh being issued when it is clicked. This closes the pop-up dialog and displays the parent page but does not use PPR for the component refresh.*

Reaching Beyond the Event Root Using PPR

To enhance the sample shown in Figure 3-3, a read-only checkbox is added to indicate visually the address information to be available or not (see Figure 3-4 a bit later). For this to work, the submit event in the dialog needs to notify the checkbox to update itself.

By referencing the component ID of the submit button in the `partialTriggers` attribute of the checkbox, the checkbox is notified to refresh upon submit. For this refresh, the full JSF lifecycle is executed for the checkbox component.

The enhanced version of the example used earlier, including the partial submit and refresh functionality, is shown here:

```
<af:selectBooleanCheckbox id="sbc1"
  readOnly="true" partialTriggers="cb3"
  value="#{PersonInput.isAddressProvided}"/>
...
<af:popup id="p1">
  <af:dialog id="d2" type="none" title="Address">
    <af:panelFormLayout id="pfl2">
      <f:facet name="footer">
        <af:commandButton text="Submit" id="cb3"
          partialSubmit="true"
          action="#{PersonInput.cb3_action}"/>
      </f:facet>
    </af:panelFormLayout>
  </af:dialog>
</af:popup>
```

The partial submit issued from the command button submits the form elements that are contained in the dialog but does not close the `af:popup` component. To do this programmatically, the following Java code stored in a managed bean needs to be referenced by the `action` attribute:

```
public String cb3_action() {
  FacesContext fctx = FacesContext.getCurrentInstance();
  ExtendedRenderKitService eks =
    Service.getRenderKitService(fctx,ExtendedRenderKitService.class);
  String _script = "AdfPage.PAGE.findComponent(\"p1\").hide();";
  eks.addScript(fctx,_script);
  return null;
}
```

The `action` method calls the `addScript` method that is exposed on the ADF Faces RC render kit to issue a JavaScript command that finds the pop-up by its component ID, p1, to call `hide` on it. The work with pop-up dialogs and JavaScript in ADF Faces RC is covered later in this book.

NOTE
If a form submit is not supposed to close the dialog, you can use the dialog type attribute to display a default button for closing the dialog.

Autosubmit

User input components such as `af:selectOneChoice` and `af:inputText` provide an `autoSubmit` attribute that, if set to `true`, submits the entered value when the focus is moved out of the component. When executing the autosubmit event on a UI component, ADF Faces limits the decoding and model updates to this component. All other component values are not getting submitted, which means that new values added to these components are not available on the server to access from Java. To submit additional component values, so decoding and model update is performed for these as well, you need to extend the event root explicitly for the autosubmit to include these components. To do so, reference the component `id` attribute value of the component that issues the autosubmit from the `partialTriggers` attribute of the components that should be included in the request.

An autosubmit event is sent as an immediate request, which means that the component validation is performed after the "apply request values" phase and that the `ValueChangeListener`, if any is set, executes before the model is updated. If the Java code executed within the `ValueChangeListener` requires accessing the updated model data for other fields submitted with the request, it fails for this reason. To be able to read the updated model values in such a use case, you need to defer the execution of the `ValueChangeListener` for this component. You do this by queuing the event back in to execute at a later time. The following code handles the `ValueChangeEvent` so that it checks for the lifecycle phase in which it is executed to queue the event until the "invoke application" phase.

```
public void handleValueChanged(ValueChangeEvent valueChangeEvent) {
  if (!PhaseId.INVOKE_APPLICATION.equals(valueChangeEvent.getPhaseId())) {
    valueChangeEvent.setPhaseId(PhaseId.INVOKE_APPLICATION);
      valueChangeEvent.queue();
  } else {
    // execute the listener code here
  }
}
```

Note that using autosubmit not only performs an immediate action on the component itself but on all other components that reference it. This means that a possible `ValueChangeListener` on these components also executes before the "update model values" phase.

Client-side Value Lifecycle

In standard JSF, input type conversion and validation are handled on the server and come with the cost of a server roundtrip even in the case of user input errors. To provide a better user experience, ADF Faces RC components support client-side input data type conversion and validation in addition to the server-side functionality. This achieves the following:

- Strongly typed client values that make it easier to work with client-side code. A date, for example, is available in the JavaScript date format instead of a string.

- Immediate validation feedback so that users don't have to wait for the server response. If client validation fails, a visual indicator is displayed on the form field causing the error and a note window with the cause is shown.

- Avoid round trips in the case of errors. Any queued server action is cancelled to avoid an unnecessary server round trip.

Figure 3-4 shows a required field validation that is performed on the client. The request is cancelled and not sent to the server until the user fixes the reported problem. Client-side conversion and validation are an addition and not a replacement for server-side functionality. Application and component developers build the client-side functionality in JavaScript and load

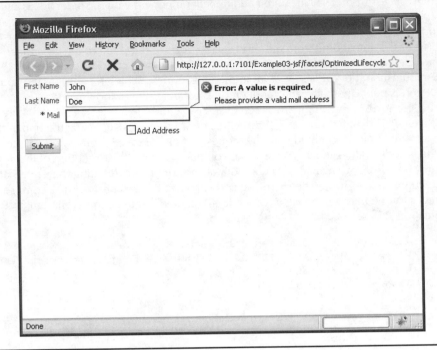

FIGURE 3-4 *Client-side validation for a required field*

it at runtime through the implementation of the `ClientConverter` or `ClientValidator` interface in their server-side implementations.

NOTE
The "Validating and Converting Input" chapter of the "Oracle Fusion Middleware Web User Interface Developer's Guide for Oracle Application Development Framework 11g" documentation, which is available online at http://otn.oracle.com, provides code examples of building client-side converters and validators.

Additional Memory Scopes

ADF Faces RC provides two additional memory scopes: `pageFlow` and `view`. The two new scopes are in addition to the existing servlet scopes, which are `request`, `session`, and `application`.

NOTE
The ADF Controller adds another memory scope, the "backingBean" scope. Because this view scope is specific to the ADF Controller we discuss it in Chapter 4.

The pageFlow scope exists for the duration of a process, which can be a set of pages that are navigated within an opened external dialog box. The memory allocated by the pageFlow scope is released when the dialog is closed. The content of a pageFlow scope is exposed in Expression Language and in Java for developers to read and write. Unlike the default scopes, accessing the pageFlow scope in Expression Language requires the prefix pageFlowScope to be used in the expression. For example, to access an attribute firstName in the pageFlow scope, the expression looks like this:

```
#{pageFlowScope.firstName}
```

If the attribute was defined in one of the standard scopes, just referencing its name could access it:

```
#{firstName}
```

To access the content of the pageFlow scope in Java, you use the Oracle AdfFacesContext object to access the exposed getPageFlowScope method:

```
AdfFacesContext adfFacesContext = AdfFacesContext.getCurrentInstance();
Map<String,Object> pageFlowScope = adfFacesContext.getPageFlowScope();
pageFlowScope.put("firstName","Larry");
```

The view scope provides a memory space for the duration that a specific view is displayed in the browser. For example, assume that a partial form submit is issued on a view. The request updates the model and refreshes some of the page components. It does not navigate away from the current view. Information stored in the view scope is available to the page content and for any subsequent partial requests in Expression Language and Java. The view scope lifetime spans multiple requests until the current view is replaced by another view as a result of page navigation. To access an attribute firstName in the view scope, the expression must be prefixed with viewScope as shown here:

```
#{viewScope.firstName}
```

Memory allocated by data written to the view scope is released upon dismissing the current view.

NOTE
Chapter 6 discusses ADF regions, which are used to render views as child areas of a parent view. ADF regions may contain other ADF regions, too. Each view exposed by an ADF region has its own viewScope.

To access the content of the view scope in Java, you use the Oracle AdfFacesContext object to access its getViewScope method:

```
AdfFacesContext adfFacesCtx = AdfFacesContext.getCurrentInstance();
Map<String,Object> viewScope = adfFacesCtx.getViewScope();
viewScope.put("firstName","Larry");
```

Both scopes are available for storing managed beans if the Oracle ADF Task Flow controller is used, as explained in Chapter 4.

NOTE
Using Expression Language to access attributes stored in the default memory scopes doesn't require a prefix to be used. The order in which the memory scopes are looked up for the attribute is from narrow to wider. So an attribute `firstName` *that is found in request scope takes precedence over the same attribute stored in session scope. This may lead to some unpredicted behavior and is also hard to read. Therefore, it is good practice to use a prefix with these scopes as well. The names available are* `requestScope`, `sessionScope`, *and* `applicationScope`.

Subform Component

A subform submits a group of form entries without impacting others. Using the `af:subform` component, parts of an input form can be validated and submitted independently from other parts with only a single page state to maintain by JSF.

Figure 3-5 shows an input form that consists of seven input text fields, one form component, and two subform components. Each subform has its own submit button to simulate the autosubmit of this part of the form. To align the input text components, each subform and the input text field that is not part of a subform are surrounded by an `af:panelFormLayout` component. The `labelWidth` attribute is used to handle the alignment difference that is caused by the subform component.

```
<af:form id="form1">
  <af:subform id="subform1" rendered="true" default="true">
    <af:panelFormLayout id="pfl2" labelWidth="70">
       ...
       <af:commandButton text="Submit 1" id="cb4"/>
    </af:panelFormLayout>
  </af:subform>
  <af:subform id=" subform2" default="true">
    <af:panelFormLayout id="pfl1" labelWidth="70">
       ...
    </af:panelFormLayout>
  </af:subform>
  <af:panelFormLayout id="pfl3" labelWidth="72">
     ...
     <af:commandButton text="Submit 3" id="cb1"/>
  </af:panelFormLayout>

</af:form>
```

Setting the `default` attribute on the `af:subform` components to `true` submits the subform not only when a component within the subform issues the submit, but also when a component that is not part of another subform issues the submit. The following table lists the submit options for the example shown in Figure 3-5:

Submit performed in	Submitted areas
subform1	Subform 1
subform2	Subform 2
form1	Form 1, Subform 1, Subform 2

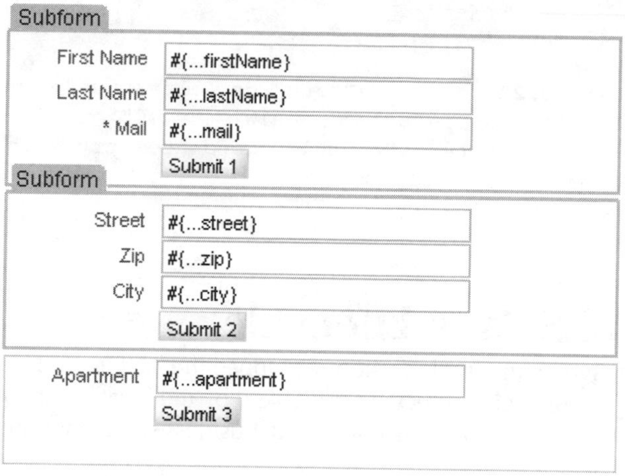

FIGURE 3-5   *Input form with subform components*

NOTE
If you try af:subform *on an ADF-bounded ADF Faces page, attribute constraint validation errors may appear in response to ADF model validation. Though submitting an* af:subform *form limits the decode and model update to its child components, the ADF binding performs the model validation on all attributes. To avoid errors, you need to prepare the ADF page lifecycle for this, which we explain in the "Usecase: Using af:subform in ADF Forms" section later in this chapter.*

Cancel Form Use Case

Setting a command component immediate attribute to true executes its action immediately and then continues with the Render Response phase. This configuration is commonly used on command components that cancel user form edits. If an input field in the edit form has the required attribute and the immediate attribute set to true, then canceling the form no longer works and instead a required field error message is shown. To solve this problem, the user needs first to provide a value for this input field before canceling the form edit. This occurs because the JSF lifecycle validates the input field after the Apply Request Values phase, which is performed before the cancel command executes. You solve this problem by wrapping the a:panelFormLayout component and the command component that cancels the form edit in different af:subform components. The cancel action now operates within the event boundary defined by the af:subform component, which does not include the form fields.

```
<af:form id="form1">
  <af:subform id=" sf1" default="true">
    <af:panelFormLayout id="pfl1" labelWidth="70">
      <af:inputText label="First Name value= … />
      <af:inputText label="Last Name" value = …/>
```

```
        <af:inputText label="Mail" value= … required="true"
                      immediate="true"/>
      </af:panelFormLayout>
    </af:subform>
    <af:subform id="sf2" rendered="true" default="true">
      <af:panelFormLayout id="pfl2" labelWidth="70">
        <af:commandButton text="cancel" immediate="true" id="cb4"/>
      </af:panelFormLayout>
    </af:subform>
</af:form>
```

Oracle ADF Page Lifecycle

From the perspective of an Oracle Fusion developer, the ADF page Lifecycle is where the rubber meets the road. The ADF page lifecycle is invoked by the JavaServer Faces lifecycle and synchronizes the ADF model and its underlying business service with data changes applied by the web request.

NOTE
The name "page lifecycle" is misleading. First of all, the lifecycle is not only executed when a page is navigated to or from, but also while a user works on the page. This is the case, for example, when scrolling in a table or setting a new current row. Second, the lifecycle executes for all activities that issue a request and therefore also for bounded method activities and operations that are added to the ADF Controller navigation.

Technically, the ADF lifecycle extends the JSF lifecycle with additional ADF page lifecycle phases that handle the ADF model interactions such as model preparation, model update, data validation, and the execution of methods and operations. The ADF model is exposed to the lifecycle through the ADF binding container, which is a live instance of the binding definition file that is associated with the current view. The binding container and its content are accessible from Expression Language using the "bindings" name in the expression.

In JSF, the lifecycle is a request lifecycle that executes one time per request. In ADF, the lifecycle may execute multiple times during a request, such as when navigation is involved. Another use case in which the ADF lifecycle is executed many times during a single request is the execution of multiple data bound activities when navigating from one view to another.

The following table lists the order in which the ADF page lifecycle phases are executed and their associated JSF request lifecycle phases. Also shown are the events raised during the ADF page lifecycle to which applications can listen and respond. The standard JSF phase events are also available in the ADF lifecycle. They are identified by their default `PhaseId` name prefixed with `JSF_`. Having the JSF standard events exposed in the ADF lifecycle allows application developers to write listeners that respond to JSF and ADF lifecycle events in the order in which they occur, which otherwise, using a separate `PhaseListener` configured in the `faces-config.xml` file, would be difficult to achieve.

JSF Phase	ADF Phase	ADF Events
Restore view	JSF Restore View	Before and after JSF restore view events
	Init Context	Before and after context initialization events
	Prepare Model	Before and after prepare model events
Apply Request Values	JSF Apply Request Values	Before and after JSF apply request values
Process Validations	JSF Process Validations	Before and after JSF process validations event
Update Model Values	JSF Update Model Values	Before and after update model values event
	Validate Model Updates	Before and after ADF model update events
Invoke Application	JSF Invoke Application	Before and after JSF invoke application events
	Metadata Commit	Before and after metadata commit events
Render Response	JSF Render Response	Before JSF Render Response event
	Init Context (only if navigation occurred)	Before and after context initialization events
	Prepare Model (only if navigation occurred)	Before and after prepare model events
	Prepare Render	Before and after prepare render events
Render Response	JSF Render Response	After JSF Render Response

Note that most of the phases have their after event immediately following their before event. The exception to this is the JSF "render response" phase, which has ADF phases executed between the events. Figure 3-6 shows how the ADF page lifecycle integrates the JSF lifecycle.

1. *JSF Restore View.* The ADF lifecycle is invoked only if the request is an ADF request identified by the ADF binding filter in the web.xml file. At the end of the JSF Restore View phase, the PageFlow scope of the ADF Controller becomes available. During this phase, the controller checks for browser back-button usage and bookmark references, which both are covered later in Chapter 5. If the request is an initial request, then the lifecycle continues with the Prepare Render phase.

2. *Initialize Context.* The associated page definition file is looked up in the DataBindings.cpx file and parsed into the binding container, which becomes available for access in Java. Internally, the `LifecycleContext` class is initialized with the request values, the binding container, and lifecycle. The `LifecycleContext` context object is passed as an argument to the ADF lifecycle phases and extends Java HashMap. It can also be used to pass custom user data between the phases. The `LifecycleContext` object lives for the duration of the current lifecycle.

3. *Prepare Model.* Iterators that are configured to refresh during this phase execute their data control to query the business service. If the ADF Faces page is built based on a page template and if this template has its own ADF binding defined, the binding definition is parsed and added to the binding context during this phase. If page parameters exist for the binding container, these are prepared and evaluated during this phase. Parameters that are defined on ADF task flows are now passed into the flow. ADF Faces uses this phase to override the `LocaleContext` on the model to the one specified in the request.

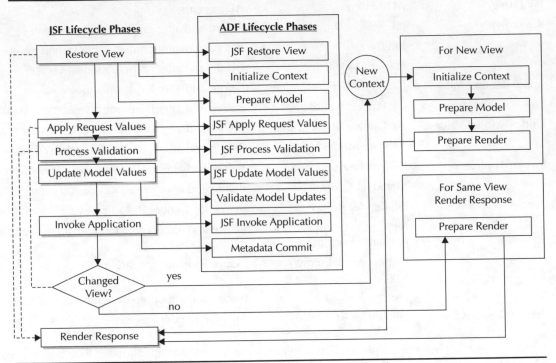

FIGURE 3-6 *ADF request lifecycle*

4. *JSF Apply Request Values.* No ADF model–specific interaction is associated with this phase and it provides only a hook point for developers to listen and respond to this phase.

5. *JSF Process Validations.* No ADF model–specific interaction is associated with this phase and it provides only a hook point for developers to listen and respond to this phase.

6. *Update Model Values.* The UI component values are used to update the business service. Values that are applied to the attribute bindings refresh their referenced iterator. The iterator refreshes if the `Refresh` or `RefreshCondition` conditions that are defined for the iterator return true. A refresh on the iterator does not force a query on the business service.

7. *Validate Model Updates.* The updated data is validated against the constraints defined on the ADF model layer. Exceptions are caught on the binding layer and cached for display to the user. The validation is performed on the binding, not the business service. In the case of ADF Business Components, this almost makes no difference because the domain validation rules defined in ADF Business Components are automatically exposed to the ADF binding layer.

8. *JSF Invoke Application.* No ADF model–specific interaction is associated with this phase and it provides only a hook point for developers to listen and respond to this phase.

9. *Metadata Commit.* This phase is important for applications that use the Metadata Service (MDS) layer to persist runtime changes.

NOTE
Information about how to leverage MDS in Fusion web applications can be found in Oracle's "Fusion Developer's Guide for Oracle Application Development Framework."

10. *Prepare Render.* After the Invoke Application phase, the lifecycle continues with the Render Response phase if no navigation is performed. Before entering this phase, the binding container object needs to be updated with the changes applied during the model update. This is when all dependent UI components are refreshed according to their current value in the binding layer. This phase is exposed to the application developers as renderModel.

11. *Render Response.* Produces the UI component visual state and sends it back to the client. This is also where the UI component Expression Language references to the ADF binding layer are evaluated.

   If application navigation is processed during the Invoke Application phase, the current binding context needs to be renewed with the binding objects of the page definition file associated with the navigation target. This is where the lifecycle performs a little detour, rerunning the Init Context and Prepare Model phases.

12. *Init Context.* Initializes the page definition file for the next ADF bound navigation stop.

13. *Prepare Model.* Sets any page parameter defined on the page definition file. For example, an ExecuteWithParams operation may have its input argument bound to a page definition parameter. So before the operation is executed, the parameter is passed in as the argument.

About Iterators and Their Refresh

An iterator binding in ADF is a reference to a rowset iterator and lives for the duration of a request. This means that for any subsequent access of the iterator binding, the binding needs to be refreshed, during which time it rebinds to the iterator that holds the record objects. If an iterator binding is never refreshed during the lifecycle, then it doesn't point to any iterator and no data is shown in the user interface.

In the case of ADF Business Components, the iterator reads its values from the business service through an implementation of the ViewObject interface. The ViewObject interface extends the RowSet and RowSetIterator interfaces. An implementation of RowSet manages a collection of view rows and is referenced by one or many rowset iterators. A rowset iterator enumerates through the rows exposed by a rowset and manages the row currency for the collection of rows. For scalability and performance reasons, the ADF Business Component application module is always released to the application module pool between requests. If a subsequent request of the same user session is issued before the application module is taken by another user session, then ADF Business Component internal algorithm tries its best to reunite the user session and its application module. When, between two requests, the application module is released to the application module pool and from there given to another user process, the application module is passivated, which means that its state is serialized and stored away for the

ADF Lifecycle Breakpoint Panel

The ADF Lifecycle Breakpoints panel, shown next, is a lightweight dialog available for the ADF Controller for developers to declaratively set debugging breakpoints to the lifecycle phases they want to analyze.

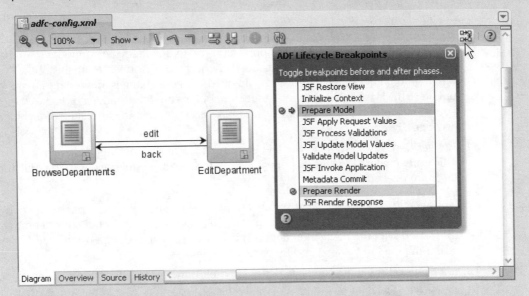

The developer sets the breakpoint for a lifecycle phase by clicking in either the left or right margin next to the phase name. Setting a breakpoint in the left margin will stop the process for debugging before the phase is entered; setting a breakpoint in the right margin stops the process for debugging at the end of the phase. The current lifecycle phase is highlighted in blue, and the phases that have a breakpoint attached are highlighted in pink. Stepping through the lifecycle enables developers to view the classes and states of the classes that are executed within the process of the current operation.

current user to recover. Part of the passivated information is the rowset iterator state so that it can be rebuilt the next time a user request comes in. A refresh of an iterator does not imply any query execution. To ensure an iterator is re-executed between requests, you explicitly need to execute it, calling the `Execute` built-in operation, which can be done in a method call activity if ADF task flows are used for the page navigation.

The two ADF lifecycle phases during which the iterator binding is refreshed are Prepare Model and Prepare Render. The condition under which an iterator binding refreshes can be specified using the `Refresh` and `RefreshCondition` properties exposed on the ADF binding definition.

Figure 3-7 shows the sequence in which the refresh condition is evaluated for an iterator. Developers use Expression Language to set the `RefreshCondition` property value to `true` or `false`.

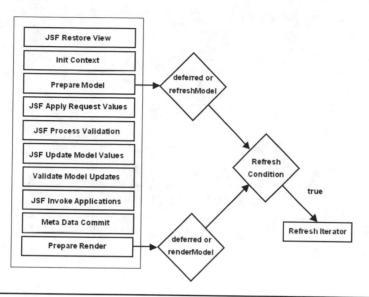

FIGURE 3-7 *Determining the default iterator refresh option*

Accessing Oracle ADF Business Components

In Fusion applications, the ADF Business Components (ADF BC) business service is accessed through the ADF application module Data Control, a thin adapter layer that obtains an instance of the BC application module from a pool of application modules at the beginning of a request for its duration. At the end of the request, the application module is released back to the ADF BC application module pool. The phases in which the ADF BC service layer is accessed during the ADF lifecycle depends on the action that is performed and the refresh settings on the iterator binding. Figure 3-8 shows the ADF BC access during the initial rendering of an ADF bound page.

The initial ADF page request accesses the ADF BC service layer during the JSF render response phase.

1. The application module is retrieved from the application module pool or created if no module exists in the pool.

2. The prepare session method is called on the application module for the framework or custom code to prepare the user session the first time the application module is referenced. For example, developers use this method to set the user context if Oracle RDBMS Virtual Private Database (VPD) security is used. The prepare session method is also executed in subsequent requests if the user's application module instance cannot be retrieved from the application module pool and instead is re-created from passivated state information.

3. The view object is executed and the iterator binding is refreshed to point to the view object default rowset iterator of the default rowset. A few ADF Faces components, such as `af:table`, expose a `contentDelivery` attribute for developers to define how

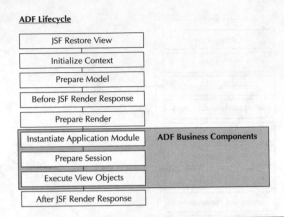

FIGURE 3-8 *ADF Business Component interaction with the ADF lifecycle during the initial page request*

the data should be fetched from the middle tier. ADF Faces components that have their `contentDelivery` attribute set to `lazy` don't reference their data in the initial request but use a deferred second partial page request to query the view object. If, for example, the `contentDelivery` attribute on a table is set to `immediate`, the data is fetched when the table renders, resulting in the lifecycle shown in Figure 3-9.

Figure 3-9 shows the ADF BC access within the ADF page lifecycle in case of a form update request. The ADF BC service is updated during the JSF Update Model Values phase. The view object is updated first before the entity object is updated and the defined validators are invoked on the updated attributes.

Notice that the Validate Model Updates phase in the ADF lifecycle is invoked after the validators on the entity object are processed. The Validate Model Updates phase performs validation on the validators defined on the ADF binding layer.

NOTE
If you're using ADF BC as a business service, you may not need to define validation on the binding layer. Best practices are to define validation on the entity object if you can. Other business services, such as POJO and Web Services, don't provide an integrated validation framework, in which case validation that is defined on the binding layer may be needed.

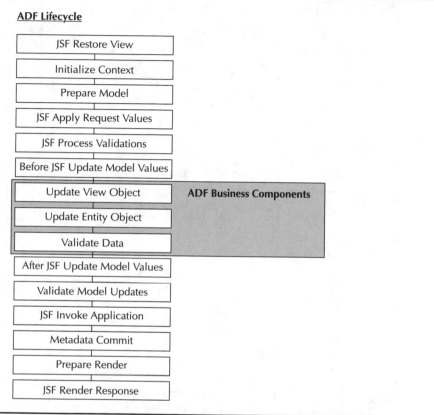

ADF Lifecycle

- JSF Restore View
- Initialize Context
- Prepare Model
- JSF Apply Request Values
- JSF Process Validations
- Before JSF Update Model Values
- Update View Object — **ADF Business Components**
- Update Entity Object
- Validate Data
- After JSF Update Model Values
- Validate Model Updates
- JSF Invoke Application
- Metadata Commit
- Prepare Render
- JSF Render Response

FIGURE 3-9   *ADF BC lifecycle integration during a form upgrade*

Oracle Fusion Page Lifecycle

Now that you've learned about individual lifecycles, let's have a look at the bigger picture, the Oracle Fusion lifecycle. As shown in Figure 3-10, any incoming HTTP request that may need access to the ADF binding layer is first processed by the ADF binding filter configured in the web .xml file. The `ADFBindingFilter` class that delegates the request to the `HttpBinding RequestHandler` class implements the binding filter. The role of the binding filter is to set up the ADF data binding context for each request and to prepare the data control instance for the incoming request. After the Java EE container calls the `doFilter` method on the `ADFBindingFilter`, the `BindingRequestHandler` object is called to initiate the ADF context. The `BindingContext` object for the request is initialized after the ADF context has been created to reset the input state, release no longer needed bindings, and call `beginRequest` on the configured data controls.

The JSF lifecycle, and the associated ADF page lifecycle, starts when the binding filter finished its initialization work. The binding container that represents the model is now ready to take the first request, which is after the Restore View phase to update the model for the request. If it is an initial request and the refresh condition on the iterator is left to the `deferred` default setting,

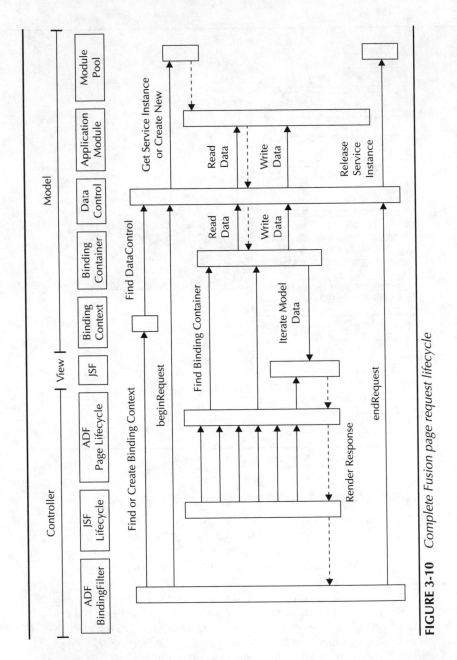

FIGURE 3-10 *Complete Fusion page request lifecycle*

then the binding layer is accessed during the Render Response phase. If the request is for update, then the binding layer is updated during the Update Model Values phase. At the end of the request, the ADF binding filter calls `endRequest` on the `BindingContext` for the data control instances to release their references to the `RowSetIterators` before the binding container is released.

Monitoring the ADF Lifecycle

Developers can create and configure custom lifecycle listeners to receive ADF lifecycle notifications at the beginning and the end of each phase to execute custom logic. Lifecycle listeners can be configured with the following scopes:

- **Global**   The page lifecycle listener is configured to execute for all lifecycle execution throughout the application.

- **Single ADF bounded page**   The lifecycle listener is configured in the page definition file, the ADF binding configuration, of an ADF bounded JSF page.

- **Programmatically**   The lifecycle listener is added programmatically from Java and remains active until it is removed or the user session is dismissed.

The following sections explain the three use cases and the creation of custom page phase listeners.

How to Create a Custom Page Phase Listener

Objects that should receive lifecycle notifications must implement the `PagePhaseListener` interface and contain implementations of the `afterPhase` and `beforePhase` methods. The method argument is an instance of `PagePhaseEvent` that passes the following information to the listener:

- **LifecycleContext**   The `LifecycleContext` object is passed to all phases of the page lifecycle. It extends `java.util.HashMap` and can be used to pass custom per-request data between the phases. It provides access to the `Lifecycle, the HttpServletRequest`, the `HttpServletResponse`, the `BindingContext`, and the `BindingContainer` objects.

- **PhaseId**   Returns the currently processed `PhaseId` as an `int` value. The `PhaseId` values are defined in the `Lifecycle` class, which is located in the oracle.adf.controller. v2.lifecycle package. To determine the current phase, developers can use one of the constants, such as `Lifecycle.PREPARE_MODEL_ID` that are defined in the `Lifecycle` class.

The following code snippet shows a simple debug listener that prints the current `PhaseId` as a translated string with whether it is printed before or after the phase:

```
import oracle.adf.controller.v2.lifecycle.PagePhaseEvent;
import oracle.adf.controller.v2.lifecycle.PagePhaseListener;

public class InteractivePagePhaseListener implements PagePhaseListener {
  public CustomPagePhaseListener() {
    super();
  }
```

```
public void afterPhase(PagePhaseEvent pagePhaseEvent) {
  String idStr = pagePhaseEvent.getPhaseId();
  System.out.println("after "+ Lifecycle.getPhaseName(idStr));
}
public void beforePhase(PagePhaseEvent pagePhaseEvent){
  String idStr = pagePhaseEvent.getPhaseId();
  System.out.println("before "+ Lifecycle.getPhaseName(idStr));
}
}
```

NOTE
When working with ADF lifecycle classes, you may see two classes with the same name stored in different packages. In such cases, make sure you reference classes located in the oracle.adf.controller.v2 package as the others are there for backward compatibility reasons only.

ADF phase listeners are configured in the adf-settings.xml file that is discussed in the next section.

How to Register Global Lifecycle Listeners

The new mechanism in Oracle JDeveloper 11*g* for developers to create and configure global lifecycle listeners is the adf-settings.xml configuration file. The adf-settings.xml file does not exist by default and needs to be created in the .adf\META-INF folder if needed. In contrast to JSF lifecycle listeners that are configured in the faces-config.xml file, the adf-settings.xml file allows developers to define the order in which page phase listeners are executed, a guarantee that does not exist in standard JSF. The order in which phase listeners execute is determined by the

Check for isDesignTime

When developing custom lifecycle listeners, it is considered best practices to check whether the listener execution environment is the Oracle JDeveloper design time. This little precaution avoids breaking or slowing down the UI rendering of the visual editor caused by missing listener dependencies or resource access latency. Here's an example:

```
public void afterPhase(PhaseEvent phaseEvent) {
  if(!isDesignTime(){
    //execute your custom code here
  }
//check if class runs in designtime
private boolean isDesignTime(){
  return Beans.isDesignTime();
}
```

`before-id-set` and `after-id-set` elements. The following table lists the metadata elements that are used to configure phase listeners in the adf-settings.xml file:

Element	Description
`lifecycle`	Beginning element of the lifecycle configuration in the adf-settings.xml file.
`phase-listener`	Start element that identifies the configuration of a phase listener. A phase listener is configured with a `listener-id` child element and a class `child` element. The value of the `listener-id` element must be unique. The `class` element references the implementation class of the listener and may be used more often within the same configuration.
`before-id-set`	This element is optional and defines the list of listeners that are executed after the current configured listener. The list of listeners is defined using multiple `listener-id` child elements.
`after-id-set`	This element is optional and defines the list of listeners that are executed before the current configured listener. The list of listeners is defined using multiple `listener-id` child elements.
`listener-id`	This references a listener by its ID. One to many `listener-id` elements may be added as child elements to the `before-id-set` and `after-id-set` elements.

The following configuration example defines three listeners. The third listener is configured to execute after the listener with the ID `AdfInteractiveAppListener1` but before `AdfInteractiveAppListener2`.

```xml
<?xml version="1.0" encoding="US-ASCII" ?>
<adf-settings xmlns="http://xmlns.oracle.com/adf/settings">
<adf-config xmlns="http://xmlns.oracle.com/adf/config">
  <adfc-controller-config
   xmlns="http://xmlns.oracle.com/adf/controller/config">
    <lifecycle>
      <phase-listener>
        <listener-id>AdfInteractiveAppListener1</listener-id>
        <class>adf.interactive.view.AdfInteractiveAppListener</class>
      </phase-listener>
      <phase-listener>
        <listener-id>AdfInteractiveAppListener2</listener-id>
        <class>adf.interactive.view.AdfInteractiveAppListener2</class>
      </phase-listener>
      <phase-listener>
        <listener-id> AdfInteractiveAppListener3</listener-id>
        <class> adf.interactive.view.AdfInteractiveAppListener3</class>
        <before-id-set>
          <listener-id> AdfInteractiveAppListener1</listener-id>
```

```
          </before-id-set>
          <after-id-set>
            <listener-id>CustomPagePhaseListener2</listener-id>
          </after-id-set>
        </phase-listener>
      </lifecycle>
    </adfc-controller-config>
  </adf-config>
</adf-settings>
```

To create the adf-settings.xml for a view layer project in Oracle JDeveloper 11*g*, choose File | New and select the XML entry in the General category. Create a new XML document, name it *adf-settings.xml*, and set the location to the .adf\META-INF directory of the current workspace. Add the file content shown above. After creation, the adf-settings.xml file is accessible from the Application Resources panel in the Oracle JDeveloper Application Navigator. It's located in the Descriptors | ADF META-INF entry.

Phase Execution Order for Multiple Listeners

The `before-id-set` and `after-id-set` child elements of the `phase-listener` element define the order in which a listener is executed compared to other listeners. Listeners are invoked twice during each lifecycle phase. The first invocation is for the `beforePhase` method, which executes at the beginning of the phase, and the second invocation is for the `afterPhase` method, which executes at the end of the phase. So if two listeners A and B are defined, with A being accessed before B, then the expected order of execution is this: "beforePhase A," "beforePhase B," "afterPhase A," and "afterPhase B." In reality, this is not the case, and instead the order of execution is this: "beforePhase A," "beforePhase B," "afterPhase B," and "afterPhase A." This order follows the rule in software development in which the order of cleanup is the opposite of the order in which initialization is performed. For example, any initialization code and resource allocation performed by listener B in its before phase method is given the chance to be cleaned up before resources used by listener A are cleaned up. If you are interested in the listener after phase execution only, without having to use any cleanup code, you should be aware about listener B firing before listener A.

How to Register Listeners for a Single ADF Bounded Page

Lifecycle listeners that should listen for a single ADF bounded page only are configured in the page definition file that is associated with the JSF page. The page definition file is created automatically for a JSF page when the data control palette is used to drag-and-drop collections or attributes as UI components to the page. To configure a page phase listener for a single ADF page, select the associated page definition file in the Application Navigator or do a right mouse click on the ADF page entry in the Application Navigator or the visual editor and choose Go to Page Definition from the context menu. Open the Structure Window and select the *<page name>*PageDef root element and open the Property Inspector. Select the Controller Class property, click the arrow icon to the right, and choose Edit to browse the class path for the custom phase listener class.

How to Register and Deregister Page Listeners Programmatically

Listeners that are configured declaratively don't have a defined scope and execute globally for all pages of an application. No declarative option exists to tell a listener under which condition, other than the lifecycle phase, it should be active and when it should stand by. A Java API is exposed on the `ADFLifecycle` class for use cases that need a listener to be set and removed dynamically. A feature of the ADF Controller in JDeveloper 11g is that it can invoke methods during page navigation, which can be used to add and remove lifecycle listeners dynamically to monitor a specific workflow within an application. As you will see later when looking at ADF Task Flow, a few event entry points exist, such as method activities, initializers, and finalizers, that can be used to add phase listeners temporarily.

ADF Lifecycle to Register Custom Listeners

The `oracle.adf.controller.v2.lifecycle.ADFLifecycle` class is a singleton that exposes the `getInstance` static method for the application developer to obtain an instance handle. The `ADFLifecycle` class extends `Lifecycle`, through which it exposes the following methods:

```
addPagePhaseListener (PagePhaseListener listener,
                      String listenerId,
                      Set<String> beforeIdSet,
                      Set<String> afterIdSet)
```

This registers a listener at a specific position within a list of listeners. The two list arguments, `beforeIdSet` and `afterIdSet`, are used to determine the position of the added listener in the execution order for a specific phase. Both, the `beforeIdSet` and `afterIdSet` arguments, can be passed in as null if there is no requirement to call the added listeners in a specific order.

```
removePagePhaseListener(String listenerId)
```

This unregisters a listener using its registration ID. The method call returns `true` if the listener ID existed and has been removed successfully.

```
getPagePhaseListeners
```

This returns the list of listener IDs for all registered listeners in the order in which they are executed. ADF internal listeners are not listed and always execute before any public listener.

```
getPagePhaseListener(String listenerId)
```

This returns the phase listener found for the provided ID. If no listener is found, then this method returns null.

These methods are exposed from the `PagePhaseListenerManager` that the `Lifecycle` class extends. Methods with the same name but different signatures exist in the `Lifecycle` class. They are deprecated and should not be used.

The following example adds a new phase listener to the set of existing listeners. If the added listener does not need to be executed in any particular order, the last two arguments in the call to addPagePhaseListener can be passed in as null. In this code example, the AdfInteractiveAppListener is configured to execute after the MyOtherPagePhaseListener.

```
public void addListener() {
    HashSet beforeListeners = new HashSet();
    HashSet afterListeners = new HashSet();
    String  listenerId = "AdfInteractiveAppListener";
    beforeListeners.add("MyOtherPagePhaseListener");
    ADFLifecycle adflifecycle= ADFLifecycle.getInstance();
    adflifecycle.addPagePhaseListener(
      new InteractivePagePhaseListener(),
      listenerId,
      beforeListeners,
      afterListeners);
}
```

The removePagePhaseListener removes a listener by its ID and returns true if the removal was successful. If the listener could not be found, then this method returns false.

```
public boolean removeListener () {
    String  listenerId = "AdfInteractiveAppListener";
    ADFLifecycle adflifecycle= ADFLifecycle.getInstance();
    return adflifecycle.removePagePhaseListener(listenerId);
}
```

Lifecycle Customization

Following up on the preceding section that discusses the available options to monitor the ADF page lifecycle, we'll next look at how the default lifecycle can be changed by application developers to adapt it to their individual needs.

Global Page Lifecycle Customization

The ADFPhaseListener class executes the ADF PageLifecycle for ADF pages, reporting all model and controller errors to the FacesContext for display. In previous releases of Oracle ADF, the ADFPhaseListener class had a public scope and was configured in the faces-config.xml file. Application developers extended the ADFPhaseListener to customize the ADF page lifecycle globally—for example, to translate system error messages into a user-friendly format or suppress them from display. In Oracle JDeveloper 11g, the ADFPhaseListener class became an internal scope and is located in the oracle.adfinternal.controller.faces.lifecycle package. Though still a public class, the createPageLifecycle method has been removed so that it can no longer be used to customize the page lifecycle. To perform global lifecycle customization in JDeveloper 11g, a custom PagePhaseListener that listens to the JSF after the Restore View phase needs to be created and registered in the adf-settings.xml file.

NOTE
The previous version of the `ADFPhaseListener` *class still exists in the* `oracle.adf.controller.faces.lifecycle` *package. The class is there for backward-compatibility reasons but is marked as deprecated for removal in a future release of Oracle JDeveloper.*

The `PagePhaseListener` code that follows registers a custom lifecycle class, `AdfInteractivePageController`, to replace the default lifecycle handling globally:

```
import javax.faces.event.PhaseId;
import oracle.adf.controller.v2.context.LifecycleContext;
import oracle.adf.controller.v2.lifecycle.PagePhaseEvent;
import oracle.adf.controller.v2.lifecycle.PagePhaseListener;

public class AdfInteractiveAppListener implements PagePhaseListener{
  public AdfInteractiveAppListener() {
    super();
  }
  //lifecycle method to listen for the RESTORE_VIEW phase
  //to set the custom controller
  public void afterPhase(PagePhaseEvent pagePhaseEvent) {
    int RESTORE_VIEW_ID = PhaseId.RESTORE_VIEW.getOrdinal();
    LifecycleContext lctx = pagePhaseEvent.getLifecycleContext();
    if (pagePhaseEvent.getPhaseId() == RESTORE_VIEW_ID){
      lctx.setPageController(new AdfInteractivePageController());
    }
  }
  public void beforePhase(PagePhaseEvent pagePhaseEvent) {}
}
```

To customize the lifecycle, developers override the methods exposed by the `PageController`, such as `validateModelUpdates`, to include custom code in the lifecycle handling or to suppress the default behavior by commenting out the call to its super class:

```
import oracle.adf.controller.v2.context.LifecycleContext;
import oracle.adf.controller.faces.lifecycle.PageController;

public class AdfInteractivePageController extends PageController {
  public AdfInteractivePageController() {
    super();
  }
@Override
  public void validateModelUpdates (LifecycleContext lifecycleContext){
    //add your custom code here and optionally suppress the
    //default behavior by commenting out the call to super
    super.validateModelUpdates(lifecycleContext);
  }
```

The extended `PageController` class implements the `PageLifecycle` functionality by delegating incoming calls to the current `PageLifecycle` instance, which in the case of ADF

Faces RC is `FacesPageLifecycle` located in the `oracle.adf.controller.faces` `.lifecycle` package. If the user interface is ADF Faces RC, then optionally the custom page controller class can extend the `FacesPageLifecycle` class directly to access or override exposed ADF Faces methods such as the following:

■ The `addError` method adds a message for each error reported by the `BindingContainer` to the `FacesContext` object.

■ The `addMessage` method is used to customize the display of error messages reported by the `BindingContainer`. The method can access the configured error handler from the data binding context by a call to `getErrorHandler`. You don't need to override this method to implement a custom error handler. To configure a custom error handler, you use the DataBindings.cpx file, as explained later in this chapter in the section "Creating a Custom Error Handler Class."

To override a method of the super class, open the code editor window and choose Source | Override Methods from the JDeveloper main menu. Select the methods to override from the opened dialog and click OK to add them to the code editor window. The methods are added so that the default functionality is not impacted until the developer changes the added method signature.

TIP
Overriding ADF lifecycle methods and classes is an advanced topic with which you should be familiar. We recommend filing a service request with Oracle customer support to obtain the ADF source code under a read-only license agreement.

Local Page Lifecycle Customization

Use cases that don't require the page lifecycle to change for all pages can apply local lifecycle customizations on the page definition level. Each page definition has a `ControllerClass` property that you can configure with the absolute class and package name of a custom page controller class that extends the `PageController` class.

To access the `ControllerClass` property for an ADF page, open the PageDef file associated with the page in the Structure window. You do this either by double-clicking the file entry in the Application Navigator, where by default it is located under <view project package name>.pageDefs, or by choosing Go To Page Definition from the page context menu.

In the Structure window, select the root node and open the Property Inspector. To browse the class path for a suitable controller class, click the arrow icon next to the ControllerClass property field and choose Edit. The custom controller class is the same class used for the global lifecycle customization. Optionally, if this class needs to be aware of the lifecycle phase in which it resides, you can implement the `PagePhaseListener` interface. A simplified stub for such a page controller is shown here:

```
import oracle.adf.controller.v2.lifecycle.Lifecycle;
import oracle.adf.controller.v2.lifecycle.PageController;
import oracle.adf.controller.v2.lifecycle.PagePhaseEvent;
import oracle.adf.controller.v2.lifecycle.PagePhaseListener;
public class AdfInteractivePageController extends PageController
```

```
                                             implements PagePhaseListener{
public AdfInteractivePageController(){
     super();
}

//add overrides here for the methods exposed by the PageController

public void afterPhase(PagePhaseEvent pagePhaseEvent){}
public void beforePhase(PagePhaseEvent pagePhaseEvent){}
}
```

Methods you may want to override based on your business requirements include `validateModelUpdates`, `validateInputValues`, or any of the ADF lifecycle methods.

NOTE
If the page definition belongs to a page fragment (.jsff) in a bounded task flow, then the controller class instead needs to be the fully qualified name of a class that implements the `RegionController` *interface.*

Use Case: Form Entry Wizard

A common use case in Oracle ADF applications are the wizard-style edit pages in which multiple pages work together to update a single collection exposed by the business service. Within a wizard, each page submits its data entry for the JSF model to be updated. As shown in Figure 3-11, submitting a wizard page often results in errors that report constraint violations that occur on ADF model attributes that are not part of the current wizard view. As mentioned earlier when discussing the `af:subform` component, the error is caused by the ADF binding layer that triggers data control validation, which then occurs on all attributes of a collection—a view object in this case—and not only those attributes that have been changed.

To avoid validation errors raised by attributes that are not updated during a partial form submit, developers need to customize the page lifecycle to suppress validation for wizard pages. This can be done by creating and configuring a custom page controller class, as explained earlier, or declaratively in the binding layer, a new feature in JDeveloper 11g.

To suppress validation declaratively, Oracle JDeveloper 11g introduces the `skipValidation` property in the page definition, the pageDef.xml file, for developers to disable ADF model validation for a page. To edit this property, right-click the ADF page in the JDeveloper application navigator or the WYSIWYG editor view and choose Go to Page Definition from the context menu. In the Structure window, select the root node of the page definition and open the Property Inspector to edit the `skipValidation` property.

The following `skipValidation` property values can be configured:

- **false** The default value setting enforces model validation on each model update.

- **true** Suppresses all model validation except the client-side binding-level attribute validations required field and type conversion errors.

- **skipDataControls** Only validates the current rows of iterator bindings that sent in changes for this page. In the view object case, the data control validation invokes

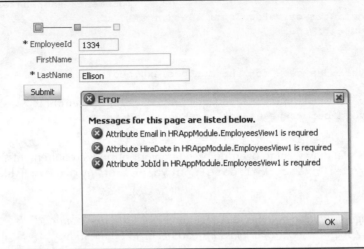

FIGURE 3-11 *Validation error for attributes not displayed on the page*

validation constraints defined on the entity level, such as the required or not null constraint that is responsible for the error shown in Figure 3-11.

- **custom** Used in combination with the `CustomValidator` property to allow developers to determine at runtime whether or not model validation should be performed. The property value is an Expression Language reference to a managed bean that implements the `oracle.binding.BindingContainerValidator` interface.

Use Case: Using af:subform in ADF Forms

As discussed earlier, the ADF Faces `af:subform` component allows developers to partition an input form so that parts of it can be submitted without causing validation errors on nonsubmitted fields. We mentioned that the subform component doesn't work well with ADF bound forms because the validation on the data control is performed for all attributes, not only those that are submitted by the subform, and it requires extra configuration. The required extra configuration is to set the `skipValidation` property in the ADF page definition file of the view that holds the subform to the `skipDataControls` value option, or to write and configure a custom page controller class that overrides the `validateModelUpdates` method to suppress validation when a subform is submitted. In addition, you need to make sure that the submit of an `af:subform` component is issued as a partial submit, either by setting the command component `partialSubmit` attribute to `true` or using the `autosubmit` attribute on an input field.

TIP
When you have a choice of how to implement a use case and one of the options is declarative, we recommend using this option. This not only simplifies development, but is also less prone to error and easier to handle when migrating to future releases. Especially when you are new to Oracle ADF, using the declarative development features is a safe bet.

Exception Handling and Error Reporting

Exceptions that occur in the context of the DCBindingContainer in Oracle ADF are handled by the DCErrorHandlerImpl framework class that implements the DCErrorHandler interface. The DCErrorHandlerImpl class contains the following public error handling methods:

- **reportException** Takes instances of DCBindingContainer and Exception as input arguments and ensures that the exception is thrown as an instance of JboException, which is the root class of all exceptions thrown by the ADF Business Component framework. You override this method in a custom error handler to analyze the exception for specific errors you want to handle yourself.

- **getDisplayMessage** Takes instances of BindingContext and Exception as input arguments to return the display message for this error. The internal error code information is not added to the message, which is important to point out since this has changed since previous releases. Override this method to change the message displayed to the client. Returning a null value suppresses the exception from displaying.

- **getDetailedDisplayMessage** Returns application-specific message details in a format suitable for the view layer used. It takes instances of BindingContext, RegionBinding, and Exception as input arguments. This method is used to provide messages that are formatted for the target display. The default error handler does not implement this method and always returns null. Override this method to provide HTML markup–formatted detail information for an error.

The DCErrorHandler handles model and business service exceptions only and does not handle exceptions thrown on the application level. Application-specific exceptions that are thrown on the view layer or the ADF Controller are handled by specific exception handlers defined on the ADF Controller. Either way, the error messages are displayed on the FacesContext so that from an user perspective, there is no difference in the way errors display on the UI.

NOTE
Errors may occur on different layers within an ADF application. The error handler defined on the ADF binding only handles errors that happen on the business service and the binding layer. Errors that occur in the ADF Controller or a managed bean in the ADF Faces RC UI must be handled extra.

Creating a Custom Error Handler Class

A custom exception handler class extends DCErrorHandlerImpl and is configured globally for an application in the DataBindings.cpx file. Users of previous versions of Oracle ADF may note that to change the error handling, a custom phase listener and lifecycle class are no longer required. A use case for a custom error handler is the handling of database errors—for example, to remove the ORA-xxx error code from the message.

```
import javax.faces.context.FacesContext;
import oracle.adf.model.binding.DCBindingContainer;
import oracle.adf.model.binding.DCErrorHandlerImpl;
import oracle.jbo.DMLException;

public class AdfInteractiveErrorHandler extends DCErrorHandlerImpl {
  public AdfInteractiveErrorHandler() {
    super(true);
  }
  @override
  public void reportException(DCBindingContainer bc, Exception ex) {
    super.reportException(bc,ex);
  }
}
```

If an exception is raised by the framework, it will be passed to the reportException method, at which point the developer can choose to suppress it, handle it, or pass it on to the default exception handler routine.

Registering a Custom Error Handler with ADF

The error handler is globally configured for the whole ADF application. To replace the existing error handler with a custom version, use the ErrorHandlerClass property of the DataBindings.cpx file to reference a custom handler class. In the Oracle JDeveloper Application Navigator, select the DataBindings.cpx file entry that is located in the same directory as the page definition files and open the Structure window (CTRL-SHIFT-S). In the Structure window, select the DataBindings root node and open the Property Inspector. In the Property Inspector, click the arrow icon next to the ErrorHandlerClass property field. This opens a dialog to browse the classpath for the custom error handler class. Choose a class and save the project.

Summary

For many web developers who come from a markup-oriented programming environment such as JSP with Struts, getting familiar with the JSF lifecycle and accepting it for what it does is a difficult learning process. If there is a steep learning curve in Fusion web application development, then it surely involves the understanding and customization of the JSF and ADF page lifecycles. As a Fusion application developer, understanding the JSF and ADF lifecycles is an important skill because it helps you understand what happens in your application at a specific time during the request. We gave a lot of hints and tips for best practices within this chapter, but we want to iterate the most important one: Always look for a declarative solution first before starting complex coding. This is less prone to error and easier to handle when migrating to future releases.

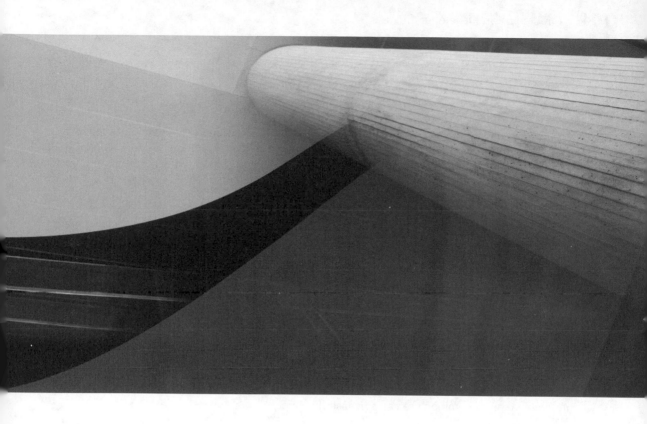

CHAPTER
4

Introduction to Oracle
ADF Task Flows

Oracle ADF bounded task flows make the juice worth the squeeze in JavaServer Faces application development. It accelerates productivity, promotes reusability, and brings ease of use to web application development.

he default page-based navigation model of the JavaServer Faces (JSF) standard in Java EE serves well for business applications that have only simple navigation requirements. However, developers who face complex routing decisions and data initialization requirements soon drive the default JSF navigation model to the edge. Missing functionality in standard JSF include the invocation of custom business logic as part of the page flow, flows within pages, declarative router decisions, declarative exception handling, reusable flows, transaction coordination, and additional memory scopes that prevent developers from abusing large scopes such as a session for temporary data holding. Luckily, JSF was designed with extensibility in mind and allows developers to change the default behavior with custom implementations, such as an extended navigation handler. To meet the expectations and the requirements of several thousand in-house developers and Oracle customers who build large-scale business applications on a day-by-day basis, the Oracle Fusion web architecture provides such an enhanced controller extension for JSF 1.2, the Oracle ADF Controller.

This chapter introduces the concepts and configuration of the new Oracle ADF Controller and its core functionalities. You'll learn about hook points and the functionality that the ADF Controller provides on top of the standard JSF navigation model. Chapters 5 and 6 dive into the implementation of common use cases by task flow type.

ADF Controller Overview

Navigation in Oracle Fusion web applications is handled by the ADF Controller, which offers a modular approach for designing application flows in JSF and ADF Faces Rich Client (RC). In contrast to the standard JSF page navigation model, which at runtime uses a single navigation graph defined in one or many copies of the faces-config.xml configuration file, the ADF Controller allows developers to break up the application flow into reusable processes. The ADF Controller term "task flow" supercedes the term "page flow" used in JSF and indicates the ability not only to navigate between pages but to also to include non-UI navigation targets such as method calls, router decisions, and calls to subflows.

ADF Controller Architecture

The ADF Controller engine is defined in the internal `NavigationHandlerImpl` class that extends the `javax.faces.application.NavigationHandler` of the JavaServer Faces framework. A `faces-config.xml` configuration file that is added to the `META-INF` directory of the ADF Controller library registers the Oracle controller with the JavaServer Faces framework at runtime. No extra configuration is required for applications to use the ADF Controller.

After successful registration, the ADF Controller handles all JSF navigation requests first. From an architecture point of view, the JSF default navigation model delegates all navigation handling to the ADF Controller. If a navigation request cannot be satisfied by the ADF Controller, control is passed back to the JSF navigation handler. Because the ADF Controller is build on top of the JSF navigation model, application developers can use the `handleNavigation` method exposed on the `javax.faces.application.Application` class to invoke navigation cases programmatically.

```
FacesContext fctx = FacesContext.getCurrentInstance();
Application application = fctx.getApplication();
NavigationHandler navHandler = application.getNavigationHandler();
navHandler.handleNavigation(fctx,<from action as String>,
                                  <outcome as String>);
```

The ADF Controller has security built-in and, for applications that have Oracle ADF Security configured, enforces access control on ADF-bound JSF pages and bounded task flows. At runtime, the ADF Controller navigation handler delegates security checks to ADF Security, which enforces user authentication if needed and authorizes resource access with the Java Authentication and Authorization Service (JAAS). For more details about ADF Security, see Chapter 21.

NOTE
Though the integration of the ADF Controller in the JSF framework allows application developers to use both the JSF and the ADF Controller navigation model, Oracle recommends that you use one of the two and use it consistently.

Two Flavors of Task Flow: Unbounded and Bounded

Two flavors of task flow exist in ADF Controller: bounded and unbounded. Leaving aside the flow control enhancements in ADF, the unbounded task flow is similar to the JSF page flow, whereas the bounded task flow does not have an equivalent in the current JSF standard.

Unbounded Task Flows

Navigation within an unbounded task flow can start anywhere in the flow by the end user pointing the browser to a specific view activity. In addition, no defined exit point exists that, when reached, cleans up the memory allocated by the user session before exiting the flow. Unbounded task flows are usually referred to as the top-level, or bootstrapping, task flow and may be used as the entry point into a Fusion web application.

Bounded Task Flows

Oracle ADF bounded task flows make the juice worth the squeeze in JavaServer Faces application development. It accelerates productivity, promotes reusability, and brings ease of use to web application development. With bounded task flows, application developers are able to modularize the application design to build process flows that execute within defined boundaries, that have their own memory scope, and that are entered through a single defined entry point.

In Fusion web applications, a bounded task flow is either called from a URL, called from other task flows, or referenced in an ADF Task Flow binding that is used with ADF regions. If called from another task flow, task flow input parameters can be used to pass data into the called task flow, preventing tight coupling of the bounded task flow to the caller context. Similar, return values are used to return data upon exiting the called task flow. It is not possible in a bounded task flow to access a page within the flow directly using the browser URL field.

NOTE
Bounded task flows can be configured to share a data control instance between the calling and the called task flow, which is also the default setting. In such a configuration, the information about the current row selection state does not need to be passed as an input parameter. However, the decision of whether or not to use shared data control scopes is a design decision and depends on how generic and reusable the called bounded task flow should be.

ADF Regions   ADF regions represent a special use case of bounded task flows in that the task flow executes within an area of a parent page. In traditional JSF applications, navigation has to be off the current JSF page to complete a subtask of the current business process to eventually return. An example for such an interruption is a login form in a self-service application in which users may log into the application, create a new account, or reset a lost password. A login flow defined in a bounded task flow and added as a region to an ADF Faces page routes the user through any of the three processes without forcing the user to leave the page. Bounded task flows that are designed to execute in regions use page fragments instead of stand-alone JSF pages.

ADF Controller Configuration Files

The configuration files used to configure ADF Controller are adfc-config.xml, adf-settings.xml and XML configuration files for the bounded task flows.

adfc-config.xml File

The adfc-config.xml file is the bootstrapping configuration file for the application unbounded task flow and is located in the public_html\WEB-INF directory of the view layer project. It contains metadata for top-level control flows, managed beans, and activities. JSF framework configurations such as converters, validators, and language settings are not configured in the adfc-config.xml. Those settings are defined in the standard faces-config.xml file.

Multiple copies of the adfc-config.xml configuration file may exist in a single application. During application startup, the ADF Controller searches the view layer project WEB-INF directory and the META-INF directories of the ADF library files available in the application classpath for copies of the adfc-config.xml configuration file.

NOTE
ADF libraries are explained in Chapter 15.

At runtime, only a single unbounded task flow instance exists and contains the configuration from all bootstrap configuration files defined for an application. Bootstrap configurations are defined in the following locales:

- The default adfc-config.xml file

- Copies of adfc-config.xml that are contained in the META-INF directory of an imported library

- Copies of the adfc-config.xml file with a different name that are created in the view layer project and referenced from the adfc-config.xml file through the metadata-resources element

In contrast to bounded task flow definitions that are lazily loaded, unbounded task flow definitions are loaded all at once. It is the responsibility of application developers to define and follow a naming scheme for activities that prevents naming collisions when multiple copies of adfc-config.xml are used.

adf-settings.xml File

The adf-settings.xml file is a shared configuration file that is not solely related to ADF task flows and is located in the .adf\META-INF directory of the application. Developers use the adf-settings.xml configuration file to extend and customize the ADF lifecycle with custom ADF phase listeners.

Multiple copies of the adf-settings.xml configuration file may exist for an application—for example, added through libraries, which are merged to a single file at runtime. The adf-settings.xml file is not created by default when starting a new application development project and needs to be created manually if needed.

Bounded Task Flow Configuration

Bounded task flows are defined in their own configuration XML files, which use the same activity flow elements as the unbounded task flow configuration plus additional elements for the bounded task flow–specific functionality such as default activity, transaction scope, reentrance condition and more. Bounded task flow configurations are stored in the project WEB-INF directory, in subdirectories of the WEB-INF directory, or in the META-INF directory of a Java Archive (JAR) file for task flows that are deployed in an ADF library.

Task Flows Don't Own the Page

Task flows don't own the pages they reference. All ADF Faces pages are located in the web project HTML root directory or a subdirectory of it. Independent of whether or not a page is referenced in a bounded or unbounded task flow, or both, it is always directly accessible from the browser URL field. Application developers should be aware of this and implement a protection strategy, such as one through ADF Security, that prevents users from directly accessing pages that they are not authorized to access. For more information, see Chapter 21. In addition, pages or page fragments may be referenced from multiple bounded task flows.

ADF Controller Activities and Control Flow Rules

Both task flow types, bounded and unbounded, consist of a group of activities and control flows. Activities are the basic ADF Controller objects and represent the starting and the end points of a control flow. Activities can be page views, or more specialized actions such as method calls, router decisions, or bounded task flow calls.

There are two options to add an activity to a task flow diagram.

- Drag and drop the activity from ADF Task Flow category of the Oracle JDeveloper Component palette and use Property Inspector to edit its configuration.

- Drag and drop a page or page fragment as a view activity from the Application Navigator, or use the Data Control palette to drag and drop methods and operations as method activities.

NOTE
If you compare your diagram view with the screen shots in Figure 4-1 and Figure 4-2, you may notice that yours displays overlay icons, indicating warnings and errors, while ours doesn't. You can switch off the display of error and warning icons by selecting the Show menu item on top of the diagrammer. From here you can specify the information for which you want icons to be displayed on your activities. This is also what we did before capturing the screen shots.

In the following sections, the available ADF Controller activity types are introduced and explained.

Design Time Icon	Activity
	View activity
	Method call activity
	Router activity
	Task flow call activity
	Return activity
	URL view activity
	Save point restore activity

NOTE
Subelements that are used to specify the configuration of activities have id attributes generated, which start with leading underlines. The ids are used internally to support ADF Task Flows customization with Oracle ADF Meta Data Services (MDS). Since the ids are not relevant for application developers to work with ADF Task Flows, for clarity, we removed them from all example configurations provided in this and the following chapters.

View Activity

View activities represent the visual end points of a navigation flow and are either pages or page fragments. JSF pages are defined as JavaServer Pages (JSP) pages or documents. JSP documents have a .jspx filename extension and use a well-formed XML syntax that makes it easy for integrated development environments (IDEs) to parse and validate the page content to ensure it is portable across application servers. In addition, using an easy-to-parse syntax allows for automated migration and upgrades of application page sources. The use of JSP documents, and thus the .jspx file extension, is preferred in JSF. Navigating between pages performs a full browser refresh.

Page fragments are JSF page includes that cannot run stand-alone. In contrast to JSF pages, which start with the f:view element, page fragments use jsp:root as the first markup element. Page fragments in ADF Faces use the file extension .jsff and can be added to a page through the jsp:include directive in a f:subview element or, if contained in an ADF bounded task flow, an ADF region.

```
<f:subview id="fragment1">
  <jsp:include flush="true" page="/fragments1.jsff"/>
</f:subview>
```

Using the JSP include tag, page fragments are added to the parent page at compile time. In this case, ADF binding references in the page fragment are expected to be defined in the ADF page definition file of the parent page.

Page fragments that are contained in a bounded task flow and referenced from an ADF region in the parent page can have their own ADF binding definitions. This is also the Oracle recommended option to include page fragments that use ADF.

NOTE
See Chapter 6 for a detailed discussion of ADF regions.

The following table shows view activity metadata elements and attributes that are commonly used in unbounded and bounded task flows.

Metadata	Description
id	A unique string that identifies the view activity in the ADF Controller configuration metadata. View activities are referenced by their id value and not the physical page name they represent, which allows the same page to be added multiple times within a flow definition. By default, the id value is set to the name of the page without the file extension.

Metadata	Description
page	Attribute that references the JSF page displayed by a view activity. The page reference always starts with a forward slash / and may contain subdirectory names for pages that don't reside directly in the public_html folder of the view layer project.

input-page-parameter	An optional configuration element that allows developers to pass data between pages upon page forward navigation. The input parameter reads its value from the request, session, or other scope and writes it to a managed bean or the ADF binding layer of the target page. Here the input parameter of the "Page2" view activity reads the value of the message attribute in the request scope to write it to the setTxtValue method of the Page2Bean managed bean:
	 `<view id="Page2">`
	 `<page>/Page2.jspx</page>`
	 `<input-page-parameter>`
	 `<from-value>`
	 `#{requestScope.message}`
	 `</from-value>`
	 `<to-value>#{Page2Bean.txtValue}</to-value>`
	 `</input-page-parameter>`
	 `</view>`
	 In Page2.jspx, a text field may be bound to this method to display the message.
	 `<af:inputText label="The input message" value="#{Page2Bean.txtValue}"/>`
	 On the page that initiates the navigation to the "Page2" view activity, a SetPropertyListener component may be used on a button to add the parameter value to the request:
	 `<af:setPropertyListener from="#{'hello world'}"`
	 `to="#{requestScope.message}" type="action"/>`
	 Page input parameters help developers build pages that are independent of others so they can be reused.
	 Note that request scope doesn't work with GET requests that are issued when setting the redirect option on an activity. In this case, use a broader scope or request parameters to pass information from one page to another.

bookmark	Optional property for view activities in unbounded task flows. The property identifies a view activity as bookmarkable by the application user. The default behavior in JSF is that pages don't show their request URL parameters in the browser URL field, which makes the URL unusable for bookmarking. Setting the bookmark property on a view activity makes the ADF Controller present the full request URL including request parameters added by the application developer and other required state information. For more information of how to set a view activity to be bookmarkable, see Chapter 5.

Metadata	Description
redirect	A significant difference between the standard JSF navigation model and ADF Controller is the flagging of a page to be accessed by a client-side redirect request. In standard JSF, the `redirect` property is added to the navigation case, the flow definition. In ADF Controller, this flag is added to the view activity that a flow is accessing next. In both cases, setting the `redirect` flag to `true` changes the page request type from postback to redirect. The default value for this property is `false`.
train-stop	A train represents a progression of related pages guiding an end user through the completion of a task. The `train-stop` element marks a view activity to become a stop in a bounded task flow train model.

NOTE
All task flow activities, including view activities, may have an optional description *and* display-name *subelement defined. The information provided by these elements is displayed when you move the mouse over an activity in the task flow diagram. You can use the Property Inspector to edit these elements.*

Method Call Activity

The method call activity enables developers to invoke Java or ADF exposed methods within control flows. Methods can take input parameters, produce results, and influence the navigation flow of an application. The method activity element can be used with methods exposed on managed beans, ADF operation bindings, and ADF method bindings.

The following table shows method activity metadata elements and attributes that are commonly used in unbounded and bounded task flows.

NOTE
In this table, the term "pageFlowScope" is used. The pageFlowScope is an additional memory scope in ADF Task Flow and is discussed later in this chapter. For now, you can look at it as a map to store and read objects.

Metadata	Description
id	Identifies a method call activity within the task flow and is used as the navigation target to abstract navigation from the name of the actual method invoked.

Metadata	Description
method	Mandatory element that takes a `method` expression as its value. The expression language either points to an ADF operation binding, such as `#{bindings.Create.execute}`, or a managed bean method, such as `#{MailBean.checkInbox}`.

```
<method-call id="checkMails">
  <method>
    #{MailBean.checkInbox}
  </method>
  <parameter>
    <class>java.lang.String</class>
    <value>#{'P1'}</value>
  </parameter>
  <return-value>
    #{pageFlowScope.message}
  </return-value>
  <outcome>
    <to-string/>
  </outcome>
</method-call>
```

The next navigation target after completing the method call activity execution is defined either statically by a fixed outcome string determined by the application developer,

```
<outcome>
  <fixed-outcome>back</fixed-outcome>
</outcome>
```

or dynamically by the result of a toString conversion of the object returned by the method,

```
<outcome>
  <to-string/>
</outcome>
```

When an object is returned as the result of a method call, make sure that the object's toString method addresses a valid navigation case.

Metadata	Description

`parameter`	Optional element that allows input arguments to be passed to a method call.
	
	`<parameter>`
	`    <value>#{'P1'}</value>`
	`</parameter>`
	
	Here the managed bean method has a single argument of type String defined. Note that the value of an input argument always is the outcome of the evaluation of an Expression Language. Even if the input argument is a static string, is has to be provided in an expression as shown here. The `input` parameter option is not available for method call activities that reference an ADF OperationBinding. For example, the `setCurrentRowWithKey` operation of a view object requires an instance of `oracle.jbo.Key` in a `java.lang.String` format. In this case, the argument value needs to be set on the ADF binding, which you access by selecting Go to Page Definition from the method activity context menu. Select the setCurrentRowWithKey operation in the Overview editor and click the pencil icon to edit the binding. Add an Expression Language reference to the `rowKey` parameter value that points to the location where the `rowKey` is stored, for example `#{pageFlowScope.key}`.
	
	The ADF Controller method activity invokes the `execute` method on the OperationBinding, which does not take arguments. Using ADF Faces RC, the OperationBinding is represented by an instance of `FacesCtrlActionBinding` class.

`return-value`	Optional configuration that determines the location where the returned object of a method invocation is stored. For example, the checkInbox method in the example may return a custom object of type `MailInfo`, which contains information such as error or status messages. In this case, you can use the `return-value` element, for example, to store the return object in the `pageFlowScope` for later use.
	
	`<return-value>`
	`   #{pageFlowScope.message}`
	`</return-value>`
	
	Though they reference the same object, the `return-value` and the outcome element are two different things.

Router Activity

A router is a switch that determines the next navigation path based on Expression Language accessible context information. Application developers define one or more evaluation criteria for a router to test from top to bottom. If an expression evaluates to `true` then the process follows its configured navigation. If multiple expressions return `true` then the navigation case of the first match is continued. If all expression evaluations return `false` then a mandatory configured default navigation path is used.

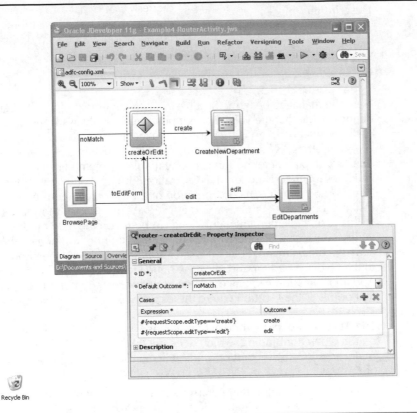

FIGURE 4-1   *Router activity flow for the edit form example*

An example use case for the router activity is an edit form for the application user to update or enter data, as shown in Figure 4-1. Before a new record can be edited, it needs to be created. In our use case, new records are created in transit when navigating the request to the edit form. To implement this, a method activity is used that executes the `create` operation exposed on the ADF Business Components (BC) view object that holds the form data. A router activity is used to distinguish between an edit request and a "create for edit" request. Given that an `in-memory` attribute exists that has its value set to `Create` or `Edit`, a router can evaluate the attribute value to decide whether to route the request to the edit form or to use a detour to the method activity to create the record first.

NOTE
The `in-memory` *attribute is stored and referenced in one of the possible memory scopes: application, session, pageFlow, view, and request. Memory scoped attributes include bean properties of managed beans that are configured in one of the listed scopes. For an efficient use of server memory, you should always use the scope with the shortest possible lifespan when storing data in memory scoped attributes.*

NOTE
The ADF BC data control exposes three operations for a view object to create a new row: `Create, CreateInsert,` *and* `CreateWithParams.` *The* `Create` *operation creates a new row for the collection but doesn't add it to the iterator.* `CreateInsert` *works the same as* `Create` *but adds the new row above the current row in the iterator.* `CreateWithParams` *works the same as* `CreateInsert` *but optionally allows developers to define default values declaratively for the row attributes. The difference between* `Create` *and* `CreateInsert` *is only relevant if the collection is displayed in a table, not for a form.*

The BrowsePage in Figure 4-1 contains two `af:commandButtons` with an `af:setPropertyListener` added on each. For the Edit button, the `from` property of the `SetPropertyListener` component is defined as `#{'edit'}` and the `to` property as `#{requestScope.editType}`. Similarly, the Create button's setPropertyListener is defined as `#{'create'}` for the `from` property and `#{requestScope.editType}` for the `to` property. So whenever the Edit button on the browse button is clicked, the `requestScope` attribute `editType` is set to `edit`. The router reads the attribute from the request and evaluates its value by comparing it with the `create` or `edit` string.

The following table shows commonly used router activity metadata elements and attributes.

Metadata	Description
`id`	Unique name of the router within the unbounded or bounded task flow.

`case`	Zero to many configuration elements that allow developers to declaratively define the condition under which a specific navigation path is followed.
	`<case>`
	`<expression>`
	`  #{requestScope.editType=='create'}`
	`</expression>`
	`  <outcome>create</outcome>`
	`</case>`
	The `outcome` element is mandatory for each case and determines the navigation case. The outcome value must be a static string.
	The `expression` element can point to an attribute in memory scopes such as request and page flow, but it can also reference a managed bean method for more complex evaluation that cannot be done within Expression Language.

`default-outcome`	Mandatory element that determines the navigation in case all evaluations of the case elements fail and return `false`.

Task Flow Call Activity

A task flow call activity integrates bounded task flows to the control flow of a calling ADF flow. Navigating to a task flow call activity in a parent control flow continues the process in the bounded flow for as long as it takes to process the subprocess. At the end of the called flow, the control is returned to the parent flow. To add a task flow call activity, you can do the following:

■ Drag-and-drop a bounded task flow definition from the JDeveloper Application Navigator to an ADF Faces page and choose between a command link and a command button control. This requires the task flows to be built with pages, not page fragments.

■ Drag-and-drop the bounded task flow definition directly to the parent flow diagram.

■ Add a task flow call activity from the ADF Task Flow entry of the Oracle JDeveloper component palette and manually configure its Task Flow Reference property.

The following table shows commonly used task flow call activity metadata elements and attributes.

Metadata	Description
id	The `id` attribute is a unique string identifier of the task flow call activity. The ADF Controller uses the call activity `id` when defining navigation cases. It does not use the physical task flow document and task flow `id` reference. This abstraction allows a bounded task flow to be referenced many times in a parent task flow.
task-flow-reference	This element contains the reference to the bounded task flow definition, which is composed out of the task flow document location and name, and the task flow definition `id`.

```
<task-flow-reference>
 <document>
   /WEB-INF/department-task-flow-definition.xml
 </document>
 <id>department-task-flow-definition</id>
</task-flow-reference>
```

The task flow referenced here is located in the WEB-INF directory of the view layer project and is defined in the department-task-flow-definition.xml file. The id of the task flow definition within this file is `department-task-flow-definition`.

Task flow references can be provided dynamically at runtime using the dynamic-task-flow-reference element instead of task-flow-reference. The value of this element is an EL expression that references a managed bean method returning the `TaskFlowId` of the task flow to navigate to. The managed bean example below returns the `TaskFlowId` for the task flow defined by the taskFlowId variable. The referenced task flow can be changed at runtime by calling the setTaskFlowId `method`.

```
public class TaskFlowIdProvider {
  private String taskFlowId =
    "/WEB-INF/employees-task-flow-definition.xml#"+
    "employees-task-flow-definition";
  ...
  public TaskFlowIdProvider () {
    super();
  }
  public TaskFlowId getDynamicTaskFlowId() {
    return TaskFlowId.parse(taskFlowId);
  }
  public void setTaskFlowId(String taskFlowId) {
    this.taskFlowId = taskFlowId;
  }
  public String getTaskFlowId() {
    return taskFlowId;
  }
}
```

This managed bean is referenced from the dynamic-task-flow-reference element as shown here

```
<task-flow-call id="showEmployees">
  <dynamic-task-flow-reference>
    #{TaskFlowIdProviderBean.dynamicTaskFlowId}
  </dynamic-task-flow-reference>
</task-flow-call>
```

Note that for future use, the design of the bounded task flow definition is such that one bounded task flow file may have multiple task flow definitions. This feature is not available in Oracle JDeveloper 11g.

Metadata	Description

remote-app-url	A bounded task flow may be available on a remote server and not within the local application. To call a task flow remotely, the `remote-app-url` element is used to specify the remote task flow URL. The URL contains the hostname, the port number, the Java EE context path, the /faces servlet mapping and the adf.task-flow access name.
	 ```<remote-app-url>```
	 ``` http://foo-server:7101/deptedit/faces/adf.task-flow?```
	 ```</remote-app-url>```
	 The resulting URL contains the information from the `task-flow-reference` element that identifies the task flow definition to call, input parameters defined for the called bounded task flow, and state information of the calling flow.
	 Calling a remote task flow redirects the call process to a different web application. This not only creates a new user session, but it also shows an initial splash screen while loading the remote task flow. You can suppress the splash screen using a custom skin definition on the remote application with the following skin selector:
	 `af|document::splash-screen{display:none;}`
	 See Chapter 16 for information about custom skin development.

input-parameter	The `input-parameter` element is used to pass input parameters to the called task flow. The name of the input parameter is the same as the parameter name defined on the task flow. In the following example, the parameter name defined on the bounded Task Flow is `keyIn`. The value of this parameter is read from the page flow scope of the calling task flow.
	 ```<input-parameter>```
	 ``` <name>keyIn</name>```
	 ``` <value>#{pageFlowScope.key}</value>```
	 ```</input-parameter>```

before-listener	Optional element that uses Expression Language to reference a public method that is exposed on a managed bean. The method does not take input arguments and does not return a result. It is invoked before the bounded task flow is called.
after-listener	Optional element that uses Expression Language to reference a public method that is exposed on a managed bean. The method does not take input arguments and does not return a result. It is invoked when the control handle is passed back to the calling task flow upon return from the called task flow.

Metadata	Description
run-as-dialog	Element that, if added by setting the `Run As Dialog` property in the Oracle JDeveloper Property Inspector to `true`, opens the task flow in a separate browser window. A control flow case is used to navigate to the task flow call activity to launch the dialog. In this example, the `run-as-dialog` metadata has a `dialog-return-value` element set that references a return value defined on the bounded task flow:

```
<run-as-dialog>
  <dialog-return-value>locationId</dialog-return-value>
</run-as-dialog>
```

The returned value is read in a return listener configured on the command item that initiated the launch of the dialog.

```
<task-flow-definition id="lookup-task-flow">
  <default-activity>Locations</default-activity>
  <return-value-definition>
    <name>locationId</name>
    <value>#{tf_selectionBean.locationId}</value>
    <class>java.lang.Object</class>
  </return-value-definition>
  ...
<task-flow-definition
```

In the next code example, the return value is read from the `ReturnEvent` and copied into an `af:inputText` component. To refresh the input text component, a call to `addPartialTarget` is issued on the `AdfFacesContext` object:

```
public void returnFromDialog
            (ReturnEvent returnEvent){
  Object location = returnEvent.getReturnValue();
  locIdField.setSubmittedValue(location);
  AdfFacesContext adfFacesContext =
    AdfFacesContext.getCurrentInstance();
    adfFacesContext.addPartialTarget(locIdField);
}
```

Metadata	Description
train-stop	Element that marks the task flow call activity as a train-stop within a bounded task flow train definition. In a train model, task flow call activities are used to group activities together as a single train stop or to call into a child train.

Task Flow Return Activity

The return activity is used in bounded task flows to exit the task flow and to pass control back to the calling task flow. Upon closing the task flow, the memory allocated by the bounded task flow pageFlowScope is released. A return activity returns an outcome for the calling flow to use to process the control flow. Optionally, a return value can be specified on the task flow definition that is written to a defined in-memory storage, such as the callers page flow scope, when exiting the called task flow.

The following table shows task flow call activity metadata elements and attributes that are commonly used.

Metadata	Description
id	Unique string identifier of the return activity instance in a bounded task flow.
name	Child element of the outcome element that defines the outcome returned to the calling task flow when exiting the called task flow. If the calling task flow has a control flow case defined for the returned outcome string, then in response to exiting the called task flow, the calling task flow is navigated to the activity that defined as the target of this control flow case.
reentry / reentry-not-allowed	Bounded task flows may allow users to re-enter the flow using the browser back button, in which case the task flow continues as if it had not exited. The decision as to whether or not a task flow can be re-entered can be defined to be dependent on the outcome returned to the calling task flow when exiting the called task flow. In this case, the reentry or reentry-not-allowed element is added as a child to the outcome element. To allow the outcome to determine the reentry behavior, the task flow must be configured with "reentry outcome dependent." If the task flow configuration allows re-entry in general, the configuration on the return activity is ignored.
rollback /commit	If the rollback child element is set for the outcome element, then, upon task flow return, the current transaction is rolled back. This option is available only if the task flow started the transaction. The rollback element is set through the Property Inspector and provides a declarative option for transaction handling. If the commit child element is set for the *outcome* element, then, upon task flow return, the current transaction is committed. The commit element is set through the property inspector and provides a declarative option for transaction handling.
restore-save-point	Ability to restore to the state stored when entering the task flow. Setting the restore-save-point child element of the outcome element requires a shared transaction to be used by the task flow and the No Save Point On Task Flow Entry option to be unchecked, which also is the default value.

NOTE
An InvalidTaskFlowReentryException *is raised when re-entering a task flow with the browser back button if the task flow is not configured to allow re-entrance. The exception is raised when the user submits a request from the reentered task flow. See Chapter 5 for information on how to handle this exception.*

URL View Activity

A URL view activity always redirects the main browser page to the page specified by the defined URL. Valid URLs are references to bounded task flows, view activities in the unbounded task flow, and external web addresses. The difference between the URL view activity and a normal view activity is that the normal view activity redirect option is ignored if performed within the context of an ADF region. The URL view activity can have parameters defined that are automatically added to the request.

The following table shows commonly used URL view activity metadata elements and attributes

Metadata	Description
id	Unique string that identifies the URL view activity instance in the task flow.
url	The `url` child element of the `url-view` element represents the navigation target to which the redirect routes the request. The URL can be absolute or relative and hard coded or dynamically derived using an EL reference to a managed bean.

```
<url-view id="goBrowseLocations">
  <url>
    /foo/faces/LocationsView.jspx
  </url>
  <url-parameter>
    <name>key</name>
    <value>
     #{pageFlowScope.keyIn}
    </value>
  </url-parameter>
</url-view>
```

Metadata	Description
url-parameter	An optional child element of the `url-view` metadata that defines request parameters that are added to the target URL. The `converter` element uses EL to point to a managed bean that implements the `UrlParameterConverter` interface to perform object-to-string and string-to-object conversion of the `url-parameter` value.

```
public class CustUrlParamsConverter implements
UrlParameterConverter {
  public CustUrlParamsConverter () {
  }
  public Object getAsObject(String value) {
   // do your string to object conversion here
   return <your Object>;
  }
  public String getAsString(Object value) {
   // do your object to string conversion here
   return <your String>;
  }
}
```

Instead of implementing the `UrlParameterConverter` interface, developers can use or extend existing converters such as `DefaultUrlParameterConverter`, which is located in the oracle.adf.controller package. This class uses regular expressions to prevent cross-site scripting (XSS) attacks and can be used as a converter on all input parameter definitions that support converters. The regular expression filter used to identify bad requests is

`[<>\'\";)(+\\\\]|&#|&(([lL]|[gG])([tT]))`

Request with a suspicious content are detected by

`[<>#&\'\"%;)(+\\\\]`

Note that, especially when security is involved, you should always check whether the protection provided by existing converters meets your requirements or whether it is better to write and use your own custom converters.

Save Point Restore Activity

The save point restore activity allows the developer to roll back all changes made in an application up to the state saved in an implicit or explicit save point. The following table shows the restore activity metadata elements.

Metadata	Description
id	Unique string identifier of the save point restore element in a task flow.
save-point-id	Child element of the `save-point-restore` element that indicates the rollback target, the `id` of the save point to which stored state should be recovered. The value can be referenced from EL.

NOTE
Savepoints are further discussed in Chapter 5.

Control Flow Rules

Control flow cases in ADF Controller define how control is passed from one activity to the next. Most of the ADF Controller activity, including activities that have no visual outcome, such as router, method, or task flow call activities, can become the starting point and end point of navigation. Because only pages and page fragments display in a browser, ADF Controller continues any navigation to non-visual activities until a visual activity is reached. This turns non-visual activities into intermediary actions that are performed on the navigation path between two views.

NOTE
Activities that cannot have control flow cases defined include URL view activity, save point restore activity, and task flow return activity.

The control flow metadata shown next is taken from the flow shown in Figure 4-2 and defines three control flow cases for the `EditDepartment` activity. Depending on the outcome of a command action, the flow is continued to the `returnCancel`, `returnCommit`, or `goBrowseLocations` activity ID. As you can see, the control flow does not indicate the

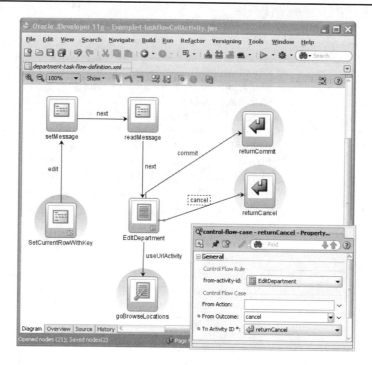

FIGURE 4-2 *Bounded task flow diagram with control flow rules*

type of activity to which it navigates, which is a wanted abstraction between the physical implementation of an activity and the flow rules.

```
<control-flow-rule>
  <from-activity-id>EditDepartment</from-activity-id>
  <control-flow-case>
    <from-outcome>cancel</from-outcome>
    <to-activity-id>returnCancel</to-activity-id>
  </control-flow-case>
  <control-flow-case>
    <from-outcome>commit</from-outcome>
    <to-activity-id>returnCommit</to-activity-id>
  </control-flow-case>
  <control-flow-case>
    <from-outcome>useUrlActivity</from-outcome>
    <to-activity-id>goBrowseLocations</to-activity-id>
  </control-flow-case>
</control-flow-rule>
```

The following table shows the metadata used to define navigation in ADF task flows.

Metadata	Description
`from-activity-id`	Specifies the unique name of the activity instance in the flow. Control flow rules with a `from-activity-id` value that contains or consists of an asterisk * character represent global navigation rules. Global navigation rules are used in page menus or to navigate to a logout link. To define a global navigation case, you first need to drag and drop a Wildcard Control Flow Rule from the Component palette to the task flow diagram. Once this is done, the Control Flow Case element can be added as the link between the wildcard icon and the target activity.
`from-outcome`	A child element of the `control-flow-case` element that determines the expected string returned from the activity action to initiate the navigation.
`from-action`	Can be used to refine the context of the navigation case by including the method name that returned the outcome to the control flow case definition.

```
<control-flow-case>
  <from-action>
     #{EditDepartmentBean.checkMemberShip}
  </from-action>
  <from-outcome>cancel</from-outcome>
  <to-activity-id>returnCancel</to-activity-id>
</control-flow-case>
```

Metadata	Description
`to-activity-id`	Defines the next destination of this navigation path.

Creating Managed Beans in ADF Controller

To create a managed bean in ADF Controller, start with creating the JavaBean class. Choose New from the Oracle JDeveloper File menu and then choose General | Java | Java Class in the JDeveloper New Gallery. Provide the requested information in the Create Java Class dialog and click OK. Make sure the class name you provided starts with an uppercase letter, which is the recommended way of doing this in Java. Oracle JDeveloper opens the newly created class in the source code editor for you to create variables with their setter and getter methods and class methods. To configure the Java class as a managed bean class, you either double-click the unbounded or bounded task flow definition file that should configure the managed bean or select the task flow definition file and open the Structure window (CTRL-SHIFT-S). In the latter case, select the ADF Task Flow entry in the Structure window and open the Property Inspector (CTRL-SHIFT-I). Navigate to the Managed Beans section. Create a new bean configuration by clicking the green plus icon. Provide the following information:

■ **Name** Provide the name that is used in Expression Language to access the JavaBean within the context of ADF Faces.

- **Class** Type the Java bean class, or browse for the class that should be accessed when the managed bean is used within the ADF Faces application.

- **Scope** Select the shortest scope possible for the bean. If the bean holds information that should be available for the page only, choose Request; if it should be available for all pages and activities in a task flow, choose Page Flow; and so on.

If you double-clicked the Task Flow definition file to create a managed bean, click the Overview tab on the launched task flow diagram to open the configuration overview panel. In the panel, select the Managed Beans entry, which displays the same configuration dialog used for the Property Inspector.

Memory Scopes

Every object of interest needs a home. In ADF, objects are stored in memory for access within the application. The most important object in Oracle ADF is the "bindings" object, which represents the Oracle ADF binding container that is available in request scope. Other objects of interest are managed beans, attributes, and state information. In JSF, memory scopes of different lifetimes exist for the developer to leverage existing server side resources sensibly. Usually, at the end of lifetime, all allocated memory by the scope is automatically freed up. As other web frameworks do, Oracle ADF provides additional memory scopes on top of the existing standard Java Servlet scopes to meet the requirements of Rich Internet Application (RIA) and Rich Enterprise Application (REA) developers. The memory scopes available in ADF are `applicationScope`, `sessionScope`, `viewScope`, `pageFlowScope`, `requestScope`, `backingBeanScope`, and `None`.

Standard JSF and Servlet Scopes

The standard memory scopes are defined as implicit objects in the JSF specification.

Application Scope

Application scoped attributes and managed beans are available for an entire application and are shared among users. Application scope information should not have session dependency since it is visible to all sessions of an application.

Session Scope

Session scoped attributes and beans are user instance–specific and exist from the time of their creation to the time they are deleted or the session ends. A use case for a session scope bean is a user info bean that stores information about a user, which is read from the database or an LDAP server, to avoid unnecessary queries. Another use case is to set a user authentication flag to indicate an authenticated user session and also to detect session expiry and renewal. To access the value of a session scope attribute from Expression Language, use `#{sessionScope.<attribute name>}`. In Java, use this:

```
FacesContext fctx = FacesContext.getCurrentInstance();
ExternalContext ectx = fctx.getExternalContext();
Map sessionScope = ectx.getSessionMap();
String attrValue = sessionScope.get("attribute_name");
```

Request Scope

The request scope is a map that represents the smallest available scope. It lasts for the time it takes to transition from one view activity to the next, or in JSF standard parlance, from one page to the next. Use the request scope, for example, to pass data between pages. Any nonvisual activity, such as router or method call activities, can access the request scope to read or write. For example, here's how to write to the request scope from a method activity:

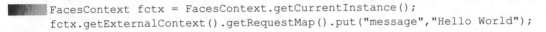

```
FacesContext fctx = FacesContext.getCurrentInstance();
fctx.getExternalContext().getRequestMap().put("message","Hello World");
```

NOTE
The request scope is not available for navigation that is performed as a redirect. In this case, data that needs to be passed from one page to the next must be added as request parameters to the URL.

None

Managed beans may provide methods that are not required to save a state. These beans don't need to remain in memory. Configuring a bean as a managed bean with a scope of None makes the bean Expression Language–accessible, instantiating it when needed and releasing it right after.

ADF-specific Scopes

Like many RIA, Fusion web applications cannot work efficiently within the boundaries of existing memory scopes defined by the Servlet specification. To address the limitations of traditional web application scopes, ADF defines three additional, explicit scopes. Unlike implicit scopes, the scope name must be contained in the Expression Language reference to a managed bean.

View Scope

The view scope stores objects used by a single page and retains the objects as long as the user works within the page. The memory scope is of type Map<String, Object> and is automatically released when the user leaves the page. A view scope instance exists for each view that the ADF Controller manages in the root browser window or in a region in the page.

Using Expression Language to Access Content Stored in a Map

Technically, all scopes are in memory instances of Java Map. Developers use maps to read and write objects, which also can be done through Expression Language. To evaluate the content of a Map such as requestScope, Expression Language can be used in its dot-notated syntax, such as #{requestScope.attribute}, or with a string argument notation, such as #{requestScope['attribute']}. Using the latter syntax allows you to access attribute keys that have a dot (.) in their name. For example, here's how to use Expression Language to write a search condition into the requestScope from an af: inputText field:

```
<af:inputText value="#{requestScope.searchCondition}" …/>
```

The lifetime of a view scope begins and ends with the change of the view ID of a view port. The view port can be either the root browser window or an ADF region that displays the current view. The view scope is accessible through Expression Language using the `viewScope` object, `#{viewScope.attribute_name}`, and in Java:

```
AdfFacesContext adfctx = AdfFacesContext.getCurrentInstance();
Map viewScope = adfctx.getViewScope();
```

PageFlow Scope

The ADF Controller pageFlow memory scope exists for the duration of a task flow, after which the allocated memory is released. If a task flow calls another bounded task flow, then the pageFlow scope of the caller flow is suspended and activated again upon return from the called task flow. The pageFlow scope of the called task flow is not available until after the JSF "Restore View" phase. This allows developers to pass values stored in the calling task flow as input parameters to the called task flow.

To access objects in the current `pageFlowScope`, developers can use Expression Language such as `#{pageFlowScope.attribute_name}`, or, using Java, the `AdfFacesContext` class:

```
AdfFacesContext adfFacesContext = AdfFacesContext.getCurrentInstance();
Map _pageFlowScope = adfFacesContext.getPageFlowScope();
String attributeValue = _pageFlowScope.get("attribute_name"));
```

Managed beans that are configured to be in `pageFlowScope` cannot contain references to UI components that are not serializable because the `pageFlowScope` is implemented as a `Map` in session scope. UI components that use binding references to a managed bean property should reference beans in request scope or backing bean scope.

To reference a managed bean that is configured in page flow scope from Expression Language, you use `#{pageFlowScope.<bean name>.<bean method>}`.

Note: The careful reader may wonder about the difference between objects that are stored in session scope and objects that are stored in the pageFlow scope of the unbounded task flow. Though both scopes last for the duration of the user session, there is an important difference in the access. In general, objects stored in the pageFlow scope are accessible only from the current task flow, which means that objects stored in the unbounded pageFlow scope are not accessible from bounded task flows. The standard session scope does not have this limitation and is accessible throughout the application. Information that is needed only within the context of a single task flow thus should be stored in the `pageFlowScope` map while information required throughout the user session could be placed into session scope or passed as parameters.

Backing Bean Scope

The backing bean scope is a special case of request scope narrowed down to a specific managed bean instance. The use cases for the backing bean scope are declarative components, regions, and page fragments that use a managed bean to hold view state information. Setting the bean scope to `backingBean` allows multiple instances of the component, and thus the bean, to co-exist on a single page. The backing bean scope is active for the current selected declarative component or fragment and is Expression Language accessible through `#{backingBeanScope.<bean name>}`.

Overview of Common Object Access

Scopes can be accessed from Expression Language and Java to perform read and write operations. The following table shows an overview of scope access for the application scope, session scope, request scope, pageFlow scope, backingBean scope, and view scope. The returned object is always of `Map<String, Object>` type.

EL Access	Java Access

`#{applicationScope}`	`FacesContext fctx = FacesContext.getCurrentInstance();`
	`fctx.getExternalContext().getApplicationMap();`
	or
	`ADFContext adfCtx - ADFContext.getCurrent();`
	`adfCtx.getApplicationScope();`

`#{sessionScope}`	`FacesContext fctx = null;`
	`fctx = FacesContext.getCurrentInstance();`
	`fctx.getExternalContext().getSessionMap();`
	or
	`ADFContext adfCtx = ADFContext.getCurrent();`
	`adfCtx.getSessionScope();`

`#{requestScope}`	`FacesContext fctx = null;`
	`fctx = FacesContext.getCurrentInstance();`
	`fctx.getExternalContext().getRequestMap();`
	or
	`ADFContext adfCtx = ADFContext.getCurrent();`
	`adfCtx.getRequestScope();`

`#{pageFlowScope}`	`AdfFacesContext adfFacesContext = null;`
	`adfFacesContext = AdfFacesContext.getCurrentInstance();`
	`Map _pageFlowScope = adfFacesContext.getPageFlowScope();`

`#{viewScope}`	`AdfFacesContext adfFacesContext = null;`
	`adfFacesContext = AdfFacesContext.getCurrentInstance();`
	`Map _viewScope = adfctx.getViewScope();`
	or
	`ADFContext adfCtx = ADFContext.getCurrent();`
	`adfCtx.getViewScope()`

`#{backingBeanScope}`	`AdfFacesContext adfFacesContext = null;`
	`adfFacesContext = AdfFacesContext.getCurrentInstance();`
	`BackingBeanScopeProviderImpl provider =`
	`adfFacesContext. getBackingBeanScopeProvider();`
	`Map backingBeanScope = null;`
	`backingBeanScope = provider.getCurrentScope();`

NOTE
The Java access to memory scope objects can also be used to look up managed bean objects by their configured name. However, it does not instantiate the managed bean and requires an existing instance. If your application requires access to a managed bean from Java but you are uncertain if this bean has been instantiated before, or if you prefer to be on a the safe side, use Expression Language in Java to obtain a handle to the managed bean instance or a managed bean property. Chapter 9 provides examples of how to invoke method and value expressions from Java.

Scopes in Action

Seeing is believing. Especially when the topic is complex, such as the lifespan of objects in memory, it is better to paint a picture. Following are two application outlines that use a mixture of ADF task flow elements.

The page flow in Figure 4-3 shows a parent task flow that contains three view activities: a router activity, a method activity, and a task flow call activity. The bounded task flow called from the parent flow has two view activities: a method activity and a return activity.

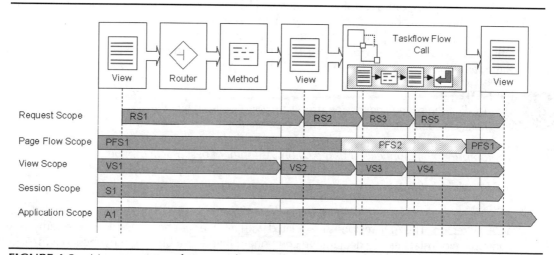

FIGURE 4-3 *Memory scopes for an application that uses a bounded task flow through a call activity*

A *request scope* starts with a request to be issued from one view to another for navigation cases that don't perform a redirect but a default server-side forward. The first request scope is from the first view activity to the second view activity. The scope spans across the router activity and the method activity, which don't have request scopes of their own. This also means that the information stored in the request scope is accessible to the router and the method. The second request scope has a lifetime starting from the second view activity to the first view activity in the called task flow. If the called task flow has no view activity defined, then the request scope lifetime lasts beyond the bounded task flow. The third request scope in this example spans from the first view activity of the bounded task flow to the second view activity. Finally, the fourth request scope exists between the second view in the bounded Task flow and the third view of the calling task flow.

A *pageFlow scope* exists for each task flow instance. The lifetime of the scope spans across all pages in a task flow, which is why the chosen name is pageFlow scope. In Figure 4-3, two task flows are shown: a parent task flow and a called task flow. The pageFlow scope of the parent task flow is suspended for the time the application spends in the second, the called task flow. It is resumed after the called task flow reaches the return activity. Information stored in a pageFlow scope is accessible only within the task flow that owns it. Therefore, input parameters need to be used to pass information from a calling task flow to a called bounded task flow.

The *view scope* exists from the beginning of a view's rendering up to the point in which a new view renders. A view scope can hold objects that are relevant for a page and that are created, removed, and updated using partial page rendering (PPR).

The *session scope* is the user scope and lasts from the user's first access to an application until the session expires, unless explicitly invalidated before. Information that is stored in session scope is accessible throughout an application with no restriction.

The *application scope* has a lifetime longer than the session and is used to share information among all instances of an application. This scope may be used to hold static objects that are the same for all users.

NOTE
Application scope and session scope are good to use when they make sense. Inexperienced developers often abuse the session scope as a registry for everything, which unnecessarily bloats the memory footprint of an application user session. As a hint of best practices, you should keep track of when and why one of these two scopes is used for which information and when the cleanup occurs.

The second use case is outlined in Figure 4-4 and shows a task flow with a view that contains an ADF region. The ADF region is associated with another bounded task flow. The same view contains two instances of a declarative component that uses a binding reference to a managed bean in backing bean scope. The request scope, session scope, and application scope usage is as explained earlier, so we can focus on the differences, which are the backing bean scope, the page flow scope, and the view scope.

The *backing bean scope* is comparable to the request scope, with the difference in that it exists for a specific client component, the declarative components in this example. Internally in ADF, a provider class that returns a backing bean scope instance for the rendered component in focus is used. Each component notifies the provider about the start and the end of it being in focus through the view layer. In general, all managed beans used in reusable components should be configured to `backingBean scope`.

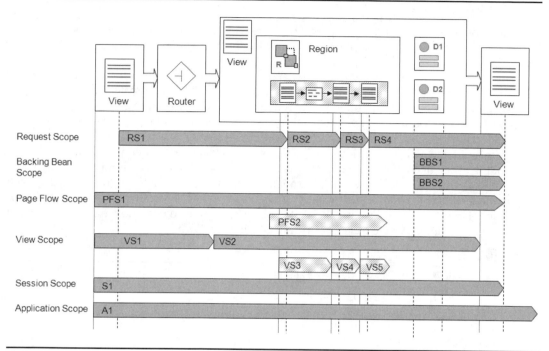

FIGURE 4-4 *Memory scopes for an application that uses a bounded task flow in a region and two declarative component on a view*

The *pageflow scope* works similar to that shown in Figure 4-3 but uses two view ports, one that holds the parent view and one that shows the bounded task flow in the ADF region. Both page flow scopes can be accessed without one of the task flows to exit and return. Note, however, that the two page flow scope instances cannot reference each other.

The *view scope* exists not only for views that are rendered by JSPX pages, but also for views rendered by page fragments, as is the case in task flows that are built to execute in a region. The view scope of the parent page is not accessible from components added to a page fragment in a region, and the view scope of a view in a region is not accessible for the parent page.

NOTE
Many of the reported problems for reusable components, such as task flows that execute in a region, declarative components, or page fragments, are caused by component binding references to broader scoped beans in request or session scope. Reusable components, especially those that are added with multiple instances on a single page, should bind to per instance scopes such as pageFlowScope, viewScope, *or* backingBean scope.

ADF Binding

Any operation or method that is added from the Oracle JDeveloper Data Controls palette to the task flow as a method activity has a pageDef file created and is mapped in the DataBindings .cpx file.

Activities such as method and router activities that are added from the Oracle JDeveloper Component Palette by default don't have associated ADF bindings created. While the request scope lasts for the duration of one view activity to the next, the binding object of an activity is available only for the lifetime of the activity itself. A developer who is not aware of this will most likely hit a NullPointerException thrown in response to accessing the binding container from a method activity that does not have its own associated page definition, unless defensive coding is practiced that frequently checks for null values. If a method or router activity needs access to the ADF binding, you can manually create a PageDef file for it by selecting the activity in the task flow diagram and choosing "Create Page Definition" from the right mouse context menu. However, if the use case allows it, a better practice is to pass the required information as an input parameter of the router or method activity, as shown here:

```
<method-call id="setCurrency">
  <method>#{DepartmentHelperBean.setCurrencyForCountry}</method>
  <parameter>
    <class>java.lang.String</class>
    <value>#{pageFlowScope.country}</value>
  </parameter>
</method-call>
```

The signature of the method in the managed bean would be similar to `public String set CurrencyForCountry(String country)`.

Customizing the Lifecycle for Operation, Method, and Router Activities

The concept of non-view activities, such as router, operation, and method activity, is new in Oracle JDeveloper 11*g* and ADF Controller. As explained earlier, these activity types can have their own ADF binding container setups. ADF bound non-view activities do not need to run through the whole page lifecycle and instead need only to execute refresh and validation. Application developers who want to customize the ADF lifecycle for non-view activities can do this by referencing a custom lifecycle class that implements the RegionController interface from the ControllerClass property of the associated page definition file.

Task Flow State Tracking

The ADF Controller automatically adds the _adf.ctrl-state request parameter to the generated page URL that holds the current ADF Controller state tracking token. The state token references a session object that keeps track of the ADF controller state and includes the pageFlowScope stacks of the running application. Using the state token, the ADF controller knows how to recover the caller state upon task flow return, including the data control instance.

Exception and Error Handling

The last thing you want to display to the application user is a blank page that contains the printed stack trace of a Java or controller exception thrown. The ADF Controller allows application developers to handle exceptions declaratively and gracefully in bounded and unbounded task flows by configuring any activity element such as view, method, or router as an exception handler. The Oracle Controller itself implements the `oracle.adf.view.rich.context.ExceptionHandler` abstract class to catch the exception and route the flow to the configured exception handler element. Once the control flow is passed to the exception handler activity, subsequent flow from the activity uses standard control flow rules. So instead of a harsh crash and burn experience, application users continue within the application based on the application developer's ability to anticipate, analyze, and handle the exception thrown at runtime.

To mark an activity as an exception handler, either right-click the activity in the task flow diagram and choose Mark Activity | Exception Handler from the context menu, or select the Task Flow entry in the Structure window to choose an exception handler from the list of activities shown for the Exception Handler property in the Property Inspector. In the task flow diagrammer, configured activity is marked with an exclamation mark (!) overlay icon to identify it as the exception handler. No navigation cases need to be drawn between the contained activities of a task flow and the exception handler activity, nor is a wild card flow required.

If a task flow does not have an exception handler defined, but one of its parent flows does, then the exception is passed to the parent handler to handle the exception. If no exception handler is found at all, the exception propagates to the Java EE container as a last resort. The following table shows the metadata added to the task flow configuration to declare an activity as the exception handler.

Metadata	Description

exception-handler	A child of the `adfc-config` element that contains the ID of the activity that is chosen to handle the exception. For example
	`<exception-handler>`
	`    RouterActivity1`
	`</exception-handler>`

The exception data is accessible from the `ControllerContext` in Java and through Expression Language to display and respond to the incident. To display the exception message on a view activity, select the "value" property of an output component in the Property Inspector and choose Expression Builder from the context menu; then click the down arrow icon at the end of the property field. Select ControllerContext | currentViewPort | exceptionData | message and click OK to build the Expression Language string that accesses the message part of the exception. To access the exception message and type, for example in a router activity marked as an exception handler, choose ControllerContext | currentViewPort | exceptionData.

To use a method activity as an exception handler, create a managed bean and add a method as shown here:

```
public void handleExceptions(){
  ControllerContext cctx = ControllerContext.getInstance();
  Exception exception = cctx.getCurrentViewPort().getExceptionData();
  //handle exception here, e.g. call a navigation handler case
}
```

One exception to the way that errors are handled in ADF Controller is for task flows that execute within an ADF region. In this case, exceptions that are not handled within the bounded task flow are not passed to the parent page's flow and instead are thrown as unhandled exceptions.

ControllerContext

The `ControllerContext` class provides per-request information about the controller state for a web application. It is one of the classes that advanced developers need to know when programming with task flows in Java. Developers obtain a handle to the context class by a call to `ContextClass.getInstance()`. The information returned by the `ControllerContext` class includes the following:

- **ViewPortContext**   Through a call to `getCurrentViewPort`. The `ViewPortContext` provides information about the current view rendered in a browser window, a modal dialog, or a region.

- **Global ViewActivity URL**   String that represents the URL of a view activity in an unbounded task flow. The URL string is obtained in Java through a call to `getGlobalViewActivityURL`. The provided argument is the view ID of the activity to navigate to. The `getGlobalViewActivityURL` method call is not supported for bounded task flows.

- **Local ViewActivity URL**   String that represents the navigation URL to a provided view ID. The URL string is obtained in Java through a call to `getLocalViewActivityURL`.

- **Task Flow URL**   String that represents the navigation URL to a task flow in the web application. The URL string is obtained in Java through a call to `getTaskFlowURL`. The first argument determines whether the URL should contain state information of the current view port. The second argument is the task flow ID, and the third argument is a Map of properties expected by the called task flow.

- **ViewActivity view ID**   String that represents a view ID of a view activity in a task flow. The view ID can be set as the new `UIViewRoot` when launching a dialog. The view ID is obtained in Java through a call to `getViewActivityViewID`.

- **Savepoint Restore URL**   String that represents the URL to a save point restore activity. The method argument is the ID of the restore activity of the save point. The URL is obtained in a call to `getSavePointRestoreURL`.

Save Points and "Save for Later"

The ADF Controller save point feature allows developers to handle those use cases in which the work of a user within an application is interrupted because of a business reason, such as missing required information, end of office business hours or a human task flow, or system failures, such as an expired session or a closed browser window. The save point that preserves the user's application state in a configured persistent storage can be created by the user, enforced by the application developer, or created implicitly by the ADF Controller. Save points that are initiated by the user, or by the application logic, are called "explicit" save points, whereas save points set by ADF are referred to as "implicit" save points. Implicit save points are created for bounded task flows that are marked as critical. The following information is stored in a save point:

- **UI component tree**   The state of an application at the time the save point is created. Note that the state within the `UIViewRoot` does include submitted form data only.

- **ADF Controller state**   The ADF controller persists the pageFlow scope with all the objects contained within the pageFlow stack, in case the save point is set from a bounded task flow. If ADF regions are used, the view port hierarchy is stored as well.

- **Model state**   The state of the Data control instance referenced by the task flows. To use save points efficiently with ADF Business Components, make sure the locking behavior is set to "optimistic" in the Application Module configuration. Otherwise chances are that a session is locked until it times out.

It is important for developers to know that no state from default scopes, such as request, session, or application, is persisted. This leads to the effect that application states that are recovered from a save point may not look exactly the same as before the save and restore operation.

When working with explicit save points, developers can store additional information with the save point to provide a meaningful context during a save point restore. To provide additional information, developers create an instance of `oracle.adf.controller.savepoint.SavePointAttributes` that is added to the save point upon creation. The additional information includes a name, a description, and user-defined attributes. User-defined attributes are grouped in a map of type `Map<String,Serializable>`. The attribute map may be used to persist information contained in the not-persisted scope mentioned earlier.

Implicit save points don't have additional information set and contain the state of the `UIViewRoot` from the last request. Save points are restored explicitly either through navigation to a `save-point-restore` element or programmatically by obtaining and redirecting to a restore URL. In both cases, it is the application developer's responsibility to restore an application state and clean up the save point if needed. For save points that are set implicitly, the save point is cleaned up from the persistent storage when the bounded task flow for which it is set completes.

Save for Later vs. Save as Draft

While the two phrases sound similar, save points is not an implementation pattern for a "save as draft" functionality in which a user temporarily saves the current state of a form document to the database. ADF Controller save points have a limited lifetime, which would lead to a loss of data if used in a "save as draft" fashion. If you use save points as "save for later", then the restore should be called before the save point expires in the persistent storage. Save points are used to restore a saved state upon application or system failure or to undo user interaction. A possible implementation of a "save as draft" functionality are polymorphic entity objects that use a discriminator column to determine the persist state of the information, such as for an unconfirmed booking.

NOTE
ADF Controller save points are not the same as save points set in the database.

SavePointManager

The `SavePointManager` class is an interface for creating, listing, retrieving, and removing save points. An instance of the `SavePointManager` is obtained in Java or Expression Language through the `ControllerContext` instance. Save points are created through a call to `createSavePoint` using one of the following options:

- **createSavePoint()**   Creates a save point with no custom attributes. The method returns the ID of the save point, or it returns null if the save point was not successfully created.

- **createSavePoint(SavePointAttributes attrs)**   Creates a save point for the current root view port and stores it. The `SavePointAttributes` argument defines attributes to describe a save point. The attributes include name, description, and any additional serializable user attribute. The save point attributes are persisted with the state manager along with a save point. The method returns the ID of the save point, or it returns null if the save point was not successfully created.

To remove a save point, developers use one of the following methods:

- **removeSavePoint(String savePointId)**   Removes the save point with a given ID. Returns null if the save point does not exist. Returns the removed save point.

- **clearSavePoints()**   Removes all save points for the current user. This method should be used only in an authenticated user context.

To access to a save point, developers use one of the following method calls:

- **getSavePoint(String id)**   Gets the save point by ID. Returns null if the save point does not exist.

- **listSavePointIds()**   Returns a `List<String>` of IDs for the save points that can be found in the state manager for the current user.

Configuring Explicit and Implicit Save Points for Oracle Fusion Web Applications

The save point feature is disabled by default and needs to be enabled for each application through a setting in the adf-config.xml file, which is located in the .adf\META-INF directory. In Oracle JDeveloper 11*g*, the adf-config.xml file can be accessed from the application Resources panel of the Application Navigator. To open the file, expand the Descriptors and ADF META-INF nodes and double-click the adf-config.xml entry or choose Open from the context menu. Select the Overview tab to enable implicit save points and to provide the JDBC datasource name for the database connection used by the ADF Controller to persist save points. After enabling save points, the following metadata is added to the adf-config.xml file:

```
<?xml version="1.0" encoding="windows-1252" ?>
<adf-config xmlns="http://xmlns.oracle.com/adf/config"
xmlns:sec="http://xmlns.oracle.com/adf/security/config">
[…]
<adf-controller-config
  xmlns="http://xmlns.oracle.com/adf/controller/config">
  <savepoint-datasource>java:comp/env/jdbc/hrDS</savepoint-datasource>
  <enable-implicit-savepoints>true</enable-implicit-savepoints>
</adf-controller-config>
</adf-config>
```

The following elements are valid child elements of the `adf-controller-config` element.

Metadata	Description
savepoint-datasource	The data source configuration for the database that is used to hold the save point storage. ADF Controller stores save points in a table with the name ORADFCSAVPT. The table is created the first time a save point is stored and has the following signature: **SAVE_POINT_ID** The primary key of the save point in VARCHAR2. **CREATED** The creation date of type DATE, which is set to SYSDATE by default and that cannot be null. **OWNER_ID** The name of the authenticated web user; the VARCHAR2 value is read from the ADF SecurityContext accessible principal name. **VERSION** VARCHAR2; versioning is not implemented and the value of this column is always null. **DESCRIPTION** Can be provided for external save points through an instance of SavePointAttributes. No API exists to add descriptions for the implicit created save points. Column type is in VARCHAR2. **EXPIRE_DT** The DATE column that holds the save point expire date. By default, the expiry data is computed as creation date + 86400 seconds, which calculates to 24 hours. **SAVE_POINT** BLOB column that holds the serialized save point.
enable-implicit-savepoints	If set to true, enables implicit save points being created by the framework. Save points are set for the entire stack if one of its bounded task flows is marked as critical.

Save Point Creation and Deletion

A single save point is created for a user that repeatedly creates explicit save points within the same browser window and session. Save points are deleted when the top level bounded Task Flow is exited, or in the case of implicit save points, the lowest Task Flow that is marked as critical is exited. Since not all save points are automatically deleted from the database, Oracle recommends application developers to implement a strategy, a script or application code, to frequently delete obsolete save points from the database.

Creating and Registering a Custom Save Point Listener

Systems that need to receive a notification on save point creation, delete, and restore complete can register a custom implementation of `SavePointListener` in the .adf\META-INF\services directory of the application workspace.

```
package adf.interactiv.listeners;
[...]
public class CustomSavePointListener implements SavePointListener{
  public CustomSavePointListener(){}
  public void savePointCreated(SavePointEvent savePointEvent) {}
  public void savePointDeleted(SavePointEvent savePointEvent) {}
  public void taskFlowCompleted(SavePointEvent savePointEvent) {}
}
```

By default, the services folder does not exist and needs to be created first. In the services folder, create a file, oracle.adf.controller.savepoint.SavePointListener, as a text file that contains the absolute name of the listeners the ADF Controller should load during application startup. For the `CustomSavePointListener`, the listener entry in this file is `adf.interactiv.listeners.CustomSavePointListener`.

> **NOTE**
> Once created, the oracle.adf.controller.savepoint.SavePointListener
> file is accessible for editing in the Application Resources panel of the
> Oracle JDeveloper Application Navigator. To open the file, expand the
> Descriptors | ADF META-INF | services entry and choose Open from
> the context menu.

SavePointListener

A public interface describes the methods that need to be implemented by custom `SavePointListener` implementations.

- **savePointCreated(SavePointEvent savePointEvent)**   Called when an explicit save point is created. The `savePointEvent` argument contains the save point ID and task flow Id of the bounded task flow on top of the stack. If no bounded task flow exists, this value is null.

- **savePointDeleted(SavePointEvent savePointEvent)**   Called when a save point is deleted. The `savePointEvent` argument contains the save point ID of the deleted save point and the task flow Id of the bounded task flow on top of the stack. If no bounded task flow exists, this value is null.

- **taskFlowCompleted(SavePointEvent savePointEvent)**   Called when a bounded task flow that was restored from a save point completes.

Summary

This chapter generally introduced the new ADF Controller in Oracle ADF 11*g*. The ADF Controller extends the JSF navigation model and introduces the concept of reusable task flows. Though using a delegation pattern that would allow developers to use the standard JSF navigation and the ADF Controller navigation in combination, best practices dictate deciding for one of the two only. Using ADF task flows, developers have the option to partition an application flow in bounded task flows. There is no rule of best practices defined other than common sense for when to use bounded and when to use unbounded task flows.

Unbounded task flows are usually used for the following:

- As the entry point to an application

- For page flows that are not restrictive on where a users enters the flow

- For pages that are bookmarkable

- For declarative page menu creation

For all other use cases, bounded task flows are the better choice. Bounded task flows should be used for flows that

- Should be reused in same or other applications

- Should run as part of a page within a region container

- Require an isolated transaction context

- Change data to then either commit or rollback on exit

- Have a requirement for a single entry point

It is important for developers to keep in mind that task flows don't own the pages they reference. This means that any ADF Faces page defined in a JavaServer Pages file can be accessed from the browser URL directly, independently of it being used in a bounded or unbounded task flow. Only page fragments are safe from direct browser access because they cannot run stand-alone.

For all state or data information that you want to keep for reference in a page or to access from client logic in a managed bean, best practice is to keep the scope of the stored information as short as possible to avoid memory leaks in your applications. For example, abusing the session scope as an integration layer between bounded task flows and regions, which are covered later in the book, bears a risk of unwanted side effects such as inadvertently tight coupling of task flows, unknown session attribute states, and memory leaks.

Another good practice is to store information not directly as in memory scope attributes but as a `HashMap` of related attributes. This not only builds an association between attributes and their context of use, but it also allows bulk clean-up of attributes in removing the `HashMap` from the scope. For example, the following Expression Language example can access attributes that are stored in a hash map in session scope:

```
#{sessionScope.hashMapAttribute.attributeName}
```

When creating managed beans, it is good practice to implement `java.io.Serializable` and to extend from a common base class.

Save points in ADF Controller help to restore lost or suspended application states and can be set explicitly by the application developer or implicitly by the framework. The save point feature should be used sensibly because there is no guarantee that the recovered state fully matches the previous state. This is because the standard scope's request, session, and application are not persisted, which is up to the developer to handle through save point attributes. As an application developer you may find explicit save points better than implicit save points, as they provide you with more control over their creation. This is why we recommend this part of the feature for your application development.

CHAPTER
5

Working with Unbounded and Bounded Oracle ADF Task Flows

There is so much to say, experience, and explore about working with ADF task flows that it probably requires a software conference of its own to touch base on all the functionality and to unveil the full power it brings to JavaServer Faces development.

he concept of unbounded and bounded task flows is new to JavaServer Faces (JSF) and is an extension exclusively available to Fusion web application developers who use the ADF Controller for their page flow handling. This chapter explains how to work with unbounded and bounded task flows in Oracle ADF with examples of common use cases and requirements.

Working with Unbounded Task Flows

Unbounded task flows are simple to use, and experienced Java EE developers soon find analogies to the standard JSF navigation model. However, there is more to unbounded task flows than meets the eye. Though the true power of the ADF Controller unfolds in the concept of bounded task flows, the unbounded ADF Task Flow contains features, such as bookmarking and menu model support that are not available in standard JSF.

There always exists a single instance of unbounded task flow at runtime, even if there is no activity added to it. The unbounded task flow base configuration file, adfc-config.xml, represents the ADF Controller bootstrapping file that may have its own activities defined. The unbounded task flow can be configured by one or many configuration files that are parsed and loaded the first time the user starts the application. Use cases for an unbounded task flow configuration include the following:

- The declarative support for building hierarchical page menus using the `org.apache.myfaces.trinidad.model.XMLMenuModel`, which builds the model of an `af:navigationPane` component. For a description of building and working with hierarchical page menus, see Chapter 7.

- Creating bookmarkable pages, which requires a view activity to be added to an unbounded task flow. Upon view activity navigation, the framework detects the bookmarking settings and renders the view URL in the browser so the user can bookmark it. Bookmarking is covered in this chapter.

- Navigation cases, which are required in the top-level task flow for developers to provide a single or multiple entry points into an application. Unbounded task flows don't have a single defined entry point, allowing the application user to access any view directly by its view activity URL.

The adfc-config.xml configuration file is automatically created when building a new application in Oracle JDeveloper 11*g*, using the Fusion Web Application (ADF) application template or when adding the ADF Page Flow Technology Scope to an existing or new web project.

Creating and Defining an Unbounded Task Flow

To design an unbounded task flow, open the task flow visual diagram by double-clicking the adfc-config.xml file in the JDeveloper Application Navigator (CTRL-SHIFT-A), or choose Open from the file's context menu. The diagram opens with a blank screen that you fill with content from the JDeveloper Component Palette (CTRL-SHIFT-P), the Application Navigator, the Data Controls panel, or the Resource palette.

- **Component palette**   Contains activities, such as view or method activities, and control flow components, such as the Control Flow Case, which developers use to define navigation between activities. To add a component to the diagram, select it in the Component palette and drag it to the diagram. The Source Elements panel contains all the metadata elements that are used in the task flow XML definition file to set up activities and flows. Usually these metadata elements are set indirectly by configuring a selected activity's properties in the Oracle JDeveloper Property Inspector (CTRL-SHIFT-I) or by adding a component from the Components palette. One element that makes an exception and is discussed in Chapter 6 is the `parent action` element, which allows a region on a page to enforce navigation on its parent page.

- **Application Navigator**   Contains ADF Faces file resources, JSPX files that are dragged and dropped to the visual diagram to create view activities. As mentioned in Chapter 4, a task flow doesn't own the page and instead references the page from a view activity. In addition, bounded task flow definitions, if they exist in the project, can be dragged and dropped to the diagram to create a call activity that references the bounded task flow.

- **Data Controls panel**   Exposes view object operations such as create, delete, and execute and application module operations such as commit and rollback, as well as client methods exposed on the application module and view object. Dragging an operation or method from the Data Controls panel to the task flow diagram creates a method call activity that executes the action when the flow navigates to it. The other option for adding method activities to a flow is to define a method in a managed bean, drag-and-drop the method call activity from the component palette, and bind it to the managed bean method using Expression Language in the PropertyInspector.

- **Resource Palette**   Contains reusable components, such as task flows that are deployed in an ADF Library file. Dragging a task flow entry to the task flow diagram adds a task flow call activity.

TIP

To zoom in and out of a task flow diagram view, press CTRL-+ or CTRl--.
If you own a computer mouse with a wheel, press CTRL and move the
wheel up or down.

The unbounded task flow in Figure 5-1 shows a mix of possible task flow activities.

Starting from the BrowseDepartments view activity, the user navigates to a bounded task flow to show and edit employees, to a save point restore activity or to an edit page to edit an existing or new department record. Until a task flow reference is configured, the task flow call activity will be flagged with a yellow warning overlay icon to indicate the missing configuration. Same for the URL view activity, which shows this warning for the missing the URL configuration. The warning overlay icons only show if they are not disabled by the developer using the visual diagrammer's Show menu option.

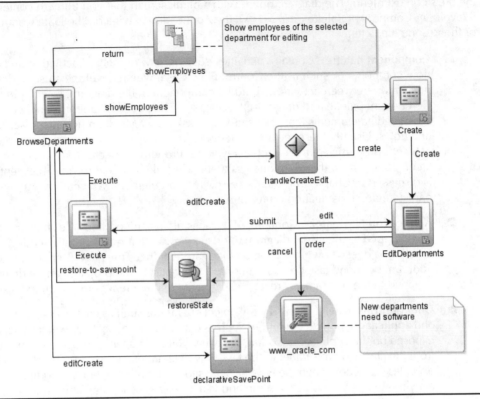

FIGURE 5-1   *Unbounded task flow diagram*

The control flow to the EditDepartments view activity has a first stop at a method call activity that sets an explicit save point and stores the save point ID as a memory scope attribute so that the user's work can be undone if needed. The next stop is a router activity that evaluates whether the request is for edit or create. For this, the router reads a value from an in-memory attribute to determine the next navigation. If the request is for a new record, the router continues with the create navigation case and the next stop is a method activity that references the ADF Business Component `Create` operation. The method call activity was added by dragging the `Create` operation from a View Object in the Data Controls panel onto the diagram. Eventually the flow reaches the EditDepartments view activity for the user to provide the data entry for the new record.

TIP
A whole application flow can be defined in the task flow diagram without any existing ADF Faces page source files. This allows developers to get early feedback from the end user about the application flow before building the application.

Note that although we referred to the intermediary activities as "stops," the navigation doesn't pause there. The end user experience is that the EditDepartments view is shown immediately after clicking the Create button in the BrowseDepartments view. If the user decides to click Cancel on the edit forum, the navigation is forwarded to the save point restore element that reads the stored save point ID from the memory to recover the saved state. The user experience is that the BrowseDepartments view is displayed with the state that existed before the save point was set. If the user clicked Submit in the edit form, a method activity is executed to refresh the BrowseDepartments view before navigating to this page. Optionally, developers may add notes to the task flow diagram, or use the description and display name elements of the task flow activities, to document what individual activities actually do.

NOTE
Two types of save points, model save points and controller save points, exist in ADF and are discussed in detail at the end of this chapter. The save point mechanism in Figure 5-1 uses an ADF Controller save point to undo changes not only on the transactional level but also changes applied to variables stored in a memory.

Bookmarking

JSF pages are difficult to bookmark because all the request parameters are passed to the server without being displayed in the browser URL field. This and the fact that the JSF postback navigation shows the URL of the previous view request means special handling is required to enable users to bookmark a page. In Oracle ADF Task Flows, view activities of an unbounded task flow can be configured bookmarkable. If so, the Oracle ADF Task Flow handler applies a special handling, which includes setting the URL parameters and their values and optionally converting data objects to their string representation, and vice versa, when the view is requested.

What happens if a view activity is marked as bookmarkable? A page is configured as bookmarkable when the optional `bookmark` element is added to the view activity metadata. You can manually set the `bookmark` element in the XML source of the adfc-config.xml configuration file or declaratively in the Property Inspector. During the rendering of the view activity, the ADF Controller constructs the bookmark URL with all the request parameters defined by the application developer to rebuild the page when dereferenced from a bookmark. To display the bookmarkable URL, the ADF Controller performs a redirect to the bookmark URL. The page state is not changed by the redirect. The constructed URL contains the name of the view activity and not the name of the physical ADF Faces page file.

_adf.ctrl-state Token and Bookmarking

The state token that is added to the bookmarked URL is usually not needed because the referenced session may no longer exist when the user dereferences the bookmark. However, ADF Controller adds the state token to all page URLs, including those pages that are marked as bookmarkable. In cases where a bookmark is dereferenced when the session referenced in the state token no longer exists, the ADF controller recognizes the invalid state token and produces a new updated token for the current user session.

How to Set Up a View Activity to Be Bookmarkable

To configure a view activity of an unbounded task flow to be bookmarkable, select the view activity in the task flow visual diagrammer or in the JDeveloper Structure window (CTRL-SHIFT-S) and open the Oracle JDeveloper Property Inspector. Expand the Bookmark category and set the Bookmark property to true, as shown in Figure 5-2.

NOTE
View activities that are configured as bookmarkable cannot have their Redirect property set to true.

How to Define Request Parameters for the Bookmark URL

To create a URL parameter for the bookmark URL, click the green plus icon next to the Bookmark URL Parameters header in the Oracle JDeveloper Property Inspector. Provide the following information:

- **Name** The name of the request parameter that is added to the bookmark URL. When the bookmark is dereferenced from a browser, the specified parameter and value are passed to the server to help rebuild the page state.

- **Value** An updateable object reference using Expression Language. The object is read when building the bookmark URL and updated when the bookmark URL is used to request the page. If the value returned by the EL resolves to NULL then the parameter is omitted from the URL

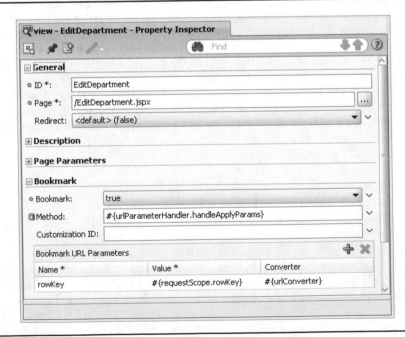

FIGURE 5-2 *Property Inspector view of a bookmarkable view activity*

■ **Converter** Optional configuration of a managed bean that implements the `UrlParameterConverter` interface. The converter is needed when the object represented by the request parameter is not of type `String`. In this case, a converter is needed that translates the objects into a `String` representation and the incoming request parameter value back to the original object. For example, an object of type `Date` adds the `String` presentation of the date to the request parameter, which, when dereferencing the bookmark, is converted back into a `Date` object.

Adding Data from the ADF Binding Layer as Values of a Bookmark Request Parameter

Let's assume a user selects a department from a list of departments and clicks an edit button to navigate to another view, an edit page to update the selected department. If the edit page view activity is marked as bookmarkable, then to rebuild the information displayed on the page from a bookmark, the row key of the edited row is required. The bookmark URL therefore would have a request parameter `rowKey` with the value obtained from the selected department row on the department's browse page.

ADF Task Flows don't have their own data binding definition, which means that the ADF data binding layer is not accessible to read the row key value from directly. Instead, the selected row key must be read from the binding before navigating to the edit page and stored in an object that is accessible for the browse and the edit pages. A scope that is accessible from both pages is the `requestScope`. Adding a `SetPropertyListener` component, located in the Operations category of ADF Faces components in the JDeveloper Component Palette, to the edit button allows you to access the current row key from the binding to write it to a managed bean or attribute in `requestScope`.

Figure 5-3 shows the SetPropertyListener configuration dialog that is shown after dragging and dropping the listener component onto a parent UI component.

In the following code example, the `af:SetPropertyListener` component reads the current `rowKey` from the `DepartmentsView1Iterator` and writes it to the `rowKey` `requestScope` attribute.

```
<af:commandButton text="Edit" id="cb1" action="edit">
  <af:setPropertyListener
    from="#{bindings.DepartmentsView1Iterator.currentRowKeyString}"
    to="#{requestScope.rowKey}" type="action"/>
</af:commandButton>
```

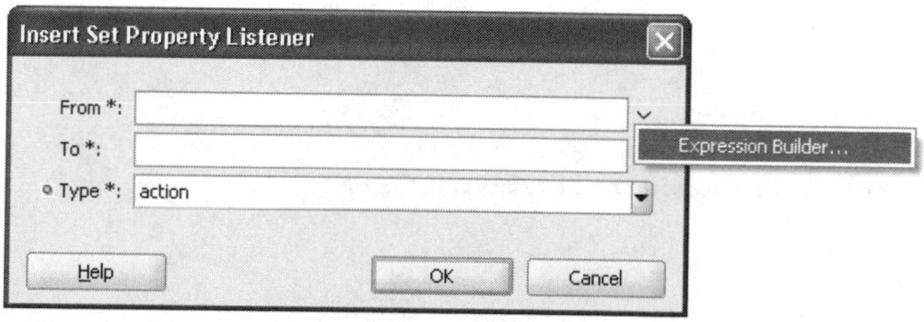

FIGURE 5-3 *SetPropertyListener configuration dialog with Expression Builder context menu option*

The bookmark definition references the request scope attribute in its URL parameter definition as shown here:

```
<bookmark>
  <url-parameter>
    <name>rowKey</name>
    <value>#{requestScope.rowKey}</value>
  </url-parameter>
</bookmark>
```

URL Parameter Converter

Optionally, the `url-parameter` element may have a `converter` element defined. A URL parameter converter is required for URL parameters that reference model values of a type different from `java.lang.String`. The converter is referenced by Expression Language and implemented as a managed bean that implements the `UrlParameterConverter` interface.

```
import oracle.adf.controller.UrlParameterConverter;
public class CustomUrlConverter implements UrlParameterConverter {
  public CustomUrlConverter() {
  }
  public Object getAsObject(String urlParam) {
    return urlParamToObject(urlParam);
  }
  public String getAsString(Object urlParamValue) {
    return urlParamObjectToString(urlParamValue);
  }
  private Object urlParamToObject(String urlParam){
    Object o = null;
    // handle urlParam to Object conversion
    return o;
  }
  private String urlParamObjectToString(Object urlParamValue){
    String sValue = null;
    // handle urlParamValue to String conversion
    return sValue;
  }
}
```

The bookmarking definition in the unbounded task flow definition shows as follows, assuming that the managed bean is configured as `urlConverter`:

```
<bookmark>
  <url-parameter>
    <name>rowKey</name>
    <value>#{requestScope.rowKey}</value>
    <converter>#{urlConverter}</converter>
  </url-parameter>
</bookmark>
```

NOTE
Because the rowKey *element used in this example is of type* String, *a converter is not needed. However, for completeness, we added a converter to show you how the configuration looks.*

NOTE
Converters are no validators. Still however they can be used to detect and filter out unwanted URL parameter values. For example, using converters you may aim for preventing SQL injection attacks in that you check the provided URL value for SQL keywords. There is no reason to trust a user.

What Happens When a Bookmarked URL Is Requested

When the ADF Controller receives a bookmarked page URL request, the controller invokes the configured parameter converters on the request parameters during the Restore View phase of the JSF lifecycle. After converting and validating the URL parameters, the *model* (from a JSF perspective, which may not be ADF) is updated using the Expression Language reference defined in the `url-parameter` metadata. The bookmark method, if configured, is then called to perform any additional action required to reconstruct the bookmarked page state before rendering it.

Referencing a URL Request Parameter from the ADF Binding

To declaratively use the request parameter of the dereferenced bookmark URL in the ADF binding of the edit page, you can either directly reference the URL request parameter, `#{param.rowKey}`, or reference the updated `requestScope` attribute, `#{requestScope.rowkey}`, from a binding parameter. The binding parameter, as shown next, is then used as an argument of an `invokeAction` executable to query the row to edit.

NOTE
Only the object that is referenced from the request parameter configuration of the bookmark definition contains the converted value. In the example shown in Figure 5-2, this is the rowKey *attribute in the* requestScope. *The* rowKey *on the URL is of type* String *and cannot be used if the binding layer expects a non-*String *object as an argument value.*

```
<pageDefinition xmlns="http://xmlns.oracle.com/adfm/uimodel"
                version="11.1.1.54.26" id="EditDepartmentPageDef"
                Package="adf.interactiv.view.pageDefs">
  <parameters>
    <parameter id="rowKey" value="#{requestScope.rowKey}"/>
  </parameters>
  <executables>
    <invokeAction Binds="setCurrentRowWithKey" id="setCurrentRowKey"
               Refresh="prepareModel"
               RefreshCondition="#{bindings.rowKey !=null}"/>
    <iterator Binds="DepartmentsView1" RangeSize="25"
           DataControl="HRAppModuleDataControl"
           id="DepartmentsView1Iterator"/>
  </executables>
  <bindings>
  ...
  <action IterBinding="DepartmentsView1Iterator"
       id="setCurrentRowWithKey"
       InstanceName="HRAppModuleDataControl.DepartmentsView1"
       DataControl="HRAppModuleDataControl"
```

```
              RequiresUpdateModel="false"
              Action="setCurrentRowWithKey">
                <NamedData NDName="rowKey" NDValue="${bindings.rowKey}"
                          NDType="java.lang.String"/>
        </action>
       </bindings>
    </pageDefinition>
```

In this example, the EditDepartmentPageDef file, the binding definition file of the target page, contains the following entries:

- **parameter**—Defines a parameter, rowKey, that reads its value from the incoming request URL. The expected URL parameter name is rowKey. Unlike binding attributes and binding variables, binding parameters are available before the model update in the ADF lifecycle, which is why a parameter is used in this example.

- **invokeAction**—Since the recommended Oracle ADF task flow is to use a method activity to initialize data queries, there are not many use cases for the invokeAction element. One use case, though, is with bookmarked pages. The setCurrentRowWithKey operation is invoked from the invokeAction entry in the executable section. This, however, is configured to occur only if the rowKey parameter is not null, using the RefreshCondition attribute.

- **setCurrentRowWithKey**—This operation is exposed on the ADF Business Component view object and added as an action binding to the pageDef file. The NDValue attribute of the NamedData element in the action binding references the rowKey binding parameter before it gets executed.

Whenever the page is requested from a URL that contains the rowKey request parameter, the setCurrentRowWithKey action is executed to prepare the model to set the row specified in the URL as current.

An example bookmark URL that invokes the action binding looks like this:

http://127.0.0.1:7101/contextPath/faces/EditDepartment?rowKey=000100000002C13300000
0050000011E350FC02F&_adf.ctrl-state=1013929944_3

Referencing URL Request Parameters from a Bookmarking Method

The coding equivalent to the preceding declarative example is a managed bean method that is referenced from the Method property of the bookmark definition and that is called when a request is issued from a bookmarked URL. The managed bean method is invoked after the optional configured converters finished their work. In the example shown in Figure 5-2, the rowKey parameter is used to set the current selected row in the page binding. The ADF page definition file of the target page contains a setCurrentRowWithKey action that expects a row key as the only argument. The rowKey parameter value is read from the requestScope attribute that is updated by the URL request parameter configured for the bookmark. Accessing the value in the requestScope attribute ensures that the obtained value is already converted to the required type.

```
public void handleApplyParams(){
    //access the request map containing all URL parameters
    //from the JSF context
```

```
FacesContext fctx = FacesContext.getCurrentInstance();
ExternalContext ectx = fctx.getExternalContext();
Map requestScope = ectx.getRequestMap();
String rowKey = (String) requestScope.get("rowKey");
if (rowKey!=null){
  BindingContext bindingCtx = BindingContext.getCurrent();
  BindingContainer bindings = bindingCtx.getCurrentBindingsEntry();
  OperationBinding setCurrentRowWithKey =
      bindings.getOperationBinding("setCurrentRowWithKey");
  setCurrentRowWithKey.getParamsMap().put("rowKey",rowKey);
  setCurrentRowWithKey.execute();
}
}
```

The bookmark method reference looks like this:

```
<bookmark>
  <method>#{urlParameterHandler.handleApplyParams}</method>
  <url-parameter>
    <name>rowKey</name>
    <value>#{requestScope.rowKey}</value>
    <converter>#{urlConverter}</converter>
  </url-parameter>
</bookmark>
```

Note that all parameters are handled within a single call to this method.

How to Visually Indicate That a Page Is Bookmarkable

How does an application user know that a particular page is bookmarkable? He does not unless the page tells him. At runtime, if a view supports bookmarking, the information is available on the `ViewPortContext` of the current view, which is accessible from the static `ControllerContext` class.

Using Expression Language, this information can be used on the *rendered* property of an image or text component that indicates that a page is bookmarkable to the user. In the following example code, formatted output text is added to ADF Faces pages and rendered if bookmarking is possible:

```
<af:outputFormatted id="cl1"
    rendered="#{controllerContext.currentViewPort.viewBookmarkable}"
    value="&lt;b>Press ctrl+D to bookmark this page&lt;/b>">
</af:outputFormatted>
```

In practice, it would be better to present a command link or an image that the user can click to create the bookmark. At the time of this writing, however, no consistent cross-browser API exists to do so in JavaScript. Most browsers, such as Microsoft Internet Explorer, Firefox, Safari, and Google Chrome, open the bookmark creation dialog when the user presses CTRL-D.

In our opinion, the only acceptable JavaScript solution for creating bookmarks programmatically exists for Microsoft Internet Explorer. If your application runs in a corporate network and IE is your browser of choice, the following script is for you:

```
<af:resource type="javascript">
  function setBookmark(evt){
```

```
    evt.cancel();
    var agentName = navigator.userAgent.toLowerCase();
    if (agentName.indexOf("msie")!=-1){
        window.external.AddFavorite(document.URL,document.title);
  }
  else {
   alert('Press ctrl+D to bookmark this page');
  }
}
</af:resource >
```

This JavaScript code opens the bookmark dialog in IE with the current selected browser URL as its value and the title string as the bookmark name. The JavaScript function `setBookmark` is called from an `af:clientListener` component, which is added as a child element of an ADF Faces component.

```
<af:commandLink
    rendered="#{controllerContext.currentViewPort.viewBookmarkable}"
    text="Bookmark this Page">
      <af:clientListener method="setBookmark" type="action"/>
</af:commandLink>
```

To ensure the `document.title` reference produces a meaningful name for the bookmark, set the `title` attribute of the `af:document` component of the ADF Faces page. The `title` attribute is not set by default.

```
<af:document id="d1" title="Edit page of the
  #{bindings.DepartmentName.inputValue} department">
```

In this example, the `title` attribute references the ADF binding layer using Expression Language to obtain the current department name value. It is also possible to read the entire `title` attribute value from a resource bundle or managed bean to implement multilanguage support. The `title` attribute also determines the default name of the bookmark that is created when the user presses CTRL-D.

> **NOTE**
> *Chapter 19 discusses the integration of custom JavaScript in ADF Faces RC, best practices, and mistakes to avoid.*

Restrictions

Declarative bookmarking works only for explicit page navigation, in which the bookmarkable page replaces the current page in the browser window. Pages that change their displayed content through partial page refresh cannot be bookmarked with their current content because the page URL in the browser does not change in this case.

> **NOTE**
> *A page that is configured as bookmarkable always shows its defined request parameters in the URL. This is independent of whether or not the user is actually bookmarking it.*

How to Pass Values Between Pages

A frequent developer requirement is to pass data from one page to the next, which can be done through memory scope attributes. To pass the value of the selected `DepartmentId` attribute from one page to the next, you use the `SetPropertyListener` as shown next:

```
<af:setPropertyListener
    from="#{bindings.DepartmentId.inputValue}"
    to="#{requestScope.deptId}" type="action"/>
```

If the `SetPropertyListener` component is added to a button, when the button is clicked, the input value of the `DepartmentId` attribute binding in the pageDefinition.xml file of the current page is read and stored in the `deptId` attribute of the `requestScope`. The `deptId` attribute is automatically created if it doesn't exist. The attribute can be accessed from the navigated page using Expression Language or Java.

> **NOTE**
> *Though we referenced the PageDef file in the explanation above, at runtime values are read from the binding container, which is the object instance created from the pageDefinition.xml file.*

> **NOTE**
> *The ADF Business Component business service is a smart layer that remembers the selected row when navigating from one page to another that uses the same view object through the ADF binding layer. In this case, you don't need to pass data between pages.*

View Activity Input Parameters

View activities may have defined input parameters that read values from a memory scope or the request parameters to store them in a memory attribute or managed bean that is accessible when the page is rendered. You can use an input parameter to copy a URL request parameter to a scope such as `requestScope`, `viewScope`, or `pageFlowScope` to make its value available when working within the page. To create an input parameter for a view activity, select the view activity in the ADF Task Flow diagram and open the Property Inspector. Expand the Page Parameters section and click the green plus icon. The From Value uses Expression Language to reference the incoming value and the To Value uses Expression Language to store away the value for later use.

The following code example copies the `deptId` request parameter value to a `pageFlowScope` attribute that makes the value available for all pages within a task flow:

```
<view id="BrowseDepartments">
  <page>/BrowseDepartments.jspx</page>
  <input-page-parameter>
    <from-value>#{param.deptId}</from-value>
    <to-value>#{pageFlowScope.deptId}</to-value>
  </input-page-parameter>
</view>
```

SetPropertyListener vs. SetActionListener

The `af:setPropertyListener` and `af:SetActionListener` components are located under the Operations section of the ADF Faces components panel in the Oracle JDeveloper Component Palette. They are used to write objects into memory or a managed bean property. While both listeners appear to have identical functionality, they are actually different. The `af:SetActionListener` responds to action events only, such as a button or link mouse click. In contrast, the `af:setPropertyListener` responds to events such as calendar, value change, disclosure, focus, launch, poll, range change, return, row disclosure, dialog, launch popup, popup fetch, query, query operation, region navigation, and return popup. The `SetPropertyListener` is new in Oracle JDeveloper 11*g* and should be used instead of the `SetActionListener`, which is included in Oracle JDeveloper 11*g* for backward compatibility.

How to Obtain the Request URL of a View Activity

Only view activities that are in the unbounded task flow can be accessed directly from a browser URL. To obtain a view activity URL, one of the following two code snippets can be used:

```
ControllerContext cctx = ControllerContext.getInstance();
String viewId = cctx.getCurrentViewPort().getViewId();
String url = cctx.getGlobalViewActivityURL(viewId);
```

Or, to obtain the URL for a non current activity, use this:

```
ControllerContext cctx = ControllerContext.getInstance();
String viewId = "/TheActivityId";
String url = cctx.getGlobalViewActivityURL(viewId);
```

An `AdfcIllegalArgumentException` is thrown if the `viewId` is not contained in the unbounded task flow. It's the developer's responsibility to ensure that the `viewId` exists when generating a view activity URL.

Working with Multiple Copies of Unbounded Task Flow Definitions

Multiple unbounded task flow definition files are merged into a single file at runtime. A use case in which multiple unbounded task flow definition files exist is when ADF libraries that have their own managed beans defined are added to an application. In this case, the library contains its own adfc-config.xml file that is located in the META-INF directory of the Java archive (JAR) file.

Another use case in which multiple definition files exist in a single web project is the declarative support for building XML menu models in Oracle JDeveloper 11*g*. To represent a page hierarchy in a site menu, developers create unbounded task flow definitions for each level in the page hierarchy from which to generate the menu model.

NOTE
The Oracle online documentation "Oracle Fusion Middleware Fusion Developer's Guide for Oracle Application Development Framework 11g Release 1" explains the creation of XML menu models for building site menus in Chapter 18.

To create additional copies of the unbounded task flow definition file, choose File | New | Web Tier | JSF from the Oracle JDeveloper menu and then select the **ADF Task Flow** entry. Unselect the Create as Bounded Task Flow checkbox and click OK. This creates the unbounded task flow definition file and references it from the adfc-config.xml file.

By default, all unbounded task flow definition files are created in the project WEB-INF directory and registered in the adfc-config.xml root configuration file:

```
<adfc config xmlns="http://xmlns.oracle.com/adf/controller" version="1.2">
  <metadata-resource>/WEB-INF/adfc-config1.xml</metadata-resource>
  <metadata-resource>/WEB-INF/adfc-config2.xml</metadata-resource>
  <metadata-resource>/WEB-INF/adfc-config3.xml</metadata-resource>
</adfc-config>
```

To define navigation cases with which to navigate from an activity defined in one unbounded task flow to an activity contained in another, you use the following strategies.

Wildcard Control Flow Rule

Also known as a global navigation rule, a wildcard control flow rule can be used to navigate from an activity in an unbounded task flow definition file to an activity in another unbounded task flow definition. To create a wildcard flow, drag the Wildcard Control Flow Rule element from the component palette onto the task flow diagram of the called flow. Create a Control Flow Case from the wildcard element to the task flow activity to call and define a name for the navigation case:

```
<control-flow-rule>
  <from-activity-id>*</from-activity-id>
  <control-flow-case>
    <from-outcome>edit</from-outcome>
    <to-activity-id>Edit</to-activity-id>
  </control-flow-case>
</control-flow-rule>
```

A wildcard is defined by an asterisk symbol (*) as the value of the `from-activity-id` element. Using the combination of an asterisk symbol and a string, such as `"browse*"`, allows you to create partial wildcard rules, in which the navigation occurs only if the calling activity name matches the defined naming pattern. In the `"browse*"` example, all activities starting with `"browse"`, such as `"browseDepartments"` or `"browseEmployees"` navigate to the activity defined in the `to-activity-id` element if the outcome of the command action is the value defined in the `from-outcome` element. If similar wildcard definitions exist, such as `"browse*"` and `"browseEm*"`, the most specific match is used.

The visual task flow editor in Oracle JDeveloper 11*g* doesn't show control flow rules that navigate across unbounded task flow definition files because it cannot resolve them. In addition, navigation cases defined in noncurrent task flow configuration files are not shown in the select list of the `action` attribute that are available for command items, such as `af:commandButton`. In this case, the action value needs to be edited manually.

The Full Name of the Calling Activity

The full name of the calling activity can be used in the `control-flow-rule` element's `from-activity-id`. To navigate from a BrowseDepartments view activity in adfc1-config.xml to an EditDepartment view activity in the adfc2-config.xml file, the control flow rule in one of the two configuration files needs to be defined as follows:

```
<control-flow-rule>
  <from-activity-id>BrowseDepartments</from-activity-id>
  <control-flow-case>
    <from-outcome>edit</from-outcome>
    <to-activity-id>EditDepartment</to-activity-id>
  </control-flow-case>
</control-flow-rule>
```

To use this configuration, you edit the task flow definition file of the source activity that initiates the navigation manually in the XML source view. Though you can use the Overview editor and Property Inspector to create the navigation case, both editors don't allow you to provide the `to-activity-id` as a free text entry.

NOTE
Oracle JDeveloper 11g does not parse multiple unbounded task flow definitions for possible naming conflicts. It is the developer's responsibility to use a naming scheme that creates unique activity names and control flow rules.

Working with Bounded Task Flows

ADF bounded task flows represent modular and reusable process flows with a defined entry and one to many defined exit points. Bounded task flows are called from other task flows, referenced from a browser URL or embedded as a region in a view. They are designed to be independent from the caller and should be implemented this way by the application developer. Input and output parameters of the bounded task flow can be used to exchange data between a calling and a called task flow. If a bounded task flow is entered from a call activity, the parent flow becomes the caller flow. If the task flow is embedded in a region, the parent flow is the task flow of the hosting view. This chapter describes bounded task flows that are accessed from a call activity, which is why, unless mentioned otherwise, the terms "parent task flow" and "calling task flow" are used to refer to the task flow that launches the bounded child flow. Bounded task flows that execute in regions on a page are subject of Chapter 6.

Bounded task flows operate within their own private memory scope, the `pageFlowScope`, that has a lifespan between request and session scope to store data and managed beans. Developers should understand that a called bounded task flow has access to its own `pageFlowScope` only and not to the scope of the calling task flow. Bounded task flows join an existing transaction or can start a new one if none exists.

TaskFlowContext

The ADF controller creates a new instance of `TaskFlowContext` each time a bounded ADF task flow is entered. The binding context manages the lifespan of all `DataControl` instances within the bounded task flow and holds information about the task flow ID and whether or not it contains uncommitted data. At runtime, the ADF Controller creates two types of task flow context, a root and a non-root context. A non-root task flow context is a child of another, which is the case when a bounded task flow is configured to reuse an existing transaction, while a root task flow context starts its own transaction. The task flow context is accessible through Expression Language using the `ControllerContext` implicit object: `#{controllerContext.currentViewPort.taskFlowContext}`.

Upon exiting a bounded task flow, the Oracle Controller calls the `release()` method on the context to free the `DataControl` resources used by the task flow.

NOTE
In Oracle ADF of JDeveloper 11g bounded task flows don't support multiple transactions when sharing the data control scope. An attempt to open a second transaction causes an `ActivityLogicException` with the error code ADFC-00020 to be thrown by the ADF Controller. To start a bounded task flow in a new transaction, always make sure the data control scope is not shared with its parent.

Creating Bounded Task Flows

Bounded task flows have their own task flow definition file that is different from the ADF Controller unbounded definition in that it has a defined entry point and zero to many defined exit points. New bounded task flow definitions can be created manually from the Oracle JDeveloper New Gallery or extracted from another bounded or unbounded task flow. The bounded task flow definition file consists of the following metadata elements, which can be added directly to the XML configuration file source or visually edited through the JDeveloper Property Inspector. In addition to the activity elements introduced in Chapter 4, you use the following elements to configure bounded task flows:

- **template-reference** Allows bounded task flows to be created from templates. If, for example, all bounded task flows should have a view to handle exceptions, this could be made a part of the template.

- **default-activity** The first activity executed when entering a task flow. The `default-activity` element can reference any activity on the bounded task flow including method and router activities. This is a mandatory element that must exist in a bounded task flow definition. At design time, the first element added to a task flow definition is marked as the `default-activity` and highlighted with a green circular background image. The default activity can be changed in the Property Inspector of the bounded task flow. To call a bounded task flow directly from a URL, the default activity must be a view activity.

- **transaction** Defines if and how the bounded task flow participates in an ADF model (ADFm) transaction. If this metadata element is set, the task flow either starts a new transaction or joins an existing transaction. Valid child elements of the `transaction` element are `requires-existing-transaction`, `requires-transaction`, and `new-transaction`. The child elements are exposed as properties in the Oracle JDeveloper Property Inspector.

■ **control-flow-rule**   Similar to unbounded task flows, the navigation within a bounded task flow is defined by named navigation cases defined by the `control-flow-rule` metadata element.

■ **input-parameter-definition**   Allows developers to pass information from the calling task flow to the called task flow. A parameter definition consists of a mandatory name, the value attribute, and an optional class attributes to provide information about the type of the passed in value in case a static string value is provided. The value attribute uses Expression Language to reference a task flow scoped managed bean or a `pageFlowScope` attribute to store the passed-in value. Optionally, an input parameter can be marked as `required` so that an exception is thrown if this parameter is missing.

■ **return-value**   Bounded task flows may return values to the calling task flow, which is done through the `return-value` element. Similar to the `input-parameter-definition` element, the `return-value` element has a required name and optional class and value attributes. The value attribute references the value object that should be returned to the caller or has a string return value defined. The `return-value` is exposed as a property in the task flow call activity for the calling task flow to map its value to a managed bean or memory scope attribute. See "Passing Values to and from Bounded Task Flows" later in this chapter for a code example.

■ **managed-bean**   Bounded task flows have their own managed bean definitions in the request and `pageFlowScope` scope, or with no scope. Defining managed beans in a task flow ensures reusability of the flow. Managed beans that are in session or application scope should be configured in the unbounded task flow definition and not the bounded task flow. Task flows that are designed to be regions on a page should use the `backingBean` scope if more than one instance of the task flow is expected to be on a single page.

■ **task-flow-reentry**   Determines the behavior when application users reenter a bounded task flow using the browser back button. By default, reentry is allowed. Valid child elements are `reentry-allowed`, `reentry-not-allowed`, and `reentry-outcome-dependent`.

■ **data-control-scope**   Determines whether the bounded task flow uses a shared data control frame or its own, isolated data control frame. The latter creates a new application module connection. The default setting is `shared`.

■ **initializer**   Managed bean method reference invoked when the bounded task flow is entered.

■ **finalizer**   Managed bean method reference invoked when the bounded task flow is exited by a return activity or exception.

- **critical**   Indicates the framework to create an implicit save point when exiting a bounded task flow. Also helps to prevent users from closing the browser window or browser tab if uncommitted data is present.

- **save-point-restore-finalizer**   Managed bean method reference invoked when the bounded task flow is restored from a save point. Developers use this element to initialize the task flow state.

- **no-save-point**   In addition to task flow save points that are created implicitly when the `critical` element is set to the task flow definition, an ADFm save point is set when entering a task flow. This allows the rollback of any data changes upon exiting the task flow. In contrast to the task flow save point, the ADFm save point does not restore `viewFlowScope` and `pageFlowScope` states.

- **use-page-fragment**   Task flows view activities either reference JSPX pages or page fragments with the .jsff filename extension. If the `use-page-fragment` element is set to `true`, all page fragments are used. Task flows that have their views built with page fragments are added to a parent page in an ADF region.

- **train**   Defines the bounded task flow as a train model and the contained view activities as train stops. Allows developers to add sequential and nonsequential navigation elements to the task flow pages.

- **visibility**   Determines if the bounded task flow can be directly accessed from a browser URL field and if it displays in ADF libraries for developers to add it to their application development. Adding a subelement of url-invoke-allowed or url-invoke-disallowed determines if the bounded task flow can be invoked directly from a browser or if it has to be called from another task flow. If none of the two subelements are set, which also is the default setting, then the ADF Controller allows direct task flow invocation if the default activity is a view activity. If using ADF Security to protect the bounded task flow, authorization is checked first. Adding the library-internal subelement hides the bounded task flow from displaying in ADF libraries.

NOTE
ADF libraries are explained in Chapter 15.

Creating a New Task Flow from the JDeveloper New Gallery

To create a new bounded task flow, choose File | New from the JDeveloper menu or press CTRL-N. In the New Gallery, select the Web Tier | JSF entry. From the available items in this category, as shown in Figure 5-4, choose the ADF Task Flow entry and click the OK button.

In the Create Task Flow dialog, provide values for the following input fields before clicking OK:

- **File Name**   The name of the task flow definition. When creating new task flows files, You should follow a naming convention, such as using an *adfc-* prefix, for unbounded task flow definition files.

- **Directory**   The directory in which the task flow definition file is stored. Task flow definition files must be located in the WEB-INF directory or in a subfolder.

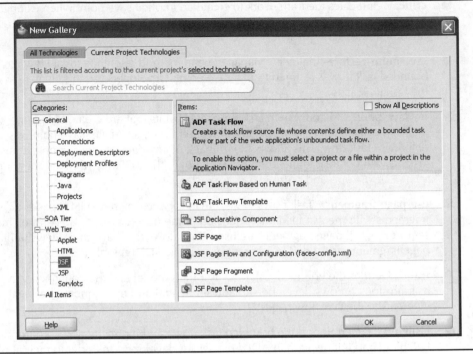

FIGURE 5-4 *New Gallery with JSF entries*

- **Create as Bounded Task Flow** Creates a bounded task flow definition as opposed to an unbounded task flow, which would be registered in the adfc-config.xml file upon creation. Since most of the task flows built by developers are bounded, this option is checked by default.

- **Task Flow ID** Identifies the task flow definition within the task flow definition file. ADF Controller is designed with regard to future extensions in which multiple task flow definitions can be hosted by a single metadata file. In preparation for this, the task flow ID is added to the definition.

- **Create with Page Fragments** Defines a task flow that executes within an ADF region on a Fusion web page. If this option is not checked, the view activities created within the flow use JSPX pages as a source file format. Note that it is possible at a later time to migrate this setting declaratively from the task flow visual diagrammer using a context menu.

- **Create Train** Creates a train model for the bounded task flow that can be used with the `af:train` UI component on the page to create a navigation bar. All view activities that are configured as a train stop are shown as navigable targets.

- **Based on Template File Name** Builds the new task flow definition file with existing entries from the referenced file.

■ **Update the Task Flow when the Template changes** Builds a new task flow definition file with existing entries from the referenced template. The template definition is contained in the file selected in the Based on Template File Name field. When this option is selected, a template-reference is added to the configuration metadata. Task flow template references and the referenced content are not displayed in the ADF Task Flow diagrammer.

In Oracle JDeveloper, the new bounded task flow definition file opens in the ADF Controller visual diagrammer for the Fusion developer to add task flow activities and control flow rules (Figure 5-5).

Extracting a New Task Flow from an Existing Task Flow

Another option in building new bounded task flows is to extract activities of existing task flows. For example, Figure 5-6 shows a bounded task flow that has a router and a view activity that represents an edit form. These two elements and the method activity to create a new record should be extracted into their own bounded task flow to be able to use ADF model save points to undo user edits.

To create a new bounded task flow, select the activities to extract (CTRL-click) in the ADF Controller visual editor and choose Extract Task Flow from the context menu. Then, in the dialog that appears, specify a name and the directory in which to store the task flow definition and click

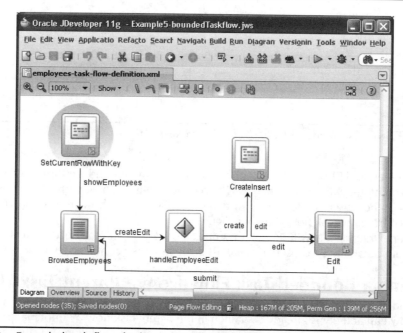

FIGURE 5-5 *Bounded task flow for browsing and editing employee data. This task flow is called from the unbounded task flow shown in Figure 5-1.*

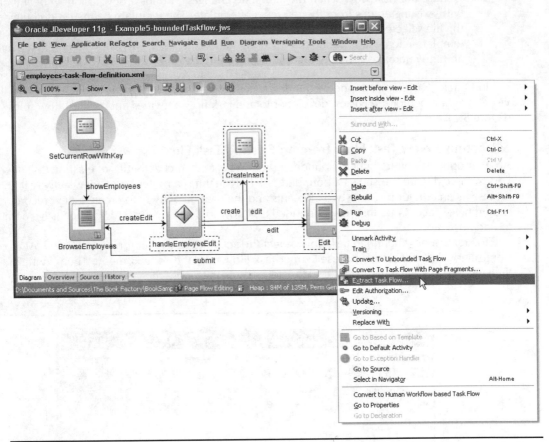

FIGURE 5-6   *Extract bounded task flow from existing flow*

OK. The new task flow is created with the selected activities and a return activity to exit the task flow to continue with the parent flow. The parent flow is updated with a task flow call activity that references the new bounded task flow definition. Figure 5-7 shows the bounded task flow that is extracted from the task flow shown in Figure 5-6.

After extracting a new task flow, the application developer may need to create input parameters and return parameters to ensure that the extracted task flow continues to work as before.

Calling a Bounded Task Flow from a Parent Task Flow

A bounded task flow is referenced by a parent task flow through the task flow call activity. If the task flow call activity is already contained in the parent task flow, but not mapped to a bounded task flow definition file, such as the showEmployees activity in Figure 5-1, then the reference to the sub–task flow definition can be created by drag-and-drop using the JDeveloper Application Navigator. Select the bounded task flow definition file in the Web Content | WEB-INF folder and drag-and-drop it onto the task flow call activity icon in the visual editor. This adds a task flow

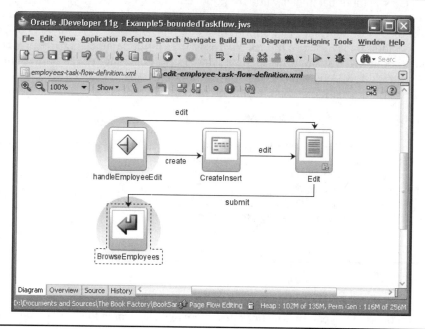

FIGURE 5-7   *Bounded task flow created from refactoring*

definition reference to the task flow call activity's `document` attribute. If the task flow has input and output parameters defined, these are also added to the task flow call activity.

If no task flow call activity exists in the parent task flow, one is automatically created when dragging the bounded task flow definition from the Application Navigator to the parent task flow in the visual diagrammer. If the called task flow has parameters defined, the parameter names are automatically added to the call activity.

Passing Values to and from Bounded Task Flows

The communication between a parent flow and a child flow occurs through input and return parameters that are defined on the task flow and referenced on the task flow call activity.

Input Parameters

Fusion web application developer access input parameters that are defined on a task flow call activity from the Property Inspector and use Expression Language to map the input parameter to a value in memory or exposed on a managed bean. The input parameter value is accessed and passed to the bounded task flow *by value* or *by reference*.

Passing values by reference passes the object itself. The associated risk of passing objects by reference is that an object may be changed in the bounded task flow and left in a mutated state when an ADF bounded task flow is abandoned. If you are concerned that this could become a problem in the application, another option is to pass the parameter by value.

To pass the input parameter value by value, check the Pass By Value option of the task flow call activity input parameter definition. If an object is passed by value, object serialization is used to make a copy of the value. This option must also be used if the input value is of a primitive type.

The default behavior in ADF Task Flow is to pass input parameters by reference. Best practice is to keep bounded task flows independent and to use input parameters only as an interface into the called task flow. Any result of the called task flow processing should be accessed from a task flow return parameter rather than relying on pass by reference.

```xml
<task-flow-call id="showEmployees">
    <task-flow-reference>
    <document>/WEB-INF/employees-task-flow-definition.xml</document>
    <id>employees-task-flow-definition</id>
  </task-flow-reference>
  <input-parameter>
    <name>departmentsRowKey</name>
    <value>#{requestScope.rowKeyStr}</value>
    <pass-by-value/>
  </input-parameter>
</task-flow-call>
```

Return Values

A bounded task flow return value is copied from the bounded task flow to a memory attribute or a managed bean of the parent flow upon task flow exit. Assuming that the edit-employee-task-flow shown in Figure 5-7 returns the row key of the last edited employee to the parent flow, the return value parameter defined for the task flow should look as shown in Figure 5-8.

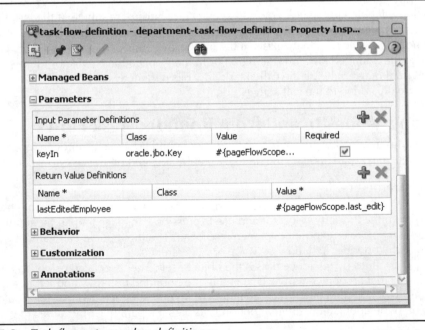

FIGURE 5-8 *Task flow return value definitions*

Following are the attribute settings:

- **Name** The name of the return value is exposed on the task flow call activity of the parent task flow.

- **Value** The returned value is read from a memory attribute or a managed bean, or is provided as a fixed string.

- **Class** Optional attribute that converts string values into object references. If the value is an Expression Language expression, it gets evaluated and the Class attribute is ignored. If the value is a String constant, it will be converted to the class specified by the Class attribute, if such type coercion is possible. For example, a value of true may be converted to the Boolean object with a value of true. The Class attribute also supports enumeration to determine the converted object.

The task flow call activity definition that received the return value from the called task flow and that writes the returned value to an object in its own memory scope looks similar to this:

```
<task-flow-call id="edit-employee-task-flow-definition">
  […]
  <return-value>
    <name>lastEditedEmployee</name>
    <value>#{pageFlowScope.last_edited_employee}</value>
  </return-value>
</task-flow-call>
```

In this example, the returned value is copied to the last_edited_employee pageFlowScope attribute of the parent task flow, where it is accessible from Expression Language.

Exception Handling

In Java Enterprise Edition (EE) application development, the web.xml file is used declaratively to configure how specific HTTP error codes or Java exceptions should be handled so as not to expose the application users to pages full of stack traces. ADF Controller uses a similar approach for handling exceptions in bounded and unbounded task flows. Application developers can declaratively specify any allowed activity, such as view, method, and router, as the exception handler for the task flow in which it is located, which is recommended. To mark an activity as the exception handler, you add the exception-handler metadata as a child element to the adfc-config element in the task flow definition, which you can do declaratively by selecting an activity and clicking the exclamation mark in the toolbar of the task flow diagrammer, as shown in Figure 5-9.

If an exception handler is configured, ADF task flow navigates to the activity ID that is specified as the value of exception-handler to take care of the problem. The ADF Controller handles exception by "navigating" to the configured handler activity, which excludes exceptions thrown during the JSF RENDER RESPONSE phase from being handled by the ADF Controller.

In Figure 5-9, a router activity is configured as the exception handler of a task flow definition, which could be unbounded or bounded. A red exclamation mark overlay icon in the visual editor indicates the configured exception handler. Selecting another activity and clicking the same icon in the toolbar of the visual editor changes the configuration.

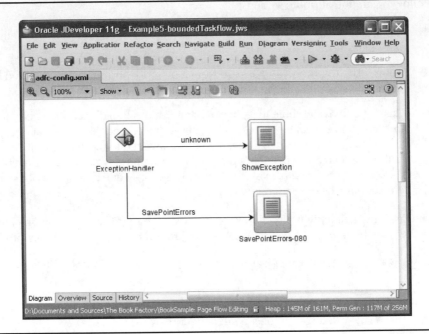

FIGURE 5-9 *Declarative Exception handling in task flow definition*

The router activity in the example uses a Java method reference to determine the type of error and how to handle it:

```
<router id="ExceptionHandler">
  <case>
    <expression>
      #{ExceptionHandlerBean.savePointException==true}
    </expression>
    <outcome>SavePointErrors</outcome>
  </case>
  <case>
  <default-outcome>unknown</default-outcome>
</router>
```

The managed bean methods that are referenced by the router access the exception object to read its message:

```
public boolean isSavePointException() {
  return errorKeyIn("ADFC-080");
}
private boolean errorKeyIn(String errorCode) {
  ControllerContext cctx = ControllerContext.getInstance();
  Exception exception = cctx.getCurrentViewPort().getExceptionData();
  String message = null;
  if (exception != null){
```

```
      message = exception.getMessage();
    }
    if (message != null && message.toUpperCase().indexOf(errorCode)>-1){
      return true;
    }
    else{
      return false;
    }
}
```

To display an exception in a page view, Expression Language can be used to access the current `ViewPort` object that is exposed on the `ControllerContext`:

```
<af:inputText id="exceptionClass" readOnly="true" columns="100"
    value="#{controllerContext.currentViewPort.exceptionData.class.name}"/>
<af:inputText id="message" readOnly="true" rows="2" columns="100"
    value="#{controllerContext.currentViewPort.exceptionData.message}"/>
```

To display the stack trace in a view, the following method in a managed bean can be used and referenced from a page:

```
public String getStackTrace(){
    ControllerContext ccontext = ControllerContext.getInstance();
    ViewPortContext viewPortCtx = ccontext.getCurrentViewPort();
    if (viewPortCtx.getExceptionData()!=null ) {
      StringWriter stringWriter = new StringWriter();
      PrintWriter printWriter = new PrintWriter(stringWriter);
      viewPortCtx.getExceptionData().printStackTrace(printWriter);
      return stringWriter.toString();
    }
    return "";
}
```

This can then be referenced from a page, as shown next:

```
<af:inputText id="exception" readOnly="true" rows="10" columns="100"
    value="#{ExceptionHandlerBean.stackTrace}"/>
```

The printed result displays as shown in Figure 5-10.

□ Unhandled Application Error	
Exception Type	javax.faces.application.ViewExpiredException
Message	viewId:/BrowseDepartments - ADF_FACES-30108:The view state of the page has expired because of inactivity. Reload the page.

Exception Trace	javax.faces.application.ViewExpiredException: viewId:/BrowseDepartments - ADF_FACES-30108:The view state of the page has expired because of inactivity. Reload the page.
	    at oracle.adfinternal.view.faces.lifecycle.LifecycleImpl._restoreView(LifecycleImpl.java:548)
	    at oracle.adfinternal.view.faces.lifecycle.LifecycleImpl._executePhase(LifecycleImpl.java:268)
	    at oracle.adfinternal.view.faces.lifecycle.LifecycleImpl.execute(LifecycleImpl.java:165)
	    at javax.faces.webapp.FacesServlet.service(FacesServlet.java:265)
	    at weblogic.servlet.internal.StubSecurityHelper$ServletServiceAction.run(StubSecurityHelper.java:227)
	    at weblogic.servlet.internal.StubSecurityHelper.invokeServlet(StubSecurityHelper.java:125)
	    at weblogic.servlet.internal.ServletStubImpl.execute(ServletStubImpl.java:292)
	    at weblogic.servlet.internal.TailFilter.doFilter(TailFilter.java:26)

FIGURE 5-10   *Displaying the exception in read-only form*

NOTE
The content of a stack trace is not for everyone's eyes, and sometimes it's not for the faint of heart either. For security reasons, stack traces should not be shown by default, or should be viewable only by authorized users. A security design pattern behind this suggestion is "limited view," which defines that users should see only what they are allowed to see. Since stack traces can contain system-related information that may make sense for an intruder to explore, you should treat this information as sensitive.

Creating and Registering a Custom Exception Handler Class

The ADF Controller exception handler class `AdfcExceptionHandler` extends `oracle.adf.view.rich.context.ExceptionHandler` to handle exceptions that are thrown during the ADF Faces lifecycle. For use cases that require a custom exception handler, developers extend the `ExceptionHandler` in their own class and register it in a text file named oracle.adf.view.rich.context.ExceptionHandler. This file doesn't exist by default and must be created manually in the .adf\META-DATA\services directory of the application workspace. The custom exception handler is registered with its full package and class name, excluding the .class file extension.

The handler code shown next listens for the "ADF_FACES-30108" error message that is thrown when the session has expired. Instead of showing the default message in case of an expired session, the user is redirected to a page that allows him or her to continue working within the application.

```
package adf.interactiv.exceptions;
import javax.faces.context.ExternalContext;
import javax.faces.context.FacesContext;
import javax.faces.event.PhaseId;
import oracle.adfinternal.controller.application.AdfcExceptionHandler;

public class CustomExceptionHandler extends AdfcExceptionHandler {
  public CustExceptionHandler() {
    super();
  }
  public void handleException(FacesContext facesContext,
                             Throwable throwable,
                             PhaseId phaseId) {
    String error_message = throwable.getMessage();
    if (error_message != null &&
       error_message.indexOf("ADF_FACES-30108")>-1) {
      ExternalContext ectx = facesContext.getExternalContext();
      ectx.redirect("faces/SessionExpired.jspx");
    }
    else{
      super.handleException(facesContext, throwable, phaseId);
    }
  }
}
```

NOTE
Although you can register a custom exception handler, this option should be a last resort. Best practice is to handle the exception using an exception handler declaratively configured in the task flow definition. In this example, the session expiry is detected by a string comparison to "ADF_FACES-30108", which can also be done in a managed bean method that is referenced by a router activity, marked as the exception handler. The class that exposes the session expiry message is `javax.faces.application.ViewExpiredException`.

ADF Controller Exception Handling vs. ADF Model Exception Handling

In Chapter 3 we introduce the Fusion application lifecycle and explained how developers can configure a custom exception handler on the DataBindings.cpx file to override the default exception handling functionality of the ADF model layer. In this chapter, we explain the concept of the ADF Controller exception handling and how to customize it. You may wonder what the difference between the two approaches is and which one is best to use. Within the Fusion development architecture are multiple layers in which exceptions can occur and in which they can be handled. Exceptions can occur and are handled in the following order:

1. Business Components service layer
2. ADF model
3. ADF Controller

If an exception is not handled in the layer in which it occurs, it continues to the next layer until, eventually, if none of the layers knows how to handle the exception, it is passed to the Java EE container.

Exceptions that occur on the Business Components service layer, as well as exceptions that are raised in the ADF model layer itself, are first reported to the configured ADF model exception handler. For example, the "JBO-26061: Error while opening JDBC connection" error is first handled by the ADF model layer exception handler before it is passed on to the ADF Controller exception handler. The ADF model exception handler is a good choice to suppress exceptions that don't need to be displayed to the user.

In ADF, exceptions that are raised in the business components and the ADF binding layer are reported to the ADF Controller declarative exception handler if not handled. In addition, the ADF controller declarative exception handling handles all exceptions that are raised within the ADF Controller and ADF Faces view layer itself. On the other hand, exceptions that occur on the ADF Faces layer or the ADF controller layer cannot be handled using exception handlers defined on the ADF binding layer, using the DataBindings.cpx file. For a better picture: exceptions always bubble up and never down.

NOTE
The ADF Controller exception handler handles all exceptions, except those that occur during the Render Response phase, which occurs too late for the controller to handle gracefully.

ADF Internals: DataControlFrame

The ADF model layer provides a scoping mechanism for data controls called a data control frame. The `DataControlFrame` interface is a mechanism that exposes a data control instance to an ADF task flow so that the task flow can interact with the ADF model layer. Bounded task flows can use the `DataControlFrame` to work within their own isolated data control instance or to share an existing instance with a caller flow. At any time, only a single active data control frame exists for the task flow. Expression Language expressions that reference the ADF binding layer always access the data control instance exposed by the current data control frame.

The ability to share a data control frame is restricted to task flows that call each other from within a browser window or an ADF region. A task flow that executes within a region can share the data control frame with its parent page.

Application developers use the `data-control-scope` element in the bounded task flow definition to specify whether the task flow should share the data control frame with a parent flow. In the Property Inspector view for the bounded task flow definition, the configuration is exposed as "Share data controls with calling task flow" in the Behavior | Transaction section.

Declarative Transaction Handling

The ADF Controller allows declarative configuration for how transactions are handled in bounded task flows. For this, all metadata explained below is created and configured through properties in the JDeveloper Property Inspector. All bounded task flows are exited through return activity elements, unless they are cancelled by back button use or a URL redirect. The return activity element defines how the bounded task flow transaction is handled. The options are to commit changes, roll back changes, or restore the transaction state back to an implicit save point created when the task flow is entered. Which option is required and which approach is used are determined by the `transaction` metadata element configuration in the bounded task flow configuration, which can be created using the Behavior category in the Property Inspector view for the selected bounded task flow. The metadata elements and their meaning are shown in the following table.

Configuration	Description
New Transaction	Defined by the *new-transaction* metadata element in the task flow configuration: ``` <transaction> <new-transaction/> </transaction> ``` The bounded task flow creates a new transaction that needs to be committed or rolled back when exiting the bounded task flow. Uncommitted data changes of the parent task flow are not visible in the called bounded task flow. The return activity used to exit the bounded task flow must be configured to commit or roll back the transaction.

Configuration	Description

Requires Existing Transaction	Defined by the `requires-existing-transaction` metadata element in the task flow configuration:
	`<transaction>`
	`  <requires-existing-transaction/>`
	`</transaction>`
	The bounded task flow expects an existing transaction to be present. The task flow must not commit or roll back the transaction when returning to the calling flow. Entering the bounded task flow creates an implicit save point that is used to restore the transaction when the return activity that leaves the task flow has the `restore-save-point` element set. Uncommitted data changes of the parent task flow are visible in the called bounded task flow.

Requires Transaction	Defined by the `requires-transaction` metadata element in the task flow configuration:
	`<transaction>`
	`  <requires-transaction/>`
	`</transaction>`
	The bounded task flow either uses an existing transaction or creates a new transaction if no transaction exists. The return activity used to exit the bounded task flow must be configured to commit or roll back the transaction. The commit and rollback operations are ignored if the transaction of the calling flow is used. Uncommitted data changes in the parent flow are visible in the called task flow because the existing transaction is used.

None	The default setting is configured by the absence of the `transaction` metadata configuration element in the task flow definition. None means that no transaction is open in the current data control frame, which also implies that no implicit save points are set to undo data changes applied in the bounded task flow and no commit or rollback operations are allowed on the return activity. Data changes of the parent flow are not visible in the called task flow until they are committed.

Browser Back Button Handling

The browser back button has two behaviors: one is for back navigation within the stacked navigation path of a nested task flow, and the other is for task flows that are reentered through the use of the back button. Using the browser back button does not raise an event on the server for a framework to respond to the user requesting a previous page. Instead, the reentered application page may be served from the browser cache. Frameworks are expected to be smart and to detect that the user browsed back to a page in time for the application developer to "do the right thing."

Navigating Back Within a Stack of Bounded Task Flows

If a user navigates from an unbounded task flow to a bounded task flow and from there to another bounded task flow, a stack of two bounded task flows exists. If the browser back button is then used to navigate back to a view of the previous bounded or unbounded task flow, then during the next user action in that view, the framework detects the abandoned bounded task flows, rolls back the transactions, and removes them from the stack. In this case, the user proceeds as if he/she never entered the bounded task flows.

Reentering a Bounded Task Flow

A bounded task flow is reentered when the use of the browser back button navigates to a view that is contained in a bounded task flow the user exited before using a return element. To respond correctly to browser back navigation in ADF bounded task flows, the application developer configures the bounded task flow and the return activity for whether reentry is allowed or not. The ADF Controller throws an `InvalidTaskFlowReentryException` exception if reentry is detected on a task flow that does not allow this. It is then the responsibility of the application developer to handle the thrown exception gracefully. The associated ADF Controller error code in the message of an invalid task flow reentry is "ADFC-06016". Since the exception instance is available from the `ControllerContext`, the invalid reentry can be detected as follows:

```
import oracle.adf.controller.InvalidTaskFlowReentryException;
...
   public boolean isInvalidtaskFlowReentry(){
      ControllerContext cctx = ControllerContext.getInstance();
      Exception exception = cctx.getCurrentViewPort().getExceptionData();
      if (exception instanceof InvalidTaskFlowReentryException){
        return true;
      } else{
        return false;
      }
   }
}
```

Configuring the Reentry Behavior of a Bounded Task Flow

The bounded task flow uses the `task-flow-reentry` element in its task flow definition to determine the kind of reentry behavior to enforce. The allowed values are `reentry-allowed`, `reentry-not-allowed`, and `reentry-outcome-dependent`. The default behavior is that reentry is allowed, which is indicated by the absence of the `task-flow-reentry` element. The following table lists the allowed metadata elements to configure the reentry behavior and their meaning.

Value	Description
`reentry-allowed`	Upon task flow reentry, the task flow is initialized as if it is entered the first time. The input parameters, if any, are populated from the current application state. If the bounded task flow requires a new transaction, this transaction is created if it doesn't exist. `<task-flow-reentry>` `<reentry-allowed/>` `</task-flow-reentry>`

Value	Description

`reentry-not-allowed`	The bounded task flow throws an exception for the user to handle. If the exception is handled, the task flow proceeds as normal. Any submitted data of the reentered page submit is ignored.
	`<task-flow-reentry>`
	`  <reentry-not-allowed/>`
	`</task-flow-reentry>`

`reentry-outcome-dependent`	A mix of the two preceding options, in that the return activity that is used to exit a bounded task flow determines its reentry behavior. Leaving a bounded task flow from a `cancel` return activity may allow reentry, but leaving a bounded task flow from a `commit` return activity may not.
	`<task-flow-reentry>`
	`  <reentry-outcome-dependent/>`
	`</task-flow-reentry>`

To configure reentrance behavior for a bounded task flow, select the task flow in the Oracle JDeveloper structure window with the task flow definition file, the XML source file, selected in the Application Navigator. Open the Property Inspector and navigate to the Behavior category. Here, a list box is provided where you can choose among the different reentry behaviors.

If the reentry behavior is configured as outcome-dependent, then either the `reentry-allowed` or `reentry-not-allowed` configuration elements must be set on each return activity.

```
<task-flow-return id="BrowseEmployees">
  <outcome>
    <name>submit</name>
    <reentry-not-allowed/>
    <commit/>
  </outcome>
</task-flow-return>
<task-flow-return id="cancelAndBrowseEmployees">
  <outcome>
    <name>cancel</name>
    <reentry-allowed/>
    <rollback/>
  </outcome>
</task-flow-return>
```

To set the reentry value on the return activity, select the return activity in the visual task flow diagram and open the Property Inspector. Navigate to the Behavior category and select the value. The default value of the return activity element is to be outcome-interdependent, which is why a visual warning is shown in the diagram for return activities that are in a task flow that is configured as `reentry-outcome-dependent`.

NOTE
If the reentry is configured to be outcome dependent, you need to make sure that the value of the name *child element of the* outcome *element in the return activity configuration is not the same; otherwise, the ADF Controller cannot detect the correct reentry policy.*

Open a Bounded Task Flow in a Dialog

Opening bounded task flows in pop-up dialogs is a frequent requirement in Fusion application development. Two implementation choices exist in ADF for this use case:

- *Open a bounded task flow in an external browser window.* A task flow call activity is used in a parent task flow to navigate to the bounded task flow that should be launched in a dialog. The call activity is configured to open the task flow in a separate browser window using the ADF dialog framework. You use this option if the bounded task flow uses JSPX pages and cannot be changed to run in lightweight dialogs.

- *Open a bounded task flow in a lightweight dialog.* ADF Faces Rich Client (RC) provides lightweight dialogs that appear on top of the current page. Developers use ADF regions to add a bounded task flow to display in a lightweight dialog. You use this option to avoid pop-up blockers to suppress the dialog to open and to create modal dialogs that work across browsers. Opening task flows in lightweight dialogs is more commonly used in Fusion applications and is explained in Chapter 6.

Open the Bounded Task Flow in an External Browser Window

Bounded task flows can be configured to launch in a modal browser dialog by adding the `run-as-dialog` element to the task flow call activity metadata. To add the metadata element, open the Property Inspector for the task flow call activity and set the Run As Dialog option to true, as shown in Figure 5-11.

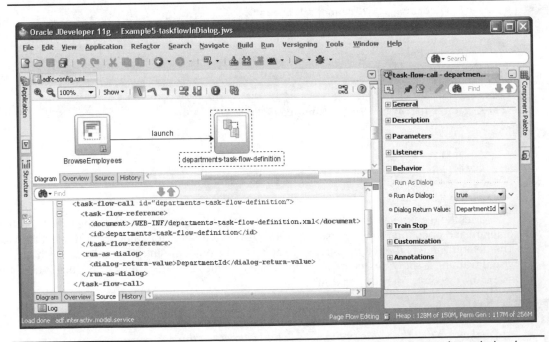

FIGURE 5-11   *Task flow diagram and source view for call activity that opens a bounded task flow in a dialog*

Split Screen: Multiple Views of a Single File Content

A handy functionality in Oracle JDeveloper is the option to split the screen of a source view. In Figure 5-11, the unbounded task flow definition, adfc-config.xml, is shown in the visual diagrammer view and the source view. To create a split screen, use the mouse to select the split handle, the horizontal line icon that in Figure 5-11 is framed by the help icon and the upward pointing error icon, and drag it halfway to the bottom. To close the split screen, double-click the middle line between the two screens.

In the example shown in Figure 5-12, BrowseEmployees.jspx contains an input form to edit the employee records from the underlying Employees database table. To create the input form, select the EmployeesView collection in the Data Controls palette and drag-and-drop it as a form onto the JSPX page. Navigating from the BrowseEmployees page to the task flow call activity launches the dialog, which is initiated from a LOV `af:commandButton` that is created for the `InputText` component that displays the `DepartmentId` attribute.

As shown in Figure 5-12, to lay out the LOV button, the `af:inputText` component and the `af:commandButton` component are configured as a child of the `af:panelLabelAndMessage` component.

The LOV command button is defined as follows:

```
<af:commandButton text="LOV" id="cb5" action="launch"
windowHeight="300" windowWidth="300"
returnListener="#{BrowseEmployeeBean.onDialogReturn}"
useWindow="true"/>
```

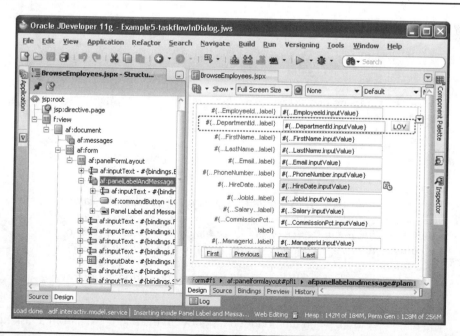

FIGURE 5-12 *Input form with LOV button to launch the dialog*

The `action` attribute has a value of `launch`, which is the name of the control flow between the browse page and the task flow call activity defined in Figure 5-11. The `windowHeight` and `windowWidth` attributes specify the size of the opened dialog, while the `useWindow` attribute ensures that the dialog will be opened in an external dialog. Optionally, the `af:commandButton` may have a `returnListener` and `launchListener` attributes specified. The `launchListener` is not needed in this example because all data that needs to be passed from the calling page to the bounded task flow in the dialog can be passed as input parameters of the bounded task flow. In the example, the `returnListener` attribute is set to receive the selected return value from the dialog. The return value `DepartmentId` is defined on the bounded task flow as the return value definition:

```
<task-flow-definition id="departments-task-flow-definition">
    <default-activity>BrowseDepartments</default-activity>
    <return-value-definition>
      <name>DepartmentId</name>
      <value>#{pageFlowScope.returnValue}</value>
      <class>oracle.jbo.domain.Number</class>
    </return-value-definition>
    [...]
</task-flow-definition>
```

You can use the Property Inspector in Oracle JDeveloper to create the return value definition.

The dialog return value is read from the `returnValue` attribute in the `pageFlowScope` of the task flow opened in the dialog. The `pageFlowScope` attribute is created by the application when the user selects a value from the list of values in the dialog.

```
<af:form>
    <af:table ...>
      ...
    </af:table>
    <af:commandButton text="Select Department" id="cb1"
                      action="return">
    <af:setPropertyListener
      from="#{bindings.DepartmentId.inputValue}"
      to="#{pageFlowScope.returnValue}"
      type="action"/>
    </af:commandButton>
</af:form>
```

NOTE
The code sample above uses a little trick to simplify reading the value of a specific column for the selected table row. The trick is to create an attribute binding in the PageDef file for the attribute that represents the column in the ADF iterator binding. The attribute binding, DepartmentId in the code example above, is synchronized with the table selection and allows the use of EL to access the current table row column value.

The dialog is closed when the bounded task flow in the dialog exits from a task flow return activity:

```
<task-flow-return id="exit">
   <outcome>
     <name>return</name>
   </outcome>
</task-flow-return>
```

An `org.apache.myfaces.trinidad.event.ReturnEvent` is propagated to the component that launched the dialog for a configured return listener to handle the payload. The configured return listener in this example is contained in a managed bean and exposed as a method:

```
public void onDialogReturn(ReturnEvent returnEvent) {
   BindingContext bindingContext = BindingContext.getCurrent();
   BindingContainer bindings = bindingContext.getCurrentBindingsEntry();
   ControlBinding control = bindings.getControlBinding("DepartmentId");
   AttributeBinding deptId = (AttributeBinding) control;
   deptId.setInputValue(returnEvent.getReturnValue());
}
```

The `returnEvent` instance contains the value of the bounded task flow return value, `DepartmentId`. The listener access the ADF binding layer to set the value on the underlying `AttributeBinding` of the `DepartmentId` attribute. Setting the input value on the `AttributeBinding` automatically refreshes the input form if the `changePolicy` property on the iterator binding is set to `ppr`.

How to Build a Task Flow URL in Java

Bounded task flows that reference JSPX page views and therefore are able to run stand-alone can be called from a URL. One example for this is when calling a bounded task flow that is deployed on a remote or local machine from a task flow call activity. The task flow call activity metadata schema has a `remote-app-url` child element that is used to configure a remote bounded task flow call. To reference the bounded task flow, developers need to know about the URL to invoke, which is in this form:

```
<host:port>/<javaEE_context>/faces/adf.task-flow?adf.tfid=<task flow definition
ID>&adf.tfDoc=<task flow definition file name>&<parameter>=<parameter value>
```

The table below describes the URL parameters and their meaning.

URL Content	Description
host:port	The remote host name or IP address and the port to which the server listens. The port information is not required for the default ports 80 and 443.
javaEE_context	The Java EE context root information of the deployed Java EE application that contains the remote task flow to call.
faces	Unless configured otherwise, faces is the default servlet mapping to access JSF applications.
adf.task-flow	A registered task flow URL mapping that indicates the URL to reference a bounded task flow.

URL Content	Description
adf.tfid	The task flow ID in the bounded task flow definition. By default the ID is the same as the task flow definition file, just without the .xml extension. However, the ID may be changed by the application developer and therefore needs to be specified.
adf.tfDoc	The name of the task flow definition file that contains the task flow ID to launch from the remote server. The filename always starts with *WEB-INF/* and contains any subfolder names used to store task flow definition files.
parameter	A list of "parameter name = value" pairs concatenated by an & that map to the defined input parameters of the task flow.

The remote URL is automatically composed when the task flow call activity element is used. To configure a task flow call activity to launch a remote bounded task flow, use the remote-app-url child element as follows:

```
<task-flow-call id="taskFlowCall1">
  <task-flow-reference>
    <document>/WEB-INF/the-task-flow-definition.xml</document>
    <id>the-task-flow-definition</id>
  </task-flow-reference>
  <remote-app-url>
    http://<remote_host>:<port>/foo_app/faces/adf.task-flow
  </remote-app-url>
</task-flow-call>
```

Replace the <remote_host> and <port> placeholders with the name of the remote server and its port. The remote-app-url can use Expression Language references, for example to a managed bean, for applications to retrieve the remote host access dynamically. The generated call URL contains the _task-flow-return parameter that contains the information required by the called bounded task flow to return to the calling task flow on exit.

Applications that need to redirect to a bounded task flow that is contained within the same application using Java can use the getTaskFlowURL method of the ControllerContext class to compose the request URL:

```
public String getRelativeTaskFlowUrl() {
    String relTaskFlowUrl = null;
    HashMap params = new HashMap();
    //rowkey from binding layer as a request parameter
    params.put("rowKey", "000100000002C133000000050000011E350FC02F");
    ControllerContext cctx = ControllerContext.getInstance();
    TaskFlowId taskFlow = new TaskFlowId(
        "WEB-INF/departments-task-flow-definition.xml",
        "departments-task-flow-definition");
    relTaskFlowUrl = cctx.getTaskFlowURL(false, taskFlow, params);
    return relTaskFlowUrl;
}
```

The returned URL is defined relative to the host and port of the server that runs the application and starts with the Java EE context path. The false argument in the call to getTaskFlowURL specifies no state information of the current view port to be added to the URL. Note that the generated URL does not contain any task flow return information, which is the case when using the task flow call activity.

How to Navigate Programmatically Among View Activities

Navigation among view activities is defined through navigation cases in standard JSF navigation and control flow cases in ADF task flows. Dependent on the outcome of an action command, the navigation is performed following the path identified by the returned action string.

For some use cases, however, developers may need to initiate navigation from a Java method that is not a command action. In these cases, you set the new view Id on the current view port as shown below

```
ControllerContext ccontext = ControllerContext.getInstance();
//define the viewId of the view in the bounded task flow
//to navigate to next
String viewId = "EditEmployees";
ccontext.getCurrentViewPort().setViewId(viewId);
```

The view activity specified by the `viewId` method argument must exist in the bounded task flow and otherwise an exception is thrown. The `viewId` method cannot be used to set a non-visual activity like router or method.

NOTE
The code example above uses an API that is available in JDeveloper 11g since version 11.1.1.2 (JDeveloper 11g R1 Patch set 1).

How to Navigate to a Specific View When Entering a Bounded Task Flow

Bounded task flows have a defined entry point, the default activity that is accessed first when requesting the task flow. A common requirement is to navigate to a specific page within a bounded task flow when entering the task flow. This requirement can be accomplished by using a router activity as the default activity and a task flow input parameter to receive information about the page to route to.

How to Determine Whether a Task Flow Contains Uncommitted Data

Though the return activity of a bounded task flow that is configured to require a new or existing transaction can commit or rollback data changes, developers need to have the user confirm that the selected option really is what he or she wants to do. The `isDataDirty` method is exposed on the `ViewPortContext` and can be accessed through the ADF Controller `ControllerContext` class in Java and Expression Language. The returned value is `true` if the current view port or one of its child view ports contains changed model data and `false` otherwise. For example, a router activity may be used within a bounded task flow to direct the request from an edit form to a confirmation page if the user clicks the cancel button to roll back the edits and uncommitted model data is detected.

```
<router id="DetectChanges">
  <case>
    <expression>
      #{controllerContext.currentViewPort.dataDirty == true}
```

```
      </expression>
      <outcome>showConfirmationPage</outcome>
    </case>
    <case>
      <expression>
        #{controllerContext.currentViewPort.dataDirty != true}
      </expression>
      <outcome>cancel</outcome>
    </case>
      <default-outcome>cancel</default-outcome>
  </router>
```

Working with ADF Controller and Model Save Points

Two types of save points exist in Oracle ADF for application developers to restore a previous state of their application and data: ADF model save points and ADF Controller save points.

An ADF model save point is implicitly set on bounded task flows if they share the data control scope with the calling task flow and have the save point functionality enabled, which it is by default. ADF model save points can also be set programmatically and save the transaction state, not the application state, to undo user data changes when exiting a bounded task flow or when the user clicks a cancel button. A good use case for ADF model save points is to undo user form edits. Model save points are valid until a commit or rollback operation completes the transaction.

The ADF Controller save point does more than the ADF model save point, and in addition to the transaction state saves the view state and the ADF memory scope state. ADF Controller save points are persisted as binary objects to the database where they are identified by a save point ID. Using an ADF Controller save point, applications can almost fully recover to a previous state, assuming that the save point in the database has not been deleted, that the save point is valid, and that other required state information was held in one of the ADF Controller memory scopes and not one of the standard memory scopes. A general use case for the ADF Controller save point feature is session expiry handling and "save for later" in which the save point ID for an open task is temporarily saved away for the user to complete later. Restoring the save point is a responsibility of an application developer and must be built in to the application.

ADF Controller Save Points

Developers set save points in unbounded and bounded task flows to store a temporary snapshot of the current user interface state, managed bean state, task flow state, and model state. Explicit save points can be set in Java or declaratively using Expression Language. To undo any work performed by the user after the save point has been created, a save point restore activity is used or the restore URL is directly accessed from a redirect call in Java. This section introduces options to create and restore explicit save points.

NOTE
Explicit save points work the same for unbounded and bounded task flows. However, explicit save points are the only save point option available in unbounded task flows. Bounded task flows can set implicit save points, for example when the session expires, if the task flow is marked as critical.

Declarative Save Point Creation Using a Method Call Activity

A method call activity can be used to reference methods exposed on an Expression Language–accessible object and to handle possible return values. The method call activity creates a new save point and writes the save point ID into the `pageFlowScope`:

```
<method-call id="declarativeSavePoint">
  <method>
    #{controllerContext.savePointManager.createSavePoint}
  </method>
  <return-value>
    #{pageFlowScope.this_save_point}
  </return-value>
  <outcome>
    <fixed-outcome>editCreate</fixed-outcome>
  </outcome>
</method-call>
```

NOTE
A save point that is repeatedly created during a user session for the same browser window does not create an additional save point entry in the database but replaces the current save point entry. As explained in Chapter 4, save points are usually removed when the top-level task flow exits. However, in the case of save points created in unbounded task flows, application developers should implement a strategy to clean up save points that are no longer needed.

Save Point Creation in Java from a Method Call Activity

When some preprocessing or post-processing is required when creating a save point, a managed bean method that is referenced from a method call activity could be used:

```
import oracle.adf.controller.ControllerContext;
import oracle.adf.controller.savepoint.SavePointManager;
...
public String setSavePoint(){
  //add pre-processing code
  ControllerContext cctx = ControllerContext.getInstance();
  SavePointManager savePointManager = cctx.getSavePointManager();
  String savePointId = savePointManager.createSavePoint();
  //add post-processing code
  return savePointId;
}
```

Building Reusable Task Flow Element Configurations

Some task flow element configurations, such as a method activity that sets a save point, may be required more often within a task flow, and you may wish that a copy brush existed to copy the configuration from one element to the other. While there is no copy brush in Oracle JDeveloper to perform this task, you can create code templates for the reoccurring configurations. To create a code template for a method call activity that sets an explicit save-point you would do the following:

1. Copy the code template source from the task flow code view into the clipboard.

2. Select Tools | Preferences | Code Editor | Code Templates.

3. Click the Add button.

4. Define a shortcut string such as `svp_mca` for save point method call activity and a short description.

5. Copy the template code and add editable variables in the form *$variable$* where data needs to be provided when using this code snippet:

```
<method-call id="$id$">
   <method>
      #{controllerContext.savePointManager.createSavePoint}
   </method>
   <return-value>
     #{pageFlowScope.this_save_point}
   </return-value>
   <outcome>
     <fixed-outcome>$outcome$</fixed-outcome>
   </outcome>
</method-call>
```

6. Open the code editor for the task flow to add the code snippet and, in this example, **type svp_mca** followed by pressing CTRL and then ENTER.

7. Provide values for the variables such as `id` and `outcome` used in the example above. Use the TAB key to forward navigate from one variable to the next and SHIFT-TAB for backward navigation.

This method call activity in the bounded or unbounded task flow looks the same as before but references the managed bean method:

```
<method-call id="managedBeanSavepoint">
   <method>
      #{DepartmentsManagedBean.setSavePoint}
   </method>
   <return-value>
      #{pageFlowScope.this_save_point}
   </return-value>
   <outcome>
      <fixed-outcome>editCreate</fixed-outcome>
   </outcome>
</method-call>
```

Java-Based Save Point Creation from an Action Method

Though the save point is easier to read if it's set in a method call activity, developers may prefer to set the save point directly from a command item. To set a save point when a command button or link is clicked, you use the component `ActionListener` property to reference a managed bean method that sets the save point and writes its ID into an attribute in memory:

```
<af:commandButton text="Create" id="cb2"
  action="editCreate"
  actionListener="#{DepartmentsManagedBean.onCreate}">
</af:commandButton>
```

The managed bean method that is referenced by the `actionListener` attribute of the command button is executed before the navigation is performed. The listener code accesses the `SavePointManager` instance to create a new save point. To store the obtained save point ID in the `pageFlowScope`, the managed bean method uses the `AdfFacesContext` object of the `oracle.adf.view.rich.context` package:

```
import javax.faces.event.ActionEvent;
import oracle.adf.controller.ControllerContext;
import oracle.adf.controller.savepoint.SavePointManager;
import oracle.adf.view.rich.context.AdfFacesContext;
...
public void onCreate(ActionEvent actionEvent) {
  ControllerContext cctx - ControllerContext.getInstance();
  SavePointManager savePointManager = cctx.getSavePointManager();
  String savePointId = savePointManager.createSavePoint();
  AdfFacesContext adfFacesContext = AdfFacesContext.getCurrentInstance();
  adfFacesContext.getPageFlowScope().put("this_save_point",savePointId);
}
```

Restoring a Save Point from a Save Point Restore Activity

Restoring a save point recovers the application state back to a specific state in time. One strategy for restoring to a save point within an unbounded task flow is to use the save point restore activity, as shown in Figure 5-1. The `restoreState` activity in this example is called from the edit form on cancel and the `BrowseDepartmentsview` activity when a button is clicked. The configuration of the save point restore activity in the adfc-config.xml is shown here:

```
<save-point-restore id="restoreState">
  <save-point-id>#{pageFlowScope.this_save_point}</save-point-id>
</save-point-restore>
```

The `save-point-id` element points to the `pageFlowScope` attribute that we use in the example to hold the most recent stored point ID. Referencing an invalid save point ID leads to an `ActivityLogicException`.

Restoring a Save Point from Java

A save point cannot be fully restored in Java itself. Instead, you determine the restore URL from the `ControllerContext` to then redirect the request. If called from an action method, the managed bean code looks like this:

```
import java.io.IOException;
import javax.faces.context.FacesContext;
import oracle.adf.controller.ControllerContext;
```

```
import oracle.adf.view.rich.context.AdfFacesContext;
...
public String restoreSavePoint(){
  String restoreURL = null;
  ControllerContext cctx = ControllerContext.getInstance();
  AdfFacesContext adfFacesContext = AdfFacesContext.getCurrentInstance();
  String savePointId =
      (String)adfFacesContext.getPageFlowScope().get("this_save_point");
  if (savePointId != null){
    restoreURL = adfFacesContext.getSavePointRestoreURL(savePointId);
  }
  try {
    if(restoreURL != null){
      FacesContext fctx = FacesContext.getCurrentInstance();
      fctx.getExternalContext().redirect(restoreURL);
      fctx.responseComplete();
    }
  } catch (IOException e) {
    e.printStackTrace();
  }
  return null;
}
```

The restore URL read from the `ControllerContext` looks similar to this: /context_path/ faces/adf.save-point-restore?adf.savePointId=70741381-01c2-4002-8416-fb7bf0bc7bd7&_adf. ctrl-state=501858238_3.

Use Case: Restoring an Application State After a Session Expiry

As mentioned when discussing the ADF Controller declarative exception handling, accessing an expired session causes a `ViewExpiredException` to be thrown, displaying an error message that has the "ADF_FACES-30108" error code in it. Application developers can configure the ADF Controller exception handler to listen to the session time-out exception and obtain the latest save point ID from the database, or a cookie, to restore the application state using a managed bean or the save point restore activity element.

The restored application state does not restore an authenticated user session, which means that a previously authenticated user needs to reauthenticate, unless single sign-on is used that implicitly performs this action. In any case, it seems to be a good practice to redirect the user to a page that informs him or her about the possibility of restoring the expired session to let the user decide how to proceed.

A good strategy for restoring user sessions after session failure include saving the save point id in a short-lived client-side cookie or a managed bean that is configured in application scope. If you use a managed bean, ensure that authenticated users can only retrieve save points they have created. In general, when working with save points you should ensure users are authenticated. Using explicit save points you may consider encrypting the save point id with information about the authenticated user as the key before saving them in a cookie, a custom database table or a managed bean.

ADF Model Save Points

The ADF model (ADFm) save point is a snapshot of the transaction state. Restoring a model save point rolls back the current transaction up to the point at which the save point was created. ADFm save points can be created explicitly by the application developer or implicit by the ADF Controller.

Configuring Implicit Save Points in Bounded Task Flows

The ADF Controller implicitly creates a save point if a bounded task flow is entered without starting its own transaction. The save point is used if the user leaves the bounded task flow, for example by clicking the browser back button, or when a return activity has the restore-save-point element set.

Bounded task flows implicitly create ADF model save points if a selected bounded task flow's "No save point on task flow entry" property in the Behavior section of the Property Inspector is unchecked, which also is the default setting.

Creating Save Points Manually

To use ADFm save points in unbounded task flows, you can manually create the save point in a managed bean method using Java. The managed bean method can be used declaratively by referencing it from a method call activity in the navigation flow. Same for restoring the save point.

Use Case: Cancel Edit Form Using an Implicit ADFm Save Point

A common use case for the declarative ADFm save point feature is to cancel a user edit in a form. In this case, the application user starts editing an input form, or deleting a row, and then decides to abandon this action by clicking the cancel button. For example, to set a save point when navigating to the edit-employee-task-flow flow shown in Figure 5-7 and to restore the save point when the user cancels the edit form, the task flow definition needs to be extended, as shown in Figure 5-13.

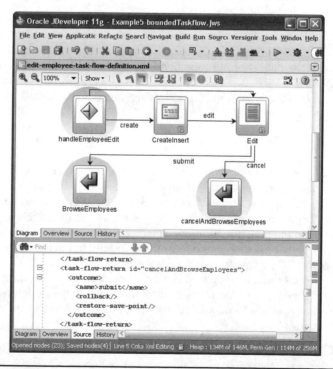

FIGURE 5-13 *Bounded task flow with cancel control flow and return activity that has the restore-save-point element set*

A return activity has been added that has the `restore-save-point` metadata element set as well as the `rollback` element. Similarly, the other return activity needs to be updated to contain the `commit` element. Note also that the outcome of both return activities is `submit`, which is OK if the implemented use case does not distinguish between a saved or cancelled from edit for the parent task flow to continue its flow. Also notice that a red overlay icon is shown on the return activity icons in the visual diagrammer until either commit or rollback is set as the value of the `End Transaction` property on the return activities.

```
<task-flow-return id="BrowseEmployees">
  <outcome>
    <name>submit</name>
    <commit/>
  </outcome>
</task-flow-return>
<task-flow-return id="cancelAndBrowseEmployees">
  <outcome>
    <name>submit</name>
    <rollback/>
    <restore-save-point/>
  </outcome>
</task-flow-return>
```

In addition, the task flow metadata itself is updated to require a transaction when entering the task flow:

```
<transaction>
  <requires-transaction/>
</transaction>
```

Also note that the data control scope needs to be shared, which is the default setting in ADF Controller. Optionally, for better readability of the application sources, you can explicitly set the data control scope to shared, adding the following metadata to the task flow definition file:

```
<data-control-scope>
  <shared/>
</data-control-scope>
```

Using a shared data control scope with the transaction metadata element set to `requires-transaction` uses an existing transaction or creates one in the parent data control frame if it doesn't exist. The `transaction` and `data-control-scope` metadata can be set declaratively in the Property Inspector. Select the task flow definition file in the JDeveloper Application Navigator and open the Structure window. Select the task flow entry in the Structure window and open the Property Inspector. Scroll to and expand the Behavior category to set the values to the Data Control Scope and Transaction property.

To cancel the edit form, a command button is added to the input form with its `action` attribute set to `cancel`, the name of the control that leads to the added return activity to restore the save point. To avoid any form validation errors, the `immediate` attribute on the command button is set to `true`.

Use Case: Cancel Edit Form Using an Adfm Save Point Set in Java

In addition to setting ADFm save points declaratively when entering a bounded task flow, you can set them explicitly in Java as well. Explicit ADFm save points not only work with bounded task

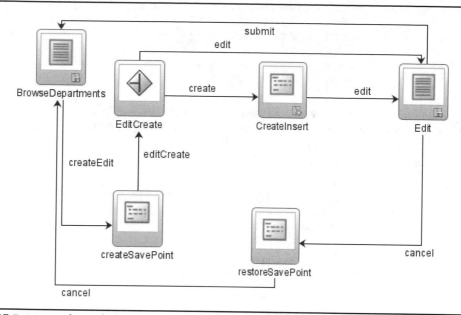

FIGURE 5-14 *Unbounded task flow with explicit save point creation and recovery through method activities*

flows but also with unbounded task flows. The example in Figure 5-14 uses two method activities to demark the save point boundaries.

The `BrowseDepartments` view activity has a create and edit button that use an `af:SetPropertyListener` component to write the selected action to an attribute in the `pageFlowScope`. The control is passed to a method activity that sets the explicit ADFm save point, which is exposed by a managed bean method. The router activity then reads the stored `pageFlowScope` attribute to determine whether the request is for edit or create. If the user decides to abandon the edit form and clicks the cancel button, the request is routed to a second method activity that restores ADFm the save point. The `restoreSavePoint` method activity references the same managed bean but a different method. The managed bean needs to be configured in the task flow definition file in which the save point is called through the method call activities. Its scope is set to `none` because there is no need for the bean to hold any state.

```
public void createAdfmSavePoint(){
   BindingContext bctx = BindingContext.getCurrent();
   DCDataControl dcDataControl = bctx.findDataControl("HRAppLocal");
   String sph = (String) dcDataControl.createSavepoint();
   AdfFacesContext adfFacesContext = null;
   adfFacesContext = AdfFacesContext.getCurrentInstance();
   adfFacesContext.getPageFlowScope().put("AdfmSavePoint",sph);
}
public void restore_action() {
   AdfFacesContext adfFacesContext = null;
   adfFacesContext = AdfFacesContext.getCurrentInstance();
   Map pageFlowScope = adfFacesContext.getPageFlowScope();
```

```
    String sph = (String) pageFlowScope.get("AdfmSavePoint");
    //clean up the memory scope
    pageFlowScope().remove("AdfmSavePoint");
    BindingContext bctx = BindingContext.getCurrent();
    DCDataControl dcDataControl = bctx.findDataControl("HRAppLocal");
    dcDataControl.restoreSavepoint(sph);
}
```

As shown in this code sample, the created save point ID is stored in a `pageFlowScope` attribute so it is accessible for a later restore if needed. Developers who need to store more than one save point would use a `java.util.HashMap` to hold the save point IDs. The method call activity references the managed bean is shown here:

```
<method-call id="createSavePoint">
  <method>#{SavePointHandler.createAdfmSavePoint}</method>
  <outcome>
    <fixed-outcome>editCreate</fixed-outcome>
  </outcome>
</method-call>
  <method-call id="restoreSavePoint">
  <method>#{SavePointHandler.restore_action}</method>
  <outcome>
    <fixed-outcome>cancel</fixed-outcome>
  </outcome>
</method-call>
```

A created ADFm save point is valid until the current transaction gets committed or rolled back.

Task Flow Templates

Bounded task flows can be based on a template, in which case the template content is copied into the task flow definition, or they can reference a task flow template, in which case the content of the template is added dynamically at runtime.

Using task flow templates, you can develop a new bounded task flow based on a set of predefined input parameters, return values, managed bean definitions, and activities. A good use case for ADF task flow templates is exception handling to enforce consistent error handling in bounded task flows. To create a task flow template, choose File | New from the Oracle JDeveloper menu and click the Web Tier | JSF category. In the list of items within the JSF category, select ADF Task Flow Template and click the OK button. The dialog to create a task flow template is the same as the dialog that appears when new task flows are created, except the proposed task flow definition filename contains the word "template" in it. A task flow template, unlike page templates that are covered in Chapter 15, can be built on top of another template.

The main difference between a bounded task flow definition and a task flow template is in the first metadata element used in the sources. The bounded task flow definition starts with the `task-flow-definition` element as the parent of all activities, managed beans, and control flow definitions. The template definition uses the `task-flow-template` element instead.

To create a new bounded task flow from a template, use the ADF Task Flow entry in the Oracle JDeveloper New Gallery to create a new task flow definition file. In the opened dialog, click the Browse button next to the Based on Template File Name field. Referencing a template from a bounded task flow definition adds the following metadata as a first child element of the `task-flow-definition` parent element:

```
<template-reference>
  <document>
    /WEB-INF/templates/excecption-handling-task-flow-template.xml
  </document>
  <id>
    exception-handling-task-flow-template
  </id>
</template-reference>
```

Referencing a template like this always ensures that at runtime, the bounded task flow works with the most up-to-date state of the template. Any change that is added to the template is automatically available to the bounded task flow referencing it. If the "Update the Task Flow when the Template Changes" option is unchecked upon task flow or task flow template creation, the referenced template content is copied directly into the new task flow definition. Later updates to the templates are not reflected in the consuming task flow.

NOTE
No visual indication exists to tell you that a bounded task flow is based on a template. If you want to perform a quick check, right-click in the visual diagrammer to open the context menu. If you see the entry Go to Based On Template, which would navigate you to the sources of the referenced template, you know that the task flow uses a template.

Refactoring Gotcha to Avoid

Templates are a means of reuse. Though theory teaches differently, in practice candidates of reusable components or artifacts most often are identified after the fact of their creation. Refactoring new components from existing components is a popular topic among developers and is supported in many ways in Oracle JDeveloper. For unbounded task flows there exists a Convert To Task Flow Template refactoring option in the context menu of the visual diagrammer. Be aware that this option turns the unbounded task flow definition as a whole into a template. To refactor only parts of an unbounded or bounded task flow into a template, no automation exists (at the time of writing), and instead you copy the content from the source task flow definition into the template definition source.

---

metadata-resource vs. template-reference
The `metadata-resources` element is used by the adfc-config.xml unbounded task flow to reference additional unbounded task flows within a project. Only one instance of unbounded task flow exists for an application, which means that the task flow definition files that are referenced by the `metadata-resources` element are merged to a single unbounded task flow graph at runtime. The `metadata-resources` element is not an option to use for bounded task flows. The `template-reference` element is used by bounded task flows only to build a live link to a template definition that is added by reference to the task flow at runtime. The `template-reference` element cannot be used with unbounded task flows.

Summary

This chapter contains introductory use cases and code samples that explain how to work with unbounded and bounded task flows. Unbounded task flows allow developers to build bookmarkable pages for users to return to a JSF page exactly where they left it. In addition, explicit save points in ADF Controller allows users to step away from their work in an unbounded task flow to continue later. Bounded task flows inherit most of the functionality of unbounded task flows, plus they provide additional functionality such as the ability to run in their own transaction context that developers set up declaratively.

The following recommendations for best practices can be derived from this chapter:

- Partition your application flows in bounded task flows.

- Ensure that no tight coupling exist between a calling and the called task flow.

- Use the ADF Controller save for later functionality to abandon a task temporarily without storing away data drafts. ADF Controller save points allow you to restore an application state, but they are not a guarantee of complete data recovery since information stored in request and session scopes are not persisted.

- Use shared data control scope in contrast to isolated to keep the resource requirements to a minimum. Use isolated data control scopes if the use case requires them, such as when a document is opened multiple times in parallel.

- Work declaratively for as much as possible, using activities and Expression Language to control application flows and accessing the ADF Controller framework. It improves readability and also simplifies application debugging through the ADF Controller task flow debugger.

- Configure managed beans in the task flow definition file from which they are referenced and use the smallest scope possible.

- Define exception handling in all task flow definitions even though exceptions propagate from bounded task flows to their parent flows. Use task flow templates to simplify this task.

There is so much to say, experience, and explore about working with ADF task flows that it probably requires a software conference of its own to cover all the functionality and to unveil the full power it brings to JSF development. The next chapter continues on this topic and introduces the work with ADF regions and bounded task flows.

CHAPTER
6

Working with Bounded
Task Flows in
ADF Regions

*ADF bounded task flows that execute in ADF regions are key enablers of enterprise Web
2.0 development with the Oracle Fusion development platform. Bounded task flows let
you build desktop-like web user interfaces that unveil the real power of Asynchronous
JavaScript and XML (AJAX) without exposing developers to the complexity of AJAX
programming.*

 special use case of bounded task flows involves ADF regions that display as
independent areas of a page or a page fragment. ADF regions represent view ports
that display the HTML markup produced by the views of an Oracle ADF Task Flow,
which executes in the ADF region without requiring a refresh of the browser page.
The concept of ADF regions enables developers to build desktop-like applications
in which the top-level page, the JSPX page in the browser, becomes the shell for areas in which
business logic executes and displays. The Oracle Applications group uses the UI shell pattern to
define a consistent application desktop for users, in which ADF regions display application
context-specific work areas. The communication between these work areas is performed through
the contextual events framework, which delivers events raised in an ADF region to event
subscribers. Information that is delivered with the event is passed in the form of a payload for
subscribers to receive and use.

This chapter explains the use of bounded task flows in ADF regions and the contextual events
framework.

NOTE
*In this chapter, the term "view" refers to page and page fragments.
The view terminology is used by the ADF Task Flow to reference the
display in the UI, which can be a physical page or page fragment.*

About View Ports

A view port holds the markup that is generated for a view and represents the browser
window or an ADF region. For each view port, an associated context object exists, an
instance of `ViewPortContext` that exposes per-request information about the current
displayed view, the executed task flow, thrown exceptions, and the transaction state to the
application developer. If a view displayed in an ADF region contains ADF regions itself, it
becomes the parent view of this region and its view port becomes the parent view port.

Helper Methods Used in This Chapter

Within the sample source code used in this chapter, we often need to execute an Expression Language method binding reference. To do this from Java, the following methods are added in and referenced by the Java classes:

```
//invoke a method from EL
private void invokeMethodExpression(String methodExprStr) {
    FacesContext fctx = FacesContext.getCurrentInstance();
    ELContext elctx = fctx.getELContext();
    Application jsfApp = fctx.getApplication();
    ExpressionFactory exprFactory = jsfApp.getExpressionFactory();
    MethodExpression methodExpr = null;
    //create method expression that doesn't expect a return type
    //(null), and that has no parameters to pass (new Class[]{})
    methodExpr = exprFactory.createMethodExpression(
                elctx,
                methodExprStr,
                null,
                new Class[]{});
    //invoke method with zero arguments
    methodExpr.invoke(elctx,new Object[]{});
}


//Return a value using EL
private Object executeValueExpression(String valueExpression){
  FacesContext fctx = FacesContext.getCurrentInstance();
  ELContext elctx = fctx.getELContext();
  Application app = fctx.getApplication();
  ExpressionFactory exprFactory = app.getExpressionFactory();
  ValueExpression valueExpr = exprFactory.createValueExpression(
                    elctx,
                    valueExpression,
                    Object.class);
    return valueExpr.getValue(elctx);
}
```

Page Fragments: .jsff

A page fragment in Oracle ADF Faces is a JavaServer Pages (JSP) document with JavaServer Faces (JSF) content that cannot run stand-alone but needs to be embedded in a parent page. The default file extension for page fragments in Oracle JDeveloper 11*g* is .jsff, which stands for JavaServer Faces Fragment. Page fragments are valid JSP documents that contain JSF components but no f:view root element. A page fragment that contains ADF bound components has its own PageDef file created and registered in the DataBindings.cpx registry.

The ADF Faces Region Tag

The ADF Faces region tag represents an instance of the `RichRegion` component and is used at runtime to add dynamic content to a parent ADF Faces view. To determine the view to display in the region, the `af:region` component uses a reference to an implementation of `oracle.adf.view.rich.model.RegionModel` in its `value` attribute. To avoid naming conflicts between content added in a region and content that exists on the parent view, ADF Faces Rich Client (RC) regions are defined as JSF naming containers that build a namespace for the UI components they expose.

Regions publish events to notify registered listeners about a change in the displayed view, a non-programmatic change of region component attributes, and disclosure of the region content area. For any change of the displayed view, identified by its `ViewId`, a `RegionNavigationEvent` is generated. Same if the region is refreshed.

NOTE
Regions cannot be used in the content created by the `af:forEach`
component iteration.

ADF Regions

ADF regions are view containers for bounded task flows that enable the modular development of desktop-like UIs without restricting the contained task flow to a specific use case or parent view. ADF regions, as shown in Figure 6-1, are ADF Faces region component instances that reference bounded task flows, which use page fragments to display views. No reasonable limit exists in the number of regions that can be added to a parent view. A region also can display views that contain other regions.

ADF Faces Regions vs. JSP Includes

Many developers with a Java EE web development background use `jsp:include` to implement page templates, build reusable page snippets, or partition JSP page development. Page source files that are referenced by a `jsp:include` tag element are compiled into the parent page, which means that their components are added to the parent page's component hierarchy before runtime.

Using ADF Faces `af:region` components, the view content is dynamically added at runtime through a reference to an instance of `RegionModel`. Content that is displayed in an ADF Faces region can be changed at runtime. Note that content that uses ADF binding references must have the bindings configured in the ADF binding definition file of the parent view. Instead of using `jsp:include` to add reusable page fragments, you could use ADF Faces declarative components, which are JSF components that can take parameters and that you can create with existing UI components. Declarative components are explained in Chapter 15 by example of a generic toolbar.

Adding a bounded task flow as a region to a .jspx or .jsff page fragment creates a task flow binding entry in the ADF binding definition file of the parent view to reference the bounded task flow. The task flow binding entry in the page definition file is referenced from the `value` attribute of the `af:region` tag by its binding ID property to obtain the region model:

```
<af:region value="#{bindings.taskflowdefinition1.regionModel}" id="r1"/>
```

Views that are exposed in an ADF region can have their own ADF binding files. The region model that is exposed on the task flow binding ensures that Expression Language references to ADF bindings in a region resolve to the pageDef.xml file of the displayed view and not the definition file configure for the parent view.

NOTE
In this chapter, we work with metadata to explain ADF region use cases and interactions. Oracle JDeveloper 11g offers two options for working with the task flow binding referenced in an ADF region. One option is to open the page definition file of the parent view that contains the task flow binding in the source editor view and the Structure Window. The other option is to select the Bindings tab at the bottom of the WYSIWYG editor displaying the parent view. For clarity, we mostly use the Structure Window and source code view of the metadata files. In your custom application development, you may find the visual editors more productive.

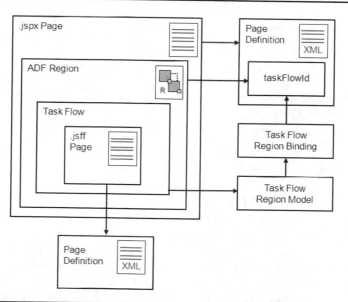

FIGURE 6-1   *ADF region architecture*

Design Considerations

Bounded task flows that are exposed in regions must use page fragments to display the view. Though it is possible first to build a bounded task flow that uses .jspx documents for the views and then refactor it to use page fragments, it is always better to build the content exposed in an ADF region by design. There are minimal differences in the use of bounded task flows that execute in a region compared to those that execute with stand-alone task flows, but these differences should be considered early on:

■ **Managed beans** Each bounded task flow that is exposed through an ADF region runs in its own instance that may or may not share the transaction and data control scope with the parent view. Views that reference managed beans should configure the beans in `backingBeanScope` if the same task flow is used in different ADF regions on the same page or page fragment.

■ **Return activities** Return activities are used to return from a called bounded task flow to the caller. Bounded task flows that execute in a region may use return activities if the return is manually handled in a navigation listener. More common though, bounded task flows in an ADF region are cyclic and don't exit.

■ **Deferred execution** ADF regions that have their execution mode set to immediate will execute the task flow even if it is not visible on the screen—for example, when added to an `af:popup` or component. The most recent version of Oracle JDeveloper 11*g* provides a deferred execution option that it also sets as the default.

■ **Communication** Region to parent view and inter-region communication may be needed for bounded task flows that are added as an ADF region to a view. This communication requires specific events to be configured and raised to pass a payload between the interested parties.

■ **Refresh** Bounded task flows in a non-region environment are refreshed when called from a call activity. Task flows in a region may never exit and thus need to be explicitly refreshed, which can be based on a change in the input parameters or a Boolean expression.

While the development of bounded task flows is the same for uses as stand-alone taskflows and in regions, the integration within the execution environment is different.

Adding ADF Regions to a View

To add a bounded task flow to a view using an ADF region, select the bounded task flow in the Oracle JDeveloper Application Navigator, where it is stored in the view controller project in the WEB-INF folder or a subfolder. Drag-and-drop the task flow entry into the WYSIWYG editor view, the page source code view, or the Structure Window (CTRL-SHIFT-S) of the opened .jspx or .jsff page. In the context menu that opens, choose the Region or Dynamic Region entry. The latter creates the task flow reference in a managed bean where it can be changed dynamically. A dialog may appear so you can map or create input parameters that are defined on the bounded task flow.

At the end of this development task, a new binding entry is created in the associated ADF page definition file and referenced from the added `af:region` tag element.

TIP
To drag-and-drop a task flow definition to the Structure Window view of a page, you need to "freeze the view" by clicking the red pin icon on top of the Structure Window before selecting the task flow entry in the Application Navigator.

NOTE
The visual WYSIWYG design time might not display the content of an added region if the first navigation item of the referenced bounded task flow is a non-view activity, such as a method or router.

Static Regions

Static regions are created by choosing the Region option from the context menu when dragging a bounded task flow onto a .jspx or .jsff page. The regions are static in that the task flow reference is hard-coded within the `taskflowId` attribute of the task flow binding.

Dynamic Regions

Dynamic regions show dynamic content in that the `taskflowId` attribute of the task flow binding references a managed bean method. The managed bean can be created or referenced when dragging the bounded task flow to a page. You use dynamic regions to change the bounded task flow reference programmatically for this region.

NOTE
In Oracle JDeveloper 11g R1, it is not possible to add a region without a corresponding af:region JSP tag. The JSP tag does most of the work of a region, not the component. Therefore, it is not possible to create a region component programmatically in Java at runtime and add it to the JSF component tree.

Task Flow Binding

The `af:region` component references the task flow binding from its `value` attribute. In the case of ADF regions, the Expression Language reference points to a binding definition stored in the ADF page definition file of the parent.jspx or .jsff file, as shown here:

```
<taskFlow id="employeesjsfftaskflowdefinition1"
    taskFlowId="/WEB-INF/employees-definition.xml#employees-definition"
    xmlns="http://xmlns.oracle.com/adf/controller/binding"
    Refresh="ifNeeded"
    parametersMap="#{pageFlowScope.paramsMap}">
  <parameters>
    <parameter id="rowKey"
    value="#{bindings.DepartmentId.inputValue}"/>
  </parameters>
</taskFlow>
```

The ADF task flow binding definition in the PageDef file exposes the following attributes for developers to configure the ADF region behavior:

- **taskFlowId** Holds the reference to the bounded task flow definition document and ID. The value can be a static string or an Expression Language expression that references a managed bean or memory attribute that returns the ID string.

- **parametersMap** Can be used to provide input parameters for the referenced task flow. Parameters defined in the `HashMap` override parameter settings of the same name that are defined within the metadata.

- **Refresh** Can be set to `ifNeeded` for the region to refresh when one of its defined parameters change.

- **activation** Determines whether the ADF region model should immediately execute the referenced task flow or not. When the ADF region model is inactive, no task flow is executed and the region always returns null for its `viewId`. The default setting is to defer task flow execution, leading to better performance during page loading when the ADF region is not initially displayed.

- **active** If the `activation` attribute is set to `conditional`, the `active` attribute must contain an Expression Language expression to determine when the task flows should become active when it is executed.

Synchronizing the ADF Region with Changes in the Parent View

ADF regions refresh when the `af:region` component `partialTriggers` attribute points to the ID of the component that should trigger the refresh. In a master-detail relationship, where the master data is displayed in the parent view and the detail is shown in the ADF region, the data synchronization is performed automatically if the bounded task flow in the region is configured to share the data control instance and transaction with the parent. If the detail view synchronization is not defined in the ADF model alone, and additional processing, such as executing a method call activity, occurs, partial page rendering alone is insufficient and the ADF region must be refreshed so that the contained task flow re-executes. For this, the ADF region has two properties, `Refresh` and `RefreshCondition`, that are explained in this chapter.

Task flow input parameters are not defined on the `af:region` tag but in the task flow binding definition, as shown in the metadata code presented earlier. Parameters are automatically created when a region is created from a bounded task flow that has input parameters defined, but they can be created manually as well. To manually create parameters for the task flow binding, do the following:

1. In the Application Navigator, select the PageDef file for the view that contains the region and open the Structure Window (CTRL-SHIFT-S).

2. Expand the executables section and select the task flow binding entry.

3. If no parameters node exists under the task flow binding node, create one by right-clicking and choosing Insert Inside taskFlow | Parameters from the context menu.

4. Select the parameters node, right-click, and then choose Insert Inside Parameters | Parameter from the context menu.

Task flow binding parameters that don't have a matching parameter on the bounded task flow don't cause any harm and are silently ignored.

ADF Task Flow Binding Refresh vs. RefreshCondition

ADF regions are initially refreshed when their parent view first displays. At that time, ADF region task flow binding parameter values are passed in from the parent page and the initial page fragment within the ADF region is displayed. The ADF region task flow binding can be refreshed at runtime based on the value setting of its Refresh and RefreshCondition attributes. By default, none of the two attributes is set, which means that the ADF region doesn't refresh after the initial load of the view.

Setting the RefreshCondition to a valid Expression Language expression that evaluates to true or false, the ADF region always refreshes when the Expression Language evaluation returns true. If the expression used in the RefreshCondition references the ADF binding layer, the binding container it accesses is the container of the parent page, not the page fragment displayed in the ADF region.

Setting the Refresh attribute to ifNeeded refreshes the ADF region with any change of the ADF region input parameter values. If the attribute value is set to default, no refresh occurs. Using the Refresh attribute with a value of ifNeeded does not refresh the ADF region when the task flow binding input parameters are passed in as a parameter Map. In this case, the RefreshCondition attribute must be used.

The RefreshCondition and Refresh attributes are mutually exclusive. If both are used in combination, the Refresh attribute, if set to ifNeeded, takes precedence over RefreshCondition.

Accessing the Task Flow Binding from Java

The task flow binding that is referenced from a region is an instance of DCTaskFlowBinding, which extends the DCBindingContainer framework class. To access a task flow binding from Java, use the following code in a managed bean:

```
BindingContext bctx = BindingContext.getCurrent();
BindingContainer bindings = bctx.getCurrentBindingsEntry();
DCTaskFlowBinding taskFlowBinding = null;
taskFlowBinding = (DCTaskFlowBinding) bindings.get("dynamicRegion1");
```

The BindingContext object returns a handle to the binding container, the live representation of the PageDef configuration of the region parent page. The task flow binding is accessed by its name, dynamicRegion1, in this example.

How to Declaratively Create a Dynamic Region That Switches Between Displayed Task Flows

This exercise steps through the creation of a dynamic region that changes the bounded task flow reference by the user clicking one of two provided command links. We start with the assumption that two bounded task flows exist in the project, departments-task-flow-definition.xml and employees-task-flow-definition.xml, that both use page fragments to display their views.

1. Drag departments-task-flow-definition.xml to a page or page fragment.
2. Choose Dynamic Region from the context menu and create a managed bean—for example, RegionBean—to hold the current task flow ID reference. The managed bean is created in backingBean scope, which we change later to use a broader scope.

3. Optionally, create input parameters that are expected by the bounded task flow and complete the region creation. This creates a task flow binding entry such as dynamicRegion1 in the PageDef file of the parent view. The task flow binding uses Expression Language to reference the created managed bean to obtain the task flow ID string to display.

4. Again, drag departments-task-flow-definition.xml to the page or page fragment. This time, in the opened context menu, choose Dynamic Region Link | *dynamicRegion1*, where *dynamicRegion1* is the task flow binding name we assume in this example to exist in the PageDef file. This creates an af:commandLink component with an Expression Language action reference to the managed bean created for the region. The reference is to a method that sets the task flow ID returned by the managed bean to the departments-task-flow-definition.xml document.

5. Repeat step 4 for the employees-task-flow-definition.xml bounded task flow and again choose *dynamicRegion1*. This creates a second command link with an Expression Language reference to the managed bean used by the region. Clicking the command link, the managed bean return ID is set to the employees-task-flow-definition.xml document, switching the task flow shown in the region.

6. Change the scope of the managed bean and run the parent page and use the created links to switch between the two bounded task flows in the region. The refresh of the region on the page is performed through partial triggers, which are configured via the region's partialTriggers attribute.

Following these steps applies changes to three files—the parent .jspx or .jsff page, the pageDef.xml file of the parent page, and the managed bean. The region tag contains a reference to the binding entry in its action attribute. Both link components have their action attribute pointing to the managed bean, which by default is created in backingBeanScope.

To switch between task flows, the managed bean must be configured in a scope broader than request, such as viewScope. When changing the bean scope, make sure you also change the managed bean Expression Language references in the page and the PageDef file. In the following code example, the page EL referenced is changed from backingBean scope to view scope.

```
<af:region value="#{bindings.dynamicRegion1.regionModel}"
     id="r1" partialTriggers="::cl1 ::cl2"/>
  <af:commandLink text="Departments"
     action="#{viewScope.RegionBean.departmentstaskflowdefinition}"
     id="cl1"/>
  <af:commandLink text="Employees"
     action="#{viewScope.RegionBean.employeestaskflowdefinition}"
     id="cl2"/>
```

The ADF task flow binding references the managed bean in its taskFlowId attributes:

```
<taskFlow id="dynamicRegion1"
     taskFlowId="${viewScope.RegionBean.dynamicTaskFlowId}"
     xmlns="http://xmlns.oracle.com/adf/controller/binding"/>
```

The managed bean has three methods—one to pass the current task flow ID to the binding and two to set the current task flow ID:

```
import oracle.adf.controller.TaskFlowId;
public class RegionBean {
```

```
private String taskFlowId = "/WEB-INF/departments-task-flow
  -definition.xml#departments-task-flow-definition";

public TaskFlowId getDynamicTaskFlowId() {
  return TaskFlowId.parse(taskFlowId);
}
public String departmentstaskflowdefinition() {
  taskFlowId = "/WEB-INF/departments-task-flow
    -definition.xml#departments-task-flow-definition";
  return null;
}
public String employeestaskflowdefinition() {
  taskFlowId = "/WEB-INF/employees-task-flow
    -definition.xml#employees-task-flow-definition";
  return null;
  }
}
```

Layout Hint: Changing a Command Link to a Tab

A common use case is to display the command links to switch between the task flows as tabs above the region. You can accomplish this with only a little change to the generated page code:

```
<af:navigationPane id="np1" hints="tab">
  <af:commandNavigationItem text="Departments" id="cn2"
    action="#{viewScope.RegionBean.departmentstaskflowdefinition}">
  </af:commandNavigationItem>
  <af:commandNavigationItem text="Employees" id="cn1"
    action="#{viewScope.RegionBean.employeestaskflowdefinition}">
  </af:commandNavigationItem>
</af:navigationPane>
```

The `af:navigationPane` is a naming container, which means that the `partialTriggers` attribute of the `af:region` tag needs to be updated, as shown next, to refresh when a panel tab is opened:

```
<af:region value="…"  partialTriggers=":np1:cn2 :np1:cn1"/>
```

NOTE
The `hints` *attribute of the* `af:navigationPane` *tag can be used to change the visual display of the* `af:commandNavigationItem` *child elements between tab (default), list, choice, buttons, and bar.*

RegionNavigationListener

Navigation listeners are implemented in a managed bean method that is referenced from the `af:region regionNavigationListener` attribute. The single listener method argument is an instance of `RegionNavigationEvent` that provides information about the ID of the current displayed view of the region and the previous view ID from which it navigated. Additionally, access is provided to the region component instance that references the listener.

To create a listener implementation in a managed bean method, select the region in the Oracle JDeveloper 11*g* visual page editor or the Structure Window and open the Property Inspector. Search for the `RegionNavigationListener` property, click the down arrow, and choose Edit. In the opened dialog, select an existing managed bean or create a new one before adding a new method to it. This creates a method signature similar to the following and an Expression Language reference from the `af:region` tag to it:

```
public void onRegionNavigated(RegionNavigationEvent event){
  //add code
}
```

Note that the `RegionNavigationListener` is not invoked during the initial load of the task flow and when switching the task flow reference in a dynamic ADF region. It is invoked only when navigation occurs within the region.

Contextual Event Framework

The contextual event framework in Oracle ADF enables the communication among ADF regions and the communication among ADF regions and their parent views. A contextual event is a notification that is sent by a region or the containing parent view to registered subscribers, which can be other ADF regions or the parent view. You use contextual events to do the following:

- Establish communication between loosely coupled ADF regions that are located on the same parent view.

- Pass messages and events notifications to an ADF region that contains an already started task flow.

- Notify an ADF region about a data change with which it should synchronize.

NOTE
If the bounded task flows referenced by ADF regions in a view share the data control scope and the transaction with the parent view, then to display the data changed in one of the ADF regions in the other, contextual events are not needed. In this case, it is sufficient to refresh the af:region *component through a partial trigger.*

How Contextual Events Work

Contextual events are a functionality of the Oracle ADF binding layer and therefore require the binding layer to be present on the producer, the dispatcher, and the consumer side. Any binding container can be configured as a contextual event dispatcher through the creation and configuration of an event map that connects an event with interested parties accessible to the container.

NOTE
In this section, the term "consumer" is used interchangeably with the term "subscriber." Events are not consumed, but observed, in which case the term "subscriber" better describes the role of the event receiver. However, because the term "consumer" is used within the JDeveloper product, we use it as well.

If an event is raised, it is passed to the binding container in which it resides for dispatch. After delivering the event to the binding container where the contextual event was raised, the event is delivered to the parent binding container for dispatch. Each PageDef file may have an event map defined that associates the event with a consumer. The event does not stop when an event map is found that contains an event mapping to a consumer. Instead, event propagation continues until the topmost parent binding container is reached. The contextual event is then dispatched to child binding containers that are referenced from one of the binding containers that received the event notification on its way up to the top-level container. Child binding container references are defined through task flow bindings or page bindings. For example, a page binding entry is automatically created for ADF bound pages that reference ADF Faces page templates that have their own ADF bindings defined.

NOTE
See Chapter 15 for more information about page templates.

If interested consumers are identified, the contextual framework event is delivered to the consumers at the end of the ADF lifecycle. The consumer of a contextual event is always a method or action binding that is defined on the ADF binding container of the consuming view. The event payload, the message object that is sent within the contextual event, can be mapped to optional input arguments of the receiving method using the event mapping dialog in Oracle JDeveloper. The payload object is Expression Language accessible through `${payLoad}` or `#{payLoad}`.

Events

Two types of events exist: events defined for an ADF binding and events that are defined for JSF component events.

ADF Binding type events are configured on the ADF control binding that is referenced by the ADF bound UI component on a page. Events are published in response to user interaction, such as a value change or a row currency change. JSF component type events, such as `ActionEvent`, `ValueChangeEvent`, or the `ClickEvent` of a data visualization component, are mapped to an `eventBinding` entry in the PageDef file associated with the JSF page. The `eventBinding` entry implements the corresponding JSF event listener interface.

In general, contextual events are defined in the PageDef file of the JSF page or page fragment that invokes it. Developers can define events by directly editing the PageDef file or declaratively, using the Publish Contextual Events dialog. When creating an event, the developer provides values for the following attributes:

- **Name** The name of the event binding entry in the PageDef file.

- **customPayload** An optional Expression Language reference to a binding or managed bean property that returns the object to pass as the event argument. Setting this property overrides the default payload. The default payload is the UI event, such as an instance of `ValueChangeEvent`, which raised the contextual event.

- **eventType** A value change, currency change, or action.

- **raiseCondition** An optional Expression Language reference to a binding or method that returns `true` or `false` to control when the event should be published and when it should be suppressed. Not setting a value for this attribute will raise the event whenever it is invoked from the UI component.

Event Map

An event finds its subscriber through event mappings that are configured on ADF binding containers. An event map is a registry that binds events to subscribers. If the producer name in the mapping is defined with a wildcard character (*), then the event is received from any producer within the binding hierarchy. Event maps that reference the producer name must be defined on a binding container that has access to the producer and the consumer page definition files, which is usually the case for parent containers. The event map can be used to define a condition when an event is passed on to the consumer. For this the event map provides a `handleCondition` property on the consumer definition. The `handleCondition` property takes an EL expression that evaluates to `true` or `false` at runtime.

How to Create and Publish Events Declaratively

Oracle JDeveloper provides a declarative editor for developers to create contextual events for ADF binding and ADF Faces component events. The editor is launched using one of the following options:

- **Property Inspector**   ADF Faces components such as `af:inputText` and `af:commandButton` publish contextual events through settings in the Behavior | Contextual Events category of the Property Inspector. To open the Publish Contextual Event dialog, click the plus icon for new events or the pencil icon for existing events.

- **Page binding editor**   At the bottom of the visual page editor in Oracle JDeveloper is a Bindings tab. Selecting this tab opens the ADF binding editor for the page. The binding editor includes a Contextual Events tab to switch the view to the contextual events editor. Clicking the plus icon for a new event or the pencil icon for an existing event opens the Publish Contextual Event dialog where you can define the event.

- **PageDef editor**   Double-clicking the ADF page definition file in the JDeveloper Application Navigator opens the visual ADF binding editor. Selecting the Overview tab at the bottom of the editor displays the ADF binding overview panel, which includes a tab to switch the view to the contextual events editor. Clicking the plus icon for a new event or the pencil icon for an existing event opens the Publish Contextual Event dialog where you can define the event.

The Publish Contextual Event dialog allows you to define a new event or select an existing event definition. It provides the following options:

- **Create New Event**   Lets you define a new event. If the editor is launched from the Property Inspector of a selected ADF bound UI component, the new event is created as a child of the ADF binding element. Otherwise, the event is created as a child of the <page_name> PageDef | events element for the developer to bind later to a UI component.

- **Select Existing Event**   Lets you associate the selected UI component with an existing event in the *<page_name>*PageDef | events entry. The events entry is automatically created for events that are built using the Publish Contextual Events editor. To find and select the event, use the search icon.

- **Name**   The name of the event to publish. This name is used as a reference when mapping it to an event consumer in the mapping editor.

- **Type** Design-time-only attribute that defines the type of event. It is not used at runtime and can be omitted.

- **Payload tab** A contextual event can have a payload that is passed to the event receiver input argument. By default, the payload is the event object, such as value changes or range changes, depending on the type of binding that publishes the event. Optionally, the default payload can be replaced with a custom payload, which can be an ADF binding reference, a return value of a method in a managed bean, or a literal value.

- **Raise Condition tab** Lets you define an Expression Language expression that returns `true` or `false` to determine when an event should be published when it is invoked. By default, events are always published when invoked.

- **Documentation** Lets you add comments an event to describe it. The description is not contained in the ADF binding file that contains the event definition, but in a separate properties file.

NOTE
Events that are created using the Publish Contextual Event dialog are defined under the events node in the PageDef file. Events in this node are not used at runtime. You can look at them as event templates that developers can reuse when defining the event publisher. If the Publish Contextual Event dialog is launched from the Property Inspector of an ADF Faces RC component, the event publisher entry is created in addition to the event template.

How to Create and Publish Events Manually

Contextual events may also be created manually by editing the ADF binding file in the Structure Window. The manual approach is recommended only for cases in which no declarative option exists, such as when contextual events are raised from a single node of a tree binding. To create an event, select the binding, for example the tree binding, in the PageDef file for which you want to create a contextual event. Right-click and choose insert inside *<binding name>* | Contextual Event | events from the context menu. Then select the events node, right-click, and choose insert inside events | event from the context menu to create an event item. Use the Property Inspector on the event item to define a name, an optional custom payload, and the raise condition. The examples provided in this chapter show both declarative and manual event definitions.

How to Create an Event Map

Event maps connect the event and producer with the subscriber. Developers have a choice of how to create the event map: declarative or manually.

How to Create an Event Map Declaratively

To create an event map declaratively, do the following:

- Select the page definition file entry of the parent view in the JDeveloper Application Navigator and choose Open from the context menu, or double-click it.

- In the opened overview editor, select the Contextual Events tab and then the Subscribers tab.

- Click the plus icon to create subscriber definition, which implicitly creates the event map definition if it does not exist yet.

- In the Subscribe to Contextual Event dialog, select the event, a publisher, and the subscriber to define the mapping. Select the Parameter tab and create a mapping between the event payload and the input argument or arguments of the subscriber method. The payload object is accessible via Expression Language: `${payLoad}` or `#{payLoad}`.

NOTE
Creating the event map declaratively allows you to configure the `handleCondition` *property in the Subscribe to Contextual Event dialog.*

How to Create an Event Map Manually

To manually create an event map, do the following:

1. Select the page definition file entry of the parent view in the JDeveloper Application Navigator and open the Structure view.

2. Select the root node, which has the same name as the page definition file, excluding the .xml file extension. From the context menu, choose Insert inside *<view name>*PageDef | eventMap to create an event map for this page definition.

3. To create an event mapping between a producer and a consumer, again select the root node of the page definition and choose Edit Event Map from the context menu. This launches the event map editor, as shown in Figure 6-2, where you can map an event producer to a consumer. If none of the event map editor buttons are enabled, then most likely no valid producer exists in the child containers or the parent container. To map an event to a consumer, make sure that the PageDef file contains a task flow binding or a page binding that links the child container.

NOTE
As shown in Figure 6-2 the `handleCondition` *property is not exposed for editing when the event mapping is created manually. In this case, after creating the event mapping, expand the event map and select the consumer node. From here, the* `handleCondition` *property can be edited using the Property Inspector.*

How to Exclude Page Definition Files from Receiving Contextual Event Notifications

The delivery of contextual events comes at the cost of ADF having to initialize all referenced child binding containers. As mentioned, an event is published from the binding container that contains the event to the parent container, and so on, until it reaches the top-level container. On the way up, the event is delivered to all event maps that have the event producer name explicitly set to the producer event binding. In addition, ADF keeps track of all child containers that are referenced from the parent containers to initialize them for event delivery when the event bubbles down from the top-level container. The event is published to event maps that have the event name defined and the producer name set to an asterisk (*). If this dynamic event propagation it is not needed by an application or a child container, you should suppress the event propagation for better

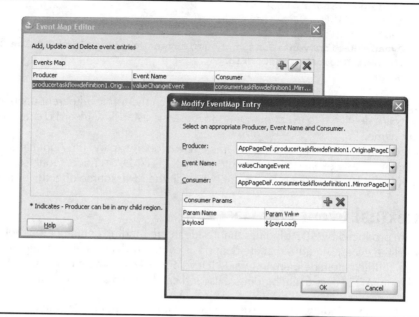

FIGURE 6-2   *Event map dialog launched from a binding definition file*

performance. At the time of writing, no programmatic option exists In Oracle JDeveloper 11*g* R1 to cancel event propagation dynamically—for example, when the first event consumer is found. However, you can configure the PageDef files not to allow dynamic event delivery to child containers. In this case, child binding containers are not registered for event delivery when the event is published to the parent containers and are therefore not initialized. To suppress wildcard event notification to child containers, add the following boldface line to the parent page definition file:

```
<pageDefinition xmlns="http://xmlns.oracle.com/adfm/uimodel"
   version="…"
   id="emp_task_flow_emp_task_flow_EditEmpPageDef"
   Package="adf.interactiv.view.pageDefs" SkipValidation="true"
   DynamicEventSubscriptions="false">
…
```

To add this line declaratively, select the root node of the PageDef file in the Structure Window and open the Property Inspector. Set the `DynamicEventsSubscriptions` property to `false`.

To prevent dynamic event propagation for an application as a whole, add the following configuration to the adf-config.xml file:

```
<?xml version="1.0" encoding="windows-1252" ?>
<adf-config xmlns=http://xmlns.oracle.com/adf/config
            xmlns:sec=http://xmlns.oracle.com/adf/security/config
            xmlns:cef="http://xmlns.oracle.com/adfm/contextualEvent">
  <sec:adf-security-child
    xmlns="http://xmlns.oracle.com/adf/security/config">
    <CredentialStoreContext
```

```
        credentialStoreClass="…"
        credentialStoreLocation="…"/>
   </sec:adf-security-child>
   <cef:DynamicRegionEventsConfig dynamicEventSubscriptions="false">
   </cef:DynamicRegionEventsConfig>
</adf-config>
```

With this setting, the event propagation stops when the top-level parent container is reached. No events are delivered to event mappings that use the asterisk wildcard character as the producer name.

To access the adf-config.xml file in Oracle JDeveloper, expand the Application Resources accordion panel and expand the Descriptors | ADF META-DATA node. Double-click the adf-config.xml file entry to open it. You need to edit the XML source directly for this entry.

Contextual Event Use Cases

Events are produced by ADF bindings that reside in the binding container that belongs to a view that raises the event. Bindings that are defined as event producers have an additional `events` metadata child element defined. In Oracle JDeveloper 11g R1, three types of ADF bindings, plus an additional ADF Faces event binding, exist and can be used as an event producer:

- **Attribute binding**   A contextual event is raised when the attribute value is successfully set or changed.

- **Range binding**   A contextual event is raised upon row currency change in a tree binding and list binding. The tree binding, for example, is used by the ADF Faces tree, table, and tree table components.

- **Action and method binding**   A contextual event is fired when the method or action executes. The method or action outcome is delivered as the contextual event payload.

- **Event binding**   An entry in the pageDef.xml file that can be invoked through an ADF Faces action or value change event.

Attribute Binding

Attributes binding producers broadcast a value change event to registered consumers. The payload contains the changed value, the row object, and the attribute definition object in an instance of `DCBindingContainerValueChangeEvent`.

The following illustration shows a use case for an attribute producer in which an attribute value change on View 2 in ADF Region 1 sends a notification to a consumer method defined in the binding definition of View 3, which is located in ADF Region 2. The event is dispatched by an event map that is configured on the parent container, View 1. View 2 contains an ADF bound input form for the Departments view and a submit button. View 3 contains an input text field that mirrors the changed value for the department name attribute binding in the Page Definition 2. To receive the change event, Page Definition 3 contains a method binding that references a method in a Java class that is exposed as a data control.

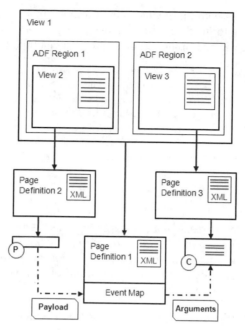

Use the following steps to implement the use case outlined above using contextual events in ADF. If you want to re-create this example, you need to do as follows:

1. Create two bounded task flows that use page fragments.
2. Create two .jsff page fragments, one for each bounded task flow.
3. Add an ADF bound input form to one of the page fragments (View 2). In our example, this is a form to edit the Departments table of the Oracle HR demo schema.
4. In the other page fragment (View 3), add an `af:inputText` field that references a managed bean property in its `value` attribute. The binding `attribute` of the text input field also needs to have a EL reference created to a managed bean property.
5. Drag the two bounded task flows as ADF region to a JSF page (View 1) that you created in the adfc-config.xml file.

Creating the Event Producer To create the event producer, do the following:

1. Open View 2 in the JDeveloper visual editor and select the DepartmentName input field. Note that the department name field is bound to ADF.
2. Open the Property Inspector and click the plus icon in the Behavior | Contextual Events section.
3. In the opened Publish Contextual Event dialog, keep the Create New Event option selected and provide a name, for example departmentNameChangeEvent, in the Name field.

4. Close the dialog, without specifying a custom payload. The default payload is sufficient to use for this use case. The event that is defined as a child element of the `DepartmentName` attribute binding in the PageDef file looks similar to the this:

```
<attributeValues IterBinding="DepartmentsView1Iterator"
                  id="DepartmentName">
   <events xmlns="http://xmlns.oracle.com/adfm/contextualEvent">
     <event name="departmentNameChangeEvent"/>
   </events>
   <AttrNames>
     <Item Value="DepartmentName"/>
   </AttrNames>
</attributeValues>
```

NOTE
*A second event entry is created under the `<page_name>PageDef |`
events element. This element is not used at runtime but exists at
design time to allow you to reuse the event definition by referencing
it from another UI component. You can delete this entry if you don't
plan to reuse the event definition.*

Creating the Event Consumer   The event consumer is a Java class that receives the event notification to look up the managed bean that exposes the setter and getter methods for the mirror text field value in View 3. The class code looks like this:

```
public class EventReceiver {
  public EventReceiver() {
    super();
  }
  public void receiveEvent(
          DCBindingContainerValueChangeEvent  incomingPayload){
    FacesContext fctx = FacesContext.getCurrentInstance();
    ELContext elctx = fctx.getELContext();
    Application app = fctx.getApplication();
    ExpressionFactory exprFactory = app.getExpressionFactory();
    ValueExpression valExpr = exprFactory.createValueExpression(
          elctx,
          //reference the managed bean that holds the mirror value
          //property displayed in the input text field
          "#{backingBeanScope.ConsumerBackingBean}",
          Object.class);
    ConsumerBackingBean consumer = null;
    consumer = (ConsumerBackingBean)valExpr.getValue(elctx);
    //get the changed attribute value from the contextual event
    //payload
    String newValue = (String)incomingPayload.getNewValue();
    //set the new value to the backing bean property that is
    //referenced by the input text field in View 3
    consumer.setMirrorValue(newValue);
    AdfFacesContext adffacesContext = null;
    adffacesContext = AdfFacesContext.getCurrentInstance();
```

```
//partially update the text field to display the new value
adffacesContext.addPartialTarget(consumer.getMirrorTxt());
    }
}
```

NOTE
The object type of the method argument is the ADF value change event, DCBindingContainerValueChangeEvent, *not the JSF component* ValueChangeEvent *object. This is because the event is raised from the value change on the binding layer, not the component.*

The managed bean that is used on View 3 is defined in the definition of the task flow referenced in ADF Region 2. It also contains a JSF binding reference to the mirror text field so the field can be refreshed in response to the event, using the AdfFacesContext.addPartialTarget method. To create a data control from the EventReceiver POJO, do the following:

1. Select the EventReceiver Java class in the Oracle JDeveloper Application Navigator, right-click, and choose Create Data Control from the context menu.

2. Create a page definition file using the Go To Page Definition context menu option for View 3 if it doesn't exist. In the PageDef file, create a new method binding in the bindings section. For this, right-click and choose insert inside bindings | Generic Bindings | methodAction from the context menu and point the opened dialog to the receiveEvent method exposed on the EventReceiver data control. The method argument is provided by the event and can be left empty when creating the method binding.

TIP
A data control can expose multiple methods. Make sure that you repeat the data control creation step whenever a method is added or a method signature has been changed.

Building the Event Map   Create an event map in the Page Definition 1 binding file. The file does exist and contains the task flow bindings used by ADF Region 1 and ADF Region 2:

1. Choose Edit Event Map from the context menu on the page definition root node and click the green plus icon in the opened dialog to create the mapping.

2. Select the DepartmentName attribute in Page Definition 2 as the producer and choose the valueChangeEvent.

3. In the Consumer field, select the receiveEvent method binding in Page Definition 3.

4. To map the incoming payload to the method argument, click the green plus icon on the Consumer Params table. The parameter name is the name of the method argument. The value of the parameter is an Expression Language reference to ${payLoad} or a JavaBean property of it: ${payLoad.<property>}. The resulting event map in the Page Definition 1 file looks similar to this:

```
<eventMap xmlns="http://xmlns.oracle.com/adfm/contextualEvent">
  <event name="valueChangeEvent">
    <producer
      region="producertaskflowdefinition1.pageDef2.DepartmentName">
```

```
        <consumer region="consumertaskflowdefinition1"
                  handler="pageDef3.receiveEvent">
          <parameters>
            <parameter name="incomingPayload" value="${payLoad}"/>
          </parameters>
        </consumer>
      </producer>
    </event>
  </eventMap>
```

TIP
*You don't need to parse the payload in the receiving Java method.
Instead, a method can have multiple arguments defined that are
populated in the event map by referencing bean properties of the
payload object. Instead of using the default payload, you can use
the event map to reference ADF binding entries or manage bean
properties as input arguments.*

How This Example Works at Runtime   When the user changes the department name's input
field value, a contextual event is raised upon form submit. The event is first handled by the
container that raised the event, which is the binding container associated to the page fragment,
Page Definition 2. From here, the event is passed on to the parent container, Page Definition 1.
This container has an event map defined that links the event to a method binding in Page
Definition 3, which is part of another ADF region. The method expects a single argument to
which we pass the change event object. This event object provides useful information to the
method—for example, the new value that is set to the attribute binding. Using EL, the method
looks up the managed bean that holds the value property for the mirror inputText field in View 3.
The method updates the field value and refreshes the inputText component instance so the value
displays in the browser.

Range Binding
Range binding producers, such as the tree binding that is used to bind the ADF Faces table, tree,
and tree table components, broadcast a selection change event to registered consumers.
    The default payload contains the selected `JUCtrlHierNodeBinding` object in an instance
of `DCBindingContainerCurrencyChangeEvent`.
    Figure 6-3 shows the runtime view of the example illustrated in Figure 6-4. An ADF Faces
tree component is located in an ADF region, which is displayed on the first facet of an
`af:panelSplitter` component. The second ADF region, displayed in the second facet of
the `af:panelSplitter`, shows an input form with information that reflects the selected node.
Depending on the user's node selection, an input form for editing department data or an input
form for editing employee data is shown.
    Figure 6-4 shows an architectural view of this use case implementation. A parent view, View 1,
contains two ADF regions: ADF Region 1 and ADF Region 2. ADF Region 1 exposes View 2, a
page fragment that displays an ADF Faces tree component that is bound to an ADF tree binding
in Page Definition 2. The tree hierarchy shows a list of departments and the employees working
within. On selection of a tree node, a contextual event is raised that sends the information about
the current selected node to the registered event consumer. In this example, the event consumer
is ADF Region 2. More explicitly, the consumer is a method binding configured in the Page
Definition 3 binding file. The method binding points to a method exposed by a POJO data
control. View 3 in ADF Region 2 contains another ADF region, ADF Region 3, a dynamic ADF

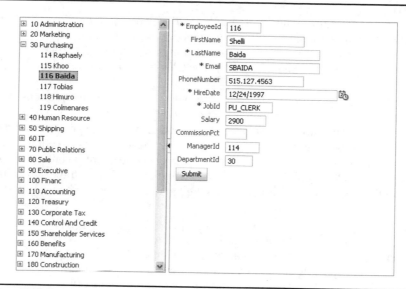

FIGURE 6-3 *ADF Faces tree component broadcasting a selection event for the ADF region to display an edit form for the selected node*

region that, depending on the selected node, shows an edit form for the Departments view or the Employees view. The event producer and consumer are linked together in an event map defined on the PageDef file of the parent view, View 1.

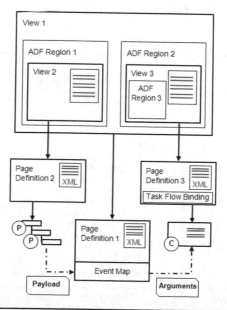

FIGURE 6-4 *Architectural view of the use case implementation*

NOTE
If the ADF Faces tree component and the ADF region displaying the detail edit form are located on the same view, contextual events are not needed; instead, you can work with partial page rendering (PPR) and ADF region input parameters only. See Chapter 9 for an example.

Creating the Event Producer   To create the event producer for the tree selection, expand the tree binding in Page Definition 2 and select the nodeDefinition entry of the node that should publish the selection event. Choose Insert inside nodeDefinition | events from the context menu. Right-click the created events entry and choose Insert inside events | event from the context menu. Type an event name, such as selectEvent. Create one events/event pair for each node for which you want to publish an event, as shown in Figure 6-5. In the example use case, the Department and Employee nodes are configured to raise an event when selected.

NOTE
If you want to pass a payload other than the currency change event object, such as an object or data accessed from the ADF binding or a managed bean using EL, you edit the `customPayload` *property of the event entry. You can also define the condition for when the selection event should be published using an EL expression that evaluates to* `true` *or* `false`.

Creating the Event Consumer   The event consumer is a method exposed on a POJO data control that is referenced from a method binding created in the page definition file of the consumer view. In the use case for this section, the consumer method receives a `DCBinding ContainerCurrencyChangeEvent` object as the argument that contains information about the selected node. The method then determines the selected node type and the node row key value that is needed to query the data form in ADF Region 3. The row key value is stored in the

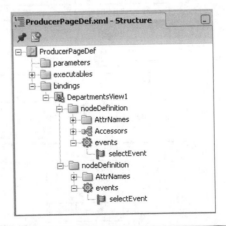

FIGURE 6-5   *Events defined on the ADF tree binding nodes*

pageFlowScope, where it is referenced from the input parameter of the bounded task flow in ADF Region 3.

```
import oracle.adf.model.binding.DCBindingContainerCurrencyChangeEvent;
import oracle.adf.view.rich.context.AdfFacesContext;
import oracle.jbo.uicli.binding.JUCtrlHierNodeBinding;
...
public class RangeEventReceiver {
  public RangeEventReceiver() {
    super();
  }
  public void receiveRangeChangeEvent(Object payload){
    //nodes are identified by the structure def name of their underlying
    //View Objects
    final String DEARTMENTS_NODE =
                      "adf.interactiv.model.queries.DepartmentsView";
    final String EMPLOYEES_NODE =
      "adf.interactiv.model.queries.EmployeesView";
    //if the method used a typed argument, or multiple typed
    //arguments then no type casting would be needed. Because
    //we defined the method argument type as Object, we do the
    //type casting below
    DCBindingContainerCurrencyChangeEvent _thisPayload = null;
    //cast the payload to the event type
    _thisPayload = (DCBindingContainerCurrencyChangeEvent)payload;
    //get the selected node type
    AdfFacesContext adfFacesContext = null;
    adfFacesContext = AdfFacesContext.getCurrentInstance();
    //get the selected node type. Based on the detected node type, if
    //it is for departments or employees, we switch the dynamic ADF
    //region that displays the input form
    JUCtrlHierNodeBinding node = null;
    node = (JUCtrlHierNodeBinding) _thisPayload.getSource();
    String nodeType = node.getHierTypeBinding().getStructureDefName();
    if (nodeType.equalsIgnoreCase(DEARTMENTS_NODE)){
      //switch the Task Flow referenced by the dynamic ADF Region
      invokeMethodExpression(
      //as explained earlier in this chapter, to change the
      //displayed bounded task flow of an ADF region, you call
      //a managed bean method to set the new task flow ID
"#{viewScope.ConsumerBacking.departmentsTaskFlow}");
      //set search key for detail search
      Map pageFlowScope = adfFacesContext.getPageFlowScope();
      pageFlowScope.put("key",node.getAttribute("DepartmentId"));
    }
    else if(nodeType.equalsIgnoreCase(EMPLOYEES_NODE)){
      //switch the Task Flow referenced by the dynamic ADF Region
      invokeMethodExpression(
      //set the new task flow ID to the employees task flow
        "#{viewScope.ConsumerBacking.employeesTaskFlow}");
      //set search key for detail search
      Map pageFlowScope = adfFacesContext.getPageFlowScope();
      pageFlowScope put("key",node.getAttribute("EmployeeId"));
    }
  }
}
```

The referenced managed bean is configured in viewScope in the task flow definition that contains the consumer view. The getDynamicTaskFlowId method is automatically created by

Oracle JDeveloper when a bounded task flow is added to a view as a dynamic ADF region. It returns the task flow ID of the current task flow referenced in the managed bean. Calling one of the other two methods, as we do in the preceding source code, sets the task flow reference.

NOTE
Remember that the managed bean that changes the bounded task flow displayed in a dynamic ADF region must be configured in view scope or a broader scope. The default managed bean scope, `backingBean`, *cannot be used for this.*

```
public TaskFlowId getDynamicTaskFlowId() {
        return TaskFlowId.parse(taskFlowId);
}
public void departmentsTaskFlow() {
  //line break is added for better readability
  taskFlowId = "/WEB-INF/departments-task-flow-definition.xml#
                departments-task-flow-definition";
}
public void employeesTaskFlow() {
  taskFlowId ="/WEB-INF/employees-task-flow-definition.xml#
                employees-task-flow-definition";
}
```

NOTE
To ensure the task flow binding in the Page Definition 3 file refreshes when the input parameter—the node key value passed into the detail task flow—changes, make sure the refresh option is set to `ifNeeded`.

Building the Event Map   Create an event map in the Page Definition 1 binding file. The PageDef file does exist and contains the task flow bindings used by ADF Region 1 and ADF Region 2. Choose Edit Event Map from the context menu on the page definition root node and click the green plus icon in the opened dialog to create the mapping. The producer list shows two producers, one for each node on which we defined the event element. You can create an event map for each event producer node, which allows you to call different consumer methods. For this, select a producer and its event name. Then, in the producer list, select the method binding of the consumer, which is Page Definition 3 in our example. Configure the input parameter of the event map to link the method input argument, `payload` in the example, to the `${payLoad}` Expression Language reference.

The event map for the example use case is shown here:

```
<eventMap xmlns="http://xmlns.oracle.com/adfm/contextualEvent">
  <event name="selectEvent">
    <producer region=
      "producertaskflowdefinition1.ProducerPageDef.DepartmentsView1.0">
      <consumer region="consumertaskflowdefinition1"
                handler="ConsumerPageDef.receiveRangeChangeEvent">
        <parameters>
          <parameter name="payload" value="${payLoad}"/>
        </parameters>
      </consumer>
```

```
      </producer>
    </event>
    <event name="selectEvent">
      <producer region=
        "producertaskflowdefinition1.ProducerPageDef.DepartmentsView1.1">
          <consumer region="consumertaskflowdefinition1"
                handler="ConsumerPageDef.receiveRangeChangeEvent">
            <parameters>
              <parameter name="payload" value="${payLoad}"/>
            </parameters>
          </consumer>
      </producer>
    </event>
</eventMap>
```

If the event producer nodes should be handled by the same consumer method, such as in our example, you can create a single event map entry and select the parent node of the two event producers. The parent node is the name of the task flow binding. The event map now looks as follows:

```
<eventMap xmlns="http://xmlns.oracle.com/adfm/contextualEvent">
    <event name="selectEvent">
      <producer region="producertaskflowdefinition1">
        <consumer region="consumertaskflowdefinition1"
                handler="ConsumerPageDef.receiveRangeChangeEvent">
          <parameters>
            <parameter name="payload" value="#{payLoad}"/>
          </parameters>
        </consumer>
      </producer>
    </event>
</eventMap>
```

In this XML code sample, the task flow binding for the event producer, the task flow with the tree view, in the PageDef file is `consumertaskflowdefinition1`. The select event is handled by the `receiveRangeChangeEvent` method binding in the PageDef of the view that is displayed in the bounded task flow referenced by the `consumertaskflowdefinition1` binding entry.

Method Binding

Method and action bindings can be created for methods and operations that are exposed on a data control. ADF Business Components expose operations on the application module and the view object level that are accessible through action bindings in ADF. Client methods that are exposed on the ADF Business Components application module or view object are accessible through method bindings. Both action bindings and method bindings can be configured as contextual event producers and consumers. Producer method return values are implicitly added to the payload passed to the consumer.

The following illustration shows an example use case for a method binding. A parent view, View 1, contains a table that lists all employees of the Employees database table, and an ADF region, ADF Region 1, that exposes a task flow. The task flow has two views between which to navigate. The first view shows a list of departments from the Departments table. In this view, the user selects a department entry and clicks a command button to create a new employee record for this department and to navigate to the second task flow view. In the second view, View 2, the user edits the new employee entry and clicks submit, which implicitly commits the new record. A new contextual event is issued from the commit operation to notify the employees table in View1 to refresh and set the new row as the current selected row.

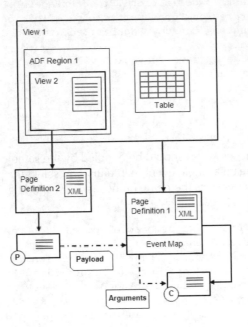

NOTE
To create a submit button that implicitly commits the edits, create an ADF input form from a view object and click the submit button. From the Data Control palette, select the Commit operation and drag it on top of the submit button. Ensure that the text *and the* disabled *attributes of the submit button are not updated by this operation.*

Creating the Producer   The event producer in this example is the commit operation that is exposed on the ADF Business Components application module. To create the event producer, open View 2 and select the command button that is bound to the commit action in the Page Definition 2 binding file. Open the Property Inspector and click the plus icon in the Behavior | Contextual Events section. Keep the Create New Event option selected and provide a new name for the event, such as newEmployeeCommit.

To refresh the employees table in View 1 and to set the new employee entry as the selected row in response to the commit action, the payload that is sent from the producer to the consumer must contain the row key of the new row. ADF Business Components actions, however, don't return a value that can be used for this. Instead, the event needs to be configured with a custom payload such as that shown in Figure 6-6. To configure the custom payload, select the Pass Custom Value From option in the Publish Contextual Event dialog. Choose Other Expression and click the calculator icon next to the Expression label to launch the Expression Builder dialog. In the Expression Builder dialog, select the iterator on which the edit form is based and choose currentRow.key.

NOTE
The `currentRow` *entry is shown in the Oracle JDeveloper Expression
Builder dialog but not the* `key` *property. You need to add this property
manually in the Expression Builder dialog. Alternatively, you can use
the* `currentRowKeyString` *entry shown for the iterator binding
after changing the receiving method to work with a String payload.*

The commit operation metadata with the associated event definition looks as follows:

```
<action id="Commit" RequiresUpdateModel="true"
        Action="commitTransaction"
        DataControl="HRAppModuleDataControl">
  <events xmlns="http://xmlns.oracle.com/adfm/contextualEvent">
    <event
      name="newEmployeeCommit"
      customPayLoad="#{bindings.EmployeesView3Iterator
                     .currentRow.key}"/>
  </events>
</action>
```

NOTE
The `customPayload` *attribute value must be provided without line
breaks. We added a line break for better readability.*

Creating the Consumer   The event consumer is a client method that is exposed on the
ADF Business Components view object. The view object method is referenced from the Page
Definition 1 binding file. The method in the custom `EmployeesViewImpl` class takes a single

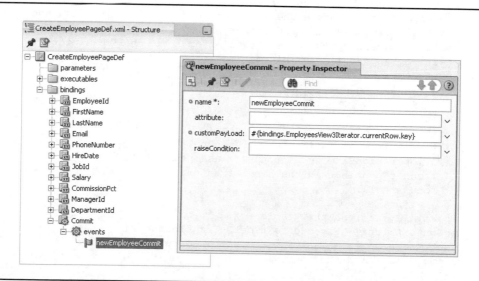

FIGURE 6-6   *Contextual event with a custom payload pointing to the current row key*

argument of type `oracle.jbo.Key` that it uses to find the first row meeting this criterion. This row then is set as the selected row:

```
public void executeWithKey(Key key){
    //refresh the collection
    //this.executeQuery();
    Row rw = this.getRow(key);
    this.setCurrentRow(rw);
}
```

The current row is set in the business service layer and not in ADF. To display the changed row selection in the ADF Faces table in the parent view, View 1, you need to partially refresh it. To avoid having to hard-code the table ID in the task flow, you can pass the table ID as an input parameter to the task flow and then in a managed bean action method, after performing the commit action, add the table to the partial refresh list using the `AdfFacesContext` object.

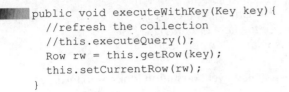

NOTE
In Chapter 1 we explained how a public method in a custom ViewImpl or ApplicationModuleImpl file is exposed as a client interface method so it can be bound to in ADF.

The following managed bean action method is referenced from the `action` property of the commit button:

```
public String submit_action() {
    //dragging the commit operation from the Data Controls palette
    //onto a command button configures an ADF binding reference to
    //the commit action binding on the button. Double-clicking the
    //button in the visual editor then allows developers to create a
    //managed bean to define the action method in. When creating the
    //managed bean, a setter and getter method is created to access the
    //binding layer, which is referenced from a managed bean property.
    //See chapter 1 for more information about managed bean properties.
    BindingContainer bindings = getBindings();
    OperationBinding operationBinding = null;
    //access the ADF commit operation in an Operation binding and
    //execute it
    OperationBinding = bindings.getOperationBinding("Commit");
    Object result = operationBinding.execute();
        if (!operationBinding.getErrors().isEmpty()) {
            //don't continue in the case of an error
            return null;
        }
    //partially refresh the  table
FacesContext fctx = FacesContext.getCurrentInstance();
    //get table id from Task Flow input parameter. Replace
    //<table id> with the id you receive
```

```
UIComponent component = fctx.getViewRoot().findComponent(<table id>);
AdfFacesContext.getCurrentInstance().addPartialTarget(component);
//call a navigation case that returns the task flow from the edit
//employee page to the departments table overview page in the bounded
//task flow
return "created";
}
```

Building the Event Map   Create an event map in the Page Definition 1 binding file. The file does exist and contains the task flow bindings used by ADF Region 1. Choose Edit Event Map from the context menu on the page definition root node and click the green plus icon in the opened dialog to create the mapping. Select the Commit attribute in Page Definition 2 as the producer and choose newEmployeeCommit. In the Consumer field, select the executeWithKey method binding in Page Definition 1.

To map the incoming payload to the method argument, click the green plus icon on the Consumer Params table. The consumer method argument name is key and needs to be mapped to the custom payload using the ${payLoad} expression. The event map in the Page Definition 1 file looks similar to this:

```
<eventMap xmlns="http://xmlns.oracle.com/adfm/contextualEvent">
  <event name="newEmployeeCommit">
    <producer
      region="createemployeetaskflow.CreateEmployeePageDef.Commit">
      <consumer region="" handler="executeWithKey">
        <parameters>
          <parameter name="key" value="${payLoad}"/>
        </parameters>
      </consumer>
    </producer>
  </event>
</eventMap>
```

Event Binding: Producing Events from ADF Faces

So far, all contextual event producers were ADF component bindings, such as attribute binding, range binding, method binding, and action binding. For use cases that require a JSF action or value change event, or a graph event of the ADF Faces Data Visualization Tool (DVT) to trigger a contextual event, developers use the eventBinding element in the ADF page definition file.

The following illustration shows an example for a contextual event raised by an ADF Faces component. The topmost parent view, View 1, contains an ADF region that displays View 2, with a table that displays a list of cities and an ADF region in it. The table and the ADF region are synchronized so that the ADF region always shows detailed information for the selected table row. The ADF region dynamically references two task flows—one to display the departments view and the other to display the employees view for the selected city. The menu component in View 1 references the event binding in Page Definition 1 to publish an event to the nested dynamic ADF region, ADF Region 2, to switch between the views. The event consumer, which switches between the views, is a method exposed on a POJO data control that is referenced from the page definition file of View 2. The consumer accesses the managed bean that is used to switch the task flow in the dynamic ADF region to set the current task flow definition according to the information in the payload.

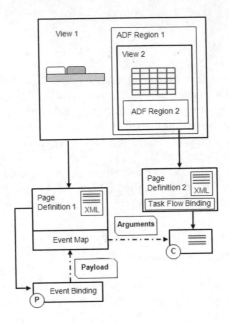

Creating the Producer If the ADF Faces component to invoke the event is an `af:inputText` or `af:commandButton`, the producer event can be created declaratively from the Property Inspector in the Behavior | Contextual Events section. In the example, we use an `af:commandNavigationItem` component to invoke the event for which the producer needs to be created manually.

To create the producer event manually, do the following:

1. Open the binding definition for the parent view, View 1 in this example, in the Structure Window and select the page definition's bindings node.

2. From the context menu, choose Insert inside bindings | Generic Bindings | eventBinding to create the event binding container.

3. Select the created event binding entry and open the Property Inspector to configure it for a JSF event such as `ActionEvent` or `ValueChangeEvent`. In the example, the event binding is called from an `ActionEvent`.

4. Define a value for the `id` attribute, such as `TaskFlowChange` in Figure 6-7, to reference the binding from Java or Expression Language.

5. To define the contextual event, select the eventBinding entry and choose Insert inside eventBinding | events from the context menu.

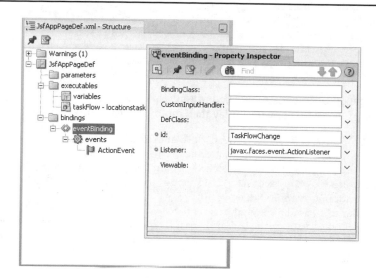

FIGURE 6-7 *Event binding configured to be invoked by a JSF action event*

6. Select the events entry and choose Insert inside events | event from the context menu to define an event entry. The name of the event in this example is `mActionEvent`. The following metadata is produced in the page definition file of the parent view:

```
<eventBinding id="TaskFlowChange"
    Listener="javax.faces.event.ActionListener">
    <events xmlns="http://xmlns.oracle.com/adfm/contextualEvent">
      <event name="mActionEvent"/>
    </events>
</eventBinding>
```

The event binding can be invoked from an ADF Faces command action component using Expression Language and Java. In the page source code shown next, we use the ADF Faces `af:commandNavigationItem` component to display two tabs, Departments and Employees. The Departments tab uses Expression Language to trigger the event, and the Employees tab, for demonstration purpose, uses a managed bean. The `af:commandNavigationItem` has a `af:clientAttribute` child component that contains the information about the task flow to show when the tab is selected:

```
<af:navigationPane id="np1">
  <af:commandNavigationItem
      text="Departments" id="cni1" partialSubmit="true"
      actionListener="#{bindings.TaskFlowChange.listener.processAction}">
    <af:clientAttribute name="type" value="departments"/>
  </af:commandNavigationItem>
```

```
<af:commandNavigationItem
  text="Employees" id=" cni2" partialSubmit="true"
  actionListener="#{JsfAppBacking.onEmployeeSelect}">
  <af:clientAttribute name="type" value="employees"/>
</af:commandNavigationItem>
</af:navigationPane>
```

The managed bean code referenced from the second `CommandNavigationItem` that changes the ADF region view to display the Employees list is shown next:

```
public void onEmployeeSelect(ActionEvent actionEvent) {
  BindingContext bctx = BindingContext.getCurrent();
  BindingContainer bindings = bctx.getCurrentBindingsEntry();
  //get access to the eventBinding node in the PageDef file
  JUEventBinding eventBinding = null;
  //get a handle to the eventBinding
  eventBinding = (JUEventBinding) bindings.get("TaskFlowChange");
  ActionListener al = (ActionListener)eventBinding.getListener();
  al.processAction(actionEvent);
}
```

NOTE
Defining `javax.faces.event.ValueChangeListener` *as the value of the Listener* `eventBinding` *attribute shown in Figure 6-7 allows the JSF value change listener to trigger the contextual event. In this case, the Expression Language string to invoke the event from an ADF Faces component* `valueChangeListener` *attribute uses the following format:* `#{bindings.<eventBinding_name>. listener.processValueChange}`.

NOTE
Defining `oracle.adf.view.faces.bi.event.ClickListener` *as the value of the Listener* `eventBinding` *attribute shown in Figure 6-7 allows the* `ClickListener` *of a graph component of the ADF Faces DVT component set to trigger the contextual event. The click event is an instance of* `oracle.adf.view.faces.bi.event. ClickEvent` *and is published as the payload of the contextual event. It contains information about the selected graph row, group, value, and rowKey. The Expression Language string to invoke the contextual event from the graph* `ClickListener` *property uses the following format:* `#{bindings.<eventBinding_name>.listener. processClick}`.

TIP
The `eventbinding` *entry can be created declaratively for all ADF Faces components, such as* `af:commandButton`, *that have a Contextual Events section in their Property Inspector view. Click the plus icon and the tool determines whether the component is ADF bound. If it is not ADF bound, an* `eventBinding` *is created. The JSF listener is also automatically configured.*

Creating the Consumer   The consumer is defined as a method binding in the ADF page definition of the view that contains the dynamic ADF region. In our example, this is Page Definition 2. The method is exposed from a POJO data control and looks like this:

```
public class EventReceiver {
  public EventReceiver() {
    super();
  }
  public void handleEvent(Object payload){
    //if event is raised from a JSF action command then the payload
    //is an instance of javax.faces.event.ActionEvent. If it is invoked
    //from a value change listener, then the payload is an instance of
    //javax.faces.event.ValueChangeEvent
    ActionEvent actionEvent = (ActionEvent) payload;
    //get the component instance that raised the event
    UIComponent navItem =  null;
    navItem = (UIComponent) actionEvent.getSource();
    //viewType is either "departments" or "employees"
    //and was added to the component using the clientAttribute
    //component
    String viewType = (String) navItem.getAttributes().get("type");
    if (viewType.equalsIgnoreCase("departments")){
      //set departments bounded task flow ID to display in the ADF
      //dynamic regions
      invokeMethodExpression(
        "#{pageFlowScope.LocationsBacking.departmentsTaskFlow}");
    }
    else if (viewType.equalsIgnoreCase("employees")){
      //set employees bounded task flow ID to display in the ADF
      //dynamic regions
      invokeMethodExpression(
        "#{pageFlowScope.LocationsBacking.employeesTaskFlow}");
    }
  }
}
```

NOTE
The refresh of the dynamic ADF region when a different table row is selected is handled using partial page refresh. This can be configured declaratively between the af:table *component and the* af:region. *The contextual event is used only to switch the ADF region view dependent on a tab component selection in the root view.*

Building the Event Map   The event map to dispatch the ADF Faces action event is defined in the page definition file of the top-level view, which in the example is Page Definition 1.

1. Choose Edit | Event Map from the context menu on the page definition root node and click the green plus icon in the opened dialog to create the mapping.

2. Select the eventBinding name, TaskFlowChange in our example, from Page Definition 1 as the producer and choose the mActionEvent.

3. In the Consumer field, select the `handleEvent` method binding contained in Page Definition 2.

4. To map the incoming payload to the method argument, click the green plus icon on the Consumer Params table.

5. The consumer method argument name is payload, which needs to be mapped to the custom payload using the `${payLoad}` expression.

NOTE
The `eventBinding`'s event entry, ActionEvent in this example, can have a custom payload configured to replace the default. Expression Language can be used to read the custom payload value from the ADF binding layer.

Producing Contextual Events from JavaScript

Every action and method binding that is accessible from a managed bean can be invoked from JavaScript. Oracle ADF Faces RC provides an operation component, `af:serverListener`, that you can use to call a managed bean method from JavaScript on the client. In the referenced managed bean method, you use the `BindingContext` object to look up the current `BindingContainer` and to access the `OperationBinding` or a `JUEventBinding` binding to invoke. The `af:serverListener` can also be used to send a message payload from the browser client to the managed bean method. Depending on the type of event that is expected by the event binding, you need to create an instance of this event in the managed bean to pass it when invoking the event.

NOTE
The `af:serverListener` component is discussed in Chapter 19, which explains how to use custom JavaScript in ADF Faces RC.

Consuming Contextual Events in Dynamic ADF Regions' Task Flows

The event mapping editor in Oracle JDeveloper 11g R1 does not help to configure the dispatch of contextual events coming from dynamic ADF regions. To consume contextual events from and in binding containers of views displayed in dynamic ADF regions, developers need to configure the event map manually. To create an event map manually in the binding container of the consumer, do the following:

1. On the root node of the page definition file that should receive the event for dispatching, choose Insert Inside <*pageDef name*> | eventMap from the context menu.

2. Select the eventMap and choose Insert Inside eventMap | event and define the event name as the name of an event to listen for, such as `mActionEvent`. The event name must match the name of the event you want to listen and respond to.

3. Right-click and select an option from the context menu to create a producer within the event. Set the producer name to an asterisk (*) or the full name of the event producer.

4. Inside of the producer, create a consumer. The consumer `handler` attribute value must be set to the binding name of the contextual event consumer.

5. Optionally, add attributes to the consumer that maps the payload or elements of the payload to method arguments.

The event mapping definition below listens for an event with the name `printActionEvent` produced by any event producer. The received event is mapped to the `printEvent` entry, which is a method or operation binding contained in the same PageDef file. A single argument is passed to the method, containing the default or custom page load defined for the event.

```
<eventMap xmlns="http://xmlns.oracle.com/adfm/contextualEvent">
  <event name="printActionEvent">
   <producer region="*">
     <consumer handler="printEvent">
       <parameters>
         <parameter name="payload" value="${payLoad}"/>
       </parameters>
     </consumer>
   </producer>
  </event>
</eventMap>
```

To change this configuration to listen to a specific producer event, you need to change the asterisk value in the `producer` attribute to a producer event name with the full task flow and page definition path in it.

NOTE
Once created, the event mapping can be edited in the declarative event mapping edit dialog. Select the page definition root node and choose Edit Event Map from the context menu. This also allows you to map the producer to a method binding in a child view or another ADF region.

ADF Region Interaction Use Cases

An ADF region that is located in a view usually does not live in isolation, but needs to integrate with the application context of the view. To enable communication, ADF regions provide hook points in addition to contextual events that developers can use to pass information in and out or to send events. Three patterns of interaction can be identified for ADF regions in Oracle Fusion application development:

- **ADF region to parent view** A region communicates back to its parent view—for example, to enforce navigation.

- **Parent view to ADF region** The parent view calls out to the ADF region to refresh it or to invoke or pass an event with or without payload.

- **ADF region to ADF region** Logically dependent regions exchange events and messages to synchronize their state.

All three patterns can be implemented with the contextual event framework introduced in the preceding section. Additional implementation choices exist for the region-to-parent and parent-to-region patterns that are introduced in the following section.

Parent View to ADF Region Interaction

Use cases, such as the navigation within an ADF region that is triggered by the parent view, are easier to implement with an interaction pattern other than contextual events.

How to Pass Parameters from a Parent View to a Region

Input parameters that are defined on the task flow binding referenced by an ADF region correspond to input parameters of the same name on the task flow definition. Input parameters are read when the ADF region refreshes, which occurs for the following conditions:

- During the initial rendering of the ADF region.

- When the referenced task flow ID changes, which may be the case for dynamic ADF regions.

- When the `af:region` component receives a PPR notification and the task flow binding of the ADF region is refreshed.

- When the `refresh method` on the `RichRegion` instance is called in a managed bean. The `RichRegion` instance is created for the `af:region` component when building a JSF component binding to the managed bean.

To refresh an ADF region in response to a partial trigger notification so that the contained task flow is re-executed, the following conditions need to be true:

- The task flow binding entry in the page definition file must have its `Refresh` attribute set to `ifNeeded`, or the `RefreshCondition` must evaluate to `true`.

- Using the `Refresh` attribute set to `ifNeeded`, the task flow binding input parameter must have a changed value for the ADF region to refresh.

Unlike contextual events that dispatch a payload to the running task flow instance in an ADF region, passing input parameters from a parent view to an ADF region requires that the referenced task flow be restarted. A use case for input parameters being passed from a parent view to the ADF region is when the ADF region is used to display an edit form for a selected data row in a read-only table. In this case, the parameter that is passed to the ADF region is the row key of the record to edit.

NOTE
Creating input parameters is explained in the section "Synchronizing the ADF Region with Changes in the Parent View" earlier in this chapter. Note that when using dynamic ADF regions, you may choose the input parameter map option instead of input parameters defined on the task flow binding.

How to Share Data and State Settings Using Data Controls

By default, the data control scope of a bounded task flow is configured so that the data control instance is shared with the parent view. If a task flow exposed in an ADF region displays data that depends on a selection in the parent view, the ADF Business Components business service automatically handles the master-detail synchronization through the shared data control layer.

To display the synchronized detail data when the master row currency changes in the parent view, you need to configure a partial refresh of the `af:region` component. To configure partial refresh on an ADF region, select the `af:region` UI component in the Oracle JDeveloper visual page editor and select the "`PartialTriggers`" property in the JDeveloper Property Inspector. Choose the Edit option in the context menu that opens after you click the arrow icon to the right to select the UI components on the parent view that should trigger a region refresh.

The partial refresh of the `af:region` component does not refresh the ADF region in that the bounded task flow is re-executed. Only the task flow current view is refreshed to show the changed data of the shared data control.

NOTE
The data control scope can be shared only if the transaction is also shared.

If the task flow execution should start with the defined default activity when the `af:region` receives a partial refresh notification, then you need to force it to re-execute. Task flow re-execution can be enforced through declarative configuration or through a Java call in a managed bean.

To configure the task flow binding declaratively to refresh and re-execute the task flow when the master row currency changes, for example when navigating in a form, the task flow binding's `RefreshCondition` attribute must evaluate to `true` and the `Refresh` attribute must be set to `default`.

The Java-based solution requires a managed bean and adds a single line of code at the end of the event that triggers the row currency change, like the action event of a command button in a toolbar. To refresh the ADF task flow binding in Java, you do the following:

1. Create a JSF binding for the `af:region` component to the managed bean to create a setter and getter method for the component.

2. Create a managed bean method to handle the navigation button action event.

3. Call the `refresh` method on the `RichRegion` instance at the end of the navigation code.

The managed bean code for a button action that refreshes the ADF region may look similar to this example:

```
public String next_action() {
  //Binding access is auto generated by JDeveloper if the managed bean
  //binding is created by a double click on an ADF bound command button
  BindingContainer bindings = getBindings();
  OperationBinding operationBinding = null;
  OperationBinding = bindings.getOperationBinding("Next");
  Object result = operationBinding.execute();
  if (!operationBinding.getErrors().isEmpty()) {
    return null;
  }
  //region1 is the JSF binding of the  af:region component in the
  //managed bean. Refresh it next
  region1.refresh(FacesContext.getCurrentInstance());
  return null;
}
```

Since both configurations, declarative and Java-based, work the same, the recommendation is to use the declarative option if the use case allows it. An example for when the ADF region refresh is better to be performed in Java is given in the next section.

How to Raise JSF Action Events in an ADF Region

The use case of a parent view to invoke a control flow in a contained ADF region can be achieved in at least two different ways:

- Using the contextual event framework to send an event to a consumer in the task flow, such as a method configured on the view bindings. See "How to Navigate Programmatically Among View Activities" in Chapter 5.

- Calling the `queueActionEventInRegion` method to queue an action event on the `af:region` component that exposes the ADF Task Flow.

Both options have their strengths. Contextual events are better to use if switching between the views implies changing the task flow referenced by a dynamic ADF region, and this example was covered earlier in this chapter. If the views are contained in the same task flow, and if control cases exist between them, then the `queueActionEventInRegion` method that is exposed on the `af:region` component's `RichRegion` implementation class is sufficient and easier to use. The `queueActionEventInRegion` method queues an `ActionEvent` as if it is queued on a command component inside the region.

Figure 6-8 shows the browser presentation of the example that we use in this chapter to explain how to navigate an ADF region from a parent view. The ADF tree component is used to select the location for which the departments and employees information should be shown. The two command buttons belong to the parent view and trigger the navigation in the ADF region. The command buttons are enabled based on the control flow choice available for the current displayed view in the ADF region.

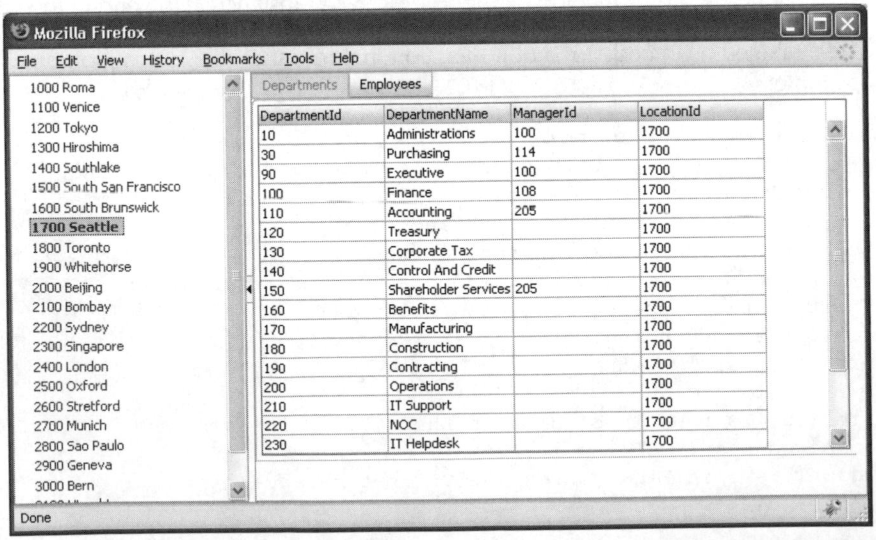

FIGURE 6-8 *A list of departments or employees based on a location selected in an ADF Faces tree*

The following illustration shows the architecture of the use case described above and shown in Figure 6-8.

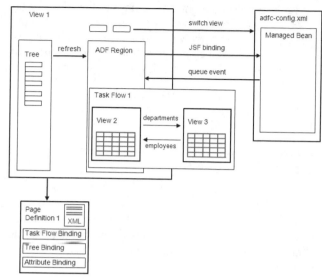

The parent view, View 1, contains the ADF region that exposes a bounded task flow, Task Flow 1. Within the task flow, two views, View 2 and View 3, exist that are linked by two control flow cases, departments and employees. The attribute binding in the page definition of View 1, Page Definition 1, exposes the location ID of the current selected tree node. The ADF Faces tree selectionListener attribute points to a managed bean that sets the selected tree entry as the current row in the iterator binding referenced by the tree binding. In addition, it refreshes the ADF region such that the contained ADF Task Flow is re-executed.

```
public void onSelection(SelectionEvent selectionEvent) {
    FacesContext fctx = FacesContext.getCurrentInstance();
    ELContext elctx = fctx.getELContext();
    ExpressionFactory expressionFactory = null;
    expressionFactory = fctx.getApplication().getExpressionFactory();
    MethodExpression methodExpression = null;
    //when building an ADF bound tree, the selection listener attribute
    //contains EL that sets the current selection as the current row in
    //the tree binding. To preserve this behavior, we call this EL
    //from the managed bean
    methodExpression = expressionFactory.createMethodExpression(
            elctx,
            "#{bindings.TreeBinding.treeModel.makeCurrent}",
            Object.class,
            new Class[]{selectionEvent.getClass()
    });
    //invoke method expression with argument. The argument is the
    //SelectionEvent object that is passed in by JSF.
    methodExpression.invoke(elctx,new Object[]{selectionEvent});
    //refresh the region based on a new node selection
    adfRegion.refresh(fctx);
}
```

The task flow binding in the page definition of View 1 has a single input parameter that writes the location ID exposed by the attribute binding to the task flow input parameter to query the detail data. The `af:region` component that belongs to the ADF region has its `binding` attribute referencing the setter and getter methods of a managed bean variable of type `RichRegion`. The managed bean uses the region instance variable, `adfRegion`, to queue the action event that triggers the navigation in the ADF region. The action listener methods of the two buttons, one to display the departments view and one to display the employees view, are shown here:

```
public void switchToDepartmentView(ActionEvent actionEvent){
    outcome = "departments";
    switchView();
}
public void switchToEmployeeView(ActionEvent actionEvent){
    outcome = "employees";
    switchView();
}
```

The `outcome` variable is defined as private in the managed bean instance and is accessible from outside the managed bean through the defined setter and getter methods only. The `switchView()` method also is private and queues the action event in the `af:region` for the ADF region to perform the navigation:

```
private void switchView(){
    FacesContext fctx = FacesContext.getCurrentInstance();
    ExpressionFactory expressionFactory = null;
    expressionFactory = fctx.getApplication().getExpressionFactory();
    ELContext elctx = fctx.getELContext();
    //we need to create a method expression that is queued in the region.
    //The setter / getter methods of the outcome variable are EL accessible.
    //LocationBean is the configured name of the managed bean in JSF
    MethodExpression methodExpression = null;
    methodExpression = expressionFactory.createMethodExpression(
        elctx,
        "#{LocationBean.getOutcome}",
        String.class,
        new  Class[]{});
    adfRegion.queueActionEventInRegion(
        methodExpression,
        null,null,false,0,0,
        PhaseId.INVOKE_APPLICATION);
}
```

The method expression references the managed bean that contains the method that returns the `outcome` variable, which is `getOutcome()` in the example. In the example, the managed bean is the same as the bean that holds the `af:region` instance reference. The managed bean is defined in the task flow configuration file of the parent view. This also can be the adfc-config.xml file.

The `queueActionEventInRegion` method signature expects the following arguments:

■ **actionExpression** A reference to an action method or the static outcome of an action.

- **launchListenerMethodExpression**   A method expression that references a launch listener method that is called if the `actionExpression` opens an external dialog window. In the example, the views are not contained in a dialog and the listener expression is set to null.

- **returnListenerMethodExpression**   If the `actionExpression` opened the view in an external dialog, then upon closing the dialog, the referenced return listener method is called to pass the dialog return values to the calling page.

- **useWindow**   Defines whether the navigated view should open in an external dialog window. Set to `false` in this example because the views don't display in a dialog window.

- **windowWidth and windowHeight**   Define the size of the opened external window.

- **phaseId**   The ID of the phase in which the action event should be executed.

The command buttons to switch from one view to another are enabled or disabled based on the availability of the navigation case they trigger.

```
<af:commandButton text="Departments" id="cb1"
   actionListener="#{LocationBean.switchToDepartmentView}"
   disabled="#{!LocationBean.adfRegion.regionModel.capabilities
           ['departments']}"
   partialSubmit="true" partialTriggers="r1"/>
<af:commandButton text="Employees" id="cb2"

   actionListener="#{LocationBean.switchToEmployeeView}"
   disabled="#{!LocationBean.adfRegion.regionModel.capabilities
           ['employees']}"
   partialSubmit="true" partialTriggers="r1"/>
```

The decision whether or not a button is disabled is made by the outcome of a call to the `getCapabilities` method that is exposed on the `RegionModel`. The `getCapabilities` method returns a not modifiable `Set` of outcomes for the current state of the `RegionModel`. Each capability is a string representing a control flow case. If the current view displayed in the ADF region is View 2, then the capability for the departments control flow returns `true`, whereas the capability for the employees control flow returns `false`.

The submit buttons perform partial submits. To refresh the `af:region` component and the buttons, partial triggers are used.

NOTE
A queued action event performs navigation only in the ADF region for which it is queued. It does not trigger navigation in contained child ADF regions. If this is a requirement, contextual events must be used.

ADF Region to Parent View Interaction

ADF regions can force navigation on the parent view with one of the two interaction patterns explained in this section. Again, contextual events may be used, but are not needed.

How to Cause Navigation in the Parent View from an ADF Region

The Oracle ADF Controller provides a parent action activity element that allows developer to declaratively initiate navigation of the immediate parent view of an ADF region. A use case for the requirement to navigate the parent view from an ADF region is a shopping cart, as shown in Figure 6-9, in which the line items of a selected order are shown in an ADF region. Within the ADF region, users can edit the existing line items or create new items. When the user is done editing the parent view—the order page—it should navigate to a summary page where the user can confirm his or her changes.

Dragging the parent activity element from the Oracle JDeveloper component palette (CTRL-SHIFT-P) to a bounded task flow that executes in an ADF region creates the following metadata:

```
<parent-action id="goParentSummary">
    <parent-outcome>summary</parent-outcome>
    <outcome>noParentControlFlow</outcome>
</parent-action>
```

- **id**   Unique identifier of the parent action activity instance in a task flow definition.

- **parent-outcome**   The control flow case name that is defined on the parent task flow definition of the view. The control flow case can be a wildcard navigation case (*) or a named navigation case defined for the parent view to the next activity in the parent task flow definition.

- **outcome**   If no control flow case is defined in the parent view that matches the value provided in the `parent-outcome` element, navigation continues in the task flow shown in the ADF region with the value specified in the `outcome` element, if any.

To execute the parent activity element, you create a control flow in your task flow that points to this element. If the control flow is a wildcard flow, the parent activity element is accessible from all activities in the bounded task flow.

How to Cause Navigation in the Browser Root View from an ADF Region

ADF regions may be located deeply nested in other views that are not the top-level view, which is the browser root view. If an ADF region needs to navigate to the root view, the URL view activity component should be used. A use case for this could be the shopping cart example. If the order view is contained in an ADF region that hosts the detail view in a child ADF region, then the parent action activity is of limited use to navigate the parent view.

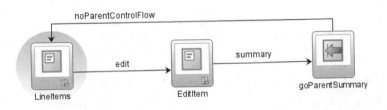

FIGURE 6-9   *Use of the parent action element in a bounded task flow*

NOTE

Of course, you could create a chain of parent action activity in all parent views for a nested ADF region that reaches through to the root view. A parent action event of the most inner ADF region would then call the control flow case that leads to the parent activity element of its parent view, and so on. But how far away from best practices does this sound?

To implement this use case, the ADF region that needs to navigate the browser root view directs its navigation to a URL view activity that redirects the request. The URL view activity may have parameters defined that would allow the target view in the unbounded task flow, which is where root views typically reside, to display a specific state. To compose the URL of a view in the unbounded task flow, you can use the `getGlobalViewActivityURL` method in the `ControllerContext` object using Expression Language.

The URL view activity in the following example references the `OrderSummary` view activity defined in the unbounded task flow. The `DetailTaskFlowBean` is a helper bean that we configured as a managed bean. Since the bean does not keep any state, its scope can be set to none.

```
<url-view id="showSummary">
  <url>#{DetailTaskFlowBean['OrderSummary']}</url>
</url-view>
```

NOTE

Managed beans can be accessed by other managed beans only if their scope matches or outlives the scope of the referencing bean or if its scope is set to none. Managed bean with a scope of none are universally accessible.

The `DetailTaskFlowBean` extends `java.util.Hashmap` and overrides the get method to allow Expression Language to use arguments:

```java
public class GlobalReturnActivities extends HashMap {
  public GlobalReturnActivities() {
    super();
  }
  /*
   * Generate a URL for a view activity in the unbounded task flow.
   * The view activity being referenced must be in the unbounded task
   * flow. URL access to view activities within bounded task
   * flows is not supported
   */
  @Override
  public String get(Object key) {
    ControllerContext cctx = ControllerContext.getInstance();
    String globalUrl = cctx.getGlobalViewActivityURL(key.toString());
    return globalUrl;
  }
}
```

How to Refresh the Parent View from an ADF Region

To refresh a parent view in response to an action or navigation in an ADF region, a partial refresh event needs to be sent from the region to its parent view.

PPR Parent View Components in Response to an ADF Region Action In addition to contextual events, another solution exists to refresh a parent view component from an ADF region for task flows that share the data control instance with their parent view. The solution is based on a `MethodExpression` in the ADF region that invokes a method in a managed bean of the parent view to execute the partial refresh. A suitable use case is a parent view that displays a list of departments in a table. The ADF region in this view contains a bounded task flow with an input form to edit the selected table row. After editing the selected row, upon submit, the table list is updated with the changes. One of the advantages of exposing the detail edit form in an ADF region is security. Using ADF Security, which we introduce in Chapter 21, ADF regions can be declaratively secured so that only authorized users are able to edit the table data.

By design, bounded task flows that are exposed in an ADF region should not have dependencies to the parent view in which they reside, other than the sharing of data controls. Instead, all information required by the task flow should be provided through input parameters on the task flow and the task flow binding created by the ADF region.

To implement the proposed solution, you create an Expression Language reference from the ADF Faces component `binding` property in the parent view to a public managed bean method. In the use case example of a departments table, the component to refresh is an ADF Faces table and the managed bean binding creates a pair of setter and getter methods for the `RichTable` instance:

```
<af:table value="#{bindings.DepartmentsView1.collectionModel}" var="row"
          rows="#{bindings.DepartmentsView1.rangeSize}"
          ...
          rowSelection="single" id="t1"
          binding="#{DepartmentsBean.departmentstable}">
```

In the same managed bean that holds the table reference, you create a public method that partially refreshes the table instance when called. The managed bean needs to be configured in `requestScope` and contain methods similar to the example shown next:

```
public class DepartmentsBean {
  private RichTable departmentstable;
  public DepartmentsBean() {}
  public void setDepartmentstable(RichTable departmentstable) {
    this.departmentstable = departmentstable;
  }
  public RichTable getDepartmentstable() {
    return departmentstable;
  }
  public void pprDepartmentsTable(){
    AdfFacesContext adfFacesContext = null;
    adfFacesContext = AdfFacesContext.getCurrentInstance();
    adfFacesContext.addPartialTarget(departmentstable);
  }
}
```

On the bounded task flow that is exposed by the ADF region, you create an input parameter, such as `refreshExpression`, to pass in the Expression Language string of the managed bean method that refreshes the component. The input string needs to be stored in the task flow `pageFlowScope` for later use, as shown here:

```
<input-parameter-definition>
  <name>refreshExpression</name>
  <value>
    #{pageFlowScope.refreshExpression}
  </value>
</input-parameter-definition>
```

To pass the Expression Language string from the parent view to the ADF region, which then passes it on to the task flow, you create an input parameter on the task flow binding in the parent view's page definition file as explained earlier in this chapter. The task flow binding metadata should look similar to this:

```
<taskFlow id="edittaskflowdefinition1" taskFlowId="…"
          xmlns="http://xmlns.oracle.com/adf/controller/binding">
  <parameters>
    <parameter id="refreshExpression"
               value="#{'#{DepartmentsBean.pprDepartmentsTable}'}"
               xmlns="http://xmlns.oracle.com/adfm/uimodel"/>
  </parameters>
</taskFlow>
```

Note the `value` attribute of the `parameter` element. The value is provided as an Expression Language expression that passes a fixed string. The string is passed to the input parameter of the bounded task flow where it becomes available in a `pageFlowScope` attribute. To refresh the table from the submit button on the edit form, you create and reference the following method from the command button `action` attribute:

```
public String submit_action() {
  AdfFacesContext adfFacesContext = AdfFacesContext.getCurrentInstance();
  //read EL string from Task Flow page flow scope
  Map pageFlowScope = adfFacesContext.getPageFlowScope();
  String expression = (String) pageFlowScope.get("refreshExpression");
  if (expression!=null){
    //call the helper method explained at the beginning of this
    //chapter
    invokeMethodExpression(expression);
  }
  return null;
}
```

NOTE
This solution allows you to send a PPR refresh notification only for the component to refresh. Because the accessible binding container is for the page fragment in the ADF region, you cannot perform actions on the parent view container, such as re-executing an ADF iterator.

Refreshing the Parent Component from a RegionNavigationListener   If the refresh should be performed in response to navigation in the ADF region, you use a managed bean method bound to the `RegionNavigationListener` property of the `af:region` component:

```
<af:region value="#{bindings.edittaskflowdefinition1.regionModel}"  id="r1"
regionNavigationListener="#{DepartmentsBean.onRegionNavigation}"/>
```

This not only allows you to partially refresh the parent view table component, but also to re-execute the ADF iterator of the table if needed. Re-executing the iterator is needed if the bounded task flow in the ADF region and the parent view don't share the same data control instance. For example, to re-execute the iterator binding used by a table component from a managed bean, you use code similar to this:

```
//JSF component reference from the af:table "bindings" property
Private RichTable departmentstable = null;
...
//Method that is referenced from the RegionNavigationListener property
//of the af:region component
public void onRegionNavigation(
    RegionNavigationEvent regionNavigationEvent) {
  //optionally check the new viewId value of the view
  //displayed in the ADF Region before calling refresh
  //on the table iterator
  executeDepartmentsTableIterator();
}
//Method that when called adds the table component to the ADF Faces
//list of partial targets to refresh
private void pprDepartmentsTable(){
  AdfFacesContext adfFacesContext = null;
  adfFacesContext = AdfFacesContext.getCurrentInstance();
  adfFacesContext.addPartialTarget(departmentstable);
}
//Method that accesses the ADF iterator binding of a table to re-query
//the iterator
private void executeDepartmentsTableIterator(){
  BindingContext bctx = BindingContext.getCurrent();
  BindingContainer bindings = bctx.getCurrentBindingsEntry();
  DCIteratorBinding dciter = null;
  dciter = (DCIteratorBinding)bindings.get("DepartmentsView1Iter");
  //memorize the current row key
  Key currentRowKey = dciter.getCurrentRow().getKey();
  dciter.executeQuery();
  //restore the current row to where it was before executing the
  //query
  dciter.setCurrentRowWithKey(currentRowKey.toStringFormat(true));
  //ppr refresh table component
  pprDepartmentsTable();
 }
```

ADF Regions in Lightweight Dialogs

We've saved the best for last! Displaying ADF regions in lightweight pop-up dialogs is a common use case in Oracle Fusion application development.

As shown in Figure 6-10, the ADF Faces parent view contains a table component that displays a list of employees. To edit an employee record, the user clicks the edit icon in the last table column or clicks the New Employee button to create a new employee row. In response to the user action, a lightweight pop-up dialog is displayed that shows the edit form in an ADF region.

The illustration on the right shows the outline view of the architecture of this use case.

With the opening of the pop-up dialog, the task flow binding setting in Page Definition 1 is changed from an empty task flow reference to referencing the task flow showing the edit view. For this, the ADF region in the pop-up dialog is added as a dynamic region.

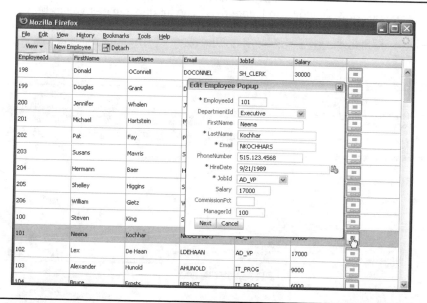

FIGURE 6-10 *ADF region opened in a lightweight dialog to edit the selected employee data row*

NOTE
The empty task flow reference is needed to re-execute the task flow when the pop-up is opened.

The state of the input form, to show existing data or an empty form, is determined by an input parameter that is defined on the bounded task flow and ADF region task flow binding. The task flow starts with a router activity that reads the input parameter and invokes a method activity either to query the employee record for edit or create a new one. The user is then presented with an edit form. When the user finishes working in the edit form, he or she exits the dialog by clicking the submit or cancel button. Both actions navigate the control flow to a return activity that either rolls back or commits the changes. Using return activities in ADF regions is not a common practice, but it is needed in the dialog use case to indicate the end of the form edit. In response to processing the return activity, the pop-up dialog is hidden and the ADF region task flow binding is reset to point to an empty task flow. In the last step, the table is refreshed to show the changed values.

Creating the Task Flow and the ADF Region

The ADF region for this use case references a bounded task flow that has two input parameters defined. The first input parameter, `keyValue`, is an optional parameter and, if provided, contains the row key of the table row to edit. The second input parameter, `type`, is mandatory and indicates whether the requested operation is a row `'edit'` or `'create'`. After dragging the task flow definition from the JDeveloper Application Navigator to the parent view, you choose the Dynamic Region entry from the context menu. This allows you to define the two input parameters required by the task flow. The input parameters are created for the task flow binding entry in the page definition file of the parent view, as shown in Figure 6-11. The input parameter values become accessible in the `pageFlowScope` of the task flow. For simplicity, in this example, the names of the input parameters are also chosen as the names of the `pageFlowScope` attributes.

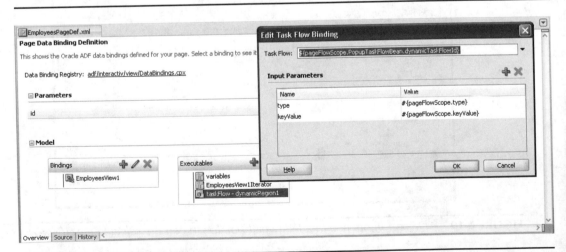

FIGURE 6-11   *Task flow binding parameters accessed from the visual binding editor in Oracle JDeveloper*

Figure 6-12 shows the Property Inspector for the bounded task flow definition with the defined input parameters and the settings for data control instance sharing and transaction settings. Note that it is also possible to not share the data control instance between the parent view and the task flow. In this case, upon exiting the task flow, the table in the parent view needs to be refreshed and the query re-executed.

To create the task flow content, you create a page fragment for the edit form and drag the `Create` and `SetCurrentRowWithKeyValue` operations from the data control palette of the Employees view object to the task flow diagrammer. The `SetCurrentRowWithKeyValue` argument value is set to `#{pageFlowScope.keyValue}`. The default activity of the task flow is a router element that you drag from the component palette. The router has the following decision cases defined that navigate the request to the `Create` or `SetCurrentRowWithKeyValue` activity and then to the view that displays the Employees view object in an editable form:

```
<router id="createOrEdit">
  <case>
    <expression>#{pageFlowScope.type=='edit'}</expression>
    <outcome>edit</outcome>
  </case>
  <case>
    <expression>#{pageFlowScope.type=='create'}</expression>
    <outcome>create</outcome>
  </case>
  <default-outcome>edit</default-outcome>
</router>
```

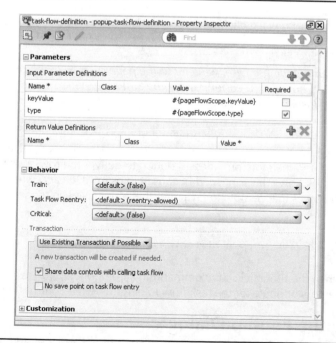

FIGURE 6-12 *Input parameters defined on the bounded task flow that is referenced from the ADF region*

Add two return activities and choose Behavior | End Transaction to set their properties to `rollback` and `commit` using the Property Inspector.

Creating the Pop-up Launcher in the Table

The ADF Faces table is created as a read-only table in a drag-and-drop operation of the Employees view object to the parent view. An extra column is added for the image link that launches the dialog using the `af:showPopupBehavior` component.

```
<af:column id="c12">
   <af:commandImageLink id="cil1" icon="/dialog.gif"
                         partialSubmit="true">
   <af:showPopupBehavior popupId-":::popup1" triggerType="action"
     align="endAfter" alignId="cil1"/>
     <af:clientAttribute name="rowKeyValue" value="#{row.EmployeeId}"/>
     <af:setPropertyListener from="#{'edit'}"
                             to="#{pageFlowScope.type}"
                             type="action"/>
   </af:commandImageLink>
</af:column>
```

The `af:showPopupBehavior` component launches the `af:popup` component identified by the `popupId` attribute value. The leading colons in the ID name indicate the search path that ADF Faces uses to find the pop-up component. While it is possible to type the `popupId` attribute value manually into the metadata, we recommend using the Property Inspector. Select the `af:showPopupBehavior` component in the Structure Window and use the Property Inspector's Edit option in the context menu of the `PopupId` property to look up the pop-up component. To avoid a full table refresh when clicking in the image link, set its `partialSubmit` attribute to `true`.

> **NOTE**
> *While explaining the use case, we refer to the page sources for clarity. Development, however, is easier if using the Structure Window and the Property Inspector for editing.*

The `af:clientAttribute` component adds a custom attribute, `rowKeyValue`, to the command image link. The `af:commandImageLink` instance becomes accessible in the launched dialog and therefore provides an option to deliver the row-specific data information needed by the task flow. This is needed because tables in ADF Faces are built so that row information becomes inaccessible to Java after the table has been rendered.

> **NOTE**
> *The ADF Faces table component is covered in Chapter 9.*

Finally, when the user clicks the command link component, the `'edit'` string reference is stored in a memory attribute for the task flow to determine the control flow path.

Creating the Pop-up Dialog

The pop-up dialog is built using the `af:popup` component and a nested instance of the `af:panelWindow` component.

NOTE
Chapter 10 explains the development and use of dialogs in ADF Faces RC; we won't cover this in more detail here, other than to describe what the pop-up code does in the context of this example.

```
<af:popup id="popup1" contentDelivery="lazyUncached"
  launcherVar="source"
  eventContext="launcher" clientComponent="true"
  popupCanceledListener=
    "#{pageFlowScope.PopupTaskFlowBean.onCancelPopup}">
  <af:panelWindow id="pw1" modal="false" title="Edit Employee Popup">
   <af:region value="#{bindings.dynamicRegion1.regionModel}" id="r1"
    regionNavigationListener=
     "#{pageFlowScope.PopupTaskFlowBean.onRegionNavigation}"/>
  </af:panelWindow>
  <af:setPropertyListener
      from="#{pageFlowScope.PopupTaskFlowBean.popupTaskFlowId}"
      to="#{pageFlowScope.PopupTaskFlowBean.dynamicTaskFlowId}"
      type="popupFetch"/>
  <af:setPropertyListener from="#{source.attributes.rowKeyValue}"
                          to="#{pageFlowScope.keyValue}"
                          type="popupFetch"/>
</af:popup>
```

The following sections explain the components contained in the pop-up dialog and their provided functionality in the context of the ADF region dialog use case.

af:popup

The af:popup component lazily loads its content without caching to ensure that each launch of the pop-up shows new content. The launcher attribute value source allows access of the UI component instance that launched the dialog, which in our example is the image link with the custom rowKey attribute defined.

The clientComponent attribute is set to true to make the pop-up accessible from JavaScript on the client, which is needed to close the pop-up in response to the return activity exiting the task flow. The popupCanceledListener attribute references a managed bean method that handles the case in which the user closes the dialog with the close icon of the panelWindow.

af:region

The af:region component displays the pop-up dialog content. It references the task flow binding in the view page definition file:

```
<taskFlow id="dynamicRegion1"
    taskFlowId="${pageFlowScope.PopupTaskFlowBean.dynamicTaskFlowId}"
    xmlns=http://xmlns.oracle.com/adf/controller/binding
    Refresh="ifNeeded">
  <parameters>
    <parameter id="type" value="#{pageFlowScope.type}"
      xmlns="http://xmlns.oracle.com/adfm/uimodel"/>
    <parameter id="keyValue" value="#{pageFlowScope.keyValue}"
      xmlns="http://xmlns.oracle.com/adfm/uimodel"/>
  </parameters>
</taskFlow>
```

The task flow binding references a managed bean in `pageFlowScope` to return the task flow ID of the task flow definition to display. When the pop-up is hidden, the task flow binding references an empty string.

NOTE
The managed bean is set to `pageFlowScope` *so the ADF region task flow reference is not set back to the empty task flow after the initial request.*

NOTE
The task flow is refreshed if needed for any change on the input parameters. Since either the `type` *input parameter or the* `rowKey` *parameter always changes, this is a reliable option to use.*

The `regionNavigationListener` that is defined on the `af:region` component notifies a managed bean method about the user navigation in the ADF region. The managed bean method evaluates the current view ID for each navigation event. If the `viewId` is received as `null`, a return activity has been processed and the pop-up dialog needs to close, which is also handled by the `regionNavigationListener` method.

af:setPropertyListener

The pop-up dialog uses two instances of `af:setPropertyListener`. The first listener changes the task flow reference from an empty task flow to the task flow that has the edit view in it. The second listener reads the custom `rowKey` attribute value from the launching component, the image command link, to write it to a `pageFlowScope` attribute from where it is accessible for the ADF region and task flow binding input parameters.

Managed Beans

With the page source and task flow set up, we now look at the two managed beans that are used within the example:

- **EmployeesBacking** A backing bean that is referenced from the ADF Faces table component `binding` attribute. In addition to hosting the setter and getter methods for the table instance, the bean also exposes a method that we use to partially refresh the table in response to the close of the pop-up.

- **PopupTaskFlow** A managed bean in `pageFlowScope` that returns the `TaskFlowId` reference to the task flow binding. It also contains other methods used in this example.

Backing Bean That Referenced and Refreshes the Table Instance

The backing bean contains two methods that are referenced from the `RegionNavigationListener` method to refresh the employees table. The first method refreshes only the ADF Faces table using a partial refresh. This method is sufficient to use when the task flow shares the data control scope with the parent view.

```
public void pprEmployeeTable(){
    AdfFacesContext adfFacesContext = AdfFacesContext.getCurrentInstance();
    adfFacesContext.addPartialTarget(employeesTable);
}
```

The second method also performs a partial refresh of the table, but it also queries the ADF iterator binding that is referenced from the table model. This method is needed to show data changes if the task flow does not share the data control scope with the parent view.

```
public void pprEmployeeTableWithDBRefresh(){
   //get iterator binding from table definition and execute the query
   CollectionModel collectionModel = (CollectionModel)employeesTable.getValue();
   JUCtrlHierBinding tableBinding = (JUCtrlHierBinding) collectionModel
.getWrappedData();
   DCIteratorBinding dciter = null;
   dciter = tableBinding.getDCIteratorBinding();
   //memorize the current table row
   Key currentRowKey = dciter.getCurrentRow().getKey();
   dciter.executeQuery();
   //set the current table row back to where it was
   dciter.setCurrentRowWithKey(currentRowKey.toStringFormat(true));
   //ppr table view
   pprEmployeeTable();
}
```

Managed Bean Methods Used Within the Pop-up Use Case

The `PopupTaskFlow` managed bean is defined in the task flow definition that contains the parent view. In our example, the parent view is in an unbounded task flow so the managed bean is configured in the adfc-config.xml file. A part of the managed bean code is generated when you create the dynamic ADF region.

Methods to Set the Task Flow ID to Display in the ADF Region   The following methods are referenced from the task flow binding and from the `af:setPropertyListener` in the view to read and set the task flow ID:

```
private String popupTaskFlowId =
      "/WEB-INF/popup-task-flow-definition.xml#popup-task-flow-definition";
private String emptyTaskFlowId = "";
private String taskFlowId = null;
//constructor
public PopupTaskFlowBean() { }

//Method referenced from the Task Flow binding "taskFlowId" property
public String getDynamicTaskFlowId() {
  if(taskFlowId != null && taskFlowId.length()>0){
    return taskFlowId;
  }
  else{
    return emptyTaskFlowId;
  }
}
//Method called by the setPropertyListener when the popup is launched to
//set the Task Flow id to the non-empty Task Flow definition.
public void setDynamicTaskFlowId(String newTaskFlowId){
  taskFlowId = newTaskFlowId;
}
```

```
//Called by the setPropertyListener that sets the Task Flow reference
//to the non-empty Task Flow
public String getPopupTaskFlowId(){
  return popupTaskFlowId;
}
```

Method Called When the User Navigates in the ADF Region   The region listener is called whenever the view ID changes in the ADF region due to a control flow. If the current `viewId` changes to `null`, the user exited the task flow performing a commit or rollback defined by the return activity elements. In this case, the region listener method attempts to get a handle to the `af:popup` component instance to close the dialog:

```
public void onRegionNavigation(
        RegionNavigationEvent regionNavigationEvent) {
  String viewId = regionNavigationEvent.getNewViewId();
  //viewId is null if the popup is exited by a return activity
  if(viewId == null){
    //get the ADF Region instance
    RichRegion region = (RichRegion) regionNavigationEvent.getSource();
    //indicate popup found
    boolean popupFound = false;
    //component to hold popup instance if exists
    UIComponent component = region.getParent();
    //search for popup component to close
    while (!popupFound && component != null){
      if(component instanceof RichPopup){
        popupFound = true;
        break;
      }
    component = component.getParent();
    }
    if (popupFound){
      //close popup using JavaScript sent from the server to the client
      closePopup(component);
      //set the Task Flow reference to empty Task Flow id
      this.setDynamicTaskFlowId(this.emptyTaskFlowId);
    }
  }
}
```

Through its Apache Trinidad base component set, ADF Faces RC provides a Java API to send JavaScript calls from the server to the client. The following method uses the Trinidad `ExtendedRenderKitService` and `Service` class to add JavaScript to the JSF response:

```
private void closePopup(UIComponent component) {
    FacesContext fctx = FacesContext.getCurrentInstance();
    //access RenderKit service in Trinidad util package to issue JavaScript
    //close command for popup
    ExtendedRenderKitService service =
        Service.getRenderKitService(fctx,ExtendedRenderKitService.class);
    //build JavaScript
    StringBuffer strbuffer = new StringBuffer();
    strbuffer.append("popup=AdfPage.PAGE.findComponent('");
```

```
//add popup client ID for JavaScript access
strbuffer.append(component.getClientId(fctx));
strbuffer.append("');popup.hide();");
//execute client side script
service.addScript(fctx,strbuffer.toString());
//Refresh the table to show the changed values. In production
//use input parameters to pass the EL string
invokeMethodExpression(
    "#{EmployeesBacking.pprEmployeeTable}");
}
```

NOTE
Don't worry about the AdfPage.PAGE *reference in the JavaScript example. This is explained in Chapter 19 when we discuss the use of JavaScript in ADF Faces.*

Method Called When Closing the Pop-up with the Close Icon   The following method is referenced from the popupCanceledListener attribute of the af:popup component. It is called when the user cancels the pop-up by clicking the close icon and sets the task flow ID reference to the empty task flow:

```
//Method called when user closes the popup window
public void onCancelPopup(PopupCanceledEvent popupCanceledEvent) {
    this.setDynamicTaskFlowId(emptyTaskFlowId);
}
```

Use Case Summary
The following actions are required to build the ADF region dialog use case:

- You need to defer the execution of the bounded task flow so the input parameters are read when the dialog is launched and not earlier. In addition, the task flow must be executed for each launch of the pop-up dialog. This is best achieved through an empty task flow reference.

- The table row key needs to be available when the dialog is launched. A client attribute is used to persist this information on the dialog launcher component.

- The dialog is closed on the client side by a JavaScript call from the server in response to the ADF region navigation listener recognizing the end of the user edit in the dialog. For this, the bounded task flow must be exited by a return activity.

- The table needs to be refreshed to show the value changes. This is achieved in a call to the AdfFacesContext.

Summary
ADF bounded task flows that execute in ADF regions are key enablers of enterprise Web 2.0 development with the Oracle Fusion development platform. Bounded task flows let you build desktop-like web user interfaces that unveil the real power of Asynchronous JavaScript and XML (AJAX) without exposing developers to the complexity of AJAX programming. Compared to task

flows that are called from a task flow call activity, the communication from the ADF region to its parent view requires contextual events or a shared data control instance.

Dynamic ADF regions are good to use when the task flow that is executed in a specific area of a view needs to change based on the application context. In this chapter, we showed you examples in which the ADF region displays different views for the Locations table, an example that showed dependent department information, and an example that showed the dependent employees. Static regions have a fixed task flow reference, which executes when the page loads. Use cases that need to defer task flow execution should use dynamic regions with an empty task flow reference.

The contextual event framework is the best way to establish bidirectional communication between the parent view and its contained ADF regions, as well as communication between ADF regions that reside on the same view. Be aware that events don't stop their propagation when a consumer is found.

When working with ADF regions, ensure that the task flows are not tightly bound to any knowledge about the context in which they execute and instead use input parameters to pass in information.

Accessing the ADF binding container from an ADF region using the `#{bindings}` Expression Language reference always accesses the binding of the current view in the region, not the binding container of the parent view.

CHAPTER
7

Page Navigation
in Oracle ADF

At its core, application navigation must be easy for the developer to maintain, functionally appropriate for the task at hand, and easy for the user to understand.

he first implementation of the Model-View-Controller (MVC) design pattern in web applications occurred with the Struts framework. This framework allowed the navigation from page to page to be configured in metadata for an application, rather than defining page navigation within pages themselves. Before MVC, web pages defined navigation in the `action` tag of a form component—here's an example:

```
<form action="page2.html">
```

This type of navigation discouraged reuse, because the navigation is hard coded. The Struts framework changed that by defining navigation rules in the struts-config.xml file so that pages refer to a navigation activity (called a *forward*). Pages can conditionally call forward activities so that dynamic navigation is possible, and the navigation from page to page can be modified without your needing to modify existing pages. JavaServer Faces (JSF) applications extend this MVC pattern, using faces-config.xml as the metadata file for the application. (Navigation activities are called navigation *cases* in JSF applications.) However, as discussed in Chapter 4, the ADF Controller framework provides additional capabilities such as task flows. Task flow definitions and the adfc-config.xml are used to configure the application and also define navigation logic, using the same principles that originated in the Struts framework.

Navigation Components

The primary means of defining navigation in ADF applications is via the adfc-config.xml. JDeveloper provides a visual diagram for creating these navigation rules, called *control flow cases*, as shown in Figure 7-1. The figure shows several cases: register, success, go, and a global control flow case named help.

The simplest form of navigating involves the use of a command item, such as a button, that calls the control flow case by a defined name. For example, the following JSPX contains two command components that call the success and help control flow cases, respectively:

```
<af:form>
  <af:commandButton text="Login" action="success"/>
  <af:commandLink text="Go to Help" action="help"/>
</af:form>
```

Command Items

As shown, command buttons (`af:commandButton`) and links (`af:commandLink`) provide the simplest form of navigation. In the example, the `action` attribute refers directly to the name of the navigation case. Alternatively, a method can be used to add logic upon navigation, as is commonly needed when additional validation or business logic should be called when a submit button is clicked. For example, the `action` attribute for a button can point to a backing bean method that returns a string:

```
<af:commandButton text="Login" action="#{NavBean.cb1_action}"/>
```

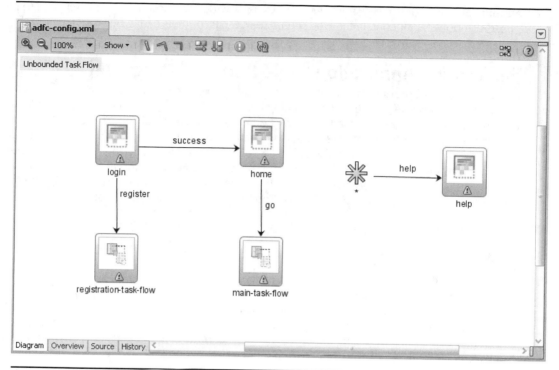

FIGURE 7-1   *Configure navigation in the adfc-config.xml*

The action method is defined as follows, where additional application logic can be added as necessary:

```
public String cb1_action() {
  //call some logic here
  return "success";
}
```

Finally, the action method can also provide conditional navigation, as shown next:

```
public String cb1_action() {
  //call some logic here
  if (someCondition){
    return "success";
  } else {
    return "register";
  }
}
```

While the various ADF Faces components that perform navigation differ in their appearance at runtime, the discussed concepts hold true for each type of navigation component. Therefore, in addition to af:commandButton and af:commandLink components, af:commandImageLink and af:commandNavigationItem components also provide a means to specify an action attribute and use control flow rules defined in task flow definitions to navigate from page to page. These components all contain the word *command* as part of their name, because they fire the `javax.faces.event.ActionEvent` event.

Performing Application Logic Prior to Navigation

An additional attribute is common across command components—the `actionListener` attribute. This attribute can be set to a backing bean method that returns `void` (and therefore does not perform navigation based on a string outcome). The method can be used in conjunction with the `action` attribute, so that the backing bean method that the `actionListener` points to performs application logic, and then the `action` command is called. In addition to accessing backing bean logic, defining both `action` and `actionListener` attributes for a command component is commonly used in ADF applications. For example, a button in a form might perform an ADF commit action and then navigate to another page, as shown in the following code:

```
<af:commandButton actionListener="#{bindings.Commit.execute}"
    text="Commit" action="go"/>
```

Go Navigation Components

The `af:goLink`, `af:goImageLink`, and `af:goButton` components are navigation components, but they navigate without delivering the `javax.faces.event.ActionEvent` event and so are best suited for navigation outside of an application. The navigation for these components is defined by setting the `destination` attribute. Additionally, these components can specify the `targetFrame` attribute to open the destination URL in a new, parent, self, or top window in relation to the launching page.

Building Bread Crumbs

The `af:breadCrumbs` component provides a container for navigation components that are listed with greater than symbols (>) between each component. The `af:commandLink` and `af:commandNavigationItem` components are best suited for the child components of `af:breadCrumbs`, because they are visually easier to read and follow common web application standards. These standards also dictate that the list of bread crumbs for a page include each of the previous pages visited (whether they are part of a train or simply part of a logical series of views). The last `af:commandNavigationItem` for a particular view is typically defined with the `selected` attribute set to `true` and the `disabled` attribute set to `true`. This enables the user to identify which views have been visited as well as where the current page resides in the chain.

The actionListener Attribute as a Means of Navigation

While it is possible to define a backing bean method that performs navigation and binds the method to the `actionListener` attribute, this is not best practice. Instead, application logic should be placed in the backing bean method to which the `actionListener` is bound. Following successful execution of that method, the ADF Faces lifecycle will call the method or control flow case specified by the `action` attribute. If the method bound to the `actionListener` fails, developers can change the action outcome to suppress navigation so that the user has the opportunity to correct the issue.

The `af:breadCrumbs` component can be used with the XMLMenuModel to display the previously visited views dynamically for a hierarchical navigation model. This is covered later in the chapter.

Menu Components

Menu components are useful for creating groups of common commands. They typically consist of three components: an outer container for the menu (`af:menuBar`), an optional vertical menu component for grouping purposes (`af:menu`), and the individual menu components (`af:commandMenuItem`) for performing actions.

Building Consistent Page Menus with Templates   Menus are excellent candidates for inclusion in a template, because they are typically standard across an application's pages. The `action` attribute for a menu item in a template is defined just as if it were included in the page directly. For navigational menu items, this means that the control flow cases for each menu item need to be defined for each page that will use the template. For example, consider the case where the following navigational menu item is defined in a page template:

```
<af:commandMenuItem text="Home" action="home"/>
```

In this example, each page that uses the template will need to contain a control flow case for `home`; otherwise, clicking the menu item will silently fail and no navigation will be performed. This leads to the use of global control flow cases. As shown in Figure 7-1, any view in the unbounded task flow can access the help control flow case, and it is common practice to have multiple global control flow cases defined for an application. However, the main-task-flow.xml definition doesn't have the help or home control flow case defined. Therefore, if a view within the main-task-flow uses a template that contains navigational items for the help and home control flow cases, clicking those action components from within a main-task-flow view would silently fail and no navigation would be performed.

Navigation in Fusion Web Applications

The `af:navigationPane` component is useful for creating multiple levels of navigation, unless they can be more easily represented by an XMLMenuModel, covered in the next section. The `af:navigationPane` component contains a `hint` attribute that is used to specify the style of component that is rendered for the nested `af:commandNavigationItem` components. These can be tabs, bars, buttons, lists, or choice components. For example, the following JSPX in the highest level of a hierarchy might have the following navigation pane:

```
<af:navigationPane hint="tabs">
  <af:commandNavigationItem text="View A" action="gotoViewA"
    selected="true"/>
  <af:commandNavigationItem text="View B" action="gotoViewB"/>
</af:navigationPane>
```

The `af:commandNavigationItem` is a generic component that can be rendered in various ways depending on the `hint` attribute value of the surrounding `af:navigationPane` component. As previously stated, this can be exploited to show various levels of navigation. For example, if the View A page should contain navigation to additional views View A1 and View A2, then the

FIGURE 7-2   *Multi-level navigation components at runtime*

`af:navigationPane` components for that page can be defined as shown next. Figure 7-2 shows the page at runtime.

```
<af:panelGroupLayout>
  <af:navigationPane hint="tabs">
    <af:commandNavigationItem text="View A" action="gotoViewA"
      selected="true"/>
    <af:commandNavigationItem text="View B" action="gotoViewB"/>
  </af:navigationPane>
  <af:navigationPane hint="bar">
    <af:commandNavigationItem text="View A1" action="gotoViewA1"/>
    <af:commandNavigationItem text="View A2" action="gotoViewA2"/>
  </af:navigationPane>
</af:panelGroupLayout>
```

> **NOTE**
> *The* `af:commandNavigationItem` *component can be used without the surrounding* `af:navigationPane`. *In this case, the component renders as a link object where the text is underlined to highlight to the user that this is a navigation component. The only valid child components of the* `af:navigationPane` *are the* `af:separator` *and* `af:commandNavigationItem` *components.*

The methodology discussed here relies upon global control flow rules defined for each view. For example, the following control flow rules are defined in the unbounded task flow for the preceding navigation:

```
<control-flow-rule>
  <from-activity-id>*</from-activity-id>
  <control-flow-case>
    <from-outcome>gotoViewA</from-outcome>
    <to-activity-id>viewA</to-activity-id>
  </control-flow-case>
  <control-flow-case>
    <from-outcome>gotoViewA1</from-outcome>
    <to-activity-id>viewA1</to-activity-id>
  </control-flow-case>
  <control-flow-case>
    <from-outcome>gotoViewA2</from-outcome>
    <to-activity-id>viewA2</to-activity-id>
  </control-flow-case>
  <control-flow-case>
    <from-outcome>gotoViewB</from-outcome>
```

```
    <to-activity-id>viewB</to-activity-id>
  </control-flow-case>
</control-flow-rule>
```

Obviously, this method of defining navigation can become difficult to maintain, and some of the readability of the task flow diagram is lost when only global control flows are used. One way to increase maintainability of the views themselves is to include the `af:navigationPane` components for each level of navigation in page fragments or templates, so that both the content and location of the navigation components remains consistent across pages. Another way to increase maintainability, as well as reuse, is to create an XMLMenuModel, discussed in the following section. Defining how a user navigates in an application is a functional, procedural, and design-based decision. At its core, application navigation must be easy for developer to maintain, functionally appropriate for the task at hand, and easy for the user to understand. Thus, a combination of the navigation methodologies discussed in this chapter is typically required for Fusion applications.

Creating Reusable Menus

An XMLMenuModel is a unique feature that provides a declarative, reusable way to create navigation components for complex navigation hierarchies. The menu model is defined in metadata and automatically keeps track of the current view in the menu model. By doing so, navigation components can be created once for multiple views in a hierarchy and dynamically modified at runtime to display appropriately (`selected` and/or `rendered` attribute) for the particular view that is current. This is especially helpful for large applications with complex navigation hierarchies. For example, consider an application that contains two or three parent functions at the first level of the hierarchy. Each of these functional categories is represented by a view in an unbounded task flow (or a starting view in a bounded task flow), which allows the user to navigate to the subsequent views within each task flow. To provide navigation for this scenario, each parent view would need to include navigation controls to each of its subsequent (child) views, and those controls would be manually defined such that the page developer must know where the page is located within a hierarchy and which child pages are navigable from the parent page. If subsequent views defined yet another level in the hierarchy, defining navigation would become especially difficult to maintain without the use of metadata. The XMLMenuModel allows for each of these parent-to-child navigation rules to be defined in metadata, and page developers add reusable navigation controls to the page that refer to the menu model, rather than manually creating navigation controls for each rule. Therefore, the XMLMenuModel should be used in Fusion applications to define navigation in a way that is easy to maintain.

To build an XMLMenuModel, you must define global control flow cases for each view in an unbounded task flow, as discussed in the preceding section. Right-click inside the diagram and choose Create ADF Menu. In the resulting dialog, provide a name for the metadata file (root_menu by default). JDeveloper will create XML elements called item nodes in the root_menu.xml file for each of the global control flow cases, but the hierarchy of these cannot be determined by the integrated development environment (IDE), so they must be nested appropriately. To nest item nodes, use the structure window to relocate child item nodes within their appropriate parent node. Figure 7-3 shows the result of rearranging nodes for a hierarchical navigation scenario.

If the global control flow cases are defined properly before creating the ADF Menu, no further configuration is required in the generated XML file. However, to add item nodes, specify the `action` and `focusViewId` attributes of the item node to the control flow case name and the view to which the item belongs, respectively.

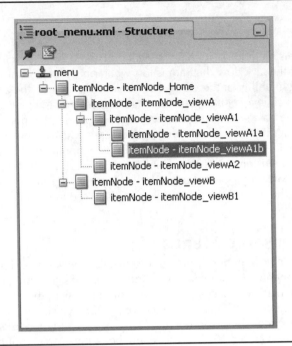

FIGURE 7-3 *Hierarchical item nodes in an XMLMenuModel*

TIP
For internationalizable applications, define a resource bundle in the menu model XML file for the labels of each item node.

Configuring the XMLMenuModel Managed Bean

In addition to the XML file, JDeveloper generates a managed bean reference in the unbounded task flow definition that points to the managed bean that provides the XMLMenuModel functionality. The managed bean reference is defined using a managed attribute that is set to the same name of the XML file by default. Additionally, the managed bean defines the `createHiddenNodes` attribute, which should be set to `true` (the default value) so that all nodes will be created for the model, even if they are not visible for a particular view. The XML code for an unbounded task flow definition containing a menu model reference is shown here:

```
<?xml version="1.0" encoding="windows-1252" ?>
<adfc-config xmlns="http://xmlns.oracle.com/adf/controller" version="1.2">
  <view id="viewA">
    <page>/viewA.jspx</page>
  </view>
<!--Other defined views -->
  <control-flow-rule>
    <from-activity-id>*</from-activity-id>
      <control-flow-case>
        <from-outcome>gotoViewA</from-outcome>
        <to-activity-id>viewA</to-activity-id>
      </control-flow-case>
```

```
      </control-flow-rule>
  <!--Other defined global control flow cases -->
    <managed-bean>
      <description>Menu Model Managed Bean</description>
      <managed-bean-name>root_menu</managed-bean-name>
      <managed-bean-class>oracle.adf.view.rich.model.MDSMenuModel
        </managed-bean-class>
      <managed-bean-scope>request</managed-bean-scope>
      <managed-property>
        <property-name>createHiddenNodes</property-name>
        <value>false</value>
      </managed-property>
      <managed-property>
        <property-name>source</property-name>
        <property-class>java.lang.String</property-class>
        <value>/WEB-INF/root_menu.xml</value>
      </managed-property>
    </managed-bean>
</adfc-config>
```

TIP
*Use the groupNode element in the XMLMenuModel metadata file to
group related itemNode elements where the group node provides a
label for the grouping, but performs no navigation. Submenus are also
possible in the XMLMenuModel—a sharedNode element can also be
used in the metadata file to access another defined XMLMenuModel.*

Using XMLMenuModel Definitions in Views

To use a menu model in a hierarchical set of views, create an af:navigationPane in either a
view or a template as previously discussed, and set the value attribute to the managed-bean-
name value in the task flow definition. Specify a value for the var attribute so that the menu
model can be referenced by that value in nested components. In the following navigation pane
component, the value attribute is set to the default root_menu managed bean name, and the
var attribute is set to menuModel. Thus, navigation components within this component will refer
to the attributes of the menu model using expression language starting with #{menuModel}:

```
<af:navigationPane hint="tabs" value="#{root_menu}" var="menuModel"/>
```

To add navigation components to the pane, right-click the navigation pane component in the
structure window and choose Facets | Navigation Pane | Node Stamp to enable the tree node
stamp for the menu model. Within the node stamp, add a single af:commandNavigationItem
component and specify the text, action, visible, and rendered attributes using the var attribute
value created in the af:navigationPane component. Here's an example:

```
<af:navigationPane hint="tabs" value="#{root_menu}" var="menuModel">
  <f:facet name="nodeStamp">
    <af:commandNavigationItem text="#{menuModel.label}"
      action="#{menuModel.doAction}" visible="#{menuModel.visible}"
      rendered="#{menuModel.rendered}"/>
  </f:facet>
</af:navigationPane>
```

Continue adding `af:navigationPane` components and nested
`af:commandNavigationItem` components for each level of the hierarchy as necessary.
Set the `level` attribute to the node's level in the hierarchy, and use the `hint` attribute to
change the rendering style of the nested navigation items as desired. The following code
renders a three-level menu hierarchy of tabs, buttons, and list components:

```
<af:navigationPane hint="tabs" value="#{root_menu}" var="menuModel">
  <f:facet name="nodeStamp">
     <af:commandNavigationItem text="#{menuModel.label}"
        action="#{menuModel.doAction}" visible="#{menuModel.visible}"
        rendered="#{menuModel.rendered}"/>
  </f:facet>
</af:navigationPane>
<af:navigationPane hint="buttons" value="#{root_menu}" var="menuModel"
  level="1">
  <f:facet name="nodeStamp">
    <af:commandNavigationItem text="#{menuModel.label}"
       action="#{menuModel.doAction}" visible="#{menuModel.visible}"
       rendered="#{menuModel.rendered}"/>
  </f:facet>
</af:navigationPane>
<af:navigationPane hint="list" value="#{root_menu}" var="menuModel" level="2">
  <f:facet name="nodeStamp">
    <af:commandNavigationItem text="#{menuModel.label}"
       action="#{menuModel.doAction}" visible="#{menuModel.visible}"
       rendered="#{menuModel.rendered}"/>
  </f:facet>
</af:navigationPane>
```

This code can be copied to each view in the task flow. However, for maximum reuse, add the
components to a page fragment and include the fragment in each view.

At runtime, TreeModel and XMLMenuModel objects are created that determine the current
view and set the rendered and selected attributes of the command navigation items for the
`nodeStamp` appropriately. The view in the third level of the hierarchy, within the viewA
itemNode, appears at runtime, as shown in Figure 7-4. Default labels are used in the figure to
illustrate the various levels, but these would of course be modified in the metadata to provide
meaningful labels.

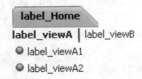

FIGURE 7-4   *Runtime view of command navigation items for a menu model*

Working with Train Components

The use of the term "train" in the ADF framework is not accidental. The rules that apply to actual trains also apply in the case of the train functionality in ADF applications. Trains have a defined series of stops, in a particular order, and each stop should be visited in sequence. Therefore, trains are a useful means to define that a task flow follows a predetermined series of steps (although ADF trains also have the ability to stop nonsequentially). ADF Faces contains components that are useful for working with train models defined for a task flow. The `af:train` component renders as a series of navigable stops, depicted as square icons, to show the user where they are in the process. This component allows for navigation to the previously visited train stops or the next unvisited train stop, but it doesn't allow for skipping over a train stop (except where explicitly defined). A train model defines the rules for train navigation and is used within each view of the train to determine that view's placement in the train process.

Additionally, the `af:trainButtonBar` component can be used to create Back and Next buttons that allow the user to navigate between views in a train. This component can be used in conjunction with an `af:train` component, but it is also helpful for navigating among stops in a train that are not statically defined. For example, if train stops may be skipped depending on application logic, using an `af:train` component that lists all train stops, even those that might be skipped, could be confusing. An `af:trainButtonBar` with only the Back and Next navigation defined will eliminate this confusion but still provide a declarative means of navigation.

Defining Trains

Trains are defined for bounded task flows because they have defined entry and exit points. You can create a train model for a series of views in a bounded task flow diagram by right-clicking in the diagram and choosing Train | Create Train. This action will create dotted lines in the diagram to indicate the order in which the views can be visited. JDeveloper automatically creates these lines and the train model according to the order that the views are defined in the XML for the task flow (typically the order in which the views are defined in the source). Alternatively, a train can be created by selecting the Create Train checkbox in the Create Task Flow dialog.

To add navigation to a train, add the `af:train` component to each view, and specify the Expression Language expression `#{controllerContext.currentViewPort`
`.taskFlowContext.trainModel}` as the `value` attribute. This creates a train stop indicator and navigation component that highlights the current train stop and provides navigation for the previous and next stops in the train model, as shown in Figure 7-5. In this example, the current view is the second stop in the process, the first and third stops in the train are navigable, and the last stop in the train is visible to show the user how many stops remain, but it is not enabled for navigation until the third stop has been visited.

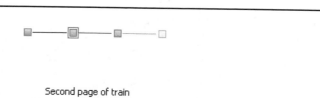

Second page of train

FIGURE 7-5   *The* `af:train` *component at runtime*

Opening Views in a Browser Dialog

The use of the `useWindow`, `windowHeight`, and `windowWidth` attributes allow command components to open new browser dialogs for a specific type of control flow case. To enable the use of this dialog feature, create a control flow case prepended with `dialog:`. For example, Figure 7-6 shows a control flow case named `dialog:go`.

When the `navtodialog` view calls the `dialog:go` action, the `dialogView` view will be opened in a separate browser window. The command component that calls the action is defined as follows:

```
<af:commandButton text="Launch Dialog" action="dialog:go" useWindow="true"
windowHeight="50" windowWidth="100"/>
```

This is different from the pop-up dialog defined in Chapter 10, where the `af:dialog` component is used to create a modal pop-up. In the case of the dialog framework, the `useWindow` and initial `windowHeight` and `windowWidth` are specified in the component that launches the dialog, which is not inline in the page but rather in a separate browser window, as shown in Figure 7-7.

Uncommitted Data Warning Support

When you're using the dialog framework, the launched page is modal, meaning that users should not be able to navigate away from the calling page. However, this cannot be explicitly enforced on the browser, so a warning dialog is displayed to the user if navigation away from the calling page is attempted. Figure 7-8 shows the result of attempting to navigate within the calling page without first closing the dialog.

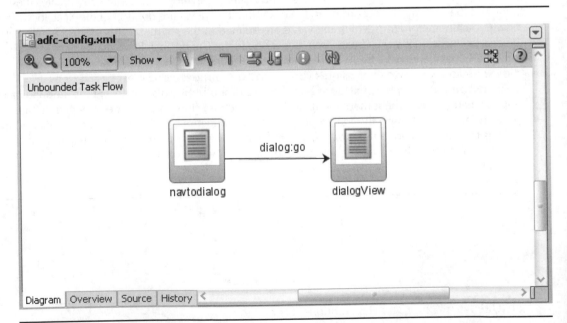

FIGURE 7-6 *Navigation definition for a dialog*

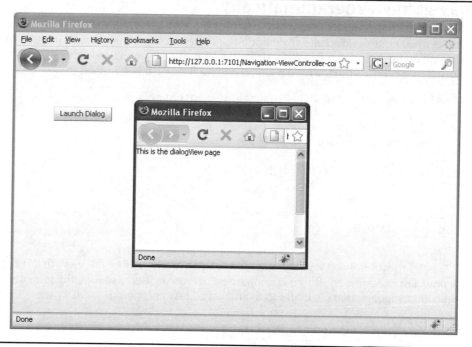

FIGURE 7-7 *View launched as a dialog at runtime*

The uncommitted data warning dialog appears when the user navigates away from a calling page, including navigating directly by typing into the URL. It also appears when navigating away from critical task flows, as discussed in Chapter 5. For example, if, after entering data on a page, the user attempts to navigate away from the page without submitting data to the server, the uncommitted data warning dialog will warn the user so that the correct action can be taken. The functionality is provided automatically in ADF applications that use critical task flows or the dialog framework. Additionally, an `af:document` can define the `UncommittedDataWarning` attribute. If this attribute is set to `true` (it is `false` by default), the behavior will be the same as if the view is part of a critical task flow or launched dialog.

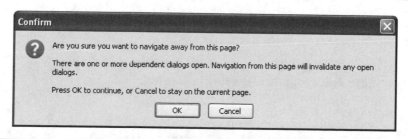

FIGURE 7-8 *The uncommitted data warning dialog*

Navigating Programmatically

As discussed, a command component can call a backing bean method that performs navigation using defined control flow rules. Additionally, navigation can be performed programmatically by retrieving defined activities from the ADF controller. The `ControllerContext` object is used in this case, as shown next, where a global control flow case is accessed programmatically:

```
import oracle.adf.controller.ControllerContext;
...
public String loginNav =
  ControllerContext.getInstance().getGlobalViewActivityURL("login");

public void setLoginNav(String loginNav) {
  this.loginNav = loginNav;
  }
public String getLoginNav() {
  return loginNav;
  }
```

This `loginNav` object can then be used to dynamically define the view that is called in a task flow. For example, a URL View component can be defined dynamically for a task flow using Expression Language that evaluates to the managed bean property:

```
<url-view id="login">
  <url>#{myManagedBean.loginNav}</url>
</url-view>
```

NOTE
A URL View is similar to a view activity except that it is bookmarkable.

Retrieving the Current View Programatically

The view ID for a page can be programmatically retrieved, so that phase listeners and other application logic (such as error messages) can be written generically for all views. For example, a utility class commonly used in ADF Faces applications includes a method for adding ADF error messages to a view. The following code defines a new `FacesMessage` and adds the message to the current view using the root component ID:

```
import javax.faces.application.FacesMessage;
import javax.faces.component.UIViewRoot;
import javax.faces.context.FacesContext;

public class JSFUtils {
  public static void addFacesErrorMessage(String msg) {
    FacesContext fctx = getFacesContext();
    FacesMessage fm =
      new FacesMessage(FacesMessage.SEVERITY_ERROR, msg, "");
      fctx.addMessage(getRootViewComponentId(), fm);
  }
```

```
public static String getRootViewComponentId() {
  return getFacesContext().getViewRoot().getId();
}
public static FacesContext getFacesContext() {
  return FacesContext.getCurrentInstance();
}
}
```

Programmatically Expiring the User Session

Another technique commonly used in web applications is the programmatic cleanup of resources and end the user's session. This is typically done upon the user logging out of the security implementation in the application, as shown in the code sample that follows:

```
import java.io.IOException;
import javax.faces.context.ExternalContext;
import javax.faces.context.FacesContext;
 import javax.servlet.http.HttpServletResponse;
import javax.servlet.http.HttpSession;
...
public String logoutButton_action() throws IOException{
  ExternalContext ectx =
    FacesContext.getCurrentInstance().getExternalContext();
  HttpServletResponse response = (HttpServletResponse)ectx.getResponse();
  HttpSession session = (HttpSession)ectx.getSession(false);
  session.invalidate();
  response.sendRedirect("Home.jspx");
  return null;
}
```

Partial Page Navigation

In traditional web applications, navigating from one page to another means that a full-page transition is performed for the called page; JavaScript libraries for a page are re-executed and the called page is initialized. In ADF Faces, however, navigation can be made much faster by using Asynchronous JavaScript and XML (AJAX) technologies to call the new page, which skips the initialization steps. This feature is called *partial page navigation*, and it allows the called page to share the same HTTP request object as the page that called it. This manifests itself to the user in two ways: First, the URL does not change; the user will see the same view Id in the URL line of the browser. Second, navigation is much quicker. The hourglass icon that appears normally when page navigation is invoked will essentially disappear and called pages will be presented much more quickly.

Partial page navigation is not the default in ADF Faces applications, due to some subtle differences that may not be expected by application developers. For instance, when using partial page navigation, JavaScript libraries and Cascading Style Sheets (CSS) files are not re-executed; thus, any variables and functions defined globally in JavaScript will not be reloaded, and page-specific CSS skins are not possible. Additionally, the use of page anchors is not supported because the hash portion of the URL is overridden by the partial page navigation functionality. The use of the back, forward, and refresh buttons in the browser, as well as bookmarking of pages, is supported in partial page navigation just as it is for the default full page navigation.

TIP
To use partial page navigation with global JavaScript variables, use the
AdfPage.getPageProperty *and* AdfPage.setPageProperty
methods to set and store variables. This will enable the variable values
to be loaded and unloaded properly even if the JavaScript library is
not re-executed.

Enabling Partial Page Navigation

To enable partial page navigation in ADF Faces applications, add a context parameter to the application's web.xml file as follows:

```
<context-param>
    <param-name>oracle.adf.view.rich.pprNavigation.OPTIONS</param-name>
    <param-value>onWithForcePPR</param-value>
</context-param>
```

The valid values for the `param-value` element are `off`, `on`, and `onWithForcePPR`. This last value enables partial navigation (as with the `on` value) and also forces all action events, even those that do not perform navigation, to use the feature.

HTTP Redirects and ADF Controller

It is possible to define that an HTTP redirect is used to call a view in a task flow. To do so, set the `redirect` attribute to `true` for a view definition in the `adfc-config.xml` or other task flow configuration file. This does enable somewhat faster page navigation, but JavaScript libraries must still be loaded anew. A better option is to use partial page navigation.

NOTE
When redirect *is set to* true *for a view, partial page navigation*
will be skipped for that particular view.

Summary

Whether navigating by using a menu component, button, or link—and whether that navigation is based on a train task flow, programmatic evaluation of a navigation rule, or an absolute URL—controlling the way that the user navigates throughout an application is an important step in both the design and development phases of application development. Creating these navigation rules by using templates and the XMLMenuModel allows developers to define the navigation declaratively for an application, maintain it easily, and ensure a consistent look and feel for navigation components across the application.

CHAPTER
8

Working with Input
Components

*Input text fields are the weakest link in the chain of preventing "garbage in, garbage out."
Therefore, the most important things to validate in an input form are the types and quality
of data that a user can enter.*

I nput components are perhaps the most straightforward components to understand, and the easiest to use. Their simplicity doesn't diminish their usefulness, however. They are key to allowing end users to add and modify data, which of course has many implications for data-bound web applications. Input components can be divided into three categories: components for inserting text, components for inserting special values such as dates and numbers, and components for selecting one or more values from a list. All input components support the use of labels, validators, converters, and value change events.

This chapter covers the attributes and several common scenarios that are used with input components. Special considerations are needed for list components, and they are covered in Chapter 11.

The most basic input form looks a lot like a Google search form and contains one input text field and one button, as shown in Figure 8-1.

Here is the source code of the JSPX file in Figure 8-1:

```
<af:form>
  <af:inputText value="#{aBoundValue}"/>
  <af:commandButton actionListener="#{}" text="Go" />
</af:form>
```

Note that in a standard HTML form, the `<form>` tag would contain the `action` attribute that performs an action when the submit button is clicked. However, in a JavaServer Faces (JSF) application, the command button submits the form, along with the form values, and the `doSomething` method is called, as shown in this code sample.

Types of Input Components

When you create input components by dropping a data control object onto the JSF page editor and selecting ADF Form or ADF Table as the type of component to bind to the data control (and not their read-only equivalents), input components are created according to the following rules:

- **String and number bindings**   Input text fields with `value`, `required`, `label`, `columns`, `maximumLength`, and `shortDesc` attributes are set to the equivalent attributes in the data model for the data control attribute. Additionally, a server-side validator component (`f:validator`) is nested within each input text component, which is bound to any validation that has been defined on the data model.

FIGURE 8-1   *Basic input form*

- **Number bindings** In addition to the attributes for string-bound input components, an `af:convertNumber` component is added within the input component to include any formatting defined for the component on the data model, such as a number with a fixed number of digits or with a specific currency format.

- **Date bindings** The `af:inputDate` component includes a text field for entering dates, as well as a pop-up calendar launched from a button click for choosing the date. Additionally, an `af:convertDateTime` component is added by default when creating data components that are bound to date types.

Label attributes bound to ADF data model components will be set by default to the `label` attribute for the data control attribute. For non–data-bound components, the `label` attribute should be specified using Expression Language to refer to the resource bundle for the application or page, rather than to a literal string. This allows for creating an internationalizable application and follows best practices. Chapter 18 covers internationalization in full detail.

TIP

An additional type of input component is `af:inputColor`. This component can be used to allow users to select a color from either standard or custom color palettes, which are automatically generated by the component. The default format is a hexadecimal value.

Input Forms

As explained, form components serve as a container for input components and the buttons that submit their values. Forms cannot be nested, but the `af:subform` component can be used to define a nested context for buttons that are used to submit values in an input form. This is typically used when an independent part of a page needs to be submitted, without validating components defined outside of the subform. However, this technique has been largely superceded by the use of page fragments and regions, which are favorable techniques for managing multiple input forms on a page.

In most cases, JDeveloper adds a form component (or prompts you to do so) when you add input components to a page. For typical applications, the only attribute for an `af:form` component that you'd modify would be the `defaultCommand` attribute. Use this attribute to specify the ID of the component that should fire its action (typically the Submit button) when the user presses the ENTER key, as shown in the following code listing:

```
<af:form defaultCommand="submit_btn">
  <af:panelFormLayout>
    <af:inputText label="Enter a username"/>
    <af:inputText label="Enter password:" secret="true"/>
    <af:commandButton text="Login" id="submit_btn"
      action="#{ register.submit_action}"/>
  </af:panelFormLayout>
</af:form>
```

The Input Text Component

The input text component is the most basic of components. The `value` attribute of the input text component is most often defined with Expression Language and can of course refer to a backing bean or the binding layer of ADF.

Entering Multiple Lines of Text

The input text component's sister component in the JSF reference implementation is *input text area*. In ADF Faces, the functionality of the input text area component is achieved by setting the Rows and Wrap attributes of af:inputText to allow multi-row editing of the component. The Wrap attribute is honored only if the Rows attribute (essentially the input text field's height) is greater than 1, and, by default, it allows the user to enter carriage returns in the visual display of the value but does not save the carriage returns to the value of the field. Setting the Wrap attribute to hard saves carriage returns to the input text value.

The rich text editor component also allows multi-line editing but provides more formatting capabilities than the input text field. The rich text editor allows formatting of font styles and sizes, paragraph justification, colors, and indentation. It's a useful component for creating letters, for example, as it supports HTML tags for styling text. Use the rows and columns attributes of the af:richTextEditor component to specify the amount of editing space displayed, and use the editMode attribute to default the view of the text to either the source or WYSIWYG views.

Displaying Tool Tips and Hints

Tool tips and hints help the user understand what types of values should be included for a particular input component. By default, the formatting of a date is included as a tool tip for ADF data model-bound components.

To alert the user when a value has been updated, use the changed and changedDesc attributes. The following listing demonstrates an example of displaying a small change icon when the value of the department name is changed and displaying a message that includes the previous value in a tool tip for the icon.

```
<af:inputText value="#{bindings.DepartmentName.inputValue}"
    label="#{bindings.DepartmentName.hints.label}"
    changed="#{bindings.DepartmentName.hints.valueChanged}"
    changedDesc="#{bindings.DepartmentName.hints.changedMessage}" >
</af:inputText>
```

In this example, the changed icon will appear when the custom hint named valueChanged is true, and the tool tip displayed will be the value of the changedMessage hint. These two hints are defined in the ViewRowImpl class as follows, where the valueChanged hint is a Boolean value based on the attributeChanged attribute, and the changedMessage hint is constructed from the entity status and previous value, so that the tool tip displays "Attribute Modified: was Administration" for a data control attribute that is modified and that has an unmodified value of Administration.

This example hard codes the attribute for which the original value is retrieved but could be adapted to accept the attribute name as an argument—or, alternatively, the original values could be stored in a backing bean.

```
import oracle.jbo.LocaleContext;
import oracle.jbo.server.AttributeDefImpl;
import oracle.jbo.server.Entity;
import oracle.jbo.server.ViewRowAttrHintsImpl;
import oracle.jbo.server.ViewRowImpl;
...
@Override
protected ViewRowAttrHintsImpl createViewRowAttrHints(AttributeDefImpl attrDef) {
    return new CustomViewRowAttrHints(attrDef,this);
}
```

```java
class CustomViewRowAttrHints extends ViewRowAttrHintsImpl {
  protected CustomViewRowAttrHints(AttributeDefImpl attr, ViewRowImpl
    viewRow) {
      super(attr,viewRow);
  }
  @Override
  public String getHint(LocaleContext locale, String sHintName) {
    if ("changedMessage".equals(sHintName)) {
      ViewRowImpl vri = getViewRow();
      if (vri != null) {
        Entity e = vri.getEntity(0);
        byte b = e.STATUS_UNMODIFIED;
        String origValue = vri.getAttributeInternal(1, b).toString();
        if (e != null) {
          String rowState = translateStatusToString(e.getEntityState());
          return "Attribute " + rowState + ": was " + origValue;
          }
        return null;
        }
      } else if ("valueChanged".equals(sHintName)) {
      ViewRowImpl vri = getViewRow();
      if (vri != null) {
      boolean changed =
        vri.isAttributeChanged(getViewAttributeDef().getName());
      return changed ? "true":"false";
      }
    }
    return super.getHint(locale, sHintName);
  }
  private String translateStatusToString(byte b) {
  String ret = null;
  switch (b) {
    case Entity.STATUS_DELETED: {
      ret = "Deleted";
      break;
    }
    case Entity.STATUS_INITIALIZED: {
      ret = "Initialized";
      break;
    }
    case Entity.STATUS_MODIFIED: {
      ret = "Modified";
      break;
    }
    case Entity.STATUS_UNMODIFIED: {
      ret = "Unmodified";
      break;
    }
    case Entity.STATUS_NEW: {
      ret = "New";
      break;
    }
  }
  return ret;
  }
}
```

Input Components for Numbers

In a typical order entry scenario, a quantity attribute is defined on the data model as an integer. Providing an input text field for the user to enter a quantity for a product would allow the user to enter negative numbers and decimals, which obviously wouldn't be valid values for a quantity attribute. An easy way to deter this is to use the `af:inputNumberSpinbox` component and define the `minimum`, `maximum`, and `stepValue` attributes to limit the values that the user can enter.

Like the `af:inputNumberSpinbox`, the `af:inputNumberSlider` and `af:inputRangeSlider` components limit the values that a user can enter. The increment steps can be set for each component, and the slider components can display vertically or horizontally. The following code sample defines each type of number input:

```
<af:inputNumberSlider value="#{bindings.UnitPrice.inputValue}"
  minimum="#{bindings.CostPrice.inputValue}"
  maximum="#{bindings.ListPrice.inputValue}"
  majorIncrement="#{(bindings.UnitPrice.inputValue)/2}"
  minorIncrement="#{(bindings.UnitPrice.inputValue)/10}"/>
<af:inputNumberSpinbox value="#{bindings.Quantity.inputValue}"
  label="#{bindings.Quantity.hints.label}"/>
<af:inputRangeSlider value="#{bindings.MinPrice.inputValue}"
  majorIncrement="#{(bindings.ListPrice.inputValue -
    bindings.CostPrice.inputValue) / 5}"
  maximum="#{bindings.ListPrice.inputValue}"
  minimum="#{bindings.CostPrice.inputValue}"/>
```

Figure 8-2 shows the runtime of this code listing. Note that in the code sample, the `ListPrice`, `CostPrice`, and `UnitPrice` attributes are defined in the data model as integers instead of the default `oracle.jbo.domain.Number` type. This is due to the fact that the `minimum` and `maximum` attributes for these components accept `java.lang.Number` types, which cannot be converted from `oracle.jbo.domain.Number`. Alternatively, backing bean methods could be created to convert the values before using them as range values, or transient attributes of type `java.lang.Number` or `java.lang.Integer` could be created on the data model to provide the values.

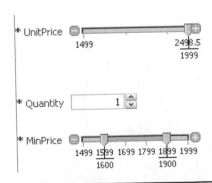

FIGURE 8-2   *Input number slider, input number spinbox, and input range slider*

The Input Date Component

The `af:inputDate` component includes attributes for specifying specific days, days of the week, and/or months that should display as disabled. Additionally, minimum and maximum values can be specified. The values for this component are formatted for the ISO 8601 format of *yyyy-MM-dd*. The `af:inputDate` component automatically provides conversion between the string that is entered and displayed in the browser and the date data type that is used by the underlying data model.

Uploading Files

To upload files, use the `af:inputFile` component and a command button to initiate the upload once a file is entered into the input component. A browse button is displayed next to the input file component to allow the user to select a file from his or her local file system for uploading.

The following example shows a form that includes an input file component. Note that the form component has the `usesUpload` attribute set to `true` to support this activity.

```
<af:form usesUpload="true">
  <af:inputFile label="File to Upload:"/>
  <af:commandButton text="Upload"/>
</af:form>
```

The "Web User Interface Developer's Guide for Oracle ADF" contains an example of using the value change listener to notify the user when a file has been uploaded successfully, and Chapter 12 discusses the use of `af:inputFile` in more detail.

Restricting Input

Many methods can be used to restrict input. The pros and cons of each are shown in Table 8-1.

Restrict Input By	Pros	Cons
Setting the read-only attribute for an input text component	Works well with ADF security; an EL expression can be evaluated to determine whether the item is updatable.	The input component can receive focus (for example, as the user tabs through the components on the form), which may be confusing for users.
Using an `outputText` component	Simplest solution for values that are not updatable on a particular page.	Least maintainable; if the component needs to be modified to an input component, validators and other attributes would need to be added to the component.
Change the attribute settings on the ADF data model to non-updatable	Offers maximum reuse for values that will never be updatable—each page that uses the attribute will default to a read-only input field.	Components bound to the attribute are never updatable.

TABLE 8-1 *Pros and Cons of Methodologies for Restricting User Input*

Implementing Password Fields

A common scenario for user registration includes supplying a username and password. When used for passwords and other similar values, input text fields should set the secret attribute to true to hide user input. Additionally, a confirmation field may be used to prevent typos creating a hidden password—for example, "password" and "confirm password" fields. This type of validation is typically not performed on the model, because the confirmation field is a user interface–specific task. To handle the processing of the input text values, a backing bean method can be used to compare the values of the input text fields, and the reset button component allows the user to reset these values (or indeed any input form values) to their previous state, which is generally their default value on the data model.

To augment this behavior further, especially in the case of the registration scenario, it is preferable to reset the values only if validation failed. The following code listing assumes that the two input text fields are bound to af:inputText components named pw1 and pw2 and demonstrates displaying an error and resetting the password fields to empty strings when the values are not equal:

```
public String commandButton1_action() {
    if (!pw1.getValue().equals( pw2.getValue())){
        FacesContext fctx = FacesContext.getCurrentInstance();
        FacesMessage message = new FacesMessage("Password fields must match");
        fctx.addMessage("pw2", message);
        pw1.setValue("");
        pw2.setValue("");
        return null;
    }
    return "go";
}
```

Easing Navigation Within an Input Form

"Head-down" data entry applications have historically been difficult to emulate in web applications. However, a combination of various ADF components and attributes can enable productive data entry. Data entry forms need to assist the user in navigating in the form to minimize mouse movements. For example, a typical input form can be augmented to include keyboard navigation among input components. The accessKey attribute can be used to specify the mnemonic, or key stroke, that will navigate to the component when the browser-specific modifier is used. In Firefox 2 and 3, the modifier keys are ALT-SHIFT. In Internet Explorer 7, the modifier is simply ALT, and in Safari, the modifier is the CTRL key. Typically, though, the labelAndAccessKey attribute is used to set both the label of the component, as well the mnemonic. Append the ampersand character (&) to the character in the label that will serve as the mnemonic, and that character will be underlined at runtime so that the user can easily see the character used to navigate to the component. For example, in the Property Inspector, enter Depar&tment Id for the LabelAndAccessKey attribute, and the first t character will be underlined at runtime. In the source code, the property value will be encoded to use the & value, such as Depar&tment Id.

For fixed-length components such as those used to enter codes, set the AutoTab attribute to true. This navigates to the next component when the value of the MaximumLength attribute of the component is reached. Optionally, use the AutoSubmit attribute to submit the enclosing form when the value is changed for a particular component. For date components, using the component instead of the pop-up component allows quick selection of a date value.

Converters and Validators

Validators and converters work together to minimize the chance that a user would see an error message and maximize the chance that a user is able to enter valid values. As such, if a converter fails for a component, validation is skipped. When the conversion succeeds, the required attribute for the component will be validated. If the required attribute is set to true and the value of the component is a non-null empty string, any other validators are skipped. Validators are executed only when the converter and `required` attribute succeed, and as previously mentioned, all validators are executed in the order in which they are declared. In this way, multiple validation error messages can be displayed for the component so that the user can understand what to enter in the input field to pass all validation, instead of seeing one error message each time an invalid value is submitted.

Additional server-side validators are provided in the JSF core library, including `f:validateDoubleRange`, `f:validateLength`, and `f:validateLongRange`. These are basic validators that accept minimum and maximum numbers to compare with the value in the field.

The ADF Faces validators include the following:

- `validateByteLength`

- `validateDateRestriction`

- `validateDateTimeRange`

- `validateDoubleRange`

- `validateLength`

- `validateLongRange`

- `validateRegExp`

These components include a tool tip or hint that you can modify using the `hintMinimum`, `hintMaximum`, and `hintNotInRange` attributes, and you can modify the `messageDetailMinimum`, `messageDetailMaximum`, and `messageDetailNotInRange` attributes to alter the message displayed when the value is invalid.

Validating User Input

Input text fields are the weakest link in the chain of preventing "garbage in, garbage out." Therefore, the most important things to validate in an input form are the types and quality of data that a user can enter. Selection and list of values components are one of the most straightforward ways to specify the values that a user can enter in an input component. Those types of components are covered in Chapter 11.

When creating data bound input forms, ADF will embed an `f:validator` component for each input component, which refers to the validator defined on the data model. Here's an example:

```
<f:validator binding="#{bindings.FirstName.validator}"/>
```

This allows the input component to inherit any validators defined on the data model. Note the use of the `f:` prefix—this is the JSF core component's validator component; the `binding` attribute can refer to any method on the data model.

Deciding Where to Include Validation

There's a balance to be achieved when considering what validation should be included only on the user interface layer and what should be duplicated from the validation already implemented on the data model. The benefit of including validation primarily on the data model layer of an application is reuse—any page or user interface implementation for that matter will contain the same validation rules. However, for usability of the application, it's important to give the user more immediate feedback and provide some validation on the user interface layer.

Several techniques can be used to validate user input on the user interface. Several component attributes can be set to require a value and enforce that rule on the client side, for example. Further, both client-side and server-side validators can be used, or custom validators can be applied to components. ADF Faces validators provide server-side validation, meaning that the value of a component is first converted and then passed to the validator method on the server, during the Process Validations phase of the JSF lifecycle. This method validates the value according to the order in which validators for the converter are declared.

Requiring Values

The `required` attribute for an input component is introspected from the data model when the component is created. By default, the error message for a required attribute is "Error: A value is required" along with the detail message "You must enter a value." To customize this, you can specify the `requiredMessageDetail` attribute for the component, which optionally allows a substitution of the component's label in the error message, as follows:

```
<af:inputText value="#{bindings.DepartmentName.inputValue}"
label="#{bindings.DepartmentName.hints.label}"
required="#{bindings.DepartmentName.hints.mandatory}"
requiredMessageDetail="{0} is required">
```

In this example, the `{0}` evaluates to the `label` attribute for the component (which evaluates to `DepartmentName` in this case), so that the error message displayed when the user navigates out of the component without entering a value reads "DepartmentName is required."

To modify the default error message and detail error message globally for all input text components in an application, add `org.apache.myfaces.trinidad.component.UIXEditableValue.REQUIRED` and `org.apache.myfaces.trinidad.component.UIXEditableValue.REQUIRED_detail` to the resource attributes file for the view project. Here's an example for a resource property file named ViewControllerBundle.properties:

```
org.apache.myfaces.trinidad.component.UIXEditableValue.REQUIRED=Error - This value is required.
org.apache.myfaces.trinidad.component.UIXEditableValue.REQUIRED_detail=Please enter a value.
```

To use this file, configure the `faces-config.xml` to point to the properties file using the `message-bundle` element. Here's an example:

```
<message-bundle>view.ViewControllerBundle</message-bundle>
```

This ensures that all required error messages for input text fields will be set to the custom values defined in the properties file, unless the `requiredMessageDetail` attribute is explicitly defined for a component.

Canceling Validation

A common validation rule applied to component values is the `required` attribute. However, in some cases, especially in the case of the creation form, you'll want to allow the user to cancel validation of the form values because not doing so would mean that the empty values would fail validation. For example, if you use a button on a page to create new records and you need to cancel that action without performing validation, setting the `immediate` attribute to `true` for a cancel or rollback button skips validation for the form, because the action fires before the Apply Request Values phase of the JSF lifecycle. Thus, to cancel validation, use the reset button component or set the `immediate` attribute to `true` for a command button or navigation component that might need to skip validation before navigating away from the page.

Custom Validators

Custom validators can be applied to a component using the `f:validator` component. These validators aren't declarative—instead, they're implemented in a backing bean, and are best used when you are creating validation that compares multiple values on the page. The best way to register a validator to a page is to double-click the input component to launch the validator dialog. In the validator dialog, specify the backing bean and a method name for the validator.

NOTE
Custom validators registered to a component and enforced on the client are not as reusable as validators included on the model. Most validation logic should be included in the data model, with client-side validators providing supplemental validation.

For custom validators that need to be reused by multiple pages, a JSF validator class can be created and registered with the application. The class should implement the `javax.faces.validator.Validator` and interfaces and thus must contain a `validate()` method that includes validation logic and adds any failure messages to the `FacesContext`. An ADF Faces version of that validator can be created for the JSF validator class, which allows the validator to run on the client and throw messages using JavaScript. The "Web User Interface Developer's Guide for Oracle ADF" contains details on how to register the validator and optionally create a tag for the validator instead of specifying the registered ID of the validator in the validator component's `validatorId` attribute.

Providing Messages for Validation and Conversion

To specify failure messages for validation and conversion, the ADF Faces components provide Message Detail attributes that allow you to customize the message displayed for tool tips and validation failures. Any associated validation error messages are added to the `FacesContext`, whether they are initiated by the ADF Faces validators in the Process Validations phase or the backend data model validation. Thus, a user could see duplicate error messages displayed within the `af:messages` component for invalid values that have duplicated validation rules.

To modify the way that messages are displayed, set the `inline` attribute of the message component to `true`, and optionally set the `text` and `message` attributes. This will disable the error message pop-up and allow customization of the error that is displayed, as shown in Figure 8-3. Additional techniques for specifying validation messages, including the use of custom placeholders in messages, are covered in Chapter 18.

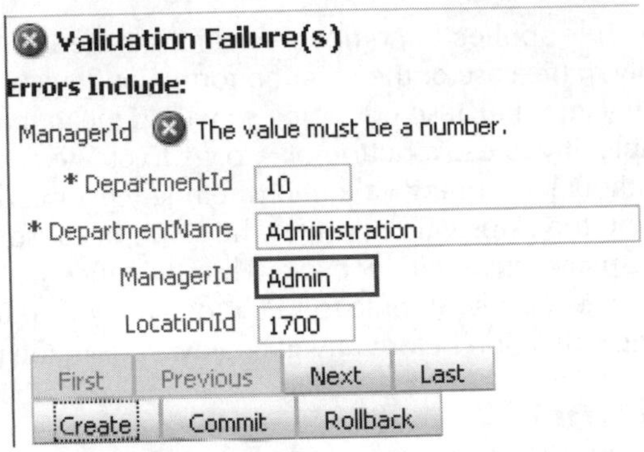

FIGURE 8-3 *Customized message strings in inline messages*

Converting Input

ADF Faces will automatically create converters based on data types such as Number, Integer, Byte, Float, Double, and Color types. For other data types, or to explicitly create a converter, you can add an ADF Faces or JSF converter to an input component.

Converting input allows user-supplied values to be transformed into values that the application accepts. This frees the user from ensuring that he or she enters date values in certain formats, for example. The JSF component set includes converters for common data types, and the ADF Faces converters allow conversion of `java.awt.Color`, `java.util.Date`, and `java.lang .Number` objects to `java.lang.String`, via the `ConvertColor`, `ConvertDateTime`, and `ConvertNumber` ADF Faces components. Multiple formats can be declared for these components so that multiple values are allowable and can be converted to the exact format that the data model accepts. You can also create custom converter classes to convert custom data types and similar to custom validation classes, register those classes with the application, and use the JSF converter component or the converter attribute to apply the converter to the component. For example, the following code listing shows how to accept multiple date formats, support both date and time formats, and display the converted date in a specified length:

```
<af:inputDate value="#{bindings.HireDate.inputValue}"
   label="#{bindings.HireDate.hints.label}">
   <f:validator binding="#{bindings.HireDate.validator}"/>
   <af:convertDateTime pattern="#{bindings.HireDate.format}" type="both"
      dateStyle="medium" timeStyle="short" secondaryPattern="yyyy/M/d"/>
</af:inputDate>
```

Creating Custom Converters

For maximum reusability, custom converter classes can be registered for a particular data type, and JSF will automatically use the converter for all components of that data type. Custom converters should implement the `javax.faces.converter.Converter` and interfaces and as such, the getAsObject() and getAsString() methods. The getAsObject method accepts the FacesContext, UIComponent, and String value of the component for conversion. The sister method, getAsString, converts the object back to a string for display. You may need to register a custom converter earlier in application development than you did in the past, because the Expression Language engine has become stricter in its type conversion in the most recent release. The Expression Language engine will now accept only values from which the target expression type is assignable. To create a converter in this case, you would create a custom converter as follows:

```
import javax.faces.component.UIComponent;
import javax.faces.context.FacesContext;
import javax.faces.convert.Converter;

public class MyCustomConverter implements Converter {
  public Object getAsObject(FacesContext facesContext, UIComponent
    uIComponent, String string)
  {
  Double d = null;
  if("ONE".equals(string))
    d = new Double(1);
  else if("TWO".equals(string))
    d = new Double(2);
  else
    d = new Double(string);
  return d;
  }

  public String getAsString(FacesContext facesContext, UIComponent
    uIComponent, Object object) {
    if(object instanceof Double){
      String doubleValue =((Double) object).toString();
    if(doubleValue.equals("1.0"))
      doubleValue = "ONE";
    else if(doubleValue.equals("2.0"))
      doubleValue = "TWO";
    return doubleValue;
    } else
      return object.toString();
    }
}
```

You can then register this converter in the faces-config.xml and apply it to an input text field:

```
<af:inputText … />
  <f:converter converterId="MyCustomConverter"/>
</af:inputText>
```

Summary

As a user interface page developer, you will spend a great deal of time defining the layout, functionality, and behavior of input components. The more time you spend developing logical, easy-to-understand input components in pages, the less time you will spend training application users. For example, by using an appropriate type of input component for a particular type of user input, you can avoid causing a great deal of user error and confusion. Additionally, by using combinations of the validation and conversion techniques covered in this chapter, typos and ill-formatted entries are caught at the user interface layer, thereby reducing the amount of user input errors that could seep into the data model.

CHAPTER
9

Working with Table, Tree, and TreeTable Components

The best thing about working with ADF bound ADF Faces table, tree, and treeTable components is their similarity, which allows reuse of skills and code samples.

ollections are lists of data objects in web applications that often represent results of database queries. Using ADF Business Components as the business service layer, collections are represented by View Objects that are displayed in the ADF Data Controls panel. When dragging a View Object to a page, developers can choose from the following UI components:

- **ADF form**   Read-only and updatable forms that contain UI components that bind to ADF attribute bindings. Chapter 8 explains how to work with input components.

- **Data Visualization Tools (DVT)**   Gantt charts, geographic maps, gauge charts, hierarchy viewer, and graphs belong to the ADF Faces DVT component set and visually present data in a collection. DVT components are covered in Chapter 13.

- **Navigation**   Components that navigate the underlying collection. Use these components to scroll a form or to build master-detail selection—for example in using a navigation list as the master component of a shuttle component displaying the detail list.

- **Single and multi-select**   Select components that display the collection in a list from which the user can choose a component. Choosing an entry in the list does not navigate the collection but holds the selected value for the application developer to access and use.

- **Tables and trees**   Presents structured data in a selectable and updatable tree and table form. The pivot table is part of the DVT component set and is a special case of table that allows users to move columns within the table to render different views to the data.

This chapter focuses on the three most commonly used UI components for collections: ADF Faces table, tree, and treeTable.

ADF Tree Binding

At runtime, the ADF table, tree, and treeTable components reference an instance of `FacesCtrlHierBinding`, which extends `JUCtrlHierBinding` to access the ADF model. An ADF tree binding is always created in the ADF page definition when you drag an ADF

ADF Faces Component Documentation

The "Oracle ADF Faces Tag Reference" is accessible following the References and APIs link in the The Oracle Fusion Middleware documentation, which is available online at http://download.oracle.com/docs/cd/E12839_01/index.htm. It provides an overview of attributes and methods exposed by the components, as well as useful background information and hints. A complete site dedicated to the development of Rich Enterprise Applications (REA) is at http://rea.oracle.com/. This site hosts tutorials and online demos for ADF Faces Rich Client components, DVTs, and Oracle WebCenter.

Business Components View Object from the Data Controls panel and drop it as a table, tree, or treeTable component to a page. Chapter 1 introduced the ADF Faces binding classes as extensions of the generic framework classes. The ADF Faces binding classes implement the component models and provide additional, Expression Language accessible, functionality. The FacesCtrl* classes are located in an ADF internal package, indicating that developers should not directly use them from Java.

To execute methods exposed by the internal binding objects, such as the makeCurrent method on FacesCtrlHierBinding, developers should use the Expression Language MethodExpression and ValueExpression objects. In this chapter, we use two helper methods to simplify our code examples: invokeMethodExpression and executeValueExpression.

The invokeMethodExpression method uses a MethodExpression to invoke methods on the ADF bindings object.

```
/**
 * overloaded method as a convenience for the common case in which only
 * a single argument is passed
 */
public Object invokeMethodBinding(String methodExpression,
                                  Object event,
                                  Class eventClass){
    //call method shown below
    return invokeMethodBinding(methodExpression,
                     new Object[]{event},
                     new Class[]{eventClass});
}
/**
 * Method that creates and executes a MethodExpression for the provided EL * string
 * @param methodExpression java.lang.String that represents a valid EL
 * string
 * @param parameters An array of Objects or null that provides the
 * arguments for the executed method
 * @param expectedParamTypes An array of <ClassType>.class or empty array
 * describing the types of the expected parameters
 * @return Object returned by the invoked method
 */
private Object invokeMethodExpression(
                String methodExpression,
                Object[] parameters,
                Class[] expectedParamTypes){
    FacesContext fctx = FacesContext.getCurrentInstance();
    ELContext elctx = fctx.getELContext();
    Application app = fctx.getApplication();
    ExpressionFactory exprFactory = app.getExpressionFactory();
    MethodExpression methodExpr = exprFactory.createMethodExpression(
                elctx,
                methodExpression,
                Object.class,
                expectedParamTypes);
    return methodExpr.invoke(elctx,parameters);
}
```

The second helper method, `executeValueExpression`, returns a result object for the value expression that is passed in as an argument:

```
/**
* Method that executes the value expression that is passed as an argument
* @param elExpression Valid value expression string that references a
* property on an object like ADF "bindings"
* @return ValueExpression result as Object
*/
private Object executeValueExpression(String valueExpression){
  FacesContext fctx = FacesContext.getCurrentInstance();
  ELContext elctx = fctx.getELContext();
  Application app = fctx.getApplication();
  ExpressionFactory exprFactory = app.getExpressionFactory();
  ValueExpression valueExpr = exprFactory.createValueExpression(
                             elctx,
                             valueExpression,
                             Object.class);
  return valueExpr.getValue(elctx);
}
```

TIP
These two methods are generic and can be added as public methods to a managed bean base class for all managed beans in an application subclass. Using a managed bean base class is comparable to using a static helper class but follows the same recommendation that we expressed for extending the ADF Business Components framework classes.

ADF Faces Table Component

As shown in Figure 9-1, the ADF Faces table component provides rich functionality such as scrolling, data filtering, data sorting, context and component menus, drag-and-drop, column reordering, and column freeze. The data displayed in the table columns can be rendered read-

PanelCollection Component

The `af:panelCollection` component can be used as a parent component for the ADF Faces table, tree, and treeTable components. It provides standard menu, toolbar, and status bar items for the contained child component. The panel collection is customizable and, for example, allows developers to switch functionality off, using the `featuresOff` attribute, or add their own menu and toolbar items using the menus and toolbar facets. Figure 9-4, later in this chapter, shows the `PanelCollection` component for a table that supports column selection and freeze. As soon as functionality like this becomes available on the table, the `PanelCollection` component reflects this in its toolbar.

only or updatable, as shown in Figure 9-1. An ADF Faces table is built using the `af:table` component tag that is the parent container for one or many instances of `af:column`. The `af:column` component contains the cell-rendering component, such as `af:inputText`, `af:outputText`, `af:goLink`, `af:commandButton`, and many other more. The runtime behavior and appearance of the table is configured through component properties of the `af:table` and `af:column` components.

By default, data shown in the ADF Faces table is lazily fetched, which means that in response to the initial request, the table renders without the data and then issues subsequent partial requests to read the data from the model. The number of rows that are fetched by each request is defined by the table `fetchSize` attribute, which has a default value of 25. The table height, which is defined by the `inlineStyle` property using Cascading Style Sheets (CSS) or the parent layout container's stretch behavior, determines the number of requests that need to be sent to the server during the initial rendering and later when the user scrolls through the table data.

To display data in a table, the ADF Faces table internally iterates over a collection of row objects that are queried from the ADF model through the binding reference in the table `value` attribute. The ADF Faces table ADF binding reference refers to an instance of the `FacesCtrlHierBinding` object that reads from the hierarchical tree binding in the page definition file. When rendering the table, the ADF Faces table component repeatedly calls the column and cell renderer child component instances, such as `af:column`, to produce the HTML markup for the row to render. The technique used to render the ADF Faces table UI is referred to as "stamping," because only single instances of the UI child components are used on a column to produce the markup output for all its rows. Any modifications applied to an instance of a table child component impact the column as a whole when the table is partially refreshed. For example, using an `af:forEach` component to render a list of values in a table is not executed per row but once for the column so that it cannot display a different select list for each table row.

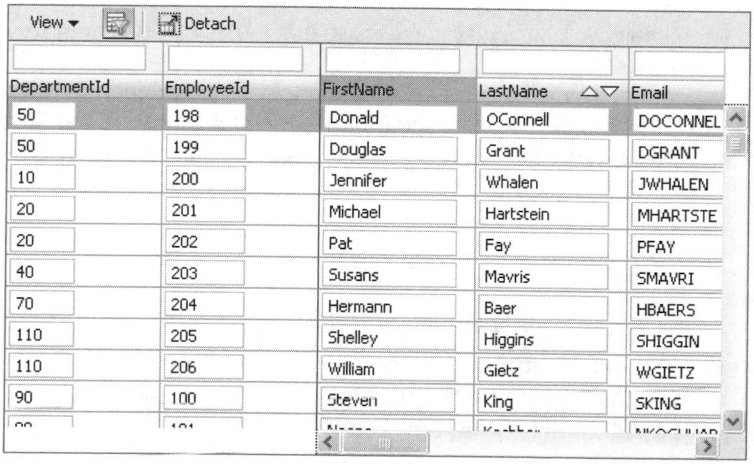

FIGURE 9-1 *Rich ADF Faces table with data filter, component menu, "frozen" columns, and scroll bars*

About the Table var Attribute and Its Default row Value

The ADF Faces table component model, which is an ADF binding instance for Fusion developers, is referenced from the table's `value` attribute. The name of the variable that holds the current row object during table rendering is defined by the table `var` attribute. By default, the value for this variable is defined as "`row`" and is accessible from Expression Language and is used in the `af:column` child components to reference the row data:

```
<af:table var="row" …>
   <af:column>
      <af:outputText value="#{row.bindings.EmployeeId}" id="ot5"/>
   </af:column>
   …
</af:table>
```

The "`row`" variable is available only during the time the table renders, which means that row data that is accessed through it needs to be stored as a custom attribute using the `f:attribute` attribute tag or a listener component to become accessible later.

How to Define the Maximum Number of Rows Displayed in a Table

The `af:table` component exposes a `rows` attribute that, according to the component documentation, allows developers to define the maximum number of rows to display in a table. The `rows` attribute does not belong to the ADF Faces Rich Client (RC) table component, but is part of the Apache Trinidad base component set and has no effect in ADF Faces. The `rows` attribute cannot be hidden from the Property Palette, which often leads to confusion among developers. To define the maximum number of rows to display in an ADF Faces RC table, you use the table's `inlineStyle` attribute to set the height of the table using CSS, so that a specific number of rows fit into the table data content area.

Here's an example using the Oracle "blafplus-rich" look and feel: To display 10 table rows, you need 16 px for each row, 14 px for the non-wrapped table header, and 16px for the horizontal scroll bar, if it is displayed. The `af:table inlineStyle` attribute value needs to be set as shown here:

```
inlineStyle="height:190px;"
```

NOTE
If you use a custom look and feel that you define through skinning, as explained in Chapter 16, the height of a table row is defined by the `af|table::data-row` *skin selector. If you use the Oracle defined "blafplus-rich" look and feel, the row height is 16 px.*

How to Size the Table Height to Fit the Number of Rows

Another use case for sizing the `af:table` component is to reduce the table size when the number of rows does not reach a defined threshold. The default behavior of the ADF Faces table component is that its height is independent from the number of rows it displays. If the number of

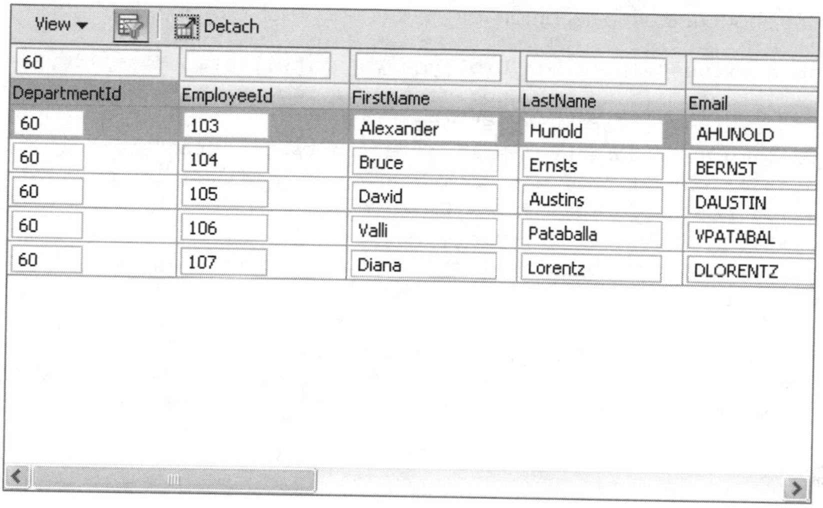

View ▼ 📑 ☑ Detach				
60				
DepartmentId	EmployeeId	FirstName	LastName	Email
60	103	Alexander	Hunold	AHUNOLD
60	104	Bruce	Ernsts	BERNST
60	105	David	Austins	DAUSTIN
60	106	Valli	Pataballa	VPATABAL
60	107	Diana	Lorentz	DLORENTZ

FIGURE 9-2   *ADF Faces table displaying fewer rows than can be displayed*

data rows exceeds the number of rows that can be displayed due to the table height, the table automatically adds a vertical scrollbar for the user to navigate to the hidden rows. If the number of queried data rows is less than what can be displayed, by default the table does not shrink its size, as shown in Figure 9-2.

Developers who need the table to reduce its height in this situation can set the `contentDelivery` attribute to `immediate` and the `autoHeightRows` attribute to the value of rows until when the table height is reduced.

The value of the `autoHeightRows` attribute cannot exceed the value set for the `fetchSize` attribute. Also, the table height must not be set using CSS in the `inlineStyle` attribute. Both the `autoHeightRows` and the `contentDelivery` attributes support Expression Language to define their values. Using the `estimatedRowCount` method that is exposed on the ADF iterator, developers can change the table behavior dynamically.

NOTE
If you want to combine the auto size functionality with defining the maximum size of table rows displayed, you can use Expression Language to set the `inlineStyle height` *value. Depending on the outcome of the estimated row count method, you can set the* `inlineStyle` *height from a managed bean method.*

Creating ADF Bound ADF Faces Tables

You create ADF bound tables by dragging a collection, such as an ADF Business Components View Object instance, from the Data Controls panel to the JSF page. Doing so displays a menu with the available rendering choices. Selecting the ADF Table or ADF Read-only Table option opens a dialog for the developer to perform basic table configure—for example, to choose whether the table rows are selectable, to change the order of the attributes shown in the columns, or to enable the column filter option, which is shown in Figure 9-1. The following sample code shows the shortened table definition for the Read-only Table option:

```
<af:table value="#{bindings.EmployeesView1.collectionModel}" var="row"
          rows="#{bindings.EmployeesView1.rangeSize}" …
          rowSelection="single" id="t1">
  <af:column sortProperty="EmployeeId" sortable="true" id="c1"
      headerText="#{bindings.EmployeesView1.hints.EmployeeId.label}" … >
    <af:outputText value="#{row.EmployeeId}" id="ot1">
      <af:convertNumber groupingUsed="false"
          pattern="#{bindings.EmployeesView1.hints.EmployeeId.format}"/>
    </af:outputText>
  </af:column>
  <af:column sortProperty="FirstName" sortable="true" id="c2"
      headerText="#{bindings.EmployeesView1.hints.FirstName.label}" … >
    <af:outputText value="#{row.FirstName}" id="ot3"/>
  </af:column>
  <af:column …>
    …
  </af:column>
  …
</af:table>
```

For each table, an ADF tree binding is created in the page definition file and referenced from the `bindings` object to provide the table data. In this example, the hierarchical tree binding is named EmployeesView1. The "`row`" variable points to the current row of the EmployeesView1. collectionModel. As you can see, all table information, including header labels, are read from the binding layer, which, in the case of ADF Business Components, reads the information from the business service.

NOTE
ADF Faces tables are bound to ADF using the ADF tree binding. This might be confusing to new developers or developers coming from a previous release of Oracle JDeveloper, which used a separate table binding definition. You can look at tables as trees that consist of a single node level. Using the ADF tree binding to populate tables does not remove any of the table functionality, but instead allows you to use a consistent binding for all collection models.

The ADF Read-only Dynamic Table option creates a table that uses the `af:forEach` component as a child to dynamically determine the attributes to show in the table columns:

```
<af:table rows="#{bindings.EmployeesView1.rangeSize}" var="row"
          value="#{bindings.EmployeesView1.collectionModel}"
          rowSelection="single" id="t1" … >
  <af:forEach items="#{bindings.EmployeesView1.attributeDefs}" var="def">
    <af:column headerText="#{bindings.EmployeesView1.labels[def.name]}"
               sortable="true" sortProperty="#{def.name}" id="c1">
      <af:outputText value="#{row[def.name]}" id="ot1"/>
```

```
    </af:column>
  </af:forEach>
</af:table>
```

Using Expression Language, developers can reference UI hints, such as width, height, label, or display hint, that are defined on the ADF Business Components View Object attributes. For example, to conditionally hide columns based on the setting of the View Object `displayHint` property, you'd use an expression like the one shown next in the `rendered` attribute of the `af:column` component:

```
rendered=
  "#{bindings.EmployeesView1.hints.Salary.displayHint!='Hide'}"
```

This code is used for tables that define their columns at design time. In this case, you reference the View Object attribute name, here using the `Salary` reference, to access the view hints. If the table is a dynamic table, the View Object attribute is dynamically determined as shown next:

```
rendered=
  "#{bindings.EmployeesView1.hints[def.name].displayHint!='Hide'}"
```

How to Configure Table Row Selection

The ADF Faces table supports single- and multi-row selection through its `rowSelection` attribute. Developers set the initial value in the Edit Table Columns dialog that opens when creating a table by dragging a collection, such as an ADF Business Components View Object, from the Data Controls panel. Selecting the Row Selection checkbox of the dialog sets the `rowSelection` attribute value to `single`. Leaving the checkbox unchecked sets the `rowSelection` attribute value to `none`. Tables that are configured for the single row selection have their `selectedRowKeys` attribute configured pointing to the binding layer. The `makeCurrent` method that is referenced from the table `selectionListener` attribute makes sure that the selected row shown in the table corresponds to the current row in the ADF iterator binding.

To configure a table for multi-row selection, in which users can select multiple rows by pressing the CTRL or SHIFT key when clicking a row, developers change the `rowSelection` attribute value to `multiple` using the Property Inspector. If the preceding table configuration was for single-row selection, then the `selectedRowKeys` attribute value must be cleared for the multi-row use case to work. This is because in JDeveloper 11*g* R1, the ADF binding layer does not support multiple current rows. If you don't clear the `selectedRowKeys` attribute in the table, the selected row keys always contain a single entry, which is the key of the last row you selected.

How to Create New Table Rows as Copies of an Existing Row

The ADF Faces table component does not expose an API to create or delete table rows. To create new rows in a table, Fusion developers use the `CreateInsert` or `Create with parameters` operations that are exposed in the Operations node of the View Object collection entry in the Data Controls panel. The `CreateInsert` operation creates a new row and adds it to the existing transaction, which is a requirement for the row to show in the table. The `Create with parameters` operation works similarly but allows developers to define default values dynamically for some or all of the row attributes. A typical use case for the `Create with parameters` operation is to create a new row as a duplicate of a selected row.

To implement the `Create with parameters` operation, drag the `Create with parameters` operation of the View Object that is used with the table from the Data Controls panel and drop it on the page as a button, link, or menu item. A new operation binding with the default name `CreateWithParams` is created in the page definition file. Alternatively you can use the Bindings tab to create the bindings manually to reference it from an existing command button.

NOTE
You can change the default name of the operation binding to a more meaningful name using the Property Inspector. When doing so, make sure you also change the button `actionListener` *attribute reference to it.*

Select the binding in the JDeveloper Structure window and choose Insert inside CreateWithParams | NamedData for each attribute for which you want to define a default value. The `NamedData` element has the following editable properties.

- **NDName** The attribute name for which you want to provide the default value.

- **NDType** The class of the data, such as `java.lang.String`.

- **NDValue** An Expression Language reference to the object that provides the default value. Clicking the arrow icon next to the property field and choosing the Edit option from the context menu opens the Expression Builder dialog.

The ADF Faces table component needs to be partially refreshed after the new row is created. This can be configured manually at the table `partialTriggers` attribute, referencing the `Id` attribute of the command component that invokes the delete operation.

To define the default value as the duplicate of an attribute in the current row, you first need to create an attribute binding for the attribute to copy the value from. Then in the `NDValue` property of the `NamedData` element, you use an expression such as `#{bindings.<attribute name>.inputValue}`. To create an attribute binding, you select the Bindings tab at the bottom of the JSF page and click the green plus icon in the Bindings category and choose the attribute Values entry. Alternatively you can open the PageDef file in the Structure window, select the bindings node, and choose Insert inside bindings | Generic Bindings | attribute Values. In the opened dialog, select the iterator used by the table and choose the attribute you want to access from the `NDValue` property.

NOTE
The use case described above works for tables that are configured for single-row selection. If the table supports multi-row selection, you need to iterate over the set of selected rows programmatically to create the duplicates. In the iteration, you call the `CreateWithParams` *action binding as an* `OperationBinding` *and set its* `NamedData` *items through the parameter map. The section "How to Delete Table Rows" contains the managed bean code to access the selected table rows in a table.*

How to Create New Table Rows Using Deep Copy

If you need to copy multiple rows of a View Object, then instead of creating the copy on the binding layer, you can use the deep copy feature on the ADF Business Components ViewObjectImpl class for better performance. The deep copy feature is exposed as a method, deepCopy, on the RowSet class and can be used to copy all rows of a View Object or only those in the current range. Using deep copy, to avoid unique constraint violations, the values of the key attributes are not copied and need to be added manually to the copied rows. Developers can also decide which of the copied row attributes copy their values to the new row. The result of the copy is a rowset that contains the new rows. Optionally, the deepCopy method can also be used to copy dependent children of a copied row, which are referenced by a view link.

The deepCopy method takes two arguments: a list of attribute values that are copied to the new row and a hint of how many rows to copy. Specifying null as the first argument copies the values of all row attributes, except the value of those attributes that are part of the row key. To explicitly define a list of attributes from which to copy the values, you create a HashMap containing a name value pair of an ADF Business Components View Object name and an array of AttributeDef objects or an array of attribute names. For the second argument, use RowSet.COPY_OPT_LIMIT_RANGE to copy all rows in range or RowSet.COPY_OPT_ALL_ROWS to copy all rows of the View Object.

As an example, assume that you need to copy all records of the employee table that are in the current range. In a master-detail relationship, you use this to copy all employee records of a selected parent department. To implement this use case, you create a method like that shown next in the Employees View Object implementation class, EmployeesViewImpl, which you create from the Java option in the View Object editor:

```
import oracle.jbo.RowSetIterator;
import oracle.jbo.RowSet;
import oracle.jbo.server.ViewRowSetImpl;
import oracle.jbo.domain.Number;
...
public void copyEmployeeRows(){
  ViewRowSetImpl vrs =  null;
  vrs = (ViewRowSetImpl) this.deepCopy(null,
                              RowSet.COPY_OPT_LIMIT_RANGE);
  RowSetIterator rowIterator = vrs.getRowSetIterator();
  while(rowIterator.hasNext()){
    Row rw = rowIterator.next();
    Number newPkValue = ... derive new PK value ...
    rw.setAttribute("EmployeeId", newPkValue);
  }
  //for this example, add the copied rows to the View Object
  this.addRowSet(vrs);
}
```

You then expose the method as a client interface of the View Object so it becomes available in the Data Controls panel. From the Data Controls panel, you can add the client interface method as a command component, such as a button or link, to the JSF page. On the command component, you set the partialSubmit attribute to true and the partialTriggers attribute of the table to point to the command component id attribute value so the table is refreshed in response to executing the method.

Additional examples of the deepCopy method are provided in the Java API documentation of the RowSet class available at http://otn.oracle.com. To access the documentation, choose Documentation | Fusion Middleware | View Library | References and APIs | Oracle ADF Model | RowSet starting from the main menu.

NOTE
The deep copy feature is not restricted to use in combination with tables but can be used when ever you need to create a copy of existing View Object row sets.

How to Delete Table Rows

Several options are available to delete rows in a table. In this section, we introduce three choices: a declarative option that uses the binding layer, a code-based solution that accesses the binding layer through the table row itself, and a solution that uses a client method on the business service to remove rows. Similar to creating new rows, the table needs to be partially refreshed after the operation.

How to Delete a Row from a Command Link in the Table

A popular use case is for a user to delete a table row by clicking a link contained in a column of the same row.

To implement this use case, you add an empty column to the table. In the JDeveloper Structure window, select the table entry and choose Insert inside af:table | Column from context menu option. From the Data Controls panel, drag-and-drop the removeRowWithKey operation of the View Object entry that you used to build the table into the column. From the opened context menu, choose Operation | ADF Link.

NOTE
If the dragged operation does not require input parameters then the context menu directly lists the possible command item options, like ADF Link.

In the opened action binding dialog, define an Expression Language value for the rowKey parameter, pointing to an attribute in memory scope. For example, using #{requestScope. key} reads the rowKey value from the request scope.

Select the command link in the column and set its PartialSubmit property to true. From the ADF Faces Component Palette, expand the Operations accordion panel and choose the Set Property Listener entry. Drag-and-drop the Set Property Listener component on top of the command link and provide the following information in the opened dialog:

Field	Value
From	#{row.rowKeyStr}
To	#{requestScope.key}
Type	"action"

When clicked the command link writes the rowKey of the row in which it is located to the request scope attribute from where it is accessible for the ADF action binding. If the change policy is set to PPR for the ADF tree binding and the iterator binding, then there is no need to refresh the table explicitly. If your page has a commit or rollback command added, for example as buttons, you use a Partial Triggers property reference on these buttons pointing to the command link in the table to refresh so they become enabled after deleting a row. The table column definition should look like this:

```
<af:column id="c5">
  <af:commandLink text="delete" id="cl1" partialSubmit="true"
                  disabled="#{!bindings.removeRowWithKey.enabled}"
                  actionListener="#{bindings.removeRowWithKey.execute}">
    <af:setPropertyListener from="#{row.rowKeyStr}"
                            to="#{requestScope.key}"
                            type="action"/>
  </af:commandLink>
</af:column>
```

Deleting Multiple Rows from a Managed Bean

ADF Faces table components that have a component binding set to a managed bean through their `binding` attribute are accessible from action methods in the same managed bean. In the example, we created a component binding with the name table1, which created a managed bean property `table1`, with its getter and setter methods, as an instance of `RichTable`. Because we want to delete only the selected rows and not navigate off the page, we use the `actionListener` attribute on a button that has its `partialSubmit` attribute set to `true` to invoke the managed bean method. The action listener method is shown here:

```
import java.util.Iterator;
import javax.faces.event.ActionEvent;
import oracle.adf.view.rich.component.rich.data.RichTable;
import oracle.adf.view.rich.context.AdfFacesContext;
import oracle.jbo.Row;
import oracle.jbo.uicli.binding.JUCtrlHierNodeBinding;
import org.apache.myfaces.trinidad.model.RowKeySet;
...
public void onDelete(ActionEvent actionEvent) {
  //access the RichTable from the JSF component binding
  //created for the table component
  RichTable _table = this.getTable1();
  RowKeySet rks = _table.getSelectedRowKeys();
  //iterate over the set of selected row keys and delete
  //each of the found rows
  Iterator selectedRowIterator = rks.iterator();
  while (selectedRowIterator.hasNext()){
    //get the first key
    Object key = selectedRowIterator.next();
    //make the row current
    _table.setRowKey(key);
    //the row is an instance of the ADF node binding class
    JUCtrlHierNodeBinding rowWrapper = null;
    rowWrapper = (JUCtrlHierNodeBinding) _table.getRowData();
    //get the actual oracle.jbo.Row object
    Row row = rowWrapper.getRow();
```

```
      row.remove();
   }
   //partially update the ADF Faces Table
   AdfFacesContext adfFacesContext = AdfFacesContext.getCurrentInstance();
   adfFacesContext.addPartialTarget(_table);
}
```

This approach allows you to write generic code because it requires only an instance RichTable to operate on. Though this solution works for single- and multi-row selections, if you are striving for best performance, you should have a look at the next section.

How to Implement Multi-Row Delete

Deleting multiple selected rows in a multi-select table should be implemented using a client method exposed on the ADF Business Components model instead of recursively iterating over the RowKeySet of selected rows to call remove on it. In addition, deleting row data is a business service operation that does not belong in the view layer. To implement the multi-row delete use case using the business service layer, the table must be configured for multi-row selection and the table selectionListener attribute and selectedRowKeys attribute values must be cleared.

To implement multi-row delete, you could create an action binding for the Delete or RemoveWithKey operations that are exposed in the Data Controls panel for a View Object and then repeatedly call the operation binding from a managed bean. While this works, it is not considered a best practice.

Instead, we recommend creating a client method on the business service that you expose as a method binding in the ADF page definition. This encapsulates the business service layer functionality and also promotes reuse.

The example in this section uses a client method that is exposed on the ADF Business Components View Object. The client method is configured as a method binding in the ADF binding layer and expects a java.util.List argument. The list contains the row keys of the selected table rows for the business service to process.

```
/**
 * Method that performs a bulk delete of all employees that are
 * referenced by the keys in the list
 * @param employees The list of employee keys
 * @return void.
 */
public void processEmployeeBulkDelete(List employees){
  if (employees != null){
    for (Object employee : employees) {
      Key k = (Key)employee;
      Row[] rowsFound = this.findByKey(k,1);
      //if the key returns more than one row then the provided
      //key obviously is not unique. Ignore in this sample
      if (rowsFound != null && rowsFound.length == 1) {
        //get the first entry in the array of rows found
        Row employeeRow = rowsFound[0];
        employeeRow.remove();
      }
    }
  }
}
```

NOTE
Chapter 1 explains how to configure an ADF Business Component View Object to create a <ViewObject>Impl *method and how to expose it as a client method.*

To invoke the method from a command component, you need to do the following:

■ Create a request scoped manage bean that contains a method to produce the list of selected row keys. The example in this section uses a method with the name getSelectedAdfRowKeys.

■ Create a JSF component binding for the table to the managed bean. This is done using the JDeveloper Property Inspector and the Binding property.

The managed bean has the following content:

```
import java.util.ArrayList;
import java.util.List;
import oracle.adf.view.rich.component.rich.data.RichTable;
import oracle.jbo.Key;
import oracle.jbo.uicli.binding.JUCtrlHierNodeBinding;
...
public List getSelectedAdfRowKeys() {
  List<Key> retVal = new ArrayList<Key>();
  //get the selected row keys from the table instance
  for (Object rowKey : employeesTable.getSelectedRowKeys()) {
    //make the row the current row
    employeesTable.setRowKey(rowKey);
    Object o = employeesTable.getRowData();
    //table rows are represented by the JUCtrlHierNodeBinding
    //binding class
    JUCtrlHierNodeBinding rowData = (JUCtrlHierNodeBinding)o;
    //add the row key to the list
    retVal.add(rowData.getRow().getKey());
  }
  return retVal;
}
//JSF component binding of the table
public void setEmployeesTable(RichTable employeesTable) {
  this.employeesTable = employeesTable;
}
public RichTable getEmployeesTable() {
  return employeesTable;
}
```

To invoke the multi-row delete method and to create a method binding for the ADF Business Component client method, drag the processEmployeeBulkDelete method entry from the Data Controls panel to the page and choose a command action component from the Method option in the opened context menu. This opens a dialog where you can configure the input argument for the method. Use the Expression Builder to reference the getSelectedAdfRowKeys method in the managed bean. The ADF binding looks like the following after clicking OK to close the dialog:

```
<methodAction id="processEmployeeBulkDelete" RequiresUpdateModel="true"
  Action="invokeMethod" MethodName="processEmployeeBulkDelete"
  IsViewObjectMethod="true" DataControl="HRAppModuleDataControl"
  InstanceName="HRAppModuleDataControl.EmployeesView1"
  IterBinding="EmployeesView1Iterator">
  <NamedData NDName="employees"
    NDValue="${MultiRowDeleteBean.selectedAdfRowKeys}"
    NDType="java.util.List"/>
</methodAction>
```

The command button that we created for this example uses the following configuration:

```
<af:commandButton
  actionListener="#{bindings.processEmployeeBulkDelete.execute}"
  text="Delete Rows"
  disabled="#{!bindings.processEmployeeBulkDelete.enabled}"
  id="cb1" partialSubmit="true" partialTriggers="t1"/>
```

Note the `partialSubmit` attribute that ensures the delete operation is executed as a partial request. To refresh the table, using the Property Inspector you need to configure the `PartialTriggers` property of the table component to point to the command button `id` value.

NOTE
The server-side code of the multi-row delete works the same for trees and treeTables components. The required modification is to create client methods for each View Object used by a tree. You then call the method of the View Object to which the row keys you want to delete belong. Later in this chapter in the section "Use Case: How to Show Additional Information in a Pop-up," we'll show you how to determine the View Object referenced by a node using the `JUCtrlHierTypeBinding` *information.*

How to Assign a Keyboard Shortcut to the Delete Operation

Often, instead of clicking a button with the mouse or navigating to it using the tab key, users want to perform an action using a keyboard shortcut. You can set the `accessKey` or `textAndAccessKey` attribute on the command button to define a mnemonic, which is a key that you use in combination with the ALT key to perform the command button's action. One problem with mnemonics is that the application-specified mnemonic may be the same mnemonic defined on the browser, in which case the browser function is invoked. Using JavaScript, you can work around this problem by defining your own keyboard shortcuts.

In the following example, we add an `af:clientListener` behavior tag to the `af:table` component to invoke a JavaScript function to execute the action defined for the delete button shown in the preceding section. The JavaScript function invokes only the command button action if the pressed keyboard key combination is CTRL-DELETE.

To invoke a client-side JavaScript function when the user presses a key on the table, you add the `af:clientListener` behavior tag to the table, as shown next:

```
<af:table value="#{bindings.EmployeesView11.collectionModel}" var="row"
          partialTriggers="::cb1" … >
  <af:clientListener type="keyUp" method="performDeleteFromKeyBoard"/>
  …
</af:table>
```

If the user presses a key while the focus is on the `af:table` component, the `perform DeleteFromKeyBoard` JavaScript function is called. The JavaScript function can be added anywhere on the page using the `af:resource` tag, as shown next. Note that the JavaScript uses only the APIs exposed on the ADF Faces client framework and never performs any direct Document Object Model (DOM) access.

```
<af:resource type="javascript">
   function performDeleteFromKeyBoard(evt){
      //invoke delete command button action if ctrl+delete key is pressed
      keyPressed = evt.getKeyCode();
      //get the pressed modifiers shift, ctrl and alt
      modifiers =  evt.getKeyModifiers();
      if (keyPressed == AdfKeyStroke.DELETE_KEY){
        if(modifiers == AdfKeyStroke.CTRL_MASK){
           //delete key is pressed, go find the command button by its
           //"id" property value and id of possible naming containers
           deleteButton = AdfPage.PAGE.findComponentByAbsoluteId('cb1');
           partial = true;
           //create new action event
           deleteEvent =  new AdfActionEvent(deleteButton);
           //queue command button action
           deleteButton.queueEvent(deleteEvent,partial);
        }
      }
   }
</af:resource>
```

NOTE
The ADF Faces RC JavaScript client framework is explained in Chapter 19, as well as the `af:clientlistener` *and the* `af:resource` *tags. Chapter 19 also explains how to invoke a managed bean method from JavaScript using the* `af:serverListener` *tag when you don't want to invoke a command action programmatically on the page but you want to use a method on the server.*

How to Display the Selected Row When the Table Renders

The table `displayRow` attribute determines the row that is displayed in the table view when the table initially renders or re-renders. The default setting is to always show the value range of the first table row, which is not optimal to use if the table refreshes after the user selected a row for which he scrolled the table. To always show the table range of the selected row, set the `displayRow` attribute value to `selected`. To always show the range of the last record, choose `last`.

How to Navigate to a Specific Row in a Table

The Oracle JDeveloper integrated development environment (IDE) provides a convenient functionality in the source code editor that allows developers to access a specific code line quickly by pressing the CTRL-G shortcut. This functionality may also be useful if provided by an application for the user to specify a row number to which to navigate. The use case is shown in Figure 9-3.

The implementation shown in Figure 9-3 consists of two parts: the launch of the pop-up dialog from JavaScript immediately when the user presses CTRL-G with the focus set into the table, and the server-side code handling the user row selection. The pop-up dialog contains an `af:inputNumberSpinner` component that has a JSF component binding reference to the managed bean that handles the dialog submit. On dialog submit, the use-specified row number is read and set as the range start of the data range shown in the table, which forces the table to fetch additional data if the row index is outside of the current displayed table range. The pop-up dialog is defined as shown here:

```
<af:popup id="p1">
  <af:panelWindow id="pw1" modal="true" inlineStyle="width:250px;"
    title="Go to table row">
    <af:panelGroupLayout id="pgl1" layout="horizontal">
      <af:inputNumberSpinbox label="Row number" id="ins1" minimum="1"
        maximum="#{bindings.EmployeesView1.estimatedRowCount}"
        value="#{SearchRowBean.rowNumber}"/>
      <af:commandButton text="Go" id="cb1" partialSubmit="true"
        actionListener="#{SearchRowBean.onRowSearch}"/>
    </af:panelGroupLayout>
  </af:panelWindow>
</af:popup>
```

NOTE
Chapter 10 explains how to work with the `af:popup` component. In this chapter, we keep the focus on the work with the `af:table` component, which is why we aren't discussing the details of working with pop-up dialogs here.

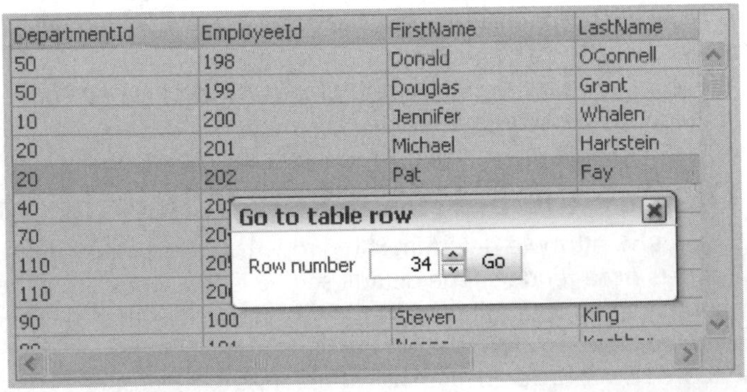

DepartmentId	EmployeeId	FirstName	LastName
50	198	Donald	OConnell
50	199	Douglas	Grant
10	200	Jennifer	Whalen
20	201	Michael	Hartstein
20	202	Pat	Fay
40	20		
70	20		
110	20		
110	20		
90	100	Steven	King

Go to table row

Row number   34 ⇕   Go

FIGURE 9-3   *Table that uses a pop-up dialog for the user to specify a row number to which to navigate*

To launch the pop-up when the user presses CTRL-G, the af:table component has the following af:clientListener defined:

```
<af:table
      rowSelection="single" id="t1"
      inlineStyle="height:190px; width:400.0px;"
      displayRow="selected" binding="#{SearchRowBean.table1}">
   <af:column ...>
      ...
   </af:column>
      ...
   <af:clientListener type="keyDown" method="launchTableRowScroller"/>
</af:table>
```

The launchTableRowScroller JavaScript function is called when the user presses a key with the table set in focus. But only if the key combination is CTRL-G will a dialog open for the user to specify the row to which to navigate.

```
<af:resource type="javascript">
   function launchTableRowScroller(evt){
      //stop server propagation
      evt.cancel();
      //keyboard code for the g character
      G_KEY = 71;
      //call delete command if ctrl+g key is pressed
      keyPressed = evt.getKeyCode();
      modifiers = evt.getKeyModifiers();
      if (keyPressed == G_KEY){
        if(modifiers == AdfKeyStroke.CTRL_MASK){
          //find popup by is id attribute value
          popup = AdfPage.PAGE.findComponentByAbsoluteId('p1');
            //display popup in the center of the screen
            var hints = {};
            popup.show(hints);
        }
      }
   }
</af:resource>
```

The managed bean code that is referenced from the actionListener attribute of the af:commandButton component in the dialog searches the table row and also closes the pop-up dialog:

```
import oracle.adf.model.binding.DCIteratorBinding;
import oracle.adf.view.rich.component.rich.data.RichTable;
import oracle.adf.view.rich.context.AdfFacesContext;
import oracle.jbo.Key;
import oracle.jbo.Row;
import oracle.jbo.uicli.binding.JUCtrlHierBinding;
import org.apache.myfaces.trinidad.model.CollectionModel;
import org.apache.myfaces.trinidad.model.RowKeySetImpl;
...
public void onRowSearch(ActionEvent actionEvent) {
```

```
//get ADF Faces RC table model. The "table1" reference is created
//when creating the JSF component binding for the table using its
//binding property
CollectionModel collectionModel = (CollectionModel)table1.getValue();
//the CollectionModel provides access to the ADF Binding for this
//table
JUCtrlHierBinding tableBinding = null;
tableBinding = (JUCtrlHierBinding) collectionModel.getWrappedData();
//access the iterator that populates the ADF binding with data
DCIteratorBinding iteratorBinding = tableBinding.getDCIteratorBinding();
//set the range start to the row number specified by the application
//user. Reduce the provided value by 1 because the table row index is
//zero based. The rowNumber is the variable that is referenced from the
//af:inputNumberSpinner component "value" attribute
iteratorBinding.setRangeStart(rowNumber-1);
//the first row in the new range is the row the user wants to access
Row currentRow = iteratorBinding.getRowAtRangeIndex(0);
//get the oracle.jbo.Key of the row to make it current
Key rowKey = currentRow.getKey();
//the ADF Faces RC table row key is defined as a List
ArrayList tableRowKey = new ArrayList();
//add the oracle oracle.jbo.Key to the table rowKey
tableRowKey.add(rowKey);
//mark the found row as selected
RowKeySetImpl rks = new RowKeySetImpl();
rks.add(tableRowKey);
table1.setSelectedRowKeys(rks);
//close the popup dialog. See "Calling a JavaScript function from a
//managed bean" in chapter 19 for the programming details of the
//closePopup method
closePopup("p1");
//PPR the table
AdfFacesContext.getCurrentInstance().addPartialTarget(table1);
}
```

How to Display Row Numbers

The table varStatus attribute defines the name for the table context variable that exists for the time the table is rendered. In the Property Inspector, the attribute is listed as a property in the Columns category. The default value of the varStatus is defined as vs. The status variable allows developers to access the row index and the table CollectionModel within the table child components. An example of how this information can be used is the display of the row number in front of the table row.

To add a column to display the row number, do the following:

1. Select the table in the Structure window (CTRL-SHIFT-S) and choose Insert inside af:table | Column from the context menu.

2. Still in the Structure window, select the new column and drag it on top of the other columns so it becomes the first column in the table.

3. Open the context menu and choose Insert inside af:column | Output Text.

4. Select the Output Text component in the Structure window and set the value attribute to #{vs.index+1} using the Property Inspector. The row index is zero based, hence the +1.

NOTE
The vs *and the* row *attribute are also accessible from the Expression Builder that you can launch from the context menu of the selected property after clicking the arrow icon. The attribute values are listed under the JSP Object node.*

How to Create and Customize Table Query Filters

When creating an ADF bound table, the table configuration dialog shows a Filtering checkbox option to enable application users to query the table by example (QBE). Enabling the table filter functionality, the following happens:

- A search binding is added to the executables section in the ADF page definition file of the containing page. The binding is configured by the <searchRegion> metadata element.

- The queryListener attribute is set to reference the processQuery method that is exposed by the <searchRegion> implementation class.

- The filterModel attribute is set to point to the query descriptor exposed on the ADF hierarchical binding that exists for the table.

- The filterVisible attribute is set to true to display the filter input components above the table header, as shown in Figure 9-4. The filterVisible attribute value can be set using Expression Language, allowing the application developer to dynamically control when a user is and isn't allowed to filter the table.

- The filterable attribute is set to true on the contained columns. To exclude a column from query-by-example, set this property to false.

When the filter option is enabled for a table, the af:table component definition appears as follows:

```
<af:table value="#{bindings.EmployeesView1.collectionModel}" var="row"
    ...
        filterModel="#{bindings.EmployeesView1Query.queryDescriptor}"
        filterVisible="true" varStatus="vs"
        queryListener="#{bindings.EmployeesView1Query.processQuery}">
...
</af:table>
```

Figure 9-2 shows the default table filter component added on top of the table header. In the following section, we explain how the default filter can be customized.

NOTE
By default, case sensitivity of QBE is model-dependent. Case sensitivity can be explicitly set for a column using its FilterFeatures property. Allowed values for this property are caseSensitive *and* caseInsensitive.

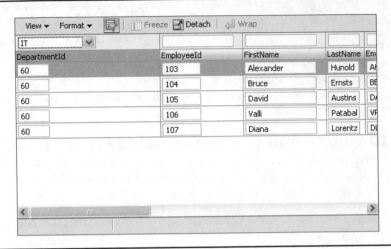

FIGURE 9-4 *Custom table filter input component with a user-friendly label*

How to Create a Table Filter as a Select List

Developers who want to guide their users who are entering query filter conditions can customize the filter input component by adding an ADF Faces UI component to the `af:column` filter facet. For example, to enforce valid user input for the DepartmentId filter shown in Figure 9-2, an `af:selectOneChoice` component can be used to display a list of allowed values, as shown in Figure 9-4. Using the `af:selectOneChoice` component, you can also display user-friendly labels for the filter values.

To implement an `af:selectOneChoice` component for a table filter, perform the following steps:

1. Select the ADF page definition file of the page that contains the table in the JDeveloper Application Navigator and choose Open from the context menu.

2. If the page definition file opens in the source view, select the Overview tab at the bottom of the editor.

3. Click the green plus icon and choose the tree binding from the list.

4. Click the Add button to create a new Root Data Source reference or select from a list of existing iterators. The root data source provides the list data and should point to a View Object that you created for the data lookup. Don't use any View Object that you use for data input within your application. Ideally, though not mandatory, the View Object for the data lookup is created read-only.

5. Click the green plus icon next to the Tree Level Rules title and choose the AddRule menu option. This creates a rule entry for the top-level View Object of the selected root data source.

6. From the list available attributes, select an attribute for the list value and, optionally, one for display. In the example, we choose the DepartmentId for the list value and the DepartmentName for a user-friendly label.

7. In the JDeveloper Structure window, select the table column to customize the filter for and expand the Column facets node so you can access the filter facet. Ensure the page containing the table is opened in the Oracle JDeveloper visual editor.

8. From the JDeveloper Component Palette, drag-and-drop a Select One Choice component into the filter facet. In the opened dialog, click Finish without performing any configuration.

9. Select the Select One Choice Component in the filter facet using the Structure window, remove the f:selectItems child component and choose Insert inside af:selectOneChoice | ADF Faces | For Each from the right mouse context menu.

10. Select the `af:forEach` component and open the Property Inspector. Click the arrow icon next to the Items property and select the tree binding `rangeSet` method entry. The returned Expression Language expression should look like this: `#{bindings. DepartmentsView1.rangeSet}`.

11. Still in the Property Inspector for the `af:forEach` component, set the `Var` property value to `li`. The `Var` property defines the name for the variable that at runtime is used to populate the list.

12. Select the `af:forEach` component in the Structure Window and choose Insert inside af: forEach | JSF Core | Select Item. Make sure you choose Select Item and not Select Items.

13. In the Structure window, select the `f:selectItem` component and edit its label and value properties with the attributes defined in the tree binding. In our example, these attributes are `DepartmentName` and `DepartmentId`.

   - Item label: `#{li.DepartmentName}`
   - Item value: `#{li.DepartmentId}`

14. In the Structure window, select the `af:selectOneChoice` component and open the Property Inspector, if not already open. Configure the `value` property to point to the filter item to populate with the selected data. In our example, this is the `DepartmentId` item. The value therefore is set to `#{vs.filterCriteria.DepartmentId}`. Note the `vs` reference that points to the table status variable explained earlier. The filterCriteria and the vs entry are also accessed from the Expression Builder JSP Objects node.

With this configuration applied, the table `af:column` definition looks like this:

```
<af:table …
            filterModel="#{bindings.EmployeesView1Query.queryDescriptor}"
            queryListener=" #{bindings.EmployeesView1Query.processQuery}">
  <af:column sortProperty="DepartmentId" filterable="true" … >
    <af:inputText … > … </af:inputText>
    <f:facet name="filter">
      <af:selectOneChoice id="soc1"
        value="#{vs.filterCriteria.DepartmentId}">
        <af:forEach items="#{bindings.DepartmentsView1.rangeSet}"
          var="li">
        <f:selectItem id="si1" itemLabel="#{li.DepartmentName}"
            itemValue="#{li.DepartmentId}"/>
        </af:forEach>
      </af:selectOneChoice>
    </f:facet>
  </af:column>
  …
</af:table>
```

How to Configure the Table Filter Functionality for an Existing Table

What if the table filter functionality wasn't selected when you initially created the table? In this case, you can add this manually:

1. To prepare the ADF binding layer, select the ADF page definition file in the Structure window and open it by choosing Open from the context menu.

2. Select the Overview tab if the file opens in the source code view.

3. Click the green plus icon in the Executables section and select the searchRegion entry and provide a unique value for the `id` property, for example `DepartmentsTableFilter`.

4. With the new search region selected, open the Property Inspector and add the name of the ADF iterator, for example `DepartmentsView1Iterator`, that the table is bound to as the value of the `Binds` property.

5. Type **oracle.jbo.uicli.binding.JUSearchBindingCustomizer** as the value of the `Customizer` property. If the customizer setting is missing, an `IllegalStateException` is thrown at runtime. Keep the default values for all the other properties.

6. Select the table component in the visual editor or the Structure window, and edit the following properties in the Property Inspector:

   ■ QueryListener: #{bindings.DepartmentsTableFilter. processQuery}

   ■ FilterModel: #{bindings. DepartmentsTableFilter.queryDescriptor}

   ■ FilterVisible: True

7. To display the filter input fields for the table columns, press and hold down the CTRL key and click any column for which you want to display the filter. In the Property Inspector, set the `Filterable` property to `true`.

How to Handle Table Events

In response to user interaction, the ADF Table publishes JavaServer Faces events for which the application developer can configure event listeners. To implement the listener, you reference a managed bean method that has the required listener signature defined.

Query Event

A query event is published for the Query, QuickQuery, and Table components. Developers can register a query listener on the components to handle the event. In ADF, the query listener is implemented through the search binding `processQuery` method. Custom implementations use a managed bean method and reference it from the QueryListener property using Expression Language.

A custom query listener is required if, for example, you want to enhance the example shown in Figure 9-4 to use an `af:selectManyChoice` component to filter the table data by more than one criteria value, as shown in Figure 9-5.

The `af:selectManyChoice` component returns the selected values in an instance of `java.util.List`. To use this with the ADF search binding, the `List` needs to be translated into a search string that uses an *or* between the values. The custom listener method in the example shown in Figure 9-5 is shown next:

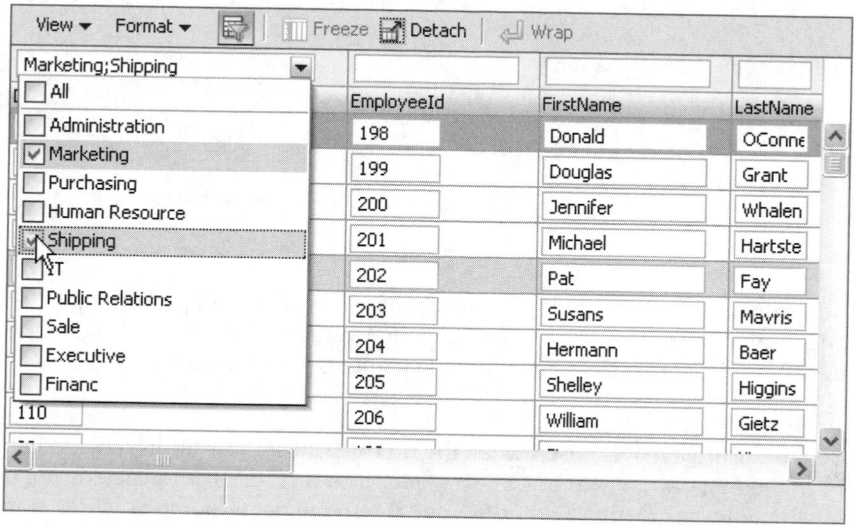

FIGURE 9-5 *ADF table with an* `af:selectManyChoice` *component to filter the DepartmentId column*

```
public void onQuery(QueryEvent queryEvent) {
  ArrayList<Number> departmentIdList = null;
  FilterableQueryDescriptor descriptor =
              (FilterableQueryDescriptor) queryEvent.getDescriptor();
  Map filterCriteriaMap = descriptor.getFilterCriteria();
  //get the filter entry for the DepartmentId.
  Object departmentIdObject = filterCriteriaMap.get("DepartmentId");
  //When the values are selected using the selectManyChoice component,
  //then parse the List. Otherwise remove the DepartmentId filter value
  //because it is empty
  if (departmentIdObject instanceof List){
    departmentIdList = (ArrayList<Number>) departmentIdObject;
  }
  else{
    filterCriteriaMap.remove("DepartmentId");
  }
  if (departmentIdList != null && departmentIdList.size()>0){
    //iterate over the list and "OR" together the values
    String departmentsSearchString;
    Iterator departmentsIter = departmentIdList.iterator();
    departmentsSearchString =
      ((Number)departmentsIter.next()).toString();
    while  (departmentsIter.hasNext()){
      //DepartmentId values are of type oracle.jbo.domain.Number
      departmentsSearchString = departmentsSearchString+" OR "+
                    ((Number)departmentsIter.next()).toString();
    }
```

```
    filterCriteriaMap.put("DepartmentId",departmentsSearchString);
    //execute processQuery on the ADF binding, passing the queryEvent
    //object as an argument
    invokeMethodExpression(
        "#{bindings.EmployeesView1Query.processQuery}",
            queryEvent, QueryEvent.class);
    //restore DepartmentId filter List value to preserve
    //user filter selection
    filterCriteriaMap.put("DepartmentId",departmentIdList);
  }
}
```

The configuration of the table filter is the same as in the example for Figure 9-4. The only difference is that the `QueryListener` property references the custom listener method. EmployeesView1Query is the search binding name used in this example.

Row Disclosure Event

The row disclosure event is raised when the user expands a row to display the UI components located in the `af:table detailStamp` facet. The `detailStamp` facet is not used by default, as you can see by comparing Figures 9-5 and 9-6. If the detail stamp contains components, each table row shows a leading column with a plus icon the user clicks to disclose the detail information. Figure 9-6 shows a modified version of the table shown in Figure 9-5 that uses an `af:panelFormLayout` to display additional table information in `InputText` components for update. Disclosing the `detailStamp` information issues a partial page rendering (PPR) request to the server and does not refresh the page.

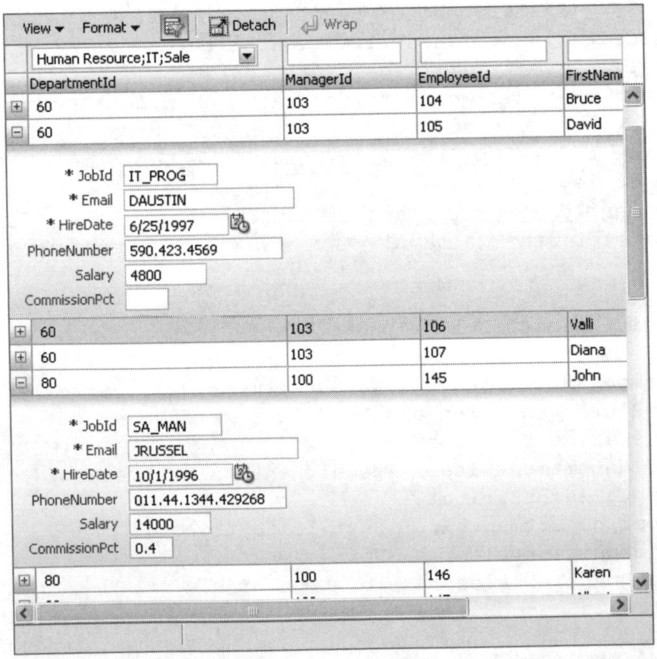

FIGURE 9-6 *Table showing a detailStamp facet with an inputForm*

To add content to the table `detailStamp` facet, expand the af:table | Table facets nodes in the Oracle JDeveloper Structure window and drag-and-drop UI components from the Component Palette into the window.

NOTE
The Table facet node only shows in the Structure window when the JSF page containing the table is opened in the Oracle JDeveloper visual page editor. To add the detailStamp facet without opening the visual page editor, select the table component in the Structure window and choose Insert inside <table> | JSF Core | Facet detailStamp.

To build the table in Figure 9-6 from the table in Figure 9-5, you add an `af:panelFormlayout` component to the `detailStamp` facet. Then drag the cell render component from the columns you want to hide from the table into the form layout component. After this, delete the `af:column` elements that are no longer used.

To respond to the disclosure of the table detail information, the developer can configure the `rowDisclosureListener` table attribute to reference a managed bean method. The managed bean method as well as the Expression Language reference to it can be created declaratively by clicking the arrow icon next to the `RowDislosureListener` property in the Property Inspector and choosing Edit from the context menu.

As shown in Figure 9-6, by default, users can disclose the detail information on multiple rows. A disclosure listener can be used to enforce that detail information for only one row is displayed at any time. An example disclosure listener method for this is shown here:

```
public void onDiscloseDetailInfo(RowDisclosureEvent rowDisclosureEvent) {
    RichTable table = (RichTable)rowDisclosureEvent.getSource();
    RowKeySet disclosedRowKeySet = table.getDisclosedRowKeys();
    RowKeySet lastAddedRowKeySet = rowDisclosureEvent.getAddedSet();
    Iterator lastAddedRowKeySetIter= lastAddedRowKeySet.iterator();
    //verify that this is a disclosing event
     if (lastAddedRowKeySetIter.hasNext()){
       disclosedRowKeySet.clear();
       //add the set that was added last
       Object lastRowKey = lastAddedRowKeySetIter.next();
       disclosedRowKeySet.add(lastRowKey);
       //make the disclosed row the current row
       makeDisclosedRowCurrent(table,lastAddedRowKeySet);
       AdfFacesContext adfFacesContext = null;
       adfFacesContext = AdfFacesContext.getCurrentInstance();
       //refresh the parent component - the PanelCollection
       //in this example - to refresh the table
       adfFacesContext.addPartialTarget(table.getParent());
    }
}
```

How to Make the Disclosed Row Current   Disclosing a table row does not make it the current row in the binding. As shown in the following code sample, you need to explicitly set the disclosed row as the current row in the binding and the table:

```
private void makeDisclosedRowCurrent(RichTable table, RowKeySet keySet){
    //set the disclosed row as the current row in the table
```

```
table.setSelectedRowKeys(keySet);
//set the disclosed row as the current in the binding
BindingContext bctx = BindingContext.getCurrent();
BindingContainer bindings = bctx.getCurrentBindingsEntry();
DCIteratorBinding dcIteratorBinding =
    (DCIteratorBinding) bindings.get("EmployeesView1Iterator");
Iterator keySetIter =  keySet.iterator();
//always use the first key in the list
List firstKey = (List) keySetIter.next();
//get first entry as this example assumes a single key
oracle.jbo.Key key = (oracle.jbo.Key) firstKey.get(0);
//set the current row in the binding based on the disclosed row
dcIteratorBinding.setCurrentRowWithKey(key.toStringFormat(true));
}
```

NOTE
In this example, the EmployeesView1Iterator reference is hard-coded in the method. Later in this chapter, we demonstrate how to derive the binding reference from the table model. This allows you to write generic code that works with all tables in an application.

Sort Event

Setting the `sortable` attribute of an `af:column` component to `true` and its `sortProperty` attribute to the model attribute to sort displays clickable ascending and descending sort icons in the column header. The `sortProperty` attribute value is passed to the table model as the sort criteria and contains the name of the ADF binding attribute to sort for. To sort a table using the keyboard, application user pressed CTRL-SHIFT-UP ARROW to sort ascending and the CTRL-SHIFT-DOWN ARROW for descend sorting.

NOTE
If the application runs in accessibility mode, hyperlinks are added to the table header for the screen reader to discover the sort action.

An example of implementing a custom sort behavior is performing the sort on multiple columns when clicking the table header icon. To implement multi-column sorting in an ADF Faces table, two changes need to be applied to the table shown in Figure 9-6. The first change is in the table column headers, which expose checkboxes for the user to select to indicate the columns that should be added to the sort. The second change is a sort method in a managed bean to modify the default sorting behavior. The table shown in Figure 9-7 is sorted by the DepartmentId column, where the user selected the sort icon. Secondary sorting is performed on the ManagerId and EmployeeId columns.

To add the checkbox components to the table header, you use the `af:column` header facet, which replaces the settings in the column `headerText` attribute, which is used in the earlier examples to define the header labels.

The following page code shows the `af:SelectBooleanCheckbox` element that is added to the column header facet. Note the use of the `f:attribute` component as a child of `af:SelectBooleanCheckbox`. The `f:attribute` component adds a custom property to the `af:SelectBooleanCheckbox` with the information about the column that should be added to the sort operation when the user checks the checkbox. To ensure the checkbox value is accessible

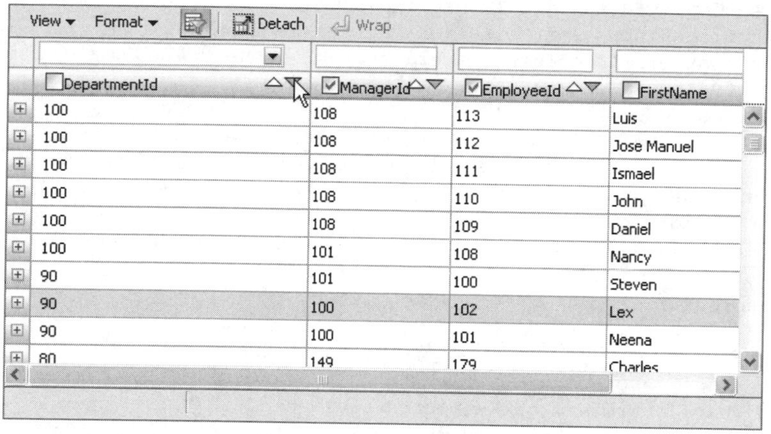

FIGURE 9-7 *ADF Faces table that supports multi-column sorting*

when the use performs the sort, the autoSubmit attribute on the af:
SelectBooleanCheckbox is set to true.

```
<af:column sortProperty="DepartmentId" sortable="true" …>
  <af:outputText value="#{row.bindings.DepartmentId.inputValue}"id="it3">
    …
  </af:outputText>
  …
  <f:facet name="header">
    <af:selectBooleanCheckbox id="sbc0" autoSubmit="true"
        text="#{bindings.EmployeesView1.hints.DepartmentId.label}">
      <f:attribute name="sortAttribute" value="DepartmentId"/>
    </af:selectBooleanCheckbox>
  </f:facet>
</af:column>
```

The ADF Faces table component references the sort method in a managed bean. To create this method, open the Property Inspector and click the arrow icon next to the QueryListener property. In the context menu, select the Edit option to create the method in a managed bean.

The method implementing the sort listener for the table shown in Figure 9-7 accesses the table instance and its columns through the sortEvent object that is passed in as the method argument. The column header facet is looked up to access the checkbox component instance in the header. If the checkbox is selected, its custom sortProperty, the f:attribute usage, attribute value is added as sort criteria to the table sorting:

```
public void onSort(SortEvent sortEvent) {
    //get the sort criteria produced by the user click on the
    //sort icon in the header
    RichTable table = (RichTable)sortEvent.getSource();
    List<SortCriterion> sortCriterionList = sortEvent.getSortCriteria();
    //obtain the attribute name of the selected column. This is the
    //column the user chose for the primary sorting
```

```
String selectedColumnHeader = sortCriterionList.get(0).getProperty();
//all secondary sorting will use the same order direction
boolean direction = sortCriterionList.get(0).isAscending();
//get a list of all column headers that have the checkbox selected
//the getSelectedHeaders method is shown next
List<String> columns = null;
columns = this.getSelectedHeaders(table,selectedColumnHeader);
//extend the default sort definition with the information from the
//selected headers
for(String column : columns){
  sortCriterionList.add(new SortCriterion(column,direction));
}
table.setSortCriteria(sortCriterionList);
}


/**
* Method that determines the selected table headers for the
* columns that need to be added to the sort
*/
private List<String> getSelectedHeaders(RichTable table,
                                        String sortedColumn){
  ArrayList<String> columns = new ArrayList<String>();
  //iterate over the table columns
  List<UIComponent> childList = table.getChildren();
  for(Object child : childList){
    //make sure child component is a column
    if (child instanceof RichColumn){
      RichColumn col = (RichColumn)child;
      RichSelectBooleanCheckbox headerCheckBox = null;
      //access the column "header" facet. Note that the assumption is
      //that the only child of this facet is the checkbox. If the child,
      //for example, is an af:panelGroup component that contains the
      //checkbox then the type casting must be to RichPanelGroup
      headerCheckBox = (RichSelectBooleanCheckbox)col.getFacet("header");
      //If the checkbox is selected, determine the value of the
      //"sortAttribute" attribute added by the f:attribute element
      if(headerCheckBox.isSelected()){
        Map columnAttributes = headerCheckBox.getAttributes();
        String header = (String) columnAttributes.get("sortAttribute");
        //Ensure the primary sort column isn't added twice
        if (!sortedColumn.equalsIgnoreCase(header)){
          columns.add(header);
        }
      }
    }
  }
  return columns;
}
```

The configuration changes applied to the table are shown here:

```
<af:table ... queryListener="#{BasicTableBean.onQuery}">
    ...
</af:table>
```

NOTE
If the table is a child of the `af:panelCollection` *component, then an implementation of the multiple column sort use case already exists using the Panel Collection View | Sort | Advanced menu option.*

Attribute Change Event

The attribute change event is raised for the `af:table` and the `af:column` components in response to attribute changes that are performed by the renderer. The change event is not published for programmatic changes. A use case that can be implemented with the `AttributeChangeListener` is to detect when the user hides or displays a table column using the `af:panelCollection` component menu. The `AttributeChangeListener` can be implemented through a managed bean reference from the column or table `attributeChangeListener` attribute. The method signature, shown next, provides information about the component that raised the event and the attribute that has changed the new attribute value and the old value.

```
public void onColumnAttributeChange(
            AttributeChangeEvent attributeChangeEvent) {
  //add custom code here
}
```

Selection Event

Developers can create and reference a custom `SelectionListener` implementation by clicking the arrow icon next to the SelectionListener property in the Property Inspector. By choosing the Edit option in the opened context menu, you can create a managed bean method that implements the listener interface.

A common use case that developers implement using a custom selection listener is to add pre- or post-processing instructions, such as showing an alert if the previous row edit wasn't completed, to the default single-row selection behavior. For this, the default functionality that is configured by an Expression Language string, as shown here, needs to be preserved in the custom listener:

```
<af:table value="#{bindings.EmployeesView1.collectionModel}" var="row"
  selectionListener=
  "#{bindings.EmployeesView1.collectionModel.makeCurrent}"
  rowSelection="single" id="t1" ...>
...
</table>
```

The `makeCurrent` method is exposed on the `FacesCtrlHierBinding` internal binding class. To access this functionality, you use the same expression string that was used in the table `selectionListener` attribute:

```
public void onSingleRowSelect(SelectionEvent selectionEvent) {
  //add pre-processing instructions here
  invokeMethodExpression(
     "#{bindings.EmployeesView1.collectionModel.makeCurrent}",
     selectionEvent,
     SelectionEvent.class);
  //add post processing instructions here
}
```

How to Export Table Data to Excel

A common requirement for web application developers is to export table data displayed on the screen to MS Excel. In ADF Faces RC, this use case can be implemented declaratively with the `af:exportCollectionActionListener` component. The export listener component can be used with the ADF Faces tree, table, and treeTable components and is added as a child component of a command button or command link. To add the export listener to a command button, select the Export Collection Action Listener entry in the ADF Faces Operations category in the JDeveloper Component Palette and drag it onto the command button. In the opened dialog click the arrow icon next to the ExportedId field and then choose the Edit option in the opened context menu. Browse to the table, tree, or treeTable component for which data should be exported and select it. The Type field currently supports only the export to Excel, so choose excelHTML as the value.

You can now access the `af:exportCollectionActionListener` element in the JDeveloper Structure window and open the Property Inspector to set additional export information such as a filename and title. Further, the data export can be configured to export either all rows of a component or only those that are selected on the screen.

Here is the configuration used to export the data from the table shown in Figure 9-8:

```
<af:commandToolbarButton text="MS Excel" id="ctb1">
  <af:exportCollectionActionListener
      exportedId="t1"
      type="excelHTML"
      title="Employees Table Data Export"
      filename="EmployeesOverview.xls"/>
</af:commandToolbarButton>
```

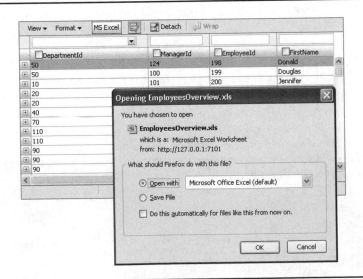

FIGURE 9-8   *Table with Excel export functionality*

HINT
The CommandToolbarButton *component always performs a partial submit. If you're using the export functionality from a command button or command link, make sure you set the* PartialSubmit *property to* true.

What You Should Know About the Data That Is Exported to Excel

The ExportCollectionActionListener component exports only the data of those columns that display their row values by a UI component that implemented the JSF ValueHolder interface, which are all components with a value attribute. Other components, such as a command link or command button, which are added to a table for displaying column data, don't export their display data to Excel. In addition, data contained in columns that are hidden by the time the table data is exported to Excel are also not part of the export. In the example shown in Figure 9-8, only the data displayed in the table columns, not the information contained in the detailStamp facet, is exported to Excel.

Table columns that use a list, such as af:selectOneChoice, to render the cell data, display a label in the browser view but export the actual cell value to Excel. For example, if an af:selectOneChoice component is used to display the DepartmentId column value in an Employees table, then in the browser view the displayed value may be Sales, whereas the exported Excel sheet shows the value as 80.

Finally, when exporting columns that contain long numeric values, Excel may interpret this as a number instead of a string and apply scientific formatting to it. To avoid this problem, you can embed an Excel formula to the rendered table column output, as shown here:

```
<af:column headerText="Some wide label">
  <af:panelGroupLayout layout="horizontal">
    <af:outputText value="=TEXT(" visible="false"/>
    <af:outputText value="#{row.bigNumberValue}" rendered="true">
      <af:convertNumber groupingUsed="false"/>
    </af:outputText>
    <af:outputText value=",0)" visible="false"/>
  </af:panelGroupLayout>
</af:column>
```

Note the two additional instances of af:outputText that are set not to render in the application runtime view. When exporting the column to Excel, the Excel formula defines the column cell content format as text.

How to Exclude Table Columns from Horizontal Scrolling

Figure 9-1 showed a table that has the DepartmentId and EmployeeId excluded from the horizontal table scrolling. The configuration for this is defined on the af:column component using the frozen attribute. Setting this attribute to true will exclude the column from horizontal scrolling. If the af:table component has its columnSelection attribute set to true, and if the table is contained in an instance of af:panelCollection, then a toolbar button is displayed for the user to use to determine which columns to freeze when working with the table.

NOTE
Configuring a column as frozen that is not the leading column in the table will also freeze the columns to its left.

How to Color Highlight Table Cells Conditionally

In this example, conditional cell highlighting is implemented through a CSS string that is returned from a managed bean method. The managed bean is referenced from the `inlineStyle` attribute of the `af:panelGroupLayout` component that surrounds the cell `af:outputText` component. In the next example, the returned CSS is used to color the EmployeeId column background in light blue for rows with a salary value of 10,000 or higher, in light pink for those with a salary value of 5000 or higher, and light yellow for all the others. To determine the row salary value, Expression Language is used to reference the row variable of the table. The visual result is shown in Figure 9-9.

```
public String getConditionalBackgroundColor(){
  String _css ="width:100%; ";
  String lightBlue    = "#9bc8e7";
  String lightYellow  = "#fbfac9";
  String lightPink    = "#fde1fd";
  Number rowSalary = (Number) executeValueExpression("#{row.Salary}");
  if (rowSalary.intValue() >=10000){
    _css = _css+"background-color:"+lightBlue+";";
    return _css;
  }
  if (rowSalary.intValue() >=5000){
    _css = _css+"background-color:"+lightPink+";";
    return _css;
  }
  _css = _css+"background-color:"+lightYellow+";";
  return _css;
}
```

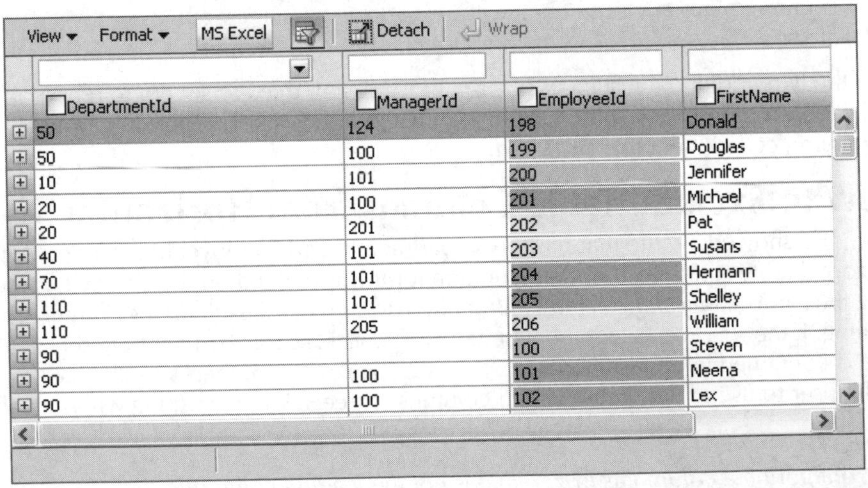

DepartmentId	ManagerId	EmployeeId	FirstName
50	124	198	Donald
50	100	199	Douglas
10	101	200	Jennifer
20	100	201	Michael
20	201	202	Pat
40	101	203	Susans
70	101	204	Hermann
110	101	205	Shelley
110	205	206	William
90		100	Steven
90	100	101	Neena
90	100	102	Lex

FIGURE 9-9 *Conditional cell color coding in a table*

Here's the table column definition:

```
<af:column sortProperty="EmployeeId" filterable="true" …>
  <af:panelGroupLayout id="plam3" layout="horizontal"
  inlineStyle="#{BasicTableBean.conditionalBackgroundColor}">
    <af:outputText … />
  </af:panelGroupLayout>
  …
</af:column>
```

Using a managed bean method to determine the color coding of a table cell has the advantage of being able to be used with complex conditions that optionally may require accessing the ADF binding layer. In addition to this, logic stored in a managed bean is reusable within an application.

Other possible solutions to render table cells conditionally include the use of an `af:switcher` component or a ternary expression that is added directly to the `inlineStyle` attribute. Using an `af:switcher` component is useful if the conditional layout change goes beyond the coloring of the rendered cell output, but it bears the risk of cluttering the page source code if more than a few conditions are to be handles. The use of a ternary expression that is added to the `inlineStyle` attribute is of good readability and useful for decisions that don't have many options to evaluate. To add a red background color to table cells that show values lower than 5000, you'd use an expression like this:

```
inlineStyle="#{row.Salary.value lt 5000?'width:100%;background-color:red'
          : 'width:100%;'}"
```

How to Implement List of Values

Using select lists as a column renderer in a table is a frequent use case that can be implemented through manual configuration or through a model-driven list of values defined on the View Object.

Model-driven Lists

Model-driven lists of values are the easiest and also the recommended option to use for developers who use ADF Business Components as the business service. Not only that they are truly easy to use and maintain, they present the most consistent approach for building select lists across an application. A model-driven list of values is defined on the View Object attribute that should render as a list when added to an ADF Faces form or table. The list of values references the View Object that provides the list values and also configures the return value. Note that this approach allows multiple attributes to be updated through a single value selection. The component to render the attribute is specified as a UI hint on the LOV definition. No additional configuration is needed by the page developer, ensuring a consistent look of the list across pages.

NOTE
Lists are covered in Chapter 11.

The `af:column` definition for a model-driven list is shown here:

```
<af:column id="c4" …>
  <af:selectOneChoice
    value="#{row.bindings.DepartmentId.inputValue}" id="soc1">
```

```
    <f:selectItems value="#{row.bindings.DepartmentId.items}" id="si1"/>
    </af:selectOneChoice>
...
</af:column>
```

NOTE
Choosing a model-driven list of values to update multiple attributes of a table requires a partial refresh on the af:column *that displays the dependent attributes. For this, you need to set the* autoSubmit *attribute of the select list to* true *and reference its* id *from the* partialTriggers *attribute of the dependent column.*

Manual Configuration

In a manual configuration, a list component, such as af:selectOneChoice, is added as the child of the af:column component. The list component updates the table row attribute using an Expression Language reference such as #{row.bindings.attribute_name.inputValue} in its value attribute. The list of values is created by a f:selectItems component, which is added as a child component of the af:selectOneChoice component. The f:selectItems component references a managed bean method that returns a List of SelectItem containing the list labels and values.

Instead of using the f:selectItems component to query the list data, you can use an af:forEach component that directly accesses the ADF binding layer. The af:forEach component iterates over the range set exposed by an ADF tree binding and uses a f:selectItem child component to build the list. If you're using the tree binding to populate the list, set the RangeSize property of the iterator binding it depends on to −1 to ensure all list values are queried. The af:column definition for the af:forEach example is shown here:

```
<af:column id="c8" ...>
  <af:selectOneChoice value="#{row.bindings.DepartmentId.inputValue}"
    id="it8" valuePassThru="true" ...>
    <!-- Accesses the ADF tree binding "DepartmentView1" that exists -->
    <!-- for the Departments View Object -->
    <af:forEach items="#{bindings.DepartmentsView1.rangeSet}" var="list">
      <f:selectItem id="si1"
    <!- Read the label values from the ="list" variable -->
        itemLabel="#{list.DepartmentName}"
        itemValue="#{list.DepartmentId}"/>
    </af:forEach>
  </af:selectOneChoice>
...
</af:column>
```

For both configurations, ensure that the valuePassThru attribute on the af:selectOneChoice component is set to true. If the valuePassThru attribute is not set, the returned value is the index number of the selected choice.

NOTE
The binding used must be a tree binding and not a list binding, which usually gets created when dragging an attribute as a list.

How to Implement a Dependent List of Values

Dependent lists in a table are best implemented through model-driven list of values, which also is the recommended way to do if the business service is ADF Business Components. In this case, a page developer, after adding the View Object as a table to a page, needs to configure the dependent list to refresh when the selection changes in the parent list. For this, you configure the `partialTriggers` attribute on the `af:column` component of the dependent list to point to the parent list and set the `autoSubmit` attribute of the parent list to `true`.

NOTE
We explain how to create model-driven dependent list of values in Chapter 11.

How to Generically Access the ADF Tree Binding Used by a Table from Java

A motivation for a generic Java access to the ADF binding layer is to create reusable managed beans that can be shared by tables in an application. Another is to protect application client logic code from the impact of refactoring in the binding layer. For example, rebinding a table or renaming a binding require that the developer change the Expression Language or binding name reference in the managed bean code. This can be avoided if the managed bean has access to the table instance, for example through a call to `getSource()` on an event object such as `SelectionEvent` or `QueryEvent`.

The table model in ADF is an instance of `FacesModel`, which is an inner class of the `FacesCtrlHierBinding` binding object that resides in a private package. As mentioned earlier, you should avoid accessing classes that are in private ADF packages and instead use the public binding APIs. To program generic access to the ADF tree binding of an `af:table` component, you use the `value` attribute of the `RichTable` instance. The following code listing assumes a handle to the `RichTable` instance through the `departmentstable` variable:

```
import org.apache.myfaces.trinidad.model.CollectionModel;
...
RichTable departmentstable;
...
//Obtain the ADF tree binding reference from the table model,
//which requires no knowledge about the binding name
CollectionModel tableModel = departmentstable.getValue();
JUCtrlHierBinding tableBinding = null;
tableBinding = (JUCtrlHierBinding)tableModel.getWrapppedData();
```

ADF Faces Tree Component

The ADF Faces tree component displays hierarchical data in which each tree node represents the data of a specific level in the hierarchy. Using ADF Business Components, tree hierarchies are defined through dependent View Objects that are referenced through the ADF tree binding. The best thing about working with ADF bound ADF Faces table, tree, and treeTable components is their similarity, which allows reuse of skills and code samples.

What You Should Know About the ADF Tree Binding

When building ADF bound ADF Faces tree components, a single iterator binding for the root collection is created in the executable section of the PageDef file, as well as a tree binding definition in the bindings section that defines the node hierarchy of the tree. While the ADF Faces table component also binds to an ADF tree binding, it uses a single-node hierarchy, which allows the synchronization of the selected table row with the selected row in the ADF binding. In contrast, trees have a multi-node hierarchy, which means that the ADF root iterator binding does not maintain the current row selection for each of the nodes. Especially when creating new tree nodes, deleting tree nodes, or updating the information in a tree, you cannot use the operations exposed on the top-level View Object. Instead, you need to create bindings explicitly for the dependent View Objects, or work from Java. Both approaches are explained in the use cases contained in this section.

Building ADF Bound Trees

You create ADF bound trees by dragging an ADF Business Components View Object from the Data Controls panel and adding it as an ADF tree to the JSF page or page fragment. The Edit Tree Binding dialog shown in Figure 9-10 automatically opens for you to define the tree node hierarchy and display attributes.

ADF Faces Tree Binding Classes

At runtime, the tree component model is represented by an instance of `FacesCtrlHierBinding`, which extends the generic `JUCtrlHierBinding` binding class. Tree nodes are instances of the `FacesCtrlHierNodeBinding` class, which extends the generic `JUCtrlNodeHierBinding` class.

Fusion developers who work declaratively with Oracle ADF are not exposed to the binding classes but use them indirectly in their Expression Language references to the ADF binding layer. Developers who use Java to access the binding layer use the framework classes mentioned earlier to access the tree data and to perform actions on the tree and tree nodes.

Note that Figures 1-7 in Chapter 1 shows a class diagram of the ADF binding classes and how they relate.

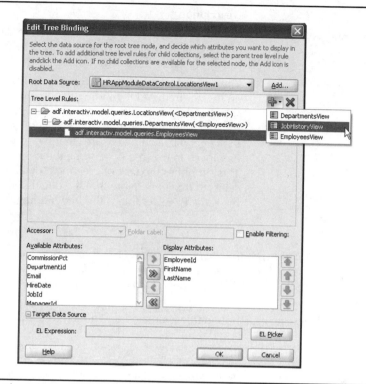

FIGURE 9-10   *The Edit Tree Binding dialog lets you configure the tree hierarchy in the ADF binding metadata.*

The Edit Tree Binding dialog allows declarative configuration of the hierarchical tree structure, which is written as metadata into the ADF page definition file of the current page or page fragment. The binding dialog provides the following options for the developer to configure:

Option	Description
Root Data Source	The View Object reference used in the top level nodes. In most cases you don't need to set this value, as this is done implicitly when creating the tree.
Tree Level Rules	Each level in the tree hierarchy is defined by a rule that selects the referenced View Object from a list of view accessors that exist for the parent node View Object.
Enable Filtering	Developers can specify a node-level attribute and value to restrict data displayed in the tree. View Objects that have a discriminator attribute, such as an employee type attribute that helps distinguishing between temporary and permanent employees, can be used to display trees for one of the allowed discriminator values.

Option	Description
Available/Display Attributes	All attributes of a node's View Object are displayed in the list of available attributes so the developer can choose those that are displayed as the tree node entry.
Target Data Source	The target data source is an Expression Language reference to an iterator in the ADF binding that is synchronized with the selection in the tree. If, for example, an employee tree node references an iterator that exposes a collection of employees, the target data source ensures that the row key of the selected employee in the tree is set to be the current row in the iterator. This simplifies the task of creating a detail edit form for the selected tree item. Note that the detail iterator must reside in the same PageDef file as the tree binding.

NOTE
To re-enter the Edit Tree Binding dialog, you select the Bindings tab at the bottom of the ADF Faces page. Selecting the tree binding entry in the Bindings category and clicking the pencil icon opens the dialog.

Finishing the dialog, an ADF bound tree is created and added to the page as shown here:

```
<af:tree value="#{bindings.DepartmentsView1.treeModel}" var="node"

   selectionListener="…"  rowSelection="single" id="t1">
   <f:facet name="nodeStamp">
     <af:outputText value="#{node}" id="ot1"/>
   </f:facet>
</af:tree>
```

The ADF Faces af:tree component, an instance of RichTree, builds the UI tree root that references the collection model in its value attribute to populate the nodes with data. The var attribute defines the name for an internal iterator variable that is referenced from Expression Language upon tree rendering to populate the tree and leaf nodes. Like tables, trees use a single instance of the UI components that are contained in the nodeStamp facet to render the nodes through stamping. The following facets are also supported:

- **pathStamp**   If the currently displayed top-level node in a tree is not the root node, but a node selected through the focusRowKey attribute, then the components located in the pathStamp are rendered in the pop-up that opens when you select the Show Hierarchy icon. The pathStamp shows the location of the current top-level node in the context of the original tree hierarchy and allows users to navigate within this path. The quickest way to define a pathStamp facet is to create a copy of the nodeStamp facet and rename the copy pathStamp. When doing so, make sure the contained UI components' id attribute values are changed to unique strings as well.

- **contextMenu**   Expects an af:popup component as its child component. The af:popup component must contain an af:menu component to display the context menu when the user selects the tree by clicking the right mouse button.

NOTE
Adding an `af:panelGroupLayout` *or similar layout component as the child of the* `nodeStamp` *facet allows developers to add multiple UI components to render the nodes. For example, a folder image may be added in front of the node label using the* `af:image` *component. An example for this is shown as a part of the Oracle ADF Faces component demo that is available online at http://www.oracle. com/technology/products/adf/adffaces/index.html for viewing and download.*

Customizing the Tree Node Display

All attributes that are selected in the tree node rule are displayed as the node label at runtime using the default `nodeStamp` rendering. Only the attributes that are selected for display are accessible from Expression Language. Use cases, such as displaying the node detail information in a pop-up, require additional attributes to be selected that should not be displayed in the node label. To implement this use case, developers can customize the node rendering of the tree.

Use Case: How to Show Additional Information in a Pop-up

Figure 9-11 shows a tree that displays a note window when the user moves the mouse over a tree node. The information displayed in the pop-up is dependent on the node and the hierarchy level of the node in the tree. The node window is closed when the mouse is moved off the node. The node label displays a single attribute for the location and department nodes and the first and last name for the employee node.

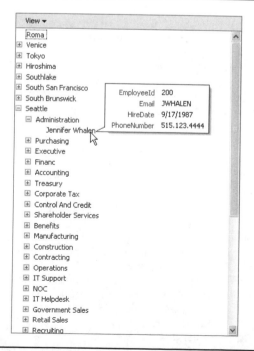

FIGURE 9-11   *Tree component with note window to display additional node information*

All attributes that are selected for display in the tree editor are Expression Language accessible. An attribute `FirstName` can be accessed through `#{node.FirstName}`, assuming the tree `var` attribute has a value of `node`. The employee node in Figure 9-11 is defined as shown here:

```
<f:facet name="nodeStamp">
  <af:outputText value="#{node.FirstName} #{node.LastName}" id="ot3"/>
</f:facet>
```

Only a single `nodeStamp` facet exists in a tree. To render the nodes with customized labels, the `nodeStamp` facet contains an `af:switcher` component that determines the node to render and the attributes to display. It works like the switch statement in Java. The following page source is taken from the tree shown in Figure 9-11 and shows how the `af:switcher` component is used by example of the locations node. The department and employee nodes are modified copies of this node and are not contained in the source. The line numbers are added for reference.

```
01. <af:tree value="#{bindings.LocationsView1.treeModel}" var="node"
02.        contentDelivery="lazy">
03.  <f:facet name="nodeStamp">
04.    <af:switcher facetName="#{node.hierType.structureDefName}">
05.      <!-- render the locations node -->
06.      <f:facet name="adf.interactiv.model.queries.LocationsView">
07.        <af:panelGroupLayout id="pgl1">
08.        <!-- display the City name as the node label -->
09.          <af:outputText value="#{node.City}" id="ot1">
10.            <!-- hide the popup on mouse out -->
11.            <af:clientListener method="popupHide" type="mouseOut"/>
12.            <!-- pass the name of the popup to close to JavaScript -->
13.            <af:clientAttribute name="callPopup" value="popup1"/>
14.            <!-- open popup dialog when the mouse is moved over -->
15.            <!-- the node -->
16.            <af:showPopupBehavior popupId="popup1"
17.                                  triggerType="mouseOver"
18.                                  align="endAfter" alignId="ot1"/>
19.          </af:outputText>
21.          <!-- popup to show the node detail information -->
22.          <af:popup id="popup1" contentDelivery="lazyUncached"
23.                    eventContext="launcher" launcherVar="source">
24.            <af:noteWindow id="nw1">
25.              <af:panelFormLayout id="pfl1">
26.                <af:inputText value="#{node.LocationId}" id="ot4"
27.                    label="#{node.bindings.LocationId.label}"
28.                          readOnly="true"/>
29.                <af:inputText value="#{node.StreetAddress}" id="ot5"
30.                    label="#{node.bindings.StreetAddress.label}"
31.                    readOnly="true"/>
32.                <af:inputText value="#{node.PostalCode}" id="ot6"
33.                    label="#{node.bindings.PostalCode.label}"
34.                          readOnly="true"/>
35.              </af:panelFormLayout>
36.            </af:noteWindow>
37.          </af:popup>
38.        </af:panelGroupLayout>
```

```
39.        </f:facet>
40.        <f:facet name="adf.interactiv.model.queries.DepartmentsView">
41.        <!-- create the node definition for the department node -->
42.          ...
43.        </f:facet>
44.        <f:facet name="adf.interactiv.model.queries.EmployeesView">
45.        <!-- create the node definition for the employee node -->
46.          ...
47.        </f:facet>
48.      </af:switcher>
49.    </f:facet>
50.  </af:tree>
```

At runtime, the `af:switcher` component in line 04 uses Expression Language to reference the getHierType method of the JUCtrlHierNodeBinding node instance to return an object of type JUCtrlHierTypeBinding that is used to determine the package and name of the View Object providing the node data. If the `af:switcher` component contains a facet (line 06) with a name matching the current node View Object, this is used to render the node.

The node label is the City attribute and is referenced in the `af:outputText` component shown in line 07. Using the `af:switcher` component, you can render each tree node hierarchy with different UI components—for example, using command links, input text fields, select lists, or checkboxes. As shown in line 07, adding a PanelGroupLayout component or similar layout container allows you to define multiple UI components to render the node.

Line 11 defines an `af:clientListener` component that calls a JavaScript function to close the pop-up window when the user moves the mouse off the node. The `af:showPopupBehavior` in line 16 provides a declarative option to launch a client-side pop-up, which in our case displays the additional information for the node. The pop-up and its content are defined between lines 22 and 37. For the data display, we use read-only `af:inputText` components because they can have an implicit label defined, which nicely aligns using the `af:panelFormLayout` component. The label is read from the node attribute, using the "#{node.bindings.<attribute>.label}" expression syntax. If you defined UI hint labels for the View Object or Entity Object attributes, these labels are displayed in the pop-up.

NOTE
Using UI hints not only ensures consistent labeling, but also allows you to provide translations for the labels.

Line 40 starts the node renderer definition for the DepartmentsView node. You create the content similar to the content of the LocationsView facet. When copying and pasting from an existing facet definition, make sure you rename the id properties to unique names. For example, the af:popup definition would have its id attribute set to popup2, which explains the importance of the `af:clientAttribute` to make the current pop-up id value accessible from the component source in JavaScript.

The JavaScript function to close the pop-up when moving the mouse off the node is optional and useful only if no action items are contained in the opened note window. For completeness, the JavaScript source is shown here:

```
<af:resource type="javascript">
  function popupHide(evt)
  {
```

```
        //cancel event from from further propagation
        //since we handle it here
        evt.cancel();
        var treeNode = evt.getSource();
        //reference af:clientAttribute value
        var popupString = treeNode.getPropertyValue("callPopup");
        var popup = treeNode.findComponent(popupString);
        if (popup.isPopupVisible()){
            popup.hide();
        }
    }
</af:resource>
```

NOTE
The code samples used in this section contain content that we did not explain in detail but is covered in one of the following chapters: Chapter 10 explains pop-ups and dialogs, including the af:popup *component and the* af:noteWindow *component. Chapter 17 explains how to build layouts in ADF Faces RC, covering the* af: panelFormLayout *and* af:panelGroupLayout *components. Chapter 19 explains the use of JavaScript in ADF Faces, with details about the use of the* af:clientListener *and* af:resource *elements.*

How to Mark a Node as Selected When Disclosing It

If a requirement is to select the node that the user expands by clicking its disclosure icon, you can use a managed bean method that is referenced from the RowDisclosureListener property in the Oracle JDeveloper Property Inspector to implement this use case. The managed bean method listens to the node disclosure and expects a single input argument of type RowDisclosureEvent that provides information about the disclosed node set and the tree component that raised the event. The following code example handles the node disclosure for a single select tree, also synchronizing the selected node with the ADF binding layer if the Target Data Source attribute reference is defined for the selected node:

```
public void onRowDisclosure(RowDisclosureEvent rowDisclosureEvent) {
    RichTree tree = (RichTree)rowDisclosureEvent.getSource();
    RowKeySet disclosedRows = rowDisclosureEvent.getAddedSet();
    RowKeySet selectedRows = tree.getSelectedRowKeys();
    //single select usecase
    selectedRows.clear();
    //only select a node when the user explicitly clicked
    //on the expand icon. Ignore bulk disclosures
    if (disclosedRows.size() == 1){
        Object disclosedNode = disclosedRows.iterator().next();
        selectedRows.add(disclosedNode);
        //optional: set the selected tree row as current in the
        //tree binding.
        makeCurrent(tree, disclosedRows);
    }
}
```

```
    tree.setSelectedRowKeys(selectedRows);
    //refresh the tree to display the changes
    AdfFacesContext adfFacesContext =
        AdfFacesContext.getCurrentInstance();
    adfFacesContext.addPartialTarget(tree.getParent());
}
```

Programmatically selecting a node does not automatically make it become the current row in the ADF Faces tree model data collection. To make the selected row become the current row in the collection, the preceding example uses the custom `makeCurrent` method shown here:

```
private void  makeCurrent(RichTree tree, RowKeySet disclosedRows){
    //To make a row current, we need to create a SelectionEvent which
    //expects the following arguments: component, unselected_keys,
    //selected_keys. In our example, we don't have unselected keys and
    //therefore create an empty RowSet for this
    SelectionEvent selectionEvent = new SelectionEvent(
        tree,
        new RowKeySetImpl(),
        disclosedRows);
    //Calling the helper method introduced for this chapter. The
    //"LocationsView1" reference is the tree binding definition
    //our example tree has in the ADF PagDef file.
    invokeMethodExpression(
        "#{bindings.LocationsView1.collectionModel.makeCurrent}",
        selectionEvent,
        SelectionEvent.class);
}
```

NOTE
The ADF binding supports only a single current row for its iterators. If you work with a tree that is configured for multiple node selection, you need to keep this in mind if you plan to reuse this code example.

How to Disclose a Tree Node with a Mouse Click

Chapter 19 discusses the JavaScript client framework of the ADF Faces RC architecture. All ADF Faces RC UI components have a client-side JavaScript component that allows developers to access them on the client. A use case for the client programming framework is to change the disclosure state of a tree node when selecting it with a mouse click. So instead of clicking the disclosure icon of a tree node to expand it, you can select the item. To implement this use case, you use a JavaScript function in the page that accesses the tree object on the client to invert the disclosure state when selected. The selection event is configured on the `af:tree` component using the `af:clientListener` component. The ADF Faces tree component that is represented by an instance of `RichTree` in Java is represented with similar functionality by the `AdfRichTree.js` object in JavaScript.

```
<af:document id="d1">
    ...
  <af:resource type="javascript">
    function expandNode(evt){
```

```
                //Get instance of AdfRichTree.js
                var tree = evt.getSource();
                var rwKeySet = evt.getAddedSet();
                var firstRowKey;
                for(rowKey in rwKeySet){
                  firstRowKey = rowKey;
                  //we are only interested in the first
                  //node and break here
                  break;
                }
                if (tree.isPathExpanded(firstRowKey)){
                 //close node if it is disclosed
                  tree.setDisclosedRowKey(firstRowKey,false);
                }
                else{
                  //disclose node if it is closed
                  tree.setDisclosedRowKey(firstRowKey,true);
                }
            }
        </af:resource>
        <af:form id="f1">
          <af:tree value="#{bindings.LocationsView1.treeModel}" var="node"
                   selectionListener="…" rowSelection="single" id="t1">
            <f:facet name="nodeStamp">
              <af:outputText value="#{node}" id="ot1"/>
            </f:facet>
            <af:clientListener method="expandNode" type="selection"/>
          </af:tree>
          …
        </af:document>
```

NOTE
*The ADF Faces RC architecture is covered in Chapter 19 with
additional code examples. For this chapter, you should realize that a
client-side API exists for the ADF Faces tree component that may be
used to implement client-side use cases.*

How to Search in Trees

Especially when trees become complex and big, users often ask for a search functionality that
parses the tree for a specific search string to expand and highlights matching nodes. The search,
however, must not only be within the displayed node labels, but can include all attributes of the
collection model, as we will show in this example. Figure 9-12 shows an ADF bound ADF Faces
tree that is searchable by the user selecting the attribute names to search in and specifying the
search condition and string.

Defining the Tree

The tree definition is contained in an `af:panelCollection` layout container that contains
an `af:selectManyChoice` component with a static list of attribute names to search in, an

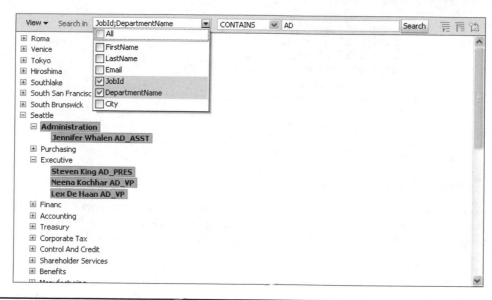

FIGURE 9-12 *Searchable ADF Faces tree*

`af:singleSelectChoice` list for the search condition, and an `af:inputText` field component for the search string in its toolbar.

```
<af:panelCollection id="pc1" inlineStyle="width:700px; height:400.0px;">
  <f:facet name="toolbar">
    <af:toolbar id="t2">
      <af:selectManyChoice label="Search in" id="sml1"
                  value="#{TreeSearchBean.searchAttributes}">
        <af:selectItem label="FirstName" value="FirstName" id="si4"/>
        <af:selectItem label="LastName" value="LastName" id="si2"/>
        <af:selectItem label="Email" value="Email" id="si6"/>
        <af:selectItem label="JobId" value="JobId" id="si1"/>
        <af:selectItem label="DepartmentName" value="DepartmentName"
                    id="si5"/>
        <af:selectItem label="City" value="City" id="si3"/>
      </af:selectManyChoice>
      <af:selectOneChoice label="" id="soc1"
                      value="#{TreeSearchBean.searchType}">
        <af:selectItem label="CONTAINS" value="CONTAIN" id="si7"/>
        <af:selectItem label="STARTS WITH" value="START" id="si8"/>
        <af:selectItem label="ENDS WITH" value="END" id="si9"/>
      </af:selectOneChoice>
      <af:inputText label="Search" id="it1" simple="true"
                  value="#{TreeSearchBean.searchString}"/>
      <af:commandToolbarButton text="Search" id="ctb1"
        actionListener="#{TreeSearchBean.onSearch}"/>
```

```
        </af:toolbar>
    </f:facet>
    <f:facet name="statusbar"/>
    <af:tree value="#{bindings.LocationsView1.treeModel}" var="node"
             rowSelection="multiple" id="t1"
             binding="#{TreeSearchBean.tree1}">
      <f:facet name="nodeStamp">
        <af:outputText value="#{node}" id="ot1"/>
      </f:facet>
      <f:facet name="pathStamp">
        <af:outputText value="#{node}" id="ot2"/>
      </f:facet>
    </af:tree>
</af:panelCollection>
```

Note the `binding` attribute on the `af:tree` component, which references the managed bean that performs the search. The bean uses the binding reference to set the selected `rowKeys` property according to the list of keys that are found that match the search condition.

Searching the Tree

The ADF Faces tree is a hierarchical structure of nodes that can be parsed in a recursive method, which in the example is called from the action listener method that is defined for the search button shown in Figure 9-12:

```
public void onSearch(ActionEvent actionEvent) {
    //Get the JUCtrlHierBinding reference from the PageDef
    JUCtrlHierBinding treeBinding = null;
    treeBinding = (JUCtrlHierBinding)executeValueExpression(
                 "#{bindings.LocationsView1}");
    //Read the attributes to search in from the "searchAttributes" variable
    //referenced from the value attribute of the SelectManyChoice component
    String searchAttributeArray[] = (String[]) searchAttributes.toArray(
                                    new String[searchAttributes.size()]);
    //Define a node to search in. In this example, the root node is used as
    //the starting point
    JUCtrlHierNodeBinding root = treeBinding.getRootNodeBinding();
    //Retrieve the tree node keys that match the search criteria
    RowKeySet resultRowKeySet =
      searchTreeNode(root,searchAttributeArray,searchType,searchString);
    //build the list of row sets for the full path that leads to the
    //nodes that match the search condition
    RowKeySet disclosedRowKeySet =
    buildDiscloseRowKeySet(treeBinding,resultRowKeySet);
    //expand the tree using the tree component JSF binding reference to
    //display the found nodes
    tree1.setSelectedRowKeys(resultRowKeySet);
    tree1.setDisclosedRowKeys(disclosedRowKeySet);
    //PPR the tree to show the changed disclosure state
    AdfFacesContext.getCurrentInstance().addPartialTarget(tree1);
}
```

NODE
For a single search match, you could set the focusRowKey *attribute with the key value of the matching node. This does not expand the node but instead makes the referenced node the top-level node, reducing the tree to the size of the node branch. Clicking the Show Hierarchy icon that is displayed when the* pathStamp *facet is defined, users can then switch back to the full path or navigate within the tree structure.*

The first of two private methods used by this sample performs the recursive tree search. It reads the bean properties defined for the search attributes, the search condition, and the search string, which setter and getter methods are referenced from the toolbar components using Expression Language:

```
private String searchString = "";
private String searchType = "CONTAIN";
private List searchAttributes = new ArrayList();
```

The search method first looks at the current node to check if its attributes match the search string. After this, the current node is checked for child nodes. If child nodes are found, the search method is recursively called for each of the child nodes. The returned RowKeySet of the child nodes is added to the parent node's RowKeySet until the top-level node, the starting point of the search, is reached. The returned RowKeySet is set as the selected keys on the tree component.

```
/**
 * Method that parses an ADF bound ADF Faces tree component to find
 * search string matches in one of the specified attributes. Attribute
 * names are ignored if they don't exist in the searched node. The method
 * returns a RowKeySet with the row keys of all nodes that match the
 * search string
 * @param   node The JUCtrlHierNodeBinding instance to search
 * @param   searchAttributes An array of attribute names to search in
 * @param   searchType defines where the search is started within the
 *                      text. Valid values are START, CONTAIN, END.
 * @param   searchString  The search condition
 * @return RowKeySet row keys
 */
private RowKeySet searchTreeNode(JUCtrlHierNodeBinding node,
                    String[] searchAttributes, String searchType,
                    String searchString){
    RowKeySetImpl rowKeys = new RowKeySetImpl();
    //set default search condition
    String _searchType = searchType == null?
            "CONTAIN" : searchType.length()>0?searchType:"CONTAIN";
    /*
     * optional: Perform sanity checks on the values passed for the method
     * arguments
     */
    //read the row data from the instance of JUCtrlHierNodeBinding
    Row nodeRow = node.getRow();
```

```
if (nodeRow != null) {
  //iterate over the search attributes and check if these are contained
  //in the node row. Ignore if attribute name does not exist
  for (int i = 0; i < searchAttributes.length; i++) {
    String compareString = "";
    try{
      Object attribute = nodeRow.getAttribute(searchAttributes[i]);
       //if attribute is found, get its value to compare
      if(attribute instanceof String){
        compareString = (String) attribute;
      }
      else{
        //try the toString method as a simple fallback
        compareString = attribute.toString();
      }
    }
    catch(oracle.jbo.JboException attributeNotFound){
      //attribute not found. Exclude from search
    }
    //perform case insensitive search using the defined search
    //condition
    if (_searchType.equalsIgnoreCase("CONTAIN") &&
    compareString.toUpperCase().indexOf(searchString.toUpperCase())>-1){
      //save row key
      rowKeys.add(node.getKeyPath());
    }
    else if (_searchType.equalsIgnoreCase("START") &&
    compareString.toUpperCase().startsWith(searchString.toUpperCase())){
      rowKeys.add(node.getKeyPath());
    }
    else if (_searchType.equalsIgnoreCase("END") &&
    compareString.toUpperCase().endsWith(searchString.toUpperCase())){
      rowKeys.add(node.getKeyPath());
    }
  }
}
//Check if this node has children and if so, recursively call
//this method for all of them
List<JUCtrlHierNodeBinding> children = node.getChildren();
  if(children != null){
    //child nodes have a type of JUCtrlHierNodeBinding
    for(JUCtrlHierNodeBinding _node : children){
      //Each child search returns a row key set that must
      //be added to the row key set returned by the overall
      //search
      RowKeySet rks = searchTreeNode(
                        _node,
                        searchAttributes,
                        this.searchType,
                        searchString);
      //if a matching rowKeySet is found for the child node and its
      // sub nodes add its content
```

```
         if(rks != null && rks.size()>0){
            rowKeys.addAll(rks);
         }
      }
   }
//row keys of the nodes that match the search string and condition
return rowKeys;
}
```

The second method takes a RowKeySet argument that contains the row keys of the found nodes. To expand a node fully in the tree, we need to add its parent node keys to the RowKeySet that is then set as the disclosed row keys on the tree in a call to tree1. setDisclosedRowKeys.

```
/**
 * Helper method that returns a list of parent node for the RowKeySet
 * passed as the keys argument. In this example the RowKeySet is used
 * to disclose the folders in which the nodes reside that meet the search
 * condition and string.
 *
 * @param  treeBinding ADF tree binding instance read from the
 *         PageDef file
 * @param  keys  RowKeySet containing List entries of oracle.jbo.Key
 * @return RowKeySet of parent keys to disclose
 */
private RowKeySet buildDiscloseRowKeySet(JUCtrlHierBinding treeBinding,
                                RowKeySet keys){
  //create a new empty RowKeySet
  RowKeySetImpl discloseRowKeySet = new  RowKeySetImpl();
  //get the iterator for the RowKeySet of found nodes in the search
  Iterator iter =  keys.iterator();
  while(iter.hasNext()){
    List keyPath = (List) iter.next();
    //find the node by its keyPath
    JUCtrlHierNodeBinding node = treeBinding.findNodeByKeyPath(keyPath);
    //if a node is found and if it has a parent node, add the parent node
    //rowKey to the disclosedRowKeySet
    if(node!=null &&node.getParent()!=null &&
                !node.getParent().getKeyPath().isEmpty()){
      discloseRowKeySet.add(node.getParent().getKeyPath());
      //call method recursively for the parent of the parent node
      RowKeySetImpl parentKeySet = new  RowKeySetImpl();
      //the parent node is the start for the recursive search
      parentKeySet.add(node.getParent().getKeyPath());
      //call recursive method
      RowKeySet rks = buildDiscloseRowKeySet(treeBinding,parentKeySet);
      //add all parent row keys to the RowKeySet of this node
      discloseRowKeySet.addAll(rks);
    }
  }
  return discloseRowKeySet;
}
```

Improving the Search for Better Performance

The `FocusRowKey` property of the ADF Faces tree components takes an `ArrayList` argument of `oracle.jbo.Key` for developers to define another tree node than the root node as the top-level node of the tree. This property is also set when the users selects a tree node and then chooses the Show as Top option in the context menu. The following addition to the `onSearch` method, explained earlier, ensures that we search only in the visible branches of the tree and not in the whole tree, which also leads to better performance:

```
public void onSearch(ActionEvent actionEvent) {
  ...
  //Define a node to search in. In this example, the root node is used as
  //the starting point
  JUCtrlHierNodeBinding root = treeBinding.getRootNodeBinding();
  //However, if the user used the "Show as Top" context menu option to
  //shorten the tree display, then we start the search from here
  List topNode = (List) this.getTree1().getFocusRowKey();
  if (topNode != null){
    //make top node the new root node for the search
    root = treeBinding.findNodeByKeyPath(topNode);
  }
  ...
}
```

NOTE
For the user to be able to use the Show as Top context menu option, the ADF Faces tree component must have the `pathStamp` *facet defined.*

How to Read the Search String from the ADF Binding

If the search string is the value of an ADF binding attribute, you can access it using the ADF `JUCtrlAttrsBinding` binding class, as shown here:

```
JUCtrlAttrsBinding attributeBinding =
   (JUCtrlAttrsBinding) bindings.get("<attr_binding_name>");
String searchString = (String) ctrlBinding.getInputValue();
...
```

How to Use an Edit Form to Create, Edit, and Delete Tree Nodes

A common use case in Oracle ADF is to display a detail input form that is synchronized with the selected node in the tree. The form should be used to insert new tree nodes and to edit existing nodes.

In the following sections, we explain how to build the implementation of the use case shown in Figure 9-13. It reuses some of the code samples and techniques explained earlier in this chapter, but it also has its specialties. The tree is created so that selecting a tree node does not synchronize the edit form. For this, users need to click one of the icons that are associated with the node. Clicking the create icon inserts a new sibling node in the tree with a default value set for the foreign key. The tree node selection when clicking the edit button is set programmatically to ensure that the row selection does not "swallow" the mouse click onto the icons, which are part of the tree node.

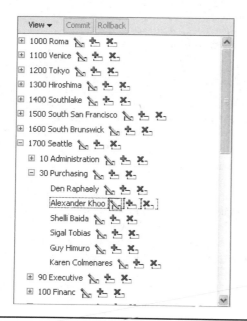
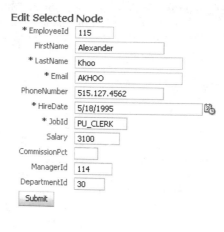

FIGURE 9-13   *ADF tree with synchronized edit form and command links for edit, create, and delete*

NOTE
An interesting alternative layout to that shown in Figure 9-13 is to place the icons in a pop-up using the note window as explained earlier. In this case, you would keep the note window open until the user clicks one of the icons.

The Target Data Source ADF Tree Binding Option

The ADF iterator that is created for the ADF tree binding references the View Object of the top-level node. The ADF tree binding uses view link accessors instead of data model view link instances to work with detail rows. This means that the child node iterators are implicit and not explicitly defined in the ADF page definition file. To synchronize the node selection in the tree with an iterator that is manually created in the PageDef file, you use the Target Data Source option that exists for all tree rules in the Edit Tree Binding dialog shown in Figure 9-10. To use the Target Data Source attribute, you do the following:

1.   Open the Bindings tab at the bottom of the ADF Faces page or page fragment to create a new iterator binding in the Executables section for the View Objects that render the nodes, or implicitly create one by dragging and dropping a View Object as an input form or table to the page. Choose View Object instances that are not dependent on other View Objects to ensure it will synchronize with all node data.

2.   In the Edit Tree Binding dialog, click the EL Picker button on the node and use the opened Expression Editor dialog to select the iterator binding.

NOTE
See the "Advanced View Object Techniques" chapter of the "Oracle Fusion Middleware Fusion Developer's Guide for Oracle Application Development Framework 11g Release 1" to learn more about view link accessors.

Building the Tree

As shown in Figure 9-13, the tree is built for the Locations, Departments, and Employees view. Because the tree node selection is required only for the form edit option, `rowSelection` attribute is set to `none`. In the edit use case, the node selection is set programmatically. In addition, setting the `rowSelection` attribute to `none` prevents node selection when the user clicks a node. The icons in the tree nodes are rendered by the `af:commandImageLink`, which uses a partial submit to execute a managed bean method referenced from the `actionListener` attribute. The `f:attribute` component that is defined on all link components makes the node object, an instance of `JUCtrlHierNodeBinding`, available to the action listener method in the managed bean. An `af:SetPropertyListener` is used on the edit and create links to memorize the selected tree node type to determine the edit to display. The tree has a JSF component binding reference to the managed bean, which is used to partially refresh the tree instance when deleting a node.

Note that the selected node type is stored in the view scope, which preserves the information between requests. The complete tree page source is shown here:

```
<af:tree value="#{bindings.LocationsView1.treeModel}" var="node"
    rowSelection="none" id="t1" binding="#{EditFormBean.tree1}"
    partialTriggers=":::cb1 :::cb2 :::cb3" displayRow="selected">
  <f:facet name="nodeStamp">
    <af:panelGroupLayout id="pgl6">
      <af:outputText id="ot1" value="#{node}"/>
      <af:commandImageLink id="cil1" icon="/images/editrec.gif"
          partialSubmit="true" actionListener="#{EditFormBean.onEdit}">
        <af:setPropertyListener from="#{node.hierType.structureDefName}"
                                to="#{viewScope.formView}"
                                type="action"/>
        <f:attribute name="node" value="#{node}"/>
      </af:commandImageLink>
      <af:commandImageLink id="cil2" icon="/images/addnew.gif"
          partialSubmit="true" actionListener="#{EditFormBean.onCreate}">
        <af:setPropertyListener from="#{node.hierType.viewDefName}"
                                to="#{viewScope.formView}"
                                type="action"/>
        <f:attribute name="node" value="#{node}"/>
      </af:commandImageLink>
      <af:commandImageLink id="cil3" icon="/images/deleterec.gif"
          partialSubmit="true" actionListener="#{EditFormBean.onDelete}">
        <f:attribute name="node" value="#{node}"/>
      </af:commandImageLink>
    </af:panelGroupLayout>
  </f:facet>
</af:tree>
```

Building the Detail Form

A detail form needs to be built for each of the nodes. To show only the detail form for the selected node, we use an `af:switcher` component to hide the other forms. An `af:switcher` component uses custom-defined facets to hold the UI components to display for a specific condition. The condition in this example is defined by the `viewScope` attribute that is set in the tree when selecting a node icon.

To create an edit form, drag-and-drop the View Object that is used by a node from the Data Controls panel to the page. Make sure the View Object shows as a top-level View Object in the Data Controls panel so it is not restricted in the set of data it can query. Adding a View Object as an edit form creates an iterator binding in the ADF page definition, which we reference from the matching tree node definition to synchronize the tree selection with the current selected row in the View Object.

To build this synchronization declaratively, open the tree binding in the Edit Tree Binding editor and expand the Target Data Source option, as shown in Figure 9-10. Use the EL Picker button to create the expressions to bind a node to the iterator binding of the edit form.

The `af:switcher` component page source for this example is shown next. Note the use of the `defaultFacet` and `facetName` attributes to define the default and the display facet based on the existence of valid values in the `viewScope` attribute. In this example, the name of the facets that contain the edit forms is defined as the name of the View Object and its package, which is the node information retrieved using the `#{node.hierType.viewDefName}` expression in the `af:setPropertyListener`.

```
<af:panelHeader xmlns:af=http://xmlns.oracle.com/adf/faces/rich
     id="pgl5" text="Edit Selected Node"
     <!-- PPR refresh the contained switcher component when the edit -->
     <!-- or create image link is clicked -->
     partialTriggers="pc1:t1:cil1 pc1:t1:cil2">
  <af:switcher id="s1" defaultFacet="None"
               facetName="#{viewScope.formView}">
    <f:facet name="None">
      <af:outputText value="Please Select Node for Edit" id="ot2"/>
    </f:facet>
    <f:facet name="adf.interactiv.model.queries.LocationsView">
      <af:panelFormLayout id="pfl1" partialTriggers="cb1">
        <af:inputText …>
           …
        </af:inputText>
        …
        <f:facet name="footer">
          <af:panelGroupLayout id="pgl2" layout="horizontal">
            <af:commandButton text="Submit" id="cb1"
                              partialSubmit="true"/>
          </af:panelGroupLayout>
        </f:facet>
      </af:panelFormLayout>
    </f:facet>
    <f:facet name="adf.interactiv.model.queries.DepartmentsView">
```

```
        <af:panelFormLayout id="pfl2" partialTriggers="cb2">
          …
        </af:panelFormLayout>
      </f:facet>
      <f:facet name="adf.interactiv.model.queries.EmployeesView">
        <af:panelFormLayout id="pfl3" partialTriggers="cb3">
          …
        </af:panelFormLayout>
      </f:facet>
    </af:switcher>
  </af:panelHeader>
```

Edit Use Case

The edit use case is implemented by the `onEdit ActionListener` method in the managed bean. The method source code shown next uses the `makeCurrent()` method explained earlier in this chapter to set the current tree node programmatically:

```
public void onEdit(ActionEvent actionEvent) {
  //get the reference to the af:commandImageLink
  RichCommandImageLink link = null;
  link = (RichCommandImageLink) actionEvent.getSource();
  //obtain the node instance reference from the "node"
  //f:attribute definition
  JUCtrlHierNodeBinding node = null;
  node = (JUCtrlHierNodeBinding) link.getAttributes().get("node");
  //Create a RowKeySet for this node and make it the selected node.
  RowKeySet rks = new RowKeySetImpl();
  rks.add(node.getKeyPath());
  //make row current. The edit form is PPR'ed and picks up the change
  makeCurrent(tree1, rks);
}
```

Create Sibling Node Use Case

The sibling node is created in the View Object that is referenced in the tree node Target Data Source option. The parent node is looked up for the foreign key value to set as a default in the form. To create a new row with a default value, we created an action binding for the `Create with parameters` operation for each of the View Objects.

NOTE
The `Create with parameters` *operation was explained earlier in this chapter in the section "How to Create New Table Rows as Copies of an Existing Row."*

```
public void onCreate(ActionEvent actionEvent) {
  //get a handle to the RichCommandLink that raised this event
  RichCommandImageLink link = null;
  link = (RichCommandImageLink) actionEvent.getSource();
  //obtain the node instance reference from the "node"
  //f:attribute definition
  JUCtrlHierNodeBinding node = null;
  mode = (JUCtrlHierNodeBinding) link.getAttributes().get("node");
```

```
    //call a helper method to create the new node
    createRowForNode(node);
}

  private void createRowForNode(JUCtrlHierNodeBinding node){
   String vo = "";
   BindingContainer bindings = node.getBindingContainer();
   //Determine the View Object for this node and invoke the create method
   //binding we created in the PageDef file
   vo="adf.interactiv.model.queries.LocationsView";
   if(vo.equalsIgnoreCase(node.getHierTypeBinding().getStructureDefName())){
    //call method binding that we created for the create with parameters
    //View Object operation
    OperationBinding oper =
       (OperationBinding)bindings.get("CreateLocationwithParameters");
    oper.execute();
    return;
   }
   vo="adf.interactiv.model.queries.DepartmentsView";
   if(vo.equalsIgnoreCase(node.getHierTypeBinding().getStructureDefName())){
    OperationBinding oper =
        (OperationBinding) bindings.get("CreateDepartmentwithParameters");
    //set the foreign key. Get the value from the parent node
    oper.getParamsMap().put("LocationId",
                            node.getParent().getAttribute("LocationId"));
    oper.execute();
    return;
   }
   vo="adf.interactiv.model.queries.EmployeesView";
   if(vo.equalsIgnoreCase(node.getHierTypeBinding().getStructureDefName())){
   OperationBinding oper =
        (OperationBinding) bindings.get("CreateEmployeewithParameters");
   //set the foreign key. Get the value from the parent node
   oper.getParamsMap().put("DepartmentId",
                           node.getParent().getAttribute("DepartmentId"));
    oper.execute();
    return;
   }
}
```

Delete Node Use Case

As we did when creating new nodes, an action binding is created for each View Object,
referencing the RemoveRowWithKey operation. This operation is called when the delete
image link is clicked for a node:

```
public void onDelete(ActionEvent actionEvent) {
    //delete the node the user clicked on
    RichCommandImageLink link = null;
    link = (RichCommandImageLink) actionEvent.getSource();
    //"node" is a custom attribute defined on the link component
    //using the f:attribute tag
    JUCtrlHierNodeBinding node =
```

```
        (JUCtrlHierNodeBinding) link.getAttributes().get("node");
  removeRowForNode(node);
  //refresh the tree using the JSF component binding to show the changes.
  AdfFacesContext.getCurrentInstance().addPartialTarget(tree1);
}

private void removeRowForNode(JUCtrlHierNodeBinding node){
 String vo = "";
 BindingContainer bindings = node.getBindingContainer();
 vo="adf.interactiv.model.queries.LocationsView";
 if(vo.equalsIgnoreCase(node.getHierTypeBinding().getStructureDefName())){
  OperationBinding oper =
      (OperationBinding) bindings.get("removeLocationRowWithKey");
  //The keyPath returns a List. For the LocationsView node, only
  //a single node exists
  Key nodeKey = (Key)node.getKeyPath().get(0);
  //pass the rwoKey argument to the action binding
  oper.getParamsMap().put("rowKey",nodeKey.toStringFormat(true));
  oper.execute();
  return;
 }
 vo="adf.interactiv.model.queries.DepartmentsView";
 if(vo.equalsIgnoreCase(node.getHierTypeBinding().getStructureDefName())){
  OperationBinding oper =
      (OperationBinding) bindings.get("removeDepartmentRowWithKey");
  //Two nodes exist in the path to the DepartmentsView. The department is
  //identified by the second key in the path
  Key nodeKey = (Key)node.getKeyPath().get(1);
  oper.getParamsMap().put("rowKey",nodeKey.toStringFormat(true));
  oper.execute();
  return;
 }
 vo="adf.interactiv.model.queries.EmployeesView";
 if(vo.equalsIgnoreCase(node.getHierTypeBinding().getStructureDefName())){
  OperationBinding oper =
    (OperationBinding) bindings.get("removeEmployeeRowWithKey");
  //Three nodes exist in the path to the EmployeesView. The employee is
  //identified by the third key in the path
  Key nodeKey = (Key)node.getKeyPath().get(2);
  oper.getParamsMap().put("rowKey",nodeKey.toStringFormat(true));
  oper.execute();
  return;
 }
}
```

TreeTable Component

The ADF Faces treeTable component brings it all together. It is a mix of the ADF Faces tree and the ADF Faces table components and uses the same ADF tree binding and binding editor. Like the af:table component, the af:treeTable component requires instances of af:column as its immediate child components. Like the af:tree component, the af:treeTable contains a nodeStamp facet that is used to stamp the UI components HTML for the top-level node, which presents the data of the View Object for which you build the treeTable. The following component definition gets created in the JSF page when you close the Edit Tree Binding dialog that opened after the View Object drag-and-drop for you to configure the tree binding:

```
<af:treeTable value="#{bindings.LocationsView1.treeModel}" var="node"
    selectionListener="#{bindings.LocationsView1.treeModel.makeCurrent}"
    rowSelection="single" id="tt1">
    <f:facet name="nodeStamp">
      <af:column id="c1">
        <af:outputText value="#{node}" id="ot2"/>
      </af:column>
    </f:facet>
    <f:facet name="pathStamp">
      <af:outputText value="#{node}" id="ot1"/>
    </f:facet>
</af:treeTable>
```

So, by default, the ADF Faces treeTable component is created with a single column that is defined in the `nodeStamp` facet and that presents the hierarchical data structure as a tree. The column does not show a column header.

The `pathStamp` facet is created for the user to navigate in the tree if the currently displayed top-level node is not the root node. The top-level tree node can be changed at runtime through application logic programmatically setting the ADF Faces treeTable `focusRowKey` attribute or the user selecting the Show As Top context menu option on a TreeTable node. The component does not yet look like a real treeTable, but we are going to change that.

Beautifying the ADF TreeTable

The ADF treeTable uses instance of `af:column` as its immediate children. Only a single column can be added to the `nodeStamp` facet; others are added to the `af:treeTable` component directly. To insert columns to the `af:treeTable`, select the component in the Oracle JDeveloper Structure window and choose Insert inside af:treeTable | Column from the context menu. Do the same to insert the column cell-rendering component, such as `af:outputText`. Also, for each column, choose Insert inside af:column | JSF Core | Facet header to create the table header. Add an `af:ouputText` component into each of the header facets.

Like the `af:tree` component, the `node` variable iterates over the tree hierarchy and stamps the nodes that are rendered in the columns. You access the attributes that are configured for display in the ADF tree binding from the `node` variable using an expression such as #{node.attribute_name}. Finishing your work, the beautified treeTable component source looks similar to this:

```
<af:treeTable value="#{bindings.LocationsView1.treeModel}" var="node"
                selectionListener="…" rowSelection="single" id="tt1">
  <f:facet name="nodeStamp">
    <!-- renders the top level node attribute(s) -->
    <af:column id="c1">
      <f:facet name="header">
        <af:outputText id="ot18" value="Department"/>
      </f:facet>
      <af:outputText id="ot2"
          <!-- render the City name and the Department name -->
          <!-- sharing the same column -->
```

```
        value=" #{empty node.City? node.DepartmentName : node.City}"/>
    </af:column>
  </f:facet>
  <!-- create the table grid -->
  ...
  <af:column id="c2">
    <f:facet name="header">
      <af:outputText id="ot3" value="Mail"/>
    </f:facet>
    <af:outputText value="#{node.Email}" id="ot4"/>
  </af:column>
  <af:column id="c3">
    ...
  </af:column>
<af:treeTable>
```

The resulting treeTable, shown in Figure 9-14, is rendered like the ADF Faces tree in that each level in the data hierarchy has a disclosure icon that the application user clicks to expand the hidden child information.

How to Display Total and Subtotal Values

Showing total and subtotal summaries for data displayed in table and treeTable components is a common requirement in business applications. Summary values can be displayed

- In line with the parent record, as shown in Figure 9-14

- In a separate summary row that is displayed below the data rows, as shown in Figure 9-15

- In its own column

Example: Displaying Subtotal Values Using Groovy in a Transient View Object Attribute

Figure 9-14 shows the result of a treeTable in which the total of the employee salary attribute is shown exposed by a transient attribute added to the DepartmentsView Object.

How to Create the Transient Attribute to Calculate the Totals   Transient attributes don't persist their values and instead calculate them dynamically. Calculation is a good use case for transient attributes because the result of the calculation can always be reproduced from the data queried by the View Objects. Transient attributes can be created on the Entity Object and the View Object level. To create a transient attribute for the Departments View Object, do the following:

1. Select the View Object in Oracle JDeveloper and open the editor using the context menu option or a double-click.

2. Select the Attributes category and click the green plus icon to create a new attribute.

3. In the New View Object Attribute editor, provide a name, such as SalaryTotal, and a type, such as Number; then set the Value Type radio group to Expression.

4. In the Value field, add the following Groovy expression:

```
EmployeesView.sum("Salary")
```

View ▾ 🗗 Detach ⛶ ⛶ ⛶					
Department	Salaries	First Name	Last Name	Salary	Mail
⊞ Roma					
⊞ Venice					
⊞ Tokyo					
⊞ Hiroshima					
⊞ Southlake					
⊞ South San Francisco					
⊞ South Brunswick					
⊟ Seattle					
⊟ Administration	**Salaries : 4,400**				
		Jennifer	Whalen	4,400	JWHALEN
⊞ Purchasing	**Salaries : 24,900**				
⊟ Executive	**Salaries : 36,500**				
		Steven	King	2,500	SKING
		Neena	Kochhar	17,000	NKOCHHARS
		Lex	De Haan	17,000	LDEHAAN
⊞ Financ	**Salaries : 51,600**				
⊞ Accounting	**Salaries : 20,300**				
⊞ Treasury					
⊞ Corporate Tax					
⊞ Control And Credit					
⊞ Shareholder Services					
⊞ Benefits					
⊞ Manufacturing					
⊞ Construction					
⊞ Contracting					
⊞ Operations					
⊞ IT Support					
⊞ NOC					

FIGURE 9-14   *Salary total values shown for departments in a treeTable*

This expression accesses a `ViewLink` accessor that is created for the View Object when a parent detail relationship exists to another View Object, Employees in this example. The name of the accessor can be looked up in the Structure window for the selected View Object, where it is listed under the ViewLink Accessors node. The Groovy expression accesses the detail View Object and calls the summary function for the Salary attribute on it. You can close the View Object attribute editor after creating the expression.

NOTE
Groovy is an open-source scripting language for Java that simplifies the development with ADF Business Components View Objects and Entity Objects. It provides declarative access to objects and attributes in the ADF Business Components framework and helps developers avoid coding in Java. Refer to the "Oracle Fusion Middleware Fusion Developer's Guide for Oracle Application Development Framework 11g Release 1" product documentation for more information about Groovy. It is truly worth a look.

Displaying the Summary Attribute in the TreeTable   To display the `SalaryTotal` transient attribute in the treeTable, you first need to add it to the list of attributes selected for display in the Tree Binding Editor. Once the `SalaryTotal` attribute is selected, it becomes accessible from Expression Language using the following expression:

```
#{node.SalaryTotal}
```

In Figure 9-14, the total salary of a department is rendered in its own column. Here is the source for the column:

```
...
<af:column id="c2">
  <f:facet name="header">
    <af:outputText value="Total Salary" id="ot3"/>
  </f:facet>
  <f:facet name="footer"/>
   <!-- layout the SalaryTotal field to stand out
   <af:panelGroupLayout layout="horizontal" id="pgl1"
          inlineStyle="width:100%; font-weight:bold;
          background-color:#c0c0c0;"
          rendered="#{not empty node.SalaryTotal}">
     <af:outputText value="Salaries :" id="ot19"/>
     <af:spacer width="10" id="s1"/>
     <af:outputText value="#{node.SalaryTotal}" id="ot17"/>
   </af:panelGroupLayout>
</af:column>
...
```

In the component code above, the `SalaryTotal` attribute column renderer is printed only if the `SalaryTotal` attribute exists in the currently rendered node and if its value is not null.

NOTE
Chapter 16 discusses look-and-feel customization through "skinning." The ADF Faces skinning framework provides a better solution for component- and instance-specific color coding than hard-coding the CSS definition as shown in this example.

Example: Displaying Subtotal Values Using a Summary Row

Figure 9-15 shows the visual output for the use case in which an additional row is appended to the employee rows to displays the summary salary for each department.

Creating the Extra Row   One option for creating the extra View Object row for this example is to use a database view that contains the aggregated salaries for the departments. To use the database view in the View Object displayed by the tree node, make sure the column names of the view match the columns of the Employees table. The database view may look as shown here, using the Oracle HR demo schema:

```
SELECT
  DEPARTMENT_ID, null as "EMPLOYEE_ID",
  '' as "FIRST_NAME", '' as "LAST_NAME",
  sum(EMPLOYEES.SALARY) "SALARY",
  '' as "EMAIL", null as "HIRE_DATE"
FROM
  EMPLOYEES, DEPARTMENTS
WHERE
  EMPLOYEES.DEPARTMENT_ID(+) = DEPARTMENTS.DEPARTMENT_ID
GROUP BY
  DEPARTMENTS.DEPARTMENT_ID
```

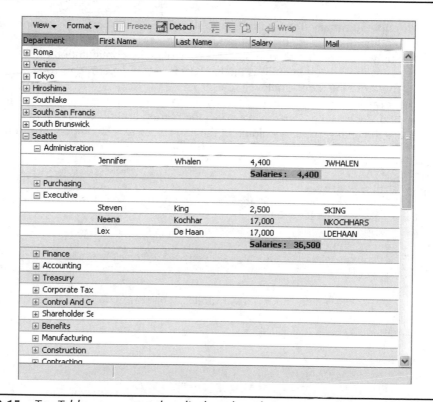

FIGURE 9-15   *TreeTable component that displays the salary summary below the employees records for each department*

Next step is to change the View Object query to include the database view. For this, open the View Object in the editor and select the Query category. Click the pencil icon to edit the query. In the query editor, change the SQL Mode option to Expert and provide a query similar to the one shown here:

```
SELECT
    DEPARTMENT_ID,EMPLOYEE_ID,FIRST_NAME,LAST_NAME, SALARY, EMAIL, HIRE_DATE
FROM EMPLOYEES
UNION
SELECT
    DEPARTMENT_ID, EMPLOYEE_ID, FIRST_NAME, LAST_NAME, SALARY, EMAIL,
    HIRE_DATE
FROM SALARY_SUMMARY_VIEW
```

Note the UNION expression that combines the result set of the Employees table query with the result from the database view query.

Displaying the Summary Row in the TreeTable   The af:treeTable component and the ADF tree binding that is used to query the ADF Business Component business service are the same. The only changes that need to be applied involve the configuration of the salary column, which contains the salary summary as the last row for each department. You can distinguish the summary row from the other employee rows because the EmployeeId attribute is empty. To not render the formatting of the salary row for nodes that also don't have an EmployeeId attribute value defined, such as the Departments node, the second criteria is that the salary value must exist. here is the changed Salary column of the af:treeTable component configuration:

```
<af:treeTable value="#{bindings.LocationsView1.treeModel}" var="node"
    selectionListener="#{bindings.LocationsView1.treeModel.makeCurrent}"
    rowSelection="single" id="tt1" displayRow="selected"
    verticalGridVisible="false" columnSelection="single">
    <f:facet name="nodeStamp">
      <af:column id="c1">
        <f:facet name="header">
          <af:outputText value="Department" id="ot18"/>
        </f:facet>
        <af:outputText id="ot2"
            value="#{empty node.City? node.DepartmentName : node.City}"/>
      </af:column>
    </f:facet>
    ...
    <af:column id="c8" >
      <f:facet name="header">
        <af:outputText value="Salary" id="ot15"/>
      </f:facet>
      <!-- show inline style only if employeeId is null  -->
      <!-- and salary is not null -->
      <af:panelGroupLayout layout="horizontal" id="pgl1"
          inlineStyle="#{empty node.EmployeeId and not empty node.Salary?
          'width:100%; font-weight:bold; background-color:#c0c0c0' : ''};">
        <!-- show the next two components only if employeeId is null  -->
        <!-- and salary is not null -->
```

```
      <af:outputText value="Salaries :" id="ot19"
         rendered="#{empty node.EmployeeId and not empty node.Salary}"/>
      <af:spacer width="10" id="s1"
         rendered="#{empty node.EmployeeId and not empty node.Salary}"/>
      <af:outputText value="#{node.Salary}" id="ot17"/>
    </af:panelGroupLayout>
  </af:column>
  ...
</af:treeTable>
```

Summary

Collections are what application developers work the most with when building business applications with the Oracle Fusion development stack. In this chapter, we introduced three of the many component options that the ADF platform provides to display multi-row data. The ADF Faces table, tree, and treeTable components, and many others, are bound to ADF using the same tree-binding metadata and framework classes. This not only means that a single skill set is sufficient to work with the different components, but also means that code samples can be reused. We also explained solutions for use cases that exist for many components.

CHAPTER
10

Working with Menus, Dialogs, and Pop-ups

Web application real estate is a precious thing; users need to be able to see vast amounts of information in a small space. Using layered components such as pop-ups and context menus provide a creative way to maximize space.

his chapter discusses several techniques for creating pop-up components in an ADF Faces application, including a specialized type of pop-up called a dialog. These components allow their nested components to be displayed in a secondary window, which is useful for maximizing the amount of available space on a particular page; users need not navigate to a different page in the application to update data, for example. Another type of pop-up is the menu pop-up, used to create context (right-click) menus. Context menus are discussed in this chapter, while menu components in general and menus as navigation components are discussed in Chapter 7.

Creating Pop-ups

There are four basic types of pop-ups. Their appearance at runtime is explained in Table 10-1.

The inline pop-up appears as a window with rounded corners that the user dismisses by clicking outside the pop-up. This type of pop-up is added to a page simply by dropping the Popup component from the Common Components section of JDeveloper's component palette onto the visual editor, structure, or source view of a page. A pop-up can be defined nearly anywhere on a page and is typically defined outside of other data bound components. For readability at design time, defining pop-ups toward the top of the source of a JSPX file (but within an `af:form` component) is recommended, but there are exceptions to this, outlined later in this section.

A note pop-up contains a nested `af:noteWindow` component and includes a callout icon next to the component that launches the pop-up. It behaves similarly to an inline pop-up in that it is dismissed when the user clicks outside the pop-up.

More robust pop-ups that enable more functionality can be built by nesting additional components within the pop-up, such as `af:dialog` and `af:panelWindow`. These pop-ups are generally referred to as floating windows, and by default will not disappear, but are instead made inactive when the user clicks outside the pop-up.

The fourth type of pop-up is a menu pop-up, which is similar to the inline pop-up in its dismissal behavior, but appears with straight edges and contains nested menu components. Figures 10-1 to 10-4 show each type of pop-up at runtime.

Popup Type	Visual Description
Inline	Pop-up with no chrome and only a faint border
Note	Inline pop-up with callout positioned next to calling component
Floating window	Window with header and footer chrome, including a close icon
Menu	Pop-up with no chrome, a faint border, and right-angled corners

TABLE 10-1 *Types of Pop-ups and How They Appear at Runtime*

FIGURE 10-1   *Inline pop-up*

FIGURE 10-2   *Note pop-up*

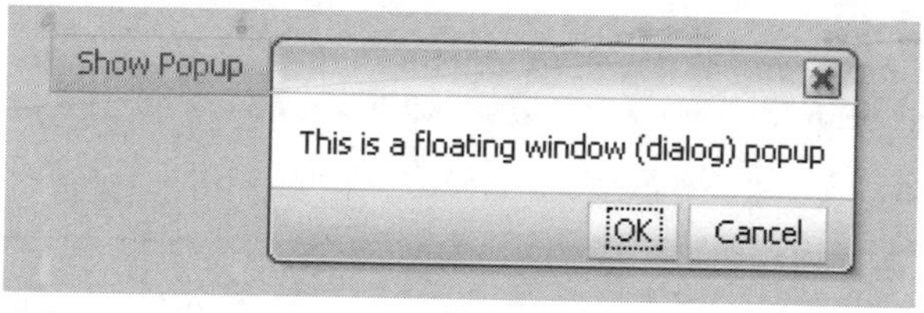

FIGURE 10-3   *Floating window pop-up*

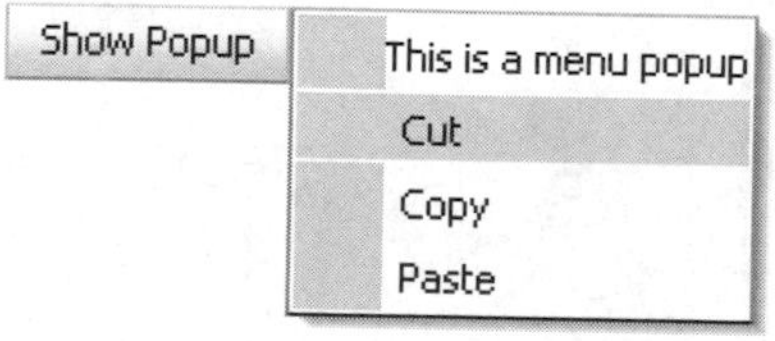

FIGURE 10-4   *Menu pop-up*

Exceptions to the rule regarding defining pop-ups outside of data bound components in a `JSPX` include cases where a pop-up facet is available. For example, the `af:commandToolbarButton` component has a pop-up facet (`f:facet name="popup"`) that can be used to add menu components to toolbar buttons easily. Additionally, context menu pop-ups should be defined within `contextMenu` facets, discussed later in this chapter.

Design Time vs. Runtime Positioning of Pop-ups
Except for cases where a pop-up is nested within an `f:facet` component, the location of an `af:popup` component in a JSPX will have no bearing on its location at runtime. The positioning of a pop-up at runtime is defined by its attributes, nested components, and the attributes of the component that launches it.

When editing a page that contains a pop-up, JDeveloper's visual editor will display the pop-up component when it is selected in the source (if the editor is shown in split view), the Structure window, or the shortcut links at the bottom of the editor. The pop-up will be displayed visually, with the rest of the page grayed out. For example, to edit a pop-up, open the page in the visual editor and select the `af:popup` component in the Structure window. The visual editor will display the pop-up component as shown in Figure 10-5, and components can then be added to the pop-up visually by dragging them from the Component Palette or Data Control Palette.

TIP
To easily add menu and dialog components within a pop-up, right-click the `af:popup` *component and select Insert Inside af:popup.*

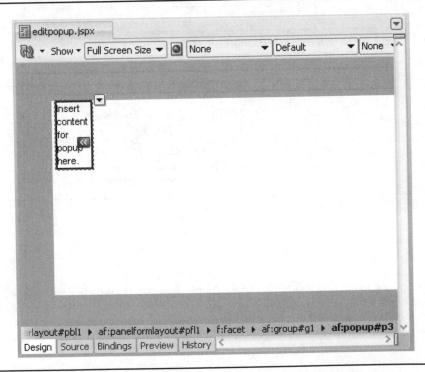

FIGURE 10-5   *Visually editing pop-up components*

Reusing Pop-up Components

Pop-ups and menus are good candidates for declarative components; you may want to define a common look and functionality for these components that developers can customize for the particular page they are developing. For example, if several pages of your application will include read-only tables of data that can be edited via a context menu, you might create a menu pop-up that defines a common look and feel and that is populated dynamically with a row key from the calling table. A custom "Edit Popup Menu" component could then be made available to page developers who would reuse the component by adding it to a page and passing in the row context. Declarative components are covered in Chapter 15.

Launching Pop-ups

Pop-ups, whether inline, menu, or floating window types, may be launched using an `af:showPopupBehavior` component, an `af:clientListener` that calls a JavaScript method on the page, or by calling a backing bean method that accesses or adds JavaScript to the calling event. Each of these methods is shown in the code listing that follows, and the methods called by the `clientListener` and `actionListener` attributes are discussed in detail later in the chapter.

```
...
<af:commandButton text="Launch via showPopupBehavior">
  <af:showPopupBehavior popupId="p1"/>
</af:commandButton>
<af:outputText value="Click to view popup">
  <af:clientListener method="launchPopup" type="click"/>
</af:outputText>
<af:commandButton text="Launch via Managed Bean"
  actionListener="#{PopupBean.launchPopup}"/>
...
<af:popup id="p1">
  <af:outputText value="Example Popup"/>
</af:popup>
...
```

You should use the `af:showPopupBehavior` component wherever possible. This component provides the most declarative way to launch a pop-up and includes attributes such as `align` and `alignId` to provide the positioning of the pop-up. Internally, these are known as pop-up hints. If these hints are not specified by the `af:showPopupBehavior` component, the pop-up will be behave according to the positioning and functionality specified by any nested components. Dialogs, for example, will be modal and aligned to the middle of the browser window by default.

Launching Pop-ups via JavaScript

To launch pop-ups via JavaScript, create a JavaScript function in the page that contains the pop-up. Best practices dictate that the `af:resource` component should be used to define script within pages. This provides better performance than adding a `script` tag within an `f:verbatim` tag. The `af:resource` tag allows for inclusion of JavaScript or Cascading Style Sheets (CSS) in pages, either nested directly within the component or defined in a `.js` or `.css` file. To add

JavaScript to a page, drop an `af:resource` component from the component palette onto the page and specify `javascript` as the value of the `type` attribute. The following code can be used to launch a pop-up with an `id` of `p1` within a page:

```
<af:resource type="javascript">
   function launchPopup(evt) {
      var source = evt.getSource();
      var popup = source.findComponent("p1");
      popup.show();
   }
</af:resource>
...
<af:popup id="p1">
   <af:outputText value="Example Popup"/>
</af:popup>
...
<af:outputText value="Click to view popup">
   <af:clientListener method="launchPopup" type="click"/>
</af:outputText>
...
```

You can add alignment hints to the JavaScript function and launch the pop-up with those values applied. For example, to display the pop-up aligned after the end of the component with an `id` of `cb2`, you would modify the `launchPopup` method as follows:

```
<af:resource type="javascript">
   function launchPopup(evt) {
      var source = evt.getSource();
      var popup = source.findComponent("p1");
      var hints = {align:"after_end", alignId:"cb2"};
      popup.show(hints);
   }
</af:resource>
```

NOTE
As in all cases where components are referred to by id, the proper use of naming containers applies here. A component is referred to by its naming container(s), if applicable, followed by the component id. Naming containers are covered in Chapter 19.

Additional pop-up hints can be used to augment pop-up behavior. However, these JavaScript hints are intended for use by nested components to define the functionality of the pop-up according to that component's needs (as in the aforementioned dialog example). Therefore, as a matter of best practice, you should use JavaScript to define pop-up hints only in cases where other components don't contain the functionality you need. This makes the application developer's job easier by providing declarative development, rather than having to write JavaScript code, which is more difficult to maintain than when using component-based development.

Launching Pop-ups via a Backing Bean

Launching a pop-up via a backing bean involves appending JavaScript to the `FacesContext` using the `ExtendedRenderKitService` class. This method for invoking pop-ups is typically used only when you need to determine programmatically whether the pop-up should be displayed. The following code adds JavaScript to the faces context that launches the pop-up. The fully qualified client ID of the pop-up is retrieved from the backing bean using `mypopup .getClientId(fctx)`, where `mypopup` is the backing bean property to which the pop-up is bound.

```java
import javax.faces.context.FacesContext;
import javax.faces.event.ActionEvent;
import oracle.adf.view.rich.component.rich.RichPopup;
import org.apache.myfaces.trinidad.render.ExtendedRenderKitService;
import org.apache.myfaces.trinidad.util.Service;
...
private RichPopup mypopup;
  public void setMypopup(RichPopup mypopup) {
    this.mypopup = mypopup;
}
public RichPopup getMypopup() {
  return mypopup;
}
...
public void launchPopup(ActionEvent actionEvent){
  FacesContext fctx = FacesContext.getCurrentInstance();
  StringBuilder script = new StringBuilder();
  String popupId = mypopup.getClientId(fctx);
  script.append("var popup = AdfPage.PAGE.findComponent(\"")
    .append(popupId)
    .append("\");")
    .append("var hints = {align:\"after_start\", alignId:\"")
    .append("cb3")
    .append("\"};")
    .append("popup.show(hints);");
  Service.getRenderKitService(fctx),
    ExtendedRenderKitService.class).addScript(fctx,
    script.toString());
}
...
```

The `JSPX` that uses this backing bean method to launch the pop-up is defined as follows:

```xml
<af:commandButton text="Launch via Managed Bean"
  actionListener="#{PopupBean.launchPopup}"/>
<af:popup id="p1" binding="#{PopupBean.mypopup}">
  <af:outputText value="Example Popup"/>
</af:popup>
```

Calling Methods Before a Pop-up Is Launched

As previously stated, you should use the `af:showPopupBehavior` component when possible. However, when you want to "double up" the functionality of a button by calling an `actionListener` method when the button is clicked, in addition to launching a pop-up, you cannot use the `af:showPopupBehavior` component. This is because a pop-up is a client event and is designed to be lightweight, so launching a pop-up cancels all server-side event handling. This makes the pop-up a favorable component for use with static notes and menus, but for more dynamic functionality, further consideration is required. For example, if you want to create a pop-up that contains a form for creating new rows in a collection, you might be inclined to write the following code to launch the pop-up:

```
<af:commandButton text-"Create"
 actionListener="#{bindings.Create.execute}">
   <!-- This will not work as expected because launching the popup with a
      showPopupBehavior cancels the button's actionListener -->
   <af:showPopupBehavior popupId="createpopup"/>
</af:commandButton>
```

This code will launch the pop-up, but the `Create.execute` method on the binding layer is never called. The result of this is typically a pop-up that is launched with the current row's values populated in the text fields of the "create" form.

A common misconception is that calling a pop-up that has its `contentDelivery` attribute set to `lazyUncached` will cause the newly created row to appear in the form, but, indeed, launching the pop-up canceled the create operation, so no newly created row exists, even on the server. (For more information, refer to the "Including Content in an `af:popup`" section later in this chapter.) Therefore, to use a button that calls a method before the pop-up is launched, use the JavaScript method of launching a component, either by calling the JavaScript method from a backing bean or from an `af:clientListener`, as shown:

```
<af:commandButton text="Create"
   actionListener="#{bindings.Create.execute}" partialSubmit="true">
   <af:clientListener method="launchPopup" type="action"/>
</af:commandButton>
```

You could also use a pop-up listener to call a server-side method to perform the same functionality, but doing this is less declarative than using an `af:clientListener`. The "Creating Server-Side Events for Pop-ups" section later in this chapter covers this technique, which would be used when the method that the pop-up should call before launching is not defined in the PageDef, thus resulting in the need to include a managed bean method anyway.

Another technique for calling a server-side method when launching a pop-up is by using regions. For example, a series of steps in a bounded task flow could be displayed in a pop-up. This method relies on the use of bounded task flows (covered in Chapter 5) and the use of regions on a page (covered in Chapter 6). Developing a pop-up in this way is less declarative, but it provides a bit more reusability in that the region can be reused across pages. The technique is covered in full in Chapter 6.

Programmatically Hiding Pop-ups

You may find a need to programmatically hide pop-ups, especially when using pop-ups for editing, inserting, or querying data. For example, consider a search pop-up that performs a `QueryEvent` when the user clicks a Search button. A dialog could be used to include OK and

Cancel buttons that would close the dialog, but if the query results are returned to the page and not the pop-up itself, it makes sense to close the pop-up after the search is performed, instead of expecting the user to click a query button and then an OK button. To show or hide a pop-up programmatically, a small amount of JavaScript can be called to perform this task, as shown in the following code sample:

```
<af:resource type="javascript">
function hidePopup(popupId){
  var popup = AdfPage.PAGE.findComponent(popupId);
  popup.hide();
}

function showPopup(evt) {
  var source = evt.getSource();
  var popup = AdfPage.PAGE.findComponent(source.getProperty("PopupId"));
  popup.show();
}
</af:resource>
```

These JavaScript methods could then be called from an `af:clientListener` to hide or show the pop-up when a button or link is clicked. Further, the pop-up could be closed programmatically using a backing bean method as in the following code example. The `processQuery` method executes the query that is fired by clicking the Search button for an `af:query` component (bound to a view criteria defined in the model as FindByDeptNameCriteria in this case), and subsequently calls the `hidePopup()` JavaScript function to close the dialog. The pop-up containing the `af:query` component is bound to the bean's `querypopup` property, and the `queryListener` attribute of the `af:query` component is set to the `processQuery` method.

```
import oracle.adf.view.rich.event.QueryEvent;
import oracle.adf.model.BindingContext;
import oracle.adfinternal.view.faces.model.binding.FacesCtrlSearchBinding;
import oracle.binding.BindingContainer;
import org.apache.myfaces.trinidad.render.ExtendedRenderKitService;
import org.apache.myfaces.trinidad.util.Service;
import javax.faces.context.FacesContext;
...
public void processQuery(QueryEvent queryEvent) {
  BindingContext bindingctx = BindingContext.getCurrent();
  BindingContainer bindings = bindingctx.getCurrentBindingsEntry();
  FacesCtrlSearchBinding queryBinding = (FacesCtrlSearchBinding)
    bindings.get("FindByDeptNameCriteriaQuery");
  queryBinding.processQuery(queryEvent);
  FacesContext fctx = FacesContext.getCurrentInstance();
  String popupId = querypopup.getClientId(fctx);
  ExtendedRenderKitService service = Service.getRenderKitService(
    fctx, ExtendedRenderKitService.class);
  service.addScript(fctx, "hidePopup('" + popupId + "')");
}
...
private RichPopup querypopup;
public void setQuerypopup(RichPopup querypopup) {
  this.querypopup = querypopup;
```

```
}
public RichPopup getQuerypopup() {
  return querypopup;
}
```

Controlling the Size and Position of Pop-ups

Pop-ups are essentially dummy containers. They size themselves according to the content included in them and cannot be manually resized by default. A pop-up's display is largely controlled by the `af:showPopupBehavior` component and by several JavaScript hints that can be used to launch the pop-up using JavaScript. However, the `af:showPopupBehavior` component enables more functionality than the JavaScript hints. For example, the `popupFetchListener` for a component is called only when the pop-up is launched from an `af:showPopupBehavior` component. Still, two hints are exposed in the documentation, `HINT_ALIGN` and `HINT_ALIGN_ID`, which can be used to position the pop-up when it is called via JavaScript.

Aligning pop-ups refers to setting the starting location of the pop-up's top left corner (in a left-to-right, or LTR, language setting in the browser). There are several options for setting a pop-up's location. For example, if you want to display a pop-up when the user hovers over a particular input component, you add an `af:showPopupBehavior` component within the input component and set the `triggerType` attribute to `mouseOver`. By default, a pop-up will be positioned at the top, start position on the page (this would be the top left for an LTR language). Use the `align` and `alignId` attributes to position the pop-up.

The following example shows a pop-up that is launched when the user hovers over the DepartmentName input field. The pop-up displays just after the input field:

```
<af:inputText value="#{bindings.DepartmentName.inputValue}"
  id="it3">
  <af:showPopupBehavior popupId="p1" triggerType="mouseHover"
    align="endAfter" alignId="it3" />
</af:inputText>
<af:popup id="p1">
  <af:table value="#{bindings.DepartmentsView1.collectionModel}" var="row">
    <af:column
      headerText="Department Id">
      <af:outputText value="#{row.DepartmentId}" />
    </af:column>
    <af:column
      headerText="Department Name">
      <af:outputText value="#{row.DepartmentName}"/>
    </af:column>
  </af:table>
</af:popup>
```

The mouseHover Trigger Type

Note that the code example uses `mouseHover` as the `af:showPopupBehavior` trigger type. At the time of writing, this `triggerType` is not exposed via the Property Inspector or tag insight. However, this is a valid value, and using this trigger type instead of `mouseOver` will cause a short delay before the pop-up is rendered.

In the preceding example, simply clicking outside the pop-up window dismisses the pop-up. This results from defining a pop-up that contains content without a nested `af:noteWindow`, `af:panelWindow`, `af:dialog`, or `af:menu`.

NOTE
If an `af:table` component includes a value for the `selectionListener` attribute, clicking a row would initiate a server event to set the current row value. The `mouseHover` trigger type shown would not catch this event, but a `doubleClick` event would—the first click of the double-click would fire the server-side event, and the second click would launch the pop-up with the appropriate row currency, provided the pop-up's `contentDelivery` attribute was set to `lazyUncached`.

Including Content in an af:popup

Including content in a pop-up is relatively straightforward. You simply drop data members (collections, attributes, or methods) or ADF Faces components within an `af:popup` component onto the visual editor, Structure window, or source of a page. The tricky part about including content in a pop-up is knowing when that content will be delivered to the component.

"Content delivery" refers to the point at which the content of a pop-up is delivered to the client. Three options can be used for defining when content is delivered in a pop-up: `immediate`, `lazy`, and `lazyUncached`. By default, the `contentDelivery` attribute is set to `lazy`, meaning that the content in a pop-up will be delivered once, the first time the pop-up is rendered (`contentDelivery="immediate"` will also deliver the content once, when the page is first loaded). This minimizes trips to the server but is really only useful for delivering static content. To deliver dynamic content in a pop-up, set the `contentDelivery` attribute to `lazyUncached`. This ensures that the content will be re-rendered each time the metadata for the pop-up is loaded.

The following example shows a pop-up that displays content in the context of the current department in the form. The pop-up content delivery is set to `lazyUncached`, and since the Next and Previous buttons initiate a server-side event, the current department name in the binding container is displayed.

```
<af:form>
  <af:panelFormLayout>
    <af:panelLabelAndMessage label="Department Id"
      id="plam4" clientComponent="true">
      <af:outputText value="#{bindings.DepartmentId.inputValue}"/>
    </af:panelLabelAndMessage>
    <af:panelLabelAndMessage label="Department Name">
      <af:outputText value="#{bindings.DepartmentName.inputValue}"/>
      <af:showPopupBehavior popupId="deptpopup" align="endAfter"
        alignId="plam4" triggerType="click"/>
    </af:panelLabelAndMessage>
    <f:facet name="footer">
      <af:panelGroupLayout layout="horizontal">
        <af:commandButton text="Previous" partialSubmit="true"
          actionListener="#{bindings.Previous.execute}"/>
        <af:commandButton text="Next" partialSubmit="true"
          actionListener="#{bindings.Next.execute}"/>
```

```
      </af:panelGroupLayout>
    </f:facet>
  </af:panelFormLayout>
  <af:popup id="deptpopup" contentDelivery="lazyUncached">
    <af:outputText value="#{bindings.DepartmentName.inputValue}"/>
  </af:popup>
</af:form>
```

In this code, the current department name is displayed because a server-side event is called to navigate to the next or previous row, and the pop-up content is refetched when the pop-up is opened, so the new value of `#{bindings.DepartmentName.inputValue}` is used to populate the value of the `outputText` component in the pop-up. If `contentDelivery` in the preceding example was set to `lazy` or `immediate`, the pop-up wouldn't be refreshed when the page was reloaded, so even though the current value of `#{bindings.DepartmentName .inputValue}` would change on the server each time the user navigates to a different row, the pop-up content that was initially loaded with the page would be cached and therefore would display the first department name in the collection by default. Additionally, since pop-ups are embedded in a browser window, a full page submit would re-initialize the pop-up and dismiss all open inline pop-ups. Thus, to ensure that the pop-up is not re-initialized, the command components (`af:commandButton` in this case) include `partialSubmit="true"`.

Creating Server-side Events for Pop-ups

If no server-side event is present that would cause a pop-up to refresh its content, you can create one using a `PopupFetchEvent`. This event is called when the pop-up is queued for delivery. To configure a `PopupFetchEvent`, set the `launcherVar` attribute to a variable name such as `"launchSource"`. This value will store the component that launched the event so that it can be retrieved from Expression Language, or from the request object via `RequestMap. get("launchSource")`. Additionally, the context of the launching component can be found only if the `eventContext` attribute of the `af:popup` is set to `launcher`.

The following example demonstrates using the `PopupFetchEvent`. In this example, the page uses a table to display data, so more than one row is shown, and no navigation components or `selectionListener` are included in the table.

The pop-up is defined as follows, with the `launcherVar` and `eventContext` set appropriately, and the `popupFetchListener` attribute set to a method in the backing bean. Additionally, the pop-up includes an `outputText` component that gets its value from the `deptNameValue` property of the backing bean.

```
<af:popup id="p1" contentDelivery="lazyUncached"
  popupFetchListener="#{PopupFetchBean.fetchPopup}"
  launcherVar="launchSource" eventContext="launcher">
  <af:outputText value="#{PopupFetchBean.deptNameValue}"/>
</af:popup>
```

Caveats When Using a PopupFetchEvent

The `PopupFetchEvent` is called when the pop-up is delivered. Thus, it can be used only with pop-ups that have a `contentDelivery` of `lazy` or `lazyUncached`. Additionally, the event will fire only when the pop-up is called via an `af:showPopupBehavior` component.

The `af:outputText` component that calls the pop-up is defined within a table. The component includes two nested components: the `af:showPopupBehavior` that calls the pop-up and an `af:clientAttribute` component that copies the current row's DepartmentName value to a client attribute.

```
<af:form>
  <af:table value="#{bindings.DepartmentsView1.collectionModel}"
    var="row" …>
    <af:column …>
      <af:outputText value="#{row.DepartmentId}"/>
    </af:column>
    <af:column …>
      <af:outputText id="ot1" value="#{row.DepartmentName}">
        <af:showPopupBehavior popupId="::p1" triggerType="mouseHover"
          align="afterEnd" alignId="ot1"/>
        <af:clientAttribute name="deptName"
          value="#{row.DepartmentName}"/>
      </af:outputText>
    </af:column>
  </af:table>
</af:form>
```

The backing bean then defines the `popupFetchListener` method and uses the attributes specified by the `af:clientAttribute` to retrieve the desired content. In the code that follows, the method simply sets the bean property to which the `af:outputText` value attribute in the pop-up is bound. However, you could also use the `launchSource` attribute values to pass arguments to a method on the binding container, which would then retrieve the desired data.

```
import java.util.Map;
import javax.faces.component.UIComponent;
import javax.faces.context.FacesContext;
import oracle.adf.view.rich.event.PopupFetchEvent;
…
public void fetchPopup(PopupFetchEvent popupFetchEvent) {
  FacesContext fctx = FacesContext.getCurrentInstance();
  Map requestMap = fctx.getExternalContext().getRequestMap();
  UIComponent component = (UIComponent) requestMap.get("launchSource");
  String value = (String) component.getAttributes().get("deptName");
  setDeptNameValue(value);
}
…
```

Another way to set values when the pop-up is launched is to nest an `af:setPropertyListener` on the pop-up component. The pop-up only needs to include a `contentDelivery` of `lazyUncached` to retrieve the correct value for a data-bound component. In this case, the `from` property is bound to a binding in a form, instead of a table collection, but the technique is the same:

```
<af:popup id="p1" contentDelivery="lazyUncached">
  <af:outputText value="#{PopupFetchBean.deptNameValue}"/>
  <af:setPropertyListener from="#{bindings.DepartmentName.inputValue}"
    type="popupFetch" to="#{PopupFetchBean.deptNameValue}"/>
</af:popup>
```

Another server-side event for pop-ups, `PopupCanceledListener`, is called when the pop-up is closed. It is useful for re-initializing form values when a pop-up is closed. It is most typically used with dialog pop-ups and is discussed in the "Overriding the Built-In `af:dialog` Buttons" section a little later in this chapter.

The af:dialog Component

An `af:dialog` component can be used to create a modal pop-up. This is useful when the user must perform some action before dismissing the pop-up (in lieu of the inline pop-up, where the dialog can be dismissed simply by clicking outside of the pop-up area). The dialog component must be included within a pop-up component, and it uses several features of the pop-up to include behavior unique to dialog windows. For example, a dialog automatically hides itself when the close icon or cancel button is clicked, unless there are `FacesContext` error messages on the page. Additionally, a dialog appears in the middle of the window by default, but it inherits any alignment hints provided by the surrounding `af:popup` component.

Typically, `af:dialog` components are used for some type of input components; otherwise, modal functionality wouldn't be required, so an inline pop-up could be used instead. A basic dialog component is defined as follows:

```
<af:popup contentDelivery="lazyUncached">
  <af:dialog title="Dialog Window Title" type="okCancel"
    modal="true" closeIconVisible="true">
    <af:inputText label="Enter a Value" required="true"/>
  </af:dialog>
</af:popup>
```

In this example, the dialog would close if the OK or Cancel button was clicked, unless no value was supplied for the nested `af:inputText` component. Setting the `af:inputText` value to `null` and clicking OK in the dialog sends a server event that submits the form and therefore validates the input text component. Thus, as shown in Figure 10-6, the required validation fails, the error is displayed in the pop-up dialog, and the dialog is not dismissed.

Dialog Buttons and Events

By default, a dialog displays OK and Cancel buttons. These buttons are internationalized and will display localized labels according to the browser's language setting. You can specify the type of buttons that will be used in the dialog by setting the `type` attribute of the `af:dialog` component. This attribute accepts several values that are iterations of the OK, Cancel, Yes, and/or No buttons.

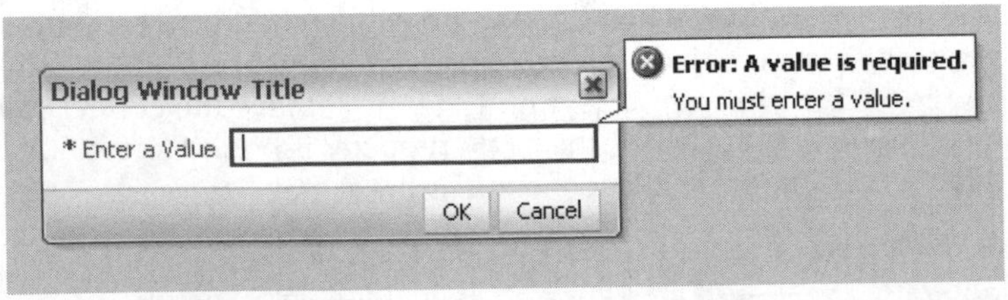

FIGURE 10-6 *Failed validation prevents a dialog from closing*

Only the OK, Yes, and No dialog buttons propagate events to the server. Clicking the Cancel button or the close icon on the dialog will close the surrounding pop-up component and raise a popupCanceled event. You can also set the type attribute to none and create your own buttons within the buttonBar facet of an af:dialog.

Overriding the Built-in af:dialog Buttons

To allow the dialog's OK, Yes, or No button to perform an operation such as a commit or rollback, you use a dialog listener. For example, the following pop-up dialog includes a backing bean method for handling when the pop-up is canceled via the Cancel button or close icon (popupCanceledListener) or the dialog is closed via the OK button (dialogListener):

```
<af:popup contentDelivery="lazyUncached"
  popupCanceledListener="#{DialogBean.handlePopupCancel}">
  <af:dialog dialogListener="#{DialogBean.handleDialogClose}">
  <!-- Input form defined here -->
  </af:dialog>
</af:popup>
```

The backing bean implements the handlePopupCancel and handleDialogClose methods, as shown in the following code sample. Note that to determine which button was clicked, the handleDialogClose method uses the getOutcome method of DialogEvent.

```
import oracle.adf.view.rich.event.DialogEvent;
import oracle.adf.model.BindingContext;
import oracle.binding.BindingContainer;
import oracle.binding.OperationBinding;
import oracle.adf.view.rich.event.PopupCanceledEvent;
...
public void handleDialogClose(DialogEvent dialogEvent) {
  if (dialogEvent.getOutcome().equals(DialogEvent.Outcome.ok)) {
    BindingContext bindingctx = BindingContext.getCurrent();
    BindingContainer bindings = bindingctx.getCurrentBindingsEntry();
    OperationBinding operationBinding =
      bindings.getOperationBinding("Commit");
    Object result = operationBinding.execute();
  }
}
...
public void handlePopupCancel(PopupCanceledEvent popupCanceledEvent) {
  BindingContext bindingctx = BindingContext.getCurrent();
  BindingContainer bindings = bindingctx.getCurrentBindingsEntry();
  OperationBinding operationBinding =
    bindings.getOperationBinding("Rollback");
  Object result = operationBinding.execute();
}
```

Creating Client Events for Pop-up Dialogs

You can prevent actions on dialogs by calling the cancel method for an event. For example, suppose you require a response in a dialog before the user can continue. To intercept the outcomes in a dialog, use an af:clientListener within an af:dialog that has the type attribute set to `dialog`. The listener will fire a method when the OK, Cancel, Yes, or No buttons are clicked.

```
<af:popup>
  <af:dialog closeIconVisible="false" type="ok">
    <af:panelStretchLayout>
      <f:facet name="center">
        <af:panelGroupLayout layout="scroll">
          <af:outputText value="A long list of terms and conditions"/>
        </af:panelGroupLayout>
      </f:facet>
    </af:panelStretchLayout>
    <af:selectBooleanCheckbox id="sbc1" clientComponent="true"
      label="I agree to the Terms and Conditions"/>
      <af:clientListener type="dialog" method="closeTermsDialog"/>
  </af:dialog>
</af:popup>
```

Remember that only the OK, Yes, and No dialog buttons propagate events to the server. The Cancel button and close icon on the dialog window raise a client `DialogEvent`, so to block that event, call `evt.cancel()`. Therefore, the following JavaScript can be used to handle the `clientListener` and call `evt.cancel()` to block the dialog from closing:

```
function closeTermsDialog(evt){
  var checkbox = evt.getSource().findComponent("sbc1");
  if(checkbox.getSubmittedValue()==false){
    evt.cancel();
  }
}
```

The Dialog Framework

In addition to the `af:dialog` component, which must reside within an `af:popup` component and is therefore launched within the same browser window that called it, there is also a facility for launching secondary windows. This is known as the ADF Faces dialog framework. The dialog framework is useful when a process external to the calling page needs to be accessed without affecting the transaction on the calling page. Thus, the dialog framework is often used for launching auxiliary bounded task flows. This method of launching bounded task flows is covered in depth in Chapter 5.

The method to launch a page as a separate window involves prefixing navigation outcomes with `dialog:` and setting the `useWindow` attribute of the component that launches the page to `true`. For example, the following button launches the page to which the `dialog:callDialog` outcome refers. The dialog is displayed in a separate page that is sized according the `windowHeight`

Handling the Enter Key

By default, pressing the ENTER key while a dialog is open defaults to the dialog's OK or Yes button. If you need to override this behavior, use the `clientListener` method of closing a pop-up dialog to handle conditionally closing the dialog.

and `windowWidth` attributes. Additionally, setting the `partialSubmit` attribute to `true` for this button ensures that the page is not reloaded and won't flicker when the button is clicked.

```
<af:commandButton text="Launch Dialog Window" partialSubmit="true"
    action="dialog:callDialog" useWindow="true"
    windowHeight="100" windowWidth="200"/>
```

The `dialog:callDialog` action outcome is defined in the adfc-config.xml, as shown in Figure 10-7. This code would reside in the launchDialog page and the dialog page could be defined as any other page; no `af:dialog` components are necessary to launch a page using the dialog framework. Of course, the button action could also be bound to a backing bean method to call the `dialog:callDialog` outcome conditionally.

When using the dialog framework, you must define an end point in the dialog page so that the ADF Faces lifecycle continues after the dialog page is dismissed. To do this, add an `af:returnActionListener` to buttons that close the dialog without requiring additional processing.

Passing Values to and from a Dialog Window

To pass values to and from a dialog window, include a `launchListener` and `returnListener` on the component that calls the dialog. For example, consider the following page that launches a dialog window:

```
<af:form>
  <af:table value="#{bindings.DepartmentsView1.collectionModel}" id="t1" ...>
    <af:column headerText="Department Id" id="c1">
      <af:outputText value="#{row.DepartmentId}">
        ...
      </af:outputText>
    </af:column>
    ...
  </af:table>
  <af:commandButton text="Launch Dialog Window" useWindow="true"
    windowHeight="100" windowWidth="200" partialSubmit="true"
    launchListener="#{LaunchDialogBean.handleDialogLaunch}"
    action="dialog:callDialog"
    returnListener="#{LaunchDialogBean.handleDialogReturn}">
  </af:commandButton>
</af:form>
```

The Launch Dialog Window button calls the `handleDialogLaunch` method when the dialog is launched. As shown in the following code example, the `handleDialogLaunch`

launchDialog   dialog:callDialog   dialog

FIGURE 10-7 *Dialog outcome defined in adfc-config.xml*

method retrieves the selected `DepartmentId` value from the current row in the `DepartmentsView1Iterator` and passes the value to the dialog via `LaunchEvent.getDialogParameters`:

```
import oracle.adf.model.BindingContext;
import oracle.adf.model.binding.DCIteratorBinding;
import oracle.binding.BindingContainer;
import org.apache.myfaces.trinidad.event.LaunchEvent;
...
public void handleDialogLaunch(LaunchEvent launchEvent) {
  BindingContext bindingctx = BindingContext.getCurrent();
  BindingContainer bindings = bindingctx.getCurrentBindingsEntry();
  DCIteratorBinding deptIter =
    (DCIteratorBinding)bindings.get("DepartmentsView1Iterator");
  Object deptAttr = deptIter.getCurrentRow().getAttribute("DepartmentId");
  launchEvent.getDialogParameters().put("theDeptId", deptAttr);
}
```

The page that is launched as a dialog window can then retrieve this value via Expression Language using `#{pageFlowScope.theDeptId}`. The code listing for the dialog window page follows. Note that the dialog includes an `actionListener` for the Save button that closes the dialog but requires further processing, and an `af:resetActionListener` for the Cancel button that closes the dialog and requires no further processing:

```
<af:form>
    <af:outputText value="Editing department #{pageFlowScope.theDeptId}:"/>
      <af:panelFormLayout>
        <af:inputText value="#{bindings.DepartmentId.inputValue}" ...>
          ...
        </af:inputText>
        <af:inputText value="#{bindings.DepartmentName.inputValue}" ...>
          ...
        </af:inputText>
      </af:panelFormLayout>
    <af:commandButton text="Save"
      actionListener="#{LaunchDialogBean.save_action}">
      <af:setPropertyListener from="#{bindings.DepartmentName.inputValue}"
        to="#{LaunchDialogBean.savedDeptName}"type="action"/>
    </af:commandButton>
    <af:commandButton text="Cancel">
      <af:returnActionListener/>
    </af:commandButton>
</af:form>
```

Figure 10-8 shows the dialog box launched in a separate window, including the value of the `outputText` component that is set in the `handleDialogLaunch` method and retrieved via `#{pageFlowScope.theDeptId}`.

To retrieve return values from a dialog box, use an `actionListener` for the button that closes the dialog, and in the corresponding backing bean method, call `AdfFacesContext.returnFromDialog` to include a return value with the `ReturnListener`. The save_action method in the following example calls a `Commit` binding to commit any changes made to the form values in the dialog, and then the value of the `savedDeptName` property (which was set via

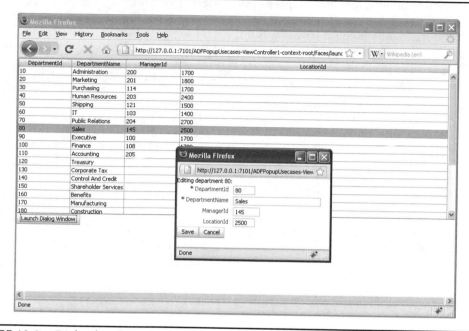

FIGURE 10-8 *Dialog box launched in a separate window using ADF dialog framework*

the setPropertyListener nested within the Save button component) is included in the call to the dialog's ReturnListener. The save_action method is defined as follows:

```
import javax.faces.event.ActionEvent;
import oracle.adf.model.BindingContext;
import oracle.adf.view.rich.context.AdfFacesContext;
import oracle.binding.BindingContainer;
import oracle.binding.OperationBinding;
...
  private String savedDeptName;
...
public void save_action(ActionEvent actionEvent) {
  BindingContext bindingctx = BindingContext.getCurrent();
  BindingContainer bindings = bindingctx.getCurrentBindingsEntry();
  OperationBinding operationBinding =
    bindings.getOperationBinding("Commit");
  Object result = operationBinding.execute();
  AdfFacesContext adfFacesContext = AdfFacesContext.getCurrentInstance();
  adfFacesContext.returnFromDialog(savedDeptName, null);
}
public void setSavedDeptName(String savedName) {
  this.savedDeptName = savedName;
}
public String getSavedDeptName() {
  return savedDeptName;
}
```

Recall that the button that launched the dialog included both a `launchListener` (that passed the current `DepartmentId` to the dialog) as well as a `returnListener`. The `returnListener` is called when the dialog returns—in this example, after the `save_action` method calls `AdfFacesContext.returnFromDialog`. The following code retrieves the return value of the dialog via `ReturnEvent.getReturnValue`, and uses that to perform further processing; in this example, the value is simply displayed in an inline pop-up:

```
import javax.faces.context.FacesContext;
import oracle.adf.view.rich.component.rich.RichPopup;
import org.apache.myfaces.trinidad.event.ReturnEvent;
import org.apache.myfaces.trinidad.render.ExtendedRenderKitService;
import org.apache.myfaces.trinidad.util.Service;
...
private RichPopup messagePopup;
private String editedDeptName;
...
public void handleDialogReturn(ReturnEvent returnEvent) {
  editedDeptName = (String)returnEvent.getReturnValue();
  FacesContext fctx = FacesContext.getCurrentInstance();
  StringBuilder script = new StringBuilder();
  String popupId = messagePopup.getClientId(fctx);
  script.append("var popup = AdfPage.PAGE.findComponent(\"")
    .append(popupId)
    .append("\");")
    .append("var hints = {align:\"after_end\", alignId:\"")
    .append("t1:c1")
    .append("\"};")
    .append("popup.show(hints);");
  Service.getRenderKitService(fctx,
    ExtendedRenderKitService.class).addScript(fctx,
    script.toString());
}
public void setMessagePopup(RichPopup messagePopup) {
  this.messagePopup = messagePopup;
}
public RichPopup getMessagePopup() {
  return messagePopup;
}
public void setEditedDeptName(String editedDeptName) {
  this.editedDeptName = editedDeptName;
}
public String getEditedDeptName() {
  return editedDeptName;
}
```

The inline pop-up is defined in the page that launches the dialog as follows:

```
<af:popup binding="#{LaunchDialogBean.messagePopup}"
  contentDelivery="lazyUncached">
  <af:outputText
    value="Department #{LaunchDialogBean.editedDeptName} has been edited"/>
</af:popup>
```

This example shows that we've come full circle; we have created a dialog that is launched from a button on a page. That dialog is displayed in a separate window using the dialog framework, as opposed to a pop-up dialog. When the dialog is closed, an inline pop-up is displayed within the page. Terrific! Now it's time to throw another component into the mix.

Creating Context Menus

Menu components are discussed thoroughly in Chapter 7. Once you have created a menu, you can create a context menu simply by surrounding the menu with an `af:popup` component. In JDeveloper's structure window, right-click the menu component and choose Surround With. In the Surround With dialog, choose Popup and click OK. You can then add an `af:showPopupListener` to a visual component as explained previously in this chapter, specifying `contextMenu` as the `triggerType`, as shown in the following code example:

```
<af:outputText value="#{row.DepartmentName}">
  <af:showPopupBehavior triggerType="contextMenu" popupId="::menupopup"/>
</af:outputText>
```

The pop-up menu would then be invoked whenever the context menu command is issued, which when using a Windows operating system is a right-click. Note that the `contextMenu` trigger will override the default browser functionality. Figure 10-9 shows a context menu that is launched from an `af:outputText` component.

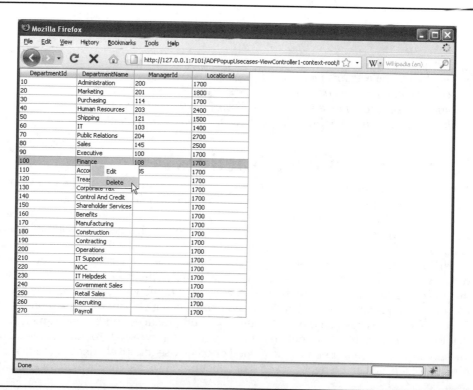

FIGURE 10-9 *Context menu launched from* `af:outputText` *component.*

Defining Context Menus in Facets

Including an `af:showPopupBehavior` for an `af:outputText` component requires that the user click the actual text (not the surrounding whitespace) to launch the pop-up. To allow the user to right-click anywhere within a row of a table or tree to launch the pop-up, insert a `contextMenu` facet in the table or tree, and to allow the user to right-click anywhere within a table or tree (outside of a row), add the `bodyContextMenu` facet. To add these facets, right-click the table or tree component in the structure and choose Insert Inside [`af:tree` or `af:treeTable`], and then choose the facet to add from the list. Then add the pop-up menu directly within the `f:facet`, as follows:

```
<af:table…>
…
  <f:facet name="contextMenu">
    <af:popup>
      <af:menu text="menu 1">
        <af:commandMenuItem text="Edit">
          <af:showPopupBehavior popupId="editPopup"/>
        </af:commandMenuItem>
        <af:commandMenuItem text="Delete"
          actionListener="#{bindings.Delete.execute}"    />
      </af:menu>
    </af:popup>
  </f:facet>
</af:table>
…
```

TIP
To disable the row in a table from being shown as selected when a context menu is invoked, set the `contextMenuSelect` *attribute of an* `af:table` *component to* `false`*. The row will still be selected in the collection, but the row will not show as selected or highlighted.*

Summary and Best Practices

Web application real estate is a precious thing; users need to be able to see vast amounts of information in a small space. Using layered components such as pop-ups and context menus provides a creative way to maximize space. Inline pop-ups are useful for read-only or auxiliary information, while pop-up dialogs are a way to ensure that the user enters input data before continuing on a page via the modality of the dialog. For a transaction that has its own scope, the dialog framework can be used to launch that transaction in a completely separate browser window. Doing so requires that the user does not have pop-ups blocked in browser settings and that the client supports pop-ups. Therefore, the dialog framework should be used sparingly when the application is intended for external customers or client devices other than browsers.

Context menus have their own unique set of best practices. Since context menus are hidden—that is, the functionality they contain cannot be seen unless the appropriate context area is right-clicked on a page—the user must be trained or otherwise intuitively understand that a particular element of a page can be right-clicked. For better or worse, the intuitive use of context menus is largely dictated by the most popular operating system, Windows. Users of an external-facing application may be inclined to right-click an element in a tree component because they are familiar with the look of a tree in Windows Explorer. They might expect functionality such as cut, copy, and paste to be available for a tree component. That inclination diminishes significantly when considering an element in a table or form, however. Thus, unless users can be trained to right-click a particular component to perform certain functions or that functionality is intuitive, context menus should be limited to inconsequential functions, and more important functionality should be obvious to the user via a command component such as a button, link, or toolbar icon.

When developing business applications for internal (or, more descriptively, trainable) users, many of the caveats regarding pop-ups, dialogs, and context menus are moot. In that case, the use of these components can create an application that has the same convenience features as a thick client application and can avoid the need to devote large areas of a page to command components. Additionally, the use of these components improves the user experience by lessening the amount of page navigation required, instead providing a more concise, one-page view of related parts of an application. This also improves the maintainability of the application; all related actions for a particular page are contained in one JSPX file, eliminating the need for developers to search for related pages and functionality.

CHAPTER
11

Looking Up Data

Displaying data in lists of values is fundamental to all user-facing applications; even character mode applications from yesteryear contained functionality to display lists of values with actual text instead of obscure IDs. Thankfully, we've come a long way in improving the user interface to help users navigate the "ID is king" world of database applications.

As discussed in Chapter 8, standard input components can be useful for advanced application users who have memorized codes and can type them in directly. However, for users not familiar with an application's codes, input fields can create a usability issue. This chapter discusses specialized types of components, including the list and query components, that allow web application developers to limit typing mistakes and invalid values by providing limitations to what can be inserted into a text field. For example, consider the input form shown in Figure 11-1. This form contains input text fields for critical fields such as JobId, Salary, and DepartmentId. As you can guess, these fields should contain a fair amount of restriction to ensure that the JobId and DepartmentId that are entered do actually exist in the system, and valid Salary values should be entered, perhaps limited to the values allowed by the selected JobId.

Whatever the business rules for the application, it's easy to see why using restrictive list components are favorable over building complex validators for each of the fields. This also eliminates the chance that the application user can enter invalid data for these fields in the first place. Thus, a better version of the input form is shown in Figure 11-2, where various select components are used to display valid data and, in some cases, provide context for that data (such as displaying a department name in a list instead of the nonintuitive DepartmentId).

The first section of this chapter discusses looking up data via the ADF Faces Rich Client (RC) list components. You can wire these components in several ways to display values in a list. Values may be directly defined in the components themselves, defined in a managed bean (either statically or by looking up values in the managed bean in a dynamic way), or defined by binding to an iterator or list binding on the ADF model layer.

The first thing to consider when you're building a list component is where the data values will come from and how tightly integrated they are to the business rules for the application. Data values, such as foreign key values, that are tightly integrated with the underlying model should be defined using model-driven lists, as covered later in this section. For values that are less related to the

FIGURE 11-1 *Input form without data lookup*

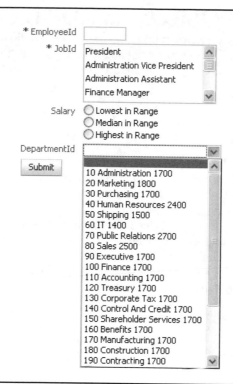

FIGURE 11-2   *Input form containing data lookup components*

data model and more related to the user interface or application navigation logic (such as menu options or color choices for a particular page or component), defining the data in the user interface layer via ADF Faces makes the most sense.

Further, when you're defining data in the user interface layer, consider whether the component will be reused. For menu-style or other components that will be reused across various pages in the application, list values should be defined in a managed bean, as this is more reusable than duplicating a particular list element with statically-defined values in each page that uses it. Alternatively, lists used for user interface logic can be defined in the database, and therefore the ADF Faces list components would be bound to the data model—this is a common method used by developers to provide a more centralized way to maintain the value of the lists. However, this database-centric method requires more flexibility in the data model to accommodate changes should another application require a different set of user interface rules.

Finally, internationalization concerns should be considered when defining list values. If an application needs to be configured for internationalization, then defining list values statically is not translatable and a data model or resource bundle should be used to provide the values instead. Internationalization concerns are covered in Chapter 18.

Creating List Objects via ADF Faces

The simplest form of a list binding is bound to a static list. In the following example, the `af:selectOneChoice` component is not bound to an ADF list binding or managed bean values; instead, `af:selectItem` components are used to create the individual items in the list:

```
<af:selectOneChoice label="Static List">
  <af:selectItem label="Yes" value="Y"/>
  <af:selectItem label="No" value="N"/>
</af:selectOneChoice>
```

This hard coding of list values is clearly the least dynamic form of creating a list, but it could be useful for very simple list options (provided no translations are necessary). Also note that this simple example does not actually store the values "Y" or "N", because the `af:selectOneChoice` component does not define a `value` attribute.

The next code listing stores the selected value and retrieves list values via a managed bean. The list is set to submit automatically when a value is selected, and this value is stored in the `choiceValue` property of the managed bean. The `af:outputText` component displays the selected value accordingly, without refreshing the page, because the `partialTriggers` attribute is set to the ID of the `af:selectOneChoice` component.

```
<af:selectOneChoice value="#{listBean.choiceValue}" id="smc1"
    autoSubmit="true" label="List from Managed Bean">
  <f:selectItems value="#{listBean.selectItems}"/>
</af:selectOneChoice>
<af:outputText value="You selected: #{listBean.choiceValue}"
    partialTriggers="smc1"/>
```

The managed bean is implemented as follows:

```
import javax.faces.model.SelectItem;

public class ListBean {
  private SelectItem[] selectitems;
  private String selectedvalue;

  public ListBean() {
    super();
  }
  public SelectItem[] getSelectItems() {
    if (selectitems == null) {
      selectitems = new SelectItem[4];
      selectitems[0] = new SelectItem(new Integer(1), "A", null, false);
      selectitems[1] = new SelectItem(new Integer(2), "B", null, false);
      selectitems[2] = new SelectItem(new Integer(3), "C", null, false);
      selectitems[3] = new SelectItem(new Integer(4), "D", null, false);
    }
    return selectitems;
  }

  public String getChoiceValue() {
```

```
      return selectedvalue;
  }
  public void setChoiceValue(String value) {
    selectedvalue = value;
  }
}
```

Note that these examples use both `af:selectItem` and `f:selectItems` components to display the list values. A discussion of the differences in these components is provided later in the chapter. These examples also use only the ADF Faces layer of technology to define list items. In most applications that use the Fusion technology stack, the ADF model layer will be employed to minimize dependence on managed beans and thus enable declarative development. The next section explains how to populate list items using the ADF binding layer.

Binding List Objects to ADF List Bindings

List items can be bound to values directly in the `f:selectItems` component. When using the ADF model layer, however, it is favorable to bind the `f:selectItems` component to a list binding, even in the case of static values, because the bindings are stored in a PageDef file like any other binding (thus separating UI logic from the binding layer) and can be defined without using code. The binding is also more reusable because it can be bound to multiple types of components. This is best described using an example. Figure 11-3 shows the list binding dialog for a PageDef, used to create a static list binding.

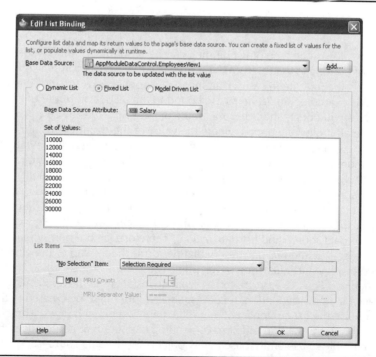

FIGURE 11-3   *List binding dialog for a static list*

The XML for this list binding in the PageDef is shown here:

```
<list IterBinding="EmployeesView1Iterator" id="Salary"
   DTSupportsMRU="true" StaticList="true">
   <AttrNames>
     <Item Value="Salary"/>
   </AttrNames>
   <ValueList>
     <Item Value="10000"/>
     <Item Value="12000"/>
     ...
     <Item Value="30000"/>
   </ValueList>
</list>
```

The benefit of this binding is that it can be reused for multiple types of list components. For example, the following three input components are bound to the same "Salary" binding:

```
<af:selectOneListbox value="#{bindings.Salary.inputValue}">
   <f:selectItems value="#{bindings.Salary.items}"/>
</af:selectOneListbox>
<af:selectOneChoice value="#{bindings.Salary.inputValue}">
   <f:selectItems value="#{bindings.Salary.items}"/>
</af:selectOneChoice>
<af:selectOneRadio value="#{bindings.Salary.inputValue}">
   <f:selectItems value="#{bindings.Salary.items}"/>
</af:selectOneRadio>
```

Of course, this same type of list binding can be used for dynamic values as well. The most direct way of binding to values from the model layer is via a dynamic list. Figure 11-4 shows the list binding dialog for creating a list binding that is populated from attribute values in the data model. In this example, the list items are bound to the `JobId` attribute of the `JobsView` iterator, and the values will update the `JobId` attribute of the `EmployeesView` iterator. This is most useful for master-detail lookup scenarios, where the value of the detail view's attribute must exist as a corresponding value in the master view. Additionally, choosing a display attribute such as JobTitle provides a more user-friendly label to be displayed in the UI component, rather than an ID. The ability to use display labels in addition to list values is a significant benefit of the dynamic list, because the static list does not provide a way to define both the list and display values.

Note that the iterators defined for a dynamic list must be based on different ADF view object instances, as shown in Figure 11-4. For example, you cannot use the `EmployeesView` iterator as both the base data source and list data source. Therefore, a common practice is to create read-only view objects defined using a query that performs the lookup of the attribute (such as JobId) and desired display attribute (such as JobTitle). These view objects could be defined in a separate package such as `view.lov` or created as separate instances in the application module data model.

However, if a new dependent record (such as a Job) might be created in the same transaction that uses the list, the list contents will not reflect any pending changes. Therefore, for scenarios in which the current transaction might have pending changes that could affect the contents of the list, it is preferable to use entity-based view objects for list data sources.

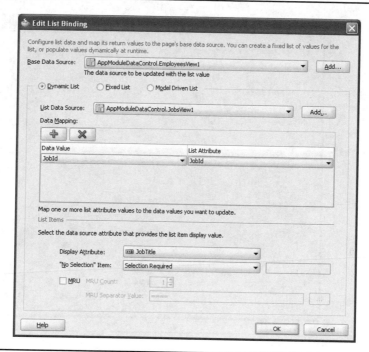

FIGURE 11-4   *List binding dialog for a dynamic list*

Model-driven List Bindings

A third type of list binding is a model-driven binding. This binding relies upon the view object's attribute definition containing a view accessor that refers to the lookup value. In this way, model-driven bindings are more reusable than dynamic list iterators because the lookup value and display value are maintained in the model, rather than being defined in a PageDef for a particular page. For example, consider the case where a department ID is added to an employee record. The department ID should be set in the user interface as a list, using the department name as the displayed value. Due to the strong relationship between the employee's and department's `DepartmentId` attributes (and because no other attributes will be populated using the list), a model-driven binding is recommended. The first step is to define the list of values metadata for the DepartmentId attribute in the `EmployeesView` object. *Oracle Fusion Middleware Web User Interface Developer's Guide for Oracle Application Development Framework 11g Release 1 Framework* explains this in detail, but an example is shown in Figure 11-5.

Note that the name of this list of values is LOV_<*attributeName*> by default (`LOV_DepartmentId` in this example). The list binding editor can then be used to specify the base data source and attribute that will be used to populate the list items. In this case, only one iterator is used on the view layer, so this would seem to be a violation because of the base data source and list data source being bound to the same view instance. But, indeed, the lookup is correctly performed on the model layer because a view accessor to the `DepartmentsView` was created from the `EmployeesView` view object when the list of values was defined. The list binding editor for a model driven list is shown in Figure 11-6.

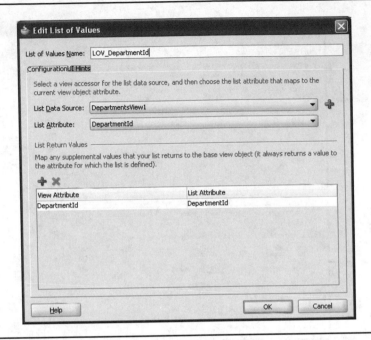

FIGURE 11-5   *List of Values definition*

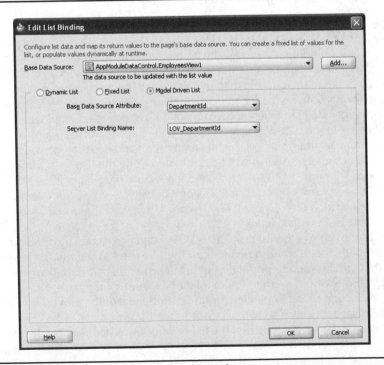

FIGURE 11-6   *List binding dialog for a model-driven list*

When defining a list of values definition for an attribute, a default list type can also be defined in the model layer. This aids UI development by predetermining the default UI component that is used when dragging the attribute onto the JSF editor. For example, a list of values attribute that is specified with Combo Box as the default list type will be bound to an `af:selectOneChoice` component by default, as shown in Figure 11-7. Of course, a different UI component can be selected in the binding editor, or a component may be converted to another component, but this predefining of list of values components saves the UI developer from having to guess the preferred way to display a list of values.

Table 11-1 shows each default list type in the model and the corresponding default UI component that will be selected when dropping a collection containing the LOV attribute onto the visual editor.

FIGURE 11-7   *Component binding editor for a collection containing a list of values attributes*

Default List Type	Default UI Component Used (tag name)
Choice List	ADF Select One Choice (`af:selectOneChoice`)

TABLE 11-1   *Default List Types and UI Components*

Default List Type	Default UI Component Used (tag name)	
Combo Box	ADF Select One Choice (`af:selectOneChoice`) Same as Choice List, except that Most Recently Used (MRU) values may appear in the list.	See Choice List
Combo Box with List of Values	ADF List of Values Choice List (`af:inputComboboxListOfValues`)	
Input Text with List of Values	ADF List of Values Input (`af:inputListOfValues`)	
List Box	ADF Select One Listbox (`af:selectOneListbox`)	

TABLE 11-1 *Default List Types and UI Components* (continued)

Default List Type	Default UI Component Used (tag name)	
Radio Group	ADF Select One Radio (af:selectOneRadio)	

Radio Group
DepartmentId
- 10 Administration
- 20 Marketing
- 30 Purchasing
- 40 Human Resources
- 50 Shipping
- 60 IT
- 70 Public Relations
- 80 Sales
- 90 Executive
- 100 Finance
- 110 Accounting
- 120 Treasury

TABLE 11-1 *Default List Types and UI Components* (continued)

For `af:selectOneChoice`, `af:selectOneListbox`, and `af:selectOneRadio` components, the binding used is a list binding, as shown in the following code snippet:

```
<list IterBinding="EmployeesView1Iterator" StaticList="false"
  Uses="LOV_DepartmentId" id="DepartmentId" DTSupportsMRU="true"/>
```

In all three types of list bindings—dynamic, fixed, and model-driven—any of the ADF Faces "select one" components can be used to display the value in the user interface: `af:selectOneChoice`, `af:selectOneListBox`, `af:selectOneRadio`, and `af:selectOneBoolean`. Two additional components are available for selecting a value from a list; both use the model-driven list binding and are covered in the next section.

ADF Faces LOV Components

Two ADF Faces components are especially useful when you're creating model-driven lists: `af:inputListOfValues` and `af:inputComboboxListOfValues`. When deciding whether or not to use these components, you must first understand the definition of an LOV and how it differs from `af:selectOneChoice`. In Fusion application development, an LOV allows users to search among not only the list attribute values, but also among values associated with the list attribute. The search is performed within a separate pop-up window that is automatically generated by the component. The runtime view of the `af:inputListOfValues` and `af:inputComboboxListOfValues` components is shown in Table 11-1. The query components that the list of values components use can also be created explicitly and are covered later in this chapter.

Both the `af:inputListOfValues` and the `af:inputComboboxListOfValues` components enable users to type directly into the field and thus, both contain nested `f:validator` components by default. This ensures that if the user elects not to select a value from the list, and instead types the value manually, the entered value is validated against the underlying business logic rules. The real difference between these two components is the way they display the list elements: The `af:inputListOfValues` displays an magnifying glass icon that the user clicks to launch a pop-up dialog. This allows the user to query the list values by using the attributes defined in the list of values binding. The `af:inputComboboxListOfValues` component contains a drop-down list icon that, when clicked, executes the underlying iterator automatically and displays all the values in a typical drop-down list. Thus, the `af:inputListOfValues` is better suited for larger data sets where query criteria are required to filter the rows in the iterator, whereas an `af:inputComboboxListOfValues` is useful for allowing the user either to type in or select a value from a list. The latter is typically used when a list box is used by so-called "power-users," who have memorized valid values and can enter them manually more quickly than selecting the value from a list.

The ADF Faces LOV components rely upon the list of values definition that is created in the model and are used primarily with models that are defined using ADF Business Components. In the preceding section, a list of values definition was created for the `DepartmentId` attribute of the Employees view object, named `LOV_DepartmentId`. Of course, the default pre-pended name "LOV_" doesn't mean that the specialized attribute must be used with an LOV component, but the naming convention came about because of the definition's primary use with the LOV components.

Creating List of Values Components

Binding list elements to ADF Faces LOV components is largely a matter of defining lists of values properties for an attribute on the data model. Creating the component on the UI is easily done by dropping the attribute onto the JSF editor and choosing either ADF LOV Input or ADF LOV Choice List from the List Of Values pop-up menu. (The List Of Values menu option will appear only for attributes whose list of values are defined on the data model.) This results in the following code in the JSF page:

```
<af:inputListOfValues id="departmentIdId"
   model="#{bindings.DepartmentId.listOfValuesModel}"
   popupTitle="Search and Select: #{bindings.DepartmentId.hints.label}"
   value="#{bindings.DepartmentId.inputValue}"
   label="#{bindings.DepartmentId.hints.label}"
   required="#{bindings.DepartmentId.hints.mandatory}"
   columns="#{bindings.DepartmentId.hints.displayWidth}"
   shortDesc="#{bindings.DepartmentId.hints.tooltip}">
   <f:validator binding="#{bindings.DepartmentId.validator}"/>
   <af:convertNumber groupingUsed="false"
     pattern="#{bindings.DepartmentId.format}"/>
</af:inputListOfValues>
```

The binding for this component is a specialized type of list binding, defined in the PageDef is as follows:

```
<listOfValues StaticList="false" IterBinding="EmployeesView1Iterator"
                Uses="LOV_DepartmentId" id="DepartmentId"/>
```

This same binding can be used to create an `af:inputComboboxListOfValues`. The default component definition is created as follows:

```
<af:inputComboboxListOfValues
   id="inputComboboxListOfValues"
   model="#{bindings.DepartmentId.listOfValuesModel}"
   popupTitle="Search and Select: #{bindings.DepartmentId.hints.label}"
   value="#{bindings.DepartmentId.inputValue}"
   label="#{bindings.DepartmentId.hints.label}"
   required="#{bindings.DepartmentId.hints.mandatory}"
```

```
columns="#{bindings.DepartmentId.hints.displayWidth}"
shortDesc="#{bindings.DepartmentId.hints.tooltip}">
<f:validator binding="#{bindings.DepartmentId.validator}"/>
<af:convertNumber groupingUsed="false"
  pattern="#{bindings.DepartmentId.format}"/>
</af:inputComboboxListOfValues>
```

TIP

The `popupTitle` *attribute for the* `af:inputListOfValues` *and*
`af:inputComboboxListOfValues` *components is set to the text*
`Search and Select:` *followed by the label for the attribute. This*
value should be replaced with Expression Language that refers to a
resource bundle value so that it is internationalizable.

One of the most desirable features of the ADF Faces LOV components is their built-in search functionality. The query forms that are used for this are formatted the same as the `af:query` component, so that users should be familiar with the layout and functionality of the component if a search is required for the component. Furthermore, the criteria that can be defined for the query and whether or not a search is even enabled for the LOV can be specified in the list of values binding editor for the data model attribute.

Implementing Auto-suggest Functionality

Google users are familiar with the auto-suggest functionality of the search input text field, where the user types a few characters and a pop-up appears with common search values. This same type of functionality is available via the `af:autoSuggestBehavior` component.

This component adds a client-side behavior to the input component within which it is nested, so that when the user types a character in the field, the values included in the `suggestedItems` attribute are displayed. The values in the list are `javax.faces.model.SelectItem` elements, and can be defined declaratively when the `af:inputListOfValues` and `af:inputComboboxListOfValues` components are bound to an LOV attribute on the model. For example, the following code snippet includes the `af:autoSuggestBehavior` component in an `af:inputListOfValues` bound to an LOV defined for `DepartmentId`. The `suggestedItems` attribute is bound to `#{bindings.DepartmentId.suggestedItems}`:

```
<af:inputListOfValues value="#{bindings.DepartmentId.inputValue}"
  label="#{bindings.DepartmentId.hints.label}"
  model="#{bindings.DepartmentId.listOfValuesModel}"
  columns="#{bindings.DepartmentId.hints.displayWidth}">
  ...
  <af:autoSuggestBehavior
    suggestedItems="#{bindings.DepartmentId.suggestedItems}"/>
</af:inputListOfValues>
```

At runtime, a pop-up appears for the component when the user types in a value—the suggested items in that list include the attributes defined as the display attributes for the component and are narrowed by the values typed into the field. For example, if "1" is typed into the field, the pop-up displays all departments that start with a *1* as the DepartmentId—10, 100, 110, and so on, as shown in Figure 11-8. If a value is typed that is not included in the list attributes, such as "M", the pop-up simply displays the default list items. This is true even if any

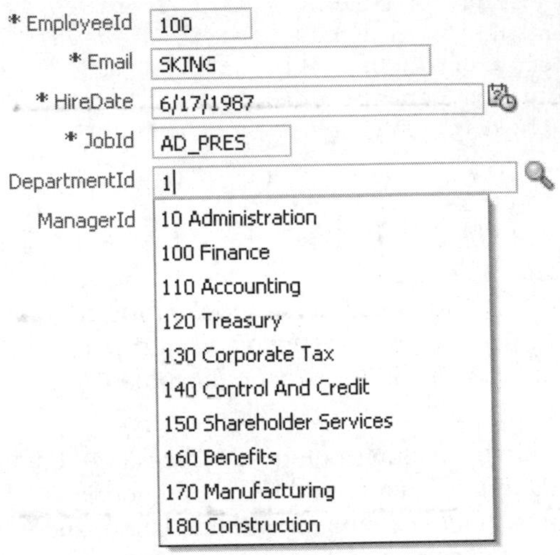

FIGURE 11-8   *Runtime view of auto-suggest behavior*

display attributes start with the value (such as the department name "Marketing"), because the `suggestedItems` list is populated based on the list attributes and not on display attributes.

Predefining Filtering for LOV Search Functionality

A common use case for augmenting the LOV components is the need to filter the search functionality by some value, such as the user's own department or manager ID. This can be accomplished by defining a view criteria on the view object that is defined as the list data source. Once defined, the view criteria can be applied to the LOV by adding it to the view accessor definition that the LOV uses. This has the affect of prefiltering the LOV, so that both the drop-down list and the query results will display only the filtered values from the view accessor.

Another technique is to select a defined view criteria in the Filter Combo Box Using drop-down list on the UI Hints tab of the Edit List of Values dialog, as shown in Figure 11-9. View criteria can be selected only for those list attributes defined with a default list type of Combo Box With List Of Values. The latter filtering method will filter only the drop-down contents; users will still be able to search and select any value that the view accessor retrieves when the search pop-up is invoked. In this way, the two methods of filtering LOVs can work together: a stricter filter can be applied on the view accessor so that those values are never displayed in the LOV drop-down or search pop-up, and another view criteria filter can be applied to limit only the drop-down list results, for convenience.

Creating Cascading Lists

The same techniques covered in the preceding section for filtering lists can also be used to create cascading lists, also known as dependent lists. For example, a view object based on the JOB_HISTORY table in the HR schema contains both `EmployeeId` and `DepartmentId` attributes. To create a list for the `EmployeeId` attribute that has values dependent upon the value chosen in the list for the `DepartmentId` attribute, first implement list of values definitions for both attributes as previously explained. This will mean that two view accessors are created in the `JobHistory` view object—one for each of the attributes. To implement the dependency between the two, you create a view criteria for the view object to which the dependent attribute belongs (`EmployeesView` in this case).

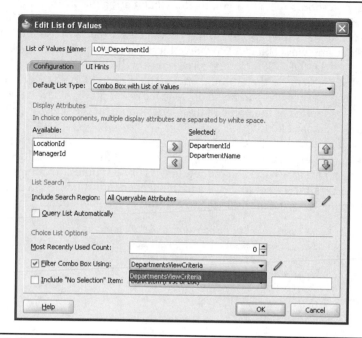

FIGURE 11-9 *Defining view criteria for a list of values attribute*

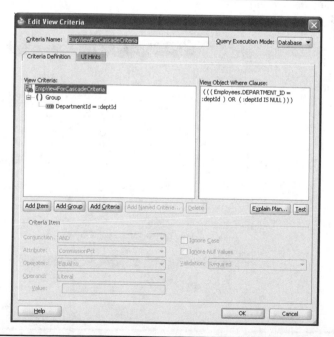

FIGURE 11-10 *View criteria definition for dependent lists of values*

The view criteria should include a criteria item that maps a bind variable to the dependent object (`DepartmentId` in this case). A view criteria defined in this way is shown in Figure 11-10.

This view criteria is then applied to the view accessor that will use it for the dependent LOV in the `JobHistory` view object. (The view object containing the new view criteria may need to be rebuilt before the IDE will pick it up.) The value of the bind variable can be defined using Groovy, so that the name of the attribute on which the secondary list will depend is supplied as the value. In this example, the primary attribute in the `JobHistory` view object is `DepartmentId`, so that name is supplied as the value of the bind variable for the view accessor of the `EmployeeId` list, as shown in Figure 11-11.

The code that defines the two lists is shown next. Note that a combination of UI list objects is used. This works as expected with the department ID list filtering the values in the employee ID list, because both lists are based on model-driven LOV attributes. In addition, the primary list has the `autoSubmit` attribute set to `true` and the dependent list has its `partialTriggers` property set to the ID of the attribute list so that no refresh is needed.

```
<af:inputListOfValues id="departmentIdId"
   value="#{bindings.DepartmentId.inputValue}"
   label="#{bindings.DepartmentId.hints.label}"
   model="#{bindings.DepartmentId.listOfValuesModel}"
   autoSubmit="true">
   ...
</af:inputListOfValues>
<af:selectOneChoice value="#{bindings.EmployeeId.inputValue}"
   label="#{bindings.EmployeeId.label}"
   partialTriggers="departmentIdId">
   <f:selectItems value="#{bindings.EmployeeId.items}" />
</af:selectOneChoice>
```

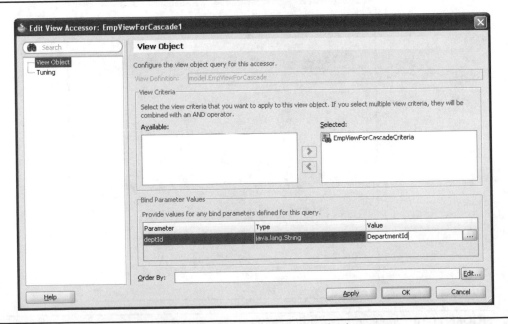

FIGURE 11-11   *View accessor definition for dependent list of values*

Now that you understand the ways that data can be populated using "select one" components, the next section will explain how to use the "select many" components of ADF Faces.

Multiple Select Components

ADF Faces includes four multiple select components: af:selectManyCheckbox, af:selectManyChoice, af:selectManyListbox, and af:selectManyShuttle. These components are useful for performing functions such as adding multiple rows to a collection or selecting multiple values from a list to modify a query. Regardless of the component used, the multiple select components are defined with nested af:selectItem or f:selectItems components, as shown in the following example:

```
<af:form>
  <af:selectManyChoice value="#{selectMany.listValue}"
    label="#{bindings.JobsView1.label}" id="smc1" autoSubmit="true">
    <af:selectItem label="select item: President" value="President"/>
    <af:selectItem label="select item: Vice President"
      value="Vice President"/>
    <f:selectItems value="#{bindings.JobsView1.items}"/>
  </af:selectManyChoice>
  <af:outputText partialTriggers="smc1" value="Jobs Selected:
    #{selectMany.listString}"/>
</af:form>
```

The backing bean that defines the values is defined as follows, and a runtime view of this component is shown in Figure 11-12:

```
public class SelectMany {
  private Object[] listValue;

  public void setListValue(Object[] listvalue) {
    this.listValue = listvalue;
  }
  public Object[] getListValue() {
    return listValue;
  }
  public String getListString() {
    return createString(listValue);
  }
  public String createString(Object[] arr) {
    if (arr != null) {
      String values = "[";
      for ( int i = 0; i < arr.length; i++) {
        values = values + arr[i];
        if ( i < arr.length - 1)
          values = values + ",";
      }
      values = values + "]";
      return values;
    }
    return null;
  }
}
```

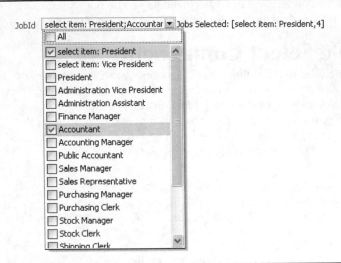

FIGURE 11-12 `af:selectManyChoice` *with* `f:selectItems` *and* `af:selectItem` elements

f:selectItems versus af:selectItem

In the preceding example, `af:selectItem` components are used to populate part of the list, and an `f:selectItems` component that is bound to a list binding populates the remainder. In this case, the `af:selectItem` label and value are hard coded, but this could also be bound to a backing bean method that used `oracle.adf.view.rich.component.rich.input` `.RichSelectItem` to create the items; the label and value attributes could then be defined using Expression Language. A select many component wouldn't typically have mixed types of list items, but their mixed use here is done to show you how the components differ and why in most cases, `f:selectItems` is preferred. Note that the `f:selectItems` component is bound to the values from `JobsView1`. This binding is defined as a list binding in the PageDef:

```
<executables>
  <iterator Binds="JobsView1" RangeSize="-1"
    DataControl="AppModuleDataControl" id="JobsView1Iterator"/>
</executables>
<bindings>
  <list IterBinding="JobsView1Iterator" ListOperMode="multiSelect"
    ListIter="JobsView1Iterator" id="JobsView1">
    <AttrNames> <Item Value="JobId"/> </AttrNames>
    <ListDisplayAttrNames>
      <Item Value="JobId"/>
      <Item Value="JobTitle"/>
    </ListDisplayAttrNames>
  </list>
</bindings>
```

Note that the `ListOperMode` attribute for this list is set to `multiSelect`. This is an important setting that will allow the model to participate in a multiple select component. Failing to set this results in a `javax.faces.convert.ConverterException: Unsupported model type` error at runtime. The attribute will be set appropriately by a list binding that is created by dragging and dropping a collection onto the JSF editor and choosing Multiple Selections, and then selecting the desired multiple select component. However, the default value for `ListOperMode` attribute is `setAttribute`, so this attribute should be changed when you're manually creating bindings for multiple select components.

A Practical Use of the Select Many Components

In some cases, it is favorable to query a view object by using the "IN" argument in a query. This lends itself nicely to the UI's use of a select many component because multiple values can be selected to build the IN part of the query. Some setup is required on the ADF Business Component view object to do this, so an example is warranted here.

1. Create a database type that will contain the value types used to populate the query. Here's an example:

   ```
   create or replace type NUMTABTYPE as table of number;
   ```

2. Configure the query and bind variable for the view object that will be used in the query. Unfortunately, the view object's declarative query editor doesn't support this; the steps must be performed separately. First, a bind variable of type `oracle.jbo.domain.Array` should be created. To do this, click the green plus sign in the Bind Variables node of the Query tab in the View Object editor.

3. Select Array as the type and define other properties as desired.

4. Click OK to exit the bind variable editor, but with the bind variable still selected in the Query tab, set the `ColumnType` property to your type (such as NUMTABTYPE) and set the `ElemType` property to the type of object you will be passing to the IN argument (such as `oracle.jbo.domain.Number`). A bind variable with these properties (named `ArrayVar`) is defined as follows in the source of the view object:

   ```
   <Variable Name="ArrayVar" Kind="where" Type="oracle.jbo.domain.Array"
     ColumnType="NUMTABTYPE" ElemType="oracle.jbo.domain.Number"/>
   ```

5. Now define the where clause by creating a view object class for the view object and overriding the create method. For example, to set the where clause to contain the `ArrayVar` bind variable using the database type NUMTABTYPE in the EmployeesView view object, the following is added to the `EmployeesViewImpl.java` file:

   ```
   @Override
   protected void create() {
     super.create();
     setWhereClause("department_id in
       (SELECT * FROM TABLE(CAST(:ArrayVar AS NUMTABTYPE)))");
   }
   ```

6. Finally, in the view object class, create a method that will accept the array of argument values and assign them to the bind variable (the accessors for the bind variable will be created automatically when adding the variable via the View Object editor):

   ```
   public void setDeptsToFind(oracle.jbo.domain.Number[] deptIds) {
     Array arr = null;
     arr = new Array(deptIds);
     if (arr != null)    {
   ```

```
        setArrayVar(arr);
    }
}
```

After adding the method to the client interface, the data model configuration is complete and setting the bind variable and executing the query in the UI are declarative. In this example, the department_id is used as the query's criteria. Therefore, a select many component containing a list of department IDs is used to set the ArrayVar bind variable. The following code defines an af:selectManyListbox that contains a list of departments and a button that executes the view object's client interface method:

```
<af:selectManyListbox value="#{bindings.DepartmentsView1.inputValue}"
  label="#{bindings.DepartmentsView1.label}" id="sml2">
  <f:selectItems value="#{bindings.DepartmentsView1.items}" id="si3"/>
</af:selectManyListbox>
<af:commandButton text="setDeptsToFind" id="cb1" action="getEmployees"
  actionListener="#{bindings.setDeptsToFind.execute}"/>
```

The bindings are defined in the PageDef as follows:

```
<executables>
  <iterator Binds="DepartmentsView1" RangeSize="-1"
    DataControl="AppModuleDataControl" id="DepartmentsView1Iterator"/>
</executables>
<bindings>
  <methodAction id="setDeptsToFind" RequiresUpdateModel="true"
    Action="invokeMethod" MethodName="setDeptsToFind"
    IsViewObjectMethod="true" DataControl="AppModuleDataControl"
    InstanceName="AppModuleDataControl.EmployeesView1">
    <NamedData NDName="deptIds" NDType="oracle.jbo.domain.Number[]"
      NDValue="${bindings.DepartmentsView1.selectedValues}"/>
  </methodAction>
  <list IterBinding="DepartmentsView1Iterator" ListOperMode="multiSelect"
    ListIter="DepartmentsView1Iterator" id="DepartmentsView1">
    <AttrNames> <Item Value="DepartmentId"/> </AttrNames>
    <ListDisplayAttrNames>
      <Item Value="DepartmentName"/>
    </ListDisplayAttrNames>
  </list>
</bindings>
```

Notice that the list binding is defined as shown in the previous select many example. The values that the user selects in the component are passed to the setDeptsToFind method action using the Expression Language ${bindings.DepartmentsView1.selectedValues}, and the type is set to the appropriate array of oracle.jbo.domain.Number[]. Department names are displayed in the list, but the underlying value is actually the DepartmentId, which is of type oracle.jbo.domain.Number, to match the type expected by the method. The runtime view of this page is shown in Figure 11-13.

In the preceding JSF page code listing, the button that calls the setDeptsToFind view object method also navigates to a page after the method is called. The page referred to by the getEmployees navigation case is simply a table bound to the EmployeesView instance. Since

FIGURE 11-13 `af:selectManyListBox` *for specifying an array of values for a bind variable*

the where clause is defined when the view object instance is created and the `ArrayVar` bind variable is set via the method action binding on the calling page, the resulting Employees table on the referenced page displays employees for the selected department ID.

Creating a Shuttle Component

Nearly every example that Oracle has produced regarding the shuttle component has included the use of managed bean properties to specify the iterator and attribute that is used for a `af:selectManyShuttle` component and its nested `f:selectItems` component. This allows a more declarative approach to building shuttle components, but it isn't the most useful example for showing how a shuttle component works. Therefore, the following example uses hard-coded iterator names to demonstrate the use of the component more clearly.

A basic `af:selectManyShuttle` component consists of "leading" values—values that are listed on the left side of the shuttle and are therefore available for selection—and "trailing" values—values that are already selected by way of the iterator to which they are bound, or values that are moved to the right side of the shuttle from the leading list.

Consider a scenario in which department data are displayed in a list, and application users can add or remove employees from departments by using a shuttle component. All employees are listed on the leading side of the shuttle. Existing employees for a department are listed on the trailing side of the shuttle, and employees can be added to the current department by clicking the shuttle or one of the many icons included in the components. A basic `af:selectManyShuttle` component for this scenario might look like the following:

```
<af:selectManyShuttle value="#{shuttleBean.selectedEmployees}">
  <f:selectItems value="#{shuttleBean.allEmployees}"/>
</af:selectManyShuttle>
```

This component displays values in the leading list from a managed bean that retrieves values from an underlying iterator, as follows:

```
import java.util.List;
import java.util.ArrayList;
import oracle.adf.model.BindingContext;
import oracle.adf.model.binding.DCBindingContainer;
import oracle.adf.model.binding.DCIteratorBinding;
import oracle.jbo.Row;
import javax.faces.model.SelectItem;
```

```
public class shuttleBean {
  List allEmployees;

  public List getAllEmployees() {
    if (allEmployees == null) {
      allEmployees =
        selectItemsForIterator("EmployeesView1Iterator",
          "EmployeeId", "Email");
    }
    return allEmployees;
  }
  public static List<SelectItem> selectItemsForIterator(String
    iteratorName, String valueAttrName, String displayAttrName) {
    BindingContext bc = BindingContext.getCurrent();
    DCBindingContainer binding =
      (DCBindingContainer)bc.getCurrentBindingsEntry();
    DCIteratorBinding iter = binding.findIteratorBinding(iteratorName);
    List<SelectItem> selectItems = new ArrayList<SelectItem>();
    for (Row r: iter.getAllRowsInRange()) {
      selectItems.add(new SelectItem(r.getAttribute(valueAttrName),
      (String)r.getAttribute(displayAttrName)));
    }
    return selectItems;
  }
}
```

The `EmployeesView1Iterator` is defined in the page definition file as a simple iterator binding that includes a `rangesize` of −1 so that all rows are selected.

```
<iterator id="EmployeesView1Iterator" Binds="EmployeesView1"
  DataControl="AppModuleDataControl" RangeSize="-1"/>
```

The iterator binding and `getAllEmployees()` method ensure that the leading list of values included in the shuttle component displays the e-mail for each employee in the iterator. For the trailing list of the shuttle component, the values are taken from another iterator. The `EmployeesInDeptIterator` iterator binding is based on the employees view instance nested within the departments iterator, so that only the employee e-mail values for the current department are shown in the trailing items list of the shuttle component. This iterator is used to populate the selected items for the current department as follows:

```
import javax.faces.event.ValueChangeEvent;
public class shuttleBean {
  List selectedEmployees;
  private boolean refreshSelectedList = false;

  public List getSelectedEmployees() {
    if (selectedEmployees == null || refreshSelectedList) {
      selectedEmployees =
      attributeListForIterator("EmployeesInDeptIterator","EmployeeId");
    }
    return selectedEmployees;
  }
}
```

```
public void setSelectedEmployees(List selectedValues) {
  this.selectedEmployees = selectedValues;
}

public static List attributeListForIterator(String iteratorName,
  String valueAttrName) {
  BindingContext bc = BindingContext.getCurrent();
  DCBindingContainer binding =
    (DCBindingContainer)bc.getCurrentBindingsEntry();
  DCIteratorBinding iter =
    binding.findIteratorBinding(iteratorName);
  List attributeList = new ArrayList();
    for (Row r: iter.getAllRowsInRange()) {
      attributeList.add(r.getAttribute(valueAttrName));
    }
  return attributeList;
}

public void refreshSelectedList(ValueChangeEvent event) {
  refreshSelectedList = true;
}
}
```

Note the use of the Boolean `refreshSelectedList` variable. To ensure that the selected employees are retrieved when the user selects a new department value in the drop-down list, a `valueChangeListener` is used to set the `refreshSelectedList` value to `true`:

```
<af:selectOneChoice id="nl1" autoSubmit="true" label="Departments"
  value="#{bindings.DepartmentsList.inputValue}"
  valueChangeListener="#{shuttleBean.refreshSelectedList}">
  <f:selectItems value="#{bindings.DepartmentsList.items}"/>
</af:selectOneChoice>
```

In addition, the `partialTriggers` attribute of the `af:selectManyShuttle` component should be set to the ID of the `af:selectOneChoice` component, which is set to submit the form automatically. Figure 11-14 shows the shuttle component at runtime.

The final step in a shuttle includes adding a command component to process the values that are shuttled. In this example, employees that are shuttled to the trailing values would be considered added to the current department and therefore removed from another department. Employees that are shuttled from the trailing values to the leading values list would no longer belong to any department. Therefore, the processing of the shuttled components is unique to each use case and the requirements cannot be assumed here. However, some general guidelines include the use of an application module method to relocate members of a collection on the data model, and the use of the `valuePassThru` attribute on the

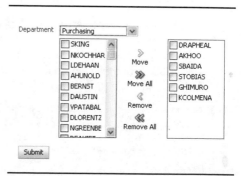

FIGURE 11-14 *The shuttle component with leading and trailing values*

shuttle component to pass the values of the component to the client so that they can be used for processing on the client. In our example, the values are processed via an action method on a button, so the values can be obtained once the button is clicked:

```
public String cb3_action() {
    for(Object employee : selectedEmployees){
      System.out.println("Employee " + employee);
    }
    return null;
}
```

NOTE
The checkboxes listed in the leading and trailing sections of an `af:selectManyShuttle` *are not used to restrict values in any way. Instead, they are used for selecting multiple values and using the single Move or Remove buttons of the component to move multiple values simultaneously.*

Building Query Components

In addition to the two LOV components covered in the preceding section, two components used for querying were added for ADF Faces RC version 11 that are especially useful for use in business applications: `af:query` and `af:quickQuery`. Like the LOV components, these components are model-driven, and thus will appear only in the drop-down list of available ADF Faces components when the underlying data model is defined to support them. In the case of the query components, a named view criteria must be defined for a view object. Thankfully, all view objects include an implicit named criteria called All Queriable Attributes, which can be bound to a query component using a specialized type of binding called a `searchRegion`. The PageDef for an implicit view criteria is defined as follows:

```
<executables>
   <iterator Binds="JobsView1" RangeSize="25"
     DataControl="AppModuleDataControl" id="JobsView1Iterator"/>
   <searchRegion Criteria="__ImplicitViewCriteria__"
     Customizer="oracle.jbo.uicli.binding.JUSearchBindingCustomizer"
     Binds="JobsView1Iterator" id="ImplicitViewCriteriaQuery"/>
</executables>
```

The All Queriable Attributes data control for a collection can be bound to the `af:quickQuery` component declaratively. This creates a drop-down list containing each attribute and an input text field to enter criterion. A clickable arrow icon is used to execute the search. Each of these elements is built into the component, so that the entire component is defined using the following code:

```
<af:quickQuery label="Search" searchDesc="Search" id="qq1"
    value="#{bindings.ImplicitViewCriteriaQuery.quickQueryDescriptor}"
    model="#{bindings.ImplicitViewCriteriaQuery.queryModel}"
    queryListener="#{bindings.ImplicitViewCriteriaQuery.processQuery}"
    />
```

The look of the component can be modified somewhat by setting the layout component and by enabling the advanced search link (which is defined within the `af:quickQuery` component

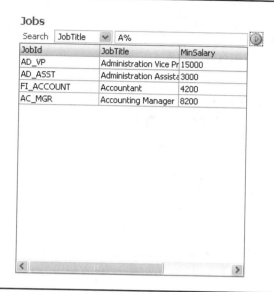

FIGURE 11-15 *The* `af:quickquery` *component at runtime*

when it is created declaratively, but set to `rendered="false"`). Figure 11-15 shows the `af:quickQuery` component at runtime, along with a table component that displays results.

NOTE
Named criteria from the view object cannot be used to create an `af:quickQuery` *component, because the operators used in the* `af:quickQuery` *component are hard coded and do not honor operators specified in the view criteria itself. However, the implicit criteria (represented by All Named Criteria in the Data Control palette) can be used both for* `af:quickQuery` *and* `af:query` *components. If a simple query form is desired but the* `af:quickQuery` *component cannot be used due to this limitation, a functionally equivalent component can be declaratively created by dragging the* `ExecuteWithParams` *operation from the Data Control palette, dropping it onto the JSF visual editor, and choosing Parameters | ADF Parameter Form. The* `ExecuteWithParams` *operation is available for view objects containing bind variables in a defined where clause.*

The advanced search link can be used to initiate the full `af:query` component, which allows more sophisticated searching by using advanced criterion such as Equal To, Less Than, Between, Is Not Blank, and so on. An `af:query` component is bound to named view criteria on a view object and the default attributes that are defined for the criteria are displayed in the basic mode of the query component at runtime. Figures 11-16 and 11-17 show the basic and advanced modes of the query component, respectively. Note that in the advanced mode, all attributes from the underlying view object that are marked as Queryable can be added to the query.

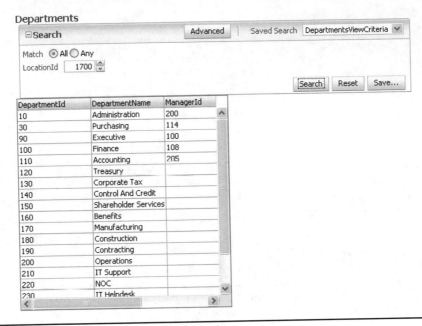

FIGURE 11-16 *Query component in basic mode*

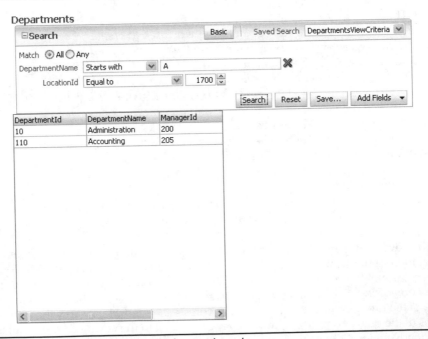

FIGURE 11-17 *Query component in advanced mode*

A table or tree table for displaying the results of the query is typically required, and the declarative drag-and-drop binding provide options to create this automatically. For an `af:quickQuery` component, the results table is bound to the view object iterator, and the `partialTriggers` attribute for the table will be set to the ID of the `af:quickQuery` component. In the case of the `af:query` component, the table is bound to the view object iterator, but instead of explicitly setting the `partialTriggers`, JDeveloper will automatically set the `resultComponentId` attribute of the `af:query` component to the ID of the table or tree table when the component is created declaratively.

Modifying Query Components at Runtime

The processing that is performed when the Search button is clicked for a query component, including the attributes, criteria, and conjunctions for the query, can be augmented by setting the `queryListener` attribute of the `af:query` or `af:quickQuery` component to a backing bean method that accepts the `oracle.adf.view.rich.event.QueryEvent`. This is useful for cases where criteria need to be appended to the values entered by the user, or when further processing is required, such as alerting the user to a long-running query. Additionally, specifying a method that accepts an `oracle.adf.view.rich.event.QueryOperationEvent` in the `queryOperationListener` attribute can be used to intercept the user's interaction with the reset and saved searches portion of the `af:query` object. An example of accessing the `QueryEvent` so that a query component that is shown in a pop-up can perform the search and then close the pop-up dialog programmatically is provided in Chapter 10.

Summary

Together, the list and query components provide a great deal of useful features for application users. The most notable feature is the ability to insert, edit, and query data by using values, rather than IDs that are synonymous with database applications. Additionally, defining view criteria and lists of values on the data model provide a declarative (and reusable) development experience for UI developers, while building guidelines for how particular data should be viewed and modified. Finally, the use of these lookup components saves application developers from duplicating business logic in the view layer—when only valid values are displayed in a list, no coding is necessary to provide meaningful error messages should the user type in an erroneous value.

Displaying data in lists of values is fundamental to all user-facing applications; even character mode applications from yesteryear contained functionality to display lists of values with actual text instead of obscure IDs. Thankfully, we've come a long way in improving the user interface to help users navigate the "ID is king" world of database applications. You can use the techniques described in this chapter to bridge the gap from the backend data model IDs to the more user-friendly descriptive text of the user interface. By using features of ADF Business Components and ADF Faces together, application developers can declaratively create interactive, dynamic-lookup fields that the meet the needs of power users and neophytes alike.

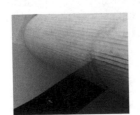

CHAPTER
12

Working with Images and Media

If a picture is worth a thousand words, then a high-definition video is priceless.

lassic business applications, such as those used for data entry, are notoriously boring in the visual sense. Part of the goal of user interface components such as the ADF Faces Rich Client (RC) library is to give users a more visually stimulating experience. Providing information to the user in the form of images, audio, and video can significantly increase the usefulness of an application, and at the very least, it provides context for the textual data included on a page.

Consider the case of online shopping. You probably wouldn't purchase a product that you couldn't see via a photo, no matter how descriptive the accompanying text. Add to that the capability to see the product in use in a video, hear a review in an audiocast, or browse the product specifications via a PDF file, and the amount of information provided to you increases greatly. All these pieces of multimedia provide a more robust user experience, and the same concepts can be applied whether you are building an external-facing online shopping portal or an internal business application.

Many options are available for including media in ADF applications. Media could be stored on the file system or in the database, and it could be stored as binary data or as special object types provided by the database. This chapter explains how to work with various types of media files from various sources.

Including Images and Media

The simplest form of including images in a page is the following:

```
<af:image source="/images/1.jpg" shortDesc="myimage"/>
```

The `af:image` tag includes attributes to specify the source of the image file to be displayed, and the alt text for the image (via the `shortDesc` attribute). Of course, more dynamic implementations of this tag are possible by using Expression Language to bind the source and other attributes of the image tag to backing bean values or ADF bindings. In the case of ADF bindings, the image source might be stored in the database as either a Large Object (LOB) or `ORDIMAGE` type; handling for these special types is covered later in this chapter in the section "Working with Oracle Multimedia Types."

Another option for displaying images or other media is by using the `af:media` component. If you know that the type of content will always be an image, it is best to use `af:image`, but if the type of content is audio or video, or could be determined dynamically, then the `af:media` component should be used.

The `af:media` component accepts a `source` attribute to define the media content that will be displayed in an embedded player, as shown in Figure 12-1. The component determines the MIME-type of the media source and will automatically choose the best media player for the content if one is not defined in the `player` attribute of the component or if the specified player is not available in the browser. Additionally, the size of the player will be determined from the content type.

The following example plays a Windows movie file that starts automatically (that is, the user does not have to click a play icon) and in a loop. The `innerHeight` and `innerWidth` attributes are used to size the content itself, with the total width and height determined by the size of the controls and chrome for the particular player that is used.

```
<af:media source="/intro.wmv"
   standbyText="Please wait while the movie loads" id="m1"
   autostart="true" playCount="0"
   innerHeight="500" innerWidth="600"/>
```

NOTE
The `af:objectmedia` *tag from the 10.1.3 version of ADF Faces has been replaced with the* `af:media` *tag for ADF Faces RC version 11.*

Uploading and Downloading Files

Uploading and downloading files is especially common for business applications where users need to work with additional files and resources to complete a task. The ADF Faces library provides several options for uploading and downloading files, discussed here. Whenever external resources are used, care should be taken to ensure security of the operation, such as when allowing users to upload files to a shared directory or download potentially sensitive information that would no longer be protected by the application's security policies.

Downloading Files

To download files, an `af:goLink` component can be used. This component provides a simple way to download content in a static manner, as shown in the following code snippet:

```
<af:goLink text="Download resource" destination="/resource.zip"/>
```

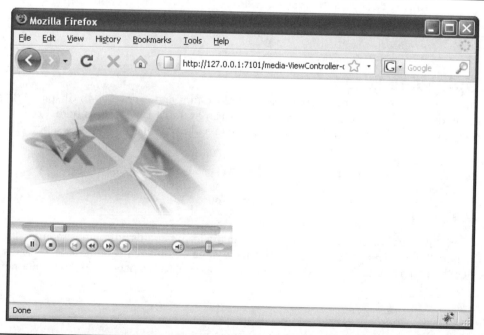

FIGURE 12-1 *Embedded video player in a JavaServer Faces (JSF) page*

A special component, `af:fileDownloadActionListener`, can be added to a command component such as a button or link. This component offers more flexibility than an `af:goLink`, in that the content can be modified after it is downloaded. Include the `contentType` and `filename` for the listener, and define the file that should be downloaded using the `method` attribute of the component. The following example demonstrates the use of this component to download a file named helloworld.html that is of type `text/html`:

```
<af:commandLink text="Download File">
  <af:fileDownloadActionListener contentType="text/html"
    filename="helloworld.html" method="#{DownloadBean.fileToDownload}"/>
</af:commandLink>
```

The `fileToDownload` method specifies the file to download (or in the code example that follows, the file is actually created):

```
import java.io.IOException;
import java.io.OutputStream;
import java.io.OutputStreamWriter;
import java.io.UnsupportedEncodingException;
 import javax.faces.context.FacesContext;
public class DownloadBean {
  public void fileToDownload(FacesContext facesContext,
    OutputStream outputStream) throws UnsupportedEncodingException,
      IOException {
    OutputStreamWriter writer =
      new OutputStreamWriter(outputStream, "UTF-8");
    writer.write("<html><body><h1>Hello world!</h1></body></html>");
    writer.flush();
  }
}
```

Uploading Files

The `af:inputFile` component is used to upload files and is covered in Chapter 8. It is commonly used with documents and media, so an example is warranted here. Consider a scenario in which a user will upload an image to a file system. The page is defined as follows:

```
<af:form usesUpload="true">
  <af:inputFile label="Image" value="#{ProcessFileUpload.file}"/>
  <af:commandButton text="Process Upload"
    action="#{ProcessFileUpload.processUpload}"/>
</af:form>
```

Note the use of `usesUpload="true"` in the form tag; this attribute is required for forms that contain the `af:inputFile` component and will be automatically added to the enclosing form tag when an `af:inputFile` component is dropped onto the page from the Component Palette.

The value of the file and the action that processes the upload are specified in a backing bean, defined as follows:

```
import java.io.InputStream;
import java.io.PrintStream;
import javax.faces.application.FacesMessage;
import javax.faces.context.FacesContext;
import org.apache.myfaces.trinidad.model.UploadedFile;

public class ProcessFileUpload {
  private UploadedFile _file;
  public ProcessFileUpload() {
  }
  public UploadedFile getFile() {
    return _file;
  }
  public void setFile(UploadedFile file) {
    _file = file;
  }
  public String processUpload() {
    UploadedFile myfile = this.getFile();
      try {
        PrintStream newFile = new PrintStream("c:/temp/" +
        myfile.getFilename());
        InputStream inputStream = myfile.getInputStream();
        long length = myfile.getLength();
        byte[] buffer = new byte[(int)length];
        inputStream.read(buffer);
        newFile.write(buffer);
        newFile.close();
        } catch (Exception ex) {
          // handle exception
        }
    FacesContext fctx = FacesContext.getCurrentInstance();
    FacesMessage message = new FacesMessage(
      "Successfully uploaded file " + myfile.getFilename() +
      " (" + myfile.getLength() + " bytes)");
    fctx.addMessage(null, message);
  return null;
  }
}
```

This backing bean method simply copies the uploaded image to a location on the file system. However, the method could be augmented to upload the image to a network resource as well. Figure 12-2 shows the runtime result of a successful file upload.

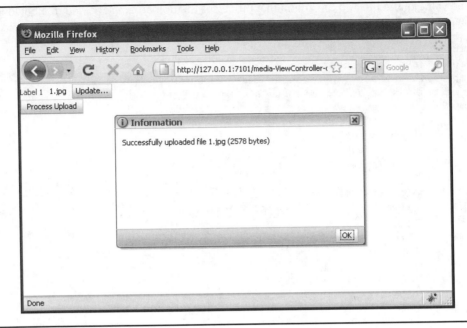

FIGURE 12-2 *Uploading a file*

Uploading Images

The preceding example is useful for smaller, unencrypted files, such as text files. For more complex files, such as images, the `af:inputFile` component can still be used, but some slightly different code is required in the backing bean. This example is useful for the common scenario in which an image (such as an employee photo) needs to be uploaded to the server for inclusion on a deployed page. Consider a JSPX file defined as follows:

```
<af:form usesUpload="true">
  <af:panelFormLayout>
    <af:panelLabelAndMessage label="#{bindings.EmployeeId.hints.label}">
      <af:outputText value="#{bindings.EmployeeId.inputValue}"/>
    </af:panelLabelAndMessage>
    <af:panelLabelAndMessage label="#{bindings.Email.hints.label}">
      <af:outputText value="#{bindings.Email.inputValue}"/>
    </af:panelLabelAndMessage>
    <af:inputFile label="Employee Photo" value="#{ImageUpload.file}"/>
    <af:commandButton text="Upload"
      action="#{ImageUpload.processUpload}"/>
    <af:image source="/#{bindings.EmployeeId.inputValue}.jpg" />
  </af:panelFormLayout>
</af:form>
```

In this example, the image displayed on the page needs to be located in the same directory as the JSPX file. To accomplish this, the HTML root of the application can be found using the

`ServletContext` class. For example, the `ImageUpload` bean that processes the file upload is defined as follows:

```java
import java.awt.image.BufferedImage;
import java.io.File;
import java.io.InputStream;
import javax.faces.context.FacesContext;
import javax.imageio.ImageIO;
import javax.servlet.ServletContext;
import org.apache.myfaces.trinidad.model.UploadedFile;

public class ImageUpload {
  private UploadedFile _file;

  public UploadedFile getFile() {
    return _file;
  }
  public void setFile(UploadedFile file) {
    _file = file;
  }

  public String processUpload(){
    UploadedFile myfile = this.getFile();
    FacesContext fctx = FacesContext.getCurrentInstance();
    ServletContext servletCtx =
      (ServletContext)fctx.getExternalContext().getContext();
    String imageDirPath = servletCtx.getRealPath("/");
    try {
      InputStream inputStream = myfile.getInputStream();
      BufferedImage input = ImageIO.read(inputStream);
      File outputFile = new File(imageDirPath + myfile.getFilename());
      ImageIO.write(input, "JPG", outputFile);
    } catch (Exception ex) {
      // handle exception
    }
  return null;
  }
}
```

This code enables the image to be uploaded to the root runtime directory of the JSPX file. To enable the root path to be navigable, an entry in weblogic.xml is required:

```xml
<container-descriptor>
  <show-archived-real-path-enabled>true</show-archived-real-path-enabled>
</container-descriptor>
```

Note that you may need to create a weblogic.xml for the user interface project, as JDeveloper does not automatically create this file. To do so, choose Deployment Descriptors from the New Gallery category and select WebLogic Deployment Descriptor. Click OK to select the weblogic.xml as the type of descriptor to create.

Working with Oracle Multimedia Types

Oracle Multimedia is a feature of the full-featured Oracle Database (it is not available in Oracle Express Edition). Oracle Multimedia allows the storing of images, audio, video, and other media types as special object types from the ORDSYS Multimedia schema, as shown in Table 12-1.

NOTE
The Oracle Multimedia feature was called Oracle interMedia prior to Oracle Database version 11.

The advantage of using one of the Oracle Multimedia types instead of Binary Large Objects (BLOBs), Character Large Objects (CLOBs), or file system repositories is that not only is the content itself stored, but metadata about that content is maintained in the database as well. Thus, information such as audio compression type or image height and width can be accessed via methods belonging to the various multimedia types. In the end, the content can be stored in a BLOB, BFILE, or outside the database in a server-based URL, but that is transparent to the application developer. If database portability is required, it is best to use a file system repository.

Consider the following example, in which a table uses the ORDIMAGE type to store an image:

```
SQL> desc image_table;
SQL>
Name              Null        Type
----------------  --------    ----------------------------------
IMAGE_ID          NOT NULL    NUMBER(15)
DESCRIPTION                   VARCHAR2(20)
IMAGE                         ORDSYS.ORDIMAGE
```

When an ADF Business Component entity object is created for this table, the Image attribute will be defined as type oracle.ord.im.OrdImageDomain. This domain provides seamless use with the OrdSys.OrdImage database type. Other Oracle Multimedia mapping types for ADF Business Component attributes include OrdVideoDomain, OrdAudioDomain, OrdImageSignatureDomain, and OrdDocDomain.

Oracle Multimedia Object Type	Supported Formats
ORDSYS.ORDAudio	.aff, .aft, .au, .3gp, .mpg, .mp4, .ra, .rm, .ram, .wav
ORDSYS.ORDImage	.bmp, .cal, .dcm, .fpx, .gif, .jpg, .pbm, .pgm, .ppm, .pnm, .pcx, .pct, .png, .rpx, .ras, .tga, .tif, wbmp
ORDSYS.ORDVideo	.mov, .avi, .3gp, .rm, .mpg, .mp4

TABLE 12-1 *Supported Formats for Oracle Multimedia Types*

Enabling a Project for Use with Oracle Multimedia Attributes

Regardless of the Oracle Multimedia type defined for an attribute, the JSF project must be configured to read and write the special attribute types. Add the "BC4J HTML" library to the view project (Project Properties | Libraries and Classpath). Additionally, add the `OrdPlayMediaServlet` servlet to the web.xml file to enable reading and writing of these types, as shown here:

```
<servlet>
  <servlet-name>ordDeliverMedia</servlet-name>
  <servlet-class>oracle.ord.html.OrdPlayMediaServlet</servlet-class>
  <init-param>
    <param-name>releaseMode</param-name>
    <param-value>Stateful</param-value>
  </init-param>
</servlet>
<servlet-mapping>
  <servlet-name>ordDeliverMedia</servlet-name>
  <url-pattern>ordDeliverMedia</url-pattern>
</servlet-mapping>
<filter-mapping>
  <filter-name>adfBindings</filter-name>
  <servlet-name>ordDeliverMedia</servlet-name>
</filter-mapping>
```

Uploading Image Files to OrdImageDomain Attributes

To upload a file as the content for an `OrdImageDomain`-typed attribute, use an `af:inputFile` tag with a nested `binding:convertOrdDomain` tag that handles the conversion of the file to the `OrdImageDomain` type. This converter is provided with the most recent release of JDeveloper 11 in the ADF Faces Data Binding library. As mentioned, the `af:inputFile` component requires the enclosing of the `af:form` component to include `usesUpload="true"`. Thus, the following JSPX code creates a record in the `image_table` via an `OrdImageDomain` attribute:

```
<af:form usesUpload="true">
  <af:panelFormLayout>
    <af:inputText value="#{bindings.Id.inputValue}"
      label="#{bindings.Id.hints.label}">
      <f:validator binding="#{bindings.Id.validator}"/>
      <af:convertNumber groupingUsed="false"
        pattern="#{bindings.Id.format}"/>
    </af:inputText>
    <af:inputText value="#{bindings.Description.inputValue}"
      label="#{bindings.Description.hints.label}">
```

```
      <f:validator binding="#{bindings.Description.validator}"/>
    </af:inputText>
    <af:inputFile value="#{bindings.Image.inputValue}">
      <binding:convertOrdDomain bindingRef="#{bindings.Image}" />
    </af:inputFile>
    <f:facet name="footer">
      <af:panelGroupLayout layout="horizontal">
        <af:commandButton actionListener="#{bindings.Create.execute}"
          text="Create" disabled="#{!bindings.Create.enabled}"/>
        <af:commandButton text="Commit"
          actionListener="#{bindings.Commit.execute}"/>
      </af:panelGroupLayout>
    </f:facet>
  </af:panelFormLayout>
</af:form>
```

Notice the use of the `binding:` prefix for the `convertOrdDomain` tag. This requires adding the ADF Faces Databinding 1.0 library to the view project in Project Properties | JSP Tag Libraries. Dropping this component from the component palette onto the page will include the tag library definition at the top of the file:

```
xmlns:binding=http://xmlns.oracle.com/adf/faces/databinding
```

In addition, to ensure that the `Image` attribute is bound to the UI layer appropriately, a custom input handler should be used. This is a manual step but it is best done by augmenting the binding code generated by the typical drag-and-drop binding gestures, as shown in the following steps:

1. Drag a collection that contains an `OrdImageDomain` attribute from Data Controls palette and drop it onto the JSF visual editor as an ADF form. Accept the default component binding types.

2. Note that this creates an input text component for the `Image` attribute, and the default binding in the PageDef.

3. In the PageDef, add `CustomInputHandler="OrdDomainValueHandler"` to the `attributeValues` definition as follows:

```
<attributeValues IterBinding="ImageTableIterator"
  id="Image" CustomInputHandler="OrdDomainValueHandler">
  <AttrNames>
    <Item Value="Image"/>
  </AttrNames>
</attributeValues>
```

4. Next, replace the `af:inputText` component for the `Image` attribute with the `af:inputFile` and nested `binding:convertOrdDomain`, as explained earlier.

The `af:inputFile` component will display an Update button for those attributes that have a value or for those attributes that have a default value in the case of newly created records, as shown in Figure 12-3. For new records without a default, the button is labeled Browse.

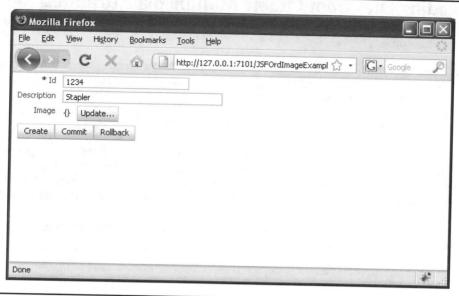

FIGURE 12-3 *The* `af:inputFile` *component in a form with default values*

Figure 12-4 shows the pop-up that is launched when the user clicks either the Update or Browse button. For security reasons, the first 100KB of the file will be stored in memory, and the remaining amount is stored on the file system. The *Oracle Fusion Middleware Web User Interface Developer's Guide for Oracle Application Development Framework 11g Release 1* explains how to specify the directory that is used for temporary file storage.

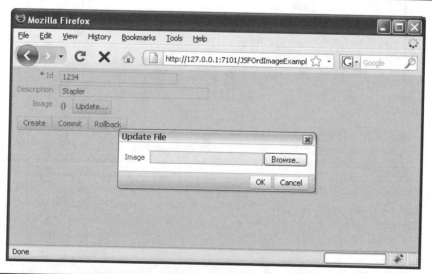

FIGURE 12-4 *Click the button to update or browse for a file.*

Reading Files from Oracle Multimedia Attributes

As for other media types, the `af:media` component is used to read Oracle Multimedia attributes.
Here's an example:

```
<af:panelLabelAndMessage label="#{bindings.Image.hints.label}">
  <af:media contentType="#{bindings.Image.inputValue.media.mimeType}"
    source="#{bindings.Image.inputValue.source}"/>
</af:panelLabelAndMessage>
<af:outputText value="#{bindings.Image.inputValue.media.width}"/>
```

The implicit property `media` is not recognized by the JDeveloper design time, but when
used with an attribute that has `CustomInputHandler="OrdDomainValueHandler"`
defined in the attribute binding, this property can be used to access all the metadata that
is available with the defined Oracle Multimedia type, such as `mimeType` and `width`, in
this example.

Figure 12-5 shows the runtime view of the form that displays the image source, as well as the
value of the `width` attribute.

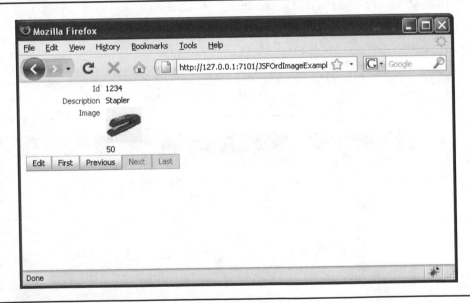

FIGURE 12-5   *Form that uses* `af:media` *to display an image*

Working with Large Object Types

To read and write from LOB types such as CLOBs and BLOBs, you must ensure that the corresponding `oracle.jbo.domain` class is mapped for the attribute in the ADF Business Components layer. Then, when using these special types in an ADF Faces RC application, several components can be used to display the content of these attributes.

Reading Images from CLOB and BLOB Types

To read images from CLOB and BLOB types, a servlet can be used to parse the raw data and display it in a valid image content type. The following servlet issues a query based on the `id` parameter of the HTTP request and transforms the CLOB column data for display:

```java
import java.io.BufferedInputStream;
import java.io.IOException;
import java.io.OutputStream;
import java.sql.Blob;
import java.sql.Connection;
import java.sql.PreparedStatement;
import java.sql.ResultSet;
import java.sql.SQLException;
import javax.naming.Context;
import javax.naming.InitialContext;
import javax.servlet.*;
import javax.servlet.http.*;
import javax.sql.DataSource;

public class ImageServlet extends HttpServlet {
  private static final String CONTENT_TYPE = "text/html; charset=windows-
    1252";

  public void doGet(HttpServletRequest request, HttpServletResponse
    response) throws ServletException, IOException {
    response.setContentType(CONTENT_TYPE);
    String productId = request.getParameter("id");
    OutputStream os = response.getOutputStream();
    Connection conn = null;
    try {
      Context ctx = new InitialContext();
      //Datasource as defined in <res-ref-name> element of weblogic.xml
      DataSource ds = (DataSource)ctx.lookup("java:comp/env/jdbc/myDS");
      conn = ds.getConnection();
      PreparedStatement statement = conn.prepareStatement(
        "SELECT ProductImage.PRODUCT_ID, ProductImage.IMAGE " +
```

```
        "FROM  PRODUCT_IMAGES ProductImage " +
        "WHERE ProductImage.PRODUCT_ID = ?");
      statement.setInt(1, new Integer(productId));
      ResultSet rs = statement.executeQuery();
      if (rs.next()) {
        Blob blob = rs.getBlob("IMAGE");
        BufferedInputStream in = new
          BufferedInputStream(blob.getBinaryStream());
        int b; byte[] buffer = new byte[10240];
        while ((b = in.read(buffer, 0, 10240)) != -1) {
          os.write(buffer, 0, b); }
        os.close();
      }
    } catch (Exception e){
      System.out.println(e);
    } finally {
      try{
        if (conn != null){
          conn.close();
        }
      } catch (SQLException sqle){
        System.out.println("SQLException error");
      }
    }
  }
}
```

The servlet is mapped in the web.xml file as follows, which allows the URL /imageservlet to access the doGet() method of the ImageServlet class:

```
<servlet>
  <servlet-name>ImageServlet</servlet-name>
  <servlet-class>ImageServlet</servlet-class>
</servlet>
<servlet-mapping>
  <servlet-name>ImageServlet</servlet-name>
  <url-pattern>/imageservlet</url-pattern>
</servlet-mapping>
```

The af:image component can then be used to display the image in a JSF page, by accessing the servlet and passing in a value for the id request parameter. To display an image in a form, use the following, assuming that ProductId is a bound value in the form:

```
<af:image source="/imageservlet?id=#{bindings.ProductId.inputValue}"/>
```

To display the image in a table, use the following code:

```
<af:column sortProperty="Image" sortable="false"
  headerText="#{bindings.ProductImagesView1.hints.Image.label}">
  <af:image source="/imageservlet?id=#{row.ProductId}"/>
</af:column>
```

To display the image in an interactive scrolling component, use the `af:carousel` component:

```
<af:carousel currentItemKey="#{bindings.ProductImagesView1.treeModel.rootCurrencyRowKey}"
value="#{bindings.ProductImagesView1.treeModel}" var="item"
  orientation="vertical">
  <f:facet name="nodeStamp">
    <af:carouselItem>
      <af:image source="/imageservlet?detail=#{item.ProductId}"/>
    </af:carouselItem>
  </f:facet>
</af:carousel>
```

Summary

In general, the way that you work with media in web applications will be greatly determined by the way in which the media is stored. In any case, the ADF Faces components provide ways to read and upload various types of media stored directly as files or in a database as a LOB or Oracle Multimedia object. The Oracle Multimedia types provide the most declarative way of displaying and uploading media files and are therefore more convenient to use than other storage options.

CHAPTER
13

Visualizing Data with DVT Components

The usefulness of numeric data can be obscured by the way it is represented. The human mind is certainly capable of processing numeric data represented by row after row of numbers. But when a chart or another graphical component conveys the same information, the categories, trends, and thresholds for a data set are immediately obvious and can be used to make determinations about the data much more quickly.?

epresenting data graphically is one of the best ways to augment traditional forms of data display such as tables to enhance the functionality and usefulness of an application. The ADF Faces library of components includes a subset of components called Data Visualization Tool (DVT) components, which are used to visualize data display.

Many DVT components are included in the ADF Faces library, including a hierarchy viewer, geographic map, four types of gauges, a pivot table, three types of Gantt charts, and twelve types of graph components. Further, each graph type contains subtypes, for about 50 graphical components in total. The *Web User Interface Developer's Guide for Oracle ADF* provides insight into each of the components and their accompanying tags. Additionally, *Oracle JDeveloper 11g Handbook: A Guide to Fusion Web Development* (by Mills, Koletzke, and Roy-Faderman, McGraw-Hill, 2009) provides an excellent description of the hierarchy viewer component. In this chapter, typical scenarios that are encountered when graphically representing data are discussed, such as changing data and graphical elements at runtime.

Using DVT Components

Several declarative features in JDeveloper help to ease development of pages that contain DVT components. For example, a simple chart can be built to show employee salaries by following these declarative steps:

1. Drag-and-drop a view object instance (such as EmployeesView) from the Data Control palette to the visual editor.

2. In the resulting context menu, choose Graph as the type of component to which you want to bind.

3. In the graph component editor, choose a graph type (such as bar or line), and optionally choose a layout for the placement of the title and legend of the graph.

4. In the graph binding editor, drag an attribute from the available attributes and drop it into the Axis area of the binding editor to serve as the label for the graph. Then drag a numeric attribute and drop it into the series value area of the binding editor (bars, lines, or slices, for example) to serve as the data value for the lines or bars.

The resulting graph component would be defined in the JSPX file follows:

```
<dvt:barGraph id="barGraph1" value="#{bindings.EmployeesView1.graphModel}"
   subType="BAR_VERT_CLUST">
  <dvt:background>
    <dvt:specialEffects/>
  </dvt:background>
  <dvt:graphPlotArea/>
```

```
    <dvt:seriesSet>
      <dvt:series/>
    </dvt:seriesSet>
    <dvt:o1Axis/>
    <dvt:y1Axis/>
    <dvt:legendArea automaticPlacement="AP_NEVER"/>
</dvt:barGraph>
```

In the bar graph component definition, the default values for the layout, colors, theme, format, background, and axis attributes (among many others) are used. These defaults can be augmented by defining the attribute values statically at runtime, dynamically through the use of Expression Language (EL), or programmatically by using the DVT component APIs. In the example that follows, the defaultColor and color attributes of the dvt:seriesSet and dvt:series components are used to define the static default color and EL-defined color used for a graph, respectively. In this example, an af:inputColor component renders a color chooser component on the page and the color attribute of the dvt:series component uses EL to determine the selected value and apply that color to the graph's series (which are bars in this example):

```
<af:inputColor id="ic1" binding="#{backing_barGraph.inputColor}"
  autoSubmit="true"/>
<dvt:barGraph id="barGraph1" value="#{bindings.EmployeesView1.graphModel}"
  subType="BAR_VERT_CLUST" partialTriggers="ic1" >
...
  <dvt:seriesSet defaultColor="#00ffff">
    <dvt:series color="#{backing_barGraph.inputColor.value}"/>
  </dvt:seriesSet>
...
```

The page definition file for the JSPX in the preceding examples contains the graphModel binding, which defines the attribute used for the data value (Salary in this case) and the attribute used for the grouping component, or the O1 axis in the case of a vertical bar chart.

```
<graph IterBinding="EmployeesView1Iterator" id="EmployeesView1" xmlns="http://
xmlns.oracle.com/adfm/dvt" type="BAR_VERT_CLUST">
  <graphDataMap leafOnly="true">
    <series>
      <data> <item value="Salary"/> </data>
    </series>
    <groups> <item value="Email"/> </groups>
  </graphDataMap>
</graph>
```

The dvt: prefix
Note that the DVT components are included as a subset of the ADF Faces component library and are contained within their own Java archive (JAR) libraries. Therefore, the DVT components use a unique namespace and default tag library prefix, dvt:, defined in a JSPX file as

```
xmlns:dvt="http://xmlns.oracle.com/dss/adf/faces"
```

The backing bean used in this example simply contains accessors for the `af:inputColor` component and is defined as follows. Figure 13-1 shows the chart at runtime.

```
import oracle.adf.view.rich.component.rich.input.RichInputColor;

public class BarGraphBean {
  private RichInputColor inputColor;

  public void setInputColor(RichInputColor inputColor) {
    this.inputColor = inputColor;
  }

  public RichInputColor getInputColor() {
    return inputColor;
  }
}
```

NOTE
The O1 axis refers to the ordinal axis. This is displayed similarly to an X axis in generic graph terminology, meaning that it is displayed as a horizontal line for a vertical bar chart. However, the X axis is specified in DVT only for scatter, bubble, and continuous time axis graphs where no grouping of data is used. The ordinal axis is used for most graph types because it relates not to the actual data values, but to the groups to which the data values belong.

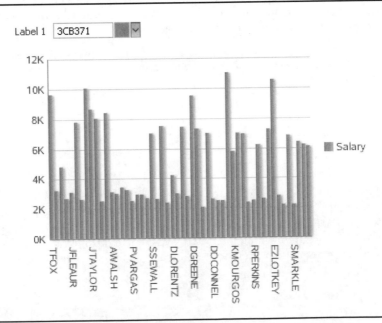

FIGURE 13-1 *Bar graph with dynamic bar colors*

Shaping Data for Use in DVT Components

When you're building DVT components, one of the first things you must determine is the shape of the data that you want to represent graphically. For basic data display in a chart component, using default view object queries and attributes will be all that is necessary, given that at least one of the attributes in the query is numeric. Here, the term "default query" relates to the select * from `<tablename>` query that is generated by the ADF Business Components wizard when building view objects based on entity objects. Each attribute of the entity object is represented by an updatable attribute in the view object, and no join or ordering clauses are included in the query.

Adding transient attributes or modifying view object queries to display groups of data is commonplace when working with DVT components. For example, consider the case of a pie chart, where percentages of a total are displayed graphically. When you're using a pie chart, a value that represents a percentage of a total is usually desired. The pie chart automatically calculates percentages of a total, but when the values are not contained in the same view object on which the graph is based, or for other types of graphs where the aggregate value is not automatically calculated, total values can easily be added to the view object by creating a transient attribute. The Groovy scripting language is helpful for performing a calculation to define the value for the transient attribute. For example, adding a `SalaryTotal` attribute to the default Departments view object and defining the attribute's default value as a Groovy expression `EmployeesView.sum("Salary")` enables the value to be used as part of a total, because the Salary attributes from the nested EmployeesView instance for the Department are added; the `SalaryTotal` attribute value is the total of the employee salaries for each department row. The data can then be used to create a graph binding, as shown in the graph binding editor in Figure 13-2.

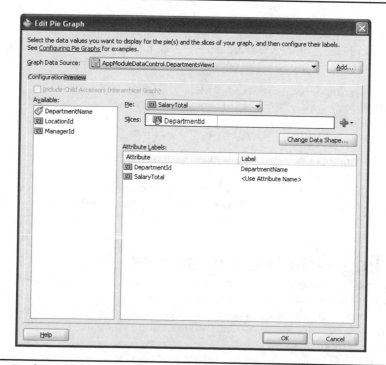

FIGURE 13-2 *Binding a calculated attribute for a pie chart*

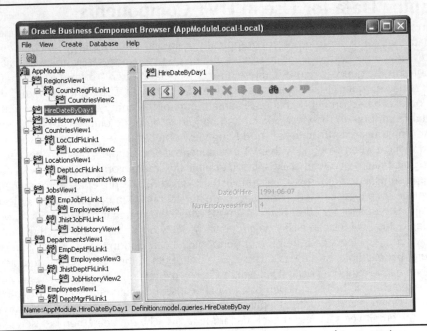

FIGURE 13-3 *Using the Business Component Browser to test view object queries*

Another common requirement for shaping data for chart components is the use of group by and order by clauses in view object queries. When queries are modified in this way, you can create read-only view objects that are defined specifically for graphical display. For example, the following query is used to select employees hired on the same date:

```
select trunc(hire_date) "Date of Hire",
  count(employee_id) "Number of Employees Hired"
from employees
group by trunc(hire_date) order by trunc(hire_date)
```

As a best practice, you should test modifications made to view objects, whether by changing the query or adding attributes, by using the ADF Business Component Browser. To do so, right-click an application module and choose Run. Double-clicking a view object instance in the resulting business component browser executes the query and displays rows, as shown in Figure 13-3.

Building Graph Components

The usefulness of numeric data can be obscured by the way it is represented. The human mind is certainly capable of processing numeric data represented by row after row of numbers. But when a chart or another graphical component conveys the same information, the categories, trends, and thresholds for a data set are immediately obvious and can be used to make determinations about the data much more quickly.

Twelve chart types are included in the DVT library, and each of these contains several subtypes and several different layouts. General-use graphs for charting one value include the familiar line, bar, and area graphs. These charts can also be configured to chart more than one series of data, including stacked line, bar, or area graphs, as well as scatter, bubble, and radar charts. Specific-use charts include the Pareto, funnel and stock chart types.

Wiring Components to Selected Chart Values

To enable selection of chart values, you can set row currency for the ADF iterator by using the built-in `processClick` method of a graph binding. For example, the following code contains a graph bound to the `DepartmentsView1` iterator. The `processClick` method for the graph's is specified in the `clickListener` attribute of the graph, and because the `partialTriggers` attribute is set for the related form, clicking a value in the graph (in this case, a pie slice) causes row currency to be set and the corresponding form to be updated accordingly.

```
<af:form>
    <dvt:pieGraph id="pieGraph1"
    value="#{bindings.DepartmentsView1.graphModel}" subType="PIE"
    clickListener="#{bindings.DepartmentsView1.graphModel.processClick}">
    ...
    </dvt:pieGraph>
    <af:panelFormLayout id="pfl1" partialTriggers="pieGraph1">
      <af:panelLabelAndMessage label="#{bindings.DepartmentId.hints.label}">
        <af:outputText value="#{bindings.DepartmentId.inputValue}"/>
      </af:panelLabelAndMessage>
<!-- Additional attributes defined here -->
    </af:panelFormLayout>
</af:form>
```

Creating Components Within Tables

Data visualization components are not only useful as separate components that are displayed separately from other content on a page, but they can be very useful as a visual aid within tables as well. Gauges are particularly suited to this use because they can be displayed in a smaller area and can thus be inline within textual table data. The following JSPX code listing is built by creating an ADF Read Only Table based on a collection (EmployeesView in this case), adding a column to the table by right-clicking the table component and choosing Insert Inside af:table | Column, and then dropping a gauge component into the new column. The gauge is not bound to a new iterator binding, but instead reuses the `SalaryTotal` attribute binding that is created when the table is bound to the collection.

```
<af:table value="#{bindings.DepartmentsView1.collectionModel}"
    var="row" rows="#{bindings.DepartmentsView1.rangeSize}">
    <af:column headerText="DepartmentId">
      <af:outputText value="#{row.DepartmentId}"/>
    </af:column>
<!--Other defined columns -->
    <af:column headerText="SalaryTotal">
      <af:outputText value="#{row.SalaryTotal}" />
    </af:column>
```

```
<af:column headerText="SalaryTotal Meter">
  <dvt:gauge id="gauge1" value="#{row.SalaryTotal}"
    gaugeType="STATUSMETER" imageHeight="50">
    <dvt:gaugeBackground>
      <dvt:specialEffects fillType="FT_GRADIENT">
        <dvt:gradientStopStyle/>
      </dvt:specialEffects>
    </dvt:gaugeBackground>
    <dvt:thresholdSet>
      <dvt:threshold text="Low" fillColor="#d62800"
        thresholdMaxValue="5000.0"/>
      <dvt:threshold text="Medium" fillColor="#ffcf21"
        thresholdMaxValue="80000.0"/>
      <dvt:threshold text="High" fillColor="#84ae31"
        thresholdMaxValue="100000.0"/>
    </dvt:thresholdSet>
    <dvt:gaugeFrame/>
    <dvt:indicator/>
    <dvt:indicatorBase/>
    <dvt:gaugePlotArea/>
    <dvt:tickLabel/>
    <dvt:tickMark/>
    <dvt:topLabel position="LP_NONE"/>
    <dvt:metricLabel position="LP_INSIDE_GAUGE"/>
    <dvt:bottomLabel position="LP_NONE"/>
  </dvt:gauge>
</af:column>
</af:table>
```

Notice that the value attribute for the gauge is set to #{row.SalaryTotal}, so that the gauge will display the same value as the text component just before it. The gauge type used here is a horizontal LED meter, and the imageHeight attribute is specified so that the default height does not take too much space in the table. Finally, threshold limits are set for the gauge, which could of course be set using EL for more dynamic gauges. The runtime view of the table is depicted in Figure 13-4.

Building Pivot Tables

Pivot tables are a useful way to display groups of data that can be reordered at runtime. Calculations such as totals can be configured for rows and columns of data, so that dynamic analysis of the data can be performed at runtime. To define a pivot table, drag-and-drop a collection containing at least one numeric attribute onto the visual editor. Then choose Table | ADF Pivot Table as the type of object to create. In the resulting Create Pivot Table wizard, configure the pivot table as follows:

1. In step one of the wizard, drag attributes from the collection onto the row and column edges as necessary. The first attribute dropped onto the column or row edge will serve as the first layer of grouping, and any attributes dropped thereafter will be the secondary grouping. Values dropped into the data body area will be the cells in the pivot table. Figure 13-5 shows this step for the default EmployeesView view object.

DepartmentId	DepartmentName	ManagerId	LocationId	SalaryTotal	
10	Administration	200	1700	1999	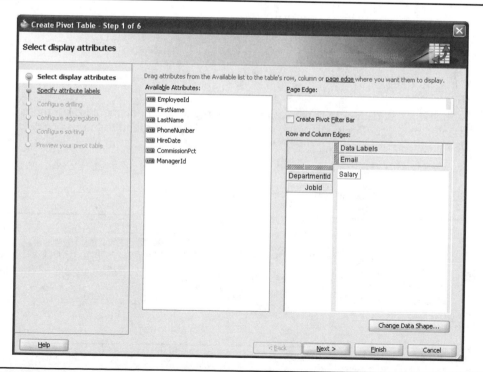
20	Marketing	201	1800	19000	
30	Purchasing	114	1700	24900	
40	Human Resources	203	2400	6500	
50	Shipping	121	1500	156400	
60	IT	103	1400	28800	
70	Public Relations	204	2700	10000	

FIGURE 13-4   *Table containing inline gauge components*

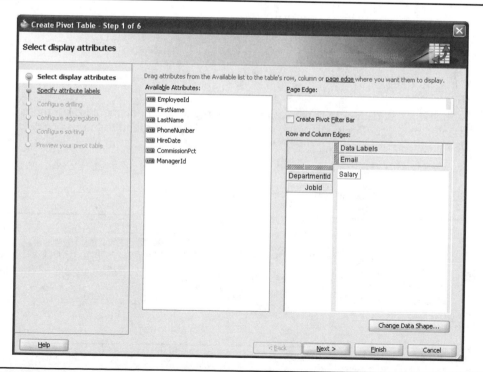

FIGURE 13-5   *Page 1 of the Pivot Table wizard*

2. In step two of the wizard, specify labels as necessary for each of the attributes defined for the pivot table, including the category and data values.

3. In steps three and four of the wizard, specify drilling (either to insert a row or column, or to filter the data), when the user clicks a row or column edge, and any aggregation rules. Aggregation is possible for both the data and categories values, where values can be aggregated by various functions including totals, averages, and minimum and maximum values.

4. In step five of the wizard, specify which attributes should be used to sort the data. Finally, preview the pivot table in the last step of the wizard.

Pivot tables are largely defined by a special `pivotTable` binding in the pageDef file, as shown next:

```
<pivotTable IterBinding="EmployeesView1Iterator" id="EmployeesView1"
  xmlns="http://xmlns.oracle.com/adfm/dvt">
  <pivotTableDataMap>
    <columns>
      <data aggregateDuplicates="true" defaultAggregateType="SUM">
        <item value="Salary"/>
      </data>
      <item value="Email"/>
    </columns>
    <rows>
      <item value="DepartmentId"/>
      <item value="JobId"/>
    </rows>
    <pages />
  </pivotTableDataMap>
</pivotTable>
```

The JSPX that defines the pivot table can be very simply implemented. For the preceding example, the `value` attribute for the `dvt:pivotTable` is bound to the `pivotTableModel` in the pageDef:

```
<dvt:pivotTable value="#{bindings.EmployeesView1.pivotTableModel}"/>
```

Figure 13-6 shows the runtime view of this pivot table.

		Salary									
		TFOX	WTAYLOR	VPATABAL	JSEO	JFLEAUR	JMURMAN	RMATOS	HBLOOM	JTAYLOR	COLSEN
80	SA_REP	9,600							10,000	8,600	8,000
50	SH_CLERK		3,200			3,100					
	ST_CLERK				2,700			2,600			
60	IT_PROG			4,800							
100	FI_ACCOUNT						7,800				

FIGURE 13-6 *pivotTable component*

The pivot table can also be defined by using the very same `graphModel` that is defined for other DVT components. For example, the following pivot table is implemented using the same `graphModel` binding that is used for the bar chart in the chapter's first example:

```
<dvt:pivotTable value="#{bindings.EmployeesView1.graphModel}"/>
```

Changing Graphs at Runtime

The graphing components are visually impressive when created at design time. However, adding functionality to change their type or to display more details depending on a selected value or interaction with another component can greatly enhance both the visual representation of the data being displayed and the chart's usefulness.

Adding Reference Objects

A bar, line, or area graph can contain a reference object to provide a visual reference line or area for a set of values. This can be specified at design time using the `dvt:referenceObjectSet` and nested `dvt:referenceObject` components, as shown in this bar graph example:

```
<dvt:barGraph binding="#{backingBeanScope.backing_dynamicrefs.graph}"
    value="#{bindings.EmployeesView1.graphModel}" subType="BAR_VERT_CLUST"
    clickListener="#{backingBeanScope.backing_dynamicrefs.click}">
  <dvt:referenceObjectSet>
    <dvt:referenceObject lineValue="2000"/>
  </dvt:referenceObjectSet>
</dvt:barGraph>
```

To set the reference object value programmatically, use the ADF Faces APIs for the graph components within the `oracle.adf.view.faces.bi` package. For example, the preceding bar graph definition includes a binding attribute that binds the graph to the graph attribute of type `oracle.adf.view.faces.bi.component.graph.UIGraph` in a backing bean. The example also includes a method binding for the `clickListener` attribute. This method can be used to retrieve the value of the bar that the user has clicked at runtime and change the reference

Parent Components in the ADF DVT Library

Many components in the ADF DVT library require the use of a parent "Set" component that contains only the corresponding components that relate to it, as shown in the example where `dvt:referenceObject` is nested within `dvt:referenceObjectSet`. Each of the following components should be nested within their corresponding "Set" component: `dvt:annotation`, `dvt:alert`, `dvt:referenceObject`, `dvt:series`, `dvt:shapeAttributes`, `dvt:threshold`, `dvt:mapBarSeriesItem`, and `dvt:mapPieSliceItem`.

object's value to the value for the clicked series programmatically, as shown in Figure 13-7. The `backing_dynamicrefs` backing bean is implemented as follows:

```
import oracle.dss.dataView.ComponentHandle;
import oracle.dss.dataView.DataComponentHandle;
import oracle.adf.view.faces.bi.event.ClickEvent;
import oracle.adf.view.faces.bi.component.graph.UIGraph;
import oracle.adf.view.faces.bi.component.graph.ReferenceObject;
import oracle.adf.view.faces.bi.component.graph.ReferenceObjectSet;

public class Dynamicrefs {
  private UIGraph graph;

  public void setgraph(UIGraph graph) {
    this.graph = graph;
  }
  public UIGraph getgraph() {
    if (graph == null) {
      graph = new UIGraph();
      }
    return graph;
  }

  public void click(ClickEvent event) {
    ComponentHandle handle = event.getComponentHandle();
    if (handle instanceof DataComponentHandle){
      DataComponentHandle dhandle = (DataComponentHandle)handle;
      Long clickedValue =
        (Long)dhandle.getValue(DataComponentHandle.UNFORMATTED_VALUE);
      ReferenceObjectSet ros = graph.getReferenceObjectSet();
      ReferenceObject ro = ros.getReferenceObject(0, true);
      ro.setLineValue(clickedValue);
    }
  }
}
```

Changing Graph Types at Runtime

Provided that your data can be displayed logically in different chart types, you can allow users to select the type of chart display at runtime. In the example that follows, an `af:selectOneChoice` list component is used to display the available graph types for the data display. A `dvt:areaGraph`

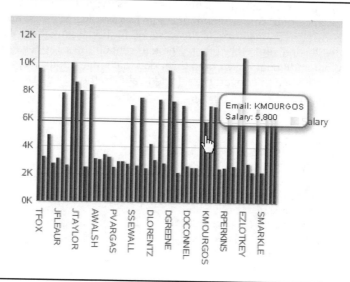

FIGURE 13-7   *Setting the value of a reference object programmatically*

component is defined at design time, and the action method for a button is used to change the type of graph that is displayed.

```
<af:form>
  <af:selectOneChoice label="Select Graph Type"
    binding="#{backingBeanScope.backing_changeType.soc1}">
    <af:selectItem label="Pie" value="PIE" />
    <af:selectItem label="Horizontal Bar" value="BAR_HORIZ_STACK" />
    <af:selectItem label="Horizontal Line" value="LINE_HORIZ_STACK" />
    <af:selectItem label="Vertical Line" value="LINE_VERT_STACK" />
    <af:selectItem label="Combination" value="COMBINATION_VERT_ABS" />
  </af:selectOneChoice>
  <af:commandButton text="Change" id="cb1"
    action="#{backingBeanScope.backing_changeType.cb1_action}"/>
  <dvt:areaGraph id="ag1" value="#{bindings.JobsView1.graphModel}"
    subType="AREA_VERT_STACK"
    binding="#{backingBeanScope.backing_changeType.ag1}">
  ...
  </dvt:areaGraph>
</af:form>
```

The button's `action` method is defined as follows, with the `dvt:areaGraph` component bound to an instance of `UIGraph` and the `af:selectOneChoice` component bound to a `RichSelectOneChoice` instance. In this case, no further augmenting of the graph is required; the graphModel, legend, and other graph elements remain the same regardless of the type of graph chosen, but additional logic could be added to change additional graph attributes. A converter method is used to convert the selected value in the `af:selectOneChoice` component to the `oracle.dss.graph.GraphConstants int` value required by the `setGraphType()` method.

```java
import oracle.dss.graph.GraphConstants;
import oracle.adf.view.faces.bi.component.graph.UIGraph;
import oracle.adf.view.rich.component.rich.input.RichSelectOneChoice;

public class ChangeType {
  private UIGraph ag1;
  private RichSelectOneChoice soc1;

  public String cb1_action() {
    String selectedValue = soc1.getValue().toString();
    int newType = convertGraphType(selectedValue);
    ag1.setGraphType(newType);
    return null;
  }
//accessors for graph and select components
  public int convertGraphType(String stringValue){
    int convertedValue = GraphConstants.AREA_VERT_ABS;
    if(stringValue.equals("LINE_HORIZ_STACK"))
      { convertedValue = GraphConstants.LINE_HORIZ_STACK; }
    if(stringValue.equals("BAR_HORIZ_STACK"))
      { convertedValue = GraphConstants.BAR_HORIZ_STACK;  }
    if(stringValue.equals("LINE_VERT_STACK"))
      { convertedValue = GraphConstants.LINE_VERT_STACK;  }
    if(stringValue.equals("PIE"))
      { convertedValue = GraphConstants.PIE; }
    if(stringValue.equals("COMBINATION_VERT_ABS"))
      { convertedValue = GraphConstants.COMBINATION_VERT_ABS; }
    return convertedValue;
  }
}
```

Adding Annotations to a Chart

The `dvt:annotation` component is used to highlight values on a chart via a callout-style indicator. An annotation can be defined at design time, as in the following example, where static text is used to annotate the graph. The `dvt:graphFont` component is used here to provide some limited formatting to the text:

```xml
<dvt:barGraph id="barGraph1"
    value="#{bindings.EmployeesView1.graphModel}" subType="BAR_VERT_CLUST">
  <dvt:annotationSet>
    <dvt:annotation series="0" group="2" text="Some annotation text">
      <dvt:graphFont bold="true"/>
```

```
      </dvt:annotation>
    </dvt:annotationSet>
...
</dvt:barGraph>
```

To define an annotation programmatically at runtime, the `oracle.adf.view.faces.` `bi.component.graph.UIGraph` class is used to retrieve and manipulate annotations on the graph. The following backing bean code removes any annotations previously defined, either declaratively or programmatically, and creates a new annotation using the attributes of the clicked value in the graph to set the text of the new annotation. The `GraphFont` class is also used to apply some formatting to the annotation text.

```java
import java.util.Map;
import oracle.dss.dataView.Attributes;
import oracle.dss.dataView.ComponentHandle;
import oracle.dss.dataView.DataComponentHandle;
import oracle.adf.view.faces.bi.component.graph.Annotation;
import oracle.adf.view.faces.bi.component.graph.AnnotationSet;
import oracle.adf.view.faces.bi.component.graph.GraphFont;
import oracle.adf.view.faces.bi.component.graph.UIGraph;
import oracle.adf.view.faces.bi.event.ClickEvent;

public class DynamicAnnotations {
  private UIGraph graph;

  public void setgraph(UIGraph graph) {
    this.graph = graph;
  }
  public UIGraph getgraph() {
    if (graph == null){
      graph = new UIGraph();
    }
  return graph;
  }

  public void click(ClickEvent event) {
    ComponentHandle handle = event.getComponentHandle();
    String clickedLabel = null;
    Long clickedValue = null;
    if (handle instanceof DataComponentHandle) {
      DataComponentHandle dhandle = (DataComponentHandle)handle;
      clickedValue =
        (Long)dhandle.getValue(DataComponentHandle.UNFORMATTED_VALUE);
      Attributes[] attrs = dhandle.getGroupAttributes();
        for (Attributes attr : attrs){
          clickedLabel = (String)attr.getValue(Attributes.LABEL_VALUE);
        }
      AnnotationSet as = graph.getAnnotationSet();
      Map asMap = as.getAnnotationMap();
      asMap.clear();
      int group = dhandle.getGroup();
      int series = dhandle.getSeries();
```

```
            Annotation note = as.getAnnotation();
            note.setGroup(group);
            note.setSeries(series);
            note.setText(clickedLabel + ": " + clickedValue.toString());
            GraphFont gf = new GraphFont();
            gf.setBold(true);
            gf.setItalic(true);
            note.setGraphFont(gf);
        }
    }
}
```

NOTE
The `DataComponentHandle` *class is used in this code to access the value of the clicked series; you can also retrieve the current* `oracle.jbo.Key` *from this class to perform further processing using*
`Key row =`
`(Key)dhandle.getValue(DataComponentHandle.ROW_KEY);`

The binding attribute of the graph is set to the `UIGraph` instance on the backing bean, and the `clickListener` attribute calls the `click()` method. The runtime result of the user clicking a value is shown in Figure 13-8.

```
<dvt:barGraph id="barGraph1" subType="BAR_VERT_CLUST"
   binding="#{backingBeanScope.backing_dynamicannotations.graph}"
   value="#{bindings.EmployeesView1.graphModel}"
   clickListener="#{backingBeanScope.backing_ dynamicannotations.click}">
```

Note that in the previous examples, the `oracle.adf.view.faces.bi.component.graph.` `UIGraph` class was used to retrieve the graph attributes (`UIGraph.getAnnotationSet()`, and

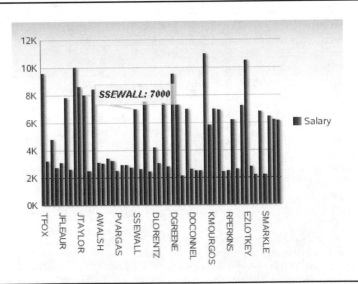

FIGURE 13-8 *Adding an annotation programmatically*

so on). This class comes from the ADF Faces API of the data visualization components and should be used wherever possible. However, the more generic `oracle.dss.graph.CommonGraph` class can also be used to manipulate graph attributes. This class is typically used only by the graphing engine, but a few methods are only available via `CommonGraph` that warrant its use—for example, `exportToSVGWithException (OutputStream os, int mode, String charEnc)`. This method is useful for exporting a graph to the Scalable Vector Graphics (SVG) format so that it is suitable for printing.

Adding a Time Selector Component to a Chart

The `dvt:timeSelector` subcomponent is available for vertically-aligned bar or line graphs, and it is useful for selecting a range of values at runtime that contain dates on the X axis, as shown in Figure 13-9.

To use the `timeSelector` component, drag it from the Graph-Type Specific section of the Graph category of the Component Palette and drop it within a `dvt:barChart` or `dvt:lineChart` definition. Specify the starting points of the time selector by setting the `explicitStart` and `explicitEnd` attributes, and optionally specify the border and fill colors for the time selector. The following example displays a time selector on a line graph according to the backing bean values for `startDate` and `endDate`, respectively:

```
<dvt:lineGraph id="lg1" value="#{bindings.HireDateByDay.graphModel}"
  subType="LINE_VERT_ABS" imageFormat="AUTO" timeAxisType="TAT_IRREGULAR">
  <dvt:seriesSet defaultMarkerType="MT_CURVE_LINE">
    <dvt:series id="a0" color="#FDB026"/>
  </dvt:seriesSet>
  <dvt:timeSelector explicitStart="#{backing_selecttime.startDate}"
    explicitEnd="#{backing_selecttime.endDate}" mode="EXPLICIT"/>
</dvt:lineGraph>
```

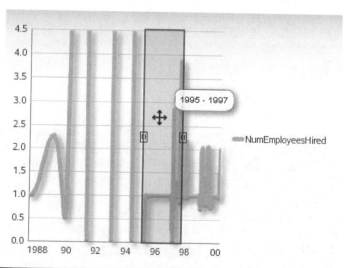

FIGURE 13-9 *The timeSelector component at runtime*

The `HireDateByDay` view object is defined using the following "expert mode" query, which results in two attributes, `DateOfHire` and `NumEmployeesHired` that are used in the graph's binding as the X axis (the group item in the page definition) and lines (the series data in the page definition).

```
select
   hire_date "Date of Hire",
   count(employee_id) "Num Employees Hired"
from employees
   group by hire_date order by hire_date
```

NOTE
The `dvt:timeSelector` *component works best with contiguous data. For data that is spread intermittently over a range of dates, the* `timeSelector` *will simply not appear at runtime. However, when using the* `timeSelector` *in conjunction with a* `dvt:lineGraph` *component, this can be remedied to some extent by setting the* `timeAxisType` *attribute of the line graph to* `TAT_IRREGULAR`.

The backing bean values for the `startDate` and `endDate` attributes are specified in the backing bean as follows:

```
import java.sql.Date;

public class Selecttime {
   private Date startDate = Date.valueOf("1994-06-07");
   private Date endDate = Date.valueOf("1994-06-08");
   public Date getStartDate() {
      return startDate;
   }
   public void setStartDate(Date date) {
      startDate = date;
   }
   public Date getEndDate() {
      return endDate;
   }
   public void setEndDate(Date date) {
      endDate = date;
   }
}
```

However, to define the `explicitStart` and `explicitEnd` attributes based on the minimum and maximum thresholds in the underlying data, the query for the `HireDateByDay` view object can be changed slightly to select these minimum and maximum values, as follows:

```
select
   hire_date "Date of Hire",
   count(employee_id) "Num Employees Hired",
   (Select min(Hire_Date) from Employees) as minHireDate,
   (Select max(Hire_Date) from Employees) as maxHireDate
from employees
group by hire_date order by hire_date
```

In this case, two additional calculated attributes are added to the view object: Minhiredate and Maxhiredate. These attributes are not used in the graphModel binding, but if they are added explicitly as attribute value bindings in the page definition, they can be used to set the explicitStart and explicitEnd attributes programmatically. Since the Minhiredate and Maxhiredate attributes effectively select the beginning and ending dates, the time selector defaults to cover the entire range of data at runtime. Naturally, calculations could be performed on the date values to modify this behavior. The required backing bean code to set the explicitStart and explicitEnd values to the values from the underlying view object attributes is as follows:

```java
import java.sql.Date;
import oracle.adf.model.BindingContext;
import oracle.binding.BindingContainer;
import oracle.jbo.uicli.binding.JUCtrlAttrsBinding;

public class Selecttime {
  private Date startDate;
  private Date endDate;

  public BindingContainer getBindings() {
    return BindingContext.getCurrent().getCurrentBindingsEntry();
  }

  public void setStartDate(Date startDate) {
    this.startDate = startDate;
  }

  public Date getStartDate() {
    BindingContainer bindings = getBindings();
    JUCtrlAttrsBinding sd =
      (JUCtrlAttrsBinding)bindings.getControlBinding("Minhiredate");
    oracle.jbo.domain.Date oracleDate =
      (oracle.jbo.domain.Date)sd.getAttributeValue();
    java.sql.Date startDate = oracleDate.dateValue();
    return startDate;
  }

  public void setEndDate(Date endDate) {
    this.endDate = endDate;
  }

  public Date getEndDate() {
    BindingContainer bindings = getBindings();
    JUCtrlAttrsBinding ed =
      (JUCtrlAttrsBinding)bindings.getControlBinding("Maxhiredate");
    oracle.jbo.domain.Date oracleDate =
      (oracle.jbo.domain.Date)ed.getAttributeValue();
    java.sql.Date endDate = oracleDate.dateValue();
    return endDate;
  }
}
```

The key elements of the page definition for this example are shown next:

```
<executables>
  <iterator Binds="HireDateByDay1" RangeSize="-1"
    DataControl="AppModuleDataControl" id="HireDateByDay1Iterator"/>
</executables>
<bindings>
  <graph IterBinding="HireDateByDay1Iterator" id="HireDateByDay1"
    xmlns="http://xmlns.oracle.com/adfm/dvt" type="LINE_VERT_ABS">
    <graphDataMap leafOnly="true">
      <series> <data> <item value="NumEmployeesHired"/> </data> </series>
      <groups> <item value="DateOfHire"/> </groups>
    </graphDataMap>
  </graph>
  <attributeValues IterBinding="HireDateByDay1Iterator" id="Minhiredate">
    <AttrNames> <Item Value="Minhiredate"/> </AttrNames>
  </attributeValues>
  <attributeValues IterBinding="HireDateByDay1Iterator" id="Maxhiredate">
    <AttrNames> <Item Value="Maxhiredate"/> </AttrNames>
  </attributeValues>
</bindings>
```

Using a Time Selector Listener to Update Related Data

Extending on the preceding example, a time selector listener can be added to the line graph so that the start and end points of the time selector created at runtime by the user can be used to narrow another binding on the page. In the example that follows, a simple table binding is used to display related data for the selected range in the time selector. The underlying view object for this table contains two bind variables, startHireDate and endHireDate, that are used to select the hire date between these two values by adding a where clause to the default query statement for the EmployeesView view object:

```
where Hire_Date between :startHireDate AND :endHireDate
```

The table and related ExecuteWithParams method to execute the query using the parameter values are defined in the page definition as follows:

```
<executables>
  <iterator Binds="EmployeesView1" RangeSize="-1"
    DataControl="AppModuleDataControl" id="EmployeesView1Iterator"/>
</executables>
<bindings>
  <tree IterBinding="EmployeesView1Iterator" id="EmployeesView1">
    <nodeDefinition DefName="model.queries.EmployeesView">
      <AttrNames>
        <Item Value="EmployeeId"/>
        <Item Value="Email"/>
        ...
      </AttrNames>
    </nodeDefinition>
  </tree>
  <action IterBinding="EmployeesView1Iterator" id="ExecuteWithParams"
```

```
      RequiresUpdateModel="true" Action="executeWithParams">
      <NamedData NDName="startHireDate" NDType="oracle.jbo.domain.Date" />
      <NamedData NDName="endHireDate" NDType="oracle.jbo.domain.Date" />
   </action>
</bindings>
```

A time selector listener cannot be added declaratively to most graph types, but a programmatic approach is available. This involves setting the binding attribute of the `dvt:lineGraph` to a backing bean method (`binding="#{backing_selecttime.lg1}"`) in this case, and defining the `getLg1()` method as shown in the following code:

```java
import java.util.Map;
import java.sql.Date;
import oracle.adf.view.faces.bi.component.graph.UIGraph;
 import oracle.adf.view.faces.bi.event.TimeSelectorListener;
import oracle.adf.view.faces.bi.event.TimeSelectorEvent;
import oracle.binding.BindingContainer;
import oracle.binding.OperationBinding;

public class Selecttime implements TimeSelectorListener {
   private UIGraph lg1;
   public void setLg1(UIGraph lg1) {
      this.lg1 = lg1;
   }
   public UIGraph getLg1() {
      if (lg1 == null){
         lg1 = new UIGraph();
         lg1.addTimeSelectorListener(this);
      }
      return lg1;
   }

   public void processTimeSelector(TimeSelectorEvent event) {
      BindingContainer bindings = getBindings();
      Date sdate = new Date(event.getStartTime());
      Date edate = new Date(event.getEndTime());
      oracle.jbo.domain.Date startHireDate =
         new oracle.jbo.domain.Date(sdate );
      oracle.jbo.domain.Date endHireDate =
         new oracle.jbo.domain.Date (edate);
      OperationBinding ob =
         bindings.getOperationBinding("ExecuteWithParams");
      Map params = ob.getParamsMap();
      params.put("startHireDate", startHireDate);
      params.put("endHireDate", endHireDate);
      ob.execute();
   }
}
```

Finally, setting the `partialTriggers` attribute of the table results in the table data being updated when the graph is updated by way of the user selecting a new time selector range. The runtime result of modifying the time selector range is shown in Figure 13-10.

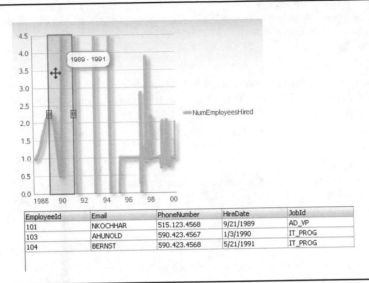

Data table below graph:

EmployeeId	Email	PhoneNumber	HireDate	JobId
101	NKOCHHAR	515.123.4568	9/21/1989	AD_VP
103	AHUNOLD	590.423.4567	1/3/1990	IT_PROG
104	BERNST	590.423.4568	5/21/1991	IT_PROG

FIGURE 13-10   *Runtime view of time selector range and corresponding data table*

The dvt:graph component

The `dvt:graph` component can be more difficult to use than the specialized `dvt:barGraph`, `dvt:lineGraph`, and so on, components, due to its complex nature. Still, it is sometimes necessary to use the component if attributes are not available for the specialized types of components. For example, the `customToolTipCallback` and `timeSelectorListener` attributes are available only for the `dvt:graph` component, so to add a custom tool tip or time selector declaratively to a graph, the `dvt:graph` component should be used instead of a specialized component. The `dvt:graph` component is not available from the component palette and therefore cannot be defined declaratively, but it is still possible to define this component in the source of a JSPX file.

Summary

Regardless of the specific graph component that is used, the ADF Faces DVT components provide a sleek set of components for graphing numeric data. For developers, using the DVT components is more favorable to using other library's graphing components because the DVT components are developed declaratively, using dialogs and even a visual previewer. These components provide a way for you to display additional useful information to the user at a glance, such as annotations and reference lines. Additionally, interactivity can be easily built into the components, allowing for the user to customize the graph display at runtime or to provide insight for a particular graph value by interacting with other components on a page. Of course, for more complex visualization of data, the hierarchy viewer, pivot table, Gantt chart, and geographical map components are also built declaratively and bound to a data model using the same drag-and-drop techniques. Finally, what cannot be achieved declaratively by using attributes of the DVT components can be achieved by using the data visualization APIs to augment the runtime engine or the way in which the component is displayed in an ADF Faces application.

CHAPTER
14

Implementing Drag-and-Drop Functionality

Drag-and-drop: the rich web must support it because desktops do!

he ability for users to input, modify, or rearrange data with a move of the mouse is a common gesture in desktop and web application user interface (UI) design. ADF Faces provides a drag-and-drop framework for developers to declaratively implement drag-and-drop in Oracle ADF Faces web applications. At runtime, users can use drag-and-drop to copy, link, and move attribute values, collections, and UI components on an ADF Faces page. Figure 14-1 shows the Oracle Fusion Order Demo (FOD), which uses drag-and-drop to add products to a shopping cart.

In this chapter, we focus on drag-and-drop use cases for UI components that display ADF bound data. However, it is important to note that the drag-and-drop functionality is provided by ADF Faces and therefore does not require that the ADF binding layer be used.

TIP
A general introduction to drag-and-drop is provided in the "Adding Drag and Drop Functionality" chapter of the Oracle Fusion Middleware Web User Interface Developer's Guide for Oracle Application Development Framework 11g Release 1.

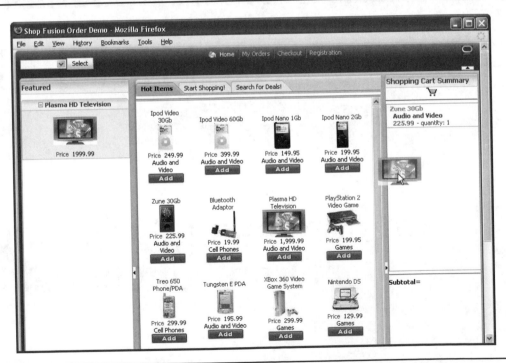

FIGURE 14-1 *Fusion Order Demo home page showing an active drag-and-drop action*

Introduction to Drag-and-Drop in ADF Faces Rich Client

At design time, drag-and-drop is declaratively configured on the server-side components, whereas at runtime, drag-and-drop executes as a client-side event. If not cancelled on the client using JavaScript, the event propagates to the server, where it invokes server-side drop listeners, passing an object, the transferable, as the payload of the drag-and-drop action. The starting point of a drag-and-drop action, the component that initiates the drag, is referred to as the "drag source," whereas the end point, the component that accepts the drop, is referred to as the "drop target."

The type of drag-and-drop action to process, whether the dragged value shall be copied, moved or referenced as a link, is defined on the ADF Faces behavior tags that configure the drag-and-drop operation. To define components declaratively as a drag source or drop target, developers use the following ADF Faces drag-and-drop behavior tags, which are located in the ADF Faces | Operations category of the Oracle JDeveloper Component Palette:

- `af:attributeDragSource`
- `af:attributeDropTarget`
- `af:dragSource`
- `af:dropTarget`
- `af:calendarDropTarget`
- `af:collectionDragSource`
- `af:collectionDropTarget`
- `af:componentDragSource`

The drag-and-drop functionality works within a single window and is cancelled when the drag exceeds the window's boundaries. It is possible, however, to drag content from an `af:popup` dialog to its base page or from a parent page to an ADF Region. In the latter case, you need to make sure that the managed bean that holds the drop handler is configured so it is accessible to the ADF Region.

TIP

To design applications that remain accessible when drag-and-drop is not available, make sure you always provide alternative access options for application functionality that uses drag-and-drop. Make the alternative access options a part of your UI design and make sure they are always shown.

NOTE

At the time of writing, there is no public API to define UI components programmatically as drag source or drop targets. Drag-and-drop must be configured at design time using the ADF Faces behavior tags described in this chapter.

Drag-and-Drop Actions: COPY, MOVE, and LINK

A drag-and-drop operation may copy, move or reference the dragged content as a link. *Copy, move,* and *link* are only semantics for the drag-and-drop type and are not implemented by the drag-and-drop framework. Application developers use the information about the drag type to then implement the functionality in Java. Components such as `af:collectionDragSource`, `af:dragSource`, `af:dropTarget`, `af:collectionDropTarget`, and `af:calendarDropTarget` tags provide an *actions* attribute for developers to define how a drop should be handled and when it should be rejected. A drop is rejected when none of the actions defined on the drag source match one of the actions defined on the drop target. If the drag source and the drop target support multiple actions, and if the application user does not provide a hint of how he or she wants to have the drop handled, then the framework tries to find a single matching action to perform. If it cannot find a single match, it tries to perform a copy, move, or link—in this defined order.

Users can provide a hint of how they want the drag to be handled by pressing the SHIFT, CTRL-SHIFT, or CTRL key while dragging the data:

- SHIFT = move
- CTRL-SHIFT – link
- CTRL = copy

Users can cancel a drag operation in action by pressing the ESC key during the drag. (See the "How to Move/Copy/Link the Dragged Content" section later in this chapter for more information.)

af:attributeDragSource

The `af:attributeDragSource` tag implements the simplest form of drag-and-drop and is used to mark a component as the drag source for transferring one of its attributes or an added `af:clientAttribute` value. For example, to drag the value of an `af:inputText` component, you add the following configuration:

```
<af:inputText ...>
  <af:attributeDragSource attribute="value"/>
</af:inputText>
```

At design time, when you drag the Attribute Drag Source entry from the component palette onto a component, such as `af:inputText`, a list of available attributes is shown. The value of the attribute developers choose is then copied to the drop target at runtime. The `af:attributeDragSource` always copies the value to the drop target and cannot "move" or "link" it. The displayed "ghost," the visual indicator that is shown during the time that a component is dragged to its target, is the actual component itself. So if the `af:attributeDragSource` is added to an image, this image indicates the drag. In the preceding example, the ghost is the input text component. The component that accepts the attribute drop must have an `af:attributeDropTarget` or `af:dropTarget` tag defined.

Using the Client Attribute Tag to Define Transferable Data Objects

It is possible to read the `af:attributeDragSource` attribute value from a client attribute that is added to the drag source. For example, if the drag source is an image in a product catalog, as shown in Figure 14-1, then the client attribute tag can be used to add product information, such as the product ID, to the drag-and-drop action. The FOD shown in Figure 14-1 can be downloaded from http://otn.oracle.com and uses the following page code in its home.jspx page to drag the product ID, represented by the `DragId` attribute, to the shopping cart:

```
<af:forEach varStatus="stat">
  …
  <af:image clientComponent="true" source="…" id="prodimage">
    <af:clientAttribute name="DragId"
      value="#{bindings.MostPopularProductsByCategories.children
          [stat.index].DragId}"/>
    <af:attributeDragSource attribute="DragId"/>
  </af:image>
  …
</af:forEach>
```

With this page code, the product image is shown as the drag ghost, whereas the dragged value is read from another attribute of the collection containing the product information.

NOTE
The FOD home page displays a list of popular products to drag-and-drop to the shopping cart using an `af:forEach` *loop tag. The* `varStatus` *attribute that provides contextual information about the state of the component is referenced as* `stat`*. For components such as* `af:forEach` *that iterate over lists of data,* `varStatus` *also provides loop counter information. Using the current row index of the* `af:forEach` *tag, the product ID information, namely* `DragId`*, is read from the child array of the* `MostPopularProductsByCategories` *collection that is exposed on the ADF binding.*

af:attributeDropTarget

The `af:attributeDropTarget` is the drop peer of the attribute drag component and copies the drag object to the attribute that it specifies on the receiving component. For example, to use drag-and-drop to copy the `value` attribute of an `af:inputText` component to the `value` attribute of an `af:outputText` component, you use the following tag definitions:

```
<af:inputText value="Hello World">
  <af:attributeDragSource attribute="value"/>
</af:inputText>
…
<af:outputText value="Drag it here !" …>
  <af:attributeDropTarget attribute="value"/>
</af:outputText>
```

At design time, when you drag the Attribute Drop Target entry from the component palette onto a UI component, a list of attributes shows where the transferrable object can be copied.

NOTE
The af:attributeDragSource *behavior can also be handled by the* af:dropTarget *tag, which is introduced later in this chapter. You use the* af:attributeDropTarget *when the value of a property just needs to be copied to another component property. The* af:dropTarget *is suitable when you need to perform computing on the dragged value or convert it, if for example the dragged object is an array.*

af:dragSource

The af:dragSource tag is a generic tag to define components as a drag source. It supports four attributes: action, defaultAction, dragDropEndListener, and discriminant. The action and defaultAction attributes of the af:dragSource define whether the drop should be performed as a copy, move, or link. The dragDropEndListener attribute allows developers to create and reference a server-side listener that receives a notification at the end of the drop event to clean up resources if required. The single argument that is passed to the managed bean listener method is an instance of DropEvent. To enable a drop target to listen for specific drag events only, ensuring that the drag source and the drop target are compatible, the discriminant attribute is set on the drag source tag to identify the drag event. Drag and drop can only be performed between compatible drag sources and drop targets. Compatible drag sources and drop targets share the same discriminant value.

```
<af:table …>
    …
    <af:dragSource actions="MOVE COPY" defaultAction="COPY"
                   dragDropEndListener="#{EmpTableBean.dndEndListener}"
                   discriminant="emptable"/>
</af:table>
```

The method signature of the dragDropEndListener attribute reference is shown next. You create the method in Oracle JDeveloper by selecting Edit from the context menu that opens in the Property Inspector after you click the arrow icon next to the DragDropEndListener property field.

```
public void dndEndListener(DropEvent dropEvent) {
    // Add event code here…
}
```

NOTE
The af:dragSource *tag can be used with UI components that display collections, such as* af:tree, af:table, *and* af:treeTable. *It replaces component specific drag tags, such as* af:collectionDragSource.

NOTE
The discriminant *attribute is used only when working with collection data. The* af:dragSource *behavior does not work when dragging attributes or components.*

oracle.adf.view.rich.event.DropEvent

The `DropEvent` class represents the drop within a drag-and-drop operation and is passed as the argument to drop event listeners configured on the `af:dropTarget`, `af:collectionDropTarget`, or `af:dragSource` component. The `DropEvent` class exposes the following information that application developers use to handle the drop:

- **getDropComponent**   Returns the UI component instance on which the drop occurred.

- **getDragComponent**   Returns the UI component that initiated the drag operation. There is no guarantee that this information is always available, so this method can return null. Another option to obtain the drag component is from the drag-and-drop payload, the transferable.

- **getDropAction**   Returns the drop action actually performed by the drop target. The action is returned as `DnDAction.COPY`, `DnDAction.MOVE`, or `DnDAction.LINK`. The performed action is determined by the action types supported by the drag source, the action types supported by the drop target, and the user-proposed action.

- **getProposedAction**   Returns the `DnDAction` that the user requests the drop target to perform in response to a drop. Users use the keyboard modifiers CTRL, SHIFT, and CTR-SHIFT to choose between the copy, move, and link action. Note that users can choose only from the supported actions built from the intersection of the actions supported on the drag source and the drop target. If no further action is specified, copy is chosen as the default.

- **getDropOrientation**   Returns the orientations relative to the `dropSite` for which the drop occurred. Valid values are `ON`, which is returned for components that don't have inner drop targets; `INSIDE`, which is returned when the drop component is a UI container accepting the dropped component as a child; and `BEFORE` or `AFTER`, indicating where, relative to the location of drop site, the dropped component should be added.

- **getDropSite**   Returns the drop-target–specific site within the drop component relative to which the drop occurred. If the drop site returns null and the drop orientation is `ON`, this indicates that the drop occurred outside of the data portion and therefore is treated as a drop on the entire component. If the drop site returns null and the drop orientation is `AFTER`, the drop occurred on an empty collection indicating that the transferred object needs to be appended.

- **getDropSiteIndex**   Returns the index of the position where the component drop occurred within a drop target. Later in this chapter, you'll see an example in which we persist the layout change of an `af:panelDashboard` using the information about the drop index. A value of –1 is returned for drop sites that don't index their child components.

- **getDropY, getDropX**   Returns the X and Y coordinates of the drop, relative to the origin of the drop component on the client.

Note that although it still exists, the `af:collectionDragSource` is deprecated. Instead, developers should use the `af:dragSource` tag.

af:dropTarget

The `af:dropTarget` tag is a generic drop handler for UI components that don't show location-specific drop feedback. The expected data type of the drop target is defined by the `af:dataFlavor` child tag. The `af:dropTarget` component tag accepts drop events that are initiated from the drag source, collection drag source, and the attribute drag source tags. Page developers can set the following attributes on the `af:dropTarget`: `actions`, `clientDropListener`, and `dropListener`. The `actions` attribute specifies the types of the drop actions accepted by this tag, which can be one or a combination of COPY, MOVE, and LINK.

The `clientDropListener` attribute allows developers to reference a client-side JavaScript function that is called prior to the event server propagation. The JavaScript function takes four arguments of type `AdfDnDContext` and `int` that receive their value from the drag-and-drop framework. The function returns an `AdfDnDContext` action, such as ACTION_NONE, ACTIONS_ALL, ACTION_MOVE, ACTION_COPY, ACTION_LINK, and ACTION_COPY_OR_MOVE. The skeleton of a JavaScript function to handle client-side drop event is shown next:

```
function handleDropClientEvent(adfDndContext, int_proposedAction,
                     int_pos_x, int_pos_y){
  //get the AdfBasicDropTarget
  dropTarget = this;
  //get the AdfDragSource
  dragSource = adfDndContext.getDragSource();
  //add custom code here
  ...
//return drag and drop outcome
  return AdfDnDContext.ACTION_COPY;
}
```

NOTE
JavaScript is not as restrictive as Java when calling a function. If the information provided by the function arguments is not needed, then you can define the function without arguments or a subset of them. In the latter case, you remove arguments from right to left as you cannot arbitrarily remove only some of them.

To reference the JavaScript function from the `af:dropTarget` tag, use a configuration similar to this:

```
<af:dropTarget dropListener="#{DragAndDropHandler.dropHandler}"
  actions="COPY"
  clientDropListener="handleDropClientEvent">
```

Using client-side JavaScript, developers are able to perform client-side logic in response to a drag-and-drop action, which also may lead to developers canceling the drop action by returning `AdfDnDContext.ACTION_NONE` as the outcome of the function call. The X and Y position values that are passed in to the function provide information about the location in the component in which the drop occurred.

NOTE
Chapter 19 discusses JavaScript in ADF Faces Rich Client (RC) and the client-side JavaScript component architecture. Please refer to this chapter to learn about how to add custom JavaScript function on an ADF Faces page.

The `dropListener` attribute of the `af:dropTarget` tag uses Expression Language (EL) to reference the managed bean method that implements the drop event listener. The event listener method accepts a single argument of type `DropEvent` and returns one of the following actions to acknowledge the success or failure of the drop operation:

■ `DnDAction.COPY`

■ `DnDAction.MOVE`

■ `DnDAction.LINK`

■ `DnDAction.NONE`

The Oracle FOD defines the following drop handler as a child component of the shopping cart table to process a purchase:

```
<af:table ... >
  <af:dropTarget dropListener="#{shoppingCartBean.handlePkDrop}">
    <af:dataFlavor flavorClass="java.lang.String"/>
  </af:dropTarget>
  ...
</af:table>
```

The drop handler that is referenced in the `af:dropTarget` tag reads the transfer object to update the shopping cart with the purchase:

```
public DnDAction handlePkDrop(DropEvent dropEvent) {
  try {
    DataFlavor<String> df = DataFlavor.getDataFlavor(String.class);
    String droppedValue = dropEvent.getTransferable().getData(df);
    if (droppedValue == null) {
      _logger.info("Dropped value is null.");
      return DnDAction.NONE;
    }
    invokeUpdateOp(new Integer(droppedValue));
    return DnDAction.COPY;
  } catch (Exception ex) {
    _logger.severe("Drop failed", ex);
    return DnDAction.NONE;
  }
}
```

NOTE
When NONE *is returned on the client or the server, the drop event is cancelled. However, all changes that are applied by custom code, either in JavaScript or Java, are not rolled back.*

af:dataFlavor

The af:dataFlavor tag is a required child of the af:dropTarget component tag that allows page authors to add an "allowed" DataFlavor to a drop target. The DataFlavor encapsulates a Java type that the drop target will accept as well as an additional discriminant on this Java type. The Java type is defined by the flavorClass attribute and can be specified as the name of a Java class. The discriminant attribute is used to handle cases in which the Java class alone is insufficient to discriminate between allowed and disallowed data. A drop event is accepted only if the DataFlavor and the value of the discriminant attribute match the drop event. It is possible to define multiple af:dataFlavor tags for a single af:dropTarget tag, in which case a drop is allowed if the drop contains any of the specified flavors and discriminant values.

NOTE
If a drag is initiated by an af:attributeDragSource *tag, no discriminator is defined, in which case it should not be set on the* af:dropTarget *tag if used.*

Marshalling Data Between JavaScript and Java   Data that is exchanged between the server and the client needs to be converted into a suitable format so that it can be optimally exchanged between client-side JavaScript and server-side Java. For browser-based clients, the two data transport formats that are commonly used for marshalling data is JavaScript Object Notation (JSON) and XML. ADF Faces uses a mix of both, with the information sent from the server to the client mostly as JSON and information sent from the client to the server as XML. Because the supported data types of the two languages are different, data objects are converted, bearing the risk of precisions getting lost. This is the case, however, only when transferring specific data objects, not when working with collections, in which case the RowKeySet is passed.

The following table lists the conversion types for JavaScript objects that are passed to the server.

JavaScript	Java
Boolean	java.lang.Boolean
Number	java.lang.Double
String	java.lang.String
Date	java.util.Date
Array	java.util.ArrayList
Object	java.util.Map

For the conversion from Java to JavaScript, the following mapping is performed:

Java	JavaScript
java.lang.Boolean	Boolean
java.lang.Double	Number
java.lang.Integer	Number
java.lang.Float	Number
java.lang.Long	Number
java.lang.Short	Number
java.lang.Character	String
java.lang.CharSequence	String
java.util.Collection	Array
java.util.Date	Date
java.util.Map	Object
Array	Array

NOTE
for an example that works with passing a RowKeySet, *see the "How to Move Tree Nodes Under a New Parent" section later in this chapter.*

af:collectionDragSource

The af:collectionDragSource tag is specific for components, such as af:table, af:treeTable, and af:tree, that render collections. Using this tag, developers are able to drag-and-drop the values of selected rows or nodes. In recent versions of JDeveloper 11*g*, this tag has been deprecated and is available for backward compatibility only. Developers should use the af:dragSource tag instead.

af:collectionDropTarget

The af:collectionDropTarget tag is a specialized drop handler for components such as af:tree, af:table, and af:treeTable that work with data collections. The tag provides the same functionality as the generic af:dropTarget tag. The difference is that the af:collectionDropTarget exposes a modelName attribute instead of the discriminant attribute of the af:dropTarget tag, and it does not require the data flavor to be specified.

The dropListener attribute of the af:collectionDropTarget tag uses EL to reference the managed bean method that implements the drop event listener. The event listener method accepts a single argument of type DropEvent and returns one of the following actions to acknowledge the success or failure of the drop operation. The returned action value defines the action that is performed in response to the drop operation.

- DnDAction.COPY

- DnDAction.MOVE

■ DnDAction.LINK

■ DnDAction.NONE

```
<af:tree … >
…
<af:collectionDropTarget dropListener="#{TreeBean.onDrop}"
    actions="MOVE" modelName="relocateEmployees"/>
</af:tree>
```

NOTE
The af:collectionDropTarget *component is a valid child of the* af:tree, af:table, *and* af:treeTable *components. Other components should use the* af:dropTarget.

af:componentDragSource

The af:componentDragSource tag can be used to move components on a page or within layout containers such as af:panelDashBoard for users to personalize the layout of a page. It may also be used to define the drag ghost image to indicate drag-and-drop since it is the drop listener method that decides whether the dragged component is moved or some other data is updated instead. For example, the single row copy use case shown in Figure 14-4 can be implemented with the af:componentDragSource component, with a few changes applied to the drop handler code of this example.

Drag-and-drop is allowed only between compatible drag sources and drop targets. If the discriminant attribute is used, then the value of the discriminant attribute on the target and the source must match.

In this section, we provide three examples for configuring drag-and-drop of components:

■ Drag-and-drop of child components in an af:panelDashBoard component

■ Drag-and-drop within an ADF Faces layout containers; as a result the child components are reordered

■ Drag-and-drop of a child component between different layout containers, in which case the dragged component is removed from the drag container and added to the drop target container

The use case for users to move components on a page to personalize the layout is quite common and is addressed in Oracle ADF Faces and ADF by the change-persistence framework and the Oracle ADF Metadata Services (MDS) functionality. In the following examples, the user defined changes are saved for the duration of the user session. However, using MDS, the same can be persisted for the application, meaning that the component reordering remains beyond closing and restarting the application.

NOTE
The MDS and runtime customization in Fusion web applications is the subject of the "Customizing Applications with MDS" and "Allowing User Customizations at Runtime" chapters in Oracle Fusion Middleware Fusion Developer's Guide for Oracle Application Development Framework 11g Release 1 *that is available as a part of the Fusion Middleware 11g documentation at http://otn.oracle.com.*

Enabling Change Persistence in ADF Faces RC Projects

In moving components on a page, users change the server-side object tree that is held in memory for the displayed JSF page. To keep the changes for the duration of the user session, you need to enable change persistence for the web application, which is done through a context parameter setting in the web.xml file:

```
<context-param>
  <param-name>
    org.apache.myfaces.trinidad.CHANGE_PERSISTENCE
  </param-name>
  <param-value>session</param-value>
</context-param>
```

You set this context parameter declaratively from the project properties. Open the project properties and choose ADF View | Enable User Customizations | For Duration of Session.

Drag-and-Drop Within an af:panelDashBoard Component

The `af:panelDashBoard` component is a layout container that aligns its children in a grid and that natively supports reordering of its child components using drag-and-drop. You use the `af:componentDragSource` behavior tag on the `af:panelDashBoard` child component, which in Figure 14-2 are instances of `af:panelBox`, to enable drag-and-drop. As shown in 14-2, moving a component of the `af:panelDashBoard` moves the other child components to the left or right, depending on the drag component location relative to the drop location.

```
<af:panelDashboard id="pd1"
    dropListener="#{ComponentDragHandler.panelDashBoardHandler}">
  <af:panelBox text="Area 1" id="pb3">
    ...
    <af:componentDragSource/>
  </af:panelBox>
  <af:panelBox text="Area 2" id="pb4">
    ...
    <af:componentDragSource/>
  </af:panelBox>
  <af:panelBox text="Area 3" id="pb5">
    ...
    <af:componentDragSource/>
  </af:panelBox>
</af:panelDashboard>
```

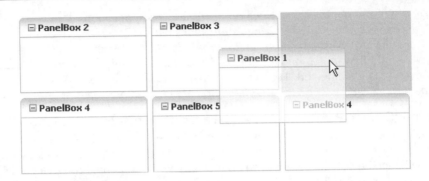

FIGURE 14-2 *Drag-and-drop within an* `af:panelDashBoard` *component*

Using the `af:componentDragSource` tag allows users to move the child components of the `af:panelDashBoard` to personalize the component layout. To persist the changes in the panel dashboard layout, you use the `ChangeManager` and the `ReorderChildrenComponent Change` object of Apache Trinidad in a drop listener method referenced by the `dropListener` attribute:

```
public DnDAction panelDashBoardHandler(DropEvent dropEvent) {
  FacesContext fctx = FacesContext.getCurrentInstance();
  //get panelDashBoard component as the drop target
  UIComponent dropComponent = dropEvent.getDropComponent();
  //get the moved child component (panelBox) as the drag source
  Transferable transferable = dropEvent.getTransferable();
  UIComponent dragComponent = null;
  dragComponent = transferable.getData(DataFlavor.UICOMPONENT_FLAVOR);
  //get a list of direct child UI components of the af:panelDashboard
  List<UIComponent> childComponents = dropComponent.getChildren();
  //the drop index gives us the information where the moved
  //component should be added in the list of children. From
  //this information we derive the child component in the
  //af:panelDashboard component that received the drop event
  int dropIndex = dropEvent.getDropSiteIndex();
  //perform reorganization only if valid drop index is found
  if (dropIndex > -1) {
    UIComponent dropChildComponent = childComponents.get(dropIndex);
    List<String> reorderedComponentList = new ArrayList<String>();
    //iterate over children to create new component order list
    for (UIComponent currComponent : childComponents) {
      String currComponentId = currComponent.getId();
      if (!currComponentId.equals(dragComponent.getId())) {
        reorderedComponentList.add(currComponentId);
        //if the current component is the child component that
        //the drop index points to then add the dragged component
        if (currComponentId.equals(dropChildComponent.getId())) {
          reorderedComponentList.add(dragComponent.getId());
        }
      }
    }
```

```
    //use the Apache Trinidad change specialization class for
    //reordering children
    ReorderChildrenComponentChange reorderedChildChange =
        new ReorderChildrenComponentChange(reorderedComponentList);
    //persist the change for the session, using the Apache Trinidad
    //ChangeManager class
    ChangeManager cm = null;
    //RequestContext in Apache Trinidad is comparable to the
    //AdfFacesContext class in ADF Faces.
    cm = RequestContext.getCurrentInstance().getChangeManager();
    cm.addComponentChange(fctx, dropComponent, reorderedChildChange);
  }
  //the panelDashboard component does not need to be refreshed so that
  //we should return DnDAction.NONE
  return DnDAction.NONE;
}
```

Drag-and-Drop Components Within a Container

Layout containers that don't provide native support for dragging their child components require developers to use a drop listener to perform the component move. Figure 14-3 shows the runtime view of the example explained in this section and the next. Users can move a picture and its associated information details within an `af:panelBox` component or between two different `af:panelBox` components.

In this section, we explain how to use drag-and-drop to reorder components within a layout component such as `af:panelBox`. As indicated by the first arrow in Figure 14-3, the user drags an image on top of another image in the same layout component to place it below the drop target.

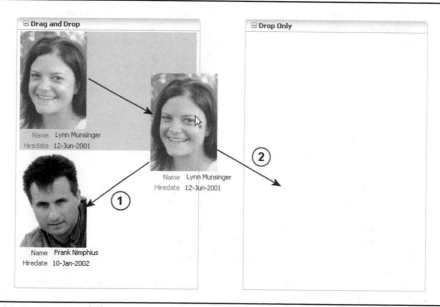

FIGURE 14-3 *Drag-and-drop UI components within a component container and between containers.*

In our example, the drag source has an `af:componentDragSource` child tag and the drop target an `af:dropTarget` tag that performs the reordering. The transferable object is an UI component, which is why the `flavorClass` attribute of the `af:dataFlavor` must be set to `javax.faces.component.UIComponent`.

The `af:componentDragSource` always performs a move operation. To handle the drop action, the `actions` attribute of the `af:dropTarget` tag is set to MOVE.

NOTE
Though `af:componentDragSource` *performs a move action, the dragged UI component is not physically moved. To move a component, developers have to program the change in a drop listener.*

The page source for the Drag and Drop panel box shown in Figure 14-3 defines an `af:panelGroupLayout` component as the drag source, as shown next:

```
<af:panelBox text="Drag and Drop" id="pb1" contentStyle="height:500px;"
    inlineStyle="width:300px;">
  <af:panelGroupLayout id="pgl1" layout="vertical">
    <af:image source="images/lynn.png" id="i1"/>
    <af:panelFormLayout id="pfl1">
      <af:inputText label="Name" id="it1" value="Lynn Munsinger"
        readOnly="true"/>
      <af:panelLabelAndMessage label="Hiredate" id="plam1">
        <af:outputText value="12-Jun-2001" id="ot1"/>
      </af:panelLabelAndMessage>
    </af:panelFormLayout>
    <af:componentDragSource/>
    <!-- call handleContainerDrag drop listener method -->
    <af:dropTarget
        dropListener="#{ComponentDragHandler.handleContainerDrag}"
        actions="MOVE">
      <af:dataFlavor flavorClass="javax.faces.component.UIComponent"/>
    </af:dropTarget>
  </af:panelGroupLayout>
  <af:panelGroupLayout id="pgl2" layout="vertical">
    <af:image source="/images/frank.png" id="i2"/>
    <af:panelFormLayout id="Pfl2">
      <af:inputText label="Name" id="it2" readOnly="true"
        value="Frank Nimphius"/>
      <af:panelLabelAndMessage label="Hiredate"
        id="plam2">
        <af:outputText value="10-Jan-2002" id="ot2"/>
      </af:panelLabelAndMessage>
    </af:panelFormLayout>
    <af:componentDragSource/>
    <af:dropTarget
      dropListener="#{ComponentDragHandler.handleContainerDrag}"
      actions="MOVE">
      <af:dataFlavor flavorClass="javax.faces.component.UIComponent"/>
    </af:dropTarget>
  </af:panelGroupLayout>
</af:panelBox>
```

Each af:panelGroupLayout component is defined as a drag source and drop target. When an af:panelGroupLayout component is dropped on top of another, the listener code in the handleContainerDrag method is invoked to change the order of the components so that the dragged component is placed below the drop target.

```java
public DnDAction handleContainerDrag(DropEvent dropEvent) {
    FacesContext fctx = FacesContext.getCurrentInstance();
    Transferable transferable = dropEvent.getTransferable();
    UIComponent dragComponent = null;
    dragComponent = transferable.getData(DataFlavor.UICOMPONENT_FLAVOR);
    UIComponent dropComponent = dropEvent.getDropComponent();
    //since the drag and drop is performed in the same container, the
    //drag parent is the same as the drop parent. We need this component
    //to reorder its children and to refresh at the end
    UIComponent dropComponentParent = dropComponent.getParent();
    //make sure the drag is successful and the drag component is not the
    //same as the drop target
    if (dragComponent != null && dragComponent != dropComponent){
        //create a list of String to take the new order of components within
        //the layout component
        List<String> reorderedComponentList =
            new ArrayList<String>(dropComponentParent.getChildCount());
        //iterate over the child components to compare them with the
        //dragged component
        for (UIComponent currComponent : dropComponentParent.getChildren()){
            String currComponentId = currComponent.getId();
            //if the current child is not the dragged component, add it
            //to the list of children
            if (!currComponentId.equals(dragComponent.getId())){
                reorderedComponentList.add(currComponentId);
                //if the current component is the drop target, then add the
                //the dragged component as the next sibling so it shows below it
                if (currComponentId.equals(dropComponent.getId())) {
                    reorderedComponentList.add(dragComponent.getId());
                }
            }
        }
    }
    //use the Apache Trinidad change specialization class for
    //reordering children
    ReorderChildrenComponentChange reorderedChildChange =
        new ReorderChildrenComponentChange(reorderedComponentList);
    reorderedChildChange.changeComponent(dropComponentParent);
    //persist the change for the session, using the Apache Trinidad
    //ChangeManager class
    ChangeManager cm = null;
    //RequestContext in Apache Trinidad is comparable to the
    //AdfFacesContext class in ADF Faces. In fact, AdfFacesContext
    //delegates most of its calls to this class
    cm = RequestContext.getCurrentInstance().getChangeManager();
    cm.addComponentChange(fctx,
                          dropComponentParent,
                          reorderedChildChange);
```

```
      AdfFacesContext adfFacesCtx = AdfFacesContext.getCurrentInstance();
      adfFacesCtx.addPartialTarget(dropComponentParent);
      //refresh container
      return DnDAction.MOVE;
    }
    return DnDAction.NONE;
}
```

NOTE
The ChangeManager, ReorderChildrenComponentChange, *and* MoveChildComponentChange *used in this example and the next also exist in the ADF Faces package. However, the ADF Faces classes delegate only to the Apache Trinidad equivalents and are deprecated. We therefore recommend that you use the Apache Trinidad classes directly.*

Drag-and-Drop Components Between Containers

The second use case shown in Figure 14-3 is the ability for users to move components from one parent component to another. As it was earlier, the drop area is defined by the af:dropTarget tag and the af:dataFlavor has its flavorClass attribute set to javax.faces.component.UIComponent.

The following page source shows the content of the Drop Only panel box in Figure 14-3. The example does not use a discriminant attribute value so that the same drag component defined in the first example can be used.

```
<af:panelBox text="Drop Only" id="pb2" inlineStyle="width:300px; "
    contentStyle="height:500px;">
  <af:panelGroupLayout id="pgl3" layout="vertical"
    inlineStyle="height:630px;width:300px;">
    <af:dropTarget
        dropListener="#{ComponentDragHandler.handleExternalContainerDrag}"
        actions="MOVE">
      <af:dataFlavor flavorClass="javax.faces.component.UIComponent"/>
    </af:dropTarget>
  </af:panelGroupLayout>
</af:panelBox>
```

This time, when the drop occurs, the handleExternalContainerDrag drop listener method is called to move the dragged component out of its current parent container to the target container.

NOTE
In the example, the drop target is af:panelGroupLayout, *which must have a size defined or stretched by its parent component for the drag to find it.*

The handleExternalContainerDrag drop listener code is shown here:

```
public DnDAction handleExternalContainerDrag(DropEvent dropEvent) {
    FacesContext fctx = FacesContext.getCurrentInstance();
    Transferable transferable = dropEvent.getTransferable();
    UIComponent draggedComponent = null;
```

```
draggedComponent = transferable.getData(DataFlavor.UICOMPONENT_FLAVOR);
if (draggedComponent != null) {
  //get the component that received the drop
  UIComponent dropTarget = dropEvent.getDropComponent();
  //use specialized change class to move a child from one container to
  //another. The MoveChildComponent instance must be registered on a
  //parent component that is common to the moved component and the
  //destination container component
  MoveChildComponentChange moveChildComponentChange =
      new MoveChildComponentChange(draggedComponent, dropTarget);
  //Access the session change manager instance to persist the
  //move
  ChangeManager cm = null;
  //RequestContext in Apache Trinidad is comparable to the
  //AdfFacesContext class in ADF Faces.
  cm = RequestContext.getCurrentInstance().getChangeManager();
  UIComponent commonComponentParent = null;
  //get the component that is a parent for the moved and the receiving
  //component. The add() method is a convenience method that ensures the
  //change is getting persisted by the Change Manager
  commonComponentParent = moveChildComponentChange.add(fctx, cm);
  moveChildComponentChange.changeComponent(commonComponentParent);
  AdfFacesContext adfFacesCtx = AdfFacesContext.getCurrentInstance();
  adfFacesCtx.addPartialTarget(commonComponentParent);
  return DnDAction.MOVE;
}
return DnDAction.NONE;
}
```

Drag-and-Drop Use Cases

In this section, we provide sample use cases to demonstrate different ways to work with drag-and-drop in ADF Faces RC applications.

How to Create a Table Row as the Copy of an Existing Row Using Drag-and-Drop

In the example shown in Figure 14-4, users can drag-and-drop a table row onto the Create toolbar button to create a new table row as a copy. Row attributes that are not set by this operation can be edited by the user in a pop-up dialog that is opened programmatically when the new row is created. If the user clicks the Create toolbar button, an empty table row is created without the default values. In this case, the user can click the Edit button to enter the row data in a pop-up dialog or drag the new row onto the Edit button. For this use case, the af:table component is configured for single-row selection.

NOTE
The green background color on the drop target is implemented using the
:drop-target pseudo class on the af|commandToolbarButton
skin selector. The ADF Faces RC skinning framework for a pluggable
application look and feel is explained in Chapter 16.

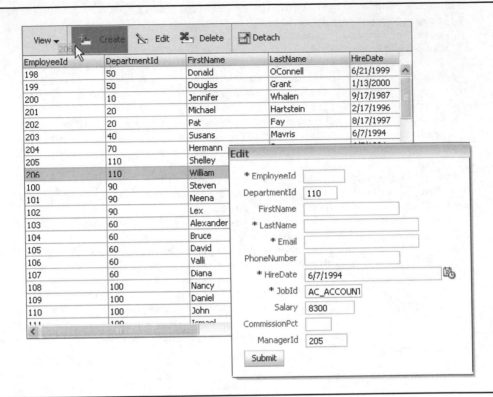

FIGURE 14-4 *Drag-and-drop action in an ADF Faces table*

The drag operation is defined on the `af:table` component using the `af:dragSource` tag that implicitly adds the row key set of the selected table row, or rows if the table is configured for multiple row selection, to the transferrable data. The `discriminant` attribute value is added to distinguish the drag event from other drag-and-drop events that may be added to the table.

```
<af:table …>
   <af:dragSource actions="MOVE COPY" defaultAction="COPY"
     discriminant="empdata"/>
</af:table>
```

The drop event is defined using the `af:dropTarget` tag added as a child component to the `af:commandToolBarButton` components. The toolbar buttons accept drag events that propose a move action and call a managed bean method to handle it.

```
<af:commandToolbarButton text="Create" id="ctb1"
     icon="/images/addnewr.gif"
     actionListener="#{bindings.CreateEmployeesWithParams.execute}">
   <af:dropTarget dropListener="#{EmpTableBean.createDropListener}"
     actions="MOVE">
   <af:dataFlavor flavorClass="org.apache.myfaces.trinidad.model.RowKeySet"
     discriminant="empdata"/>
   </af:dropTarget>
</af:commandToolbarButton>
```

The `af:dropTarget dropListener` attribute references a listener method in a managed bean that determines the selected table row and that adds the default values for the new row to create.

At runtime, the toolbar button references the view object Create with parameters operation through an action binding `CreateEmployeesWithParams` created in the binding container. The action binding definition in the PageDef file is shown next and contains attributes to define default values for the `DepartmentId`, `ManagerId`, `HireDate`, `JobId`, and `Salary` attributes of the new row.

```
<action IterBinding="EmployeesView1Iterator"
    id="CreateEmployeesWithParams"
    RequiresUpdateModel="true" Action="createWithParams">
  <NamedData NDName="DepartmentId" NDType="oracle.jbo.domain.Number"/>
  <NamedData NDName="ManagerId" NDType="oracle.jbo.domain.Number"/>
  <NamedData NDName="HireDate" NDType="oracle.jbo.domain.Date"/>
  <NamedData NDName="JobId" NDType="java.lang.String"/>
  <NamedData NDName="Salary" NDType="oracle.jbo.domain.Number"/>
</action>
```

NOTE

How to bind to and work with the Create with parameters operation is explained in Chapter 9.

The listener handling the drop event accesses the transfer object from the drop event to look up the `RowKeySet` object, which contains the row keys of the dragged table rows.

```
public DnDAction createDropListener(DropEvent dropEvent) {
  //get the transferable object
  Transferable transferable = dropEvent.getTransferable();
  //get the RowKeySet object that contains the row keys of the
  //selected rows added to the drag and drop
  DataFlavor<RowKeySet> rowKeySetFlavor =
        DataFlavor.getDataFlavor(RowKeySet.class, "empdata");
  RowKeySet rowKeySet = transferable.getData(rowKeySetFlavor);
  if (rowKeySet != null)
  {
    //get a handle to the collection model used by the table. Instead of
    //looking up the ADF binding for the JUCtrlHierBinding, we get the
    //information from the transferable
    CollectionModel dragModel = null;
    dragModel = transferable.getData(CollectionModel.class);
    if (dragModel!=null) {
      //in the single selection usecase, get the first row key.
      Object firstRowKey = rowKeySet.iterator().next();
      //use the row key to make the row it references the current row in
      //the collection
      dragModel.setRowKey(firstRowKey);
      //we are working against the ADF binding layer as a model. The table
      //row is represented by an instance of FacesCtrlHierNodeBinding,
      //which we cast to JUCtrlHierNodeBinding, the public binding class
      //to use
      JUCtrlHierNodeBinding rowNode = null;
```

```
rowNode = (JUCtrlHierNodeBinding) dragModel.getRowData();
//The row object is an instance of oracle.jbo.Row
Row row = rowNode.getRow();
//We have the row to copy the attribute from. Next we need to access
//the "create with parameters" operation to define the default
//values as copies of the current row
BindingContext bctx = BindingContext.getCurrent();
BindingContainer bindings = bctx.getCurrentBindingsEntry();
OperationBinding oper = null;
oper = (OperationBinding)bindings.get("CreateEmployeesWithParams");
//the operation is executed by the toolbar button actionListener
//attribute reference. So all we need to do is to set the default
//values as parameters.
Map params = oper.getParamsMap();
params.put("DepartmentId",row.getAttribute("DepartmentId"));
params.put("ManagerId",row.getAttribute("ManagerId"));
params.put("HireDate",row.getAttribute("HireDate"));
params.put("JobId",row.getAttribute("JobId"));
params.put("Salary",row.getAttribute("Salary"));
oper.execute();
if (oper.getErrors().isEmpty()){
  //if no errors, then show popup dialog to edit the values. See
  //chapter 10 to learn how to launch a client side popup from
  //server side Java
  showEditEmployeePopup();
}
//handle error case
else{
  //if needed, add code to display message to user, then
  //return NONE as the outcome of the action
  return DnDAction.NONE;
}
}
return DnDAction.COPY;
}
else{
//if the operation failed, no need to refresh the drop source
return DnDAction.NONE;
}
}
}
```

NOTE
The table is partially refreshed when the pop-up dialog is closed. A code example for how to close a pop-up dialog programmatically from Java in a managed bean is provided in Chapter 19.

How to Move Tree Nodes Under a New Parent

A common use case when working with trees is to move child nodes under a new parent node—for example, to relocate employees. To implement this use case, you use an `af:dragSource` tag and an `af:collectionDropTarget` tag on the `af:tree` component. This makes all tree nodes becoming a drag source and drop target so that the drop listener logic needs to check for valid operations.

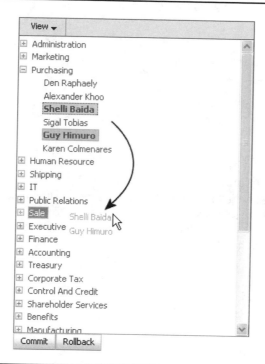

FIGURE 14-5 *Drag-and-Drop within an* af:tree *component*

The example we use to demonstrate this use case is shown in Figure 14-5. An af:tree component displays departments and associated employees. The user is able to drag employees from one department and drop them in another. If the drop is on a department node, the employees are added to this department. If the drop is on another employee node, the department node for the employee is looked up before the new employees are assigned to it. Dragging a department node to another node is not allowed and will be ignored.

Building the Tree

The tree is built by dragging the parent view object from the data control palette to the ADF Faces page, as explained in Chapter 9. An af:switcher component is used to define the information displayed on each node level individually.

```
<af:tree value="#{bindings.DepartmentsView1.treeModel}" var="node"
    selectionListener="#{bindings.DepartmentsView1.treeModel.makeCurrent}"
    rowSelection="multiple" id="t1">
  <f:facet name="nodeStamp">
    <af:switcher facetName="#{node.hierType.structureDefName}" id="s1">
      <f:facet name="adf.interactiv.model.queries.DepartmentsView">
        <af:outputText value="#{node.DepartmentName}" id="ot2"/>
      </f:facet>
      <f:facet name="adf.interactiv.model.queries.EmployeesView">
        <af:outputText value="#{node.FirstName} #{node.LastName}"
```

```
                                          id="ot3"/>
                   </f:facet>
             </af:switcher>
        </f:facet>
        <af:dragSource actions="MOVE"
             dragDropEndListener="#{TreeBean.onDragEnd}"
             discriminant="relocateEmployees"/>
        <af:collectionDropTarget dropListener="#{TreeBean.onDrop}"
             actions="MOVE" modelName="relocateEmployees"/>
   </af:tree>
```

The allowed drag-and-drop action in this example is MOVE.

The Drop Listener Code

The dropListener code that handles the drop event is shown next. Since the component initiating the drag is the same as the component that receives the drop, the DropSite is used to determine the row key of the node that received the drop event. The DropSite may return null if the drop is performed in an area that does not take data.

```
import oracle.adf.view.rich.component.rich.data.RichTree;
import oracle.adf.view.rich.datatransfer.DataFlavor;
import oracle.adf.view.rich.datatransfer.Transferable;
import oracle.adf.view.rich.dnd.DnDAction;
import oracle.adf.view.rich.event.DropEvent;
import oracle.jbo.Row;
import oracle.jbo.domain.Number;
import oracle.jbo.uicli.binding.JUCtrlHierBinding;
import oracle.jbo.uicli.binding.JUCtrlHierNodeBinding;
import org.apache.myfaces.trinidad.model.CollectionModel;
import org.apache.myfaces.trinidad.model.RowKeySet;
...
public DnDAction onDrop(DropEvent dropEvent) {
   RichTree dropComponent = (RichTree) dropEvent.getDropComponent();
   //variable that holds the new department Id for the dragged
   //employees
   Number newDepartmentId = null;
   //get the keyPath of the node that received the drop. The key path is
   //an object of type List
   List dropRowKey = (List) dropEvent.getDropSite();
   //if no dropsite then drop area was not a data area
   if(dropRowKey == null){
      return DnDAction.NONE;
   }
   //set the current row to the node that received the drop
   dropComponent.setRowKey(dropRowKey);
   //get the drop node. If the node is a child node (employees), get the
   //parent node if it is a department node use it
   JUCtrlHierNodeBinding dropNode = null;
   dropNode = (JUCtrlHierNodeBinding) dropComponent.getRowData();
   //the structureDef information allows us to determine the node level
   //that the drop occurred on
   String dropNodeStuctureDefname =
           dropNode.getHierTypeBinding().getStructureDefName();
```

```
String employeeDef = "adf.interactiv.model.queries.EmployeesView";
//check if drop is on employee node. If, get the parent node's
//departmentId to relocate employee
if (dropNodeStuctureDefname.equalsIgnoreCase(employeeDef)){
  newDepartmentId =
    (Number) dropNode.getParent().getRow().getAttribute("DepartmentId");
}
//the drop is on a department node. Get departmentId to relocate
//employee
else{
  newDepartmentId =
    (Number) dropNode.getRow().getAttribute("DepartmentId");
}
//now that we are clear on the drop target, we read the dragged content
Transferable transferable = dropEvent.getTransferable();
//the drag content is of type RowkeySet with a discriminator set to
//"relocateEmployees"
DataFlavor<RowKeySet> rowKeySetFlavor =
  DataFlavor.getDataFlavor(RowKeySet.class, "relocateEmployees");
RowKeySet rowKeySet = transferable.getData(rowKeySetFlavor);
if (rowKeySet != null){
  //the collectionModel is the tree model, which points to the ADF
  //binding layer
  CollectionModel dragModel = null;
  dragModel = transferable.getData(CollectionModel.class);
  if (dragModel!=null) {
    //using ADF Faces with ADF binding as the component model, the
    //dragged CollectionModel is an instance of FacesModel, which is
    //an inner class of FacesCtrlHierBinding. Using the getWrappedData
    //method of the CollectionModel interface, we can obtain an instance
    //of JUCtrlHierBinding, representing the ADF tree binding
    JUCtrlHierBinding binding = null;
    binding = (JUCtrlHierBinding) dragModel.getWrappedData();
    //create iterator of keyPath
    Iterator rowKeySetIterator = rowKeySet.iterator();
    if (binding != null) {
      while (rowKeySetIterator.hasNext()) {
        //get tree node by the key path in the RowKeySet and ensure
        //that only  employee nodes are dropped
        List nodePath = (List) rowKeySetIterator.next();
        //avoid NPE because of empty node entries due to
        //a failed drag action
        if(nodePath != null){
          JUCtrlHierNodeBinding node = null;
          node = binding.findNodeByKeyPath(nodePath);
          //get the View Object definition that represents the node.
          //the structure def name contains the VO name and package
          String stuctureDefname =
              node.getHierTypeBinding().getStructureDefName();
          if (stuctureDefname.equalsIgnoreCase(employeeDef)) {
            //employee node is found. Get the oracle.jbo.Row
            Row rw = node.getRow();
```

```
                //relocate employee
                rw.setAttribute("DepartmentId", newDepartmentId);
            }
          }
        }
      }
      //drop was successful, return MOVE so the drag source is refreshed
      return DnDAction.MOVE;
    }
  }
}
//if no drop operation could be handled, return NONE
return DnDAction.NONE;
}
```

How to Move/Copy/Link the Dragged Content

Dragged content is copied, moved, or linked to the drop target. The type of action is determined by the behavior tag, such as `af:componentDragSource`, and the `actions` attribute defined on the drag source and drop target. In addition, using the keyboard modifiers CTRL, SHIFT, and CTRL-SHIFT, users can decide the action to use if the drag source and drop target are configured for more than a single action type.

The example shown in Figure 14-6 shows a table that has an `af:dragSource` behavior tag added that supports the copy, move, and link actions. The drop target is an `af:selectOneListbox` component that has an `af:dropTarget` tag defined. The drop target also supports the COPY, MOVE, and LINK actions. When the user drags a row from the table to drop it on the `af:selectOneListbox`, the user controls the performed action using the keyboard modifiers. If no keyboard modifier is pressed, the default action performed is copy.

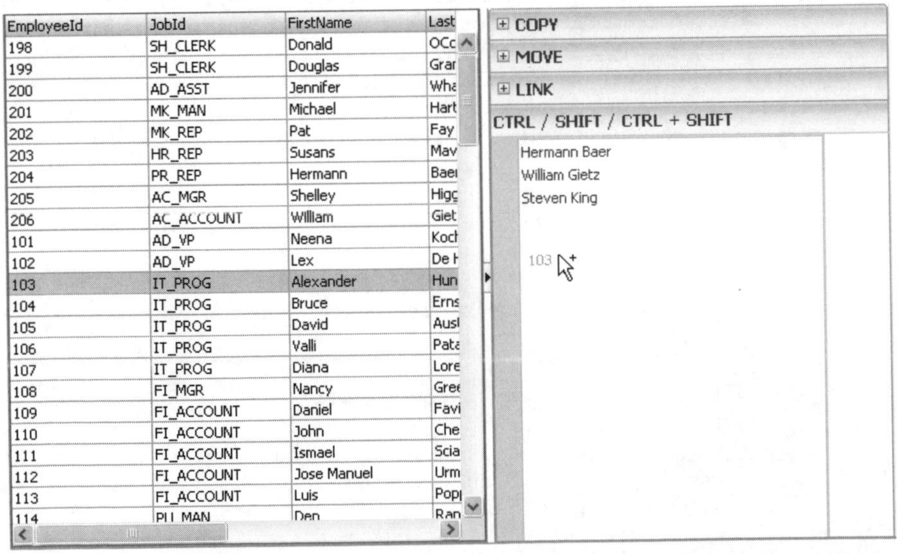

FIGURE 14-6 *Copy, move, and link example using a table as the drag source and a* `selectOneListbox` *as the drop target*

Note that in the sample code shown next, the af:selectOneListbox is bound to a managed bean to hold the drop data.

```
<af:table value="#{bindings.EmployeesView1.collectionModel}"
          rowSelection="multiple" … >
  <af:dragSource
          actions="COPY MOVE LINK" discriminant="tabledrop"
          dragDropEndListener="#{DragAndDropHandler.onDragEnd}"/>
</af:table>
```

The page code of the af:selectOneListbox is shown next.

```
<af:panelAccordion id="pa1" inlineStyle="height:500.0px;">
  <af:showDetailItem text="COPY" id="sdi1"/>
  <af:showDetailItem text="MOVE" id="sdi2"/>
  <af:showDetailItem text="LINK" id="sdi3"/>
  <af:showDetailItem text="SHIFT / CTRL+SHIFT / CTRL" id="sdi4">
    <af:selectOneListbox size="20" id="sol4" … >
      <f:selectItems
        value="#{pageFlowScope.SelectItemsArrayBean.selectList}"
        id="selectItems3"/>
      <af:dropTarget dropListener="#{DragAndDropHandler.dropHandler}
        actions="MOVE COPY LINK">
        <af:dataFlavor
          flavorClass="org.apache.myfaces.trinidad.model.RowKeySet"
          discriminant="tabledrop"/>
      </af:dropTarget>
    </af:selectOneListbox>
  </af:showDetailItem>
</af:panelAccordion>
```

In Figure 14-6, note that the EmployeeId "100" in the table is missing, which belongs to Steven King that you see in the select list. This is the result of a move action, while the other employees were copied to the list.

The dropHandler method that is referenced in the dropListener attribute of the af:dropTarget tag is shown here:

```
public DnDAction dropHandler(DropEvent dropEvent) {
  DnDAction proposedAction = dropEvent.getProposedAction();
  DnDAction returnAction = DnDAction.NONE;
  //the allowed DnDAction options are defined in an enumeration.
  //enumerations are used in a switch statement without adding
  //the class name they are defined in (DnDAction.class)
  switch(proposedAction){
    case COPY:
      returnAction = handleCopy(dropEvent);
    break;
    case MOVE:
      returnAction = handleMove(dropEvent);
      break;
    case LINK:
      returnAction = handleLink(dropEvent);
```

```
      break;
   default:
      returnAction = handleCopy(dropEvent);
   }
   return returnAction;
}
```

The `handleCopy`, `handleMove`, and `handleLink` methods are similar, so we provide the code example for only one case:

```
/**
* Method that handles the drag and drop MOVE action. It updates the drop
* target list and refreshes the drag source after removing the dragged
* table row
* @param dropEvent the input argument received by the drop handler method
* @return DnDAction.NONE or DnDAction.MOVE depending on the success of the
* operation
*/
private DnDAction handleMove(DropEvent dropEvent){
   //get the row keys of the dragged table rows. Note that the
   //row key is not the oracle.jbo.Key but the key path of the
   //node in the tree binding, which in case of a table consists
   //of a single entry
   Transferable transferable = dropEvent.getTransferable();
   DataFlavor<RowKeySet> rowKeySetFlavor =
     DataFlavor.getDataFlavor(RowKeySet.class, "tabledrop");
   RowKeySet rowKeySet = transferable.getData(rowKeySetFlavor);
   if (rowKeySet != null)
   {
      //get the ADF binding for the tree component
      CollectionModel dragModel = null;
      dragModel = transferable.getData(CollectionModel.class);
      if (dragModel!=null) {
         JUCtrlHierBinding binding =
           (JUCtrlHierBinding) dragModel.getWrappedData();
         //since the table is configured for multi row select, we
         //iterate of the row keys to handle the MOVE
         Iterator rowKeySetIterator = rowKeySet.iterator();
         if (binding != null) {
           while (rowKeySetIterator.hasNext()) {
             List rowKey = (List)rowKeySetIterator.next();
             JUCtrlHierNodeBinding nodeBinding = null;
             nodeBinding = binding.findNodeByKeyPath(rowKey);
             //oracle.jbo.Row instance found
             Row rw = nodeBinding.getRow();
             //add the FirstName and LastName as the list label and
             //the row object as the list value.
             String label = rw.getAttribute("FirstName")+" "
                         +rw.getAttribute("LastName");
```

```
                //in our example, the list bean that holds the dropped
                //values is configured as a managed bean in
                //a scope larger than request scope so it survives
                //the end of a request.
                //The list bean is injected to the managed bean that
                //contains this method using a managed bean property
                //see Chapter 1 for more information about managed
                //properties)
                listBean.addItem(label,rw);
                //For move operation, delete entry from the table
                //source
                rw.remove();
            }
            //refresh Drag Source. The drag and drop COPY and MOVE action
            //automatically refresh the drop target so that this does not
            //need to be programmed explicitly
            AdfFacesContext adfFacesCtx = AdfFacesContext.getCurrentInstance();
            adfFacesCtx.addPartialTarget(dropEvent.getDragComponent());
            //since the move was successful, we return the MOVE action. This
            //ensures the DragDropEndListener is called on the af:dragSource
            return DnDAction.MOVE;
        }
    }
}
//no drop is not performed
return DnDAction.NONE;
}
```

The managed bean that is referenced by the `af:selectOneListbox` component to populate the list is configured in `pageFlowScope` in the example we built. The source code is shown next:

```
public class SelectListBean {
    ArrayList<SelectItem> selectList = new ArrayList<SelectItem>();
    public void setSelectList(ArrayList<SelectItem> selectList) {
        this.selectList = selectList;
    }
    public ArrayList<SelectItem> getSelectList() {
        return selectList;
    }

    //convenience method to add a list item
    public void addItem(String label, Object value){
        SelectItem item = new SelectItem();
        item.setLabel(label);
        item.setValue(value);
        selectList.add(item);
    }
}
```

Summary

Application users who worked with desktop-based applications are accustomed to moving or copying data with the mouse and expect the same functionality to work on the Web. In other words, the rich Web must support drag-and-drop because desktops do! The Oracle ADF Faces RC framework supports drag-and-drop at runtime without requiring application developers to implement the functionality manually. Instead, ADF Faces provides drag-and-drop behavior tags that developers declaratively add to the UI components to drag data from or drop data to. The Java interface with which developers work is consistent and not dependent on the components involved.

CHAPTER
15

Working with Oracle ADF
Reusable Components

Necessity is the mother of invention; reuse is the godfather of developer productivity.

he Oracle Fusion development stack promotes the reuse of application logic, user interface components, and page layouts to simplify your work with recurring tasks. In addition to the patterns of reuse in Java and Java EE, Oracle ADF allows developers to define groups of components and business logic declaratively as reusable units and to register them in custom component catalogs for easy reuse during application development.

NOTE
In this chapter the term "view" refers to pages and page fragments. The view terminology is used by the ADF task flow to reference the display in the user interface (UI), which physically can be a page or page fragment.

ADF Library JAR

The delivery vehicle for deploying reusable components across applications and projects in Oracle JDeveloper 11*g* is the ADF library JAR. ADF library JARs are standard Java archive (JAR) files with built-in discovery functionality. To reuse the components in an ADF library JAR, developers import the ADF library JAR file to the Oracle JDeveloper Resource Palette, from where it can be added to Oracle JDeveloper projects. ADF components that can be reused through ADF libraries include ADF Business Component models, data controls, bounded task flows, page templates with or without ADF bindings, declarative components, and resource connections.

NOTE
Additional information about ADF libraries is available in the Oracle Fusion Middleware Fusion Developer's Guide for Oracle Application Development Framework 11*g* Release 1 *online product documentation.*

Creating ADF Libraries

Two options are available in Oracle JDeveloper for creating an ADF Library JAR deployment profile for a project that contains components that should be reused and shared:

■ Double-click the project node, or choose the Project Properties option from the project node context menu, to open the project properties. In the project Properties dialog, select Deployment and click the New button. Select ADF Library JAR File in the Archive Type list and enter a name for the library. Click OK to close the dialog and return to the project.

■   Choose File | New to open the Oracle JDeveloper New Gallery. There, select General | Deployment Profiles and choose the ADF Library JAR File option.

Both options create the ADF library JAR deployment profile as a named entry in the project properties. To edit the ADF library JAR definition after creating it, you open the project properties and select the Deployments node. The ADF library JAR Creation dialog contains the following configuration options:

■   **Library Dependencies**   Allows developers to specify the dependencies of an ADF library JAR to referenced projects and their configured libraries.

■   **Connections**   Lets the user decide which application connections to include in the ADF library JAR and whether to include connection details or just connection names. By default, all application connections are selected. Note that connections are not only for database access but may also exist for Service Oriented Architecture (SOA) server references.

■   **JAR options**   The default Java JAR configuration options that allow developers to add manifest files and decide whether or not to compress the archive.

■   **ADF Validation**   Lets the user decide whether to stop JAR processing or ignore errors when validation fails. The validation checks package names for potential conflicts, such as components that are created in the root package or that use common naming. Lacking a good package naming structure increases the risk that content combined in an ADF library will not be uniquely referenced and will therefore collide with files that share the same names.

To deploy a project to an ADF Library, select the project node with the right mouse button and choose Deploy from the context menu. By default the ADF Library JAR file gets created in the deploy directory of the project file structure on the file system.

Reusable Components Must Be Given Unique Names

An ADF Library JAR does not represent a namespace that ensures unique names when it is added to a project. To avoid naming conflicts between libraries and the content of the project to which the libraries are added, you should work on a consistent enterprise-wide naming scheme that enables everyone in the development team to build unique naming for class packages, Java classes, pages and page fragments, database connections, application modules, task flow definitions, page templates, declarative components, and library JAR filenames.

You can increase your development productivity by defining a naming schema before building your first reusable component. Better to spend some time up front defining a naming standard than to have to fix issues later on.

When conflicting naming exists between the content of an imported ADF library JAR and content that already exists in a project, the existing project content is used. For example, if an ADF library JAR has a connection defined that uses the same name the connection uses in the project, this conflict is reported in the Oracle JDeveloper log window but the project's connection information is used.

How Data Bindings Are Deployed in ADF Libraries

If an ADF library JAR project contains ADF bindings, and the DataBindings.cpx file is included in the JAR file, the name of the data binding registry file does not need to be changed. However, the contents of the DataBindings.cpx registry file, such as page mappings and data control definitions, should be uniquely named to avoid conflicts.

For all web projects that contain ADF bindings, the DataBindings.cpx file is automatically registered in the project adfm.xml file that is located in the project's /adfmsrc/META-INF/ directory. If the project gets deployed in an ADF library JAR, the adfm.xml file is stored in the META-INF/ directory of the generated JAR file. Applications that consume ADF libraries search the class path for copies of the adfm.xml registry file to discover metadata references, such as DataBindings.cpx, dynamically and to append their content to the application configuration.

Note that other registry files that are deployed in an ADF library JAR, if needed, are bc4j.xcfg, <bc4j_project>.jpx and DataControls.dcx. The bc4j.xcfg and <bc4j_project>.jpx files are deployed with ADF libraries that contain ADF Business Components objects.

Dependent Third-party Library Handling

The content of an ADF library JAR may have dependencies to third-party libraries that are not part of the default ADF library JAR set. For example, a declarative component may be built that shows RSS feeds or provides Google search capabilities for an ADF Faces page. Both solutions require additional libraries to perform their work. ADF libraries, however, cannot contain other JAR files, which means the JAR files that are shipped with the ADF library JAR must be separate files. To ensure that the third-party libraries are deployed with the application web archive (WAR) file of the project that consumes the ADF library JAR content, we recommend that you define the libraries as Oracle JDeveloper libraries. An Oracle JDeveloper library is a named reference to JAR files or sources that you can add to a project using the Tools | Manage Libraries option in the JDeveloper project properties. Content that is added through a JDeveloper library is automatically added to the project dependencies for deployment.

Here's how to create an Oracle JDeveloper library:

1. Choose Tools | Manage Libraries.

2. Click the Load Dir button.

3. In the opened dialog, select the directory that holds the third-party libraries.

4. Select the new Libraries entry and click the New button.

5. In the opened dialog, define a meaningful name for the library.

6. Select the Class Path entry and click the Add Entry button to select the JAR files to include in this library.

7. Check the Deployed by Default checkbox to ensure that the libraries are added to the deployment when they are added to a project.

To deploy this Oracle JDeveloper library with the web project that imports the ADF library JAR with the dependency to the contained third-party JAR files, do the following:

1. Open the project properties dialog.
2. Select the Libraries and Classpath node.
3. Click the Add Library button.
4. Select the JDeveloper library entry you created.

The third-party libraries are automatically added to the list of deployed libraries when you're building the web application WAR file.

How to Import and Use ADF Libraries in the Oracle JDeveloper Resource Palette

To import content from an ADF Library JAR, do the following:

1. Select the project that you want to import the ADF library content to and open the Oracle JDeveloper Resource Palette (CTRL-SHIFT-O).
2. In the Resource Palette, select the folder icon next to the search field and choose New Connection | File System.
3. Provide a name for the new connection and browse to the folder that contains the ADF Library JAR file. Then click OK.

   Figure 15-1 shows the Resource Palette window in Oracle JDeveloper with two ADF libraries imported from two file system connections. The butterfly-jar connection has an ADF library JAR entry that contains a bounded task flow, ADF Business Components objects, a data control and a page template for reuse.

TIP

If you select the file system connection that contains the ADF library JAR in the Resource Palette window and open the context menu, you can filter and search the library content using either the Filter or Advanced Search menu option.

Technically, ADF Libraries Are JARs

Because the feature is called "ADF library JAR," some ADF developers believe that it is comparable to Oracle JDeveloper libraries or shared libraries. Technically, ADF library JAR files contain ADF components and metadata artifacts but no dependent third-party library files. If an ADF library JAR requires additional dependent JAR files to be around at runtime, these need to be added separately to the web project that consumes the ADF library JAR. The dependent JAR files must then be deployed in the web project's WAR file or configured as shared libraries on the deployment target.

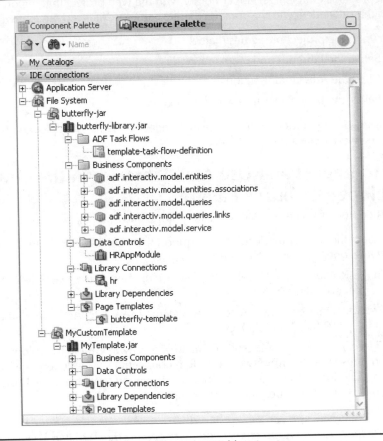

FIGURE 15-1 *Resource Palette with configured ADF libraries*

4. To import the content of an ADF Library JAR, select the ADF library JAR that contains the content to import and choose Add to Project.

5. In the opened confirmation dialog, click the Add Library button. Note that the whole ADF library JAR is imported, not just the content of interest.

What Happens When an ADF Library JAR Is Added to a Project

When adding an ADF library JAR to a web project, a new project library entry with a reference to the ADF library JAR archive file on the file system is created in the project properties. To access the ADF library JAR entry, open the project properties using the JDeveloper context menu and select the Libraries and Classpath node. In the list, a new entry ADF Library is created that you can edit by selecting it and clicking the Edit button.

ADFLibraryFilter and ResourceServlet

To load the resource content from the library archive, the web.xml descriptor in the web project that imports the ADF library JAR is extended with two servlet entries, the oracle.adf. library.webapp.ResourceServlet resource servlet and the ADFLibraryFilter servlet filter. The ADFLibraryFilter loads web resources from ADF library JAR archive files in the classpath if the content is not found in the web project public_html directory or a subdirectory. By default, resources that are handled by the ADFLibraryFilter include files with extensions .png, .jpg, .jpeg, .gif, .js, .css, .htm, and .html. Developers don't need to do anything to use this loading mechanism. Suppose, for example, that you build a declarative component that references an external JavaScript file; if the file is contained in the declarative component public_html directory or a subdirectory of it, the resource filter automatically handles the file access.

At design time, the Oracle JDeveloper component palette and data control palette are updated with content references from the ADF Library JAR. For example, if the ADF library JAR contains bounded task flows, these are listed in a separate category of the component palette using the name of the ADF library JAR. Similarly, custom declarative ADF Faces components display in the component palette in the context of a JavaServer Faces page development environment. Wizards, such as the new JSF page creation wizard, contain template references from the ADF library JAR if any exist.

TIP
ADF bounded task flows can be directly added from the Resource Palette to an ADF Faces page, page fragment, or task flow definition.

Page Templates

Page templates provide a reusable page definition for application developers to enforce a consistent branding and look and feel of pages and page fragments across the application. Because the content of a page template is referenced at design time and runtime and not compiled into the page source of a consuming page or page fragment, layouts that are defined by a template can be changed easily.

NOTE
To distinguish between the ADF Faces page that contains the template content and the pages that reference a template, we use the terms "consumer" and "consuming," respectively.

Developing Page Templates

To develop a page template, application developers or template designers build a JavaServer Pages (JSPX) document that contains the XML metadata and JavaServer Faces (JSF) layout and UI components. In Oracle JDeveloper 11*g*, page templates use the same visual and declarative development environment as stand-alone JSF pages, but they are different in that they don't have the f:view and af:document elements defined. The following section explains how you build, use, and deploy templates.

NOTE
Application developers should not add an af:form *component to the template. Use of the* af:form *component is limited to a single occurrence per page. If you need to define subforms, consider using the* af:subform *element.*

Creating Page Templates

Page templates can be developed in the view layer of a project or in a separate project, where they are made available in an ADF library JAR. To build a new template, do the following;

1. Select the root project node of the project in which you want to create the new template.

2. Choose New from the context menu and expand the Web Tier | JSF node. If the Web Tier node does not exist in the project properties, select the All Technologies tab on top of the dialog, choose the JSF Page Template, and click OK.

3. In the Create JSF Page Template screen shown in Figure 15-2, provide the following information:

   ■ **File Name**   The physical filename of the JSP document that represents the page template.

   ■ **Directory**   The directory within the project public_html folder that holds the template file. For example, placing page templates into a templates folder under the WEB-INF folder makes them unavailable for direct access from browsers.

   ■ **Page Template Name**   The display name of the template that is shown in Oracle JDeveloper when building new ADF Faces pages and page fragments.

   ■ **Use a Quick Start Layout**   Templates can be built on predefined layouts of the Oracle JDeveloper 11*g*. Click the Browse button and select the initial page design from a list of suggested layouts. The selected layout is copied into the page template definition.

   ■ **Create Associated ADFm Page Definition**   The ADFm page definition allows templates to reference ADF binding sources. Select this option for templates that need to display or access data content from the ADF data controls. ADF Faces pages that reference such a template will need a page binding reference defined in their own page definition file that points to the template binding definition file. By default, the binding ID is created as pageTemplateBinding.

   ■ **Facet Definitions**   Page templates would be of no use if the application developer could not add dynamic page content to them. Facets define areas in a template that are writable for the application developer who references the page template on a page.

   ■ **Attributes**   Page templates are referenced by the application page or page fragment and know nothing about the context in which they are used. Template attributes are named variables that are Expression Language (EL) accessible when developing the template. They can be used in the value property of a input or output component, or referenced from any other property that can use EL. Use cases for attributes are a welcome message that displays the name of the user passed in from the consuming page and skinning, in which the `viewId` of the current page is used as a value of the `styleClass` property. The latter use case, setting the styleClass property of a UI component from a template attribute is further explained in Chapter 16. Template attributes show as properties in the JDeveloper property inspector.

■ **Model Parameters** If the ADFm page definition is created for the template, optional template developers may need to define binding parameters—for example, to pass URL parameters to the execution of a query.

NOTE
Page templates cannot extend other templates because template inheritance is not supported in Oracle JDeveloper 11g R1.

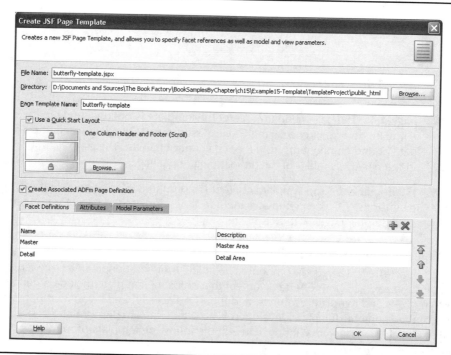

FIGURE 15-2 *Create JSF Page Template screen*

JSP Page vs. JSP Document

JSP pages are stored in files with a .jsp or .jspx extension. Files with .jsp extensions are referred to as JSP pages, whereas files with a .jspx extension are referred to as JSP documents. JSP documents were introduced by the JSP 1.2 standard and format the JSP page content using well-defined XML. Though both JSP pages and JSP documents are valid file formats in which to define JSF pages, JSP pages are harder to parse and change automatically, making application upgrade and migration mostly a manual task. When building new applications with the Oracle Fusion development stack, we recommend using the JSP document format.

Template Source and Metadata Files

Defining a page template in Oracle JDeveloper creates the following projects files:

- **page-template-metadata**   The pagetemplate-metadata.xml registration file is created in the project's src\META-INF directory the first time a page template is created in a project. The pagetemplate-metadata.xml file contains all templates that are defined in the project to display when creating new JSF pages based on a template.

```
<pageTemplateDefs
  xmlns="http://xmlns.oracle.com/adf/faces/rich/pagetemplate">
  <pagetemplate-jsp-ui-def>
    /butterfly-template.jspx
  </pagetemplate-jsp-ui-def>
</pageTemplateDefs>
```

- **pageDef**   The page definition file of the template is optional and created when the template developer checks the Create Associated ADFm Page Definition option or adds data bound components from the data control palette. The page definition file is created in the pageDefs folder of the project default package.

- **JSP document**   The template content is stored in a JSP document with a .jspx file extension. ADF page templates include XML formatted metadata and therefore cannot be stored in JSP pages with a .jsp extension.

Editing the Page Template File

The `af:pagetemplateDef` component is the JSF root component in a page template. It contains the `af:xmlContent` tag element that holds the template metadata definitions, such as custom facets and template attributes, and the ADF Faces UI and layout components that make the template content. Template developers who select the `af:pagetemplateDef` component in the JDeveloper Structure window can edit the following template properties in the Property Inspector:

Property	Description
Var	The var attribute defaults to attrs and is the EL reference to attributes defined in the page template. To reference a template attribute value from a UI component
	1. Select the UI component property that should read the attribute value.
	2. Click the arrow icon next to the property field and choose Expression Builder from the context menu.
	3. Expand the JSP Objects | attrs node to access the attributes defined in the template.
	The attributes that are accessible through the Var property value referenced include custom template attributes as well as standard attributes, such as partialTriggers, that are defined on the af:pageTemplate component that is used to reference the template in the template consumer page or page fragment.
Facet Definitions	The Facet Definitions tab panel in the Property Inspector allows developers to create, edit, and remove facets.
Attributes	The Attributes tab panel in the Property Inspector allows developers to create, edit, and remove template attributes. Template attributes are read upon initial rendering of the view that consumes the template and when partially refreshing the template reference. The attributes are not refreshed automatically when the value reference changes. Attributes are EL accessible within the page template source file through the var attribute value definition.
ComponentVar	The ComponentVar property value allows developers to obtain a Java handle to the page template instance from a managed bean at runtime. Assuming the ComponentVar value is defined as butterflyTemplateDef, then to access the template instance from Java, you can define the following method:

```
private RichPageTemplate getTemplateHandle(){
  FacesContext fctx = null;
  fctx = FacesContext.getCurrentInstance();
  ELContext elctx  = fctx.getELContext();
  Application app = fctx.getApplication();
  ExpressionFactory elFactory = null;
  elFactory = app.getExpressionFactory();
  ValueExpression valueExpr = null;
  valueExpr  = elFactory.createValueExpression(
          elctx,
          "#{butterflyTemplateDef}",
          Object.class);
  RichPageTemplate template =
    (RichPageTemplate) valueExpr.getValue(elctx);
}  return template;
```

The component variable allows template developers to search and access components contained in the template, facets created in the template area, and attributes.

Adding Facets to the Page Template

You use the af:facetRef component to add a defined facet to the template layout content. The af:facetRef provides an abstraction between the facet area and the template. Dragging the Facet Ref component entry from the JDeveloper component palette (CTRL-SHIFT-P) to the template page (Figure 15-3) displays a dialog box that lists all the available defined facets. A facet defined in a template can have only a single af:facetRef component reference to avoid naming conflicts.

Managed Beans

Page templates may reference managed beans, which can be configured in the standard faces-config.xml file or the adfc-config.xml file, if the ADF Page Flow technology scope is configured in the project. If there is a chance that a page template is added twice on a consumer page—for example, when the consumer page contains an ADF region that displays a page fragment with the same template reference—then if the template uses JSF component bindings to a managed bean, you should use the adfc-config.xml file to configure the managed bean and set the bean scope to backingBean. Using the backingBean scope isolates multiple instances of a managed bean on a page and avoids conflicts on the UI components referencing the bean. However, when following this recommendation, be aware that the project that references the page template must also have the ADF Page Flow technology scope configured as otherwise the required ADF Controller libraries are missing.

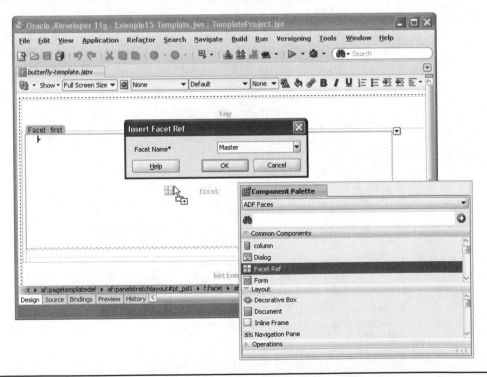

FIGURE 15-3   *Adding a Facet Ref from the component palette to the page*

NOTE
The ADF Controller scopes are explained in Chapter 4.

Deploying Page Templates

Page templates can be deployed in ADF libraries if they are created in a separate project, in which case they are not visible in the web application project. To deploy the template in an ADF library JAR, select the project node and choose Deploy | *<library name>* | to ADF Library Jar from the context menu. This creates the ADF library JAR in the deploy directory of the project containing the template.

Using Page Templates in an ADF Faces UI

Unlike the new Quick Start Layout, page templates are not added to the page source but referenced at design time and runtime. Page templates are added to the template consumer page as a whole and not in parts. As an application developer, you can add a UI component anywhere on a page before and after the template reference. Within the template, however, ADF Faces UI and layout components can be added only in designated areas that are the predefined template facets.

Importing Page Templates to a Project

Page templates can be created in the same project that uses them, or they can be imported from an ADF library JAR. To import a template from an ADF library JAR, do the following:

1. Select the project that contains the web project and open the Oracle JDeveloper resource palette.

2. In the resource palette, select the library entry for the template to import and choose Add to Project.

3. In the opened confirmation dialog, click the Add Library button to make the template available in the project.

NOTE
How to configure the resource palette to display ADF libraries for import is explained in the "ADF Library JAR" section earlier in the chapter.

Creating Template-based ADF Faces Pages

Page templates are applied to an ADF Faces page upon page creation or they can be manually configured into existing pages. The Create JSF Page dialog has a Page Template option in its Initial Page Layout and Content section that, when selected, lists all the templates accessible to the current project. Selecting a template adds an `af:pageTemplate` component to the page that referenced the template source file, similar to the following:

```
<af:pageTemplate viewId="/butterfly-template.jspx"
   value="#{bindings.pageTemplateBinding}" id="pt1">
  <f:facet name="Master"/>
  <f:facet name="Detail"/>
  <f:attribute name="Welcome" value="ADF Interactive"/>
</af:pageTemplate>
```

In the template reference, the template source file contains two facets, `Master` and `Detail`, as well as a template attribute `Welcome`. The facets show in the Oracle JDeveloper visual page editor as active areas for the application developer to add UI components. The `af:pageTemplate` `value` attribute references the ADF binding of the template, which is linked from the template consumer page's ADF page definition file.

NOTE
If the page template in the ADF library JAR contains an ADF region, this region is not rendered at design time. Instead, a placeholder region is shown that informs the developer that the ADF region cannot be rendered in design time but will be rendered at runtime. Chapter 6 explains the use of ADF regions.

How to Access the ADF Binding of a Page Template

If a page template contains ADF bound components, the ADF binding file of the page template is referenced from the ADF page definition file of the template consumer page or page fragment. Application developers can use this reference to access the template's ADF binding entry using Java or Expression Language.

NOTE
At runtime, ADF maintains a single bindings object. Pages that include external content that has its own ADF bindings defined, reference the associated PageDef file in their own binding definition. The binding content of the referenced PageDef files is initiated at runtime to become accessible to the referencing binding container. The included content could come from page templates or bounded task flows in an ADF region.

To illustrate this by an example that also contains additional programming hints, assume that a page template contains an ADF bound table that displays a list of employees. The view object that is referenced from the table has a named view criteria defined that allows filtering of the employee list. To set the named view criteria, a method binding is created in the page template PageDef file for an application to call.

NOTE
Named view criteria define dynamic where clauses for View Objects in ADF Business Components. They are explained in Chapter 1.

The search field shown in Figure 15-4 is not part of the template but belongs to the consuming view, View 1. The page definition file of View 1, Page Definition 1, has a reference to the page definition file of the template. Page Definition 2 exposes the method binding that applies the view criteria to the view object when invoked.

When creating an ADF Faces page based on a template that has its own ADF bindings, a `<page>` binding entry is implicitly added to the page definition file of the newly created page. The page binding, which is created in the executable section of the consumer page's PageDef file, points to the path of the template's ADF page definition file, as it is known by the DataBindings.cpx file. The template binding entry is uniquely identified by its `id` property value, which by default is set to `pageTemplateBinding`, as shown in Figure 15-5.

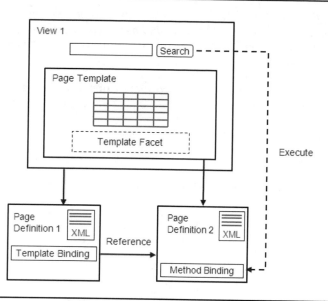

FIGURE 15-4 *Architecture diagram of the illustrated example*

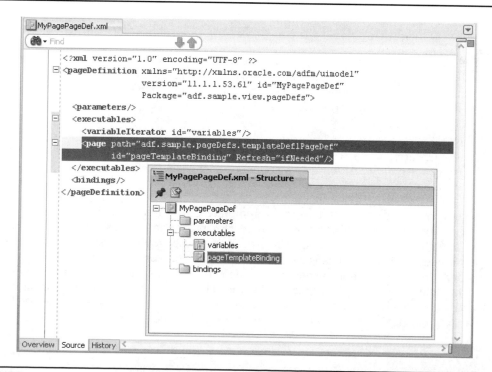

FIGURE 15-5 *ADF page definition file of the consumer view with page template binding reference*

> **NOTE**
> *Accessing the template ADF binding through its binding reference*
> *requires that you know about the ADF binding structure of the*
> *template page definition file, as it cannot be discovered at design time*
> *in Oracle JDeveloper.*

Accessing the Client Method from the Template Consumer Using EL   The method binding in the template definition is referenced in the consumer view page definition, as shown in Figure 15-5. To access the binding from an action listener property of a command button, the search button shown in Figure 15-4, you use the following expression syntax:

```
#{bindings.<template reference>.<method binding>.execute
```

Similarly, if you want to access an iterator binding, you use this:

```
#{bindings.<template reference>.<iterator binding>.<method>
```

To access a value binding from an input component, you would use this:

```
#{bindings.<template reference>.<attribute binding>.inputValue
```

To pass the search value to the method binding defined in the PageDef file of the page template, the search field component needs to be bound to a memory attribute that is also referenced by the input argument of the method binding in the template. For example:

```
#{requestScope.queryStr}
```

> **NOTE**
> *The method binding parameter reads the search string from a memory*
> *attribute, which creates a dependency that needs to be documented*
> *and communicated. In this case using a programmatic solution as*
> *shown next should be preferred.*

> **NOTE**
> *The EL cannot be created declaratively, because the Expression*
> *Language builder in Oracle JDeveloper does not resolve references to*
> *the template page definition.*

Accessing the Client Method from the Template Consumer Using Java   Though declarative programming is often preferable over code-centric programming, in some cases, you'll need to call a method binding referenced from Java. For example, you may need to perform pre- and post-processing before invoking the method action. In this case, the command button action property invokes an action method in a managed bean. The same bean has a JSF binding to the search field component to read the provided search string. Note that this approach avoids the need for using a shared requestScope attribute to pass the search value to the method binding, which is less error prone and does not require extra documentation.

```
public String search_action() {
    //get access to the current ADF binding container
    BindingContext bctx = BindingContext.getCurrent();
```

```
    DCBindingContainer bindings = null;
    bindings = (DCBindingContainer) bctx.getCurrentBindingsEntry();
    //access the template binding container by its <page> binding
    //reference with the default id of "pageTemplateBinding"
    DCBindingContainer templateBinding =
      (DCBindingContainer) bindings.get("pageTemplateBinding");
    //access the exposed View Criteria method
    OperationBinding queryMethod =
        (OperationBinding)
 templateBinding.get("qryEmployeesByNameSearch");
    //set the parameter to the value read from the search UI input
    //component
    queryMethod.getParamsMap().put("searchString",srchField.getValue());
    //execute the query
    queryMethod.execute();
    return null;
  }
```

Strategies to Partial Page Refresh Child Components in a Page Template

The search button shown in Figure 15-4 has its `partialSubmit` attribute set to `true` to avoid a full page refresh. To show the query result, the table that is contained in the page template needs to be refreshed. This refresh can be configured declaratively or programmatically invoked.

Declarative   Setting the `partialTriggers` property on the `af:pageTemplate` component to the command button `id` attribute value does not refresh the employees table contained in the template. To achieve this, the value of the `partialTriggers` attribute of the `af:pageTemplate` must become available on the `af:table` component's `partialTriggers` attribute, so the table itself gets refreshed when the button is pressed. As explained earlier, all attributes passed to the template are EL accessible through the `var` attribute on the `af:pageTemplateDef` component. The default value of this attribute is `attrs`. To reference the `partialTriggers` attribute value of the `af:pageTemplate` from the table, you use the following expression:

```
<af:table …
   partialTriggers="#{attrs.partialTriggers}">
   …
</af:table>
```

The `af:pageTemplate` component in the page or page fragment references the search button `id`, which can be done declaratively using the Edit content menu option on the `partialTriggers` attribute:

```
<af:pageTemplate viewId="/templateDef1.jspx"
   value="#{bindings.pageTemplateBinding}" id-"pt1"
   partialTriggers="::cb2">
   <f:facet name="MAIN"/>
</af:pageTemplate>
```

Programmatically   Components that are contained in a template are read-only for the page or page fragment that references the template. To partially refresh a child component of the template in Java, you access the component instance by its `id` attribute value and add it to the `AdfFacesContext` list of partial targets.

UI components that are contained in a template become a part of the sever-side JSF component tree at runtime. The component tree is searchable from its view root to access a specific component instance. To ensure that the `id` value of a component in a template is unique when added to the JSF component tree, the page template is designed to be a naming container. Naming containers are name spaces in which naming must be chosen uniquely.

At runtime, the `id` of the naming container, which is chosen to be unique in the view to which the page template it is added, becomes the name prefix of the component `id` value. A component that is located in a naming container thus always has an `id` value of `<naming container id>:<component id value>`. If you use this approach, any component that is part of a template can be uniquely addressed. Even if the same template is added twice—for example, through an ADF region referencing a view that is built based on the same template—the component is uniquely addressable in the component tree and thus partially refreshable. The following method takes two arguments: the naming container `id`, which is the `id` value of the `af:pageTemplate` component, and the component `id`.

```
private void pprTemplateTable(String templateId, String componentId){
  FacesContext fctx = FacesContext.getCurrentInstance();
  //get the view root as the start for the component search
  UIViewRoot root = fctx.getViewRoot();
  //find table component on the page
  UIComponent tableComponent =
    root.findComponent(templateId+":"+componentId);
  //partially refresh the table
  AdfFacesContext.getCurrentInstance().addPartialTarget(tableComponent);
}
```

A disadvantage of the programmatic approach is that the application developer must know about the UI component `id` attribute value. This might not be easy if the template is deployed in an ADF library JAR. The advantage of this solution is that it can refresh any component.

NOTE
Finding a child component in a page template is the same as finding components in declarative components. The approach explained here can therefore be used with declarative components as well, in which case the declarative component and not the page template represents the naming container.

How to Partially Refresh Content on the consumer Page from Content in the Template

Although a page template does not expose its read-only component areas for direct access, it allows developers to use the Expression Builder in Oracle JDeveloper to register components on the page as the partial trigger event receiver of components contained in the template. Configuring a component to get partially refreshed in response to a component event of a component in a template is therefore a purely declarative programming task.

How to Dynamically Change Templates at Runtime

The page template referenced by an ADF Faces page can be dynamically determined at runtime using EL. For example, the `af:pageTemplate` component in the following page code snippet checks a session scope attribute for the page template to use with a page. If the session attribute doesn't exist, it falls back to its default template reference.

```
<af:pageTemplate
    viewId="#{sessionScope.viewId==null?'/butterfly-template.jspx' :
            sessionScope.viewId}"
        id="pt1">
<f:facet name="Master">
  ...
</f:facet>
<f:facet name="Detail">
  ...
</f:facet>
</af:pageTemplate>
```

While switching the page template reference at runtime allows developers to change the layout of an application page per user demand, it requires some precaution:

- The names and number of facets and facet references in the page templates must be identical and match the facet names used in the consuming ADF Faces page.

- If page templates use their own ADF binding container, both templates must use the same binding definition. Changing the referenced page template dynamically is all about changing the page layout, not about changing the page's referenced data content.

- The EL expression added to the `af:pageTemplate` component `viewId` attribute is not resolved at design time. During ADF Faces page development, the page template reference must be set as a static string.

ADF Faces Declarative Components

A benefit of the JSF platform is that it lets the application developer write and seamlessly integrate his or her own UI components. Often, the motivation for developers to write a custom component is not to add functionality but to create a composite of existing components. For example, application developers could build declarative components for specific layouts they need in an application. So in addition to the use of page templates, declarative components can be used to provide pre-defined layouts for specific content areas on a page or page fragments.

Another, more functional example, is a generic toolbar that is build out of a toolbar panel, `af:toolBar`, and several instances of the toolbar button component, `af:commandToolbarButton`. Application developers could use this custom made toolbar to add standard navigation and Data Manipulation Language (DML) functionality to tables and forms without coding it. To simplify the task of building new composite ADF Faces Rich Client (RC) components, Oracle JDeveloper 11*g* provides the declarative component feature, which is a declarative approach for developers to build custom components by reusing existing UI components.

Two types of declarative components exist in ADF Faces:

- **Declarative component** A standard JSF component that is built from exiting ADF Faces components and that is deployed in an ADF library JAR. Declarative components are added to a page or page fragment at design time using JSP Tag Library Definition (TLD). TLD based declarative components are good to use for components that you plan to reusable within many applications.

■ **Dynamic declarative component**   Declarative components that are defined and contained within a web project. Dynamic declarative components don't use TLD tags but are directly referenced from a page or page fragment. Dynamic declarative components are good to use for custom components, like reusable layout definitions, that are reused within the scope of the application they are built in only.

Declarative Components

Declarative components reduce the overhead for developers who need to build a custom component out of existing JSF components. Developers build declarative components visually in Oracle JDeveloper 11*g* as if building a new ADF Faces RC page or template. The new component is deployed in an ADF library JAR after development. The component is defined in a JSP TLD, which is why we also refer to them as TLD-based declarative components.

Here we explain the declarative component creation and handling by example of a generic toolbar to navigate and manipulate an ADF iterator binding. The ADF iterator binding reference used by the declarative component is provided in a component attribute by the application developer using EL.

NOTE
For better clarity, we distinguish between component developers and application developers. Component developers build and provide reusable JSF components that application developers use in their Fusion development projects.

Creating a Declarative Component Project

We consider it a best practice to develop declarative components in their own Oracle JDeveloper project within a separate Oracle JDeveloper workspace to separate application development from component development. To create a new project in Oracle JDeveloper 11*g*, choose File | New | General | Projects and choose the Generic Project entry. The declarative component project needs to have the ADF Faces and the ADF Page Flow technology scope set, which can be selected either during or after project creation in the project properties. Oracle ADF runtime libraries are needed only if binding specific classes are used in the declarative component and can be added later.

Creating a New Declarative Component

To create a new Declarative Component, choose File | New | Web Tier | JSF and choose the JSF Declarative Component entry. In the Create JSF Declarative Component dialog, provide the following information:

Field	Value Example	Description
Declarative Component Name	`InteractiveToolbar`	The name of the component to build.
File Name	InteractiveToolbar.jspx	The source file of the new JSF component. By default, the source filename is the same as the component name.
Directory	Path to public_html directory	

Declarative Component Package	`adf.interactive.comp`	Default package structure for the created Java sources used by the declarative component. This includes managed beans.
Declarative Component Tag Library		Created after completing the Create Declarative Component Library dialog, which opens when you click the Add Tag Library button. See "Creating the Declarative Component Tag Library."
Use Custom Component Class	`InteractiveToolbar`	The custom component class is optional and allows component developers to override methods inherited from parent classes such as `UIXComponentBase` and `UIComponent`.
Facet Definitions		Facets allow application developers to add other UI components to the custom component. See "Creating Facet Definitions."
Attributes	`ShowLabels`	Attributes show as component properties in the JDeveloper property inspector. See "Creating Attributes."
Methods	`ActionEventListener`	Provides an option for the Declarative Component to call out to the consuming page. See "Creating Methods."

NOTE
Attribute and method definitions can also be added later during component development.

Creating the Declarative Component Tag Library   Declarative components are deployed in ADF libraries with the component name and attributes defined in the library TLD file. The tag library and the TLD file are created during deployment into an ADF library JAR from the declarativecomp-metadata.xml metadata file, located in the component project's src\META-INF directory on the file system. In Oracle JDeveloper 11*g*, the component metadata file is displayed in the Application Sources | META-INF folder of Application Navigator (CTRL-SHIFT-A) view. The declarativecomp-metadata.xml is declaratively created by the component developer in the Create JSF Declarative Component dialog by clicking the Add Tag Library button. In the Create Declarative Component Tag Library dialog (Figure 15-6), the component developer provides the library name, a URI that uniquely

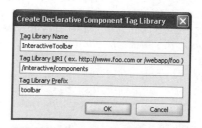

FIGURE 15-6   *Create Declarative Component tag library dialog*

identifies the tag library on a JSF page, and the tag library prefix, which the application developer uses to reference the contained JSF tag elements.

A tag library may contain multiple ADF declarative components. Each component in the library is configured by its defined component name, the generated tag class, and a list of default and custom attributes. Following are the default component attributes:

- **ID** The component unique instance reference ID on a page. The field value is either provided by the application developer or added by the JSF framework.

- **Rendered** A Boolean attribute that is used by the application developer to determine whether a component should be rendered or not. A component that is not rendered physically doesn't exist as an object in the JSF page, which is slightly different from a component that is not displayed. The default value of this attribute is `true`.

- **Binding** The JSF binding to a setter and getter pair in a managed or backing bean.

Custom attributes are created for each attribute and method that the component developer defines in the Create JSF Declarative Component dialog or later at design time in the Oracle JDeveloper Property Inspector (CTRL-SHIFT-I). All custom attributes of a Declarative Component show as component properties in the Property Inspector after adding the component to a web project.

Creating Facet Definitions In JSF, two strategies can be used by the application developer to add other JSF components: children and facets. A child component is added to the component body, which means that the parent component builds a container for the added component. The `af:table` component, for example, can have one to many `af:column` components as a child. At runtime, the parent component ensures that the child component is rendered properly by including the child rendering into its own component rendering lifecycle. A good example of a component that doesn't accept children but uses facets to layout components added by the application developer is `af:panelSplitter`. The `panelSplitter` component has two visual areas that are separated by the splitter control. It is not responsible for the rendering of the added components.

Declarative components allow component developers to define facets for the application developer to customize the component. In the generic toolbar example, a facet is used to enable application developers to add their own buttons on a page. To create a facet when creating a declarative component, select the Facet Definitions tab in the Create JSF Declarative Component dialog and click the green plus icon. Add a name for the facet and an optional description. No restrictions exist for the number of facets added to a declarative component.

NOTE
Facets, attributes, and methods can also be created declaratively in the declarative component design time. For this, select the declarative component's .jspx file in the Application Navigator of Oracle JDeveloper 11g and open the Structure window. In the Structure window, select the `af:componentDef` *entry and open the Property Inspector if it's not already open. The Property Inspector shows "Facet Definitions, Attributes and Methods tabs that you use to create additional configurations or modify existing ones.*

Creating Attributes Attributes are created similarly to facets. To create a new custom attribute when creating a declarative component, select the Attributes tab in the Create JSF Declarative Component dialog and click the green plus icon. Provide the following information:

- **Name**   A string value that is later shown as the component property name in the Oracle JDeveloper Property Inspector, and referenced within the component as `#{attrs.<name>}`. See "Building the Declarative Component UI."

- **Type**   The data type of the value added to the component. The default value is `java.lang.String`, which can be changed by typing in the package and name of another object class or using the class browser that is launched with the ellipses (…) button next to the Type field.

- **Default Value**   The attribute's value if no value is provided by the application developer. Good design dictates that you should provide smart defaults as much as possible. In the toolbar example, the `ShowLabels` attribute defaults to `false`.

- **Required**   Indicates a mandatory component property. For example, the generic toolbar must have an iterator binding configured to work properly. Setting the required attribute ensures that Oracle JDeveloper shows a configuration dialog when the component is added to a page.

There is no restriction regarding the number of attributes that can be added to a declarative component. For a description of how to create attributes at component design time, see "Creating Facet Definitions."

Attributes represent value expressions and are used on a declarative component to allow application developers to provide data input to the component. For example, in the generic toolbar example, the `ShowLabels` attribute is used for the application developer to define whether or not the labels should be shown next to the buttons in the toolbar.

Creating Methods   Declarative component methods are special cases of attribute definitions and expect the application user to provide method expression references, like a reference to an action listener method, as the value.

In JSF, components raise events to notify the application of a change or user interaction. Declarative components in Oracle JDeveloper 11*g* allow the component developer to raise component events for the consuming page to handle. A method attribute has a return type and optional arguments that are passed with the event. On the consuming page, Expression Language is used to bind the component method property to a managed bean method with the expected signature. In the toolbar example used in this chapter, an action event is passed to the page whenever a button is clicked. Application developers would configure an action listener in a managed bean to handle the event.

Method attributes can also be referenced from command component in the declarative component. For example, if a declarative component contains a button that, when pressed, should execute a method on the ADF binding or a managed bean of the consuming page, then a method attribute can be used. In this case the command component in the declarative component references the method attribute in its `ActionListener` property. When adding the declarative component to a page, the application developer configures an EL reference to the event handler as the value of the method attribute similar to that shown next:

```
<toolbar:InteractiveToolbar
    id="it5"
    CommitEventListener="#{bindings.Commit.execute}"
    ...
    ShowNavigationItems="true"/>
```

In the example code above, a `CommitEventListener` method attribute is assumed to be referenced from a button on the custom toolbar. The attribute value provided by the application developer references the `Commit` operation binding that he or she created in the ADF binding of the consuming page.

Methods are created similarly to facets. To create a new custom method when creating a declarative component, select the Methods tab in the Create JSF Declarative Component dialog and click the green plus icon. Provide the following information:

- **Name**   The name of the property as it appears in the Property Inspector for this component.

- **Method Signature**   A return value, if any, and the argument types. In the toolbar example, the `ActionEventListener` method dispatches command button action events to the consuming page and therefore has a signature defined as `void method(javax.faces.event.ActionEvent)` (see Figure 15-7). To configure the method argument types, click the ... button next to the Method Signature value field. Other possible event types include `javax.faces.event.ValueChangeEvent` for application developers to respond to value change events raised in a declarative component, or ADF Faces component specific events, like the `QueryEvent` that is raised by the `af:table` component. ADF Faces component events are defined in the `oracle.adf.view.rich.event` package.

- **Required**   Indicates a mandatory component property. Setting the required attribute ensures that Oracle JDeveloper shows a configuration dialog when the component is added to a page.

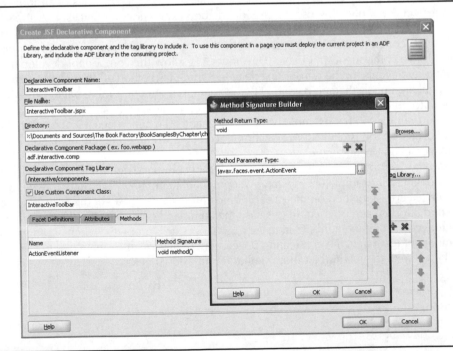

FIGURE 15-7   *Defining the signature of a declarative component method*

There is no restriction regarding the number of attributes that can be added to a declarative component. For a description of how to create attributes at component design time, see "Creating Facet Definitions."

Building the Declarative Component UI

Finishing the Create JSF Declarative Component dialog, the required metadata artifacts are created by Oracle JDeveloper and the declarative component design time opens in the visual editor. To re-open the component design time after closing the visual editor, double-click the component .jspx file in the Application Navigator.

The UI design of a declarative component is comparable to the design of an ADF Faces RC page. The developer has a visual, source code, and structured view of the component being built. All three editors are synchronized, as you would expect from Oracle JDeveloper. The component palette shows the configured tag libraries, to drag ADF Faces components into the declarative component UI. The Oracle JDeveloper Property Inspector, shown in Figure 15-8, shows the defined properties for the selected UI component. Selecting the declarative component as a whole shows the defined custom attributes, methods, and facet entries. In addition, the following two variables exist for a declarative component:

Name	Default Value	Description
ComponentVar	component	The component variable is a handle to the declarative component instance and is used, for example in a managed bean or in EL, to access the component. The toolbar sample used in this chapter has a custom method property `ActionEventListener` defined, which can be accessed using the following EL expression: `#{component.handleActionEventListener}` Developers are free to choose their own value for this property.
Var	attrs	All custom attributes that are defined on the declarative component are accessible from EL. A custom attribute in the toolbar sample is `ShowNavigationItems`, with a default value set to `true`, to show or hide the navigation toolbar buttons. This attribute is referenced from the `Rendered` property of all navigation buttons in the menu bar using an EL expression such as this: `#{attrs.ShowNavigationItems }` If the `component` attribute is set to `true`, the button is shown; if not. the button is hidden.

HINT

The `component` *and* `attrs` *variables are exposed in the Expression Language builder that you can open from the context menu in the Property Inspector. Expand the JSP Objects node to access the variables and their exposed functionality.*

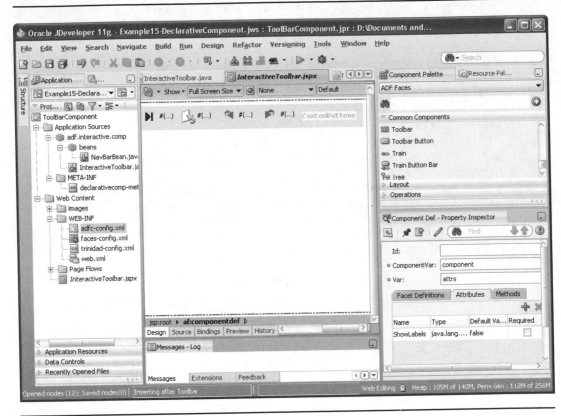

FIGURE 15-8 *Declarative component visual design time*

Creating Managed Beans

Component-specific code is added in managed beans. Depending on how the declarative component project is set up, the managed bean is created in the standard faces-config.xml file, or the adfc-config.xml file if the Oracle controller is added as a project library. Upon deployment, the configuration file is added to the META-INF directory of the ADF library JAR file. At runtime, the configuration file is automatically added to the configuration of the consuming application. Though both configuration files, faces-config.xml and the adfc-config.xml, are good to use, we recommend the adfc-config.xml file because of its "backing bean scope."

The backing bean scope has the same lifetime as the request scope but restricts the access scope of a managed bean to the instance of a declarative component, which is important if multiple instances of a declarative component co-exist on a single ADF Faces page. The JSF standard does not support this degree of isolation, limiting declarative components usage to one instance per page. To create a managed bean in a declarative component using the ADF Controller, you have a choice:

- Create a Java class to become the managed bean and open the adfc-config.xml file. In the adfc-config.xml overview editor, select the Managed Beans entry and click the green plus icon to create a new managed bean entry. Provide a managed bean name that will

be used in EL expressions and browse for the name of the created Java class. Set the
Scope property to backingBean.

■ Select the component for which you want to create a managed bean binding and
select the property for which you want to create the binding. In the toolbar sample, for
example, a managed bean method is created for the `ActionListener` property. At the
end of the property field is a control with an arrow icon pointing down. Click the icon
and choose Edit from the context menu to launch the managed bean creation dialog. This
creates the bean and the JSF binding, and sets the EL to reference the managed bean to
the property.

NOTE
*Declarative components that make use of the backingBean scope
depend on the ADF controller libraries. If a declarative component is
added to a web project that does not have the ADF controller libraries
configured, then the backingBean scope becomes unavailable and an
EL exception is thrown at runtime.*

The managed bean of the toolbar sample contains methods to handle the action event for each
of the command items displayed on the menu bar. The assumption we make is that the business
service used with the toolbar is ADF Business Components:

```
//navigate to previous record if exists
public void prevRecord_action(ActionEvent evt) {
  DCIteratorBinding iter = getIteratorBinding();
  if(iter.getViewObject().hasPrevious()){
    iter.getViewObject().previous();
  }
  //notify consumer about event
  invokeActionListenerExpression(evt);
}
//create a new record in this collection
public void newRecord_action(ActionEvent evt) {
  //access the ADF iterator binding that is provided
  //in an attribute value of the Declarative Component
  DCIteratorBinding iter = getIteratorBinding();
  Row rw = iter.getNavigatableRowIterator().createRow();
  rw.setNewRowState(Row.STATUS_INITIALIZED);
  iter.getNavigatableRowIterator().insertRow(rw);
  //notify consumer about event
  invokeActionListenerExpression(evt);
}
//delete the current selected row
public void deleteRecord_action(ActionEvent evt) {
  DCIteratorBinding iter = getIteratorBinding();
  iter.removeCurrentRow();
  //notify consumer about event
  invokeActionListenerExpression(evt);
}
```

```
//navigate to the next row in the collection
public void nextRow_action(ActionEvent evt) {
  DCIteratorBinding iter = getIteratorBinding();
  if(iter.getViewObject().hasNext()){
    iter.getViewObject().next();
  }
  //notify consumer about event
  invokeActionListenerExpression(evt);
}
//commit changes
public void commit_action(ActionEvent evt) {
  DCIteratorBinding iter = getIteratorBinding();
  ApplicationModule am = null;
  am = iter.getDataControl().getApplicationModule();
  am.getTransaction().commit();
  //notify consumer about event
  invokeActionListenerExpression(evt);
}
//rollback uncommitted changes in the transaction
public void rollback_action(ActionEvent evt) {
  DCIteratorBinding iter = getIteratorBinding();
  ApplicationModule am = null;
  am = iter.getDataControl().getApplicationModule();
  am.getTransaction().rollback();
  //notify consumer about event
  invokeActionListenerExpression(evt);
}
public void undo_action(ActionEvent evt) {
  DCIteratorBinding iter = getIteratorBinding();
  iter.getCurrentRow().refresh(Row.REFRESH_FORGET_NEW_ROWS |
                               Row.REFRESH_WITH_DB_FORGET_CHANGES);
  //notify consumer about event
  invokeActionListenerExpression(evt);
}
//navigate to the last row in the collection
public void last_action(ActionEvent evt) {
  DCIteratorBinding iter = getIteratorBinding();
  Key rowKey = iter.getNavigatableRowIterator().last().getKey();
  iter.setCurrentRowWithKey(rowKey.toStringFormat(true));
  //notify consumer about event
  invokeActionListenerExpression(evt);
}
//navigate to the first row in the collection
public void first_action(ActionEvent evt) {
  DCIteratorBinding iter = getIteratorBinding();
  Key rowKey = iter.getNavigatableRowIterator().first().getKey();
  iter.setCurrentRowWithKey(rowKey.toStringFormat(true));
  //notify consumer about event
  invokeActionListenerExpression(evt);
}
```

The declarative component managed bean methods handle the toolbar first record, previous record, last record, next record, insert, delete, undo, commit, and rollback operations. The ADF iterator binding on which the code executes is provided in an attribute of the declarative component.

NOTE
`getIteratorBinding()` and `invokeActionListenerExpression()` are private helper methods in the component that obtain a reference to the iterator binding and notify a registered `ActionListener` on the consuming page about the toolbar button action. Both methods are explained later in this chapter.

Deploying Declarative Components

Declarative components are deployed in an ADF library JAR files. You create the ADF library JAR for the project that contains the declarative component. Once the library deployment profile is created, you choose Deploy from the project node context menu to generate the ADF library JAR file.

Working with Declarative Components in Web Projects

To use a declarative component within a web project, import the ADF library JAR file that contains the component and open the Oracle JDeveloper Component Palette. The declarative component is listed in its own component panel with its name. Drag the declarative component from the JDeveloper Component Palette to the page. If the component has mandatory attributes defined, a dialog is shown for the application developer to provide the attribute values.

The declarative component is added to the page with its tag element. The tag library is automatically registered in the page header. The declarative component attributes are configurable in the page source editor or declaratively in the Property Inspector (Figure 15-9).

The toolbar example used here exposes custom attributes to show or hide each button, a mandatory attribute for the iterator reference on which the declarative component operates, and an action method to invoke a managed bean method on the consumer project.

Importing Declarative Components to a Web Project   If it's not already open, open the JDeveloper resource palette and expand the IDE Connections section. With the web project node selected, choose the ADF library JAR file entry that contains the declarative component in the resource palette and select Add To Project from the context menu. In the Confirm Add ADF Library JAR dialog, click the Add Library button. This adds the ADF library JAR to the web project and exposes the contained declarative component in the Oracle JDeveloper component palette.

NOTE
To remove an ADF library JAR from a project, select the ADF Library JAR file in the resource palette and choose Remove From Project from the context menu.

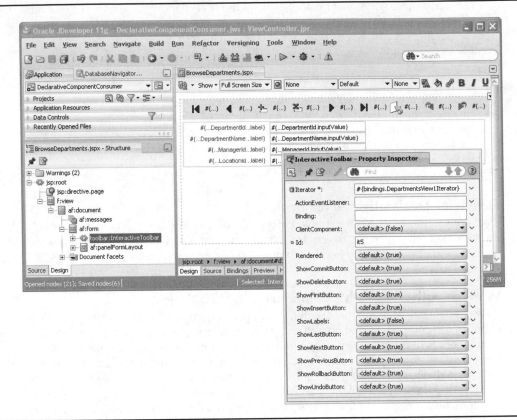

FIGURE 15-9 *Declarative toolbar component with its attribute exposed in the Property Inspector*

Notifying Consuming Pages of Component Events   Declarative components use method attributes to propagate component events to the consuming page. The toolbar declarative component example defines a method attribute `ActionEventListener` as shown here:

```
<method-attribute>
  <attribute-name>ActionEventListener</attribute-name>
  <method-signature>
     void method(javax.faces.event.ActionEvent)
  </method-signature>
</method-attribute>
```

The consuming page configures event listener methods on the declarative component instance to handle the component call. In our toolbar example, the private method `invokeActionListenerExpression` is called from the action event methods executed by the toolbar buttons. The `invokeActionListenerExpression` method uses EL to get a handle to the `ActionEventListener` method attribute that is exposed as a property to the consuming page:

```
private void invokeActionListenerExpression(ActionEvent evt){
   FacesContext fctx = FacesContext.getCurrentInstance();
   ELContext elctx  = fctx.getELContext();
   ExpressionFactory elFactory =
     fctx.getApplication().getExpressionFactory();
   //create a method expression for the component method attribute
   MethodExpression mexpr = elFactory.createMethodExpression (
                            elctx,
                            "#{component.handleActionEventListener}",
                            null,new Class[]{ActionEvent.class});
   //invoke the method and add the ActionEvent instance as an argument
   mexpr.invoke(elctx, new Object[]{evt});
}
```

NOTE
The "handle" in handleActionEventListener *is implicitly added by the ADF Faces framework.*

Referencing a Declarative Component Instance from a Managed Bean   Like any JSF component, the declarative component has a binding attribute that can be bound to a pair of setter and getter methods in a managed bean. This allows developers to programmatically access properties exposed on the declarative component. The method signature for the setter and getter methods looks similar to the following:

```
public void setToolbar(RichDeclarativeComponent toolbar) {
   this.toolbar = toolbar;
}
public RichDeclarativeComponent getToolbar() {
   return toolbar;
}
```

NOTE
Instead of using the RichDeclarativeComponent *class, you can use the optional custom component class you created for the declarative component.*

Using Multiple Instances of a Declarative Component   Multiple instances of a declarative component may be added to a single page. For this to work, the component developer must ensure component state isolation, which means that either no managed bean is used by a component instance or the bean is limited to backing bean scope.

Accessing ADF Bindings in Declarative Components

Declarative components cannot have ADF bindings of their own. To work with the ADF binding layer, you use a custom attribute on the declarative component to pass the binding reference in from the consumer page. The toolbar component example has an Iterator attribute defined as a child element of the af:xmlContent element in the component definition, which application developers use to reference the ADF iterator binding on which toolbar should operate.

```
<attribute>
   <attribute-name>Iterator</attribute-name>
   <attribute-class>
```

```
        oracle.adf.model.binding.DCIteratorBinding
    </attribute-class>
    <required>true</required>
</attribute>
```

The iterator binding is accessed by the declarative component managed bean as shown next:

```
private DCIteratorBinding getIteratorBinding(){
    FacesContext fctx = FacesContext.getCurrentInstance();
    ELContext elctx  = fctx.getELContext();
    Application app = fctx.getApplication();
    ExpressionFactory elFactory = app.getExpressionFactory();
    //get access to the component instance from within the declarative
    //component itself
    ValueExpression valueExpr =

 elFactory.createValueExpression(elctx,"#{component}",Object.class);
RichDeclarativeComponent _this = null;
 _this = (RichDeclarativeComponent ) valueExpr.getValue(elctx);
    //Access the Iterator attribute
    return (DCIteratorBinding)_this.getAttributes().get("Iterator");
}
```

> **NOTE**
> *The "component" object name used in* #{component} *references the declarative component by the value specified for its* componentVar *variable. The default value of this variable is* component.

Accessing Child Components in Facets

A custom component can have facets defined that are referenced by a facetRef element for the application developer to add child components. The toolbar example in this chapter has a facet CustomButtons to allow application developers to add more buttons. To access the content of a custom facet from Java, developers use the getFacet or getFacets method that is exposed on the UIComponent base class of the declarative component:

```
private List<UIComponent> getCustomAddedButtons(){
    FacesContext fctx = FacesContext.getCurrentInstance();
    ELContext elctx  = fctx.getELContext();
    Application app = fctx.getApplication();
    ExpressionFactory elFactory = app.getExpressionFactory();
    ValueExpression valueExpr =

 elFactory.createValueExpression(elctx,"#{component}",Object.class);
    RichDeclarativeComponent _this =  null;
    _this = (RichDeclarativeComponent ) valueExpr.getValue(elctx);
    UIComponent buttonFacet = _this.getFacet("CustomButtons");
    return buttonFacet.getChildren();
}
```

Refreshing Components on the Declarative Component Consumer View

In the toolbar example, the declarative component performs actions on the ADF iterator. To refresh UI components on the parent page or page fragment in response to a toolbar button action, you use PPR.

The declarative component can be configured as a partial trigger for other components on the same page or page fragment. To do this, the component that should be partially refreshed in response to an event on the declarative component references the declarative component `id` attribute or the `id` attribute of a child UI component in the declarative component value's `partialTriggers` attribute.

To set this up, select the UI component that should be refreshed in response to a partial update event and browse for its `PartialTriggers` property, which represents the `partialTriggers` attribute in the Property Inspector. Click the arrow icon and choose Edit. In the open dialog, browse to the declarative component entry in the view and move the entry to the list of selected components.

The declarative component sends a partial update event in response to any JSF event, such as action or value changes, that is raised by one of its child components.

Components that should be refreshed upon a specific UI component event in the declarative component can also directly register to a child UI component. To do this, use the same steps for the UI refresh explained in the preceding paragraph, but expand the declarative component node to select a child component, as shown in Figure 15-10.

NOTE

Configuring a component within a declarative component as a partial trigger breaks encapsulation in that the application developer needs to know about the functionality of the contained UI components. However, there is no other declarative option available to ensure a partial update is triggered by a specific component in a declarative component.

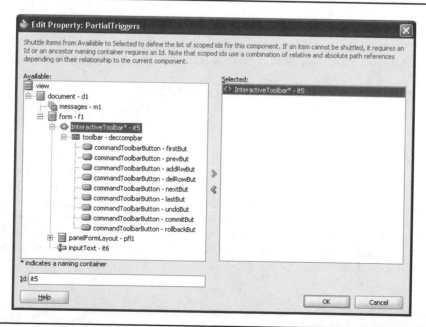

FIGURE 15-10 *Selecting a child component in a declarative component to partially refresh a component on the page*

Building a Toolbar Just for a Consistent Look and Feel

The generic toolbar example in this chapter is an advanced implementation and uses Java to access the value attribute that holds the information about the ADF iterator binding and to invoke an action on the component method attribute. A simple version of a toolbar could be created purely declarative with no Java involved. In this case, you would delegate providing the toolbar button action to the application developer. The toolbar is created as explained in this chapter, but for each toolbar button, the declarative component developer creates a method attribute, like nextAction, previousAction, createAction, deleteAction, commitAction etc. The method expressions are then referenced from the toolbar button `ActionListener` property using Expression Language. Opening the Method Expression Builder from the JDeveloper Property Inspector, all method attributes are listed under JSP Objects | component. Component developers would associate a method attribute with each button in the component palette. The application developer who uses the declarative component on a page, provides the action bindings for the method attributes, which display as component properties in the Property Inspector. For example, to provide an action binding for the createAction method property using ADF, he or she would do as follows.

1. In the PageDef file of the consuming page, create an ADF action binding for the `CreateInsert` operation of the View Object used with the form or table to use the toolbar with.

2. Manually or declaratively add the following EL as a value to the createAction property #{bindings.CreateInsert.execute}

This purely declarative approach uses the declarative component to create a consistent layout for toolbars used in an application. It requires the application developer to provide the toolbar button functionality.

Both, the generic toolbar that has the button functionality implemented in Java and the toolbar that delegates its functional implementation to the application developer are good use cases of how to use and build declarative components in Oracle JDeveloper.

Dynamic Declarative Components

Dynamic declarative components (DDC) in Oracle JDeveloper 11g R1 are lightweight versions of the declarative components we've been discussing. They can be used to create reusable components within a web project without the need to define and deploy a tag library.

DDCs are developed in a page fragments and are referenced at runtime by a page or page fragment using the `<af:declarativeComponent\>` tag. DDCs are fully integrated in the ADF Faces partial page refresh event notification architecture and can trigger partial updates on other ADF Faces components and also receive partial update notification itself. If the DDC is referenced as a partial trigger by a component, a partial event is published in response to events raised by any of child components that are contained in the DDC. You build dynamic declarative components instead of tag library based declarative components, if component reuse is required only within the application that has the component defined.

NOTE
DDC is a brand new feature in the most recent Oracle JDeveloper 11g production version. While there is good runtime support in ADF Faces for this feature, the design time experience is a manual configuration in the Oracle JDeveloper page source editor.

Dynamic Declarative Components vs. Declarative Components

The TLD-based declarative component is packaged and deployed in an ADF library JAR for reuse from the Oracle JDeveloper resource palette. TLD-based declarative components can be used outside of the project in which they are defined and are listed in the Oracle JDeveloper Component Palette for visual development. DDCs exist only in the context of the project in which they are defined and cannot be used outside. They cannot have method attributes defined, which would allow the component to invoke event listeners on the parent page. ADF Faces UI components that are contained in a DDC are visible to the parent page or page fragment, which means that the stretch behavior of an `af:panelStretchLayout`, or similar components, and the alignment in an `af:panelFormLayout` component, are correctly applied. This is not possible using the TLD-based declarative component, which is seen as a single component by the ADF Faces layout management. DDC therefore make lots of sense to be used for building application specific reusable layouts.

NOTE
Chapter 17 discusses layouts and geometry management in ADF Faces RC.

Dynamic Declarative Components vs. jsp:includes

Both DDCs and page fragments, which are added to a page using the `jsp:include` tag, cannot have their own ADF page bindings when referenced from a parent page or page fragment. Instead, the parent view's page definition file is expected to contain possible bindings required by the fragment. The benefit of using the new DDC feature is that component attributes can be used to pass ADF binding references from the parent view to the component, thus ensuring loose coupling between the parent view and its included content. Another argument against the use of `jsp:include` tags is a look ahead to what is coming in the JSF 2.0 standard. In JSF 2.0, the file format for JSF pages are Facelets, which is an open source XML rendering technique. Facelets does not support the `jsp:include` tag, causing additional migration work that can be avoided using DDCs.

DDC vs. ADF Regions

ADF regions, as explained in Chapter 6, display JSF page fragments in the context of bounded task flow. Using ADF regions is a superior solution compared to DDCs in that it allows isolated transaction handling, in-place navigation, ADF binding definitions for the page fragments, deployment in ADF libraries, reuse from the JDeveloper resource palette, and more. However, ADF regions come with the overhead of a bounded task flow and the task flow binding reference, which may not be the right choice to use for simple use cases like a reusable toolbar that operates on a single instance of `DCIteratorBinding`. So compared to ADF regions, DDC is a better choice if the included reusable content does not require its own bindings or transaction.

af:declarativeComponent Tag

The `af:declarativeComponent` tag element defines the DDC in a .jsff page fragment without the need of a TLD tag. DDC allows developers to build reusable components out of existing ADF Faces components. Like TLD-based declarative components, DDCs can define the `componentVar` and `var` attribute values for the application developer to access the component instance and optionally pass input attributes at runtime using Expression Language. DDC developers can use facets and `af:facetRef` tag reference to define areas in which page developers can add their own content to the DDC. Each facet can be referenced only once within a DDC.

Facelets

The combination of JSP and JSF has never been a marriage made in heaven, mostly because of the request lifecycle differences and the component model that exists only for JSF. Developers quickly learned that mixing JSP tags, including tags of the Java Standard Tag Library (JSTL), with JSF tags is error-prone and should be avoided. In addition, having the JSF page sources contained in JSP pages or documents adds a limitation to JSF, which is that JSF requires a Java EE servlet container to compile the JSF files before executing them.

Facelets is a XML based view definition that provides an alternative technology for hosting JSF definitions. Facelets are designed with JSF in mind and allows painless and seamless integration of markup elements in the design of JSF pages, which is more attractive to page designers than JSP ever was. The page template approach of Facelets works similarly to how page templates in ADF Faces RC work, except that Facelets have a tighter integration with HTML markup for the layout definition. Page designers use HTML markup and Facelets default tags to design the template. The templates contain named placeholders, which are defined areas for application developer to add their custom JSF page content. Developers reference the named template areas in a specific Facelets tag that surrounds the added JSF content, which is similar to using af:facetRef components in ADF page templates, which we introduced earlier in this chapter. Like DDCs, Facelets can be defined for stand-alone use, built from other Facelets, or referenced by other Facelets as they provide a subsets of the JSF component tree.

Future versions of the JSF, starting with JSF 2.0, use Facelets as the default file format. Oracle JDeveloper 11g and ADF Faces RC support both source formats, JSP and Facelets.

In addition to other attributes, the af:declarativeComponent exposes the following commonly used attributes:

- **binding** An EL reference that will store the component instance on a bean. This can be used to grant programmatic access to a component from a backing bean or to move creation of the component to a backing bean. The component instance is of type RichDynamicDeclarativeComponent.

- **partialTriggers** List of IDs of the components that should trigger a partial update. Identifiers are relative to the DDC and must account for naming containers.

- **Id** The ID of the component.

- **viewId** The component to include referenced by the view ID of the page fragment in which it is contained.

Building DDCs

Building DDCs in Oracle JDeveloper 11g R1 is a declarative task, while using them in an ADF Faces page or page fragment requires manual configuration.

To explain DDCs, we use the same toolbar example that we used to explain TLD-based declarative components. Figure 15-11 shows the DDC toolbar, which is defined in the toolbar.jsff page fragment, added to a page, DepartmentsPage.jspx, in the JDeveloper 11g design time. In the example shown in Figure 15-11, two custom attributes are used by the DDC. The first attribute, Iterator, passes an instance of DCIteratorBinding to the toolbar to perform the toolbar actions on. The other attribute, `ShowNavigationItems`, is a Boolean flag that indicates whether or not the navigation buttons in the toolbar should be displayed.

The `viewId` attribute of the `af:declarativeComponent` tag element points to the toolbar.jsff page fragment, which defines the custom reusable component.

Developing DDCs

DDCs are ADF Faces page fragments, which means that the development is visual and declarative, using existing ADF Faces UI components for the UI and managed beans for the component logic.

To build a JSF page fragment, you choose File | New from the Oracle JDeveloper menu. In the Web Tier | JSF category, choose the JSF Page Fragment entry. This creates a page fragment with a filename extension of .jsff. Finishing the creation dialog creates the page fragment as shown here:

```xml
<?xml version='1.0' encoding='windows-1252'?>
<jsp:root xmlns:jsp="http://java.sun.com/JSP/Page" version="2.1"
          xmlns:af="http://xmlns.oracle.com/adf/faces/rich">
</jsp:root>
```

Before adding ADF Faces components to the fragment to define the DDC visual appearance, the page fragment needs to be prepared to become a declarative component. The root component

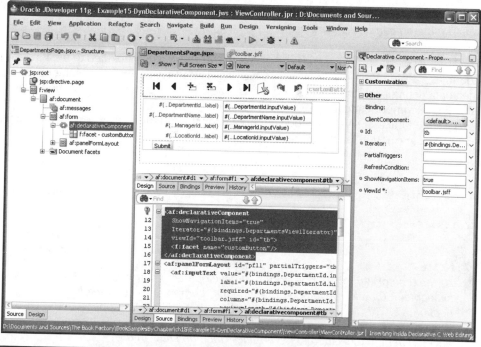

FIGURE 15-11 *DDC toolbar example for navigating and operating on ADF Faces tables and forms*

of the declarative component is the `af:componentDef` that needs to be added right after the `jsp:root` tag element:

```
<?xml version='1.0' encoding='windows-1252'?>
<jsp:root xmlns:jsp="http://java.sun.com/JSP/Page" version="2.1"
          xmlns:af="http://xmlns.oracle.com/adf/faces/rich">
  <af:componentDef var="attrs" componentVar="component">
    <af:xmlContent>
      <component
xmlns="http://xmlns.oracle.com/adf/faces/rich/component">
      </component>
    </af:xmlContent>
  </af:componentDef>
</jsp:root>
```

The `af:componentDef` element is added manually in the Oracle JDeveloper source editor. The optional `componentVar` and `var` attribute values are used to reference the component instance from Java in a managed bean and the components attributes from EL within the component.

NOTE
The `af` *namespace identifier needs to be registered before adding the* `af:componentDef` *tag. The easiest way to configure this is to drag an* `af:commandButton` *to the source editor view of the page fragment, which creates the registration in the page fragment header. The button can be removed then.*

The `af:xmlContent` tag allows arbitrary XML content to be added to a JSP page and is added as a child of the `af:componentDef` tag. The `af:xmlContent` element holds the DDC metadata definitions for attributes and facets. The `af:xmlContent` tag can be added from the ADF Faces component palette or from in the source editor.

Use the Oracle JDeveloper code editor window to add the `component` child element to the `af:xmlContent` tag, as shown below.

```
<af:xmlContent>
  <component
xmlns="http://xmlns.oracle.com/adf/faces/rich/component">
  </component>
</af:xmlContent>
```

NOTE
As the time of writing there is no visual development environment available in Oracle JDeveloper to build DDC components completely declarative. This is planned for a later release in Oracle JDeveloper. Because of the productivity benefits DDC brings to Fusion application development, we decided to nevertheless include DDC in this chapter.

TIP
The declarative component definition is always the same. To automate the DDC configuration, you can create a code template in Oracle JDeveloper using the Tools | Preferences | Code Editor | Code Templates option.

The `component` tag element is the parent element for the metadata of the DDC. The metadata that is supported by the DDC include the following:

Metadata	Example

Facet	`<facet>`
	
	`<description>`
	`Add Facet Description`
	`</description>`
	`<facet-name>`
	`name_here`
	`</facet-name>`
	`</facet>`
	The facet name is referenced from the `af:facetRef` component in the declarative component to position the facet area within the page fragment. The facet allows application developers that reuse the component to extend it with additional UI components. In the toolbar example, a facet is used to allow adding custom command buttons.

Attribute	`<attribute>`
	`<attribute-name>`
	`name_here`
	`</attribute-name>`
	`<attribute-class>`
	`absolute_class_name`
	`</attribute-class>`
	`<required>`
	`true or false`
	`</required>`
	`</attribute>`
	The `<attribute>` tag element defines named attributes that are EL accessible within the component. The attribute names also show in the Expression Builder dialog under the JSP Object
		attrs node. The `<attribute-class>` and `< required >` elements are optional.

The following source code example shows the DDC toolbar used in this section:

```
<?xml version='1.0' encoding='windows-1252'?>
    <jsp:root  xmlns:jsp=http://java.sun.com/JSP/Page version="2.1"
```

```
        xmlns:af="http://xmlns.oracle.com/adf/faces/rich">
  <jsp:directive.page contentType="text/html;charset=utf-8"/>
  <af:componentDef var="attrs" componentVar="component">
    <af:toolbar id="deccompbar"
                inlineStyle="#{attrs.ToolbarInlineStyle}">
      <af:commandToolbarButton
        icon="/toolbarIcons/firstrecr.gif"
        shortDesc="First Record"
        actionListener="#{backingBeanScope.NavBarBean.first_action}"
        id="firstBut"
        rendered="#{attrs.ShowNavigationItems}"/>
        …
    </af:toolbar>
    <af:xmlContent>
      <component
  xmlns="http://xmlns.oracle.com/adf/faces/rich/component">
        <facet>
          <facet-name>
            customButton
          </facet-name>
        </facet>
        <attribute>
          <attribute-name>Iterator</attribute-name>
          <attribute-class>
            oracle.adf.model.binding.DCIteratorBinding
          </attribute-class>
          <required>true</required>
        </attribute>
        <attribute>
          <attribute-name>ShowNavigationItems</attribute-name>
          <attribute-class>java.lang.Boolean</attribute-class>
          <default-value>true</default-value>
        </attribute>
        <attribute>
          <attribute-name>
            ToolbarInlineStyle
          </attribute-name>
          <attribute-class>
            java.lang.String
          </attribute-class>
          <default-value>
            background-color:White;
          </default-value>
        </attribute>
      </component>
    </af:xmlContent>
  </af:componentDef>
</jsp:root>
```

All toolbar buttons reference a managed bean method in their `actionListener` attribute to perform actions on the `DCIteratorBinding` instance that is passed as an attribute into the component. The `af:commandToolbarButton` component uses partial submit by default so that there is no need to set this behavior explicitly. To refresh a UI component on the view that uses the DDC in response to a toolbar action, you can reference the declarative component as a partial trigger from this component. The managed bean used with DDCs must be configured in backing bean scope to ensure that multiple instances of the custom component can be added to a page or page fragment.

The toolbar has one facet and three attributes defined. The facet is referenced by an af:facetRef component to define its location in the toolbar. The attributes are referenced from the command buttons using the attrs value in the expression, which is the value of the var attribute in the af:componentDef.

Configuring the Managed Bean

In the toolbar example, the managed bean is defined in the adfc-config.xml file or a bounded task flow definition file, depending on where the view to which the toolbar is added is referenced. The managed bean holds the toolbar logic, which is a slightly changed version of the code we used in the TLD declarative component example earlier. Here are the methods that contain changes:

```
public class NavBarBean {
  public NavBarBean() {}
  public void first_action(ActionEvent evt) {
    DCIteratorBinding iter = getIteratorBinding();
    Key rowKey = iter.getNavigatableRowIterator().first().getKey();
    iter.setCurrentRowWithKey(rowKey.toStringFormat(true));
  }
```

In the TLD-based version, at the end of the toolbar button action listener method, we called a method to invoke an action listener that the consuming page could register on the declarative component. Method attributes are not supported in the DDC, which is why this method call is removed. If you need to call back into the consuming page from a declarative component, you create a method expression using the ExpressionFactory class to reference the managed bean method used by the consumer view.

```
  private DCIteratorBinding getIteratorBinding(){
    FacesContext fctx = FacesContext.getCurrentInstance();
    ELContext elctx  = fctx.getELContext();
    ExpressionFactory elFactory =
    fctx.getApplication().getExpressionFactory();
    ValueExpression valueExpr =

elFactory.createValueExpression(elctx,"#{component}",Object.class);
    //access the declarative component reference: see the "componentVar"
    //value
  RichDynamicDeclarativeComponent  _this =
      (RichDynamicDeclarativeComponent ) valueExpr.getValue(elctx);
  //Access the Iterator attribute
  (DCIteratorBinding)_this.getAttributes().get("Iterator");
  }
}
```

The major change in the getIteratorBinding method is the use of the RichDynamic DeclarativeComponent class to type cast the #{component} EL reference, as opposed to using the RichDeclarativeComponent.

Using DDCs on ADF Faces Views

As shown in Figure 15-11, the DDC is added to a page using the `af:declarativeComponent` that references the DDC content in the page fragment in its `viewId` attribute. Custom DDC attributes can be passed to the declarative component by adding them to the `af:declarativeComponent` component tag, as shown in Figure 15-11, and in the following code snippet by example of the `Iterator` and `ShowNavigationItems` attributes.

```
<af:declarativeComponent
   ShowNavigationItems="true"
   Iterator="#{bindings.DepartmentsView1Iterator}"
   viewId="toolbar.jsff" id="tb">
     <f:facet name="customButton"/>
</af:declarativeComponent>
```

> **NOTE**
> *You can also specify attributes that are not defined in the declarative component metadata. In this case, the attributes also are accessible from the* `#{attrs.<name>}` *expression but cannot have a default value defined and are not visible in the Expression Language builder when editing the DDC.*

The facets that are defined on the DDC definition, such as the `customButton` facet in the toolbar example, don't automatically show when the declarative component is referenced from the `af:declarativeComponent` component. To display the component facets so that the application developer can add UI components to them, select the `af:declarativeComponent` node in the Structure window and choose Insert inside af:declarativeComponent | JSF Core | Facet from the context menu. The name of the facet must match a facet defined in the custom declarative components.

How to Partially Refresh UI Components of the DDC Parent View

All JSF events that occur on a child UI component of the DDC trigger a partial update notification to be sent by the DDC. Configuring the `partialTriggers` attribute of a UI component, such as `af:panelFormLayout` in Figure 15-11, to reference the ID of the DDC, refreshes the panel layout in response to any component event.

To refresh a component on the parent page or page fragment in response to a specific UI component event within the DDC, developers can reference the child component by its ID. To reference the `id` attribute value of a UI component in a DDC, you concatenate the `id` attribute value of the declarative component in the parent view with the UI component `id` attribute value, using a colon as the separator character. For example, if the `af:declarativeComponent id` attribute value is defined as `ddc_id` and the child UI component of the DDC that should trigger the partial update has its `id` attribute value set to `cbut1`, then the `partialTriggers` attribute value of the component to partially refresh needs to be set to

```
partialTriggers="ddc_id:cbut1"
```

> **NOTE**
> *The Oracle JDeveloper Expression Builder cannot be used to resolve the UI child component in a DDC.*

How to Partially Refresh Child UI Components of a DDC

Refreshing a UI component contained in the parent view of a DDC is one use case. Another use case is to partially refresh a UI component in the DDC in response to a component event on the parent view. For this, the `af:declarativeComponent` component tag also has a `partialTriggers` attribute, which can be pointed to the `id` attribute value of a UI component on the parent view to receive the update notification. This, however, does not yet refresh the child UI components of the declarative component and an additional configuration is required.

If the `var` attribute value of the `af:componentDef` tag of the DDC is set to `attrs`, then child UI components in the DDC are refreshed when the DDC refreshes, if their `partialTriggers` attribute value is set to the `#{attrs.partialTriggers}` EL expression.

For example, in the UI source that follows, the ADF Faces declarative component tag is refreshed in response to an action event of the command button component with the ID of `cb1`:

```
<af:declarativeComponent ShowNavigationItems="true"
   Iterator="#{bindings.DepartmentsView1Iterator}"
   viewId="toolbar.jsff" id="tb"
   partialTriggers="::cb1"/>
```

To refresh a child UI component, the toolbar in this example, in the DDC upon the same action event, it needs to reference the value of the `partialTriggers` of the `af:declarativeComponent` tag, which it does as shown here:

```
<af:componentDef var="attrs" componentVar="component">
  <af:toolbar id="deccompbar"
               partialTriggers="#{attrs.partialTriggers}">
  ...
  </af:toolbar>
  ...
</af:componentDef>
```

The declarative component itself is not re-rendered. Therefore, to change any attribute value of the DDC itself during a partial update, the parent component of the declarative component must be partially updated.

Summary

Necessity is the mother of invention; reuse is the godfather of developer productivity. By leveraging the Java EE Model-View-Controller (MVC) architecture, the Oracle Fusion platform provides a clean separation of duty. This allows application developers to modularize their application development and to enforce the development of reusable components. Reusable components that exist for the Oracle Fusion development platform include page templates, declarative components, task flows, ADF Business Component models, data controls, and custom skins. Using the ADF library JAR archive format for deployment, the Oracle JDeveloper Resource palette can be used to find and import components to a project for reuse. Though component reuse in Java EE is not standardized, Oracle ADF libraries are built on the existing Java Archive formatting standard with additional functionality that makes component reuse easy.

Oracle ADF Faces provides two types of custom declarative components that allow application developers to build new components as a composite of existing ADF Faces components. The tag library—based declarative component can be reused across applications, whereas the DDC is reused for the project in which it is defined. Both declarative components support partial page rendering as a partial trigger and partial target. We agree that the DDC feature looks as if it is not ready yet for prime time because of the lack of declarative development support in the JDeveloper IDE. However it is and the runtime part of it is complete and supported. Developers will find DDC components useful in their application projects and in fact, the upcoming JSF 2.0 standard has a similar functionality defined.

Some of the reusable components, particularly page templates, ADF regions, declarative components, and DDCs, appear to have similar use cases. In fact, however, they are different and allow developers and application architects to choose the right approach for individual use cases, always making sure the smallest amount of overhead is used.

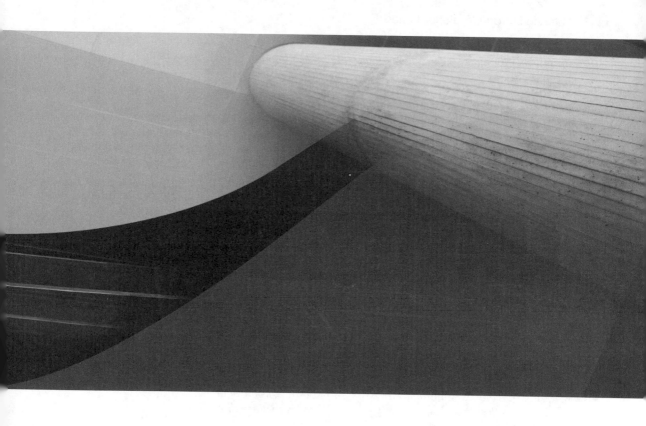

CHAPTER
16

Building Custom Look and Feel with Cascading Style Sheets and Skinning

Skinning is artwork. You cannot teach good taste, but you can demonstrate the techniques to implement some.

A user's first experience when working with web applications is the look and feel of the user interface (UI). No matter how well an application is developed, or how many Java EE design patterns and object-oriented coding principles are built in, if the UI does not impress the users, they won't like the application as a whole.

In traditional web application development, the UI look and feel is implemented through Cascading Style Sheets (CSS), a simple ASCII-based technique used to apply visual style definitions, such as sizing, colors, or spacing, to the generated HTML page markup. In ADF Faces Rich Client (RC), which uses external rendering classes to create the HTML markup at runtime, CSS is added to a page through component style properties, such as `inlineStyle` and `contentStyle`, and ADF Faces component skins.

This chapter briefly introduces CSS and shows how it can be used in ADF Faces RC to change the default component look and feel. It then discusses the ADF Faces skinning framework, an integrated CSS-based architecture used to customize the look and feel of a whole application through external skin definitions, as the preferred solution for Oracle Fusion developers.

NOTE
In this chapter, we use the term "skinning" to refer to the capabilities of the ADF Faces skinning framework and not to look-and-feel customization that is achieved through CSS styles that are directly added to the page markup.

Cascading Style Sheets

CSS are a standard of the World Wide Web Consortium (W3C) and originally helped solve the problem of web pages that had content mixed with presentation. For example, the content information of the following HTML markup is "Hello World." In addition to the content information, the markup contains information about the presentation to display the string "World" with a different font size, type, and color.

```
Hello <font color="#FF0000" size="+3" face="Arial, sans-serif">World</font>
```

The problem of mixing content with information about its presentation is in maintenance and reuse. With CSS, the information about the content's presentation moves out of the markup into the document header or an external file.

NOTE
In this chapter, CSS is covered in only as much detail as necessary to enable readers to style their Fusion web applications. For an in depth tutorial of CSS, visit the W3C School website at www.w3schools.com or the W3C web site at www.w3c.org.

CSS Syntax

A style definition consists of three parts: a selector, a property, and a value. The selector determines the target element or elements to which a specific style definition should be applied. The property defines the attribute to change, such as background color, color, or font. The value is assigned to a property by a colon, which is used instead of an equal sign:

```
selector{property: value}
```

A styling rule can have multiple properties defined, and it can also group different selectors that should have the same style definition applied. For example, to define a font color of red to all header sizes h1, h2, h3, and h4, you would define the following CSS rule:

```
H1, h2, h3, h4 {color: red}
```

To set multiple property-value pairs within a single style rule, a semicolon is used at the end of each pair. The following styling rule sets the font color, size, and font type to be used with all h1, h2, h3, and h4 header types:

```
h1, h2, h3, h4 {color:red; font-family: Arial, Helvetica, sans-serif; font-size: 16px;}
```

Note the use of the semicolon to separate the property-value pairs in this example.

Applying Styles to HTML Markup Elements

CSS is interpreted at runtime by the browser. To apply style information to HTML elements, developers either use style classes or inline style CSS.

Style Classes

A style class is a named styling rule that is declared by a leading dot (.) followed by a name and curly braces ({ and }). The style definition, the styling rule, is added between the braces. Style classes allow style definitions to be reused within a web document or across documents. At design time, style classes are defined or registered in the document header and are referenced from the class attribute of the HTML elements using it.

```
<head>
  <style type="text/css">
    .world {
       font-family: Arial, sans-serif;
       font-size: 16px;
       color: #FF0000;
       font-weight: bold;
    }
  </style>
</head>
<body>
  Hello <span class="world">World</span>
</body>
```

Style classes can be stored in an external style document that is referenced from a link in the page header to reuse style definitions across web pages:

```
<head>
  <link href="css/ora.css" rel="stylesheet" type="text/css">
</head>
<body>
  Hello <span class="world">World</span>
</body>
```

Inline Style

The other option to apply style definitions to markup is to provide the styling rules with the markup itself. For this, HTML elements have a `style` attribute that developers use to provide a list of semicolon-delimited style property/value pairs. Though inline style definitions don't help solving the problem of page content getting mixed with presentation logic, it is often used for simple fixes such as component width and height corrections.

```
Hello <span style="font-family: Arial, sans-serif;font-size: 16px;
color: #FF0000; font-weight: bold;"> World</span>
```

Styles in ADF Faces RC

The HTML `style` attribute is exposed on ADF Faces components through the `inlineStyle` attribute. CSS style classes are referenced from the component `styleClass` attribute.

In addition to using the ADF Faces RC skinning framework (explained later in this chapter), developers can use three options alone or in combination to apply traditional CSS styles to the generated component markup in ADF Faces:

- Inline style
- Local style class references
- External style class reference

In the case of overlapping style rules, CSS resolves possible conflicts by weighting in the location of the CSS definition and the length of the match in the selector definition. This is where the meaning of *cascade* in Cascading Style Sheets comes into play.

At runtime, all style documents are virtually merged into one. Styles defined on a markup element using the `inlineStyle` attribute take precedence over all other styling rules, followed by definitions that are contained in the document header. Styles stored in external files come third, preceding any browser defaults settings. Selectors that define an exact match to a component precede selectors that have only a partial match.

Using CSS in ADF Faces RC

In JavaServer Faces (JSF), style definitions are added to individual components using either the `style` or the `styleClass` attribute of the UI components. In ADF Faces RC, the `style` attribute is named `inlineStyle`. CSS styles that are added as a value to one of the two properties will be applied to the root Document Object Model (DOM) element of the rendered ADF Faces RC component. In addition to the `styleClass` and `inlineStyle` attributes, ADF Faces provides another attribute, `contentStyle`. The `contentStyle` attribute allows developers to apply CSS directly to the content area of a complex component.

inlineStyle Attribute

The `inlineStyle` attribute value is expected as a semicolon-separated list of CSS style definitions. Styling rules that are configured in the `inlineStyle` attribute are added directly to the JSF page source as part of the component markup. The following example shows style definitions that are added to the `inlineStyle` attribute of an ADF Faces table component:

```
<af:table ...  inlineStyle="width:400px; height:300px; padding:5px;">
    ...
</af:table>
```

At runtime, the styling rules are applied to the outermost HTML element of the complex HTML rendering that makes the visual appearance of an ADF Faces RC component in the browser. For the `af:table` component, the outermost HTML element is a `div` that contains a nesting of `div`, `table` and other child elements that build the rich table UI presentation.

```
<div  style="padding: 20%; outline-width: 0px; position: absolute; top: 0px; bottom:
0px; left: 0px; right: 0px; min-height: 200px; width: 100%; height: 100%;">
  <div …>
        <table>…</table>
  </div>
</div>
```

The outermost HTML element is also referred to as the DOM root element of an ADF Faces component. Style definitions added to the DOM root may not show a visual change at runtime.

Oracle JDeveloper 11g provides declarative design time support to style components using the `inlineStyle` attribute (Figure 16-1).

NOTE
Styles that are defined in the `inlineStyle` attribute cannot be reused and therefore always add to the size of the resulting HTML page at runtime.

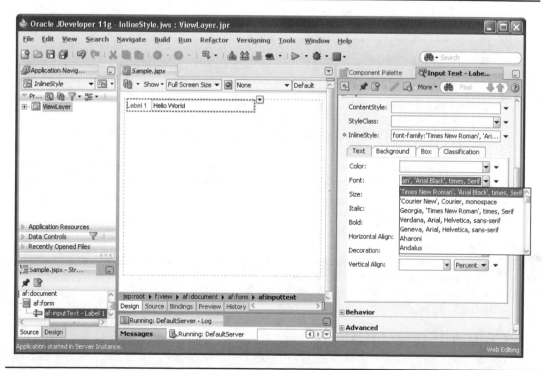

FIGURE 16-1 *Declarative design time support for editing the inlineStyle attribute in Oracle JDeveloper 11g*

styleClass Attribute

The `styleClass` attribute of an ADF Faces RC component references a style class that is defined in the page or contained in an external style sheet document that is referenced by the JSF page. As mentioned earlier in this chapter, a style class is a named configuration of styling rules. Though the style class definition has a leading dot in front of the name, this dot is not used when referencing the style class. In the following sample, the `af:inputText` field references the `backgrOrange` style class in its `styleClass` attribute:

```
<af:document>
  <af:form>
    <af:inputText … styleClass="backgrOrange"/>
  </af:form>
  <f:facet name="metaContainer">
    <af:group>
        <style type="text/css">
             .backgrOrange{background-color:orange;}
        </style>
    </af:group>
  </f:facet>
</af:document>
```

JSF 1.2 allows you to mix JSF markup—the JavaServer Pages (JSP) tag library elements that add JSF components to a page—with HTML markup. A recommendation of best practices is to add the CSS style class definition or the reference to an external style sheet document to the `metaContainer` facet of the `af:document` component, or use the new `af:resource` tag within the document, for better performance.

NOTE
Notice the `af:group` *element that surrounds the style class definition. This element is invisible in the rendered HTML page but is required to add more than one child object to the* `metaContainer` *facet. This element is not required when using the* `af:resource` *tag.*

Oracle JDeveloper 11*g* does not provide declarative design time support to define style classes on the JSF page. Still, the approach of using style classes referenced from the component `styleClass` attribute is preferable over the use of the `inlineStyle` attribute because of the option to reuse style definitions.

TIP
We recommend that you store style class definitions in external source files and referencing them at runtime. It is easier for developers to maintain and share style definitions if they are stored in a central place.

ContentStyle Attribute

The `contentStyle` attribute of an ADF Faces RC component applies the style definition to the inner content area of the component. As mentioned, CSS definitions that are applied to the `inlineStyle` or `styleClass` attribute render on the root DOM element and may not visually impact the display of the component at runtime. The `contentStyle` attribute works around this limitation to some extent.

For example, the CSS code shown next does not result in a visual impact when applied to the `inlineStyle` attribute of `af:inputText`:

```
border-color:White; border-style:none; border-width:0;
```

The same styles applied to the `contentStyle` attribute remove the input text field border. Analyzing the generated HTML output of the `af:inputText` component explains the case:

```
<tbody>
  <tr>
    <td class="xu">
      <label for="j_id_id3::content">Label 1</label>
    </td>
    <td valign="top" nowrap="" class="x187">
      <input type="text" value="Hello World" class="x25"
      id="j_id_id3::content"/>
    </td>
  </tr>
</tbody>
```

At runtime, the `af:inputText` component renders as a table body that has the `tbody` element as its root DOM element. The `inlineStyle` property applies the style rules to the root DOM element, which does not have a border property. As a result, the CSS is ignored. Adding the CSS to the `contentStyle` attribute applies the style definition to the HTML `input` element, which has a border property and the border gets hidden.

NOTE
The Oracle ADF Faces component product page on the Oracle Technology Network (OTN), http://otn.oracle.com/products/adf/ adffaces/index.html, hosts a live component demo that you can use to try the `inlineStyle` *and* `contentStyle` *attributes. The demo sources are also available for download and offline testing.*

Conditional Formatting Using Expression Language

All three attribute fields, `inlineStyle`, `contentStyle`, and `styleClass`, can use Expression Language (EL) to set their values dynamically. A use case for dynamic style definition is conditional formatting.

In the page code shown next, the `af:table` component contains an `af:column` that displays the salary of employee. The `inlineStyle` attribute of the `af:column` uses an EL reference to a managed bean method to obtain the style property/value pairs for each row.

```
<af:table value="…" var="row">
    <af:column sortProperty="Salary" headerText="Salary"
            inlineStyle="#{EmployeeUtilBean.inlineStyle}">
            <af:outputText value="#{row.Salary}">
            </af:outputText>
    </af:column>
</af:table>
```

In ADF Faces, an internal iterator navigates over a collection of row data to render the table. The collection of row data is accessible through the name specified for the `var` attribute value, which is set to `row` by default. A managed bean has access to the `row` variable through EL during the time the table renders. This way it can evaluate the row's salary value to return a CSS string based on a defined condition

NOTE
Chapter 9 contains a complete example for this use case, including the managed bean code.

Introduction to Skinning in ADF Faces RC

Skinning in ADF Faces RC is an integrated styling framework based on CSS. In the JSF architecture, UI components are display agnostic in that they don't know about their rendering on an output device. In other words, a button knows what a button is and what its expected behavior is, but it doesn't know how it looks when it's displayed on an iPhone or in a browser. The UI rendering is delegated to device-specific Java classes, the component renderers. A set of component renderers is grouped in a render kit, which is configured in the faces-config.xml configuration file, located in the WEB-INF directory of the view layer project. The browser render kit for the ADF Faces RC framework is `oracle.adf.rich`.

An ADF Faces skin is a style sheet document that contains the look-and-feel definition for an entire application. Instead of working with the W3C-defined standard style selectors, skinning uses component specific selectors, such as `af|inputText`, that are exposed on the component renderer. Component selectors allow skin developers to skin a specific content area of the component directly, which is far more powerful than skinning on the DOM root. Another benefit of skinning is that a configured look and feel can be changed at runtime with no additional coding required in the application.

Skinning is artwork. You cannot teach good taste, but you can demonstrate the techniques to implement some. Therefore, in the following, we don't present a how-to that leads you through the steps to create a stunning look and feel for an application, but we teach you the technology behind skinning so you can understand how to build your own custom look and feel.

The History of Skinning

The origin of the skinning framework is in Oracle User Interface XML (UIX), originally an Oracle internal technology that was first released to public in 2002. With the advent of JSF in 2004, UIX has been deprecated since JDeveloper 10.1.3 and replaced with ADF Faces. UIX used XML Style Sheet (XSS) language to apply styling rules to UI components and so did ADF Faces, which provided a subset of the styling capabilities available in UIX. In 2005, after the release of ADF Faces, Oracle donated the ADF Faces components to the Apache MyFaces Trinidad open source project, where skinning has been greatly enhanced. ADF Faces RC is a new JSF component set in Oracle JDeveloper 11*g* that is based on the Trinidad open source project. ADF Faces RC inherits the entire skinning framework originally started in UIX, changed in ADF Faces and enhanced in Trinidad.

ADF Faces Skinning vs. inlineStyle, contentStyle, and styleClass CSS

The difference between style definitions directly added to an ADF Faces page and the ADF Faces RC skinning framework is as significant as the difference between British and American English. Through both techniques use CSS to style the look of an ADF Faces RC application, they are different. Skinning provides fine-grained hooks to the individual ADF Faces UI components and to style areas that are not accessible to style definitions added directly to the page.

Skin documents use CSS 3 to define styling rules for the ADF Faces RC components, not the rendered HTML output. At runtime, the skinning framework interprets the skin definitions and turns them into a CSS 2 style document added to the generated HTML output. Skinning on the component and not the generated HTML output allows skin developers, also referred to as "skinners," to apply style definitions directly to a specific content area of a component.

Skin definitions can be created for a specific agent. Though standardized by W3C, style definitions are not consistent in the browser implementation, and some browsers don't support styles that other browsers do. To address the difference when developing customs skins, the skinning framework allows developers to determine the browser agent and apply styles according to this information. To skin for a specific browser type, developers prefix the style selector with `@agent` followed by one of the following identifiers: `ie`, `mozilla`, `gecko`, or `webkit`.

Skin definitions can be created for a specific client operation system using the `@platform` selector. This allows defining styles specific to Windows, Mac OS, Linux, Solaris, and iPhone.

Skin definitions can use the `:rtl` (right-to-left) pseudo elements to adapt to local reading directions. Note that this functionality can be used only with Internet Explorer.

Skinning can be used to change the default component labels and tool tips, replacing them with custom strings read from a resource bundle.

Skin selectors are automatically translated to style classes at runtime. For example, the skin selector `af|panelBox::content:default:core` translates to `af_panelBox_content p_AFCore p_AFDefault` on the uncompressed ADF Faces page output.

NOTE
The translation of skin component selectors into style classes and how to switch compression on and off for ADF Faces pages is covered later in the chapter in the "Skin Debugging" section.

Skinning enables developers to inherit style definitions from a base skin or a local style class, and it gives them control over which properties to inherit using the `-tr-inhibit` style property.

NOTE
Skinning is the Oracle recommended choice for applying custom look-and-feel definitions. However, the `inlineStyle`, `contentStyle`, *and* `styleClass` *attributes may be used as well if the look-and-feel modification is for a specific component instance only and if there is no need to change the look and feel at runtime.*

Skin Selectors

Developers who develop customs skins work mainly with global selectors, component selectors, and styleClasses.

NOTE
Theoretically, it is possible to define styling rules in the skin document that use selectors that address the generated HTML output of the ADF Faces page. This possibility should be avoided, however, since there is no guarantee that different releases of ADF Faces always generate the same HTML. Styling that is based on the generated HTML markup is fragile and not future-safe.

Global Selectors

Skinning occurs by component. All component selectors implement a set of global selector names, inheriting their style definitions, to avoid the need for unnecessary duplication of styles in custom skins. Global skin selectors are styleClasses with a `:alias` pseudo class. For example, the `.AFDefaultFontFamily:alias` pseudo class defines the default font family name and is referenced in almost all of the component selectors. Adding a line such as the following to your custom skin changes the font-family name used by input and output components to another font (here, Comic Sans MS):

```
.AFDefaultFontFamily:alias{font-family:'Comic Sans MS';}
```

Component Selectors

All ADF Faces RC components implement a skin component selector to style their content. All skin selectors names start with `af|` followed by the component tag name. The skin selector for the `inputText` component, for example, is `af|inputText`, which is similar to the tag name, which is `af:inputText`.

Component selectors may have pseudo classes and pseudo elements defined that allow developers to skin specific areas and conditions of a component.

Pseudo Class   ADF Faces RC components support the standard CSS pseudo classes such as `:hover`, `:active`, `:visited`, `:selected`, and others that exist for the component's HTML peer.

Beyond the standard pseudo classes, some components provide additional ADF Faces–specific classes. For example, the `af:panelBox` component has a ramp and background attribute that application developers use to select one of eight predefined color schemes. The ramp values `core` and `highlight`, as well as the background attribute values `default`, `light`, `medium`, and `dark`, are skinnable through pseudo classes representing the value. To skin the `panelBox` content area when the `core` ramp is chosen in combination with the `medium` background color, the skin selector looks as follows:

```
af|panelBox::content:core:medium{…}
```

Pseudo Element   Pseudo elements are component specific and identify areas within a component for skinning. To use a pseudo element, skin developers append the name of the pseudo element with a double colon (`:`) prefix to the component selector. The following pseudo elements, for example, exist for the input text selector `af|inputText`.

- **af|inputText::access-key**   Style on the access key for the label of the `af:inputText` component. For example, underline the access key. Includes `.AFFormAccessKeyStyle:alias`.

- **af|inputText::content**   Style on the content of the `af:inputText` component.

- **af|inputText::dynamic-help-icon-style**   Style the dynamic help icon. By default the `dynamic-help-icon` is null, and this style has a background-image that you can override. Available pseudo classes are `disabled:hover`, `:hover`, and `:active`. Includes `.AFDynamicHelpIconStyle:alias`.

NOTE
Component skin selectors follow a very simple naming pattern, which is <selector name>::<pseudo element>:<pseudo class>, where the pseudo element and pseudo class are optional but the selector name is mandatory to use.

Themes   Themes allow look-and-feel developers to skin ADF Faces components conditionally based on the layout container in which they are located. Layout container components in Oracle JDeveloper 11*g* R1 that support the `theme` attribute are

- `af:document`

- `af:decorativeBox`

- `af:panelGroupLayout`

- `af:panelStretchLayout`

For example, a page layout that has two nested `af:decorativeBox` components may require that the two instances have different background colors so they can be distinguished in the rendered view. If the `theme` attribute is set on a layout container, then at runtime all its contained child components are checked to determine whether they support themes. If a child component supports themes, the generated HTML markup for this component contains an additional attribute `theme="<name of theme>"`.

Themes are enabled for a component through the `-tr-enable-themes` flag. For example, to enable themes for the ADF Faces RC inputText component, the `af|inputText` selector element needs to look similar to this example:

```
af|inputText {
    -tr-enable-themes: true;
}
```

To skin an `InputText` component so it looks different when added as a child to one of the layout component that support themes and that has its `theme` attribute set to `"dark"`, you use a skin definition similar to this:

```
af|inputText::content{
    color:white;
    background-color: red;
}
af|inputText::content[theme="light"]{
    background-color: rgb(132,132,132);
}
```

With the preceding skin definition, the following markup definition renders the `InputText` component with a white font color and a dark gray background color:

```
<af:decorativeBox id="db1" theme="light">
  <f:facet name="center">
    <af:inputText label="Last Name" id="it2"/>
  </f:facet>
</af:decorativeBox>
```

Style Classes

Style classes in CSS group styling definitions use a custom name that starts with a leading dot (.). Style classes are supported in the skinning document and can be used by developers to define custom global selectors. In addition, style classes in the skinning document can be referenced from the `styleClass` attribute on the UI components, in which case the style class CSS rules are applied to the component DOM root element.

Overview of Custom Skin Development

To write custom skins, skin developers first need to become familiar with the available skin selectors for the component to skin. Though the option exists to use the Firebug plug-in in Firefox to discover skin selectors at runtime, the skin documentation provided on the OTN website is the recommended starting point for skinners.

To build and configure a custom skin, skinners complete the following tasks:

1. Create a skin source file for the style definitions under the public-html directory of the view layer project or a subdirectory of it.

2. Optionally, provide images in a directory that is accessible to the custom skin.

3. Optionally, create a resource bundle to override the default strings used by ADF Faces RC components.

4. Create a file, trinidad-skins.xml, in the WEB-INF directory to register the custom skin.

5. Edit the trinidad-config.xml file with a reference to the custom skin.

Create a Custom Skin File

Custom skin definitions use the documented skin selectors for ADF Faces RC components, as well as their pseudo classes and pseudo elements, to apply style definitions that give the custom skin the look and feel of an application. The skin definitions are stored in style sheet document, an ASCII file that has the .css file extension.

To create a new style sheet document in Oracle JDeveloper 11*g*, do this:

1. Choose File | New.

2. In the Web Tier | HTML category, select the CSS File entry to launch the file creation dialog.

3. Ensure that the style sheet gets created in the view layer project's public_html directory or a subdirectory of it.

The Oracle JDeveloper 11*g* source code editor supports skin developers with CSS-style completion and resource lookup. For example, typing **background-image:** opens a dialog where you can select the image to reference from the file system when pausing. Same for color selections, where JDeveloper opens a color picker when pausing on `color:` or `background-color`.

NOTE
Developers who are new to CSS may find it helpful to create an empty skin definition such as af|inputText{ }, *assuming they want to skin the* InputText *component. Place the cursor between the curly braces and then press* CTRL-SPACEBAR *for a list of style choices.*

Oracle JDeveloper 11*g* has a built-in ADF Faces skinning extension to assist skinners in their skin development with code completion, syntax help, and an error margin to spot and correct coding errors. The skinning extension is disabled by default and is enabled by checking the ADF Faces Extension checkbox after choosing Tools | Preferences | CSS Editor.

To work with the skinning extension in a style sheet document, type **af|** and pause for a moment, or press CTRL+SPACEBAR. This opens a list of skin selectors that you can filter by continuing typing. To see a list of predefined style classes, type a dot (**.**) and then pause until the list of alias names comes up. To learn about possible pseudo classes that exist for a skin selector, type the selector name and then add a colon (:) at the end. Do the same, appending a double colon, to see a list of component areas pseudo elements to use for skinning.

Skins in ADF Faces RC can extend an existing base skin so that there is no need to build a complete custom skin that contains styling rules for all possible skin selectors and combinations.

To navigate within a skin file, select the skin source file in the Oracle JDeveloper Application Navigator and open the Structure window (CTRL-SHIFT-S). In the Structure window, double-click the skin selector entry to edit to locate it in the code editor. You can use the Property Inspector to add CSS style definitions declaratively to the selected skin selector, as shown in Figure 16-2.

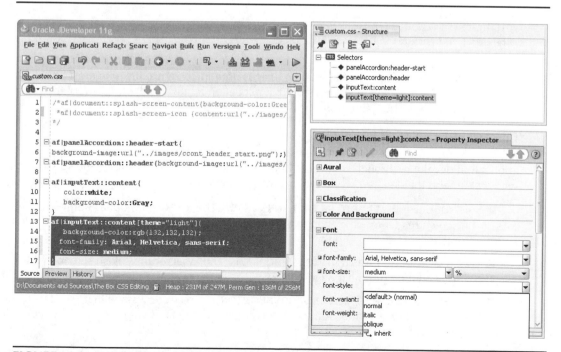

FIGURE 16-2 *Using the code editor, Structure window, and Property Inspector to add CSS to a selected skin selector*

Image location	Image reference example
Absolute	background-image:url("http:server:port/images/img1.png");
Relative to skin CSS file	background-image:url("images/ img1.png");
Relative to web application context root	background-image:url("/skins/images/ img1.png");

TABLE 16-1 *Possible Image Locations When Developing Custom Skins*

Using Images

Not all of the look and feel can be achieved with styling rules that set colors and sizes for a component. Many components in ADF Faces use images to achieve their look and feel. In the Oracle blafplus-rich look and feel, the `PanelBox` component uses the ccont_header_bg.png, ccont_header_end.png, and ccont_header_start.png image files to skin its header bar. To provide a custom look and feel, replacing the default images with custom images, add the following skin definition to the custom skin style sheet document:

```
af|panelBox::header-start:core:default{
    background-image:url("images/custom_header_start.png");
}
af|panelBox::header-center:core:default{
    background-image:url("images/custom_header_bg.png");
}
af|panelBox::header-end:core:default{
    background-image:url("images/custom_header_end.png");
}
```

You have choice of options for locating images used in custom skins. The most common implementation is to have the images stored in a location relative to the location of the skin CSS document. Table 16-1 shows the possible image locations.

Create Custom String Bundles

Most of the ADF Faces RC components use native message strings that are not configurable by the application developer through setting the component attributes. For example, the splash screen, which entertains the end user while the application loads, uses the following keys/message pairs:

- **af_document.LABEL_SKIP_LINK_TEXT** The text written out as part of the link in screen reader mode to skip to the content on the page. The default value is "Skip to content."

- **af_document.LABEL_SPLASH_SCREEN** The label for the splash screen that is displayed the first time a page is shown. The default value is "Loading...".

- **af_document.MSG_FAILED_CONNECTION** The error message that appears in an alert box when a connection to the server fails. The default value is "A connection to the server has failed."

Skinning allows the developer to style component messages by providing a custom message bundle. The message bundle does not need to contain the message strings for all ADF Faces RC components but only those that should be customized. The search order for message strings is that they are first looked up in the message bundle if configured. If a string cannot be found here, then the default component string is used.

To build a custom message bundle, extend `java.util.ListResourceBundle` and override the `getContents` method. To provide a translated bundle, duplicate the custom message bundle class, translate the contained strings, and save it under <bundle name>_<language>.java—for example <bundle name>_<de>.java for a German translation.

```
public class ButterflyMessageBundle extends ListResourceBundle {
@Override
  public Object[][] getContents() {
    return _CONTENTS;
  }

  private static final Object[][] _CONTENTS =
  {
    {"af_document.LABEL_SPLASH_SCREEN", "Fly like a Butterfly …"}
  };
}
```

The message bundle is configured in the trinidad-skins.xml file using the `bundle-name` element or the `translation-source` element.

Working with Dynamic Message Resources

A feature added to Apache MyFaces Trinidad that is inherited by ADF Faces RC is the ability to dynamically reference a resource bundle or map holding the custom strings that replace the default message strings at runtime. To use this functionality developers must do the following:

- Create a managed bean that returns a map or resource bundle.

- Configure the managed bean in the faces-config.xml file located in the WEB-INF directory of the view layer project.

- Configure the `translation-source` element in the trinidad-skins.xml file with a reference to the managed bean.

- Remove the `bundle-name` reference from the trinidad-skins.xml file in case it exists.

The managed bean that is referenced by the `translation-source` element in the trinidad-skins.xml file exposes a public method that either returns an instance of `Map<String, String>` or an instance of `ResourceBundle`.

```
public class DynamicResourceHandler {
  public Map<String, String> getContents(){
    // Add Strings to the message Map here if needed
    return _CONTENTS;
  }
  // setting default strings
  static {
    _CONTENTS.put("af_document.LABEL_SPLASH_SCREEN", "Fly like a
            Butterfly …");
  }
}
```

Messages can be added dynamically to the message map based on external conditions evaluated in the managed bean. Alternatively, developers can create multiple beans or map file references and use EL in the trinidad-skins.xml file to dynamically change the message bundle used.

To work with dynamic message bundles, configure the managed bean in the faces-config.xml file as shown here:

```
<managed-bean>
   <description>
      Bean allowing dynamic message bundles to be used</description>
    <managed-bean-name>dynamicResourceHandler</managed-bean-name>
    <managed-beanclass>
       adf.interactiv.view.bundles.DynamicResourceHandler
    </managed-bean-class>
   <managed-bean-scope>session</managed-bean-scope>
</managed-bean>
```

NOTE
If the custom label and message strings are the same across instances of an application, we recommend using `application` *as the managed bean scope.*

Creating and Configuring the trinidad-skins.xml File

The trinidad-skins.xml file is the skin registry for a Fusion web application. Only those skins that are configured directly in the trinidad-skins.xml file or added through a skin library that contains a trinidad-skins.xml file in its META-INF directory are accessible at runtime. The trinidad-skins.xml file contains the configuration for one to many skin definitions. The trinidad-skins.xml file is not needed for applications that use the Oracle default look and feel.

The trinidad-skins.xml file is not created by default and needs to be added manually to the view layer project. To create the trinidad-xml file, do this:

1. Create a new XML document in JDeveloper. Select File | New and then choose the General | XML node.

2. Select the XML Document entry and click OK.

3. In the dialog, ensure the document gets created in the public_html\WEB-INF directory of the view layer project and type the name **trinidad-skins.xml**. When done, click OK to close the dialog.

4. The trinidad-skins.xml file comes up empty in the JDeveloper source editor. Edit the document so it looks similar to the example shown here:

```
<?xml version="1.0" encoding="ISO-8859-1"?
<skins xmlns="http://myfaces.apache.org/trinidad/skin">
 <skin>
    <id>butterfly.desktop</id>
    <family>butterfly</family>
    <render-kit-id>org.apache.myfaces.trinidad.desktop</render-kit-id>
    <extends>blafplus-rich.desktop</extends>
    <style-sheet-name>skins/butterfly.css</style-sheet-name>
    <bundle-name>
```

```
      adf.interactiv.view.bundles.ButterflyMessageBundle
    </bundle-name>
    <!-- commented out: use translation-source or bundle-name. To use
         translation-source, comment the bundle-name and uncomment the
         configuration below -->
    <!-- <translation-source>
       #{dynamicResourceHandler.contents}
    </translation-source> -->
  </skin>
</skins>
```

The trinidad-skins.xml file registers custom skins within the `skin` element. You can define as many skin elements as you need. Not all elements shown in the preceding configuration are mandatory.

- **id** Every skin must have a unique ID assigned. The .desktop extension indicates that the skin is to be used with browser-based applications.

- **family** The family name of a skin is used at runtime. A skin family is a group of skins for different devices. If a skin was defined for PDA, this could be configured under the same family name, but with its own unique ID.

- **render-kit-id** `org.apache.myfaces.trinidad.desktop` is the value always used with ADF Faces applications displayed in a browser.

- **style-sheet-name** Reference to the location of the custom skin document.

- **extends** A custom skin can extend from a base skin. Being able to extend from an existing skin saves skin developers from having to build a full skin when only a few changes to the existing skin are required.

- **bundle-name** Optional. Name of the bundle for this skin. By default, the custom skin inherits the translations that are provided by the parent skin. The custom skin can override any customizable message by defining its own resource bundles. If no skin is explicitly extended, the default parent is `simple.desktop`.

- **translation-source** Optional. Uses EL to point to a method that returns an instance of `ResourceBundle` or `Map<String, String>`. The `translation-source` element can be used instead of the `bundle-name` element if there is a requirement to change the bundle dynamically based on some external conditions, such as on April 1, when everything is a bit more funny than usual. If the elements `bundle-name` and `translation-name` are both configured, the bundle name is used.

Configure trinidad-config.xml The trinidad-config.xml file holds the current skin setting for an application. Skin definitions are set for an application but are runtime specific, which means they can be changed at runtime for a user session. When developing a new Fusion Web application, the trinidad-config.xml contains only one entry, which is the family name set to `fusion`, the Oracle default look and feel.

```
<skin-family>fusion</skin-family>
```

For the screen shots in this book, we use the `blafplus-rich` Oracle look and feel. While the new `fusion` look and feel shows a more modern application UI, we chose `blafplus-rich` because it prints clearer in gray scale tones.

```
<skin-family>blafplus-rich</skin-family>
```

NOTE
If you are on the latest version of Oracle JDeveloper 11g, at design time you can switch between available look and feel definitions contained in the `trinidad-skins.xml` *file using the ADF View category in the View Layer project properties.*

To use a custom skin definition instead of the default skin, change the setting of the `skin-family` element to the name of the custom skin family; here's an example:

```
<skin-family>butterfly</skin-family>
```

In addition to setting the static configuration, you can also dynamically set the skin for an application instance so it can be changed at runtime. In the following example, an EL string is used to read the current string from a managed bean configured in the adfc-config.xml or faces-config.xml file:

```
<skin-family>
    #{skinHandler.skin eq null?'blafplus-rich': skinHandler.skin}
</skin-family>
```

Alternative options include reading the setting from a session scoped attribute, in which case the configuration looks as follows:

```
<skin-family>
    #{sessionScope.skin eq null?'blafplus-rich': sessionScope.skin}
</skin-family>
```

NOTE
To avoid parsing errors after adding EL evaluations to the `skin-family` *element, make sure that a space appears between the colon and the second expression,* `skinHandler.skin`, *in the preceding example.*

In both cases, the `skin-family` definition performs a check for `null` to show a sensible default skin in case no skin family information is available. The managed bean reference allows developers to perform complex evaluations of which skin to show or to look up the user skin preference from a table in the database.

Advanced Topics

If you can think it, you can skin it! Skinning is a wide topic to cover, and up to now, this chapter has covered the basics that enable developers to configure and use custom skins in their Fusion web applications. It's about the time to switch gears.

Working with Scopes

In a custom look and feel, the same UI component may be required to display in different styles. Skin developers can control the scope of a skin definition as global, component specific, or instance specific. A fourth scope possible is page context, which is a useful strategy for skinning templates.

Global Scope

Global scopes are defined by predefined style classes that end with :alias. So called "alias classes" don't show as style classes in the generated HTML output, but are referenced by the component-specific skin selectors. To set a default font for the whole application, skin developers could modify the style of .AFDefaultFont:alias, which automatically impacts all components that display text in the UI:

```
.AFDefaultFont:alias{
    font-size:12px;
    font-weight:normal;
}
.AFDefaultFontFamily:alias{
    font-family: font-family: Helvetica, Arial, sans-serif;
}
```

The default font setting can be changed for individual components by setting the same style properties on the component-specific selectors. The benefit of global scopes is that they simplify development, because it means fewer styles to write, and that they ease administration, because changing a style in a single place propagates to many components.

Using custom style classes in the skinning document in combination with the component -tr-rule-ref:selector property, skin developers are able to configure their own global styles.

```
/* custom alias definition */
.butterflyPanelBackground:alias{
    background-color:rgb(255,255,181);
}
/* panelBox referencing custom alias */
af|panelBox::content:default:core{
  -tr-rule-ref:selector(".butterflyPanelBackground:alias")
}
```

NOTE
The use of the :alias *extension is optional for custom global style classes and any extension, or none, does the same. However, for better readability using some kind of extension is advisable.*

Component Specific

Skin selectors that are defined for a specific UI component are in component scope, which means that a modification of this selector changes all instances of the component within an application. Skinning a component for this scope does not require any more knowledge than a look in the component skin selector document provides.

Instance Specific

Instance-specific skinning applies style definitions to selected instances of a component on a page. For example, a Fusion web page shows two instances of the panelBox component on a page. One instance should show the component disclosure icon in the component header, the other would not. Since the disclosure icon cannot be hidden through component attribute settings, instance-specific skinning must be used.

In CSS, component instances are addressed through selectors. The following selectors can be used to address an ADF Faces component instance:

- **id** A less commonly used option in ADF Faces that allows developers to reference the component instance by its unique ID attribute value. The skin selector for the ID selector looks like this: #<*id* attribute value>.

- **attribute** A styling option that is used, for example, with theme support in ADF Faces RC. Attribute selectors address an attribute value definition of the rendered HTML component output. To use an attribute selector for instance-specific skinning, append [*attribute_name*="<*condition*>"] to the ADF Faces component selector.

- **styleClass** The most commonly used option in ADF Faces RC to implement instance-specific skins. The styleClass attribute value is used to define a named identifier for a group of components that should have a specific skin definition applied.

Using Class Selectors The most commonly used option to implement instance-specific skinning is through the component's styleClass attribute. Using the styleClass attribute, developers can mark more than one component for instance-specific skinning. In the following example, the first panel box, PanelBox1, has the styleClass attribute added as hideIcon.

```
<af:form id="frm1">
    <af:panelGroupLayout id="grp1" layout="scroll"
        xmlns:af="http://xmlns.oracle.com/adf/faces/rich">
            <af:panelBox text="PanelBox1" styleClass="hideIcon"/>
            <af:panelBox text="PanelBox2"/>
    </af:panelGroupLayout>
</af:form>
```

In the generated page HTML, the style class is applied to the root HTML component:

```
<div class="hideIcon af_panelBox">
```

The additional class attribute allows skinners to address the panel box instance directly. Using style class names as a handle to the component instance to skin is not limited to a single component or a specific page, but can be used with many instances of a component across pages and components.

```
.hideIcon af|panelBox::disclosure-icon-container{display:none}
```

The advantage of using the styleClass attribute for instance-specific skinning is that its value doesn't change if the component runs in a naming container, in which case an ID selector wont work.

NOTE
The "Skin Debugging" section in this chapter explains how skinners discover how style classes are used in the generated HTML output of ADF Faces RC components.

Context Scope Skinning

For components that are contained in a template, a component may need to be styled differently based on the page with which the template is used. To meet this requirement, the page view ID of the page that references the template needs to be added to the skin definition.

NOTE
ADF page templates are covered in Chapter 15.

To implement a page context to the skin definition, configure the view ID as the value of the `styleClass` property. Since templates are generic and are used with many pages, hard-coding the view ID is not an option. In this case, using attribute definitions in the template metadata is a better option.

The next example shows the page code content of a template file that has a single attribute, `styleClassAttr`, defined. The attribute is referenced within the page template content by the `styleClass` attribute using the `#{attrs.styleClassAttr}` expression. This makes the value of the `styleClassAttr` the value of the `styleClass` attribute.

```
<af:pageTemplateDef var="attrs">
  <af:panelGroupLayout layout="scroll" …>
      <af:panelBox text="PanelBox1"
                   styleClass="#{attrs.styleClassAttr}">
          <af:facetRef facetName="mainArea"/>
      </af:panelBox>
  </af:panelGroupLayout>
  <af:xmlContent>
    <component …>
      <facet>
        <facet-name>mainArea</facet-name>
      </facet>
      <attribute>
        <attribute-name>styleClassAttr</attribute-name>
        <attribute-class>java.lang.String</attribute-class>
      </attribute>
    </component>
  </af:xmlContent>
</af:pageTemplateDef>
```

Attributes defined in a template used with a page show in the Oracle JDeveloper Expression Builder under the JSP Objects | attrs node, as shown in Figure 16-3. To reference an attribute from the `styleClass` attribute, select the component in the JDeveloper Structure window or the visual editor, open the Property Inspector (CTRL-SHIFT-I) and click the arrow icon on the right side of the `styleClass` attribute field. This brings up the Expression Builder.

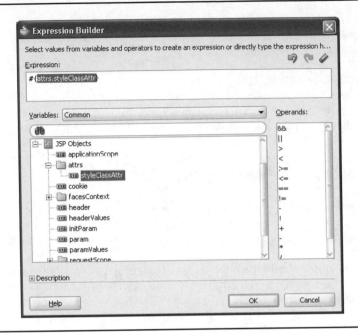

FIGURE 16-3 *Template attributes in Expression Builder*

On the ADF Faces page that references the template, template attributes show as properties in the JDeveloper Property Inspector when the af:pageTemplate element is selected in the JDeveloper Structure window (CTRL-SHIFT-S).

Application developers use a managed bean method to set the current page view ID to the template attribute at runtime. The reference to the managed bean method is added as an EL reference to the af:pageTemplate attribute.

The managed bean method looks up the FacesContext object for the current view ID. The value of the viewId, without the leading slash (/) and the page's file extension is passed back to the template attribute and added to the styleClass attribute of the component in the template that references the attribute. The managed bean code to read the current page's view ID is shown here:

```java
public class ViewContextBean {
    String currentViewId = "";
    public ContextUtil() {
    }
    public void setCurrentViewId(String currentViewId) {
    }
    public String getCurrentViewId() {
        FacesContext fctx = FacesContext.getCurrentInstance();
        String currentViewId = fctx.getViewRoot().getViewId();
        return currentViewId.substring(1,currentViewId.indexOf('.'));
    }
}
```

The managed bean method is referenced from the `af:pageTemplate` component on the ADF Faces page as follows:

```
<f:view>
 <af:document>
  <af:form>
   <af:pageTemplate viewId="/butterfly-main-template.jspx">
    <f:facet name="mainArea"/>
     <f:attribute name="styleClassAttr"
       value="#{ ViewContextBean.currentViewId}"/>
   </af:pageTemplate>
  </af:form>
 </af:document>
</f:view>
```

The `f:attribute` element is automatically added to the page at design time when choosing to build the page based on a template. The configuration of the managed bean in the adfc-config. xml file looks as follows:

```
<adfc-config ...>
  <managed-bean>
   <managed-bean-name>ViewContextBean</managed-bean-name>
   <managed-bean-class>
    adf.interactiv.view.ViewContextBean
   </managed-bean-class>
   <managed-bean-scope>request</managed-bean-scope>
  </managed-bean>
</adfc-config>
```

The skinning definition used to style a component in a template based on the page it is in contains the view ID name, which is the ADF Faces filename without the leading slash and the file extension at the end. The skin selector to apply skin definitions to instances of the `af:panelBox` component on a page with the view id page1 looks as follows:

```
page1 af|panelBox::disclosure-icon-container{display:none}
```

Using Skin Family Names in the Application Code

Though the goal of skinning is to move UI presentation code out of the application code, this is not always possible or wanted. When an application needs to respond to the selected skin family name, EL can be used to read the current skin family name from the `AdfFacesContext` object. The `AdfFacesContext` object provides access to the ADF Faces RC framework functionalities such as skinning. For example, to define an icon on a command button that references skinning-specific icon files on the file system, use the following page code:

```
<af:commandButton
   icon="/skins/images/#{adfFacesContext.skinFamily}_btnicon2.gif">
</af:commandButton>
```

A version of the command button icon btnicon2.gif needs to be available for all skin family names that are used with an application. The naming pattern for the skin-specific icons used in the code sample is *<skin family name>_<icon name>*.gif. In these code sample, the location of the images is assumed to be in the public_html\skins\images directory of the view project.

NOTE
The image URL public_html\skins\images uses relative addressing starting with a leading slash, making the browser read the image directly from the server, which may offer better performance. It is also possible to serve the image through the JSF servlet, in which case the leading slash is omitted.

Handling Client Agents and Operation Systems

In an ideal world, application UIs would render independent of browser and operation systems types. But that's not the reality. Therefore, skinning in ADF Faces RC provides two selectors to determine the user agent and the client operation system of the running user session: `@agent` and `@platform`.

To apply style definitions for Mozilla, but not for Microsoft IE, the following entry needs to be added to the skinning document:

```
@agent mozilla {
    /* skin definition here, for example … */
    af|inputText{ … }
    af|panelBox{ … }
    …
}
```

To apply style definitions to Linux clients only, use the following skin definition in the skin document:

```
@platform linux {
    /* skin definition here */
}
```

To apply style definitions to Safari browsers running on Microsoft Windows clients, use this:

```
@platform windows {
    @agent webkit {
    /* skin definition here */
}
}
```

Controlling Skin Inheritance

As documented in this chapter, custom skins can extend existing skins so the skin developer does not have to build a complete skin before an application can ship. Extending a skin, however, also allows to inhibit inheritance or add custom global selectors. In ADF Faces RC, both are possible using the `-tr-inhibit` and `-tr-rule-ref` properties.

The -tr-inhibit Property

The `-tr-inhibit` property suppresses styling rules defined on the parent skin, the base skin, or a specific selector. In addition to using `-tr-inhibit:all`, which suppresses the inheritance of all style properties defined in a base skin for a specific selector, you can inhibit style properties by exact match, which means that the exact property name must be used as in the base skin. For example, the skin definition

```
af|panelBox::content{border-left: solid thick Orange;}
```

defined in the base skin, is inhibited by the exact same property name `border-left`. Using `border` instead does not match and therefore doesn't suppress the skin definition:

```
af|panelBox::content{-tr-inhibit:border-left}
```

To use the exact match requirement, skin developers must have a good understanding of the base skin they extend.

The -tr-rule-ref Property

The `-tr-rule-ref` property references existing style classes, such as `:alias` classes, to a skin selector. While this feature is meant for component developers to use in their skin implementations, it is useful for skin developers as well. A style class, such as `.borderLeft` in the next example, that exists in the skinning document can be referenced from component selector definitions.

```
.borderLeft{border-left: solid thick}

af|panelBox::content{
 -tr-rule-ref:selector(".borderLeft");
}
```

Selecting Skins Dynamically

User interface design is the art of building applications that create happy users. Using skinning, Oracle Fusion applications can allow users to choose a custom look and feel from a list of available skins. The list can be hard coded in the application, or even better, dynamically discovered at runtime. Allowing the user to select a custom look and feel is a two-step process:

1. Discover and filter available skins at runtime.
2. Expose the list in a list choice component in the UI.

Discovering Skins at Runtime

To discover available skin at runtime, you can create and configure a managed bean that contains the following method:

```
public class SkinUtilBean implements Serializable{
   public List getSkinChoices() {
     List choices = new ArrayList();
     String skinFamily;
     String skinLabel;
     SkinFactory sf = SkinFactory.getFactory();
     FacesContext fctx = FacesContext.getCurrentInstance();
       for (Iterator i = sf.getSkinIds(); i.hasNext(); ) {
         String skinID = (String)i.next();
         Skin skin = sf.getSkin(fctx, skinID);
         // skin family also becomes the label. Alternatively
         // reference a resource bundles for translated labels
         skinFamily = skin.getFamily();
         skinLabel = skinFamily;
         if (skin.getRenderKitId().indexOf("desktop") > 0) {
           choices.add(new SelectItem(skinFamily, skinLabel));
```

```
      }
    }
  return choices;
  }
}
```

The `getSkinChoices` method obtains a list of defined skin family names from the internal `SkinFactory` class. Before adding the skin name to the list, the method checks whether the skin is defined for the desktop so it can run in browsers. This also is the location to add code that checks whether or not the evaluated skin is a base skin that may not be included in the list. A good naming scheme is needed to allow the application code to distinguish skins based on their responsibility.

The JavaBean is configured in the adfc-config.xml file or the faces-config.xml file to make it accessible to ADF Faces RC:

```
<managed-bean>
  <managed-bean-name>skinUtilsBean</managed-bean-name>
  <managed-bean-class>
    adf.interactiv.view.SkinUtilBean
  </managed-bean-class>
  <managed-bean-scope>request</managed-bean-scope>
</managed-bean>
```

Switching Skins at Runtime

The skin family name is configured in the trinidad-config.xml file using the `skin-family` element. To change the skin at runtime, you need to make the configuration dynamic and not provided as a static string. To make the configuration dynamic, use EL to read the family name string from either an attribute in the user session or a managed been in session scope.

Reading from a Session Attribute   Use the following configuration in the trinidad-config.xml file to read the skin family name from an attribute, `skin`, in the session:

```
<?xml version="1.0" encoding="windows-1252"?>
  <trinidad-config xmlns="http://myfaces.apache.org/trinidad/config">
  <skin-family>
    #{sessionScope.skin eq null?'blafplus-rich': sessionScope.skin}
  </skin-family>
</trinidad-config>
```

If the `skin` attribute is not found in the session, the Oracle default look and feel blafplus-rich is configured.

NOTE
In this configuration, a blank space appears between the colon and the `sessionScope.skin` *expression. The blank space is important, as otherwise the EL parsing will fail.*

If the skin selection is from a `af:selectOneRadio` component, then the page code for this component looks as follows:

```
<af:selectOneRadio label="Available skins" value="#{sessionScope.skin}">
   <f:selectItems value="#{skinUtilsBean.skinChoices}"/>
</af:selectOneRadio>
<af:commandButton text="Select Skin"/>
```

A full-page refresh is required to apply the new skin to the running application. By writing the skin family name directly to the session attribute, and reading it from there, it's easy for an application developer to change the name of the default skin to be used, because no Java code needs to be changed for this.

Reading from a Managed Bean   When developing reusable code, which should be self-contained, writing and reading the skin family name directly to the session appears to be error-prone. A better solution is to add this functionality to the managed bean, too:

```
public void setSkin(String skinFamily) {
   FacesContext fctx = FacesContext.getCurrentInstance();
   fctx.getExternalContext().getSessionMap().put("skin",skinFamily);
   String viewId = fctx.getViewRoot().getViewId();
    try {
       fctx.getExternalContext().redirect("faces"+viewId);
    } catch (IOException e) {
       e.printStackTrace();
    }
}
```

The setter method in the managed bean not only sets the new skin family name to the session attribute, but it also redirects the request so that no additional command button is required:

```
public String getSkin() {
   String skinFamily;
   FacesContext fctx = FacesContext.getCurrentInstance();
   Map sessionMap = fctx.getExternalContext().getSessionMap();
   Object skinFamilyObject = sessionMap.get("skin");
   skinFamily = skinFamilyObject == null?
                "blafplus-rich":(String)skinFamilyObject;
   if (skinFamilyObject == null){
     fctx.getExternalContext().getSessionMap().put("skin","blafplus-rich");
   }
   return skinFamily;
}
```

When reading the skin name, the managed bean code checks whether the `session` attribute exists, and if it doesn't, the skin falls back to a predefined default look and feel. The trinidad-config.xml file is configured as follows to call the managed bean methods:

```
<trinidad-config xmlns="http://myfaces.apache.org/trinidad/config">
   <skin-family>
    #{skinUtilsBean.skin eq null?'blafplus-rich': skinUtilsBean.skin}
   </skin-family>
</trinidad-config>
```

Because the managed bean handles the required redirect when selecting a skin, no command button needs to be added to the page source; instead, the component `autoSubmit` attribute is set to `true`:

```
<af:selectOneRadio label="Skins found" autoSubmit="true"
  value="#{skinUtilsBean.skin}">
  <f:selectItems value="#{skinUtilsBean.skinChoices}"/>
</af:selectOneRadio>
```

Deploying Skins in a Library

Skins can be deployed as part of the Fusion web application or in a library—a JAR file that has a META-INF directory added. Using a library is a good choice for skins that are to be reusable, such as base skins. Deploying skins as a library not only prevents developers from changing the look ad feel, but it also simplifies updates.

The directory structure for skins deployed in a JAR file is slightly different from skins deployed with the application. To add a skin at runtime so that the trinidad-skins.xml of the consuming application is updated, the skin definition files must be located in a directory called META-INF.

Create a directory structure similar to this on your file system:

\META-INF\adf\oracle\skin\images

\META-INF\skins\butterfly_base.css

\META-INF\trinidad-skins.xml

Note that the image directory starts with a folder named adf. Fusion web applications use a resource servlet, which is configured in the web.xml file to handle the loading of external resources. By default, the resource servlet is mapped to the adf/* URL pattern. So unless this configuration is changed by an application developer, the images must be located in a directory structure that starts with *adf* as the first folder name.

To reference an image from the style sheet document, use the following addressing:

```
content:url(../adf/oracle/skin/images/cfsortl.gif);
```

Note that the leading dots (..) in front of the image path are required to navigate from the skin directory, where the style sheet document is stored, to the META-INF root to start a search for the resource.

The trinidad-skin.xml file is located directly in the META-INF directory and contains the following entries:

```
<?xml version="1.0" encoding="ISO-8859-1"?>
  <skins xmlns="http://myfaces.apache.org/trinidad/skin">
    <skin>
      <id>butterfly_base.desktop</id>
      <family>butterfly_base</family>
      <render-kit-id>org.apache.myfaces.trinidad.desktop</render-kit-id>
      <style-sheet-name>skins/butterfly_base.css</style-sheet-name>
    </skin>
  </skins>
```

To create a JAR file from this folder structure, type the following command from the parent directory of the META-INF directory:

```
jar -cvf butterfly_base.jar META-INF/
```

Copy the resulting JAR file, butterfly_base.jar in the example, to the WEB-INF/lib folder of the ADF Faces RC view project and configure the trinidad-config.xml file, located in the WEB-INF of the same project, as shown here:

```
<?xml version="1.0" encoding="windows-1252"?>
<trinidad-config xmlns="http://myfaces.apache.org/trinidad/config">
  <skin-family>butterfly_base</skin-family>
</trinidad-config>
```

NOTE
At design time, the skin definition stored in the JAR file is not displayed in the visual editor of Oracle JDeveloper 11g, and a message appears in the log window saying that the skin family could not be found. Don't worry about this.

Skin Debugging

Skin selectors are added as style classes to the generated HTML. This makes skin debugging the art of translating the style classes used in the generated HTML output for a component to the skin selectors that produces them.

The pattern used to translate skin selectors into style class names is simple in that an underline character replaces all vertical line and colon separators. Pseudo classes are translated into their own style class name prefixed with p_AF.

- **af|panelBox**   Translates to `af_panelBox`

- **af|panelBox::header-start:core:default**   Uses two of the pseudo classes that exist for `panelBoxes` and translates to `af_panelBox_header-start p_AFCore p_AFDefault`

- **af|inputDate::content**   Translates to `af_inputDate_content`

- **af|inputDate::launch-icon-style**   Translates to `af_inputDate_launch-icon-style`

For performance reasons, the style class names are compressed by default, which means the generated style class names in the generated HTML source are shorter but also meaningless. To debug an ADF Faces RC application, the compression must be switched off, which is done by adding the following context parameter to the web application's web.xml file:

```
<context-param>
  <param-name>
    org.apache.myfaces.trinidad.DISABLE_CONTENT_COMPRESSION
  </param-name>
  <param-value>true</param-value>
</context-param>
```

NOTE
*Make sure the context parameter is removed or its value is set
to* false *before deploying your application to a production
environment; otherwise, the generated page source becomes
quite large, leading to performance degradation.*

Because the style classes are added to the generated browser output, debugging is performed
in the browser. Each browser vendor provides its own tooling or plug-in to debug web pages.
Firebug, a plug-in for the Firefox browser, provides excellent debugging functionality for HTML,
CSS, and JavaScript. Figure 16-4 shows Firebug debugging an ADF Faces RC input form. You can
see how the selected input text field is constructed using nested HTML markup and that the style
class to skin the content area is `af_inputText_content`. The style class name is the runtime
representation of the `af|inputText::content` skin selector and pseudo class. So to change
the look and feel of the `textInput` field, we use the `af|inputText::content` selector in the
skin definition.

Another useful Firefox tool is the Web Developer plug-in that allows developers to change
and test style sheet definitions instantly on the browser page. To understand how to skin a specific
area of an ADF Faces RC page, the combination of Firebug and Web Developer is very powerful.
After installing Web Developer, select Tools | Web Developer | CSS | Edit CSS to open the CSS
edit dialog. In the opened CSS editor dialog, use the skin selector class names to test your CSS styles.

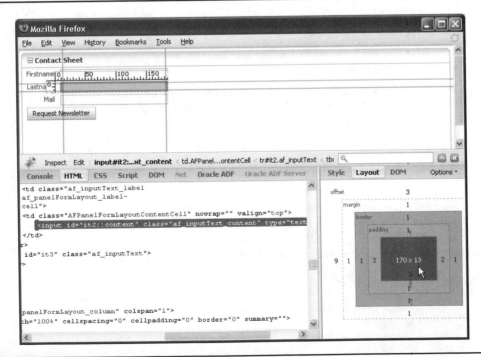

FIGURE 16-4   *Firebug inspection view of ADF Faces RC page*

Summary

Despite all the standardization underway in JSF, none exists for applying styles or a consistent look and feel across JSF components built by different vendors or open source projects. This means that application developers who look for JSF component sets to use in building their web applications not only need to look for the richness and the completeness of the components, but also for the best-of-breed implementation of UI styling.

ADF Faces RC applications are styled with CSS, which is either added directly to the JSF page source, using a semicolon-delimited list of styles in the component `inlineStyle` attribute or a style class reference added to the `styleClass` attribute, or is applied through skinning, a framework feature in ADF Faces RC.

The first rule of best practices is to avoid extensive use of the `inlineStyle` attribute because of its limited scope and its lack of existing reusable style definitions.

Style classes are good to use if they're used sensitively. A style class name added to the component `styleClass` attribute references a named style definition added to the JSF page or referenced from an external file. Avoid adding the style class definition directly to the page; add it to the skin document instead.

Style class definitions apply to the root DOM element of the ADF Faces RC component HTML. The way that CSS works is that definitions defined on a child component of the DOM tree override the same definition on the root component. Adding a style to the root document node, therefore, is no guarantee that the style has a visual impact to the rendered component. The authors recommend using style class names for addressing purposes, when implementing instance-specific skinning or as global style selectors in a skin document.

Any good application architecture is build out of layers. The recommendation for skinning is to build a layered architecture of skin documents, where inheritance goes from most generic to most specific. Start with a base skin that contains the rules of your corporate look and feel. If regional differences exist, such as logos, create a second skin document extending the global base skin. Eventually, you can extend the regional skin in an application-specific skin that contains instance- and context-specific skinning rules.

To enforce corporate look and feel standards, deploy the base skins in libraries that are added to the applications. Application-specific skins are not made for reuse and are deployed with the application. Changing a corporate look and feel becomes as easy as replacing the base skin libraries.

Define a resource bundle for each skin definition and leave it empty if there is no need to override native ADF Faces component strings.

Define naming patterns for the skin documents, such as `corporate_base`, `corporate_emea_base`, or `corporate_us_base`, to suppress base skins in the list of available skins if users are allowed to select their look and feel of choice.

Avoid skinning directly on the generated HTML output, even though it is tempting and possible to do so. For example, to skin the first DIV element of the generated output of `af:document`, the following skin definition in a skin document works:

```
af|document > div {border:medium solid Red;}
```

NOTE
There are no rock stars in software development, though some names are more familiar than others. With a custom skin in production, you certainly have evolved into a skinner, and you can put this on a t-shirt.

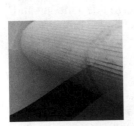

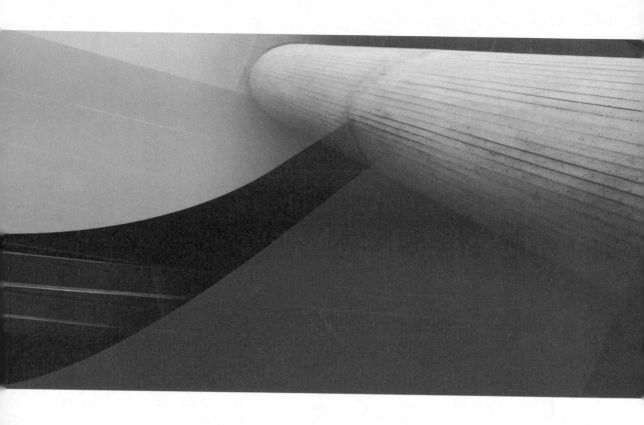

CHAPTER
17

Building Layouts
in ADF Faces RC

Application users never complain about a good layout. Even the most technically effective application will not be well received unless the layout is functional.

uilding page layouts refers to creating a grid of components for the placement of other components. The goal of building layouts is to arrange components in a logical, organized manner. This chapter is not a substitute for a formal user interface (UI) design book. However, the chapter provides several guidelines for building layouts and an explanation of each component involved.

Building Layouts

The ADF Faces library contains more than 20 layout components, as shown in Figure 17-1. Some of these components provide empty containers for other components, while others provide some level of user interactivity, such as clickable tabs and collapsible panel accordions. Still others provide what is called "geometry management," in which nested components are stretched within their outer component. Geometry management refers to how components are displayed when the page is initially rendered, when the user resizes the browser or interacts with components, or when components are updated dynamically at runtime. Geometry management is an important aspect to keep in mind while developing a layout; the process of building a layout not only includes the creation of containers for other components, but also requires an understanding of the behavior of those components as the browser is resized or as the size of the data changes.

Because browsers are not designed as robust UI containers, they should not be relied on to perform geometry management. As such, layout and style settings such as percentage dimensions differ across browsers. For this reason, the `inlineStyle` component attribute should be used sparingly. If custom styling is required, you should attempt to find a declarative approach using ADF Faces layout components. Themes, for example, can be used to apply color schemes to components declaratively. In addition, the `styleClass` attribute of components is useful for applying global styles to components, as is the use of custom skins to change the look of components for a particular organization or application. The use of style classes, skins, and themes is covered in Chapter 16.

All standalone JSF pages require the `f:view` tag. In ADF Faces applications, the `af:document` component is also mandatory, as it enables geometry management for ADF Faces layout components and creates the page infrastructure required by all ADF Faces components nested within it. Each JSF page that is created in JDeveloper will automatically include the `f:view` and nested `af:document`

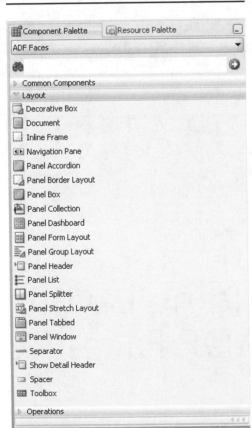

FIGURE 17-1 *Layout components in the ADF Faces library*

components and, in most cases, the `af:form` component. The document component's `maximized` attribute is set to `true` by default. This ensures that any stretchable components within the document component will be stretched.

NOTE
When building layouts in JDeveloper, many of the components are nonvisual so they do not appear in the visual editor as obviously as databound components. Therefore, using the Structure window instead of the visual editor can be helpful for building layouts in JDeveloper.

By far the most common components used to start building a layout are the panel stretch layout and panel group layout components. The `af:panelStretchLayout` component provides a stretchable container for child components nested within it, whereas the `af:panelGroupLayout` component provides a flowing component that vertically or horizontally stacks its child components. Most pages should use a mix of stretchable and flowing components, as shown in Figure 17-2.

Building Stretchable Layouts

Several main components are used to encapsulate a layout, including `af:panelStretchLayout` and `af:decorativeBox`. These components automatically stretch stretchable components that are placed within the component's center facet. The decorative box component is similar to the panel stretch layout component, but it includes a few more facets than the panel stretch layout and provides a decorative border in the form of rounded corners to its nested components. The `af:panelTabbed` and `af:panelAccordion` components will also stretch nested components within them, so they may be used as a root layout component as well.

TIP
When you're building layouts using multiple components that contain facets in the visual editor, if you nest a component into a facet that has the same facet used by the component in which it is being nested—such as including an `af:decorativeBox` in the top facet of an `af:panelStretchLayout` component—you will see only another facet named top in the editor. This is because the visual editor displays the top facet of the nested decorative box. You can remedy this by deselecting the duplicate facet in the Structure window.

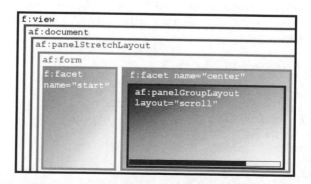

FIGURE 17-2 *Panel group layout within a panel stretch layout*

Stretching Components

Stretching components refers to enabling a child component to take up all available space that is not reserved by other components. Two conditions must be met for a component to stretch: First, the component must itself be stretchable. Second, the component must either be a direct child of a component that stretches its child components or be located within a facet of a component that stretches its child components.

The Panel Stretch Layout Component

In addition to the stretchable center facet, the `af:panelStretchLayout` component contains top, bottom, start, and end facets that are used to contain other components. By default, the dimensions of these facets are set to `auto` (via the `topHeight`, `bottomHeight`, `startWidth`, and `endWidth` attributes) and therefore do not stretch their components. With these attributes set to a value other than `auto`, the facets will attempt to stretch their components, with the remaining space allocated to the center facet.

One typical design for a page includes a fixed height area at the top of the page; a portrait-oriented area on the left side of the page for a list of navigation, operation, or menu components; a fixed height area at the bottom of the page for globally defined links or copyright information; and a large, landscape-oriented area that contains the main content of the page. The `af:panelStretchLayout` lends itself nicely to this type of layout, where the main content area of the page is located in the center facet of the component.

Of course, many types of components may be nested within the `af:panelStretchLayout` facets, but only certain components are stretchable. The `af:panelStretchLayout` component will attempt to stretch its child components, if they are stretchable. Otherwise, a transition component that is stretchable, such as an `af:panelGroupLayout` component with the `layout` attribute set to `scroll` (discussed later in this chapter), will need to be used to ensure that the user can access all the contents of the page, regardless of the size of the container. This is shown in Figure 17-2: the `af:panelGroupLayout` component is used as a transition between whatever content might be nested within it and the `af:panelStretchLayout` component. In this way, the `af:panelGroupLayout` component will be stretched within the center facet of the `af:panelStretchLayout`, and any component, stretchable or not, that is placed within the `af:panelGroupLayout` component will be accessible to the user because the `layout` attribute is set to `scroll`.

An example of the panel stretch layout component is available as one of the many Quick Start Layouts provided in JDeveloper when a new JSFF or JSPX page is created. The following code is generated if the Two Column Left Sidebar (stretched) layout is selected from the quick start layout gallery when creating a new page:

```
<f:view>
  <af:document>
    <af:form>
      <af:panelStretchLayout startWidth="100px">
        <f:facet name="start"/>
        <f:facet name="center"/>
      </af:panelStretchLayout>
    </af:form>
  </af:document>
</f:view>
```

While this layout modifies the `startWidth` size, the non-center facets of the `af:panelStretchLayout`, such as start and end, are set to 50 pixels wide (or 50 pixels high, in the case of top and bottom facets) by default. This can be modified by setting the `topHeight`, `bottomHeight`, `startWidth`, and `endWidth` attributes to a specific pixel value, or, alternatively, by setting these attributes to `auto`. However, the `auto` setting for these attributes does degrade performance somewhat, so it should be used sparingly. If the space that these facets should occupy varies, an alternative solution is to use a backing bean to determine the value and use Expression Language to specify the attribute.

TIP
If a facet does not contain content, it will not be rendered. To create blank space within a facet, use an `af:spacer` *component.*

The `af:panelStretchLayout` component is very useful for building templates. In this case, a template can contain the `af:panelStretchLayout` component, with defined content for the top and bottom facets, and facet references for the start, center, and end components. Template development is covered in detail in Chapter 15.

The Panel Splitter Component

The `af:panelSplitter` component is useful for dividing an area into two user-modifiable sections (or more, if multiple panel splitter components are used). The dividing line between the sections can be manipulated at runtime to change its location (and therefore change the amount of space displayed on either side of the line). The component's `orientation` attribute determines whether the division is horizontal or vertical, and the `splitterPosition` attribute is used to specify the initial location of the dividing line. Like the `af:panelStretchLayout` component, content for each section of the `af:panelSplitter` component is included by nesting components within the facets of the layout component.

Quick Start Layouts

More than 100 different predefined ADF Faces layouts are provided in JDeveloper. These Quick Start Layouts are available from the creation dialog when you're creating a new JSF page, JSF page template, or JSF page fragment. The layouts are categorized by the number of columns required for the page, and further categorized into types of layouts, such as whether header and footer areas are included and the orientation of side bar areas. Within each layout type are several layout variations that determine whether areas are resizable, scrollable, stretchable, and/or include splitter components. The Quick Start Layouts are not templates themselves and are fully customizable once they have been used to create a page, fragment, or template. Therefore, the layouts are a perfect way to begin creation of a template in an ADF Faces application. The following illustration shows the Quick Start menu selection for the previously mentioned Two Column Left Sidebar (stretched) layout.

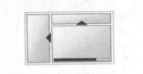

FIGURE 17-3 *A page with three splitter-divided areas*

The panel splitter contains two facets named *first* and *second*. If the orientation of the panel splitter is vertical, the first facet will be on the top and the second facet on the bottom. If the orientation of the panel splitter is horizontal, the first facet will be on the left and the second facet on the right (or the reverse for bidirectional applications). Therefore, it is necessary to nest multiple `af:panelSplitter` components to achieve a page that contains more than two splitter-divided areas, as shown in Figure 17-3.

The following code is generated if the Two Column Left Partial Header (Two splits, scrolled) quick start layout is selected when creating a page:

```
<f:view>
  <af:document>
    <af:form>
      <af:panelSplitter orientation="horizontal" splitterPosition="100">
        <f:facet name="first"/>
        <f:facet name="second">
          <af:panelSplitter orientation="vertical" splitterPosition="50">
            <f:facet name="first"/>
            <f:facet name="second">
              <af:panelGroupLayout layout="scroll"/>
            </f:facet>
          </af:panelSplitter>
        </f:facet>
      </af:panelSplitter>
    </af:form>
  </af:document>
</f:view>
```

Notice in this example that two splitters are used—one is defined with an orientation of `horizontal` (the default), and within the second facet of that splitter, another panel splitter is defined with an orientation of `vertical`. It is recommended that you set the `splitterPosition` attribute to a default size that will display both facets without scrolling, if possible. This ensures that the user can see all content before choosing to resize the amount of space devoted to each facet.

The `af:panelSplitter` component is stretchable inside an `af:panelStretchLayout`, and a panel splitter facet may wrap, truncate, or stretch when the browser is resized, depending on the components placed within it. Since the `af:panelSplitter` and `af:panelStretchLayout` components can both be stretched as well as stretch their components, these components are good choices for the outer container of a page that fills all the available browser space.

Rules for Stretching Components

ADF Faces provides components that are both stretchable and stretch their children, flowing components that are not stretchable, and transitional components that are stretchable but will not stretch their children. This allows page developers to create page layouts without specifying heights in percentage units or attempting to stretch components forcibly, as these techniques do not render reliably across multiple browsers.

Specifying Heights When Absolutely Necessary

As a general rule, the `height` attribute for all layout components should not be specified. Instead, stretchable components should be used, or, as a less favorable option, `height` attribute values can be specified in absolute units, such as pixels or `em`, which is a unit similar to pixels, except that an em unit will grow with the browser's specified font size. Specifying a height with percentage units should be avoided at all times.

The following list of components are stretchable inside an `af:panelStretchLayout` or `af:panelSplitter` facet, or inside an `af:showDetailItem` with the `stretchChildren` attribute set to `first`, nested within an `af:panelTabbed` or `af:panelAccordion` component:

- `af:panelAccordion`
- `af:panelCollection`
- `af:panelGroupLayout` (with `layout="scroll"` or `layout="vertical"`)
- `af:panelSplitter`
- `af:panelStretchLayout`
- `af:panelTabbed`
- `af:region`
- `af:table`
- `af:tree`
- `af:treeTable`

The following components cannot be stretched inside an `af:panelStretchLayout` or `af:panelSplitter`, nor can they be stretched inside an `af:showDetailItem` with the `stretchChildren` attribute set to `first`, or nested within the `af:panelTabbed` or `af:panelAccordion` components. (In the case of an `af:showDetailItem`, the `af:showDetail` and `af:showDetailHeader` components are invalid children of that component, regardless of their stretchable behavior.)

- `af:panelBorderLayout`
- `af:panelBox`
- `af:panelFormLayout`
- `af:panelGroupLayout` (with `layout="default"` or `layout="horizontal"`)
- `af:panelHeader`
- `af:panelLabelAndMessage`
- `af:panelList`
- `af:showDetail`
- `af:showDetailHeader`

It is illegal to place components that cannot stretch into facets of a component that stretches its child components, because the layout could be rendered inconsistently across multiple browsers. Instead, a component that cannot stretch should be wrapped in one that can. For example, consider a component that can stretch its children, such as an `af:panelStretchLayout` component. Within the center facet of that component, a component that is stretchable is defined, such as the `af:panelGroupLayout` with the `layout` attribute set to `scroll`. Within the panel group layout, a table component is defined, as shown in the following code:

```
<af:panelStretchLayout>
  <f:facet name="bottom"/>
  <f:facet name="center">
    <af:panelGroupLayout layout="scroll">
      <af:table value="#{bindings.DepartmentsView1.collectionModel}"
        var="row" rows="#{bindings.DepartmentsView1.rangeSize}">
        <af:column>
          <af:outputText value="#{row.DepartmentId}"/>
        </af:column>
        <!-- Other defined columns -->
      </af:table>
    </af:panelGroupLayout>
  </f:facet>
  <f:facet name="start"/>
  <f:facet name="end"/>
  <f:facet name="top"/>
</af:panelStretchLayout>
```

In this example, the `af:panelStretchLayout` stretches its children, and the `af:panelGroupLayout` with the `layout` attribute set to `scroll` is a stretchable component. However, the `af:panelGroupLayout` does not stretch its children. Therefore, even though two stretchable components are used in this example, the `af:table` component will not stretch because the parent component of the `af:table` (`af:panelGroupLayout`) does not stretch its children. To stretch the `af:table` component, it should be surrounded with a component that *does* stretch its children, such as `af:panelCollection` (this component stretches a single child table component).

The following code produces a page that displays a vertically scrolling panel group layout containing a panel collection and a fully stretched table component:

```
<af:panelStretchLayout>
  <f:facet name="bottom"/>
  <f:facet name="center">
    <af:panelGroupLayout layout="scroll">
      <af:panelCollection>
        <f:facet name="menus"/>
        <f:facet name="toolbar"/>
        <f:facet name="statusbar"/>
        <af:table value="#{bindings.DepartmentsView1.collectionModel}"
          var="row" rows="#{bindings.DepartmentsView1.rangeSize}">
```

```
        <af:column>
          <af:outputText value="#{row.DepartmentId}"/>
        </af:column>
        <!-- Other defined columns -->
      </af:table>
    </af:panelCollection>
  </af:panelGroupLayout>
</f:facet>
<f:facet name="start"/>
<f:facet name="end"/>
<f:facet name="top"/>
</af:panelStretchLayout>
```

NOTE
Learning each of the stretchable behaviors of each component can be tedious, but it is important not to attempt to shortcut the learning process by stretching components manually (such as by setting the width *attribute to 100%). This can produce inconsistent and undesirable results and should not be done. Instead, components that are not stretched (because their surrounding component does not stretch its children) should be wrapped in components that do stretch child components.*

Building Flowing Layouts

It is generally recommended that you create a combination of stretchable and flowing areas on a page. For example, a page may contain an af:panelStretchLayout as an outer component, with stretchable components in the center facet, and flowing components, such as an af:panelGroupLayout with the layout attribute set to scroll, located in the start and/or end facets of the af:panelStretchLayout. This creates a consistent page with components that are rendered reliably across browsers and browser sizes, allowing users to find relevant content easily in the page.

The Panel Group Layout Component

The af:panelGroupLayout component organizes child components into horizontally or vertically arranged sections. Horizontally arranged components can be wrapped if necessary, and can also be aligned to each other, either vertically or horizontally. As explained previously, the af:panelGroupLayout does not stretch child components, but the component itself will stretch if the component is within an af:panelSplitter or af:panelStretchLayout and the layout attribute is set to scroll or vertical.

By default, the layout attribute of the af:panelGroupLayout component is set to default. At design time, this looks similar to the layout provided by the component if the layout attribute is set to horizontal. However, the default layout attribute of the af:panelGroupLayout will not always guarantee a horizontally aligned layout at runtime (one such case is within node stamps of an af:tree component). Therefore, it is recommended that the layout attribute of af:panelGroupLayout always be explicitly set to horizontal, vertical, or scroll.

TIP
If the amount of content to be displayed in a vertically aligned af:panelGroupLayout *component is greater than the height of the screen, it is advisable that you use a* layout *attribute of* scroll, *rather than* vertical. *In both cases, the user will be able to access all the content, either via a vertical scroll bar provided by the component if the* layout *attribute is set to* scroll *or by a scroll bar provided by the browser if the* layout *attribute is set to* vertical. *However, if a modal dialog is used within the same page that contains a browser-provided scroll bar, that scroll bar will not be disabled (as it should be). Using a* scroll *layout for an* af:panelGroupLayout *component will ensure that any pop-up dialogs will not contain unnecessary scroll bars from the browser, unless these are explicitly specified by the components within the popup dialog.*

The Panel Box Component

Another useful flow component is the *panel box*. An af:panelBox component is used to highlight an area of a page with a border and a different color. It is typically used as a side container on a page, and because it has a defined border, it usually contains a small amount of content (75 × 150 pixels or so). Two color themes can be specified in the ramp attribute of the af:panelBox (core or highlight), and the background attribute can be set to none, light, medium, or dark to change the depth of the color theme used for the panel box header. An icon attribute is also available for this component, allowing developers to include images in the header of the af:panelBox component. Further changes to the look and feel of this component are common in applications and can be achieved through skinning, as discussed in Chapter 16. This component also contains a toolbar facet, and a toolbar component can be added to the facet for adding toolbar buttons to the panel box.

To arrange multiple panel box components, the af:panelDashboard component can be used. This component tiles nested panel box components according to the columns and rowHeight attributes. The dashboard component is stretchable, and because it includes listeners for dragging and dropping child components, it is frequently used as a parent component for allowing users to define the placement and visibility of panel box and region components at runtime.

The Panel Border Layout Component

The panel border layout component is similar to the panel stretch layout component in that it contains facets on the left, right, top, and bottom for placing nested components. However, the panel border layout component is a flowing component that does not stretch its children and is not stretchable. Therefore, this component is useful for flowing areas where content should be displayed on either side of a central component, as shown in Figure 17-4.

The af:panelBorderLayout component contains several facets, including inner facets located adjacent to their outer counterparts. For example, the component contains both left and innerLeft facets, where the innerLeft component is closer to the center than the left facet. For absolute placement, the left and right facets are used, and for bidirectional use, start and end facets are available. In each of these facets (left, innerLeft, right, innerRight, top, innerTop, bottom, innerBottom, start, innerStart, end, and innerEnd), the size of each is calculated based on the size of the component it contains.

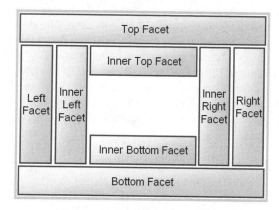

FIGURE 17-4   *Facets of the Panel Border Layout Component*

In addition to the use of facets, the `af:panelBorderLayout` component allows for direct children, which is similar to the `center` facet of the `af:panelStretchLayout` component, except that the component placed directly within the `af:panelBorderLayout` will not be stretched as it would inside the `center` facet of panel stretch layout.

Conditionally Displaying Content

Allowing users to hide and show certain areas of a page at runtime can save a great deal of space in a web application. To hide and show large areas of content, the panel tabbed component, `af:panelTabbed`, is recommended. For smaller areas of a page, the panel accordion component, `af:panelAccordion`, is useful. This section discusses each of these components in detail and provides techniques for stretching and placing components.

The Panel Accordion Component

One of the unique features of the ADF Faces components is the fact that they include built-in Asynchronous JavaScript and XML (AJAX) functionality. An obvious manifestation of this feature is shown in the `af:panelAccordion` component. This component displays one or more collapsible areas (nested within an `af:showDetailItem` component). The ability to collapse and expand accordion panels is built in to the component, as is the slick animation that highlights the collapsing or expanding of the panel.

JDeveloper will automatically create one `af:showDetailItem` component when an `af:panelAccordion` is added to a page. The `discloseMany` attribute of the panel accordion is set to `false` by default, so that only one detail item is displayed at a time. Additionally, the `discloseNone` attribute is `false` by default, so that one detail item must be disclosed at all times. *Oracle Fusion Middleware Web User Interface Developer's Guide for Oracle Application Development Framework 11g Release 1* covers the use of the `flex`, `inflexibleHeight`, and `stretchChildren` attributes of the `af:showDetailItem` component when used as a child of `af:panelAccordion`.

If show detail item components are used with an `af:panelAccordion` component, the `inflexibleHeight` attribute of `af:showDetailItem` can be used to specify the amount of pixels that the show detail item component will consume. The default value is 100 pixels. If insufficient vertical space is available to display all show detail items due to setting this value (or due to other constraints on the page), overflow icons in the form of double up or down arrows will be displayed at runtime just above and/or below the component, as shown in Figure 17-5. Note that these icons are not obvious to the user, and since the goal of accordions in general is to reuse vertical space, every effort should be made to limit the amount of content included so that the headers of each `af:showDetailItem` component can be displayed without the need for overflow icons.

The Panel Tabbed Component

The `af:panelTabbed` component displays `af:showDetailItem` components in the form of folder tabs (at the top of the component by default). Alternatively, you can use the `position` attribute of `af:panelTabbed` to display the tabs at the bottom or both the top and bottom of the component. Note that these tabs display only the `Text` attribute in the header. If other components such as buttons or links are required in the header area, consider using an `af:panelAccordion` component instead and adding a toolbar and action components to the toolbar facet of an `af:showDetailItem`.

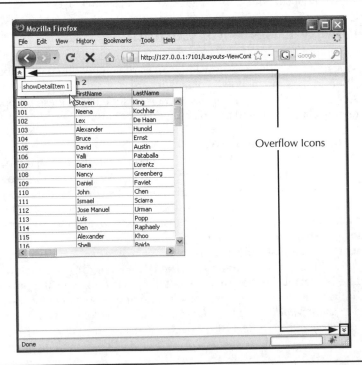

FIGURE 17-5 *Overflow icons in the panel accordion component*

The Show Detail Item Component

Show detail item components are the primary child components of `af:panelAccordion`, `af:panelTabbed`, and other layout containers. The component toggles to hide or show its content. This toggle is referred to as `undisclosed` (hide) and `disclosed` (show).

As explained previously, the `af:form` component is mandatory for enabling the built-in event functionality that is automatically enabled for components such as the `af:showDetailItem` component's hide/show functionality. The component delivers an `org.apache.myfaces` `.trinidad.event.DisclosureEvent` when the component's hide/show icon is clicked at runtime. The following example demonstrates the use of the `disclosureListener` attribute for `af:showDetailItem`. In this example, two show detail items are nested within an `af:panelAccordion`, and the `disclosureListener` attribute is set to the `showHideListener` backing bean method for both show detail item components.

```
<af:panelAccordion discloseMany="true">
  <af:showDetailItem text="First ShowDetail Item"
    disclosureListener="#{ShowHideBean.showHideListener}"/>
  <af:showDetailItem text="Second ShowDetail Item"
    disclosureListener="#{ShowHideBean.showHideListener}"/>
</af:panelAccordion>
```

The `showHideListener` method is implemented as follows, where the `disclosureEvent` raised by the hide/show toggle is used to retrieve the title and disclosed state of the `af:showDetailItem` that raised the event:

```
import javax.faces.application.FacesMessage;
import javax.faces.context.FacesContext;
import oracle.adf.view.rich.component.rich.layout.RichShowDetailItem;
import org.apache.myfaces.trinidad.event.DisclosureEvent;

public class ShowHideBean {
  public void showHideListener(DisclosureEvent disclosureEvent) {
    RichShowDetailItem sdi =
      (RichShowDetailItem)disclosureEvent.getComponent();
    boolean accordionExpanded = disclosureEvent.isExpanded();
    String title = sdi.getText();
    String state = (accordionExpanded ? "disclosed" : "undisclosed");
    FacesMessage msg = new FacesMessage(title + " is " + state);
    FacesContext.getCurrentInstance().addMessage(null, msg);
  }
}
```

Stretching Components Within Panel Accordion and Panel Tabbed Components   See the section titled "Rules for Stretching Components" earlier in the chapter for a list of components that can be stretched inside the `af:panelAccordion` and `af:panelTabbed` components. Note that in the case of an `af:panelAccordion` and `af:panelTabbed`, the stretchable components will not stretch if the nested `af:showDetailItem` component contains more than one child, or if the child has styles such as width and height specified, or if the `stretchChildren` attribute of the `af:showDetailItem` is not set to `first`.

Laying Out Forms

Good layouts are especially important when they are used to lay out data entry components. In these cases, the order and organization of nested components are especially important to ensure that the user can efficiently enter data in the form's input fields.

The af:panelFormLayout component is added by default when a data control collection is dropped onto a page as an ADF form (for both read-only or editable forms). The component doesn't have any visual attributes, meaning that no dividing lines or headers are included within it.

NOTE
The panel form layout component evenly distributes nested components, so that the amount of space between labels and text fields is consistent. In addition, the component vertically and horizontally aligns nested components, so that all labels are right-aligned and all text fields are left-aligned. For panel form layouts with multiple columns, the text fields are horizontally aligned across columns.

Typically, the contents of the form include one or more input fields that include the label attribute (or an af:panelLabelAndMessage component and an af:outputText component in the case of read-only form items). By default, the af:panelFormLayout lays out its child components in one column. This is because the rows attribute for the component is set to the maximum integer value (2147483647) by default. This ensures that all child components will be rendered in one column, with labels right-aligned and fields left-aligned.

The af:panelFormLayout component can be arranged to contain multiple columns by modifying the maxColumns and rows attributes of the af:panelFormLayout. The component will render no more than three columns in a browser by default, and the maximum number of columns can override the set number of rows. The maxColumns attribute can be set to a larger value, although this is not recommended because not all users will have large enough screen resolutions to display the data.

The amount of space between the columns can be modified somewhat by using the labelWidth and fieldWidth attributes, which will create white space around all labels and fields, unless the data in the labels or fields occupy the available space. Labels are wrapped if additional space is needed. The labelWidth and fieldWidth percentages should add up to 100%, regardless of the number of columns specified, and the component's geometry management mechanism will calculate the percentages for more than one column.

Recommendations for Building Form Layouts

In typical applications, several styles of input forms are required. In some cases, a form with two columns, each containing evenly distributed labels and input fields, is sufficient. Consider, however, the case of a registration page, where a name, address, and registration options are displayed in a form. The form might include input fields for a first name, last name, street address, city, and state, and checkboxes or radio buttons for registration options. Each of these components would include its own defined label, and it may be best to specify the rows attribute of the parent af:panelFormLayout so that the form displays two columns. However, the fields related to the address shouldn't be distributed across columns because this would be confusing to the user. To force the address components to be displayed in the same column, wrap them in a af:group component. Grouped components are always displayed in the same column, regardless of the number of rows or maxColumns specified in the af:panelFormLayout, as shown in Figure 17-6.

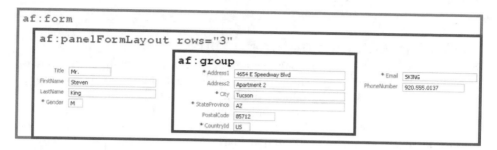

FIGURE 17-6 *Grouped components are always displayed in the same column.*

As mentioned, when dropping a collection from the Data Control palette onto the visual editor and choosing any of the selections in the Forms creation menu, JDeveloper will create an `af:panelFormLayout` component as well as nested components bound to the data collection. If ADF Read-only Form is selected as the type of form to create, `af:panelLabelAndMessage` components are created, with `af:outputText` components bound to each attribute value. If an ADF Form is selected as the type of form to create, `af:inputText` components with `label` attributes are created within the form. If you want to display multiple input components with only a single label, remove the `label` attribute from the input text component and surround the fields that require a common label with `af:panelLabelAndMessage`, as shown in the following example:

```
<af:panelFormLayout>
  <af:panelLabelAndMessage label="Department Information">
    <af:inputText value="#{bindings.DepartmentId.inputValue}" … />
    <af:inputText value="#{bindings.DepartmentName.inputValue}" … />
  </af:panelLabelAndMessage>
  <af:inputText value="#{bindings.ManagerId.inputValue}"
    label="#{bindings.ManagerId.hints.label}" … />
  <af:inputText value="#{bindings.LocationId.inputValue}"
    label="#{bindings.LocationId.hints.label}" … />
</af:panelFormLayout>
```

A footer facet is available for the `af:panelFormLayout` component, so that child components (such as a submit button) can be added beneath the form. Only one child is allowed, however, so multiple buttons (such as a reset button as well as a submit button) need to be wrapped in an `af:panelGroupLayout` or `af:group` component.

NOTE
The `af:group` *component is a nonvisual component, except when it is used in an* `af:panelFormLayout`, *a footer facet of an* `af:panelFormLayout`, *or within menus, where horizontal dotted separation lines are used to delineate the top and bottom of the grouped components.*

To align items in multiple form areas that are nested within separate `af:panelFormLayout` components, set the `labelWidth` and `fieldWidth` attributes consistently in each form. This technique can also be used to align components within individual `af:panelFormLayout` components when building forms that read across and then down, rather than down and then across.

Layout Considerations for Printing

When creating pages with layout components that allow users to modify visible areas (such as tabs, splitters, accordions, and so on), you should give special consideration to support printing. The `af:showPrintablePageBehavior` component should be placed appropriately if only a portion of the page is printable. For example, in the case of an `af:panelSplitter` component, if only one facet should be printed, the `af:showPrintablePageBehavior` component should be added to an action component within that facet. The `af:showPrintablePageBehavior` component does not actually launch the print function of the browser; instead, a new tab or window will open that contains the content to be printed, typically without scroll bars. This behavior should be tested for content of various widths, as it is possible to create a layout that will display a scroll bar when the printable page is displayed. To call the browser's print function, a `clientListener` can be added to an action component that calls the `self.print` method, as follows:

```
<af:commandButton text="Print">
  <af:clientListener type="action" method="self.print"/>
</af:commandButton>
```

Additional Layout Components

The Apache MyFaces Trinidad HTML library (prefix `trh`) provides a few additional layout components that are not available in the ADF Faces library. These include the `trh:tableLayout`, `trh:rowLayout`, and `trh:cellFormat` components. The components create a raw HTML table structure and are therefore flowing components, meaning that they do not support being stretched by their surrounding components, nor do they stretch their child components. These components should generally be avoided as the layouts they provide can typically be achieved by using ADF Faces components, which allows UI developers to work with fewer libraries to create pages.

Adding Headers to a Layout

Just like the headers used for sections in this book, headers in an application are beneficial for providing context for a particular area of a page. The header components in ADF Faces provide containers for action components that are related to content in that particular section. Menu and toolbar facets for creating action components are available for many layout components, or they can be added directly by using specific header components. As shown in Figure 17-7, the Structure window can be used to determine which facets are available and enabled for a particular component. Right-click a component in the Structure window and choose Facets to view the available facets for the component. Those that are enabled will be displayed with a checkmark.

The `af:panelHeader` component provides a well-defined structure for including components such as toolbars and menus in a header area. In `af:panelHeader`, specify the `messageType` attribute to define the icon that is used in the header (`confirmation`, `error`, `info`, `warning`, or `none`). Alternatively, supply a unique icon by setting the `icon` attribute to an image in the context root of the page. The `af:showDetailHeader` provides the same functionality as the `af:panelHeader`, except that this component can be expanded and collapsed at runtime.

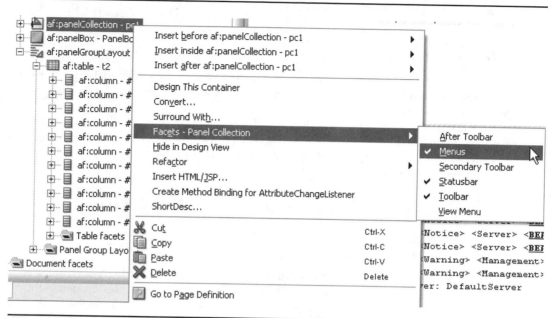

FIGURE 17-7   *Viewing available facets for a component*

When building menu and toolbar components for a page or a section of a page, the `af:toolbar` and `af:menuBar` components are used to wrap `af:commandToolbarButton` and `af:menu` components, respectively. The use of these components is covered elsewhere in this book, but a layout component should be used to define the layout of action components such as menus and toolbar buttons. The `af:toolbox` component is a parent component for panel menu bar and toolbar components, and the `af:group` component can be used to create separators between groups of related action components.

Organizing Items Within a Layout Container

Previous sections of this chapter explain how to define layouts for entire pages or portions of pages. Within those layout containers, additional components are used to lay out smaller bits of content. For example, the `af:panelList` component creates a non-interactive hierarchical list of components. For an interactive list (where components can be expanded and collapsed), use the `af:tree` component instead.

The Panel List Component

The `af:panelList` component supports both bulleted and ordered lists, and hierarchies can be created by using the `af:group` component. To specify the image used to denote the list, set the `listStyle` attribute to one of the following values:

- `list-style-type:none`
- `list-style-type:disc` (the default)
- `list-style-type:square`
- `list-style-type:circle`

- `list-style-type:decimal`

- `list-style-type:lower-alpha`

- `list-style-type:upper-alpha`

The `rows` and `maxColumns` attributes can also be specified for the panel list component. These settings are related to each other in the same way as described previously for the panel form layout component.

Consider a portion of a page that displays a list of attributes from a collection. Output text components can be defined statically within a panel list, of course, but to iterate over a collection in the data model, the `af:forEach` tag is used within an `af:panelList` component, as shown in the following example:

```
<af:panelList>
  <af:forEach var="row" items="#{bindings.EmployeesView1.rangeSet}">
    <af:outputText value="#{row.Email}"/>
  </af:forEach>
</af:panelList>
```

In the following example, the items that the `af:forEach` tag iterates through are specified in the binding layer using a tree binding. This enables each of the attributes defined in the node definition of the tree binding to be accessible from Expression Language using the value of the `var` attribute in the `af:forEach` tag (`row.Email` in this case). The tree binding definition is specified as follows:

```
<executables>
  <iterator Binds="EmployeesView1" RangeSize="25"
    DataControl="AppModuleDataControl" id="EmployeesView1Iterator"/>
</executables>
<bindings>
  <tree IterBinding="EmployeesView1Iterator" id="EmployeesView1">
    <nodeDefinition DefName="model.EmployeesView" Name="EmployeesView10">
      <AttrNames>
        <Item Value="Email"/>
      </AttrNames>
    </nodeDefinition>
  </tree>
</bindings>
```

Note the use of the `af:forEach` tag, instead of `c:forEach` from the JavaServer Pages Standard Tag Library (JSTL). In ADF Faces applications, the `af:forEach` tag should be used instead of `c:forEach`, unless the intent is to iterate over `java.util.Collection` objects.

Creating Dynamic Layouts

The same principles that apply to using the `af:forEach` tag in this example of an `af:panelList` component can be used to create custom layouts.

Recommended Layout Techniques

As described throughout this chapter, it is recommended that page layouts contain a mix of stretchable and flowing components organized in a consistent manner. This ensures maximum reuse and flexibility in an application. The root component for a page should contain a stretchable outer frame, such as af:panelStretchLayout, and should contain nested flowing areas within its facets, such as scrolling containers.

TIP
When building layouts, it is sometimes helpful to use the inlineStyle attribute as a debugging mechanism to distinguish different components at runtime. For example, specifying unique background colors for layout components (in the Style and Theme node in the Property Inspector) can help determine which component is stretching or flowing. Figure 17-8 shows the Property Inspector for an af:panelGroupLayout component that has the background color property set to Fuchsia. Another useful tool is the "debug" skin, which is included in the ADF Faces Rich Client component runtime demo web archive (WAR) file, available from Oracle Technology Network.

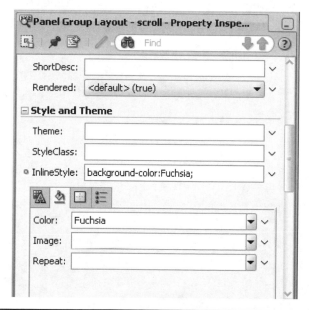

FIGURE 17-8 *Debugging layout components using background colors*

Creating Bidirectional Components

In many of the ADF Faces layout components, the terms "start" and "end" are used to describe the limits of the component's horizontal layout. For example, an `af:panelStretchLayout` component contains five facets—top, bottom, center, start, and end. The start and end facets are located on either side of the center facet and are named as such because of the localization support available in ADF Faces. If an ADF Faces application is run in a language that is read from left to right, then the start facet will be located on the left and the end facet will be located on the right. However, if the application is run in a language that is read from right to left, the facet placement is reversed. This allows developers to create an application that can be read bidirectionally. Chapter 18 covers the subject of internationalization in detail.

Summary

The success of an application depends greatly upon the user's ability to understand and efficiently utilize the content of the application. Application users never complain about a good layout. Even the most technically effective application will not be well received unless the layout is functional. Well laid-out pages enable users to be more efficient and less likely to require application training. Additionally, proper layouts and the use of templates increase the maintainability of an application.

Application logic developers should not be tasked with UI design. By using templates and layout containers effectively, the application's rules for content containers (menu areas, form layouts, table containers, and so on) are consistent and obvious to page developers, thereby reducing the time necessary to create a page, as well as ensuring consistent functionality in the application.

CHAPTER
18

Internationalization

Think of your users first! For whom are you developing? What languages do they speak? Will application training be provided, or is this a self-service application for which proper documentation must be shipped along with the product?

Internationalization is an important step in developing applications and is recommended even if an application may not be localized to support different languages. Localization is one of the last steps in application development, when an application is shaped for specific languages by translating text and number formats for languages, countries, and/or regions. Localization allows application users to interact with the application in the way that is most efficient for them—in their native language.

Creating Internationalizable JSF Applications

Regardless of the need for localizing an application for different languages or countries, every application should be configured so that it may be localized. The process of configuring an application for localization is called *internationalization*, sometimes abbreviated *i18n* (the *18* is for the number of characters between the *i* and the *n*). It is performed by the developer providing data and text labels in separate files to which the application refers by a key value, instead of hard-coding the text. For example, a Hello World message could be statically defined as follows:

```
<af:outputText value="Hello World"/>
```

However, it is preferable instead to define the value field using Expression Language (EL) that looks up a key value from a resource file. The expression used to refer to a key value is #{*bundlevar.keyname*}; here's an example:

```
<af:outputText value="#{vcb.home_greeting}"/>
```

The value associated with the key is defined in a file that serves as the resource bundle for the application. For example, the `home_greeting` key might be defined as follows:

```
home_greeting=Hello World
```

This value could then be translated and saved in an additional resource bundle for the application. For example, a resource bundle for the German language might contain the following value for the same `home_greeting` key, and the bundle would be used when the user's browser default language is set to the German language:

```
home_greeting=Hallo Welt
```

The EL defined in our example includes the use of a variable (`vcb`) and the key value, `home_greeting`. The variable can be defined in several ways. First, an `f:loadBundle` tag from the JavaServer Faces (JSF) core tag library can be used to define the resource bundle for the page, as shown:

```
<f:loadBundle basename="view.ViewControllerBundle" var="vcb"/>
```

This is the pre-JSF 1.2 way of defining resource bundles, because every page that refers to the resource file must include the `f:loadBundle` tag. In this example, `view` is the package name in which the bundle `ViewControllerBundle` resides. Another way to define resource bundles is to declare them globally in the faces-config.xml of the application, as described in the next

> **Defining Strings Using Expression Language**
>
> Our code example shows the `value` attribute of an `af:outputText` component defined using EL to retrieve the value from a resource bundle. Of course, resource strings can be used not only for output text components, and not only for the `value` attribute. Common ADF Faces components that should use EL instead of literal strings include layout component strings such as the `disclosedText` and `undisclosedText` attributes of the `af:showDetail` component, the `title` attribute for the `af:dialog` and `af:document` components, and the `text` attribute of the `af:showDetailItem` and `af:panelHeader` components. It's also very typical for all command components to use resource strings, defined in the `text` attribute of the `af:commandButton`, `af:commandLink`, `af:commandToolbarButton`, and `af:commandNavigationItem` components, for example. Additionally, components that do not have their label or value determined by EL that refers to the data model can specify one using a resource string. For example, the `label` attribute of the `af:panelLabelAndMessage` component can be defined using EL that refers to a resource string.

section. A third way is to use some functionality provided by the ADF framework called the *ADF bundle*, described later in the section "Using the ADF Bundle to Create Resource Strings."

NOTE
By default, JDeveloper sets the encoding for JSF pages to windows-1252. However, for properly internationalized applications, pages should specify an encoding that will support all languages that are intended to be supported, such as UTF-8. The default encoding can be modified by choosing Tools | Preferences in JDeveloper, selecting the Environment node, and choosing the appropriate value from the Encoding drop-down list.

Defining Resource Bundles Globally

To define resource bundles globally, use the `resource-bundle` element of the faces-config.xml file to refer to a bundle. Here's an example:

```
<resource-bundle>
  <base-name>view.ViewControllerBundle</base-name>
    <var>vcb</var>
</resource-bundle>
```

In this case, the EL used to refer to a string is similar to the EL for resource bundles that are declared for each page, but the variable is used directly and refers to a variable defined in the faces-config.xml, instead of a variable defined in the page's `f:loadBundle` tag. Here's an example:

```
<af:outputText value="#{vcb.home_greeting}"/>
```

This is the most common way for JSF 1.2 applications to be configured, and this can be easier to maintain because every page in the application refers to the resource bundle using the same variable, which makes searching for strings easier when you're trying to locate a string in a particular page at design time.

However, this global configuration is not the default way that ADF applications are configured, because ADF applications created in JDeveloper will be configured for use with the ADF bundle functionality, discussed in the next section. Due to this fact, when choosing the Select Text Resource option in the Property Inspector for a value, text, or label property, the ADF bundle functionality does not use a globally defined variable. Therefore, when using a resource bundle that is globally defined in the faces-config.xml file, do not use the Select Text Resource option when defining strings or labels in the Property Inspector. Instead, choose Expression Builder, as shown in Figure 18-1, and then choose the appropriate key to use for the string resource from the available values in the Faces Resource Bundles node of the Expression Builder dialog, as shown in Figure 18-2.

Using the ADF Bundle to Create Resource Strings

The ADF bundle functionality in JDeveloper allows developers to create customizable resource strings for applications. For example, a set of resource strings can be specified for a particular user or user role, and another set of strings might be used for another user or role. This provides a great deal of flexibility in developing customizable applications.

This functionality is typically used with XML Localization Interchange File Format (XLIFF) resource bundle types, which provide a more structured way of defining resource strings for ease in customizing resources in an application. As stated earlier, however, JDeveloper will assume the use of an ADF bundle regardless of the type of resource bundle used. Even if the additional functionality of an ADF bundle is not required, the design-time benefits to using this method far outweigh using a globally defined resource bundle in faces-config.xml, even though the use of an ADF bundle means that the resource bundle will be defined in each JSF page. (At the time of writing, there is an outstanding enhancement request for JDeveloper that will enable the Select Text Resource dialog to use the ADF bundle and thus allow the resource bundle to be defined globally.)

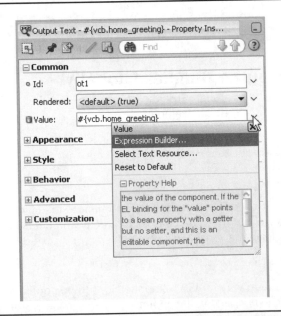

FIGURE 18-1   *Property Inspector for text, value, and label properties*

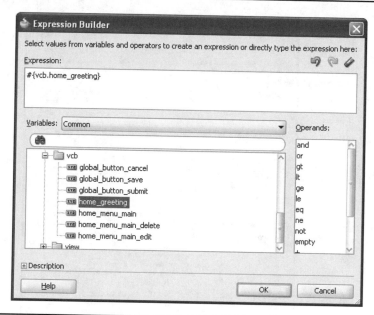

FIGURE 18-2   *Expression Builder dialog for Faces Resource Bundles*

Consider the preceding example where the Expression Builder is used to select a resource string key, as shown in Figure 18-2. In that example, only those keys that already exist are shown in the Faces Resource Bundles node. However, when using the ADF bundle, two important design-time benefits are provided, both related to creating new strings resources. The first benefit is the ability to define new resource keys and values using the Select Text Resource dialog. In the Property Inspector, click Select Text Resource in the drop-down list for a text, value, or label property to open the Select Text Resource dialog shown in Figure 18-3.

The Select Text Resource dialog allows developers to filter the list of existing strings by typing values into the Display Value or Key field, which greatly assists in selecting a string from a long list. The dialog also allows developers to create new strings directly without having to edit the resource file manually. This saves time during development; however, teams should ensure that new resource strings are created appropriately so that inconsistent labels are not generated. (For example, if the agreed-upon string for buttons that save user changes is *Save*, by using the Select Text Resource dialog, it becomes very easy for developers to create new string resources such as *Submit* or *Commit* for a button with the same functionality.)

The second benefit of using an ADF bundle is the ability for strings to be created automatically as developers enter values, labels, and text in the JSF visual editor. The Resource Bundle node of the Project Properties dialog contains the setting Automatically Synchronize Bundle, as shown in Figure 18-4. If selected, this setting will automatically create resource keys and values as they are typed into the visual editor. Note that this feature should be used only for small development projects, because the ability to create duplicate or inconsistent resource strings is significant.

Figure 18-4 also shows the Warn About Hard-coded Translatable Strings option. This option is extremely useful (whether used in conjunction with synchronization or not) for providing visual cues to developers when literal strings are entered into label, text, and value properties.

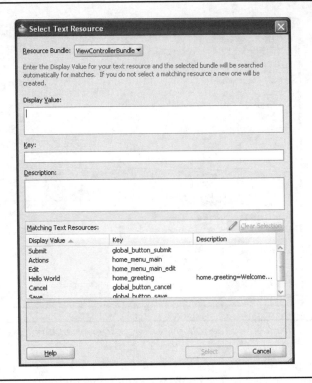

FIGURE 18-3 *The Select Text Resource dialog*

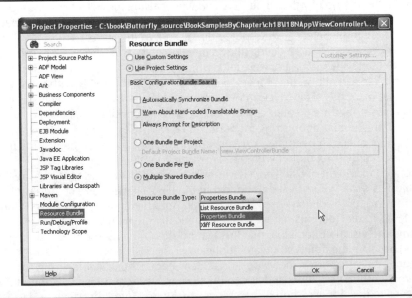

FIGURE 18-4 *Project Properties dialog for synchronizing resource strings*

When this option is selected, properties that contain literal strings will be highlighted in the Property Inspector with a warning.

As mentioned, ADF applications will use the ADF bundle functionality by default. When a value is selected from the Select Text Resource dialog, a `c:set` tag from the Java Standard Tag Library (JSTL) core library will be added to the page. Here's an example:

```
<c:set var="vcb" value="#{adfBundle['view.ViewControllerBundle']}"/>
```

The `c:set` tag refers to the implicit object `adfBundle` and defines a variable (`vcb` in this example) in each JSF page that uses a text resource. The EL syntax for referring to the bundle is the same as in previous examples:

```
<af:outputText value="#{vcb.home_greeting}"/>
```

Defining Resource Strings

In the preceding sections, the key used to refer to the resource string was `home_greeting`. The key/value mapping for this resource string can be specified in a list resource bundle, a properties file, or an XLIFF resource bundle. The options to configure the resource type are defined in the Project Properties dialog, as shown in Figure 18-4. The most common case is the use of a properties file, where key/value pairs are separated by line and contained in a text file with the extension *.properties*. For example, the `home_greeting` key would be contained in a file named ViewControllerBundle.properties, where this file is used as the default resource bundle for the entire ViewController project. As shown in Figure 18-4, multiple files may be specified for a project, or each JSF page may use its own resource bundle.

NOTE
Only strings can be defined in a resource properties file. If objects other than strings need to be internationalized for the application, a list resource bundle should be used instead.

In this example, the ViewControllerBundle.properties file would contain the key `home_greeting`, mapped to a string value, along with other key/value pairs:

```
home_greeting=Hello World
global_button_submit=Submit
global_button_cancel=Cancel
global_button_save=Save
home_menu_main=Actions
home_menu_main_edit=Edit
home_menu_main_delete=Delete
```

Resource Bundles as Marketing Tools
Defining resource bundles does not have to be done solely for the purposes of supporting multiple languages in an application. Applications that require different labels for marketing purposes, for example, can also use resource bundles so that labels can be easily replaced across the application depending on variations in promotions or seasonal sales.

Translating Access Keys

Access keys are defined by page developers to provide keyboard access to command components by using the ALT-access key (or ALT equivalent). The access key must be a letter within the string. Thus, these keys must be translated and included in the resource bundle for each supported language. For example, if the ViewControllerBundle.properties file defines the `home_menu_main_view` key as `Vie&w`, where the `w` is defined as the access key, then the ViewControllerBundle_de.properties file should contain the translated version of that key value, as well as specifying a valid access key—such as this: `home_menu_main_view=&Ansicht`

Note the use of underscores in the resource properties file. This is done for both functionality as well as readability. It is helpful to categorize types of strings by their purpose and/or specific page, especially when one properties file is used for an entire application. This helps developers maintaining the properties file to determine which labels are used for various parts of the application, and makes it much easier for page developers to find the appropriate string for a UI component. The use of dot notation in the properties file is allowed, but the EL syntax must be changed to support this. For example, suppose the `home_greeting` key was changed to the following:

```
home.greeting=Hello World
```

You might be inclined to access this key using the following expression:

```
<af:outputText value="#{vcb.home.greeting}"/>
```

However, this code would fail at runtime with a `javax.el.PropertyNotFoundException`, because the expression is attempting to evaluate the property by the name of `greeting` in the `home` object, which of course does not exist. Instead, the EL to access a key value containing a dot would need to include single quotes around the key:

```
<af:outputText value="#{vcb['home.greeting']}"/>
```

When using the Select Text Resource dialog, the syntax is generated correctly and so no effort is required on the part of the developer to modify the syntax. However, when using a globally defined resource bundle and thus selecting the expression from the Expression Builder dialog, the expression will be created without the quotes and therefore would require a manual modification. Thus, when using globally defined resource property files (instead of the default ADF bundle functionality), keys should not include the use of dot notation to delineate categories.

NOTE
Setting resource bundle preferences for a project should be performed before resource strings are used in an application. Any settings specified in the Resource Bundle node of the Project Properties dialog will be relevant from that point forward. This means that if resource bundles have already been created, configured in the project, and/ or used in UI components prior to specifying the resource bundle properties, the key/value pairs in the existing bundle file(s) will not be merged to the new file(s), and EL that refers to the original file(s) will not be modified automatically.

Using Tokens in Resource Strings

When the content of the key's value isn't known at design time, a substitution parameter, or *token*, can be provided in the string. To use tokens in a resource string, simply include a token placeholder within curly braces in the message. For example, in a properties file, the following string is specified:

```
home.param.greeting=Hello {0}. You have been logged in since {1}.
```

The values for these tokens can be applied at runtime in several ways. The easiest way is to use the h:outputFormat tag from the JSF core library and include nested f:param tags to supply the values of the tokenized strings. For example, the following tag produces the output "Hello Lynn. You have been logged in since Mon Jul 13 23:35:14 MDT 2009."

```
<h:outputFormat value="#{vcb['home.param.greeting']}">
  <f:param value="Lynn"/>
  <f:param value="#{userInfoBean.loggedInTimeFormatted}"/>
</h:outputFormat>
```

In this example, a static string is supplied for the first token value, and the value of the loggedInTimeFormatted property from a managed bean is supplied as the second value. The parameters will be processed in the order they are supplied, regardless of any value supplied for the optional name attribute of the f:param tag.

The ADF Faces equivalent af:outputFormatted component does not support the use of nested f:param tags. However, internal af:format and af:formatNamed EL functions can be used within the value attribute of ADF Faces components to supply token values. The next example shows the use of the af:format2 tag which allows two token values to be passed to the resource string:

```
<c:set var="myvar" value="#{userInfoBean.loggedInTimeFormatted }"/>
<af:outputText value="#{af:format2(vcb['home.param.greeting'], 'Lynn',
myvar)}"/>
```

In addition to the af:format2 function, several other functions are available that allow up to four substitution values to be specified. The signature for each of these methods is listed here:

- af:format(String base, String param0)

- af:format2(String base, String param0, String param1)

- af:format3(String base, String param0, String param1, String param2)

- af:format4(String base, String param0, String param1, String param2, param3)

- af:formatNamed(String base, String key0, String value0)

- af:formatNamed2(String base, String key0, String value0, String key1, String value1)

- af:formatNamed3(String base, String key0, String value0, String key1, String value1, String key2, String value2)

- af:formatNamed4(String base, String key0, String value0, String
  key1, String value1, String key2, String value2, String key3,
  String value3)

Defining Resource Strings Using XLIFF

XLIFF files (.xlf extension) allow developers to maintain a properly formatted XML structure for specifying string resources. The process for creating a resource bundle using the XLIFF format is most easily accomplished by specifying XLIFF as the resource type in the Project Properties dialog, and then choosing Select Text Resource from the Property Inspector when specifying a text value. This action creates the XLIFF resource bundle and adds the newly created element automatically. For example, the ViewControllerBundle.xlf might contain the following code:

```
<?xml version="1.0" encoding="windows-1252" ?>
<xliff version="1.1" xmlns="urn:oasis:names:tc:xliff:document:1.1">
  <file source-language="en" original="view.ViewControllerBundle"
    datatype="x-oracle-adf">
    <body>
      <trans-unit id="home_greeting">
        <source>Hello World</source>
        <target/>
      </trans-unit>
      <trans-unit id="global_button_submit">
        <source>Submit</source>
        <target/>
      </trans-unit>
    </body>
  </file>
</xliff>
```

More information about XLIFF, a project of the Oasis group, can be found at http://docs.oasis-open.org/xliff/xliff-core/xliff-core.html.

Defining Resource Strings Using Classes

List resource bundles are most commonly used when substitution parameters for resource string values do not provide enough flexibility and coding is required to determine resource values.

Like XLIFF files, the most straightforward way to configure an application to use the list resource bundle is to specify the list resource bundle resource type in the Project Properties dialog, and then use the Select Text Resource dialog to enter string resources that will then be automatically created in a list resource bundle. The file is a Java class that extends `java.util`
`.ListResourceBundle` and implements the `getContents()` method, which returns an array of key/value pairs. For example, the ViewControllerBundle.java list resource file is implemented as follows:

```
import java.util.ListResourceBundle;

public class ViewControllerBundle extends ListResourceBundle {
  private static final Object[][] contents = {
    { "home_greeting", "Hello World" },
    { "global_button_submit", "Submit" }
  };
```

```
public Object[][] getContents() {
  return contents;
  }
}
```

Note that the class is not as human-readable as the properties file and therefore might not be as easily translated by nontechnical translation specialists.

Internationalizing ADF Business Components

Internationalizing labels, date formats, error messages, and other strings such as tool tips in ADF BC is very straightforward. As with UI projects, the Resource Bundle node of the Project Properties dialog is used to define how resources will be configured for an application, including the type of resource bundle and whether one bundle will be used for the project or one bundle per file. In the case of UI projects, it is common to define one resource bundle for the entire application. However, for projects containing ADF Business Components, it may be beneficial to define one resource bundle per file (for example, a resource bundle for every entity object). The benefits of this are seen at design time; JDeveloper nests resources for a particular file with the Application Navigator (when the default Group Related Files option is selected), as shown Figure 18-5. This allows data model developers, who typically work with one entity object or view object at a time, to locate the resource bundle easily for the component with which they are working.

Another reason for using one resource bundle per file is that (especially in the case of entity objects) the labels, data formats, and other internationalizable strings are typically unique to a particular entity. For example, the appropriate `DepartmentId` attribute label for a Department entity object might be `Id`, whereas the label for the `DepartmentId` attribute for an Employees entity object might be `Department`.

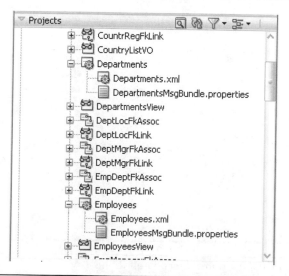

FIGURE 18-5 *JDeveloper nests resources with Application Navigator.*

Internationalizing ADF BC Attributes

When creating ADF Business Components, column names from the database are converted into appropriate attribute names for Java naming conventions. For example, the DEPARTMENT_ID column name is converted to the attribute name `DepartmentId`. This same value is used as the label for the attribute by default. To modify the label so that it is more descriptive, use the Control Hints node of the attribute editor to define a label. Figure 18-6 shows the Control Hints node for the `DepartmentId` attribute where the label and tool tip text are specified.

These control hints can also be entered in the Property Inspector, but regardless of how they are specified, corresponding entries will be automatically added (or modified if the keys already exist) to the default resource property file as shown:

```
DepartmentId_LABEL=Department Number
DepartmentId_TOOLTIP=Identifier for the Department
```

Internationalizing Date, Number, and Currency Attributes   To internationalize date, number, and currency attributes (attributes with type `Number`, `Date`, `Timestamp`, `Long`, and so on), specify a format type (`Date`, `Currency`, or `Number`) for the attribute as appropriate, and define a format if necessary. This will add an entry for the built-in ADF BC formatter to the resource bundle, as well as an entry for any format specified. For example, the following resource keys are added to a resource bundle when specifying the `Salary` attribute as type `Currency`, the

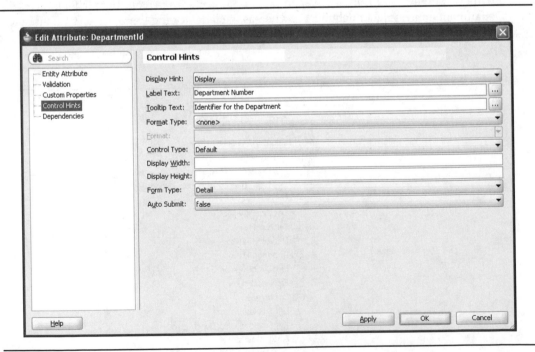

FIGURE 18-6   *Specifying control hints for attributes*

CommissionPct attribute as type Number with format of ##.##, and the HireDate attribute as type SimpleDate with a format of MM-dd-yyyy:

```
Salary_FMT_FORMATTER=oracle.jbo.format.DefaultCurrencyFormatter
HireDate_FMT_FORMATTER=oracle.jbo.format.DefaultDateFormatter
HireDate_FMT_FORMAT=MM-dd-yyyy
CommissionPct_FMT_FORMATTER=oracle.jbo.format.DefaultNumberFormatter
CommissionPct_FMT_FORMAT=\#\#.\#\#
```

The list of valid formats for an attribute with type SimpleDate is available at http://java.sun .com/j2se/1.5.0/docs/api/java/text/SimpleDateFormat.html, and the list of valid formats for an attribute with type Number is available at http://java.sun.com/j2se/1.5.0/docs/api/java/text/ DecimalFormat.html. The currency format type has a non-editable format.

TIP
To add format masks that appear in the format drop-down list for attributes, modify the formatInfo.xml file located in the o.BC4J directory of the system directory (typically C:\Documents and Settings\<user>\Application Data\JDeveloper\system11.1.1.2.x.x.x\ o.BC4J). A restart of JDeveloper is necessary to pick up the change.

Internationalizing ADF BC Error Messages

Like attribute control hints, business component error messages are automatically internationalized when an error message is added to a validator. For example, Figure 18-7 shows the Select Text Resource dialog that is launched when clicking the magnifying glass icon in the Failure Handling tab of the Validation Rule editor.

Defining an error message in this way adds the key and to the appropriate resource bundle. Here's an example:

```
INVALID_LOCATION_ID=Invalid Location Id.
```

Error messages can also be entered directly in the Failure Handling tab of the Validator dialog and will use a generated key. However, to make it easier to locate keys for reuse, use the Select Text Resource dialog to specify the value, key, and an optional description.

Built-in validators are automatically created for attributes that are based on database columns that contain constraints such as not null, precision, and so on. Custom error messages can be added for these validators (again, using

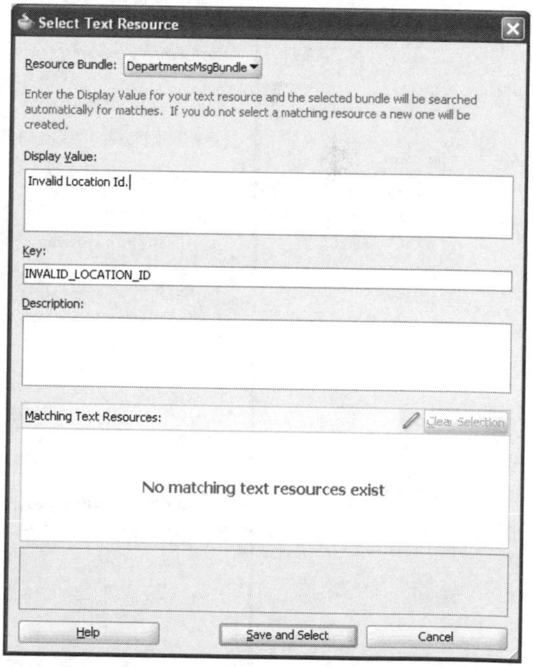

FIGURE 18-7 *Select Text Resource dialog*

the Failure Handling tab of the Validator dialog), but note that these validators are already translated into many languages, as discussed later in the section "Localizing ADF BC Applications."

Using Tokens in Validation Error Messages   Tokens can also be used in error messages and warnings for ADF BC validators. Expressions are used to evaluate the value for the token. For example, if a validator is added to the `LocationId` attribute so that it must correspond to a `LocationId` that is present in a view accessor, the error message could be defined with a token that indicates the appropriate value. First, the error message is defined as shown in Figure 18-8 (defining the string resource with a token adds the key and value to the resource bundle file as usual).

Notice in Figure 18-8 that the Message Token field accepts an expression to evaluate the value for the token. In this example, the token would be set to a Groovy expression as follows:

```
def locationvalue = []
while ( LocationsView1.hasNext() ) {
LocationsView1.next()
locationvalue.add(LocationsView1.currentRow.LocationId) }
return locationvalue
```

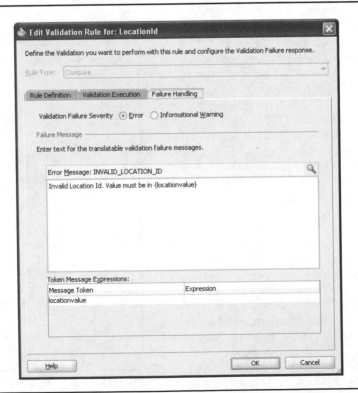

FIGURE 18-8   *Defining a validation error message that contains a token*

At runtime, the key value replaces the `locationvalue` token with the value defined in the expression, as shown here:

Localizing Applications

While internationalization of applications should be performed throughout development, localizing applications should be performed after application testing is completed using the default language. This way, resource bundle files that are defined for the application's default language can be translated and subsequently added to the project as a last step before testing, without having to synchronize multiple resource files.

Localizing ADF Faces Applications

Once internationalization for an application is completed and the resource file keys are translated, localizing an application is very straightforward. For example, to support German and French languages using properties files, save the ViewControllerBundle.properties file as ViewControllerBundle_de.properties and ViewControllerBundle_fr.properties, respectively. Follow this same convention for XLIFF files. For list resource bundles, save the ViewControllerBundle.java file as ViewControllerBundle_de.java and ViewControllerBundle_fr.java, and change the class signature to match the filename. The `de` and `fr` codes represent the ISO 639 language code. Additionally, an ISO 3166 country code can be appended if a language is used by more than one country.

Creating Properties Files for Special Character Sets

To create properties files for character sets that are outside of the ISO-8859-1 encoding (such as multibyte character sets), you need to use Unicode escaping to allow the special characters to be encoded properly—for example, `\u<char-code>`. Properties files must be saved in the 8-bit Latin-1 (ISO-8859-1) character set, and not doing so results in question marks (?) appearing at runtime rather than the proper characters. Typically, however, human translators will save a working copy of the properties file in an encoding that supports the character set for the language they are translating to, and directly type in the characters to provide the translation. It is impractical to ask translators to create the translated file using Unicode character codes instead of native characters. To solve this dilemma, use the native2ascii conversion tool provided in <JDK_HOME>\jdk\bin to convert properties files saved with encoding other than ISO-8859-1 to the Unicode format.

NOTE
List resource bundles and resource properties files can be used in parallel if required. The list bundle will be searched first for a key. If the key does not exist, then the properties file will be searched.

For a full list of the ISO 639 and 3166 country codes, refer to http://www.loc.gov/standards/iso639-2/php/code_list.php and http://www.iso.org/iso/country_codes/iso_3166_code_lists/english_country_names_and_code_elements.htm.

Specifying Supported Locales in a JSF Application

Once the values are translated, add default and supported locales for the application to the faces-config.xml file. In the Overview tab of the faces-config.xml editor, select the Application node and in the Locale Config section, and add language and/or country and region codes for the supported locales, as shown in Figure 18-9.

This adds the following code to the faces-config.xml file:

```
<locale-config>
  <default-locale>en</default-locale>
  <supported-locale>en</supported-locale>
  <supported-locale>en_US</supported-locale>
  <supported-locale>de</supported-locale>
  <supported-locale>de_DE</supported-locale>
  <supported-locale>de_AT</supported-locale>
</locale-config>
```

Typically, the user's browser settings determine the locale requested, as shown in Figure 18-10. At runtime, the application will search locales according to a restrictive match with the user's browser settings. For example, if the user's browser locale is set to `de_AT`, an exact match is found, so the `ViewControllerBundle_de_AT` resource will be used to load resource strings. If the user's browser locale is set to `de_CH`, an exact match isn't found, but the generic German locale (`de`) is supported, so the `ViewControllerBundle_de` resource will be used. Further, if a locale that is not among the list of supported locales is set in the browser, the default locale (`ViewControllerBundle_en`) will be used.

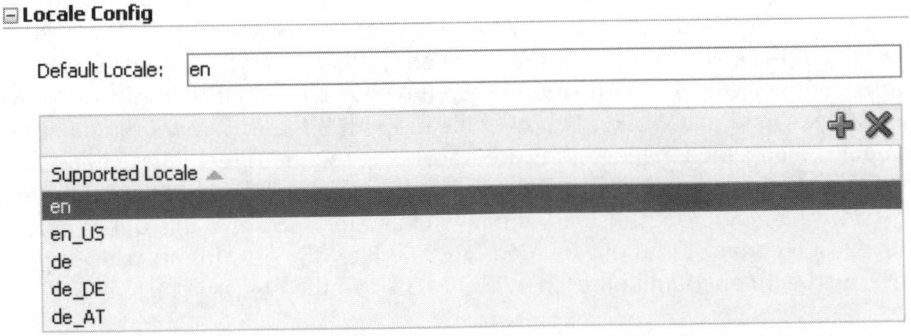

⊟ Locale Config

Default Locale: | en

| ➕ ✖ |

Supported Locale ▲
en
en_US
de
de_DE
de_AT

FIGURE 18-9   *Locale configuration in faces-config.xml*

FIGURE 18-10   *Language dialog*

Localizing ADF BC Applications

The same technique for localizing UI resource bundles is used to localize ADF BC resource
bundles, and localization can be tested in the business components browser. For example,
consider the case where key/value pairs for entity attributes are specified in a resource properties
file as shown in DepartmentsMsgBundle.properties:

```
DepartmentId_LABEL=Department Number
DepartmentName_LABEL=Department Name
ManagerId_LABEL=Manager's Employee Id
LocationId_LABEL=Location Code
```

To localize these strings, the file would be saved as DepartmentsMsgBundle_de.properties
and translated appropriately, as follows:

```
DepartmentId_LABEL=Abteilungs Nummer
DepartmentName_LABEL=Abteilungsname
ManagerId_LABEL=Vorgesetzer
LocationId_LABEL=Standort
```

As mentioned previously in this chapter, error messages for built-in validators are translated
into several languages. For example, Figure 18-11 shows the default error message dialog for an
invalid scale when an application module is run in the `de_DE` locale.

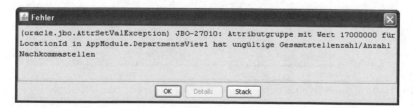

FIGURE 18-11   *Error message dialog*

To run the Business Component browser in a language other than the default `en_US` locale, specify the locale, country, and region properties of the application module configuration. Figure 18-12 shows the configuration dialog where the default locale and country properties have been modified.

Localizing Dates, Numbers, and Currencies

UI components that are created in a JSF page by dragging attributes from the Data Control palette will automatically add nested `af:convertDateTime` and `af:convertNumber` tags as appropriate. For example, if the `HireDate` and `CommissionPct` attributes in the Employees view object are created as output text components in a page, the following code results:

```
<af:outputText value="#{bindings.HireDate.inputValue}">
  <af:convertDateTime pattern="#{bindings.HireDate.format}"/>
</af:outputText>
<af:outputText value="#{bindings.CommissionPct.inputValue}">
  <af:convertNumber groupingUsed="false"
    pattern="#{bindings.CommissionPct.format}"/>
</af:outputText>
```

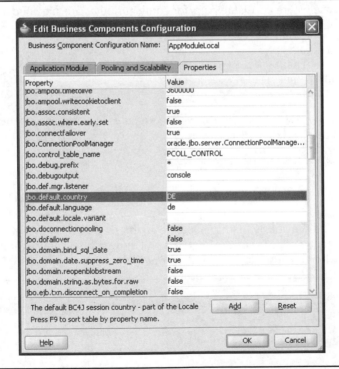

FIGURE 18-12 *Specifying a default language for an application module*

Notice that the `pattern` attribute of the converter components is set to the format property from the attribute's binding. This refers to the format specified for the attribute in the Control Hints dialog, typically defined in the entity object, and sometimes overridden by the attribute definition in the view object. When a format type and format are defined for a number or date attribute in ADF business components, formatters for these objects are added to the resource bundle, as explained in an earlier section. Decimal separators (commas versus periods) for number and currency types are automatically localized appropriately by the framework. However, date format masks are not automatically localized and should be modified for supported locales. For example, if the following entries are included in the en_US properties file, they may need to be localized appropriately for different locales:

```
HireDate_FMT_FORMAT=MM-dd-yyyy
CommissionPct_FMT_FORMAT=00.00
```

In the de_DE properties file, these formats could be modified to the following values that reflect the format style of European countries:

```
HireDate_FMT_FORMAT=dd.MM.yyyy
CommissionPct_FMT_FORMAT=00.00
```

Note that the `CommissionPct_FMT_FORMAT` value remains `00.00`. At runtime, the value will automatically display the decimal separator as a comma instead of a period for the `de_DE` locale.

Special Considerations When Localizing Currencies

If no country is defined in the supported locales, a default symbol (¤) will be used in place of an actual currency symbol. Be careful when defining locales with currencies. Consider the case where both `en_US` and `fr_FR` are defined as supported locales. If a value of 20.00 is stored in the database, the value will display as $20.00 when the browser's language is set to `en_US`. When the browser language is set to `fr_FR`, the value will display as 20,00 €, which does provide the proper formatting for the number itself, but obviously doesn't represent the same value in monetary terms.

TIP
When considering localization of currencies, the country part of the locale should be specified in faces-config.xml.

ADF Faces Components Translation

Many ADF Faces components contain text that is embedded in the component itself. For example, the `af:panelCollection` component includes View and Detach menu items as part of the component. Conveniently, this text is automatically translated into the standard languages for end-user facing products: Arabic, Brazilian Portuguese, Czech, Danish, Dutch, English, Finnish, French, German, Greek, Hebrew, Hungarian, Italian, Japanese, Korean, Norwegian, Polish, Portuguese, Romanian, Russian, Simplified Chinese, Slovak, Spanish, Swedish, Thai, Traditional Chinese, and Turkish. Figure 18-13 shows the runtime view of a page run in the German locale that contains automatically translated ADF Faces component elements.

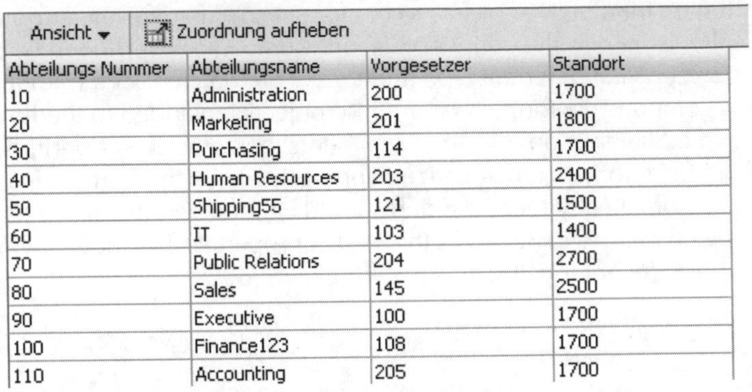

Abteilungs Nummer	Abteilungsname	Vorgesetzer	Standort
10	Administration	200	1700
20	Marketing	201	1800
30	Purchasing	114	1700
40	Human Resources	203	2400
50	Shipping55	121	1500
60	IT	103	1400
70	Public Relations	204	2700
80	Sales	145	2500
90	Executive	100	1700
100	Finance123	108	1700
110	Accounting	205	1700

FIGURE 18-13 *Runtime view of page run in German locale*

If the application needs to support a language other than those listed earlier, or if your application rules mandate that different text be used to warn the user of invalid entries due to the use of the converter and validator components of the ADF Faces library, you can globally override the default messages. To do so, locate the key value for the converter or validator component that requires an override in Appendix B of *Oracle Fusion Middleware Web User Interface Developer's Guide for Oracle Application Development Framework 11g Release 1*. For example, to override the error messages displayed for an `af:validateLength` validator when the user exceeds the maximum length, use the following keys, defining custom messages as necessary:

```
org.apache.myfaces.trinidad.validator.LengthValidator.MAXIMUM=Error: There are
too many characters.
org.apache.myfaces.trinidad.validator.LengthValidator.MAXIMUM_detail=
Attention: Enter {2} or fewer characters, not more.
org.apache.myfaces.trinidad.validator.LengthValidator.MAXIMUM_HINT=Hint:
Enter {0} or fewer characters.
```

These keys can be defined in the default properties file for the application, or they can be defined in a separate file. In either case, the file should be configured in the `message-bundle` element of the faces-config.xml file, as follows:

```
<message-bundle>view.ViewControllerBundle</message-bundle>
```

Figure 18-14 shows the runtime view of an input text field with an `af:validateLength` component where the key values above have been overridden.

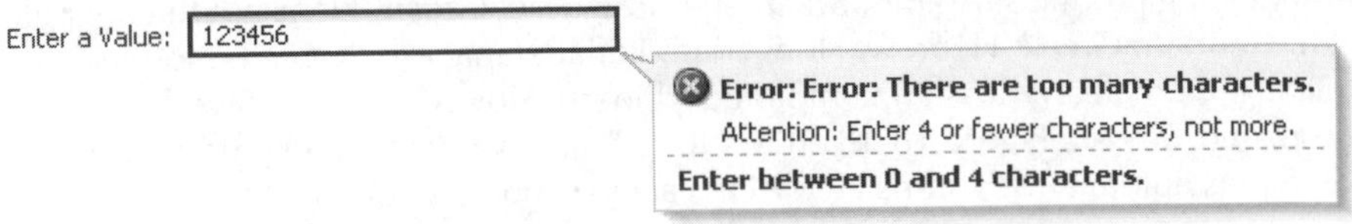

FIGURE 18-14 *Runtime view of input text field*

In addition to the built-in translation features of ADF Faces, the framework will also automatically set other locale-based features, such as bidirectional text rendering and currency symbols, based on the user's preferred locale. To alter the default functionality, modify the trinidad-config.xml file. There are several localization settings, including the following:

- currency-code

- decimal-separator

- formatting-locale

- number-grouping-separator

- right-to-left

- time-zone

Refer to *Oracle Fusion Middleware Web User Interface Developer's Guide for Oracle Application Development Framework 11g Release 1* for further information regarding these settings.

TIP
Using custom skins, you can override default ADF Faces component labels. In this case, you need to provide the translations for these labels as well. Chapter 16 covers the use of resource bundles in custom skin definitions.

Changing Locales

Typically, locales are changed by modifying a browser's default language. Developers can easily test the functionality of a localized application by adding a language to the browser and running the application. For added flexibility, applications may support changing the locale programmatically, regardless of the browser settings. The remainder of this section describes how to implement this technique.

Changing Locales Programmatically

Instead of using browser settings to control the locale that is loaded for an application, you may sometimes find it necessary to change the locale based on the user's preferred language. For example, a drop-down list can be used to allow the user to choose from languages that the application supports and programmatically change the locale in this way. This is implemented by programmatically retrieving the list of supported languages for an application and then changing the locale of the application dynamically. These two aspects can be implemented separately if desired, but the most dynamic and reusable way of changing locales programmatically is described here.

Programmatically Retrieving Supported Locales   To retrieve a list of supported locales, use the `getSupportedLocales()` method from the `FacesContext.getApplication()` method, as shown in the following managed bean code:

```
import java.util.ArrayList;
import java.util.Iterator;
import java.util.List;
import java.util.Locale;
```

```
import javax.faces.context.FacesContext;
import javax.faces.model.SelectItem;

public class ChangeLocale {

  List suppLocales;

  public void setSuppLocales(List suppLocales) {
    this.suppLocales = suppLocales;
  }
  public List getSuppLocales() {
    FacesContext fctx = FacesContext.getCurrentInstance();
    Iterator<Locale> localeIt = fctx.getApplication().getSupportedLocales();
    suppLocales = new ArrayList();
    while (localeIt.hasNext()) {
      Locale locale = localeIt.next();
      SelectItem item = new
       SelectItem(locale.getLanguage(),locale.getDisplayLanguage(locale));
      suppLocales.add(item);
    }
    return suppLocales;
  }
}
```

The list element in the JSF page is then defined as follows:

```
<af:selectOneChoice>
  <f:selectItems value="#{ChangeLocale.suppLocales}"/>
</af:selectOneChoice>
```

Changing a Locale Dynamically   Once the supported locales from the application are determined, your next step is to change the locale of the application. This can be done via various command components, but in this example, a list is used and so the `valueChangeListener` attribute of the list can be used to retrieve the locale that the user has selected. The `selectOneChoice` component would be modified as follows:

```
<af:selectOneChoice valueChangeListener="#{ChangeLocale.listChanged}">
  <f:selectItems value="#{ChangeLocale.suppLocales}"/>
</af:selectOneChoice>
```

The `listChanged` method is implemented in the managed bean and calls a method named `changeLocale` that accepts the newly selected value and sets the locale for the application appropriately:

```
import javax.faces.event.ValueChangeEvent;
import java.util.Locale;
import javax.faces.context.FacesContext;
...
public void listChanged(ValueChangeEvent valueChangeEvent) {
  changeLocale(valueChangeEvent.getNewValue().toString());
}
```

```
private void changeLocale (String language){
  Locale newLocale = new Locale (language);
  FacesContext fctx = FacesContext.getCurrentInstance();
  fctx.getViewRoot().setLocale(newLocale);
}
```

The changeLocale() method sets the locale for the application, but this isn't applied to the running page at this point. What's required is an instance variable for the user's current locale. This is provided by creating accessors as well as a command component action that sets the value to the updated locale, as shown in this managed bean code:

```
Locale preferredLocale;
  public void setPreferredLocale(Locale preferredLocale) {
    this.preferredLocale = preferredLocale;
  }
  public Locale getPreferredLocale() {
    return preferredLocale;
  }
  public String cb1_action() {
    setPreferredLocale
      (FacesContext.getCurrentInstance().getViewRoot().getLocale());
    return null;
  }
}
```

Finally, after creating a command component on the page that has the action attribute set to the cb1_action method, a phase listener is registered with the application in the adf-settings.xml file. The phase listener intercepts the ADF lifecycle before the prepare model phase and applies the selected locale to the JSF uiViewRoot of the page:

```
import java.util.Locale;
import javax.faces.component.UIViewRoot;
import javax.faces.context.FacesContext;
import oracle.adf.controller.v2.lifecycle.ADFLifecycle;
import oracle.adf.controller.v2.lifecycle.PagePhaseEvent;
import oracle.adf.controller.v2.lifecycle.PagePhaseListener;

public class CustomPhaseListener implements PagePhaseListener    {
  public CustomPhaseListener() {
    super();
  }
  public void afterPhase(PagePhaseEvent event) {
  }
  public void beforePhase(PagePhaseEvent event) {
    Integer phase = event.getPhaseId();
    if (phase.equals(ADFLifecycle.PREPARE_MODEL_ID)) {
      FacesContext fctx = FacesContext.getCurrentInstance();
      ChangeLocale changelocale = (ChangeLocale)fctx.getApplication()
        .evaluateExpressionGet(fctx, "#{ChangeLocale}", Object.class);
      Locale preferredLocale = changelocale.getPreferredLocale();
      UIViewRoot uiViewRoot =
        fctx.getCurrentInstance().getViewRoot();
```

```
    if (preferredLocale == null) {
      changelocale.setPreferredLocale(uiViewRoot.getLocale());
    } else {
      uiViewRoot.setLocale(preferredLocale);
    }
  }
 }
}
```

In this example, the `CustomPhaseListener` class retrieves the `preferredLocale` set via the command button action in the managed bean and applies that to the current page. The resulting runtime view is shown in Figure 18-15, where an `af:outputText` field that contains an internationalizable value is included in the page, as well as a form based on a localized business components data model. The ADF application lifecycle phases and the adf-settings.xml file are explained in detail in Chapter 3.

Localizing an Application Using the Database as a Resource Store

Applications with a database-centric architecture might store resource strings and translations in the database. For example, consider a database table CATEGORIES with the following values:

CATEGORY_ID	CATEGORY_NAME	LANGUAGE
1	Books	EN
2	Movies	EN
3	Magazines	EN
1	Buecher	DE
2	Filme	DE
3	Magazine	DE

NOTE
To support non–Latin-based character sets using the database, additional database configuration may be required.

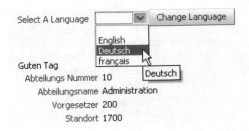

FIGURE 18-15 *Runtime view of setting the Locale programmatically*

To localize an ADF application to determine which set of these rows to use at runtime, a dynamic database parameter can be set that stores the preferred language for the current session. For example, the following procedure stores the value of a dynamic parameter (named `user_ lang`) to the built-in database procedure `dbms_application_info.set_client_info`:

```
CREATE OR REPLACE
PACKAGE BODY USER_CONTEXT_PKG IS
  PROCEDURE set_app_user_lang ( user_lang IN VARCHAR2) IS
  BEGIN
    dbms_application_info.set_client_info(user_lang);
    EXCEPTION WHEN OTHERS THEN raise_application_error (-20001, 'Error in
      user_context_pkg.set_app_user_lang: ' || SQLERRM);
  END;
END USER_CONTEXT_PKG;
```

The procedure is called by a custom application module class that extends the `ApplicationModuleImpl` class and overrides the `prepareSession` method. The following code demonstrates how to determine the default language for the application using the `jbo.default.language` property of the application configuration. Additionally, the code calls the `set_app_user_lang` procedure using the default language as the argument.

```
import java.sql.CallableStatement;
import java.sql.SQLException;
import oracle.jbo.JboException;
import oracle.jbo.common.PropertyMetadata;
import oracle.jbo.Session;
import oracle.jbo.server.ApplicationModuleImpl;
import oracle.jbo.server.DBTransactionImpl;

public class CustomApplicationModuleImpl extends ApplicationModuleImpl {
  @Override
  protected void prepareSession(Session session) {
    super.prepareSession(session);
    setCurrentUserLanguage();
  }

  public void setCurrentUserLanguage(){
    DBTransactionImpl dbti = (DBTransactionImpl)getDBTransaction();
    CallableStatement statement = dbti.createCallableStatement(("BEGIN " +
      "user_context_pkg.set_app_user_lang(?); " + "END;"), 0);
    try {
      statement.setString(1, getApplicationLanguage());
      statement.execute();
      } catch (SQLException sqlerr) {
        throw new JboException(sqlerr);
      } finally {
      try {
        if (statement != null) {
          statement.close();
        }
      } catch (SQLException closeerr) {
```

```
        throw new JboException(closeerr);
      }
    }
  }
  public String getApplicationLanguage(){
    String appLanguage = "EN";
    appLanguage = getAMLanguage();
    return appLanguage;
  }
  public String getAMLanguage(){
    PropertyMetadata langProperty =
      PropertyMetadata.findProperty("jbo.default.language");
    String amLanguage = langProperty.getProperty();
    return amLanguage.toUpperCase();
  }
}
```

View Objects that require filtering based on the user's preferred language should include a where clause to filter the query by the database parameter that has been set. This is stored in the database as `'CLIENT_INFO'` in the built-in database USERENV namespace, which describes the current session.

```
SELECT CategoriesEntity.CATEGORY_ID, CategoriesEntity.CATEGORY_NAME,
    CategoriesEntity.LANGUAGE, CategoriesEntity.ROWID
FROM CATEGORIES CategoriesEntity
WHERE CategoriesEntity.LANGUAGE = USERENV('CLIENT_INFO')
```

When running the application module with this code in place, the default language is determined by the application module configuration, and the View Object will return only those rows that have a LANGUAGE value set to that value. However, this does not handle the case when the language should be determined by the web browser, and not by the application module's jbo.default.language property (to which users might not have access). To provide this functionality, the application module class needs to be include the ability to set the language for the current user based on the browser's default language. For example, the following modified getApplicationLanguage() method determines whether the user is accessing the application via the Web, and if so, it attempts to match the user's preferred language to the supported languages of the application:

```
public class CustomApplicationModuleImpl extends ApplicationModuleImpl {
  public static String preferredLanguage;
  public static boolean isWebUser=false;
  private String[] supportedLanguages = {"EN","DE"};

  public String getApplicationLanguage(){
    String appLanguage = "EN";
    if (isWebUser){
      for (int index=0; index<supportedLanguages.length; index++){
        if (preferredLanguage.equals(supportedLanguages[index])){
          appLanguage = preferredLanguage;
          break;
        }
      }
    }
```

```
      } else{
        appLanguage = getAMLanguage();
      }
      return appLanguage;
    }
}
```

The `isWebUser` and `preferredLanguage` variables in the code can be set using a phase listener that implements the `beforePhase()` method to augment the default functionality when the model is prepared for delivery. The following code in the phase listener retrieves the locale from the `FacesContext` object (which is introspected from the browser) and sets that value to the `preferredLanguage` variable of the custom application module class:

```
import oracle.adf.controller.v2.lifecycle.ADFLifecycle;
import javax.faces.context.FacesContext;
import oracle.adf.controller.v2.lifecycle.PagePhaseEvent;
import oracle.adf.controller.v2.lifecycle.PagePhaseListener;
import model.CustomApplicationModuleImpl;

public class CustomPhaseListener implements PagePhaseListener {
  public void afterPhase(PagePhaseEvent pagePhaseEvent) {
  }
  public void beforePhase(PagePhaseEvent pagePhaseEvent) {
    Integer phase = pagePhaseEvent.getPhaseId();
      if (phase.equals(ADFLifecycle.PREPARE_MODEL_ID)) {
        FacesContext fctx = FacesContext.getCurrentInstance();
        String language =
        fctx.getExternalContext().getRequestLocale()
          .getLanguage().toUpperCase();
        CustomApplicationModuleImpl.preferredLanguage = language;
        CustomApplicationModuleImpl.isWebUser = true;
      }
  }
}
```

Providing Help Topics

ADF Faces lets you define instructional information for components in a central file, rather than hard-coding the information within the component. This allows developers to specify a pointer to help information for components, and the source of the information can be dynamically defined, localized, and reused across components as necessary. For example, an application may have many input components that are duplicated across pages but have the same function in the application. An e-mail field is a good example of this. If the login page as well as several other pages in an application contain an input text field for entering an e-mail address, helpful information for the correct format and example values could be stored in a centralized help bundle containing help text for the entire application. The various input text fields can refer to the help text dynamically, so that if a change in the help text is required, they need to be applied only in the help bundle and not in every page containing the e-mail fields.

Help text can be defined for two types of information: DEFINITION and INSTRUCTIONS. The runtime view of the help text "Enter the employee's user id without a domain." defined for the instructional help type is shown in Figure 18-16.

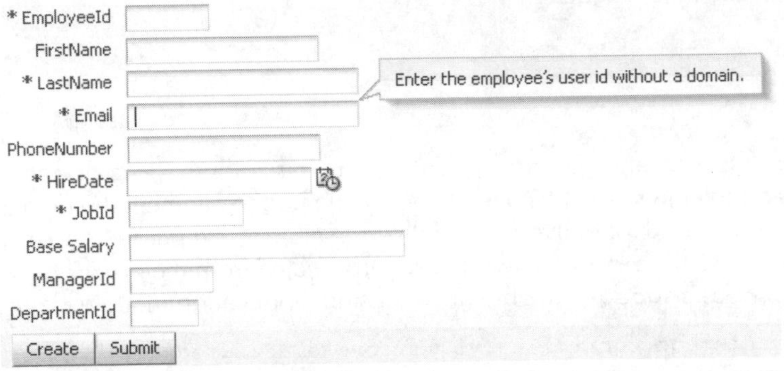

FIGURE 18-16   *Runtime view of help text*

Notice that the help text appears at runtime as a note window when the mouse hovers over the component to which the help topic is attached. This is because the instructional help type was used, and it was used with an input component (`af:inputText`). For header components, the instructional text appears beneath the header text. For definition help types, a help icon is displayed instead of the help text, and hovering over the icon displays the definition help text. The help icon appears before the label of input components, at the end of header components, next to the close icon in window and dialog components, and below table headers in table components. The runtime view of the definition help text type for an input component is shown in Figure 18-17.

The help text can be stored in resource property files, XLIFF files, managed beans, or class files. No matter which type of file is used for the help text storage, the application must configure a help provider in the adf-settings.xml file and define a prefix to be used to access the provider. For example, the following code specifies a help provider to be used across the application. The prefix for the help provider is `APP_HELP_`, the provider class is the built-in

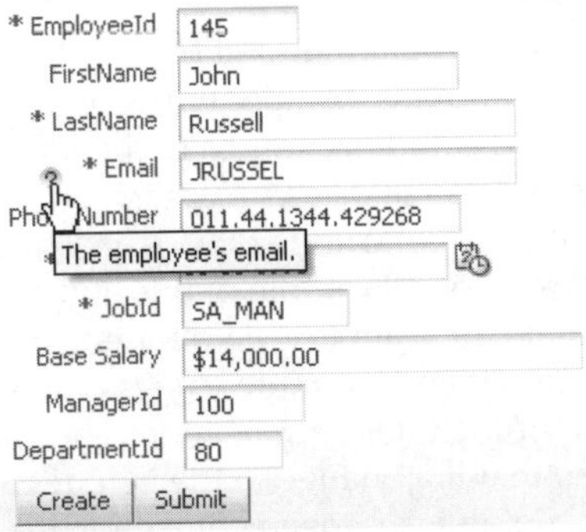

FIGURE 18-17   *Runtime view of the definition help text type*

`ResourceBundleHelpProvider` for resource property file storage, and the property for the help provider is defined with a property name and value that refer to the storage file.

```xml
<?xml version="1.0" encoding="windows-1252" ?>
<adf-settings xmlns="http://xmlns.oracle.com/adf/settings">
  <adf-faces-config xmlns="http://xmlns.oracle.com/adf/faces/settings">
    <help-provider prefix="APP_HELP_">
      <help-provider-class>
        oracle.adf.view.rich.help.ResourceBundleHelpProvider
      </help-provider-class>
      <property>
        <property-name>baseName</property-name>
        <value>view.ViewControllerBundle</value>
      </property>
    </help-provider>
  </adf-faces-config>
</adf-settings>
```

This example contains values unique to the resource properties file method of storing help text. The following tables describe what the values should be for the other types of storage files.

Storage File	`help-provider-class` Value
Resource property file	`oracle.adf.view.rich.help.ResourceBundleHelpProvider`
XLIFF	`oracle.adf.view.rich.help.ELHelpProvider`
Managed bean	Fully qualified class path to the managed bean—such as `view.MyHelpBean`
Class file	Fully qualified class path to the class—such as `view.MyHelpProvider`

Storage File	Help Provider Property `<value>`
Resource property file	Fully qualified name of the property file—such as `view.ViewControllerBundle`.
XLIFF	EL value for the XLIFF file—such as `#{adfBundle['view.ViewControllerBundle']}`. Note that the `property-name` for XLIFF-based help text storage must be `helpSource`.

Managed bean	EL value for the `helpMap` property of the managed bean. For example, if the managed bean is defined as
	`<managed-bean>`
	`  <managed-bean-name>`
	`    helpMapBean`
	`  </managed-bean-name>`
	`  <managed-bean-class>`
	`    view.MyHelpBean`
	`  </managed-bean-class>`
	`  <managed-bean-scope>`
	`    session`
	`  </managed-bean-scope>`
	`<managed-bean>`
	the property value would be `#{helpMapBean.helpMap}`.

Class file	Custom value for the custom property.

NOTE
You may need to create the adf-settings.xml file if it does not already exist in your application. To create the file, choose File | New in JDeveloper to create a new XML file, and save the file in the src\META-INF directory of the UI project. You may also need to create the META-INF directory if it does not already exist; however, any project that contains ADF data bindings will already include a META-INF directory that contains the adfm.xml file.

Specifying Help Text

Configuring help text is similar to specifying resource strings for an application. A key/value pair is entered into the help storage file, where the key contains the help provider prefix, a custom topic (such as a descriptive name of the field to which the text should be applied), and the appropriate help type (INSTRUCTIONS or DEFINITION). The generally accepted naming conventions include the use of underscores to separate the key elements. For example, the following key/value pairs are defined in a resource properties file (ViewControllerBundle.properties) and contain the help provider prefix APP_HELP_, the topic EMPLOYEE_EMAIL, and the help type:

```
APP_HELP_EMPLOYEE_EMAIL_INSTRUCTIONS=Enter the employee's user id without a domain.
APP_HELP_EMPLOYEE_EMAIL_DEFINITION= The employee's email.
```

These same values can be configured in an XLIFF (.xlf) file, as shown next:

```xml
<?xml version="1.0" encoding="windows-1252" ?>
<xliff version="1.1" xmlns="urn:oasis:names:tc:xliff:document:1.1">
  <file source-language="en" original="view.ViewControllerBundle"
    datatype="xml">
    <body>
      <trans-unit id="APP_HELP_EMPLOYEE_EMAIL_INSTRUCTIONS">
        <source>Enter the employee's user id without a domain.</source>
        <target/>
      </trans-unit>
      <trans-unit id="APP_HELP_EMPLOYEE_EMAIL_DEFINITION">
        <source>The employee's email.</source>
        <target/>
      </trans-unit>
    </body>
  </file>
</xliff>
```

NOTE
Definition text may not include any HTML formatting and is typically less than 100 characters or so. Instructional text may be longer, as it is displayed in a note component, and it may include simple HTML formatting.

Configuring Components for Use with Help Topics

Regardless of the storage mechanism used for help text, components are configured to display help topics by setting the `helpTopicId` attribute. The attribute should be set to the value of the help provider prefix and the help topic only. All available help types defined for the help topic re determined by the help provider and displayed at runtime as necessary. For example, the `af:inputText` component for the e-mail field would be defined as follows:

```
<af:inputText value="#{bindings.Email.inputValue}"
    label="#{vcb.EMAIL}"
    helpTopicId="APP_HELP_EMPLOYEE_EMAIL"/>
```

Note that this is an `af:inputText` field, which directly supports help topics by providing the `helpTopicId` attribute.

Adding Help Text for Other Components

You can display help text for a component that does not directly support help topics via the `helpTopicId` attribute. You might bind the `shortDesc` attribute of a component to a help topic, create an output text component and bind the value to the help topic, or create a command component to launch the help topic external URL (external URLs are covered in the next section). The following code shows each of these examples in practice, using EL to retrieve the help provider from the ADF Faces context:

```
<af:menuBar>
  <af:menu text="Actions">
    <af:commandMenuItem text="Edit"
shortDesc="#{adfFacesContext.helpProvider['APP_HELP_ACTIONS_MENU_EDIT']
      .definition}"/>
    <af:goImageLink text="Help for this Menu"
      destination="#{adfFacesContext.helpProvider['APP_HELP_ACTIONS_MENU']
      .externalUrl}"/>
  </af:menu>
  <af:outputFormatted
    value="#{adfFacesContext.helpProvider['APP_HELP_ACTIONS_MENU']
    .instructions}"/>
</af:menuBar>
```

Providing Help Using Web Documents

In addition to the definition and instruction types of help, a help provider may include an external URL help type. This type of help topic renders a help icon as is done for the definition help type, but the help icon will launch an external URL when clicked. Since resource bundles should not include URLs, the `ResourceBundleHelpProvider` does not provide an implementation for returning external URL values. Therefore, to create a help provider that uses external URL help types, create a class that extends `oracle.adf.view.rich.help.ResourceBundleHelpProvider` and overrides the `getExternalUrl` method, as shown here:

```
import javax.faces.component.UIComponent;
import javax.faces.context.FacesContext;
import oracle.adf.view.rich.help.ResourceBundleHelpProvider;
```

```
public class MyHelpProvider extends ResourceBundleHelpProvider{
  public MyHelpProvider() {
  }
  private static String APP_HELP_EMPLOYEE_EMAIL_URL =
    "http://<site>";
  private static String APP_HELP_DEPT_URL = "http://<anothersite>";
  private static String DEFAULT_URL = "http://www.oracle.com";

  @Override
  protected String getExternalUrl(FacesContext context,
    UIComponent component, String topicId) {
    if (topicId == null)
      return null;
    if (topicId.contains("APP_HELP_EMPLOYEE_EMAIL") )
      return APP_HELP_EMPLOYEE_EMAIL_URL;
    if (topicId.contains("APP_HELP_DEPT")){
      return APP_HELP_DEPT_URL;
    } else {
      return DEFAULT_URL;
    }
  }
}
```

Using Oracle Help for the Web (OHW)

Oracle Help for the Web (OHW) is an application that provides comprehensive online help systems via HTML files. Documentation writers create the help topics using an authoring tool, and the application is deployed as an Enterprise Java application (EAR). For more information on how to author and deploy an OHW application, refer to *Oracle Fusion Middleware Developer's Guide for Oracle Help 11g*.

OHW can be integrated with an ADF Faces application by deploying the OHW application and then referring to the front controller servlet of the OHW application in the adf-settings.xml file of the ADF Faces application. The adf-settings.xml file should be configured as follows to use OHW as the help provider:

```
<adf-settings xmlns="http://xmlns.oracle.com/adf/settings">
  <help-provider>
    <help-provider-class>
      oracle.help.web.rich.helpProvider.OHWHelpProvider
    </help-provider-class>
    <property>
      <property-name>ohwConfigFileURL</property-name>
      <value>/helpsets/ohwconfig.xml</value>
    </property>
    <property>
      <property-name>baseURI</property-name>
      <value>
        http://localhost:7100/help-ohw-rcf-context-root/ohguide/
      </value>
    </property>
  </help-provider>
</adf-settings>
```

This example contains two properties within the `OHWHelpProvider` definition. The first is `ohwConfigFileURL`. The value for this property should be set to the location of the ohwconfig. xml file that is located in the public_html directory of the accessing ADF Faces application. Thus, the entire contents of the helpsets (including the ohwconfig.xml file) should be copied into the public_html folder of the application that will use OHW. In this case, the files were copied into a new folder named helpsets. The second property, `baseURI`, should be set to the location of the OHW servlet that is deployed with the OHW application to launch the appropriate page.

Finally, to use OHW topics as the help for a component, specify the topic ID defined in the map of the OHW application as the value of the `helpTopicId` attribute for components. The help will appear as for the external URL type of help, where a user can click a help icon for a component to launch the help file.

Summary

This chapter covered two significant aspects of Web application development that enable end users to interact with an application effectively: providing instructional information and providing the ability to run an application in the end user's native language. Think of your users first! For whom are you developing? What languages do they speak? Will application training be provided, or is this a self-service application for which proper documentation must be shipped along with the product? Answering these questions early on in development will greatly affect application development policies, standards, and procedures. Failing to recognize the importance of these aspects can cause headaches later on. For example, retrofitting an application to be internationalizable is a difficult and time-consuming task. For this reason, it is recommended that every application use resource bundles, regardless of the need for multiple language support.

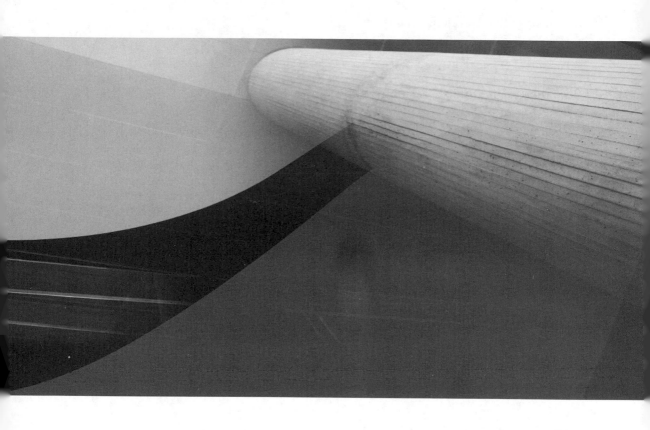

CHAPTER
19

Using JavaScript
in ADF Faces RC

Future proof applications are not developed in JavaScript. They are built using a framework that may use JavaScript in its UI rendering, but that can easily adapt to a new technology in the future without sacrificing the application you developed with it.

 he ADF Faces Rich Client (RC) component framework is an Asynchronous JavaScript and XML (AJAX)–enabled JavaServer Faces (JSF) component set that uses JavaScript in its client-side lifecycle, event handling, and dynamic component rendering. Furthermore, ADF Faces RC contains a complete JavaScript client framework as a part of its component architecture that protects ADF Faces RC component and application developers from needing to call the client browser Document Object Model (DOM) directly, providing a consistent access pattern for client-side programming.

The popularity of AJAX and the desire for rich web application clients have enticed companies to favor such scripting, and ADF Faces RC would not be possible without these companies' acceptance. This chapter introduces the ADF Faces RC client architecture and explains how developers can integrate JavaScript into their application development.

CAUTION
You should never manipulate the browser DOM directly when using JavaScript in ADF Faces. It is neither future-proof nor cross-browser compliant. The worst that could happen is that you would interfere with ADF Faces client functionality and your application would stop working.

Must You Use JavaScript to Build ADF Faces Applications?

JavaScript as a scripting language for client-side programming has been around for many years, and a lot of web application developers have gained great expertise in using it. For many web application developers who developed applications with JavaServer Pages (JSP) in the past, JSF is a fairly new technology, despite the fact that it has been available for several years as a Java EE standard. Those developers often find the solution to a problem first in JavaScript and then in JSF.

ADF Faces RC uses JavaScript in the UI component rendering and its client-side behavior, and therefore JavaScript must be enabled on the client browsers. For ADF Faces developers, however, using JavaScript in their ADF Faces RC application programming is a choice, not a design pattern. You should always prefer a solution that is programmed in ADF Faces and JSF over a solution requiring JavaScript, because future-proof applications are not developed in JavaScript. They are built using a framework that may use JavaScript in its UI rendering, but that can easily adapt to a new technology in the future without sacrificing the application you developed with it.

A few use cases require JavaScript, such as launching pop-up dialogs from command components that have an `af:setPropertyListener` tag attached, as explained in Chapter 10, or displaying a glass pane (described later in the chapter) that pauses the UI while the application processes a long-running query. For such use cases, the ADF Faces RC framework provides a public set of JavaScript APIs that developers will find useful.

A golden rule for JavaScript programming in ADF Faces RC is this: Don't use JavaScript unless there is no other solution to a problem.

The ADF Faces RC Client Framework

The ADF Faces RC platform consist of AJAX-enabled JSF UI components and framework services, such as drag-and-drop, partial request handling, validation, and more. A key characteristic of the ADF Faces RC client architecture is the use of a mixture of HTML and JavaScript to render the UI, which provides better performance and resource use than a pure JavaScript client. Three categories of components can be identified in ADF Faces:

- Components such as `af:table`, `af:tree`, and `af:menu` that have client-side functionality and therefore must have a client representation.

- Components that don't requires a client component representation unless a specific programming use case, such as changing the source reference of an image, needs it. To enforce the creation of a client component for a UI component that otherwise would not have one, developers either add an `af:clientListener` component as a child component or set the component's `clientComponent` attribute to `true`.

- Components such as `af:panelGroupLayout`, `af:spacer`, or `af:image` that do not require a client-side representation at all.

NOTE
Using client-side components adds a little performance overhead to the UI component rendering. Therefore, before enabling client component rendering for a component, you should make sure it's the most appropriate option.

ADF Faces RC Architecture

Figure 19-1 shows a simplified architecture of ADF Faces RC. The UI components of a JSF page have an in-memory Java object representation on the server. These object instances are used when a client request comes in through the Faces servlet to update the value state and to handle component events. The combination of all component objects on a page make up the page component tree, which starts from the view root.

The server-side part shown in Figure 19-1 outlines the memory tree for a user input form. ADF Faces RC component object instances are of type `Rich<UI Component>`—for example, `RichInputText` or `RichCommandButton`. UI components that have a component binding to a managed bean are Java-accessible through the created managed bean properties and the associated setter and getter methods. The ADF Faces components are display agnostic, which means that they delegate their UI rendering to a set of renderer classes that produce the content.

The ADF Faces RC client-side framework is a mirror of the server-side architecture and uses two objects, a stateless component peer object and a render object, to represent the component instance in JavaScript. ADF Faces RC UI components have a JavaScript object equivalent, which is created on an as-needed basis and that is an instance of AdfRich<*Component*>.js. For example, the `af:inputText` component that is an instance of `RichInputText` on the server side is represented by the `AdfRichInputText` object on the client.

ADF Faces client components help to abstract the DOM in that they expose a defined and consistent set of APIs for component and application developers to build portable AJAX components and applications. Only components that have a client behavior, such as table, tree, tree table, panel splitter, panel accordion, and similar components, require a JavaScript object instance to

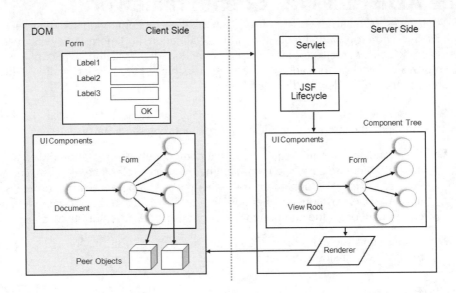

FIGURE 19-1 *ADF Faces RC architecture*

exist by default. And even those components render their static content in HTML. Like the `f:view` root on the server, the root of the client-side component tree is the browser document. ADF Faces RC provides you with access to the page document object through the `AdfPage.PAGE` static object.

NOTE
The ADF Faces RC JavaScript component and framework API documentation is available as a part of the Fusion Middleware documentation at http://otn.oracle.com.

Because the client-side components define only the public API, they often don't contain implementation codes but only JavaScript Object Notation (JSON) definitions of the component attributes they expose and the super class reference if the component is a subclass of a base component. The implementation details are contained in internal classes, which are marked as peer components, such as `AdfDhtmlInputTextPeer.js`. The peer object abstracts the client component object and handles all the browser DOM interaction and event handling, which leads to another golden rule of JavaScript programming in ADF Faces RC: Don't use peer objects in your custom JavaScript code.

As shown in Figure 19-1, the component hierarchy is similar to the hierarchy of the components on the server side. As you can use the `UIViewRoot` in JSF to search for a specific UI component on the page, you can do the same using the `AdfPage.PAGE` object.

NOTE
Though the JavaScript framework components are designed as client-side equivalents of the server-side ADF Faces components, for security reasons they don't expose setter methods for all their properties. The number of secured properties is different for each UI component. A list of components and their secured properties is documented in Chapter 3 of the "Oracle Fusion Middleware Web User Interface Developer's Guide for Oracle Application Development Framework 11g Release 1," which is available online at http://otn.oracle.com.

ADF Faces Client Component Events

When developing interactive UIs with JavaScript, developers usually listen to DOM events such as click, focus, load, and keydown. For this, they register JavaScript event listeners on the HTML elements using specific attributes such as `onclick`, `onfocus`, `onload`, and `onkeydown`.

The ADF Faces client component framework is much more sophisticated than pure HTML and raw JavaScript, and, in addition to the basic events, it provides real component events, such as `valueChange`, `action`, `query`, or `rowDisclosure` for which the developer register event listeners. ADF Faces client component events provide a consistent API for cross-browser development that abstracts custom JavaScript code from the browser-specific DOM implementation. Handling component events on the client, instead of handling them on the server, always saves a network round trip. To avoid an event propagating to the server, it can be cancelled by a call to `cancel()` on the event object. Oracle JDeveloper lists all allowed client events to listen to for a component when adding a client listener to it.

NOTE
The "Oracle Fusion Middleware Web User Interface Developer's Guide for Oracle Application Development Framework 11g Release 1" that is available online at http://otn.oracle.com as a part of the Oracle Fusion Middleware documentation prints the full list of client events in its Chapter 5.

ADF Faces JavaScript Partitioning

The last thing application users want to do is to stare at an empty page for minutes while the splash screen spins and the application loads. A requirement in AJAX, therefore, is to shorten the time it takes to download the JavaScript required for the initial page rendering. But size matters not only for the initial download of the script sources. JavaScript libraries that already exist in the browser cache need to be loaded into the JavaScript engine before they can be used, and this also delays view transition if the libraries are large.

ADF Faces RC addresses this requirement with a set of framework features that include content obfuscation and compression, the grouping of related scripts, and the ability of application developers to build their own groupings. These groupings of JavaScript are referred to as "JavaScript partitioning." Grouping reduces the number of round trips and the download page sizes. All script classes that are used to render a specific component are grouped to a "feature." Logical groups of features are created to define specialized download bundles, called the "partitions."

A feature aggregates the JavaScript files, which are also referred to as classes, of a component. In ADF Faces, UI components are defined by at least two classes—a component class and a peer class—and optionally have dependencies to a base class. The component feature is defined by the component developer adding a copy of adf-js-features.xml in the component META-INF JAR directory. Using the concept of features decouples the work of the component developer from the work of the application developer in that application developers don't need to know about how a component is built to reference it for download. Using a metadata configuration file also prevents hard-coded references in application pages for a specific component. Features exist for all the ADF Faces components shipped with Oracle ADF. The name of a feature is the same as the name of the JavaScript component it describes. For example, the feature name for the `af:inputText` component is `AdRichfInputText` because the JavaScript component class is `AdRichfInputText.js`.

A partition is a logical group of features that is configured in the default-adf-js-partitions.xml internal file, which provides the default configuration in ADF Faces. Developers can override the default settings by creating a custom configuration file, which they name adf-js-partitions.xml.

At runtime, the ADF Faces RC framework determines the features that are required by a page and attempts to map these features to defined partitions in the configuration file. If partitions are found that contain the required features, these are referenced at the end of the generated HTML page output. With this in mind, application developers are able to tune the performance of the initial page load by doing the following:

- Reducing the number of different components on a page to minimize the list of features that need to be added to the response

- Optionally, defining a custom adf-js-partitions.xml configuration file to provide custom partitions that contain only the features required by a page

Enabling JavaScript Partitioning

Application developers do nothing to enable JavaScript partitioning, because it is enabled by default. You can switch this feature off and on using the `web.xml` context parameter shown next. Setting the parameter value to `false` disables the partitioning.

```
<context-param>
  <param-name>
      oracle.adf.view.rich.libraryPartitioning.ENABLED
    </param-name>
  <param-value>false</param-value>
</context-param>
```

Developers who want to replace the default partitions with a custom version can create their own version of the adf-js-partitions.xml file and place it into the WEB-INF directory of the web project.

NOTE
Other than to measure the performance effect of custom partitions, there is really no reason to switch off the partitioning feature at runtime.

Registering the adf-js-partitions.xsd Schema   Optionally, you can register the adf-js-partitions XML schema with the integrated development environment (IDE) before creating the configuration file for JDeveloper to provide syntax help and code completion when editing the XML file. To do this, choose Tools | Preferences from the Oracle JDeveloper menu and then choose XML Schemas | Add. Click the Browse button to locate the schema in the root of the adf-richclient-api-11.jar file. The JAR file is located in <*jdev_home*>\modules\oracle.adf.view_11.1.1\, where the <*jdev_home*> needs to be replaced with the absolute path of the jdeveloper folder in the JDeveloper software installation directory. Keep the .xml value in the Extension field.

Creating the adf-js-partitions.xml File   To create an adf-js-partitions.xml configuration file, select File | New from the JDeveloper menu and choose the XML | XML Document entry, or choose the XML | XML Document from Schema if you followed the preceding section, in the New Gallery. Define the XML document name as adf-js-partitions.xml and ensure it is created in the web application project's WEB-INF directory. The XML document to start with should be created as shown here:

```
<?xml version="1.0" encoding="utf-8" ?>
<adf-js-features xmlns="http://xmlns.oracle.com/adf/faces/partition"
<partition>
  <partition-name> </partition-name>
    <feature> </feature>
  </partition>
</adf-js-partitions>
```

The `partition` element is the parent element of a partition. One or many of these partition groups are allowed in the configuration file. Each partition has only one `partition-name` element but can have multiple `feature` elements. The `feature` element values are the JavaScript names of the component to add as a feature. To add the client component of an `af:inputText` component, you use a value `AdfRichInputText`.

A custom adf-js-partitions.xml file always replaces the default JavaScript partition configuration. Therefore, when creating a custom configuration, we recommend that you start with a copy of at least the boot and core partitions of the default-adf-js-partitions.xml configuration file.

The ADF Faces default configuration is stored in the adf-richclient-impl-11.jar file that you find in the \jdeveloper\modules\oracle.adf.view_11.1.1 directory of the Oracle JDeveloper software installation directory. In addition, the file content is also available online in the "Oracle Fusion Middleware Web User Interface Developer's Guide for Oracle Application Development Framework 11*g* Release 1." The content of the default configuration file and a list of the default features are provided in Appendix A.9, "Using JavaScript Library Partitioning."

NOTE
The default partitions in ADF Faces are sensibly defined. Replacing them with a custom configuration may improve performance but can also degrade performance. Browser plug-ins, such as Firebug, guide you in the process of fine-tuning your initial page load.

Working with JavaScript in ADF Faces Applications

The ADF Faces client framework consists of components and events that developers can work with or listen to using JavaScript. In the following sections, we explain how to work with JavaScript in ADF Faces and provide example use cases. Although we've already mentioned this, it is worth reiterating: Don't use JavaScript only because you can! Use JavaScript when *necessary* or *required*, but use it sensibly to retain upgradability, to ensure cross platform execution, and to build applications that are truly future-proof.

How to Add JavaScript to a Page

When placing JavaScript, do you add it directly into the page or reference it from an external file? Adding JavaScript to the page reduces the number of round trips, as no additional fetch is required to load the JavaScript sources. However, adding JavaScript to the page content increase the page size and cannot be cached by the browsers, which might end up worse than an additional round trip. Therefore, the recommendation is to build generic JavaScript functions and store them in external files (note the plural) that you reference from the application pages as needed. This way, JavaScript content can be loaded by pages that need them and can be cached by the browser to avoid additional downloads. If you need to put JavaScript directly on a page, make sure this also references external JavaScript files. For example, Chapter 10 contains the following code sample for launching a pop-up dialog from JavaScript:

```
function launchPopup(event) {
    var source = event.getSource();
    var popup = source.findComponent("p1");
    popup.show();
}
```

We showed this function directly added to the page content. This function could easily be moved into an external JavaScript file. It does not specify any alignment hints, so it could be renamed as `launchBasicPopup(event)`. But then, how would you pass the information about the pop-up component instance to launch to the JavaScript function? Of course, there is an answer to this—and we'll get back to this use case later in this chapter in the section "How to Pass Additional Arguments to a Client Event Handler."

Also shown in Chapter 10 and in other chapters that use JavaScript in the examples, the `af:resource` tag is used to enclose the JavaScript coding:

```
<af:resource type="javascript" source="/scripts/basic_usecases.js"/>
```

Or this,

```
<af:resource type="javascript">
  function doSomething(args){
    ...
  }
</af:resource>
```

The ADF Faces `af:resource` tag optimizes the loading of JavaScript and style sheet content in an ADF Faces pages. It can be added anywhere in ADF pages and page fragments and always adds the contained or referenced content to the document header. Scripts that are referenced in the page header load before the page renders and are not executed immediately. Using the header to download JavaScript ensures better performance and ensures that the scripts are available when called in the page.

The af:clientListener Tag

The `af:clientListener` tag is located in the Operations panel of the ADF Faces category in the Oracle JDeveloper Component Palette and is used in ADF Faces to register JavaScript event handlers with a component. To handle client-side component events, the `af:clientListener` is added as a child to the component that raises the event. The `af:clientListener` tag has two attributes for which developers need to provide values:

- **type**   Contains the component event name to which the listener responds. If the component is `af:document`, then this could be `load`. If the component is `af:tree`, then this type could be `rowDisclosure` or `selection`.

- **method**   Contains the name of the JavaScript handler to call. The JavaScript handler is a function that has a single argument for the component event to be passed in. The `method` attribute value contains only the function name, without the brackets and argument.

The client listener configuration for an `af:inputText` component looks as follows:

```
<af:inputText label="Only Numbers" id="it1">
  <af:clientListener type="keyDown" method="filterForNumbers"/>
</af:inputText>
```

The JavaScript function `filterForNumbers` is defined as shown next and is either located on the page or referenced from an external JavaScript library file using the `af:resource` tag. The function filters the user keyboard input to allow only numeric data input:

```
function filterForNumbers(evt){
   //get ADF Faces event source, InputText.js
   var inputField = evt.getSource();
   var oldValue = inputField.getValue();
   var ignoredControlKeys = new Array(
        AdfKeyStroke.BACKSPACE_KEY, AdfKeyStroke.TAB_KEY,
        AdfKeyStroke.ARROWLEFT_KEY, AdfKeyStroke.ARROWRIGHT_KEY,
        AdfKeyStroke.ESC_KEY, AdfKeyStroke.ENTER_KEY,
        AdfKeyStroke.DELETE_KEY);
   //define the key range to exclude from field input
   var minNumberKeyCode = 48;
   var maxNumberKeyCode = 57;
   var minNumberPadKeyCode = 96;
   var maxNumberPadKeyCode = 105;
   //key pressed by the user
   var keyCodePressed = evt.getKeyCode();
   //if it is a control key, don't suppress it
   var ignoreKey = false;
   for (keyPos in ignoredControlKeys){
```

```
      if(keyCodePressed == ignoredControlKeys[keyPos]){
        ignoreKey = true;
        break;
      }
    }
    //return if key should be ignored
    if(ignoreKey==true){
      return true;
    }
    //filter keyboard input
    if (keyCodePressed < minNumberKeyCode ||
        keyCodePressed > maxNumberPadKeyCode){
      //set value back to previous value
      inputField.setValue(oldValue);
      //no need for the event to propagate to the server, so cancel
      //it
      evt.cancel();
      return true;
    }
    if (keyCodePressed > maxNumberKeyCode &&
      keyCodePressed < minNumberPadKeyCode){
      //set value back to previous value
      inputField.setValue(oldValue);
      evt.cancel();
      return true;
    }
}
```

The event type that is passed as an argument to the function is a browser-specific version of `AdfUIInputEvent.js`. If, for example, the browser is Safari, then the event type is `AdfSafariUIInputEvent.js`. Unlike in Java, where an object needs to be cast to access methods of an implementation class, in JavaScript this is not required because it is an untyped language. Also notice the use of the `AdfKeyStroke.js` class that provides consistent definitions for the keyboard keys.

NOTE
ADF Faces RC JavaScript objects are automatically loaded. Application developers don't have to load these objects explicitly before they can use them in their client-side programming.

Dynamically Creating a Client Listener

In the preceding example, the `af:clientListener` component is added as a child of the `af:inputText` component at design time. For use cases in which the client handler should be added dynamically at runtime, you use a Java method that obtains a handle to the `af:inputText` component instance to add an instance of `ClientListenerSet`. The Java code shown next adds the client listener to an input text field in response to a command button action event:

```
public void addClientListener(ActionEvent actionEvent) {
   addClientListener(txt1,"keyDown","filterForNumbers");
}
```

```
private void addClientListener(RichInputText component,
                              String type, String method{
  ClientListenerSet cls = new ClientListenerSet()
  cls.addListener(type,method);
  component.setClientListeners(cls);
}
```

NOTE
The client listener functionality is a feature of the ADF Faces RC framework, which is why you can't use UIComponent *in the method signature but have to use an ADF Faces component class.*

How to Pass Additional Arguments to a Client Event Handler

If client-side event handlers are JavaScript functions with a single argument, how do you pass additional information to the functions? You can use two strategies to pass extra arguments to an event handler.

Using the af:clientAttribute Component   Using ADF Faces RC components, and only within this UI component set, the af:clientAttribute tag can be used to define a name/value pair as an additional custom attribute on the component that raises the event. The client attribute is accessible on the client using JavaScript and on the server using Java or Expression Language. To access a client attributes programmatically, you call getProperty on the UI component, passing the name of the attribute as the argument.

The same method can be used to call regular component attributes if the clientComponent attribute of the component is set to true so a client-side object exists.

Here's an example: Assume that a command link is added in a column of the af:table component that displays the information of the Departments table. When the user clicks the link, a calendar component is launched to show team events and meetings for the selected department. To indicate the selected department in the dialog, JavaScript is used to set the title of the af:dialog component in the pop-up, as shown in Figure 19-2. Notice the contentDelivery attribute that needs to be set to immediate for this use case.

```
<af:popup id="popup1" contentDelivery="immediate">
  <af:dialog id="dialog1">
    <af:calendar id="c5" …/>
  </af:dialog>
</af:popup>
```

The command link in the table has an af:clientAtrribute defined to read the department name from the table:

```
<af:column id="c6" headerText="Show Calendar">
  <af:commandLink text="edit" id="cl1" partialSubmit="true">
    <af:clientAttribute name="departmentName"
                        value="#{row.DepartmentName}"/>
    <af:clientListener method="launchPopup" type="action"/>
  </af:commandLink>
</af:column>
```

Finally, the event handler that is called by the `af:clientListener` accesses the client attribute from the event's source component reference finds the `af:popup` instance and the `af:dialog` contained within. Note that before the title of the dialog can be set, the dialog component must be rendered on the client, which is done when the pop-up is opened:

```
<af:resource type="javascript">
  function launchPopup(evt){
    var commandLink = evt.getSource();
    //the popup resides outside of the table, thus the leading "::"
    var popup = commandLink.findComponent("::popup1");
    //access the client attribute
    var departmentName = commandLink.getProperty("departmentName");
    //launch the popup relative to the command link
    var dialog = popup.findComponent(":dialog1");
    var hints = {};
    hints[AdfRichPopup.HINT_ALIGN_ID] = commandLink.getClientId();
    hints[AdfRichPopup.HINT_ALIGN] = AdfRichPopup.ALIGN_END_AFTER;
    popup.show(hints);
    dialog.setTitle("Team calendar for "+departmentName);
  }
</af:resource>
```

Using a JavaScript Callback   The preceding example is not generic enough to be stored in an external library because it has the values for the client attribute name, and the pop-up and dialog *id* properties contained in the JavaScript code. To create a generic solution, the sample needs to

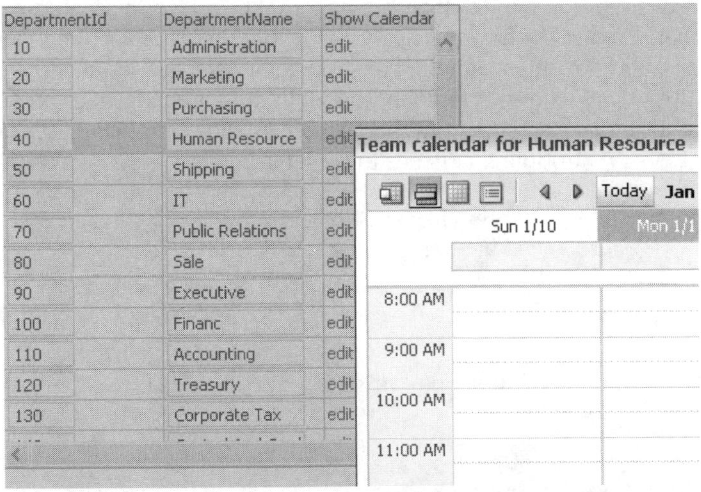

FIGURE 19-2   *ADF Faces table with command link that launches a pop-up displaying information about the selected row*

be changed so that the client attribute name and the id attribute values of the dialog and pop-up components are passed as an argument to the JavaScript function, in addition to the event object. The changed function is shown here:

```
function launchPopupWithDialog( popupId, dialogId,
                                clientAttributeName, title){
  //callback function that receives the component event
  return function (evt){
    //cancel server propagation of the event
    evt.cancel();
    var commandLink = evt.getSource();
    var popup = commandLink.findComponent(popupId);
    var departmentName = commandLink.getProperty(clientAttributeName);
    var dialog = popup.findComponent(dialogId);
    var hints = {};
    hints[AdfRichPopup.HINT_ALIGN_ID] = commandLink.getClientId();
    hints[AdfRichPopup.HINT_ALIGN] = AdfRichPopup.ALIGN_END_AFTER;
    popup.show(hints);
    dialog.setTitle(title+departmentName);
  };
}
```

The changed JavaScript code uses a callback function that defines the ADF Faces client component event handler. The af:clientListener definition on the af:commandLink component needs to be changed, too, as shown here:

```
<af:commandLink text="edit" id="cl1" partialSubmit="true">
  <af:clientAttribute name="departmentName"
                      value="#{row.DepartmentName}"/>
  <af:clientListener method="launchPopupWithDialog(
    '::popup1',':dialog1','departmentName', 'Team calendar for ')"
      type="action"/>
</af:commandLink>
```

The outcome of this change is the same as that shown in Figure 19-2, with a difference, however, in that this code can be reused if it's stored in an external library.

How to Find Components on a Page

To find a client component on an ADF Faces page, the component must exist as a client component. To ensure a client component is created, you set the component clientComponent attribute to true. At runtime, ADF Faces components are uniquely identified by their client ID, which is derived from the component id attribute value. Components that don't have an id attribute defined get a random ID assigned at runtime, in which case the values may be different between page runs. Even if components have an id attribute defined, the generated client ID is different if the component is located in a naming container.

Naming Containers and the Generated clientId

In JSF, the generated HTML markup for a component must uniquely identify the server-side object it represents so they can be matched upon postback submits. `NamingContainer` is a JSF interface that is implemented by UI containers to provide a local namespace for their contained child components. Naming containers help to avoid conflicts that may occur when external content is included on a page or when you're dynamically creating or stamping components. The unique component identification is ensured through the component renderer producing a `clientId value`, which is added as the `id` attribute to the component generated HTML output. For components that don't reside in naming containers, the `id` value added to the generated markup is the same as the component `id` defined at design time. When a component is a child component of a naming container, the component ID of all parent naming containers within the hierarchy from the page root to the component is added to the component `id` as a prefix separated by a colon (`:`).

For example, an `af:inputText` component with an `id` attribute of `txt1` appears with a client ID of `txt1` in the generated HTML output if it is not contained in a naming container. If it is contained in a naming container, with an `id` of `nc1`, then the client ID at runtime is `nc1:txt1`.

To access a component on a page without the need to parse the whole document, developers must understand and know about the client-side ID. You can obtain the client ID of a component by a call to its `getClientId` method.

ADF Faces components that implement the NamingContainer interface include the following (and many more):

`af:calendar`	`af:carousel`	`af:declarativeComponent`
`dvt:hierarchyViewer`	`dvt:map`	`af:navigationPane`
`af:panelCollection`	`af:query`	`af:quickQuery`
`af:region`	`af:pageTemplate`	`dvt:pivotTable`
`dvt:projectGantt`	`af:subform`	`af:table`
`af:train`	`af:treeTable`	`af:tree`

Searching from the Page Root

To search for a component on a page, you can perform an absolute search, starting from the page root, or a search relative from a component to which you obtain a handle. To search from the page root, you use the `AdfPage` object, the page management class that exposes three search methods:

- `AdfPage.PAGE.findComponent`

- `AdfPage.PAGE.findComponentByAbsoluteId`

- `AdfPage.PAGE.findComponentByAbsoluteLocator`

The `findComponent` and `findComponentByAbsoluteId` methods appear identical when called from the `AdfPage` component. The difference, though, is that the `findComponent` method searches the component `clientId` attribute value, whereas the `findComponentBy AbsoluteId` method searches each component mentioned in the search path individually by its `id` attribute value. For example, if a component is located in a naming container, such as `af:panelCollection`, then to locate the component, the naming container is looked up first to become the search base for the component lookup.

The format of the `clientId` attribute is not guaranteed to be consistent because it is implementation-specific to the renderer that produces the HTML output. Therefore, if you prefer using the `findComponent` method, you should not hard-code the `clientId` search string but pass it in dynamically—for example, using the `af:clientAttribute` tag.

The `findComponentByAbsoluteId` method search is comparable to the search method exposed on the JSF `UIViewRoot` and is not supposed to change its format. The `find ComponentByAbsoluteId` is recommended to be used by application and page developers:

```
Component = AdfPage.PAGE.findComponentByAbsoluteId('componentId');
```

If a component is contained in a naming container, then the call is

```
Component = AdfPage.PAGE.findComponentByAbsoluteId(
                    'containerId:componentId');
```

If a component is located in a nested naming container, then the call becomes

```
Component = AdfPage.PAGE.findComponentByAbsoluteId(
                    'containerId1:containerId2:componentId');
```

> **NOTE**
> *The structure of the* `absoluteId` *passed to this function is identical to the structure passed to* `UIViewRoot.findComponent` *on the server. No leading colons are used in the search string.*

The `AdfPage.PAGE.findComponentByAbsoluteLocator` method searches for child components in components that stamp their children, such as `af:Table`. Stamping repeatedly calls the generated markup of a child component and adds the current row's cell value. For example, a table, *table1*, is contained in a naming container, such as a subform or a page template, *nc1*. The table has a column with the ID *col1* that contains an output text, *ot1*, component as the cell renderer. To access the column value of the third row, you use the following search expression:

```
component = AdfPage.PAGE.findComponentByAbsoluteLocator(
                    'nc1:table1:2:ot1');
```

In this example, the absolute component locator ID contains the ID of the naming container, the ID of the table, a zero-based row index, and the component ID. The `af:column` ID value is missing in the component reference because the `af:column` is not a naming container. Only naming containers and the referenced component ID are part of the search string. The `af:table` component is a naming container and therefore has its ID referenced in the search string. The returned value of the search is a JavaScript component object of the cell component type, for example `AdfRichOutputText`.

> **NOTE**
> *To be able to access the cell rendered component, you must set its* `clientcomponent` *attribute to* `true` *as otherwise no client-side object exists with which you can work.*

Search Starting Relative to a Component

Within an application, you often gain access to a UI component and from there want to access a sibling, parent, or child component. For example, a button that has an `af:clientListener` component added that points to a JavaScript function like this,

```
function doIt(evt){ ... }
```

can be accessed like this:

```
var button1 = evt.getSource();
```

Starting from this instance, you can search for a component using one of the two search methods exposed on the component handle:

- `<component>.findComponent`

- `<component>.findComponentByAbsoluteLocator`

The `findComponent` method supports absolute `clientId` references, as well as search expressions in the form of leading colons (:). Table 19-1 shows examples for how a search expression needs to be built for different locations of the components. The search always starts from a button component and attempts to access an instance of an `af:inputText` component.

The use of the colons in front of the component `clientId` is comparable to the way you use double dots (`..`) when searching for folders on the command line of your operation system. A single colon always starts the search from the page root, which is the most expensive way if the searched component is not located in the root page. Using two colons (`::`) searches in the ancestor container of the component on which you perform the search. Using three colons (`:::`) starts the search in the parent container of the component's ancestor container.

NOTE
No `findComponentByAbsoluteId` function is available when starting the search for a component relative to another. Internally, however, the `findComponent` function, which is exposed on the UI component from which the search is started, performs an absolute search based on the information passed as an argument.

Dynamically Determining the Component's clientId

As you may have noticed, a search requires the `clientId` or `componentId` that identifies the component location relative to where the search is started from. So how do you obtain the `clientId` in a future-proof way that avoids hard-coding it in the JavaScript sources? A solution to this is to pass the `clientId` value of the component you need to access with the event using an `af:clientAttribute` component on the UI component that raises the event. Again, assuming that the component to access from an event is `textField1` located in a naming container `nc1`, to determine the `clientId` of the component at runtime, you would create a JSF component binding to a managed bean using the `binding` attribute of `textField1`. In the same managed bean, create a property with its setter/getter method and name it `clientIdTextField1`. Edit `getClientIdTextField1` as shown here:

```
public String getClientIdTextField1(){
    return txtField1Binding.getClientId(FacesContext.getCurrentInstance());
}
```

Component Location	Search Access

`button1` and `textField1` are located in the same naming container of page root	Start the search from the page root and only search on this level:
	`button1.findComponent(':textField1')`
	Search in the same naming container that the button is in:
	`button1.findComponent('textField');`

`button1` is located on page; `textField1` is located in a naming container `nc1`	Start the search on the page root and look into the specified naming container:
	`button1.findComponent(':nc1:textField1');`
	Search in the naming container that is a child of the naming container or page root in which the button is located:
	`button1.findComponent('nc1:textField1');`

`button1` is located on the page; `textField1` is located in a naming container `nc1` that is located in a naming container `nc2`	Start the search from the page root and look for the component in the naming container `nc2`, which is nested in `nc1`:
	`button1.findComponent(':nc1:nc2:textField1');`
	Start the search from the naming container that the button is in, which can be the page root, and look in the nested naming container `nc`:
	`button1.findComponent('nc1:nc2:textField1');`

`button1` is located in naming container `nc1`; `textField1` is located on the page root	Start the search from the page root. If the text field is located in the root then it is found:
	`button1.findComponent(':textField1');`
	Search in the ancestor naming container:
	`button1.findComponent('::textField1');`

`button1` is located in a naming container `nc1` within naming container `nc2`; `textField1` is located in the root page	Start the search from the page root. If the text field is located in the root then it is found:
	`button1.findComponent(':textField1');`
	Search in the parent container of the ancestor container of the container in which the button resides:
	`button1.findComponent(':::textField1'');`

TABLE 19-1   *How a Search Expression Needs to Be Built for Different Locations of the Components*

Drag the `af:clientAttribute` component to the launcher component that has the `af:clientListener` defined. Specify a name, such as `searchId`, and open the Expression Builder dialog from the context menu of the `value` attribute. Point the Expression Builder to the managed bean property that returns the component client ID. At runtime, in your JavaScript event handler, you'd use the following code to perform the search:

```
Function doIt(evt){
    var button = evt.getSource();
    var searchId = button.getProperty('searchId');
    var txtField = button.findComponent(':'+searchId);
    ...
}
```

Introduction to the af:serverListener Component

The `af:serverListener` tag invokes a managed bean method on the server in response to a client-side event. The server-side method returns void and takes a single input argument of type `ClientEvent`. The `ClientEvent` allows developers to access messages sent from the client. The `af:serverListener` tag has two mandatory attributes, `type` and `method`. The `type` attribute defines the name of the custom server event, and the `method` attribute references the server-side managed bean method using Expression Language.

To add an `af:serverListener` component to a page, drag it from the ADF Faces | Operations category of the component palette to a UI component on the page and set the component's `clientComponent` attribute to `true`. In the example shown next, a server listener is added to an `af:panelGroupLayout` component to echo the user input in the two `af:inputText` components to the server. Each of the `af:inputText` components has a client listener defined that raises a keyboard event.

```
<af:panelGroupLayout layout="scroll" id="pgl1" clientComponent="true">
  <af:inputText label="Send to server" id="it1">
    <af:clientListener method="echoInput" type="keyUp"/>
  </af:inputText>
  <af:inputText label="Send to server" id="inputText2">
    <af:clientListener method="echoInput" type="keyUp"/>
  </af:inputText>
  <af:serverListener type="notifyServer"
                     method="#{ClientEventBean.echoTextField}"/>
</af:panelGroupLayout>
```

NOTE
The `af:inputText` *components shown here don't need to have the* `clientComponent` *attribute set to* `true`. *Components that have a client listener added automatically get a client object created.*

The JavaScript source code that is invoked by the `af:clientListener` component is shown next. Notice how it passes the value of the input text component in its payload.

```
function echoInput(evt){
    var txtField =  evt.getSource();
    var clientId =  txtField.getClientId();
    var value = txtField.getSubmittedValue();
    var panelGroup = AdfPage.PAGE.findComponentByAbsoluteId("pgl1");
    AdfCustomEvent.queue(
        //reference the component that has the server
        //listener defined
        panelGroup,
        //specify server listener to invoke
        "notifyServer",
        // Send two parameters. The format of this message is
        //a JSON map, which on the server side Java code becomes
        //a java.util.Map object
        {echo:value, clientId:clientId},
        // Make it "immediate" on the server
        true);
}
```

The managed bean that receives the event on the server reads the message from the `ClientEvent` and prints it.

```
public void echoTextField(ClientEvent clientEvent){
    String message = (String) clientEvent.getParameters().get("echo");
    String clientId = (String) clientEvent.getParameters().get("clientId");
    System.out.println("ECHO "+clientId+": "+message);
}
```

How to Block User Input During Long-Running Queries

Another use case for using the `af:serverListener` component are long-running queries or processes during which developers want to prevent the user from submitting any additional requests, or resubmitting the sent request. The design pattern for this type of input deactivation is a glass pane. Using the glass pane pattern, a semitransparent layer is pulled over the UI so the user can still see the form but cannot use the form controls or input components. At the end of the long-running query, control is passed back to the application and the glass pane is removed.

Using the `af:clientListener` and `af:serverListener` components, developers invoke the long-running query or process from a managed bean method. The `af:clientListener` component calls the custom JavaScript that queues the action event for the `af:serverListener` component, and that blocks the user interface until the custom event completes. This source code defines a command button that, when clicked, executes a client-side JavaScript function `runLongRunningQuery`:

```
<af:commandButton text="Start long running Query" id="cb1"
  partialSubmit="true">
    <af:clientListener method="runLongRunningQuery" type="action"/>
    <af:serverListener type="invokeLongRunningQuery"
                       method="#{QueryHelperBean.executeQuery}"/>
</af:commandButton>
```

The JavaScript function that queues the event is shown next:

```
<af:resource type="javascript">
  function runLongRunningQuery(evt)
  {
    //cancel the action event so it is not propagating to
    //the server
    evt.cancel();
    //set the parameters that needs to be passed when
    //queuing the event
    var source = evt.getSource();
    var params = {};
    var type = " invokeLongRunningQuery ";
    var immediate = true;
    var isPartial = true;
    //create a new custom ADF Faces client event
    var customEvent = new AdfCustomEvent(source, type, params, immediate);
    //block all user action while the event executes. This function
    //call pulls a glass pane over the UI
    customEvent.preventUserInput();
    //queue the event to be handled by the serverListener
```

```
    customEvent.queue(isPartial);
  }
</af:resource>
```

NOTE
The `preventUserInput` *method can be called only on custom events and does not work with action events raised by command components. Attempts to re-queue an action event of a command component leads to an infinitive loop.*

Calling a JavaScript Function from a Managed Bean

In ADF Faces RC, client-side JavaScript execution can be initiated from the server in response to a request. In the example below, a managed bean method is used to close a client side popup dialog. ADF Faces RC does not provide a native Java API for closing a client side popup so that JavaScript must be used. The JavaScript should be located in a JavaScript library or, as in our example, defined in the managed bean.

```
import oracle.adf.view.rich.component.rich.RichPopup;
import org.apache.myfaces.trinidad.render.ExtendedRenderKitService;
import org.apache.myfaces.trinidad.util.Service;
...
private void closePopup(String _popupId) {
  FacesContext fctx = FacesContext.getCurrentInstance();
  //create the JavaScript expression
  StringBuffer scriptBuffer = new StringBuffer();
  scriptBuffer.append(
      "var popup = AdfPage.PAGE.findComponentByAbsoluteId('");
  //add the _popupId value from the the method argument
  scriptBuffer.append(_popupId +"');");
  scriptBuffer.append("if(popup.isPopupVisible()){");
  scriptBuffer.append("popup.hide();}");
  String script = scriptBuffer.toString();
  //execute the script on the client
  ExtendedRenderKitService extendedRenderKitService =
     Service.getRenderKitService(fctx,ExtendedRenderKitService.class);
  extendedRenderKitService.addScript(fctx,script);
}
```

To close a pop-up from a button, you create a button action method in the managed bean and call the method shown above. If the `af:popup` has a component binding defined to the same managed bean, then you can use this instance to get the search string to locate the component on the client.

```
//managed bean method to close an instance of af:popup
//on the client
public String closePopup_action(){
  FacesContext fctx = FacesContext.getCurrentInstance();
  //popup1 is the component instance variable for the
  //af:popup component in the managed bean
  closePopup(popup1.getClientId(fctx));
  return null;
}
```

NOTE
JavaScript that you add dynamically from Java is more difficult to debug than JavaScript located in a JavaScript library or contained on the page.

JavaScript Programming Use Cases

In this section, we demonstrate practical JavaScript client solutions that are in line with the golden rule we expressed at the beginning of the chapter: Don't use JavaScript unless there is no other solution to a problem. Scripts with no server-side dependencies are good to use and may help to improve the user experience when working in an ADF Faces RC application. A last golden rule we want to offer is this: Use the ADF Faces public client APIs only if you want your scripts to be future-proof. Don't use direct DOM manipulation techniques in your JavaScript code.

NOTE
ADF Faces RC provides behavior tags in the Operations category of the ADF Faces selection in the JDeveloper component palette. The tags can be used to implement functionality for which you otherwise have to use JavaScript. For example, the `af:showPopupBehavior` *can be used to open a pop-up dialog on the client instead of using JavaScript. Whenever a behavior tag exists, you should prefer this over custom JavaScript programming.*

How to Specify a Form Tab Index

In HTML input forms, you can specify the `tabindex` attribute on the input fields to determine the order in which the form is navigated when the user presses the TAB key. The default tab order in ADF Faces is from top to bottom and from bottom to top when pressing the SHIFT key. This order doesn't change if you set the `row` and `column` attributes of an `af:panelFormLayout` component to display the form with multiple columns, as shown in Figure 19-3. If you want to change the tab order, you need to set the `tabindex` attribute. Unfortunately, the ADF Faces RC components don't expose a `tabindex` attribute, because it is difficult to handle the tab index generically—for example, when the form element is contained in an ADF region or used in a page template. If the custom requirement is to change the default tab order of an ADF Faces form, developers can use JavaScript to enforce this behavior.

To specify the component tab index, you add an `af:clientAttribute` component and an `af:clientListener` component to each input component. The `af:clientAttribute` component defines the position a component has in the tab order. The `af:clientListener`

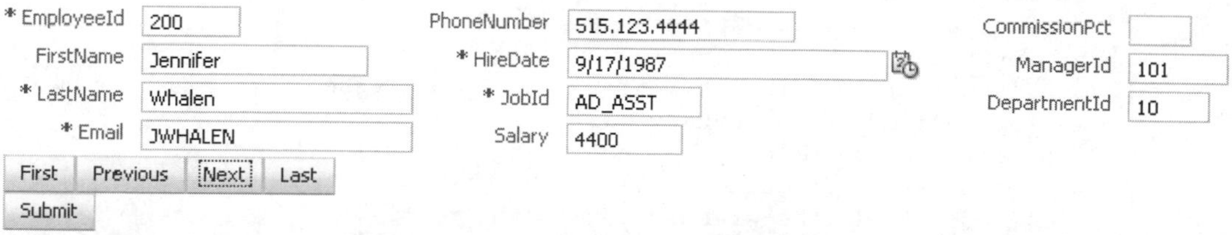

* EmployeeId	200	PhoneNumber	515.123.4444	CommissionPct	
FirstName	Jennifer	* HireDate	9/17/1987	ManagerId	101
* LastName	Whalen	* JobId	AD_ASST	DepartmentId	10
* Email	JWHALEN	Salary	4400		

First | Previous | Next | Last

Submit

FIGURE 19-3 *ADF form in an* `af:panelFormLayout` *with three columns*

invokes the JavaScript that puts focus on the next component when the TAB key or SHIFT-TAB is pressed.

The JavaScript function we provide as an example allows developers to pass three arguments from the af:clientListener configuration. The first argument is the id value of the af:panelFormLayout component that is the parent component of the input fields. The second argument defines the lowest tab index of the form, and the third argument defines the highest tab index. Specifying the panelFormLayout ID and tab index minimum and maximum values allows this script to be reusable across pages and applications.

In this example, the ADF Faces RC form consists of nine input components of type RichInputText and RichInputDate. The components are laid out in three columns and three rows.

```
<af:panelFormLayout id="pfl1" maxColumns="3" rows="3"
  clientComponent="true">
  <af:inputText value="#{bindings.EmployeeId.inputValue}"
      label="#{bindings.EmployeeId.hints.label}" … >
    <af:clientAttribute name="tabindex" value="1"/>
    <af:clientListener method="setTabIndex('pfl1',1,9)"
                       type="keyPress"/>
  </af:inputText>
  …
  <af:inputText value="#{bindings.PhoneNumber.inputValue}"
      label="#{bindings.PhoneNumber.hints.label}" … >
    <af:clientAttribute name="tabindex" value="2"/>
    <af:clientListener method="setTabIndex('pfl1',1,9)"
                       type="keyPress"/>
  </af:inputText>
</af:panelFormLayout>
```

NOTE
The af:panelFormLayout *tag must have its* clientComponent *attribute set to* true; *otherwise, no client-side object is created for this component.*

```
//function that takes the panelFormLayoutId, the min tabindex number
//and the max tabindex number as input arguments
function setTabIndex(panelFormLayoutId, min, max){
  //callback function to pass the ADF Faces RC keyboard event
  return function(evt){
    var minTabIndx = min;
    var maxTabIndx = max;
    //the actual key that got pressed
    var keyCodePressed = evt.getKeyCode();
    //the modifier - ctrl, alt, shift - that is pressed
    var keyModifiers = evt.getKeyModifiers();
    //the input component that is edited by the user
    var component = evt.getSource();
    //only operate if the pressed key is the tab key
    if(keyCodePressed == AdfKeyStroke.TAB_KEY){
```

```
      //don't allow keyboard event to be handled by the
      //browser
      evt.cancel();
      //find panelFormLayout
      var panelFormLayout =
        AdfPage.PAGE.findComponentByAbsoluteId(panelFormLayoutId);
      var tabIndx = parseInt(component.getProperty("tabindex"));
      //detect backward tab
      if(keyModifiers == AdfKeyStroke.SHIFT_MASK){
        //decrement tab index. If new tab index is lower
        //than min, set tab index to max index
        tabIndx = (tabIndx-1) < minTabIndx ? maxTabIndx : tabIndx-1;
        //check child components for index match and if, set focus
        setComponentFocus(panelFormLayout.getDescendantComponents(),
                          tabIndx);
      }
      //forward tab
      else{
        //increment tab index. If new tab index is greater
        //than max, set tab index to min index
        tabIndx = (tabIndx+1) > maxTabIndx? minTabIndx : tabIndx+1;
        setComponentFocus(panelFormLayout.getDescendantComponents(),
                          tabIndx);
      }
    }
  }
}
//shared function to set focus on the tabbed component
function setComponentFocus(childComponentArray, focusIndex){
  //iterate over all UI components
  for(indx in childComponentArray){
    var comp = childComponentArray[indx];
    //check if input component of expected type. This checking needs
    //to be extended if your form contains other input types
    if (comp instanceof AdfRichInputText ||
        comp instanceof AdfRichInputDate){
      var compIndx = comp.getProperty("tabindex");
      if (compIndx == focusIndex){
        comp.focus();
        return false;
      }
    }
  }
  return false;
}
```

User Input Count

For user convenience, applications may indicate the remaining number of characters that are allowed to enter into a text area. Using ADF Faces, this indicator can be built with JavaScript, as shown in Figure 19-4.

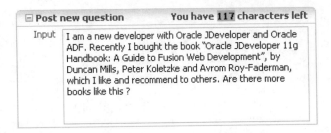

FIGURE 19-4   *Input text component with character counter*

The page code of the box shown in Figure 19-4 is shown here:

```
<af:panelBox text="Post new question" clientComponent="true" id="pb1">
  <f:facet name="toolbar">
    <af:panelGroupLayout layout="horizontal" id="g2">
      <af:outputText id="ot1" value="You have"/>
      <af:spacer width="3" height="1" id="s1"/>
      <af:outputText id="counter" clientComponent="true"
                     value="#{CharCounterBean.charCount}"/>
      <af:spacer width="3" height="1" id="s2"/>
      <af:outputText id="ot3" value="characters left"/>
    </af:panelGroupLayout>
  </f:facet>
  <af:inputText label="Input" rows="7" columns="50" clientComponent="true"
                maximumLength="400" id="it1" wrap="soft"
                binding="#{CharCounterBean.inputArea}">
    <af:clientListener method="charChecker" type="keyUp"/>
  </af:inputText>
</af:panelBox>
```

Note the `maximumLength` attribute on the `af:inputText` component that is used to determine the maximum number of characters. For this, a managed bean method is referenced from the `af:outputText` component `value` attribute. The managed bean method reads the `maximumLength` attribute value and returns it to the output text component that represents the counter.

```
public int getCharCount() {
   String txtValue = (String)inputArea.getValue();
   int maxLength = inputArea.getMaximumLength();
   int currentLength = (txtValue!= null? txtValue.length():0);
   return (maxLength - currentLength);
}
```

The script colors the counter background in green, orange, and red, dependent on the number of characters that are left to enter:

```
function charChecker(evt){
   var textfield = evt.getCurrentTarget();
   var textfield_current_content = textfield.getSubmittedValue();
   var textfield_current_content_length = textfield_current_content.length;
   var vGREEN = textfield.getMaximumLength();
   //define the condition when the background color changes
   var vORANGE = vGREEN/2;
   var vRED = vORANGE/4;
   var vBACKGROUND_COLOR ='white';
   var vCOLOR ='black';
   var counter = AdfPage.PAGE.findComponentByAbsoluteId("counter");
   var counter_value = counter.getValue();
   //determine the color based on the current value
   if (vGREEN - textfield_current_content_length  <= vGREEN &&
       vGREEN - textfield_current_content_length > 0){
     if(vGREEN - textfield_current_content_length <= vRED){
        vBACKGROUND_COLOR ='red';
        vCOLOR='white';
     }
     else{
       if(vGREEN - textfield_current_content_length <= vORANGE){
         vBACKGROUND_COLOR ='orange';
         vCOLOR='black';
       }
       else{
         vBACKGROUND_COLOR ='green';
         vCOLOR='white';
       }
     }
   }
   //set the component inlineStyle property
   counter.setInlineStyleProperty("background-color",vBACKGROUND_COLOR);
   counter.setInlineStyleProperty("color",vCOLOR);
   counter_value = vGREEN - textfield_current_content_length-1;
   }
  counter.setValue(counter_value);
}
```

How to Invoke a Command Component Programmatically

JavaScript can be used to invoke an action component on a page using the `AdfActionEvent`
object. `AdfActionEvent` takes two arguments, the command component instance and a
Boolean value, to determine whether or not the action should be executed as a partial submit:

```
//method expects the action component id attribute value as
//the argument value
function invokeCommandAction(id){
  var component = AdfPage.PAGE.findComponentByAbsoluteId(id);
  AdfActionEvent.queue(component, component.getPartialSubmit());
}
```

How to Change the Disclose State of ADF Faces Components Programmatically

ADF Faces components such as `af:panelAccordion`, `af:panelBox`, and `af:showDetailHeader` dynamically hide and disclose their child components in response to a user action, such as a click of the header or the open/disclose icon. With client-side JavaScript, you can close and disclose the components based on a client-side condition, such as a mouse event, on another component.

PanelAccordion

The `af:panelAccordion` component panels are `af:showDetailItem` components, as shown here:

```
<af:panelAccordion id="pa1">
   <af:showDetailItem text="Panel 1" id="sdi1"/>
   <af:showDetailItem text="Panel 2" id="sdi2"/>
   <af:showDetailItem text="Panel 3" id="sdi3"/>
</af:panelAccordion>
```

Note that each of the `ShowDetailItem` components has a unique `id` attribute value so it can be located on the client. You can use an `af:clientAttribute` or a JavaScript callback function to pass the `af:showDetailItem id` attribute value to the JavaScript function that closes or discloses the component. The JavaScript code that uses a JavaScript callback is shown here:

```
function toggleAccordionPanel(panelId){
   return function(evt){
     var panel = AdfPage.PAGE.findComponentByAbsoluteId(panelId);
     panel.broadcast(new AdfDisclosureEvent(panel, !panel.getDisclosed()));
   }
}
```

PanelDetailHeader, PanelBox

The `af:panelDetailHeader` and `af:panelBox` components work similarly to the `af:panelAccordion`, except that the component itself is closed and disclosed, not one of its child components. The JavaScript function to toggle the disclosure state is shown here:

```
function toggleBoxOrHeader(compId){
   return function(evt){
     var comp =  AdfPage.PAGE.findComponentByAbsoluteId(compId);
     comp.broadcast(new AdfDisclosureEvent(comp, !comp.getDisclosed()));
   }
}
```

PanelSplitter

To close and disclose the `af:panelSplitter` component, you use the `setProperty` function that exists on the ADF Faces RC client components. For example, to toggle the disclosed state of a `PanelSplitter` component, you use JavaScript similar to the following:

```
function toggleSplitter(evt){
```

```
    var psp = AdfPage.PAGE.findComponent('ps1');
    psp.setProperty("collapsed", !psp.getProperty("collapsed"));
}
```

Note that this code does not make use of the event object that is passed in by the `af:clientListener` call. However, you may use the event object to search the `panelSplitter` component relative to the component that raised the event. This example performs an absolute search starting from the page root. The `PanelSplitter id` attribute is defined as `ps1`.

NOTE
The events in these examples are not cancelled, so the server receives event notification about the disclosure change. If you don't have a server-side disclosure listener defined, you can cancel the server propagation by a call to `evt.cancel()`.

Debugging JavaScript

If custom JavaScript fails, it usually does so silently. The result is a blank, not fully rendered ADF Faces page with a continuously spinning splash screen. The reason for this, which also is the most common mistake developers make, is usually a false component reference in the custom JavaScript code. A time-saving practice to detect this is to run a page on different browsers such as Firefox, Internet Explorer, and Safari. Different browser types not only show different behavior, they also produce different error messages that range from meaningless, such as when no error messages are shown or the displayed message is ambiguous, to meaningful, when the true cause of the problem is clearly flagged. Therefore, a good recommendation for application developers is to have different browser types installed and to use them for application testing.

If the page renders but does not execute the JavaScript function, you can debug the script with the JavaScript debugger of your choice—for example, Firebug in Firefox. To be able to debug into the ADF Faces JavaScript sources, you can disable content compression in the web.xml file so it will display meaningful method and variable names:

```
<context-param>
    <param-name>org.apache.myfaces.trinidad.DEBUG_JAVASCRIPT</param-name>
    <param-value>true</param-value>
</context-param>
```

If using JavaScript debuggers such as Firebug in Firefox, make sure you don't ignore the browser native error console. Debuggers are usually sufficient to locate a problem, but sometimes the browser console provides the more detailed information.

NOTE
If you have Firebug installed on browsers that execute production ADF Faces applications, then for better performance, we recommend disabling Firebug network monitoring for the application. To do this, open Firebug while running the ADF Faces application and select the drop-down list next to the Net option. Choose the Sites entry to disable or enable monitoring. Best is to not have Firebug installed on browsers used by application end users.

Summary

The ADF Faces RC client framework exposes a consistent set of JavaScript APIs to developers to build cross-browser applications. JavaScript in ADF Faces should be used sensitively for those areas that don't have a JSF programming equivalent. Like the server-side components, ADF Faces client components provide properties and raise events and have their own client lifecycle. The client programming framework is used by component developers and application developers alike and abstracts client-side programming from browser differences. When developing with the client programming framework, you should not use direct browser DOM manipulation techniques but the ADF Faces RC client API set.

Always make sure the component you need to access from client-side code has an `af:clientListener` added or its `clientComponent` attribute set to `true`.

CHAPTER
20

Active Data Services

Good ideas need adoption. To business application developers, real-time user interface (UI) refresh in Rich Enterprise Applications appears to be an unreachable goal because of the complexity involved. Active Data Services in Oracle ADF Faces Rich Client provides a simplified and future-proof platform for real-time data UI refresh in Oracle Fusion application development that shields developers from the implementation details of the push notification in Asynchronous JavaScript and XML (AJAX).

ctive Data Services (ADS) in Oracle ADF is a software implementation of the old Hollywood saying, "Don't call us, we call you"—assuming the server is Hollywood and the client is the actor. In this chapter, we introduce ADS and show you how application developers use this functionality to push messages in real-time from the server to the client in Oracle ADF.

Overcoming the Disconnected Web

To web application users, it must appear as if the Web reinvents itself once a year—with more interactive UIs, increasing performance through partial page refreshes, and desktop-like usability patterns that allow users to become as productive using web applications as they are using real desktop clients. One technical detail, though, hasn't changed in the past and is unlikely to change in the near future: HTTP.

Hypertext Transfer Protocol is based on the request–response principle in which the client sends a query to the server and the server responds with the requested data. Between requests, no connection is maintained between the client and the server that would allow server-side logic to send more data unasked. Any changes in the underlying data layer used by an application are first detected within the next client request.

Hopefully, it doesn't come to you by surprise when we say that in the modern days of Web 2.0 and Rich Enterprise Applications (REA), the Web still is disconnected and stateless. You may object, saying that you frequently use some applications on the Web that update their client UIs with server-side changes without your needing to do anything. And right you are—there is truth in both our statement and your observation. The question, therefore, is how this was accomplished and whether you can do the same with ADF Faces Rich Client (RC).

In the following discussions, we'll have a look at the options that are available in AJAX and other implementation technologies of Rich Internet Applications (RIA) to implement automatic UI refreshes.

By Chance Approach

The "by chance" approach queues a message on the server and waits for the next client request to apply the content changes to the rendered parts of the UI. This implementation does not qualify for any real-time messaging but is good to use when model data changes between user requests. An example for this is dependent lists, in which a value change in the parent list refreshes the choice in the detail list. If this is well implemented, the user query does not need to query the changed data explicitly to mark the associated UI components as refresh candidates.

Polling

Using polling, the client frequently sends a client request to the server to check for updates. Unlike user client requests, a poll is initiated by the client and is usually configurable for the application developer. The challenge using polling is in finding the best balance between the poll frequency and network capabilities. The maximum waiting time for a server-side change before it is sent to the client is the duration between two polls. This mechanism is good for model changes that are predictable and that don't need to be displayed immediately or at least close to when they occur. Polling helps where no server-side support is available for advanced techniques. However, it tends to suffer from network latency and blocking-IO handling of the servers.

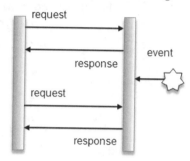

Long-polling

As in polling, with long-polling, the initial request comes from the client. Unlike with polling, using long-polling, the server response does not immediately follow the request and instead waits for a server-side event, hence its name. If an event occurs on the server, the response is sent to the client and the UI is updated. After completing the long poll, a new request is sent from the client to the server and again the response waits for an event to come.

Long-polling has its maximum delay for server-side events that occur directly after a response is sent to the client, as it takes a bit of time for the client to send the next request. Long-polling is a good choice for different network topologies, including the use of proxies. You need to be aware, though, that long-polling uses two connections—one for the push notification and one for the data. The way that long polling is implemented determines the number of opened connections to the server. In practice, though, most solutions for active data support provide channel sharing to reduce the number of opened server connections.

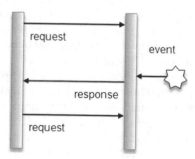

Push

Push, also known as HTTP streaming, starts with a client request opening a connection to the server. With a connection open, the server is immediately able to notify the client about server-side changes. To keep the connection alive, the server sends partial responses to the client, which are empty if no server-side update is available, or they contain a message payload if a UI change is required.

Push is more immediate than poll and long-poll and suitable for the impatient use cases when the UI needs to be refreshed as close as possible to a server-side change event. As in long-polling, two separate connections are used for data and event notification. Push may not work well if older proxies are involved that cache the HTTP content, in which case long-polling could be used as a fallback.

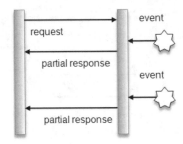

The Need for Speed

For REA applications to replace the desktop, real-time data UI refresh using push technology is a must-have feature. Being able to push messages from the server to the client is an old topic in AJAX, but it has not yet reached broad adoption in enterprise application development. One reason for this is that implementing real-time communication often involves low-level coding close to the HTTP layer, which appears to be less future-proof if technology changes, which definitively will happen.

A new technology slowly moving into its starting blocks is WebSockets, a specification of the World Wide Web Consortium (W3C). As the time of writing, WebSockets is not finalized. Once it is, it aims for native browser support, allowing RIA applications to respond closer to the server event, to use upstream and downstream messages sent over a single communication channel, to handle proxies better, and to support binary payloads such as images. Speaking of browsers—old wisdom says that a browser is a browser, but, in truth, all browsers are not equal. Business applications that require support for a range of browser versions and types need to ensure that the use of push in their web applications allows them to fall back to a technology supported by the browser version and type on which the client runs, as well as the Java EE server used.

Development frameworks that provide push functionality paired with a consistent programming API and a good range of supported browsers surely raise the adoption rate of push in RIA and REA development. We consider them as required key enablers of the interactive Web, shielding developers from fine-grained implementation details and increasing their productivity. Active Data Services (ADS) in Oracle ADF Faces RC is a big leap in this direction and shields developers from low-level coding, as we demonstrate later in this chapter.

Introduction to Active Data Services

In ADF applications, you use ADS to build dashboard-style, read-only UIs that actively notify users about data changes. Since data updates are performed only on the UI component rendering, you cannot use ADS on UI input components. To add ADS functionality to application development projects, application developers implement the `ActiveDataModel` interface or the ADS proxy framework, which decorates the component model to provide active data changes. In this chapter, we use the ADS proxy `ActiveCollectionModelDecorator` as an example for implementing ADS in ADF applications.

NOTE
To implement ADS functionality to your web applications using the ADS proxy framework you need a recent version of Oracle JDeveloper 11g no older than JDeveloper 11g R1 Patch Set 1.

NOTE
The ADS proxy decorator to use with Oracle ADF Faces DVT components is ActiveCollectionModelDecorator. In this book, we don't cover developing ADS implementations for ADF Faces DVT component models.

ADS gives developers a configurable choice of notification types they can use to push server-side events to the client. As mentioned earlier, the supported notification types in ADS are polling, long-polling, and push. In addition, the ADF Faces RC Auto-PPR (partial-page refresh) functionality allows components to automatically register themselves to be refreshed by the next incoming client request. The selling point of ADS is its flexibility and the ability to determine a notification type by configuration and not through hard-coding it into an application.

NOTE
ADS is designed to work with ADF-bound and non–ADF-bound ADF Faces component models. It does not require the ADF binding layer to be present.

ADS Architecture

As shown in Figure 20-1, the ADS architecture consists of the following core components:

- **Active Data Model**   The ADS model abstracts the active model and manages the active data received from the active service. To simplify working with the ADS model, you can implement it using the ADS proxy, a wrapper class that leaves only a few tasks to the application developer.

- **Event Manager**   Listens to events on the component model and retrieves the active data changed. It is responsible for active component registration and active data encoding, and it invokes the push service to send the data. It also adds components to a list of partial targets that get updated by the next client request if the bindings do not support push. One Event Manager always exists per browser window, which means that sessions with multiple browser windows open also use multiple event managers. Event managers are associated to a window by the session and the Window ID assigned by ADF Faces RC. If a page is dismissed, the Event Manager associated with it automatically performs resource cleanup before exiting itself.

■ **Push Service**   Dispatches between the Event Manager and the client-side Active Data Manager. It handles the data delivery to the client and manages the connection between the client and the server. To support different transport mechanisms, such as polling, long-polling, and push, a specific channel handler programming interface is used internally to isolates the implementations. This also enables ADS to add new transport mechanisms easily in the future. A single Push Service object will be created and maintained on the server for each user HTTP session. A second Push Service is created if the user opens a new browser window to displays active content and does not use CTRL-N or the browser menu to open it. Also, loading an active page on the same server but from two different browser types creates separate push channels.

■ **Render Kit**   Renders an ADF Faces component as an active component that registers itself with the event manager.

■ **Active Data Manager**   A client-side JavaScript engine that receives the active data messages from the Push Service to update the client-side ADF Faces RC component peer. A single Active Data Manager exists at runtime to update multiple browser windows and tabs initiated from the browser process running an application. To accomplish this, ADF Faces RC provides an implementation of the `WindowIdProvider` interface that exposes the current window ID and that receives notification of window open and close events. The server-side Event Manager and the client-side Active Data Manager use this API to route data change events to the target window or tab.

NOTE
Active services, in the context of ADS, are business services that know how to push change events to the component model. In this chapter, we use the terms "active services" and "business services" interchangeably

Using ADS in Custom Application Development

Figure 20-1 shows the ADS architecture in Oracle ADF. From an active services perspective, two options are available for applications to bind active business services to ADS to refresh the UI in response to a change event.

The first option is to use the Active Data Model proxy framework in ADS to decorate the JavaServer Faces (JSF) component model. In this scenario, data is directly passed on to the ADF Faces components model, without using the ADF binding layer.

The second option is to use the ADF binding layer. As of this writing, only one data control exists, which is for Business Activity Monitoring (BAM), with integrated ADS functionality. To bind active services to ADS using the ADF binding layer, you may use the POJO (Plain Old Java Objects) data control in combination with the Active Data Model proxy. As of this writing, there is no direct support for ADS push in ADF Business Components (BC). Therefore, best practice for updating the user interface in response to change events in ADF BC is to use a mix of Auto-PPR and poll.

No matter which approach you choose, ADS is defined on the ADF Faces component model, implementing the `ActiveDataModel` interface.

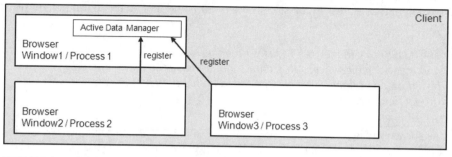

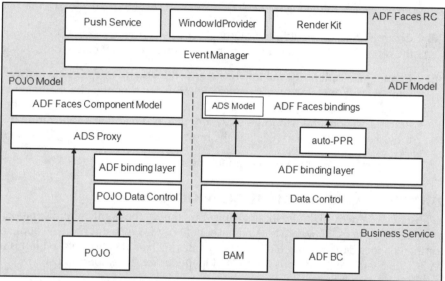

FIGURE 20-1 *ADS architecture*

Note: Though the active part of pushing data from the server to the UI is implemented on the component model, it is the component UI renderer that registers the component displayed on the client with ADS. Nevertheless, not all ADF Faces RC components support ADS registration. We provide a list of components that do support it later in this chapter in the section "Active UI Components." As shown in Figure 20-1, ADF-bound UIs have the active data model implemented in the ADF Faces–specific ADF binding classes that we introduced in Chapter 1. ADF Faces UIs that are not bound to ADF need to implement ADS in their component model, which is the recommended approach for application developers using the ADS proxy.

The ADS proxy saves developers from implementing the ADS interfaces by decorating the ADF Faces component model with ADS functionality. It delegates active data handling to a convenient implementation of the `ActiveDataModel` interface that listens to data change events from the data layer and interacts with the event manager. Using the ADS proxy, developers enable existing JSF component models for active data, which also means that application development may start without ADS in the picture and then activate it at a later point in time.

NOTE
The ADS proxy framework focuses on a dashboard-type of application, which means that data is not transformed for or filtered based on conditions. Such cases need to be handled by the data model before rendering.

As shown in Figure 20-1, on the client side, the Active Data Manager uses a single parent channel to handle all active UI updates, no matter how many browser windows or tabs are open in an application. The following framework features allow it to do this:

- **Channel sharing**   Multiple browser processes share the same ADS channel to address the limitation of browsers in the number of channels they can handle in parallel.

- **Channel migration**   If multiple browser windows and the parent window are used, the window that initialized the channel is closed, and then the channel parent window gets migrated to one of the child windows. The parent channel window may be closed by the user clicking the window's close icon, navigating off the application by pointing the browser to a new URL or clicking the browser back button, or by a browser window crash.

- **Multiplexing**   A single ADS channel is used by multiple pages.

Supported Communication Modes

ADS abstracts the active UI refresh mechanism used from the application developer building interactive ADF Faces RC web UIs. A major benefit of ADS is that it protects applications from requiring changes due to future technology updates such as WebSockets, which is in the works by W3C. Currently, ADS supports the following modes for developers to use.

By Chance with Auto-PPR

Developers are able to refresh ADF Faces components in response to the changes of another, without requiring a full browse page refresh. To enable this, the `partialTriggers` attribute on a dependent ADF Faces component is used to reference another component that, if changed, triggers the refresh. Auto-PPR automates the partial component refresh in that it integrates the refresh with change events that are raised on the server side in response to model data changes.

Technically, the Auto-PPR functionality adds UI components for which a server-side change event is raised, to the list of partial targets in the ADF Faces context for the UI to refresh by the next request. The UI is refreshed using the active data service mechanism introduced before to push changes from the middle tier of the client. For ADF Faces components that are bound to ADF, the Auto-PPR functionality is implemented on the ADF Faces–specific binding classes, which extend the generic ADF binding layer. To enable Auto-PPR for ADF-bound ADF Faces components, set the `ChangeEventPolicy` property of the component binding entry in the PageDef file to `PPR`. The benefit of using Auto-PPR over manual configuration is ease of use and administration, especially in complex applications.

Polling

Using polling, client-side JavaScript is frequently used to send requests to the server, so the server will respond with the information about events that were raised since the previous poll. Events are sent as JavaScript chunks that get executed on the client. If a poll is sent to the server while no data update is available, an empty response is sent immediately to indicate that there is no need for an UI update. Technically, a `ChannelHandler` API implementation exists in ADS for polling, which takes care of the client and server communication.

If the configuration of ADS is set up for polling, the ADS ServletFilter creates an instance of the poll channel handler.

NOTE
The ADS servlet is implemented internally using annotations and does not require any extra configuration in the web.xml file.

Long-polling

Long-polling occurs when a request is suspended to stay open until a server-side event occurs. It is implemented using a `ChannelHandler` implementation specific for long-polling. After an initial channel connection sends down the ADS configuration data to the client, the client sends an HTTP request to the server. If no data is waiting on the server, the thread is suspended to wait until new data becomes available. If new data is waiting on the server, a response is sent back to the client, which applies the payload to the client-side ADF Faces RC renderers and triggers a new poll events request. The subsequent poll events requests stay on the server until new data is available or a timeout occurs.

If the configuration of ADS is set up for long-poll or push, which is covered next, then in Oracle WebLogic Server, a specific ADS servlet is used to create the channel manager instance. Executing ADS on a non-WebLogic server uses the ADS ServletFilter instead.

NOTE
Chapter 19 explains the ADF Faces RC client architecture and client side component peers used to present data in the browser.

Pushing

Using push, the HTTP response is kept open by ADS continuously writing data to the response object. The data is written to the response in the form of JavaScript chunks that are immediately executed when rendered on the browser. As for the other options, the push implementation uses a specific `ChannelHandler` to provide the functionality. For using push, which is the default setting, and the other communication options, developers need to do nothing other than decide on a configuration.

Choosing a Communication Mechanism

Choices can be a bad thing if you don't understand what the choices mean. Active data is a continuous stream of changes that is delivered to a client using a push- or polling-based mechanism. Polling is not considered as efficient as pushing. But in cases such as server connection or browser limitation, polling might be a better choice. Good to know, then, that in ADS, the transport mechanism used is a matter of configuration and not one you need to consider during application development. On top of this, ADS provides an optimized architecture that uses available resources sensibly. The following table provides high level guidelines for when each communication type should be used.

	Polling	**Long-polling**	**Push**
Latency	Not well suited but possible if a long polling interval is chosen.	Good. The longest "blackout time" would occur between when a server event is sent to the client and the client sends a new request.	Very good. The connection is held and only partial responses are sent.
Proxy servers	No problems.	No problems.	Problems may arise if the proxy caches data, which prevents real-time client updates.
Connections	The connection exists only during the poll, so no long-lived extra connections need to be maintained.	A second connection is kept open, so the server, as well as the client, has an additional channel to maintain. Adds to the overall application overhead.	Same as for long polling; an additional channel is kept open and must be maintained.

Configuring ADS for an Application

If a push is what your application is intended to use, then no further configuration is needed.

If you want to use polling or long-polling as a communication mechanism, you need to configure the adf-config.xml file in the application .adf\META-INF directory and create the adf-config.properties file in the .adf\META-INF\services directory.

The adf-config.xml file is created by default for applications that use Oracle ADF, but it needs to be created manually for applications that don't use ADF. If it exists, the adf-config.xml in the .adf\META-INF directory is accessible from Oracle JDeveloper in the ADF META-INF folder of the Application Resources | Descriptors panel view in the Application Navigator. If the adf-config.xml does not exist for an application, it needs to be created manually in the .adf\META-INF directory, by choosing File | New | XML | XML Document. A sample configuration is shown next:

```
<?xml version="1.0" encoding="utf-8" ?>
  <adf-config xmlns="http://xmlns.oracle.com/adf/config"
  xmlns:ads="http://xmlns.oracle.com/adf/activedata/config">
  <ads:adf-activedata-config
    xmlns="http://xmlns.oracle.com/adf/activedata/config" >
    <transport>long-polling</transport>   </ads:adf-activedata-config>
  </adf-config>
```

NOTE
If you're using Oracle ADF for your application development, the adf-config.xml file is not only used to define ADS-specific settings, but it also defines Metadata Services (MDS), ADF Controller, and ADF Security settings.

The preceding configuration shows the minimum configuration required for transport mechanisms other than push if the defaults settings for other configuration parameters, such as the following, shall be used:

- **transport** The transport element defines which communication type to use to bring server-side event notification to the client. Valid values are `streaming`, `polling`, and `long-polling`. If the element is not set, `streaming` is used.

- **latency-threshold** Time in milliseconds that defines when active data is considered late. The default is set to 10000 ms. Using push, if no activity happens within the time that is defined by `latency-threshold` and `keep-alive-interval`, a request is sent out to re-establish the connection. If the `max-reconnect-attempt-time` is reached with no active connection being established, the communication channel is considered disconnected.

- **keep-alive-interval** The frequency in which ADS sends a ping to ensure the connection is not closed down if no active events are generated. The default is 10000 ms.

- **polling-interval** If polling is used, this value defines the frequency in which a poll is sent from the client to the server. The default is set to 5000 ms. If no response is received within the allowed time defined by `max-reconnect-attempt-time`, no further polling is performed and the connection is considered disconnected.

- **max-reconnect-attempt-time** Defines the maximum time that the client attempts to re-establish a broken push connection to the server. The default is set to 1800000 ms (30 minutes).

- **reconnect-wait-time** The time between reconnection attempts when using push. If the push connection fails, the client tries to re-establish the channel for the duration defined by the `max-reconnect-attempt-time` parameter. The frequency in which reconnecting the client is tried within this period is defined by this parameter. The default is 10000 ms.

In current releases of Oracle JDeveloper 11g R1, the adf-config.properties file and the .adf\META-INF\services directory don't exist by default. Developers need to create the file and the directory manually. For this, select the view layer project and choose File | New from the Oracle JDeveloper menu. In the General category, select the File entry and press OK. In the opened dialog, type adf-config.properties as the File Name value. In the Directory field, browse to the .adf\META-INF\ directory and append services for the folder containing the adf-config.properties file. Close the dialog by pressing OK. The content of the adf-config.properties file is shown below.

```
http\://xmlns.oracle.com/adf/activedata/config=oracle.adfinternal.
view.faces.activedata.ActiveDataConfiguration$ActiveDataConfigCallback
```

Add the value as a single string with no line breaks.

Active UI Components

The following ADF Faces RC components are able to register themselves to the ADS framework to receive active data updates:

- `af:activeCommandToolbarButton`

- `af:activeImage`

- `af:activeOutputText`

- `af:table`

- `af:tree`

- `af:treeTable`

- All ADF Faces RC data visualization components

A requirement for these components to refresh is a component model that supports ADS. One option to achieve such a component model is to use the ADF binding layer—for example, in combination with the Business Activity Monitoring (BAM) Data Control. Another option is to use the ADS proxy to decorate an existing model, adding active update capabilities.

Active Data Services Proxy by Example

In this section, we provide you with the knowledge you need to use the ADS proxy framework in your application development. We offer technical details of how to program with the ADS proxy framework. To understand these details fully, you need to have Java programming experience.

NOTE
A declarative example that uses Auto-PPR with ADF Business Components is provided in the next section.

The strength of ADS proxy is that it allows developers to integrate a variety of active services such as Oracle RDBMS using the JDBC 11*g* thin driver, Java Message Service (JMS), background threads, Extensible Messaging and Presence Protocol (XMPP) servers, and other push services in their ADF application development without having to deal with HTTP streaming details. This section explains development with the ADS proxy by example of pushing Oracle RDBMS updates to the UI.

Use Case: Displaying Database Change Events in ADF Faces

Using the Oracle JDBC 11*g* thin database driver and the Oracle Database, application developers can register Java listeners to receive change notifications that are published for table updates, inserts, and delete operations. The JDBC driver starts and listens to database change events in a separate thread and automatically sends Java events to registered Java listeners. To leverage change notification in ADF Faces RC applications, you need Oracle Database 10*g* Release 2

(10.2) or 11*g* and must have granted the change notification privilege to the database schema user. For example, if the application connects to the database with the HR user account, open SQL*Plus or a similar editor, connect as SYS, and issue the following command:

```
grant change notification to HR;
```

Figure 20-2 shows a block diagram of the database change notification example. A POJO is registered as a listener to the Oracle JDBC 11*g* driver to receive database event notification. The POJO allows interested clients that implement a specific interface to receive event notification and a change payload. The interface is implementation specific and defined by the developer who built the POJO.

The ADS proxy is implemented in a managed bean that is referenced by the ADF Faces component, a table in this example, which should receive active data updates. The managed bean extends the `ActiveCollectionModelDecorator`, which is an abstract class of the ADS proxy framework. In this example, the managed bean also implements the custom interface required by the POJO. Methods that are marked with an asterisk (*) are required to be implemented by the application developer. Other methods are added as helper methods—for example, to prepare and push the update notification. The ADF Faces component references the collection model exposed by the managed bean to query data.

```
<af:table value="#{MyActiveTableModel}" var="row" id="t1">
    <af:column sortable="false" headerText="Department Name" id="c3">
      <af:outputText value="#{row.departmentName}" id="ot2"/>
    </af:column>
    ...
</af:table>
```

Figure 20-2 shows the active model created as an inner class of the table model bean. The active model can also be created as an external class, which seems to be preferable for complex implementations that you want to reuse. The active model class extends `BaseActiveDataModel` and implements the contract required by the ADS framework. It receives start and stop notifications when the component referencing the model is rendered or dismissed and broadcasts the change event to ADS to perform the UI update.

Figure 20-3 shows the runtime behavior of the database change notification example. The Departments table is registered to send change notifications, which are received by the POJO implementation shown in Figure 20-2. When changes are committed to the database, they are sent as a bundle to the POJO, and from here they are passed to the active table model using the callback method that it implemented through the custom POJO interface. A handle to the managed bean is passed to the POJO upon bean registration. Note that the way beans register and the POJO keeps track of the registration is specific to the service you use and the use case in which the service is used. Oracle ADS does not manage or balance connections to the active service. With the commit of the database change and the event passed to the active model, ADS updates the UI, as shown in Figure 20-3. End users see the table cells that contain changed data twinkle so they are informed about the change. The transport mechanism, push, long-polling or polling, that is used between the server and the browser client is not programmed in the active model class, but externally configured in the adf-config.xml file.

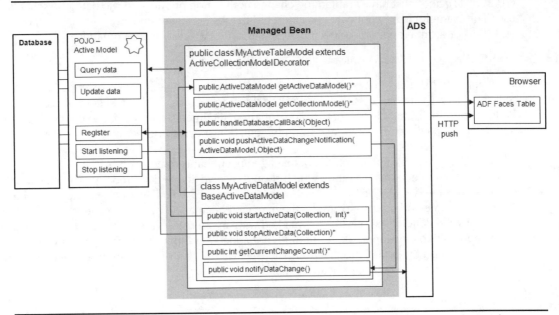

FIGURE 20-2 *Integration of Oracle Database change notification in ADF Faces RC applications using the ADS proxy*

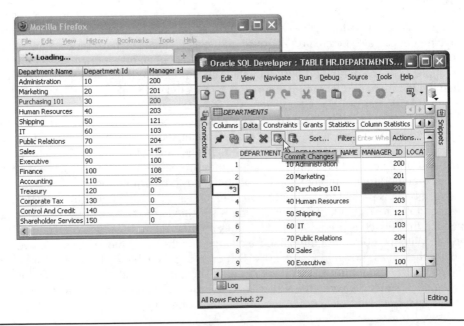

FIGURE 20-3 *Database change event notification at runtime*

NOTE
To learn about how to create a listeners that receive Java events from the database, refer to the Oracle Database JDBC Developer's Guide and Reference, 11g Release 1 *documentation available at http://otn. oracle.com.*

ADS Proxy Implementation Details

As shown in Figure 20-2, the ADS proxy framework provides a convenient implementation of the ADS active model and exposes only a few abstract methods for the application developer to implement. Application developers write two application-specific classes to implement ADS for pushing data updates to the UI:

- A class that wraps the UI component model, allowing ADS to manipulate the display of the data

- An active model that manages the active service notification and lifecycle

UI Component Model Wrapper Class

A component model is referenced by a UI component such as `af:table` to read data from the business service and, optionally, write data back.

A simple example of a component model is a managed bean property, which is defined by a private variable, which is accessible for read and write through exposed getter and setter methods. An `af:inputText` component could reference this property from its `value` attribute using Expression Language (EL). The attribute model equivalent in Oracle ADF is `FacesCtrlAttrBinding`. For developers to intercept and modify the UI to model communication, they build a wrapper class that encapsulates the model.

If the UI component is an `af:table`, the model is an implementation of `org.apache .myfaces.trinidad.model.CollectionModel`. Wrapping this model, as shown in Figure 20-2, allows developers to add ADS capabilities to the rendered ADF Faces table.

NOTE
At the time of this writing, the ADS proxy framework provides an abstract decorator class for use with collections, such as those needed for the `af:table`, `af:tree` *and* `af:treeTable` *components. An abstract decorator class for scalar component models is not yet available but will be offered in the future.*

```
public class MyActiveTableModel extends ActiveCollectionModelDecorator{
    public CollectionModel getCollectionModel() {
        return <instance of CollectionModel>;
    }
    public ActiveDataModel getActiveDataModel() {
        return <active model class>;
    }
}
```

The class extends `ActiveCollectionModelDecorator` that contains two abstract methods, `getCollectionModel` and `getActiveDataModel`. The two methods must be implemented by the application developer to expose the wrapped collection model and the active model. The `getCollectionModel` method returns the model that is encapsulated by the `MyActiveTableModel` class. Using ADF with a POJO data control, the ADF binding that is used as a component model for tables could be accessed using the following Java code:

```java
public CollectionModel getCollectionModel(){
    JUCtrlHierBinding tableBinding = null;
    CollectionModel tableModel = null;
    ..
    //access the tree binding in the ADF PageDef to read its
    //collection data
    tableBinding = (JUCtrlHierBinding) bindings.get("allDepartments");
    List<JUCtrlHierNodeBinding> nodes = tableBinding.getChildren();
    //create list of entity objects from the tableBinding
    List<EntityClass>entityList = new ArrayList<EntityClass>();
    //iterate over the ADF table binding rows to create the
    //POJO list
    for(JUCtrlHierNodeBinding node : nodes){
        DCDataRow row = (DCDataRow)node.getRow();
        entityList.add((EntityClass)row.getDataProvider());
    }
    //Create the collection model
    tableModel = new SortableModel(entityList);
    return tableModel;
}
```

`allDepartments` is the name of the tree binding in the PageDef file that is associated with the JSF page. Replace `EntityClass` with the entity object class of the row data provided by the POJO.

The `SortableModel` we use in the example above uses the row index to identify rows in a table. Especially when using ADS also to insert and delete rows in a table, you should consider using a `CollectionModel` that supports row keys.

The following example shows how to access the `CollectionModel` that is available from the `FacesCtrlHierBinding` object that represents the ADF tree binding at runtime. Because the `FacesCtrlHierBinding` class is located in a private package, we use Expression Language to access the `CollectionModel`, thus avoiding direct access from Java.

```java
public CollectionModel getCollectionModel() {
    if (tableModel == null){
        FacesContext fctx = FacesContext.getCurrentInstance();
        Application application = fctx.getApplication();
        ExpressionFactory elFactory  = application.getExpressionFactory();
        ELContext elctx = fctx.getELContext();
        //allDepartments is the tree binding definition name in the
        //PageDef file
        ValueExpression expr = elFactory.createValueExpression(
            elctx,
```

```
      "#{bindings.allDepartments.collectionModel}",
      Object.class);
    tableModel = (CollectionModel) expr.getValue(elctx);
  }
  return tableModel;
}
```

NOTE
Sample code for using the `CollectionModel` *is provided later in
this chapter in the section Implementing ADS Using the ADF POJO
Data Control. In the following, we use a pure POJO-based component
model data source.*

If the data to display in the table does not come from ADF but is a Java collection, such as
implementations of the `java.util.List` interface, then the table model can be created as
follows:

```
CollectionModel tableModel = null;
...
public CollectionModel getCollectionModel() {
  if (tableModel == null){
    //get a List with the table row data from a POJO data source by
    //referencing a method exposed on it. For example, assuming a Java
    //instance QueryService to exist that exposes a getAllDepartments
    //method, you create the table model as shown below
    List tableDataCollection = queryService.getAllDepartments();
    tableModel = new SortableModel(tableDataCollection);
  }
  return tableModel;
}
```

The second method, `getActiveDataModel`, returns an instance of the second custom class
to create—the active model. Here's an example:

```
//instantiate the custom active Data Model.
MyActiveDataModel activeDataModel = new MyActiveDataModel()
...
public ActiveDataModel getActiveDataModel() {
  return activeDataModel;
}
```

The following methods are not defined by an ADS interface or parent class but are also
needed:

- A callback handler method to handle the callback from the active service of which you
  want to receive notifications

- A method you can call from within this class to notify ADS about the active service
  notification

Callback Handler Method   To listen to an active service, you need to register to it and provide an option for the service to send back event notification and a payload. One option is to define the model wrapper class as a listener and implement the callback method used by the active model. A callback is a contract between a message sender and receiver that is usually described for the client by a Java interface. In the database update example, the custom `handleDatabaseCallback` method is called by the Java client that receives the Oracle database event notification to notify the ADS proxy implementation about the event. The callback handler of the RDBMS example in Figure 20-2 is shown here:

```
public void handleDatabaseCallback(Object object, String changeType) {
   //change type is defined on the custom ComponentModelChange
   //callback interface
   if (changeType == ComponentModelChange.TYPE_UPDATE){
    //call active model method to initiate the UI change notification
     pushActiveDataChangeNotification(
       getActiveDataModel(),(Department)object);
     }
   else if(changeType==ComponentModelChange.TYPE_INSERT){…}
   else if(changeType==ComponentModelChange.TYPE_DELETE){…}
}
```

The Oracle database change notification returns the `ROWID` of the changed table row. In our example the custom database change listener calls a helper method, notifyChange, to create a POJO object representation of the changed database row. The object type is `Department`. The changed row object is then sent as an entity within the callback, a call to the `handleDatabaseCallback` method in our example, to the active component model.

```
/**
 *Change event listener class that implements the
 *DatabaseChangeListener interface
 */
public class RdbmsChangeEventListener implements DatabaseChangeListener{
   ChangeEventHandler _eventHandler = null;
   public RdbmsChangeEventListener(ChangeEventHandler eventHandler) {
     super();
     this._eventHandler=eventHandler;
   }
   //interface method
   public void onDatabaseChangeNotification(
     DatabaseChangeEvent databaseChangeEvent){
     QueryChangeDescription [] changes =
       databaseChangeEvent.getQueryChangeDescription();
     //detect changes insert/update/delete on registered table
     if (changes != null && changes.length > 0) {
       QueryChangeDescription change = changes[0];
       TableChangeDescription[] tableChanges = null;
       tableChanges = change.getTableChangeDescription();
       TableChangeDescription tcd = tableChanges[0];
       RowChangeDescription[] rowChanges = null;
       rowChanges = tcd.getRowChangeDescription();
       //iterate over applied changes
       for (RowChangeDescription rcd : rowChanges) {
```

```
    RowChangeDescription.RowOperation operation = null;
    //determine if change is insert, update or delete
    operation = rcd.getRowOperation();
    String type =
      operation == RowChangeDescription.RowOperation.DELETE ?
      "DELETE" :
      operation == RowChangeDescription.RowOperation.INSERT ?
      "INSERT" : "UPDATE";
    //get the ROWID of the changed table row
    oracle.sql.ROWID rowid = rcd.getRowid();
    //call custom helper method that builds POJO entity for the
    //table row referenced by the ROWID. In this example, the
    //helper method also issues the call back to the registered
    //clients
    eventHandler.notifyChange(rowid, type);
      }
    }
  }
}
```

ADS Update Notification   To notify the ADS proxy to push updates to the UI, a method that is exposed on the active model class needs to be called. The single method argument is an object of type `ActiveDataUpdateEvent`. To create the event object, the ADS proxy framework provides a static utility class `ActiveDataEventUtil` that exposes a public method `buildActiveData UpdateEvent`.

```
/**
 * builds the <code>ActiveDataUpdateEvent</code>.
 *
 * @param type the change type of the event, could be UPDATE, INSERT,
 * DELETE, REFRESH, etc
 * @param changeCount the changeCount
 * @param key the key of the row (in the CollectionModel case)
 * @param insertKey the key to indicate the insert position
 * @param genericConversion param passed to the internal call of
 * <code>convertKeyPath</code>
 * @param names the names of the attributes to be changed
 * @param values the values of the attributes to be changed
 * @return the ActiveDataUpdateEvent
 */
public static ActiveDataUpdateEvent buildActiveDataUpdateEvent(
  ActiveDataEntry.ChangeType type,
  int changeCount,
  Object[] key,
  Object[] insertKey,
  String[] names,
  Object[] values)
```

The type of update pushed to the UI can be defined using static values of the `ChangeType` class, which is an inner class of `ActiveDataEntry`. For example, to indicate an update, you use the `ActiveDataEntry.ChangeType.UPDATE` value.

The changeCount value is used by ADS to detect flooding, which occurs when change events are not received by the UI in the order of their occurrence. To ensure consistency between changes applied to the model and the UI, which is not part of ADS's responsibilities, your active model class needs to generate a sequence of numbers that are used to synchronize the UI on the client with the internal component model state on the server.

The key is used to identify the position of the row in the table that should be changed in response to the active event. Using non-ADF component models, the key is an object array that contains a single numeric value that represents the zero-based row index. Updating an ADF bound row, the key is defined by an object array that contains values of type oracle.jbo .domain.Number.

The insertKey is used in the insert case and need to be set to null otherwise. It defines the position in which to include the new row.

The names parameter defines a String array of column attribute names that should have their values changed. Table cells in which data has been changed "twinkle" at runtime—that is, their background color changes for about a second.

The values object array holds the values that should be set for the attribute names listed by the names parameter.

For convenience reasons, in the RDBMS example shown in Figure 20-2, an extra method, pushActiveDataChangeNotification, is used to determine the changed column values based on the database change notification. The method is called from the callback method that receives the database event and takes two arguments—a reference to the active model and an object representing the changed database row.

```
public void pushActiveDataChangeNotification(
   ActiveDataModel model,Department department){
   MyActiveDataModel adm = (MyActiveDataModel)model;
   //call a method on the active model to increase the change
   //counter used to keep track of orders in which events are
   //fired
   adm.increaseChangeCounter();
   //perform update
   ActiveDataUpdateEvent updateEvent = null;
   //the SortableModel reference is used to get a list of current
   //departments for comparison
   List<Department> dl = departmentsCollection;
   Iterator<Department> iter = dl.iterator();
   int i=0;
   boolean rowFound = false;
   //keep track of changed values and the attribute
   ArrayList<Object> updateValueList = new ArrayList<Object>();
   ArrayList<String> attributeList = new ArrayList<String>();
   while(iter.hasNext()&&!rowFound){
      Department d = iter.next();
      //compare departments by their primary key
      if (d.getDepartmentId() == department.getDepartmentId()){
         //if there is a match, make row current to read the rowkey
         tableModel.setRowIndex(i);
         //determine the changes
         if(!d.getDepartmentName().equals(department.getDepartmentName())){
            updateValueList.add(department.getDepartmentName());
```

```
        attributeList.add("departmentName");
      }
      if (!(d.getLocationId().equals(department.getLocationId()))){
        updateValueList.add(department.getLocationId());
        attributeList.add("locationId");
      }
      if (!d.getManagerId().equals(department.getManagerId())){
        updateValueList.add(department.getManagerId());
        attributeList.add("managerId");
      }
      rowFound = true;
    }
  i++;
  }
  String[] attributeListArray = new String[attributeList.size()];
  //update the table by passing the change notification to ADS
  updateEvent = ActiveDataEventUtil.buildActiveDataUpdateEvent(
      ActiveDataEntry.ChangeType.UPDATE,
      model.getCurrentChangeCount(),
      new Object[]{tableModel.getRowKey()},
      null,
      attributeList.toArray(attributeListArray),
      updateValueList.toArray());
      //submits the event to the ADS framework. It is a method developers
      //implement on the active data model
      adm.notifyDataChange(updateEvent);
  //update the collection
  departmentsCollection = departmentsDataService.getAllDepartments();
}
```

NOTE
*While this code source is implementation-specific to the example
in this chapter, we provide it for the reader as an example of how to
update multiple attributes of a table row.*

Active Model Class

The active model class extends the ADS `BaseActiveDataModel` class and handles starting
and stopping of the active listener, listener registrations if the same class is used by multiple
component wrapper instances, as well as the data change notification to ADS. The active model
class is returned by the component wrapper `getActiveDataModel` method. Depending on the
complexity of the implemented solution and its grade of reusability, the active model class may
be implemented as an inner class or an external class.

When creating the active model class, you must implement the following methods that are
declared as abstract in `BaseActiveDataModel`:

- `public int getCurrentChangeCount()`

- `protected void startActiveData()`

- `protected void stopActiveData()`

In addition, you need to use two class variables to hold the current value of the number of listeners that are created and the number of changes to ensure consistency between the view and the component model.

getCurrentChangeCount Method   As mentioned, this method returns a sequence number that flags each change so the ADS framework can determine whether change notifications are received in the correct order to ensure that old change notifications are disregarded. You can implement this method as follows:

```
//use AtomicInteger as the type for the change event count variable
//because it is thread safe
private final AtomicInteger _currEventId    = new AtomicInteger(0);
…
/**
  * Method implementation required for BaseActiveDataModel.Returns the
  * current monotonically increasing change count for this ActiveDataModel
  * @return The current change count
*/
public int getCurrentChangeCount() {
  //identify current model change
  return _currEventId.get();
}
```

startActiveData Method   The startActiveData method is invoked by the ADS framework to start listening to the active service, which may also be the same time that you register to this source. The start method is called once per ADF Faces component instance that is bound to the custom model wrapper. Depending on the active service to which you connect, you may use this method to register with the service if no connection exists. An example implementation is shown here:

```
private final AtomicInteger _listenerCount = new AtomicInteger(0);
…
/**
  * Method implementation required for BaseActiveDataModel.
  * Start active data for the specified rowKeys and from the
  * startChangeCount
  */
protected void startActiveData(Collection<Object> collection, int i) {
  _listenerCount.incrementAndGet();
  if (_listenerCount.get() == 1)
  {
    //register to or start event notification
  }
}
```

The _listenerCount variable reference is of type AtomicInteger and is used to record the number of listener instances. So if you use multiple components with the same active model and a factory class returns the existing model instance, you may increase the listener count to ensure that you disconnect from the active service when the last listening component is dismissed.

stopActiveData Method   In a more relaxed tone, this method ensures that the last one out turns off the lights. The stopActiveData method is called for each ADF Faces component that is bound to the custom model wrapper as soon as the component instance is dismissed. This dismissal may happen because of navigation or page refresh. You use this method to keep track of the number of registered listening components and, if no listeners are left, use this information to disconnect from the active service.

```
protected void stopActiveData(Collection<Object> rowKeys) {
   //stops the counter if the count is 0
   //the last client to switch off the light
   _listenerCount.decrementAndGet();
    if (_listenerCount.get()==0) {
      //clean up
    }
}
```

ADS Proxy Framework Class Template for Starters

Following is a class template that implements the active model as an inner class. Developers may use this as a starting point for building a custom active component model. Dependent on the active service that you listen to, this code runs as a managed bean within smaller or larger scopes.

```
public class MyActiveTableModel extends ActiveCollectionModelDecorator{
   //instantiate activeDataModel to handle ADS interaction
   MyActiveDataModel  activeDataModel = new MyActiveDataModel ();
   //the UI component model
   CollectionModel tableModel = null;
   //constructor
   public MyActiveTableModel(){
     super();
     //optionally register with active service
     ...
     //get table model for component
     tableModel = new SortableModel(<add collection here>);
   }
   /**
    * Method required by the ActiveCollectionModelDecorator
    * @return ActiveDataModel
    */
   public ActiveDataModel getActiveDataModel() {
     return activeDataModel;
   }
   /**
    * Method required by the ActiveCollectionModelDecorator
    * @return Table CollectionModel
    */
   public CollectionModel getCollectionModel() {
     return tableModel;
   }
   /**
    * callback method called by an active service. The method name and
    * signature depends on the active service used, RDBMS, Asynchronous
    * Web Service, JMS etc. to listen to and the listening contract defined
    * by the developer.
    */
```

```
public void handleDataServiceCallback(<define payload arguments here>) {
  //prepare the data received from the active service to handle in ADS
  //use this method for example to convert data types to types used
  //in the collection
  pushADSChangeNotification(getActiveDataModel(),
                         <object that contains update value>);


}
//helper method that contains the ADS update notification code
private void pushADSChangeNotification(ActiveDataModel model,
                       <object that contains update value>){
  //cast to custom ActiveModel class
  MyActiveDataModel adm = (MyActiveDataModel)model;
  //increase the counter used to keep track of the sequence
  //of changes
  adm.increaseChangeCounter();
  …
  //perform ADS UI update
  ActiveDataUpdateEvent updateEvent = null;
  updateEvent = ActiveDataEventUtil.buildActiveDataUpdateEvent(
     ActiveDataEntry.ChangeType.UPDATE,
     adm.getCurrentChangeCount(),
     new Object[]{key},
     null,
     String[]{attributeName},
     Object[]{updateValue});
   //fire change event on active model class
   adm.dataChanged(updateEvent);
   //ADS does not update the business service or ADF model.
   //If this is required in response to the UI update then do
   //it now
      … add required code …
}

//Define the active data model, extending BaseActiveDataModel.
class MyActiveDataModel extends BaseActiveDataModel{
  //variable that ensures the listener is started only once
  private final AtomicInteger _listenerCount = new AtomicInteger(0);
  //change counter to ensure consistency between model data and
  //screen data.
  private final AtomicInteger _currEventId   = new AtomicInteger(0);
  //Constructor
  public MyActiveDataModel(){
    super();
  }
  /**
   * method called to increase current ID to ensure consistency
   */
  public void increaseChangeCounter(){
    _currEventId.incrementAndGet();
  }
```

```
   //Method called from MyActiveTableModel.
   public void notifyDataChange(ActiveDataUpdateEvent event){
     //method of the BaseActiveDataModel class that dispatches
     //the event to all registered listeners (UI component
     //registrations)
     fireActiveDataUpdate(event);
   }
   /**
    * Method implementation required for BaseActiveDataModel.
    * Start active data for the specified rowKeys and from the
    * startChangeCount
    */
   protected void startActiveData(Collection<Object> collection, int i) {
     //in this basic example we are not looking at the arguments that
     //are passed in as arguments
     _listenerCount.incrementAndGet();
     if (_listenerCount.get() == 1){
       … start listening to active source …
     }
   }
   /**
    * Called by the DataUpdateManager to notify the ActiveDataModel to
    * stop delivering change notifications for the collections of the
    * container identified by the given rowKeys
    */
   protected void stopActiveData(Collection<Object> rowKeys) {
     _listenerCount.decrementAndGet();
     if (_listenerCount.get()==0) {
       … stop listening to events from active source …
     }
   }
   public int getCurrentChangeCount() {
     //identify current model change
     return _currEventId.get();
   }
 }
}
```

Implementing ADS Using the ADF POJO Data Control

The example codes in this chapter so far directly access the table data, reading it from a POJO. If, for example, you receive the component data and change event notification from a POJO that is exposed through an ADF POJO data control, you need to access the data control from the active UI component model to register the component as a callback client to the change event. Assuming the POJO bean class name from which you created the data control is MyPojo, then by default the same name is used as the name of the data control. To access the POJO class through ADF, you use the BindingContext object, as shown here:

```
BindingContext bctx = BindingContext.getCurrent();
//look up the Data Control by the name. This call searches the
//DataBindings.cpx file for the data control entry to provide an
```

```
//instance of this class
DCDataControl pojoControl = bctx.findDataControl("MyPOJO");
//get access to the DataControl instance
MyPojo pojoApp = null;
if(pojoControl!= null){
    pojoApp  = (MyPojo)pojoControl.getDataProvider();
    //call a method that allows you to register this active model as
    //a callback client for the active POJO service
    pojoApp.<call any method>
}
```

NOTE
The ADS update notification is not routed through the ADF binding layer. The binding layer simply provides an easier access to the data and the POJO bean through its data control.

Modifying the RDBMS change notification example that we used in this chapter to explain how to use ADS, the `getCollection` method looks as follows:

```
public CollectionModel getCollectionModel() {
    if (tableModel == null){
        FacesContext fctx = FacesContext.getCurrentInstance();
        Application application = fctx.getApplication();
        ExpressionFactory elFactory  = application.getExpressionFactory();
        ELContext elctx = fctx.getELContext();
        //access the CollectionModel exposed by the FacesCtrlHierBinding
        //instance that represents the tree binding defined in the PageDef
        //file at runtime. The ADF tree binding name is "allDepartments"
        ValueExpression expr = elFactory.createValueExpression(
            elctx,
            "#{bindings.allDepartments.collectionModel}",
            Object.class);
        tableModel = (CollectionModel) expr.getValue(elctx);
    }
    return tableModel;
}
```

The `pushActiveDataChangeNotification` helper method that we used in the non-ADF POJO–based example to handle the active server callback needs to be changed, as shown here:

```
public void pushActiveDataChangeNotification(
    ActiveDataModel model,Department department){
    //cast the ActiveModel argument to our custom Active
    //model class
    DepartmentsActiveDataModel adm = (DepartmentsActiveDataModel)model;
    adm.increaseChangeCounter();
    ActiveDataUpdateEvent updateEvent = null;
    //the departmentId is the PK in the collection
    Long departmentId = department.getDepartmentId();
```

```
//create the collection key, which, using ADF binding is in the form
//of List<oracle.jbo.Key>
ArrayList keyEntry = new ArrayList();
//provide the key used by the table. Note that you may need to use
//the debugger for once if you are uncertain of how the key is built.
//In the RDBMS example, the key turned out to be the departmentId and
//an integer, which always showed as 0
Key key = new Key(new Object[]{departmentId, new Integer(0)});
keyEntry.add(key);
Object[]  updateValueArray = new
Object[]{department.getDepartmentName(),department.getManagerId()};
//update the departmentName and the managerId column with the data
//received from the active model
String[]  updateAttributeArray =
  new String[]{"departmentName","managerId"};
updateEvent = ActiveDataEventUtil.buildActiveDataUpdateEvent(
  ActiveDataEntry.ChangeType.UPDATE,
  model.getCurrentChangeCount(),
  new Object[]{keyEntry},
  null, updateAttributeArray,
  updateValueArray);
  adm.notifyDataChange(updateEvent);
}
```

Implementing Database Update Notification Using ADF BC

In ADF BC, the use case of updating the UI based on database updates can be declaratively implemented in a mix of Auto-PPR and client-side polling, using the `af:poll` component. Unlike using the ADS proxy framework or working with custom implementations for the ADS Java interfaces, no configuration is required in the adf-config.xml file.

The Auto-PPR functionality queues a change request for components in the ADF Faces context but requires a client request to process the UI refresh, which is what the `af:poll` component is used for. In the example in this section, a View Object that is exposed on a shared application module in ADF BC is used to listen for database table changes to update a list of values. The changes that are detected include the addition and removal of list objects.

Figure 20-4 shows a list of values that is updated with database value changes. This approach, compared to using the code-centric integration with the ADS proxy, uses a declarative approach with Auto-PPR instead of HTTP streaming. As a result, the list of values is refreshed as a whole when a change is detected on the server.

To implement this example, you need to understand the role of shared application modules in ADF BC. Not all data that is displayed in business applications changes frequently. For better performance, this data could be cached and shared across applications or within a session. Such data would be used with lookups such as LOVs. To define a shared application module in ADF BC, open the ADF BC project properties and expand the Business Components | Application Module Instances node. You use session sharing for lookup data that is instance-specific to the user session. Otherwise, share data application-wide.

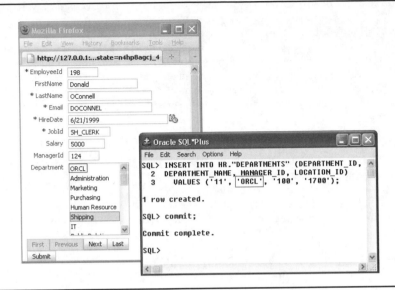

FIGURE 20-4 *ADF BC LOV refresh in response to database update*

 NOTE
Working with shared application modules in ADF BC is fully explained in the "Sharing Application Module View Instances" chapter of the Oracle Fusion Middleware Fusion Developer's Guide for Oracle Application Development Framework 11g.

To push database change notification updates to the UI, you need to share the application module in application scope. This way, the data of View Object instances that are exposed on the shared application module become accessible to all user sessions. In the example shown in Figure 20-4, the department View Object that is used to display data in the LOV is exposed on a shared application module. The LOV is model-driven, which means the departments View Object instance of the shared application module is defined as a LOV on the `DepartmentId` attribute of the `employees` View Object.

 NOTE
Model-driven lists of values are explained in detail in Chapter 11.

To refresh the model-driven list of values in response to a database change event, you need to grant the change notification privilege to the database schema user. For example, if the application connects to the database with the HR user account, open SQL*Plus or a similar editor, connect as SYS, and issue the following command:

```
grant change notification to HR;
```

To enable a View Object to respond to database change events, open the View Object in the declarative editor by double-clicking it. Select the General category and open the Property Inspector, as shown in Figure 20-5. In the Tuning category, set Auto Refresh to true. Only those View Objects instances that are defined in application modules are refreshed, and are shared on an application level.

When developing ADF applications in Oracle JDeveloper 11*g*, enable Auto-PPR on the ADF iterator binding so that only a client request is required to refresh the LOV data in response to a database change event. Auto-PPR is enabled through setting the Change Event Policy property on the iterator binding to ppr. To send a client request periodically, you add the `af:poll` component to a page, as shown:

```
<af:document>
  <af:form>
    ...
    <af:poll interval="20000" immediate="true" id="poll1"/>
  </af:form>
</af:document>
```

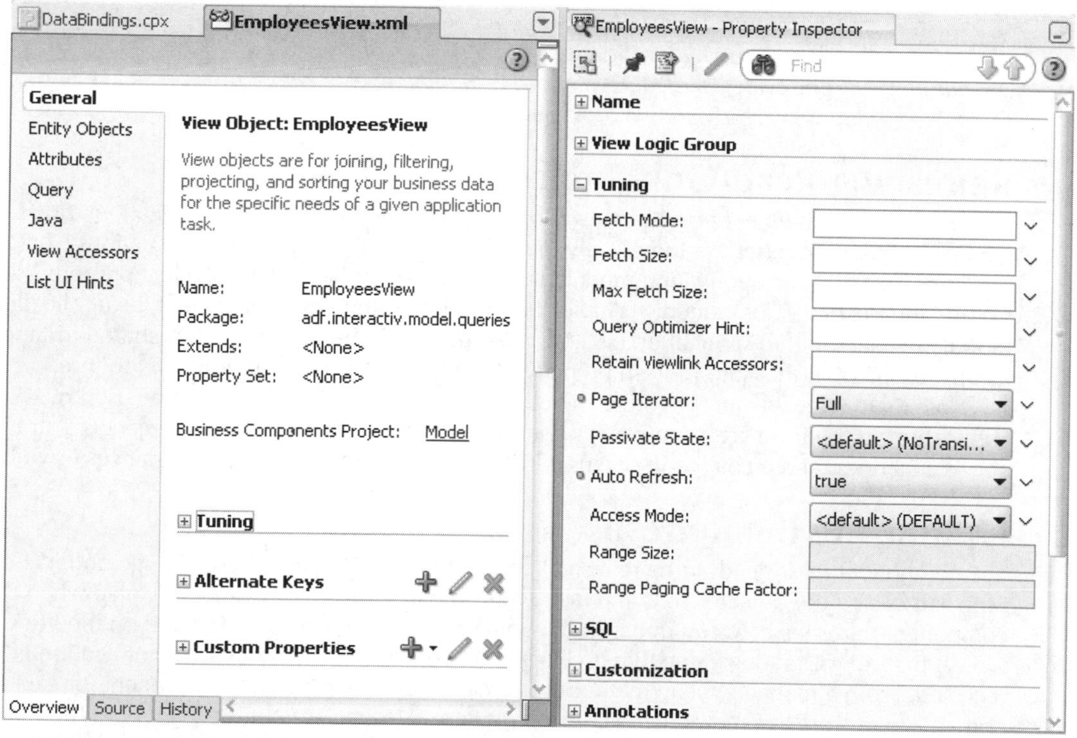

FIGURE 20-5   *View Object editor and Tuning category to set the auto refresh behavior*

The poll interval, which you define in milliseconds, should be chosen sensibly in regard to the use case requirements and the expected network latency and event rate. The longer the poll frequency, the better the performance is.

In addition, you need to reference the `af:poll` component from the `partialTriggers` attribute of the list component:

```
<af:selectOneListbox value="#{bindings.DepartmentId.inputValue}"
    label="Department" id="soc1" partialTriggers=" poll1" size="7">
    <f:selectItems value="#{bindings.DepartmentId.items}" id="si1"/>
</af:selectOneListbox>
```

NOTE
You need to PPR refresh the list so that a change event not only updates the list data, but also adjusts the selected value. Value selection in list components is managed by their index position. Just adding a new entry in a list will change the list, while the selected index remains the same and now may point to a different list value.

NOTE
The Oracle JDeveloper 11g R1 design time incorrectly shows the "ppr" as the default setting for the ChangeEventPolicy of an iterator binding. Starting with Oracle JDeveloper 11g R1 PatchSet 1, the default value is correctly shown as "none."

Refreshing Read-Only Tables

ADF Faces tables that are bound to View Objects that are exposed on an application-wide shared application module refresh automatically in response to database change notifications.

To define a shared application module in ADF BC, open the ADF BC project properties and expand the Business Components | Application Module Instances node. Select the application module to share in the Application tab and press the shuttle button to create a shared instance. Finally, ensure that the Auto Refresh property of the View Object definition is set to true.

Note that tables that are bound to shared application modules should not be used by applications to perform create, update, or delete operations. The table View Object is shared across instances, and a change in one user instance has an impact on other instances as well.

Optimizing the Refresh

The component itself needs to be refreshed only in response to a database change notification. Especially using the `af:table` component, refresh may show an unwanted twinkle when the component refreshes between updates. To avoid this, you can expose a method on the View Object that returns a long value that is changed whenever a database change notification is received. From a managed bean method that is called by the `af:poll` component for each polling, you access this method and compare it with a stored value. If the values are the same, you don't refresh the component. If they don't match, this is a clear indication that a server-side update is available and the component needs to be refreshed.

NOTE
When implementing this optimization, you don't need to set the `partialTriggers` *attribute on the list or table component.*

View Layer Changes

On the view layer, you create a managed bean that reads the long value from a client method that is exposed on the View Object and configured as a method binding in the PageDef file and compare it with a stored value. The managed bean needs a JSF component reference to the table or LOV component so it can add it to the list of partial targets that are refreshed with the poll.

```
<af:poll interval="20000" immediate="true" id="poll1">
  pollListener="#{DepartmentsPage.onPollTimerExpired}"
</af:poll>
```

The `onPollTimerExpired` method has the following content:

```
public void onPollTimerExpired(PollEvent pollEvent) {
  AdfFacesContext adfFacesCtx = AdfFacesContext.getCurrentInstance();
  //get stored query flag
  Long lastRequery = (Long)adfFacesCtx.getViewScope().get("lastRequery");
  BindingContainer bindings =
    BindingContext.getCurrent().getCurrentBindingsEntry();
  //get the current flag value from the View Object using a method
  //binding in the PageDef file
  Long lastRequeryFromVO =
    (Long)bindings.getOperationBinding("getLastRequery").execute();
  //if the query flag is not stored yet, or if it is different from
  //the current value on the View Object, refresh the UI component and
  //store the new value in the View scope as we need a scope longer than
  //request
  if (lastRequery == null || (!lastRequery.equals(lastRequeryFromVO))){
    adfFacesCtx.getViewScope().put("lastRequery",lastRequeryFromVO);
    adfFacesCtx.addPartialTarget(getTable());
  }
}
```

Binding Changes

The required change on the binding layer is to create a method binding in the "bindings" category of the PageDef file that references the client method we describe in the next section. If not set, the `ChangeEventPolicy` property on the iterator must be set to `ppr` for the Auto-PPR feature to be active.

ADF BC Changes

Using the View Object editor shown in Figure 20-5, you create a View Object implementation class from the Java Category. In the View Object implementation class, add the following methods and instance variables:

```
long lastRequery = 0;
...
public long getLastRequery() {
  return lastRequery;
}
//refresh query flag when View Object data is re-queried
@Override
protected void bindParametersForCollection(
    QueryCollection queryCollection,
```

```
    Object[] object,
    PreparedStatement preparedStatement) throws SQLException {
  super.bindParametersForCollection(
    queryCollection, object, preparedStatement);
  if (queryCollection != null) {
    lastRequery = System.currentTimeMillis();
  }
}
@Override
//Refresh query flag on database change event notification
protected void processDatabaseChangeNotification(
    QueryCollection queryCollection) {
  lastRequery = System.currentTimeMillis();
  super.processDatabaseChangeNotification(queryCollection);
}
```

Also from the Java category of the View Object editor shown in Figure 20-5, you create a client interface representation for the `getLastRequery` method that the ADF method binding will use to provide the current query flag value to the managed bean method invoked by the `af:poll` listener.

Summary

Good ideas need adoption. To business application developers, real-time UI refresh in REA appears like an unreachable goal because of the complexity involved. Active Data Services in Oracle ADF Faces RC provides a simplified and future-proof platform for real-time data UI refresh in Oracle Fusion application development that shields developers from the implementation details of push in AJAX. As we showed in this chapter, ADS helps REA developers build interactive dashboard-style features that enrich interactive web applications with on-time data change deliveries. This, and the ability of the framework to scale and to ensure its availability, invites a broader audience of business application developers to adopt AJAX push and streaming for their business applications.

For this book, we need to be careful in predicting new ADF features in regard to integration of Active Data Services. However, the combination of ADF declarative component binding and the ADS superior architecture for real-time data push look promising for REA developers to be able to abandon desktop application development completely for a future-facing technology that is an RIA development with the Oracle Fusion development platform, using Oracle ADF BC, ADF, ADF Faces RC, and AJAX.

CHAPTER
21

Oracle Fusion Web
Application Security

*The Oracle ADF Security framework in the Oracle Fusion development stack provides several
out-of-the-box features to make it easier for developers to code secure ADF applications.*

mplementing security in web applications manages the risk of data losses, data
manipulation, and system failures caused by unauthorized access from internal or
external sources. Such unauthorized access exploits the application as the weak
link within an overall protection strategy. A business application running on the
Web bypasses firewalls and peripheral security mechanisms. It is a door swung
wide open that needs guarding to avoid the worst. But applications need to be protected not only
against the malicious user. Application security is also used to enforce data and functional access
restrictions based on the user privilege. In this chapter, we introduce ADF Security, an application
protection layer within Oracle ADF and the ADF Business Components service that developers
can use to control user access within an application.

NOTE
*A single chapter about security cannot cover a complete end-to-end
solution. In the context of this book, we therefore focus on the ADF
Security framework.*

Application Security: A Part of the Whole

As shown in Figure 21-1, application security is a part of an overall security strategy that includes
network, server, and peripheral security. Building applications with the Oracle Fusion development
stack contains at least four layers on which you should apply security: view, controller, business
service, and data. A fifth layer not shown in Figure 21-1 exists when you're integrating web
applications in a Service Oriented Architecture (SOA) or simply when remote services such as
Web Services are called. In such cases, trust must be established between the two end points, the
application and the service, to authenticate the user or the application against the remote service.

- **View layer**   Security handled on the view layer includes authentication and the security-
  aware rendering of user interface components.

- **Controller layer**   The controller determines the navigation within an application, and, in
  the case of an Oracle ADF task flow, a user's access to it.

- **Business service layer**   The business service queries data from the database and
  executes the business logic of an application. Security is used to determine a user's
  access to entities and attributes, as well as the functionality the user can process.

- **Data layer**   The Oracle RDBMS system is a safe place for data, and it provides security
  functionality such as Virtual Private Database (VPD), proxy user access, and more to keep
  it safe. Applications should leverage database security and query only the data that a user
  is allowed to view.

In an end-to-end security-aware environment, security is not implemented on one of the
application layers but on all of them. Business service security may display on the view layer in
that input components that are not updateable because of missing user authorization are rendered
read-only. This can be an out-of-the-box behavior or it can be implemented by the application
developer.

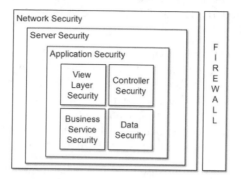

FIGURE 21-1   *Elements of application security*

Guiding Principles for Building a Secure Application

Applying security in application development requires good design. It is good and recommended practice that developers and architects follow design patterns that exist for application security as well as the recommendations published by advisories such as the Open Web Application Security Project group (OWASP), which publishes a well recognized Top 10 list of potential vulnerabilities on its web site at www.owasp.org.

Security design patterns are road-tested recommendations of best practices that are language and implementation independent in their description. They are derived from experience and are not invented. Existing patterns include the following:

- **Defense in depth**   Describes a multilayered security that redundantly enforces security on different levels within an application. For example, in Java EE application development with the Oracle Fusion stack, security can be implemented on the view layer, the binding, and the business service. The same security context object is available on all three layers to provide consistent policy enforcements. Database security should be used as a last line of defense.

- **Least privileged access**   Alerts the application developer to restrict the user privileges to those required to do their work within the application. Even if a user is a database administrator, this doesn't mean that he or she should have access to an application with database administration rights.

- **Single access point**   Controls how users access an application. For example, you may want to force authenticated users to start on a specific home page. In addition, you may want to restrict the number of pages within an application that users can directly request from a browser. In ADF, the access of pages that are directly accessible from a browser can be restricted using ADF Security and bounded task flows.

- **Check points**   Describe areas in an application that are frequently passed by the request and in which authentication and authorization checks are performed. Before a user executes sensitive code, you may want to reverify that the user is authorized to do so.

An example of this is a bounded task flow that with ADF Security being enabled, needs to be authorized for users and that can use its initialize method or default activities to perform additional checks.

- **Roles**   Abstract the individual user from the security system. Instead of granting permissions (and hundreds of them may exist) to the individual user, you grant permissions to an application role that defines a responsibility within an application. The application role is application-specific and is mapped to a group of users that have this responsibility within an enterprise. With this abstraction, administrators can change the user privileges within an application without consulting the application developer. In ADF Security, application roles, which are hierarchical roles, are used for authorization grants.

- **Limited view**   Ensures that users see only what they need to see, including the display of error message details. Note that many hacks in the past were possible because the intruder forced the system to fail, simply to learn from its error messages about the technology it used.

In addition to design patterns, less formal design principles and secure coding guides exist, and you should build and adopt your own catalog to include these. Here are some examples:

- *Applications should be secured by default.* This means that the failure of the authorization system locks the system down instead of opening it up. Security should be considered during the design phase as well, to make sure that security implementations don't interrupt the business processes.

- *Use safe defaults.* For example, the variable you use in your Java code to indicate whether a user is authenticated or not by default should have its value set to `false`.

- *Security should be implemented across the entire application, not only in parts of it.* If you need to provide public access to some areas of an application, use permissions that are granted to all authenticated or anonymous users. Note that you cannot revoke access rights that you never granted to anyone.

- *Don't take obscurity as security.* If you want to prevent users from accessing information, don't hide it; instead, remove it from the rendered page output.

- *There is no reason to trust a friend.* All users can, deliberately or not, provide malicious data input that you should filter before sending it to the database. This can be done through filters that watch the incoming traffic or components that handle validation and conversion of the user input.

- *Build usable systems.* Security is no good if it slows down the work within an application or interrupts the user in his or her job. Applied security should appear when things go wrong.

As you can see, technology alone doesn't decide whether application security turns out to be a perfect wave of perfect storm. But technology is an important factor, and this is why we dedicate the remainder of this chapter to it.

The Java EE Security Platform

The Java EE platform provides tools for application developers to include authentication, authorization, and message encryption to web applications. Security can be implemented by delegating authentication and authorization to the Java EE container or by programming it directly into the application. As you will see, a comprehensive security solution demands a combination of both.

Container-Managed Security

Container-managed security, also referred to as container-delegated security or Java EE security, is configured in the web.xml deployment descriptor file and relies on the Java EE container to perform all authentication and authorization checks. Since all the security decisions are passed on to the Java EE server, container-managed security is the most portable security implementation to use in web applications.

To configure container-managed application security, developers use the application web.xml file to specify the type of authentication they want to enforce for an application and the URL patterns to protect. Authentication in Java EE can be defined as basic, form based, or certificate based. Configuring the authentication as basic invokes the browser native login dialog for the user to provide the username and password credentials.

Form-based authentication redirects the request to a developer-created HTML or JavaServer Pages (JSP) page for authentication. The page contains j_username and j_password input fields, as well as a form element with a j_security_check action. If a user submits the form, a request is sent to the server, where it is intercepted by the security provider because of the j_security_check action. If the authentication is successful, the user is redirected to the business application page he or she originally tried to access. In case of an authentication failure, the user is redirected to an error page that is also provided by the application developer and may allow the user to retry the authentication. Note that when submitting the login form, the username and password information is not encrypted but sent to the server in plain text, which is why a Secure Sockets Layer (SSL) connection should be used.

NOTE
The Java EE standard does not provide an API that allows developers to authenticate application users programmatically. Such an API is subject of the Servlet 3.0 specification that will be released with Java EE 6. Until then, programmatic authentication requires vendor-specific extensions to the Java EE security platform that are not portable.

A Side Effect of Basic Authentication

A side effect of basic authentication is browser-based single sign-on, which means that once the user is authenticated for an application, he or she is also authenticated for all other applications that run on the same server using this security realm. This often leads to confusion by developers who want to log their users out of an application explicitly, because even when invalidating a user session, the next application request from the user is reauthenticated by the browser. For the user to be challenged for the username and password pair again, he or she needs to close the browser process. So don't use basic authentication if your application needs to support logout.

Certificate-based authentication uses a public key certificate configured on the browser to identify the user against the server. The server retrieves the user's identity and password from the certificate to authenticate the requested application.

Authorization in container-managed security is defined by access patterns that reference the Uniform Resource Identifier (URI) of the pages within an application. Access patterns can be grouped in security constraints that are granted to application roles. The application roles are then mapped to groups of users during or after deployment.

Limitations of Container-Managed Authorization

Container-managed authentication protects resources by semantic role names that don't have privileges associated that describe the permissions an authorized user has against the protected resource. To understand the protection represented by a role, you need to look at the application sources to learn how the role is used in the context of the application runtime.

In addition, authorization is coarse-grained and protects the root URI only, which does not allow you to refine protection further—for example, by including the request parameters in the security decision. User interface technology such as JavaServer Faces (JSF) also easily bypasses container-managed security by performing server-side navigation instead of sending a GET request.

Lastly, web application roles defined in the web.xml file are not hierarchical, which means that you cannot include privileges through inheritance. Instead, all roles that need to have access to a protected resource must be mentioned in the security constraint definition.

Java Authentication and Authorization Service

The central design point of Java Authentication and Authorization Service (JAAS) is that it allows the application to perform fine-grained permission checks based on the authenticated user, the action the user wants to perform, and the resource against which the action is going to be performed. Using JAAS, application developers can protect any aspect of an application based on the authenticated user role memberships. It's much more powerful than the URL constraint design of container-managed security that can't be used to protect anything beyond a simple HTTP GET request.

In addition to fine-grained access control, the benefit of JAAS is within its pluggable authentication architecture. JAAS authentication is handled by independent LoginModule instances that communicate with an application through callbacks. Using external LoginModules allows identity providers to be changed without a change required to the application.

Users in JAAS are represented by Principal classes that are stored in a Subject. Application roles are also defined as Principal classes stored in the Subject. The Subject, therefore, is what developers need to get a hold on to perform authorization checks in applications. The user access privileges are defined by permissions configured in an external configuration file or repository, the security policy store. Permissions are defined using Permission classes that are granted to user or role Principal classes. Permissions have a class name, a target, and set of actions defined. The Permission class name defines the resource object to protect, such as a file on the file system using the FilePermission class. The target name further qualifies the resource—for example, the name of the file to control access for. Last, but not least, the action defines what a user can do with the defined resource, such as to perform read, create, and delete operations. The action is specific to the permission type and therefore differs between Permission class implementations. As you can see from this brief introduction, JAAS protects resources by their object, not by a page URL, which allows finer grained authorization than container-managed authorization.

Java EE container vendors, such as Oracle, use JAAS to implement container-managed security. This implementation is not standardized, however, which means that the portability of an application depends on a comparable security infrastructure that exists on the target platform.

OPSS: A Hybrid Approach to Web Application Security

Using Java EE security in web applications provides the highest degree of portability and API consistency. However, security models that protect resources by their request URI without considering query parameters and without handling server-side page redirects fail to secure modern web applications. To handle application security properly using the standard container-managed security, developers need to implement their own authorization enforcer strategy within the application code itself, which still does not allow for fine-grained access control. Here, JAAS provides the better authorization model but does not integrate well with Java EE, in that Java EE containers are not required to manage the authenticated user subject if authentication is performed through JAAS. To overcome the limitations in Java EE security, Java EE vendors such as Oracle provide vendor-specific security platform services such as Oracle Platform Security Services (OPSS) that extend the Java EE security model.

OPSS provides an abstraction layer between security providers and Java EE applications. It is a pluggable architecture that provides a consistent, portable, and standards-based solution for authentication, authorization, auditing, and managing roles and credentials that integrates with Oracle WebLogic Server, Oracle Entitlement Server, Oracle SOA, Oracle WebCenter, and Oracle Web Service Manager in the Oracle Fusion Middleware 11*g* offering.

Interesting for application developers, OPSS combines JAAS authentication, using default and custom JAAS LoginModules, and JAAS authorization for role-based and permission-based authorization with Java EE container-managed security. Using a hybrid approach like this, application developers can use the best of both worlds—the ease of authentication provided by the container managed login and the superior authorization support of JAAS. The Oracle ADF Security framework, which is an integral part of the Oracle ADF development platform, uses OPSS to perform user authentication based on Java EE and authorization based on JAAS. ADF Security, explained next, is the recommended option for developers that develop their applications with the Oracle Fusion development platform to build secure web applications.

NOTE
The OPSS security platform provides more than just JAAS integration to web application development. For more information, see the "Oracle Fusion Middleware Security Guide 11g Release 1" documentation that is available as part of the Oracle Fusion Middleware documentation at http://otn.oracle.com.

ADF Security

The Oracle ADF Security framework in the Oracle Fusion development stack provides several out-of-the-box features to make it easier for developers to code secure ADF applications. It automatically performs a JAAS security check whenever a user tries to access a bounded task flow or a top-level page, so no coding is required to secure these artifacts. It provides an authentication servlet that delegates authentication to the container, but provides the application developer with control over exactly when login/logout is triggered. It exposes both Java and Expression Language (EL) expressions that allow application developers to get information easily about the current user, including roles and permissions. When OPSS is used as the default security platform on top of the Java EE container security, ADF Security supports file-based and Lightweight Directory Access Protocol (LDAP)–based policy stores for storing user permissions. Using Oracle WebLogic Server in Oracle Fusion Middleware 11*g*, application users are authenticated through authentication providers, which can be custom providers that use custom JAAS LoginModules or one of the default providers that include LDAP and RDBMS providers.

ADF Security Architecture

ADF Security is integrated with OPSS in Oracle WebLogic Server for authentication and authorization. Authentication is delegated to the Java EE container, whereas authorization is performed with JAAS. Figure 21-2 shows the ADF Security architecture at design time in Oracle JDeveloper 11*g* and at runtime in Oracle WebLogic Server.

The ADF Security design time in Oracle JDeveloper 11*g* provides declarative editors and a wizard to configure the associated metadata files, web.xml, adf-config.xml, jazn-data.xml, and weblogic.xml. Developers use the editors to create application users, groups, application roles, and policies for testing and deployment. User groups are also referred to as "enterprise roles" because they are not application specific.

NOTE
In this book, we use the terms "enterprise roles" and "user groups" interchangeably for clarity reasons to avoid confusion with application roles. Enterprise roles is used in ADF Security and the name you find in the Oracle product documentation.

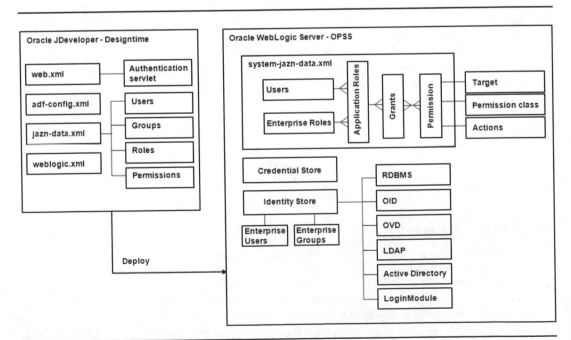

FIGURE 21-2   *ADF Security design time and runtime architecture*

ADF Security settings are stored in the application-wide jazn-data.xml file, which is located in the src\META-INF directory of the application root folder on the file system. For testing, and later for production, the application is deployed to the Oracle WebLogic Server. Upon deployment, the jazn-data.xml file content is copied to the Oracle WebLogic Server domain system-jazn-data.xml file that is located in the config\fmwconfig directory of the WebLogic Server domain. One benefit of using the jazn-data.xml local policy file during application development is that it can be source controlled and that it makes it easy for developers to zip up applications as a test case for other developers or quality testing (QA) engineers.

Application developers may run the ADF Security wizard multiple times and switch ADF Security on and off for testing purposes. Disabling security changes the settings only in the adf-config.xml file and does not remove the permissions defined in the jazn-data.xml file.

NOTE

For security reasons, avoid copying users and groups that you created for runtime testing ADF Security to production servers. You can configure the security deployment to exclude these accounts and user groups.

The system-jazn-data.xml file represents the OPSS file-based policy store and contains JAAS permissions and grants. A grant associates permissions with an application role. The application role is mapped to users and user groups defined in Oracle WebLogic Server through enterprise roles or user principals in ADF Security. Following is the entry of the system-jazn-data.xml file that defines the hr_manager_group enterprise role as a member of the app_manager application role:

```xml
<app-role>
  <name>app_manager</name>
  <display-name>Application Managers</display-name>
  <class>
    oracle.security.jps.service.policystore.ApplicationRole
  </class>
  <members>
    <member>
      <class>
        weblogic.security.principal.WLSGroupImpl
      </class>
      <name>hr_manager_group</name>
    </member>
  </members>
</app-role>
```

Permissions consist of a permission class, such as `RegionPermission`, used to protect an ADF page—a target, which is the name of the resource to protect, and an action, which defines what the user is allowed to do with the resource. Actions that are available for the `RegionPermission` include view or customize. Note that ADF Security checks only the view action, and not customize, which is what the Oracle WebCenter product uses in addition to view.

NOTE

The two permission classes in ADF Security are `PagePermission` and `RegionPermission`. They do exist in the ADF framework and don't need to be created by the application developer.

Authentication in ADF Security is handled by the Java EE container. Shown in Figure 21-2, in Oracle WebLogic Server, authentication is delegated to authentication providers, which are pluggable identity store adapters. Identity stores for which authentication providers exist in WebLogic Server include the integrated Open LDAP server, Oracle Internet Directory (OID), Oracle Virtual Directory (OVD), RDBMS, and MS Active Directory. In addition to the existing authentication providers, you can create custom providers that use a JAAS LoginModule to access the custom identity store. Upon successful authentication, the user Subject in WebLogic Server is populated with the user and use group information contained in a JAAS Subject.

OPSS provides a credential store in which sensitive information, such as database passwords for applications that use a JDBC URL connection or authentication details for accessing protected Web Services, are stored safely. The credentials are saved and deployed in a file, cwallet.sso, which is located in the config\fmwconfig directory of the Oracle WebLogic Server domain.

NOTE
The security configuration in Oracle WebLogic Server is explained in the "Oracle Fusion Middleware Securing Oracle WebLogic Server 11g Release 1" documentation that is available at http://otn.oracle.com.

At runtime, the following security sequence is performed for ADF Security protected applications:

1. A user requests an ADF bound ADF Faces page or bounded task flow.

2. The ADF Security layer in ADF checks whether security is enabled for the ADF application configuration.

3. If security is enabled, the security layer checks whether security is enabled for authentication only or for authorization, too.

4. If authorization is enforced, ADF Security checks whether an anonymous principal exists and if the permissions granted to anonymous users are sufficient to run the page or task flow. This usually is the case for public pages. However, it is important to note that page and task flow permissions must be explicitly granted to the anonymous role to make them publicly accessible.

5. If page access is not possible with the privileges of the anonymous user account, the framework triggers authentication by redirecting the request to the protected ADF authentication servlet.

6. The servlet delegates the authentication request to the Java EE container.

7. Using Oracle WebLogic Server, the container responds to the request with a login form or by sending a response header that makes the browser display its login form.

8. The user-provided credentials are checked against the identity stores that are configured for the WebLogic Server domain. If authentication is successful, the server redirects the request to the authentication servlet. The session now is authenticated and the user Subject contains the user and enterprise group principals.

9. If ADF Security is configured to use a single application entry point for authenticated users, the authentication servlet directs the request to this page. If not, it directs the user to the originally requested page.

10. ADF Security now checks whether the user Subject has permission to run the requested resource. For this, it performs permission checks for the page or task flow in the context of the authenticated user.

Protection Scope of the ADF Security Runtime

The ADF Security runtime does provides authorization checks on the binding container and the bounded task flow level. Using ADF Business Components as the business service, authorization can also be defined on the entity object. EL can be used in the UI to check authorization defined on the entity object and to declaratively check custom permissions that developers create for their applications. Binding container and task flow authorization in ADF Security is optimized for best performance and the following rules apply:

- When ADF Security is enabled, all ADF bound pages and bounded task flows are protected, including public pages.

- Application security information in the jazn-data.xml file and the system-jazn-data.xml file are defined for a specific application. Two applications that use the same policy store don't conflict with each other, even if the names of the application roles they have defined are identical.

- Bounded task flows are secured by default if authorization is enabled for ADF Security. Accessing a secured bounded task flow requires that the user have the required permission granted.

- Bounded task flows are protected through permissions in the policy store, using their unique ID as the target. No security metadata is added to the task flow definition.

- The unbounded task flow is not secured. No specific task flow permission is required to access content of an unbounded task flow.

- ADF Security authorization for pages is performed on the binding container level and therefore protects only JSF pages that contain ADF binding references.

- Binding container–level authorization is not enforced for pages and views that are contained in a bounded task flow. Pages and views inherit the authorization required to run the bounded task flow.

- Pages that are referenced within a bounded task flow and that require additional authorization checks should be in their own bounded task flow and added to other task flows using a task flow call activity.

- Binding container–level authorization is defined by permissions defined in the policy store for the associated PageDef file. It is checked for pages that are referenced from the unbounded task flow. No security definitions are defined in the PageDef file.

- An `AuthorizationException` is thrown if authorization in ADF Security fails. The ADF Controller directs such failures to the defined exception handler. If an error occurs on a page that is not referenced from the ADF controller, an error page defined as a initialization parameter on the ADF binding servlet is used.

- The ADF Controller performs a permission check on each task flow invocation and does not cache the outcome of the checks. The authorization checks also occur when navigating within a task flow to detect session expiry or permission changes.

If you need additional security checks to be performed within bounded task flows, without creating a subtask flow, you can use EL. The benefit of permission-based authorization is that access can be checked any time and anywhere in the application. In the section "Adding Extra Security Checks to Views, Methods, and Routers Contained in Bounded Task Flows," later in this chapter, we provide an example of how authorization can be used in the context of a router decision.

NOTE
Declarative exception handling in ADF task flows is explained in Chapters 4 and 5.

NOTE
To protect JSF pages that are not ADF bound, you can make them ADF bound using an empty PageDef file. To create an empty PageDef file, right-click a page and choose Go To Page Definition from the context menu. Be aware that, after this, the page is added to the ADF lifecycle, which is a minimal overhead added to the page runtime.

The oracle.security.jps.ee.http.JpsFilter

The `JpsFilter` servlet filter class is configured in the web.xml deployment descriptor file of Oracle Fusion web application projects and integrates JSF-based web applications with the OPSS policy enforcement. By default, a single filter parameter, `enable.anonymous`, is configured:

```
<filter>
  <filter-name>JpsFilter</filter-name>
    <filter-class>
      oracle.security.jps.ee.http.JpsFilter
    </filter-class>
    <init-param>
      <param-name>enable.anonymous</param-name>
      <param-value>true</param-value>
    </init-param>
</filter>
```

Other, optional, parameters can be added by the application developer, as shown in the following table:

Parameter	Description
application.name	Set this parameter if the application name reference in the jazn-data.xml policy file differs from the deployed application name. Use this name property if multiple applications should share the same policy definition.
add.application.roles	When set to `true`, the default setting, application roles are added to the authenticated subject. Use these application roles when checking user permissions in JAAS, which is also done by ADF Security.
enable.anonymous	Set this property to `true` if you want to create a JAAS subject for unauthenticated users. The subject will have the anonymous user and role principal added, allowing applications to grant permissions. Using anonymous users is similar, but not the same, as public pages. The difference is that developers have more control over what anonymous users can see on web pages that are also used by authenticated, more privileged users.
remove.anonymous.role	Keeping the default value, `true`, the anonymous user role is removed from the subject as soon as the user is authenticated. Set this parameter to `false` to keep the role in the subject. Removing the anonymous role removes the privileges of unauthenticated users. For example, the privilege to log in may be granted to anonymous users but revoked from authenticated users to prevent users from being able to authenticate twice. Note that ADF Security overrides this parameter setting to `false` so that granting a page to the anonymous role makes it accessible to all users.
add.authenticated.role	The authenticated role is added to the subject for all users that provided a valid username and password pair. Using the authenticated role, applications can enforce authentication but not authorization on pages. The default setting is `true`. Setting it to `false` will not add the role to the subject after user authentication.
oracle.security.jps.jaas.mode	The JAAS mode is set to `doAsPrivileged` by default and ensures that actions are performed in the context of the user permission. The other possible configuration option, "doAs, works similarly, but uses the `AccessControlContext` of the current thread instead of a context that is provided with the security check. The `AccessControlContext` context contains information about all the classes that are executed by an application since its initialization. If an application performs a security-sensitive action, Java platform security demands that all classes in the `AccessControlContext` must have the required permission granted for the call to succeed. Using the `doAsPrivileged` option allows security checks to be performed with a fresh `AccessControlContext`.

Public, Anonymous, and Authenticated Users

Three types of users exist in web application development: public, anonymous, and authenticated.

The public user is defined by Java EE authorization, which is when unauthenticated users enter a web page that is not constrained by any Java EE role.

Anonymous users in OPSS are unauthenticated users for which a JAAS subject is created when the user enters the application. The subject contains the anonymous role principal, which can have permissions granted. Using the anonymous role, developers can define public pages within a protected application. Users that are not authenticated are able to access all resources that are explicitly granted to the anonymous role by the developer, which is a narrower focus compared to what public users can do in Java EE.

Note that if the `remove.anonymous.role` initialization parameter is set such that the anonymous role is removed after the user is authenticated, make sure that public pages are granted to the authenticated role to remain public.

The authenticated user role is assigned to an identified user—a user that the application knows. The authenticated user, by default, has no privileges unless the user directly or indirectly has been granted privileges to a resource. If you want to make sure that specific functionality, such as online shopping, is available only to identified users, use the authenticated role.

Both the authenticated and anonymous roles are specific OPSS roles that are not explicitly defined in the jazn-data.xml file at design time and the system-jazn-data.xml file at runtime.

The ADF Security Design Time

ADF Security is well integrated in the Oracle JDeveloper 11*g* integrated development environment (IDE) and can be declaratively defined for applications. You can configure ADF Security at any time in the course of your application development. To enable ADF Security, you run the ADF Security configuration wizard that you access from Oracle JDeveloper 11*g* by choosing Application | Secure, as shown in Figure 21-3.

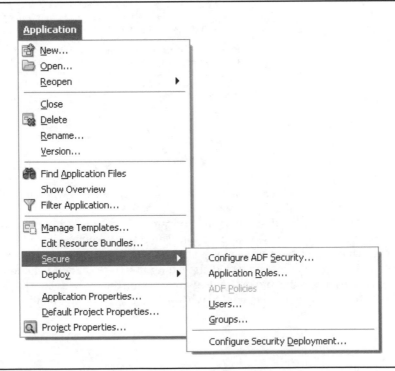

FIGURE 21-3   *Choose Application | Secure to access ADF Security*

TIP
An alternative access path is provided through the drop-down menu that opens when you click the icon next to the application select box at the top of the Application Navigator panel.

The Secure submenu provides the following security related options:

- **Configure ADF Security** Starts the ADF Security configuration wizard to enable, configure, and disable ADF Security for an application.

- **Application Roles** Application roles are created in the jazn-data.xml file for the application. In ADF Security, application roles are used to grant security permissions to authenticated users through mappings to enterprise user groups after deployment.

- **Users** For testing purpose, ADF Security allows developers to create users in the jazn-data.xml file.

- **Groups** Security is seldom granted to individual users, but is usually granted to user groups for easier administration. You can create user groups for testing purposes in jazn-data.xml.

- **Configure Security Deployment** Defines how deployed security configurations are treated if existing configurations are detected on the target WebLogic Server. In addition, test users and groups contained in the application jazn-data.xml file can be excluded from deployment.

You can start with any option you want to configure security in your application. Because users, groups, and application roles are needed only when ADF Security is enabled for an application, the most logical starting point is the Configure ADF Security option.

Enabling ADF Security for an Application

ADF Security for an application is configured by the ADF Security Wizard that you launch by choosing Application | Secure | Configure ADF Security. The wizard steps you through the five dialogs panels, explained here:

1. Step 1: Enable ADF Security: The first panel offers three options for enabling or disabling ADF Security:

    - **ADF Authentication and Authorization** Enables ADF Security for user authentication and ADF binding container and task flows access control.

    - **ADF Authentication** Enables authentication only and invokes container-managed authentication as soon as users access an ADF bound page. Choose this option and the security wizard is reduced to four steps, omitting step 3.

    - **Remove ADF Security Configuration** Disables ADF Security but does not delete the created permission. Use this option to run a previously secured application unsecured.

2. Step 2: Select authentication type: Select the web project for which you want to configure authentication. The project web.xml file is edited with the selected authentication type and the authentication servlet.

■ **HTTP basic Authentication**   Launches the browser native login dialog for users to authenticate.

■ **HTTP Digest Authentication**   Same as basic authentication with the password being encrypted. A unique number, the *nonce,* is generated for each authentication request. The nonce is sent back by the client with the user-provided password and the authentication realm. The server uses this information to create a hash that is used to authenticate the client during subsequent communication. This authentication type may be used to prevent replay attacks.

Note: Because ADF Security does not authenticate users, completing this wizard step only configures the type of login in the web.xml file and does not verify if the Java EE container supports this authentication type.

■ **HTTPS Client Authentication**   Authentication is performed by a browser-configured client certificate.

■ **Form-Based Authentication**   Authentication is performed using a HTML form embedded in a HTML, JSP, or JSF document that uses the j_security_check action and the j_username and j_password field to identify the user to the server. Optionally, the login and error page can be generated in this step.

3. Step 3: Automatic Policy Grants: Enabling ADF Security for an ADF application requires the developer to decide how, by default, ADF Security should protect the application.

■ **No Automatic Grants**   Does nothing and locks your application until all objects are manually granted to application roles defined for an application.

■ **Grant To Existing Objects Only**   ADF Security grants access to existing page and bounded task flow objects to the test-all application role, which is mapped to the anonymous role in Oracle WebLogic Server; this means that anyone can run the application. The test-all role is as if no security is applied, which is why the role should not be deployed to a production system.

■ **Grant To All Objects**   Similar to the Grant To Existing Objects Only option, except that any new object that is created in an application is automatically granted to the test-all role.

Note: The option you choose is not a question of best practices but personal preferences.

4. Step 4: Specify authentication welcome page: Configure or generate a page that you want to become the starting point for all authenticated users in an application. The user may access an application on any page; after authentication, the user will be directed to the defined starting page. If you leave this configuration empty, the authenticated user is directed back to the page he or she originally accessed.

Note: The page to which users are redirected can be dynamically provided if the login is performed through a link in the application that references the authentication servlet. This option is explained later in this chapter.

5. Step 5: Summary

The summary panel lists all the files that are changed when finishing the ADF Security wizard. The changes are discussed in the following section

Overview of the Files Changed When Enabling ADF Security

Completing the ADF Security wizard, enforces authentication and optionally authorization on ADF applications. The following files are changed with security settings:

adf-config.xml   The ADF configuration file, adf-config.xml, contains the authentication and authorization switches to enable and disable ADF Security and is accessible from the Application Resources panel in Oracle JDeveloper. In the panel, expand the Descriptors | ADF META-INF node. Select the adf-config.xml file and open the Structure Window.

Expand the adf-config | adf-security-child entry and select the `JaasSecurityContext` entry. Open the Property Inspector (CTRL-SHIFT-I) to enable or disable ADF Security. The `jaasProviderClass` property references the `SecurityContext` implementation used by the application. The `SecurityContext` is accessible from Java and Expression Language and provides developers with authentication and authorization information that they can use in programmatic security decisions.

jps-config.xml   The jps-config.xml file is the OPSS security platform configuration. The application jps-config.xml file is not used by Oracle Fusion web applications. Web applications use the jps-config.xml file of the WebLogic Server domain. This file is used, for example, when you run the Business Component tester, which is a J2SE application.

jazn-data.xml   The jazn-data.xml file is the application policy and identity store at design time. Physically, the file is located in the application src\META-INF directory. In JDeveloper, the file is accessed from the Descriptors | META-INF node of the Application Resources panel.

Enabling ADF Security for an application adds an application entry in the policy store section of the jazn-data.xml file. The initial policy store configuration contains the test-all role and anonymous role definitions, and, if the Grant To All Objects or Grant To Existing Objects Only authorization option is selected, the page and bounded task flow permissions are granted to the test-all role.

web.xml   The web.xml file is located in the web project WEB-INF directory and is updated with the information about the chosen authentication type and the ADF Security authentication servlet configuration. For example, the login type configuration for form-based authentication looks like this:

```
<login-config>
  <auth-method>FORM</auth-method>
  <form-login-config>
    <form-login-page>
       /login.html
    </form-login-page>
    <form-error-page>
       /error.html
    </form-error-page>
  </form-login-config>
</login-config>
```

In addition, the wizard adds the following initialization parameter to the JPS filter to keep authorization granted to the anonymous user in the authenticated JAAS user Subject:

```
<init-param>
  <param-name>remove.anonymous.role</param-name>
  <param-value>false</param-value>
</init-param>
```

The ADF Security authentication servlet handles, in addition to others, the direct of the login request to the container and back to the originally requested page or a specifically defined welcome page. The configuration in the web.xml is shown here:

```
<servlet>
  <servlet-name>adfAuthentication</servlet-name>
  <servlet-class>
    <!-- added with no line breaks in web.xml -->
    oracle.adf.share.security.
    authentication.AuthenticationServlet
  </servlet-class>
  <load-on-startup>1</load-on-startup>
</servlet>
```

If ADF Security is configured to redirect the authenticated user to a predefined start page, the following servlet initialization parameter is added:

```
<servlet>
  <servlet-name>adfAuthentication</servlet-name>
  ...
  <init-param>
    <param-name>success_url</param-name>
    <param-value>
        /faces/BrowseEmployees.jspx
    </param-value>
  </init-param>
  ...
</servlet>
```

Another initialization parameter, end_url, which defines the URL to navigate to after the user logged out, is not configured by the ADF Security wizard and needs to be added manually:

```
  <init-param>
    <param-name>end_url</param-name>
    <param-value>
        /faces/MyLogout.jspx
    </param-value>
  </init-param>
```

To trigger container-managed authentication, the servlet is protected by the valid-user role, which exists in the web.xml file and that needs to be mapped to a role granted to any authenticated user. Note that the ADF authentication servlet is mapped to the /adfAuthentication context path in the web.xml file.

```
<security-constraint>
   <web-resource-collection>
     <web-resource-name>
       adfAuthentication
     </web-resource-name>
   <url-pattern>
     /adfAuthentication
   </url-pattern>
   </web-resource-collection>
     <auth-constraint>
       <role-name>valid-users</role-name>
     </auth-constraint>
</security-constraint>
```

weblogic.xml   The weblogic.xml file is located in the web project WEB-INF directory and contains the mapping of the valid-users role to the users principal in Oracle WebLogic Server.

```
<security-role-assignment>
   <role-name>valid-users</role-name>
   <principal-name>users</principal-name>
</security-role-assignment>
```

As mentioned earlier, the valid-users role in the web.xml file must be mapped to a role that all authenticated users are a member of. This role is users in WebLogic Server. It is an implicit role that you don't need to create explicitly in Oracle WebLogic.

NOTE
The WebLogic security role assignment has nothing in common with application roles defined in the jazn-data.xml. Roles in the weblogic.xml file are Java EE roles defined in the web.xml file that are mapped to user groups or users in WebLogic Server.

SecurityContext

ADF Security–enabled applications are configured to use OPSS for security services by default. However, ADF Security provides a JAAS-based security plug-in architecture that does not rely purely on OPSS and that allows applications to use plain JAAS security. The `SecurityContext` interface defines programming APIs to retrieve the authenticated user's `Principal` class and JAAS `Subject` and to perform permission checking. It is implemented by the security provider and integrates ADF Security with the underlying security platform.

The default implementation configured in the adf-config.xml file is `JpsSecurityContext`, which integrates ADF Security with OPSS. The public methods exposed by the context object include the following:

- **getUserPrincipal**   Retrieves the authenticated user principal obtained from an internal call to `getUserPrincipal()` on the `HttpServletRequest` object.

- **getUsername**   Retrieves the name of the user principal obtained from the `SecurityContext`.

- **getUserProfile** Returns a `UserProfile` object with the authenticated user information. The implementation is dependent on the security provider.

- **hasPermission(Permission)** Returns `true` if the authenticated user has the permission granted that is passed as the argument.

- **isAuthorizationEnabled** Returns `true` if ADF Security is configured with authorization enabled.

- **isAuthenticationEnabled** Returns `true` if ADF Security is configured with authentication required.

- **isAuthenticated** Returns `true` if the user has been successfully authenticated.

- **isUserInRole(String)** Returns `true` if the user is a member of the specified enterprise group. The user role membership is checked on the `HttpServletRequest` object first. If this fails, the role is read from the `Principals` added to the authenticated user Subject.

- **getUserRoles** Returns a string array of user group memberships obtained from the authenticated user Subject. Note that in container-managed security, this information is not available.

- **getSubject** Returns the JAAS Subject for the authenticated user.

From Java, you access the `SecurityContext` object as shown here:

```
SecurityContext securityContext = null;
securityContext = ADFContext.getCurrent().getSecurityContext();
```

The `SecurityContext` object can be accessed from Expression Language via the Expression Builder in Oracle JDeveloper. For example, to hide UI components from unauthenticated users, you use this expression:

```
<af:inputText … rendered = "#{securityContext.authenticated}" />
```

Using Expression Language, additional functionality is exposed that allows you to check directly for page and task flows permissions.

The Fusion development platform uses ADF Business Components as the primary business services. In ADF Business Components, you can access the `SecurityContext` object using Groovy. For example, to use the name of the authenticated user as the value of a bind variable, you build the following Groovy string:

```
adf.context.securityContext.userName
```

Creating Users, Groups, and Roles

To grant permissions to ADF objects, you need to create application roles that are mapped to enterprise groups. OPSS supports the mapping of application roles to enterprise groups in the policy store configured for the WebLogic Server domain. This mapping is independent of which type of policy store, file based or LDAP, is used.

NOTE
The mapping of an enterprise user group to an application role always adds privileges for the contained users and never revokes them. The JAAS standard provides that permissions cannot be defined to exclude granted privileges from a Subject.

For testing purposes, application users and groups need to be created that simulate accounts available in the production environment. Creating the identity information also helps to define the application role to user group mappings that is required at runtime to determine the permissions indirectly granted to a user. An alternative option to create the mapping is to use the Oracle Enterprise Manager console. Oracle Enterprise Manager is not installed when Oracle WebLogic Server is installed and is contained in a separate software download. To install Oracle Enterprise Manager, download the Application Development Runtime bundle from the Oracle software site at http://www.oracle.com/technology/software/index.html. On the page, find and select the Oracle Fusion Middleware 11gR1 link to navigate to the Fusion Middleware product download area.

NOTE
Oracle Enterprise Manager runs as an ADF Faces Rich Client application deployed on Oracle WebLogic Server.

Creating Application Roles

The page and task flow access permissions are granted to application roles. To create application roles in the application jazn-data.xml file, choose Application | Secure | Application Roles from the Oracle JDeveloper menu. Figure 21-4 shows the editor provided in Oracle JDeveloper to edit application roles, users, and user groups, referred to as enterprise roles.

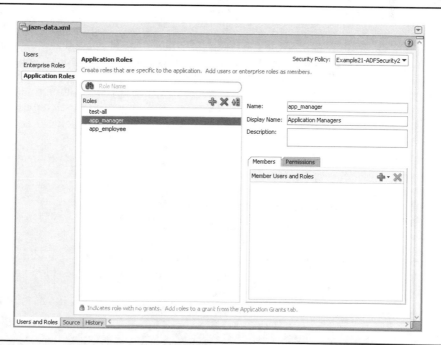

FIGURE 21-4 *Create and manage application roles, users, and user groups.*

The Application Roles editor allows developers to create, delete, and update roles and to assign users and enterprise roles as members. The Permissions tab offers a summary view on the granted resources, permission types, and allowed actions for the selected application role. If, when enabling ADF Security for an application using the ADF Security wizard, you choose the Grant To Existing Objects Only or Grant To All Objects option, the test-all role is created, and displayed in the Application Role editor. The test-all role has a single member, which is the anonymous-role principal that is defined in jazn-data.xml.

The following entry in the jazn-data.xml file is added when a new application role is created:

```
<app-role>
  <name>app_manager</name>
  <class>
    oracle.security.jps.service.policystore.ApplicationRole
  </class>
  <display-name>Application Managers</display-name>
</app-role>
```

Later, you'll see how ADF Security permissions are granted to this role.

Creating Users and Groups

Users and groups are created in the editor shown in Figure 21-4. You launch the user editing context by choosing Application | Secure | Users in JDeveloper. When creating a user, you can add the user as a member of user groups or application roles to obtain authorization privileges.

NOTE
When creating a user, make sure the password is seven characters long and that it contains at least one numeric value to comply with the default WebLogic Server password policy.

To open the security editor with the Enterprise Roles context opened to create user groups, choose Application | Secure | Groups. In the opened Enterprise Roles editor, you can create user groups and assign existing user accounts and enterprise roles as their members. From the same editor, you can add the user group as a member of one or many application roles.

For the examples in this book, we created three user accounts: sking, ahunold, and dfaviet. Here's the entry for sking in jazn-data.xml:

```
<user>
  <name>sking</name>
  <display-name>Steven King</display-name>
  <credentials>
    {903}YtOSbZTdwvp1kg3YjLLR8092k6fWKFX9
  </credentials>
</user>
```

User sking is a member of the hr_vp_group group. Users sking and ahunold are members the hr_manager_group, where sking is indirectly added through the membership in the hr_vp_group, as shown here:

```
<role>
    <name>hr_manager_group</name>
    <members>
      <member>
        <type>user</type>
        <name>ahunold</name>
      </member>
      <member>
        <type>role</type>
          <name>hr_vp_group</name>
          </member>
    </members>
</role>
```

All permissions that are granted to the hr_manager_group are added to the privileges of ahunold and sking, but not dfaviet.

Permissions are granted to application roles. For users to gain authorization, the user account, or a group of which they are a member, must be added as a member of the application role. All three configuration options shown in Figure 21-4—Users, Enterprise Roles, and Application Roles—provide an option to add users and groups to an application role. The following jazn-data.xml file content is created when assigning the hr_manager_group user group to the app_manager application role:

```
<app-role>
    <name>app_manager</name>
    <display-name>Application Managers</display-name>
    <class>
      oracle.security.jps.service.policystore.ApplicationRole
    </class>
    <members>
      <member>
        <name>hr_manager_group</name>
        <class>
        oracle.security.jps.internal.core.principals.JpsXmlEnterpriseRoleImpl
        </class>
      </member>
    </members>
</app-role>
```

The next section explains how resource permissions are granted to application roles. This, then, is the final required step to authorize users in ADF Security.

Note that the JpsXmlEnterpriseRoleImpl principal class that is used in the jazn-data.xml design time policy is changed to WLSGroupImpl in the system-jazn-data.xml runtime policy store. (An example is shown earlier in this chapter in the section "ADF Security Architecture.") You need to keep this in mind if you plan to copy and paste permissions from the design time environment to a production or testing runtime. Similar is the case for roles granted directly to user accounts, which, however, is not considered a best practice. When deploying ADF Security enabled applications to Weblogic Server, the change to WLSGroupImpl is automatically handled.

Creating and Granting Page and Task Flow Permissions

With the application roles created, we are ready to grant resources. For each resource, a
`Permission` entry is created in jazn-data.xml. The `Permission` class for protected JSF pages is

```
oracle.adf.share.security.authorization.RegionPermission
```

For task flows, the `Permission` class is

```
oracle.adf.controller.security.TaskFlowPermission
```

Figure 21-5 shows the task flow diagram of an unbounded ADF task flow that contains view,
method, router, and task flow activities. The example is a reuse of the sample used in Chapter 5,
where it is used to explain working with unbounded and bounded task flows. (Refer to Chapters 4
and 5 for more information.)

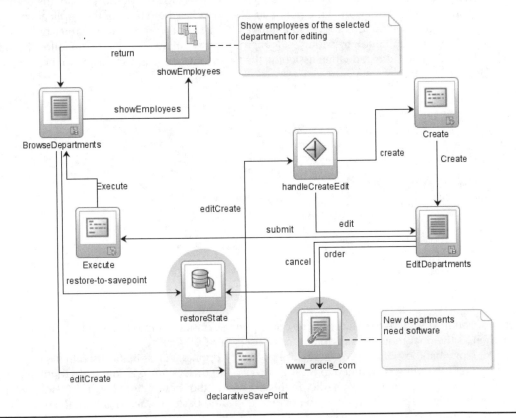

FIGURE 21-5 *Sample application flow diagram*

We'll configure the following scenario using ADF Security: The BrowseDepartments shown in Figure 21-5 should become the public home page that is accessible to authenticated and unauthenticated users. Navigation to any other view or task flow within the application requires that users authenticate first. The showEmployees task flow is not allowed for employees and requires that the user be a manager or vice president. In the task flow, only vice presidents are allowed to edit employee data.

Protecting Pages

To define page permissions, choose Application | Secure ADF Policies from the Oracle JDeveloper menu. In the policy editor, select the Web Pages tab, as shown in Figure 21-6.

TIP
To quickly open the policy editor for an ADF bound page displayed in the Oracle JDeveloper visual or page source editor, right-click and choose Edit Authorization from the context menu.

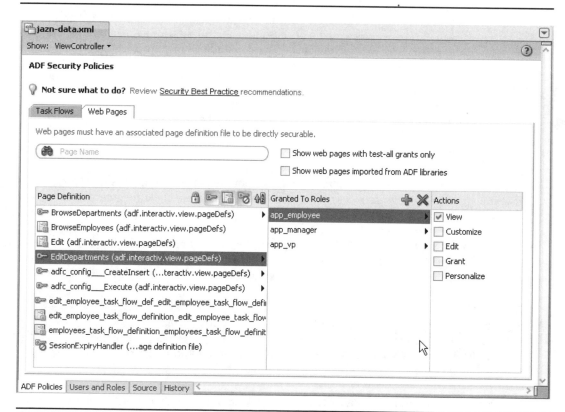

FIGURE 21-6 *Policy editor for ADF-bound JSF pages*

The policy editor shows a list of ADF-bound JSF pages, each with an associated icon, that provides information about the security state of a page. The following table lists the icon types and their meanings:

Icon	Description
Lock (not shown in Figure 21-6)	Marks pages in the unbounded task flow that have no associated grants. Pages that are not granted to an application role are not accessible.
Key	Indicates top level pages in the unbounded task flow, with associated grants. These pages are accessible only if the authenticated user has the page permission.
Task flow	Indicates pages that are referenced in bounded task flows. These pages are protected by the task flow permission and don't require explicit permission grants. Trying to access these pages outside of a bounded task flow leads to an authorization failure, unless the pages are explicitly granted to application roles.
Disabled key	The key icon with the red circle indicates pages that are not securable because they are missing an associated ADF PageDef file. The SessionExpiryHandler in Figure 21-6 is such a page.

NOTE
ADF bound pages that are referenced in a bounded task flow don't need to be granted to an application role. However, they can have grants, in which case they are accessible from bounded task flows and directly from a browser URL.

As shown in Figure 21-6, selecting a page displays the application roles to which it is granted. If you want to grant page access to additional application roles, click the green plus icon in the header. In the list displayed, you can select from the available application roles in the jazn-data.xml policy file. The choices of actions are View, Customize, Edit, Grant, and Personalize. Only the View action is used by Oracle ADF Security applied to ADF applications. The other actions are used by Oracle WebCenter, the new Oracle enterprise portal in Oracle Fusion Middleware 11*g*, which provides ready-to-use Enterprise 2.0 capabilities and is developed with Oracle ADF.

NOTE
To learn more about Oracle WebCenter, we recommend Oracle WebCenter 11*g* Handbook: Build Rich, Customizable Enterprise 2.0 Applications, *by Desbiens, Moskovits, and Weckerle, and published by McGraw-Hill.*

The iconic controls in the header of the Page Definition policy editor can be used to filter the list of pages based on their security status. In addition, a Show web pages with test-all grants only checkbox is provided to identify those pages that have grants to the test-all role. (Again, don't use the test-all role in a production environment.)

An example of a page definition is shown next. It is the permission created for the BrowseDepartments page, which is granted to the anonymous-role, so that it can be accessed by any user.

```
<grant>
  <grantee>
    <principals>
      <principal>
        <class>
          oracle.security.jps.internal.core.principals.JpsAnonymousRoleImpl
        </class>
        <name>anonymous-role</name>
      </principal>
    </principals>
  </grantee>
  <permissions>
    <permission>
      <class>
        oracle.adf.share.security.authorization.RegionPermission
      </class>
      <name>
        adf.interactiv.view.pageDefs.BrowseDepartmentsPageDef
      </name>
      <actions>view</actions>
    </permission>
  </permissions>
</grant>
```

The `permission` shown in this code sample identifies the resource, the page, by its package name, which is the directory structure that contains the PageDef file, and the name of the ADF page definition file. As you see from this XML, the jazn-data.xml file is organized such that a grant entry is created for each application role. An application role can have multiple permissions granted to access pages or task flows.

NOTE
Figure 21-6 shows an entry `adfc_config_CreateInsert`, *which is not a page but an ADF bound method activity in the unbounded task flow. In Oracle JDeveloper 11g, you can define ADF bindings for method and router activities, which can then be protected by ADF Security.*

Protecting Bounded Task Flows

To secure bounded task flows, you use the same policy editor, but select the Task Flows tab, as shown in Figure 21-7.

The security option for bounded task flows is a binary decision, as either a bounded task flow is granted to at least one application role or it is not accessible. For example, the employees task

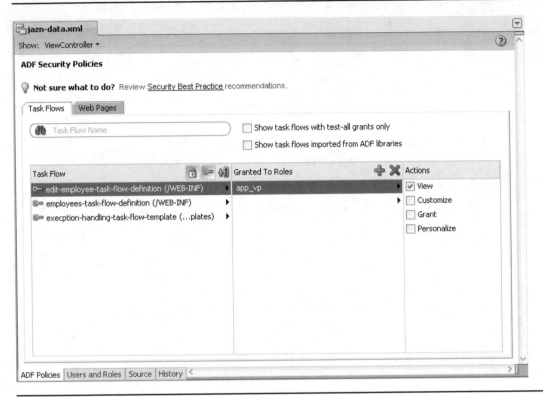

FIGURE 21-7 *Policy editor for bounded task flows*

flow definition shown in Figure 21-7 is granted to users in the app_manager role. The grant statement in the jazn-data.xml policy file is shown here:

```
<grant>
  <grantee>
    <principals>
      <principal>
        <class>
          oracle.security.jps.service.policystore.ApplicationRole
        </class>
        <name>app_manager</name>
      </principal>
    </principals>
  </grantee>
  <permissions>
    <permission>
      <class>
        oracle.adf.controller.security.TaskFlowPermission
      </class>
      <name>
        <!-- value must be on single line in jazn-data.xml -->
        /WEB-INF/employees-task-flow-definition.xml#
```

```
        employees-task-flow-definition
    </name>
    <actions>view</actions>
  </permission>
 </permissions>
</grant>
```

NOTE
The app_manager application role used in the example above is granted to enterprise roles. Enterprise roles can be hierarchical, which means that for example, the hr_vp_group enterprise role can be a member of the hr_manager_group enterprise role. If the app_manager application role is granted to the hr_manager_group enterprise role, then it is also implicitly granted to the hr_vp_group enterprise role.

The protected task flow is identified by its location, starting from the WEB-INF directory, the name of the task flow document, and the task flow ID. As for pages, the only possible action is View for ADF applications.

Bounded task flows that are referenced in other bounded task flows, using a call activity or an ADF Region in a contained view, run under their own permission granting and don't inherit the security settings of the parent task flow. This allows for fine-grained access control by breaking up large bounded task flows into smaller bounded task flows.

TIP
Bounded task flows can be protected from direct browser URL access by setting the `url-invoke-disallowed` *element for the visibility metadata in the task flow definition. You configure this setting from the Property Inspector via the URL Invoke property.*

Using Templates

Figure 21-7 shows the policy editor for task flows containing a task flow template that is referenced by other task flows to implement exception handling. Similarly, page templates that have an ADF binding reference may be referenced from other ADF pages. For ADF pages in an unbounded task flow and bounded task flows that reference templates, you need to make sure that the templates are granted to the application roles that are allowed to access the page or task flow resources, or that the templates are granted to all authenticated users.

NOTE
Page templates are explained in Chapter 15.

Using Regular Expressions and Wildcards in Granting Permission

Grant statements may use regular expression statements or wildcards to define the target resource of a permission. For example, to grant access to all bounded task flows that are stored under the WEB-INF/manager folder to the app_vp role, you use the following grant statement:

```
<grant>
  <grantee>
    <principals>
      <principal>
        <class>
```

```
       oracle.security.jps.service.policystore.ApplicationRole
     </class>
     <name>app_vp</name>
   </principal>
  </principals>
 </grantee>
 <permission>
   <class>
      oracle.adf.controller.security.TaskFlowPermission
   </class>
   <name>/WEB-INF/manager/.*</name>
   <actions>view</actions>
 </permission>
 </permissions>
</grant>
```

Similar, using regular expressions, more complex pattern filters can be defined. For example, to grant permission to all task flows that are located in the WEB-INF\manager directory and start with a lowercase *edit*, followed by a dash and either an uppercase or lowercase *e*, you use the following:

```
<permission>
  <class>
    oracle.adf.controller.security.TaskFlowPermission
  </class>
  <name>/WEB-INF/manager/(?-i)edit-[eE].*</name>
  <actions>view</actions>
</permission>
```

Using regular expressions and wildcards helps to grant permissions to a set of resources, reducing the number of individual permissions that to be defined in the policy store for an application. For the following reasons, wildcards and regular expressions should be used by experienced developers and administrators only:

- The grants don't show in the ADF Security policy editor at design time. They need to be created manually in the jazn-data.xml policy file, which is error-prone.

- Deployed on a production machine, grants that use wildcard or regular expression statements are difficult to read and require that administrators who, for example, perform a security audit understand the scope of an expression.

Creating Custom JAAS Permission Classes

The ADF Security policy editor is a declarative configuration environment for granting permissions of the `RegionPermission` and `TaskFlowPermission` types. This does not mean that the jazn-data.xml file cannot contain other permission grants, such as permissions granted to custom `Permission` classes. Oracle JDeveloper supports application developers creating custom JAAS `Permissions` to be used in the context of ADF Security.

To create a custom JAAS `Permission` class, choose File | New and select the All Technologies tab. Select the Security entry in the Business Tier node to create a new ADF `Permission` class.

The OPSS security platform however provides a generic, or multipurpose, `ResourcePermission` class that can be used to define artifact and method permissions, reducing the need for custom JAAS Permission file. In the "How to Use ADF Security on the Binding Layer" section later in this chapter, we show an example for using the `ResourcePermission` to read-protect binding attributes. This section also shows how to grant custom permissions declaratively in the jazn-data.xml file, which is the same configuration developers use with their own `Permission` classes.

Exceptions Thrown upon Failed Authorization

Users who attempt to access resources for which they are not authorized will receive an exception thrown by the ADF Controller, or an HTTP error, dependent on how the attempt is made. If the protected page or task flow is accessed in the context of ADF Controller navigation, then missing authorization is handled as follows:

■ Navigation to a bounded task flow using a task flow activity or to a stand-alone ADF page causes an `AuthorizationException` to be thrown by the controller. Developers can handle this exception using the declarative exception feature of the ADF Controller, which we explain in Chapter 5.

■ Accessing a protected ADF page directly from a browser requires the user to authenticate if he or she isn't authenticated. If the authenticated user does not have the permissions required to run the page, an HTTP unauthorized error is added to the response that can be handled through settings in the web.xml file.

■ Bounded task flows that are accessed in an ADF Region don't raise an exception but are excluded from rendering in the page in which the ADF Region is located.

NOTE
Bounded task flows that reference stand-alone ADF bound pages can be protected from direct browser access using a configuration setting in the bounded task flow definition. If the visibility node of the task flow definition has the `url-invoke-disallowed` *element set, then any attempt to invoke the task flow directly is answered with an http-403 error indicating that access to this resource is forbidden.*

Security Expression Language

To display ADF Security authorization results in the view layer, security expressions are provided for developers to use as the value of ADF Faces component attributes such as `render`, `display`, and `disabled`. Security expressions help to guide users gracefully through an application, avoiding the use of controls such as command buttons or form input fields that they are not authorized to use. Good practice in application security requires that security becomes apparent only when things go wrong. Until then, the presence of security is hidden by security-aware UI controls. Security Expression Language (EL)in ADF Security helps implement this practice.

Two categories of security expressions are available in ADF Security: global security expressions and expressions that reference ADF Security permissions in the policy store, such as the system-jazn-data.xml file. Global security expressions access information in the `SecurityContext` object and allow developers to display the name of the authenticated user or protect application menus by the enterprise roles of which the authentication user is a member. Expressions that reference permissions in the policy store check authorization for pages and task flows, allowing application developers to hide navigation controls if the user is not allowed to access one of these targets. The following table lists the supported security expressions in ADF Security:

Expression	Description
`#{securityContext.authenticated}`	Returns `true` if the user is authenticated, `false` otherwise.
`#{securityContext.userName}`	Returns the authenticated username or anonymous for unauthenticated users.
`#{securityContext.userInRole['roleList']}`	Checks if user is member of at least one of the listed enterprise or application roles. The role names are comma-separated.
`#{securityContext.userInAllRoles['roleList']}`	Checks if the user is a member in all of the listed roles. Role names are comma-separated.
`#{securityContext.taskflowViewable['target']}`	Checks if the user has permission to access the specified task flow. Returns `true` or `false`.
`#{securityContext.regionViewable['target']}`	Checks if the user has permission to access the specified PageDef file to evaluate the user access to an ADF bound page.
`#{securityContext.userGrantedPermission['permission']}`	Checks if the user has access to a specific permission defined in the policy store. This can be a custom `Permission` class.
`#{securityContext.userGrantedResource['permission']}`	Checks access to a named resource and action. Uses `ResourcePermission` class in OPSS, a multipurpose `Permission` class that saves developers from writing their own.

Using the Expression Builder, which you launch from the Property Inspector in Oracle JDeveloper, the securityContext entry is exposed under the ADF Bindings node, as shown in Figure 21-8.

Using EL to Check JAAS Permissions

The `regionViewable`, `taskflowViewable`, `userGrantedPermission` and `userGrantedResource` expressions shown in Figure 21-8 perform JAAS permission checks against permissions defined in the OPSS policy store. The single argument defines the target of the security check.

■ **regionViewable** Checks access permission for ADF bound pages using the `oracle.adf.share.security.authorization.RegionPermission` class. The function's argument is appended in the form of `['name']` and contains the ADF binding definition filename. The permission action that is checked is View. For example, to check whether the user is allowed to access the JSF page bound to the BrowseDepartmentsPageDef binding file, you use the following expression: `#{securityContext.regionViewable['adf.interactiv.view.pageDefs .BrowseDepartmentsPageDef']}`

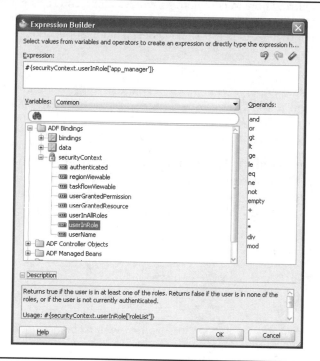

FIGURE 21-8 *Security EL in the Oracle JDeveloper Expression Builder*

- **taskflowViewable** Checks access permission for bounded task flows using the oracle.adf.controller.security.TaskFlowPermission class. The single required argument is appended in the form of ['name'] and defines the task flow by its full name, which consists of the task flow document name and id, prefixed with the WEB-INF folder and subfolder name that the task flow document is stored in. The checked action is "View". For example, to check the permission a user has to view the employees task flow shown in Figure 21-7, you use an expression like `#{securityContext. taskflowViewable['/WEB-INF/employees-task-flow-definition. xml#employees-task-flow-definition']}`

- **userGrantedPermission** Checks for arbitrary user permission, such as custom permissions or permissions defined for ADF Business Components entities. The single argument is appended in the form of `['permissionClass=<class>; target=<target>; action=<action>']` and describes the complete permission string to check. `Permission` classes must be referenced by the package and class names. Actions are provided in a comma-separated list of strings. The result is `true` if the authenticated user has the requested permission granted and `false` if not.

- **userGrantedResource** Checks user permissions to access OPSS-managed resources, implicitly using the `ResourcePermission` class located in the oracle.security.jps package. The required argument is provided in the form `['resoureType=type; resourceName = target; action=a1,a2,…']`. See the "How to Use ADF Security on the Binding Layer" section later in this chapter for an example of how to use this EL and how to configure `ResourcePermissions` permission in jazn-data. xml. Using the generic `ResourcePermission` class saves developers from having to write their own JAAS permission classes, making application security development more productive.

NOTE
Expanding the description area shown in Figure 21-8 provides an example of how to use a selected security expression. The Expression Builder in Oracle JDeveloper does not allow browsing and selecting the argument for the expression. This has to be added manually.

Disabling a Command Button Based on Missing Authorization

Here's an example of how to use security expressions in the ADF Faces view: We'll configure an `af:commandButton` so that it displays only if the user has granted view permissions for the employee task flow, which we protected in Figure 21-7:

```
<af:commandButton text="Show Employees" id="commandButton1"
    action="showEmployees"
    rendered="#{securityContext.taskflowViewable['/WEB-INF/employees-
    task-flow-definition.xml#employees-task-flow-definition']}">
</af:commandButton>
```

NOTE
In your application development, the expression must be provided in a single line with no line breaks.

The command button is located in the BrowseDepartments page that is the application entry point of the navigation flow shown in Figure 21-5. This command button is used to access the employees task flow. Earlier in this chapter, we granted the employees task flow to the app_manager and app_vp application roles. At runtime, this button is therefore hidden for unauthenticated users and authenticated users that are not members in one of the two roles.

TIP
Curiosity killed the cat! If you have a choice between hiding and disabling a component for which a user has not been granted access, choose hide. In JSF, this means not to render the component so it does not even show as hidden in the page-generated source. Showing a component as disabled in the UI can raise a user's curiosity as to what it would do if enabled and how it could be changed to become enabled. To enlarge tailor application UIs based on the authenticated user role, consider leveraging Oracle Metadata Services (MDS) seeded customization using the existing RoleCC customization layer class.

Adding Extra Security Checks to Views, Methods, and Routers Contained in Bounded Task Flows

Pages that are referenced in a bounded task flow but need additional protection can be moved into their own bounded task flow. This bounded task flow is then accessed from the bounded task flow the page originally was in using a task flow call activity. In this case, the ADF Security framework performs an additional permission check for the newly created bounded task flow, allowing finer grained authorization.

However, it is only the ADF Security runtime that does not check permissions for resources contained in a bounded task flow. That does not mean that you cannot do this explicitly using ADF Security EL. For example, if a router activity is contained in a bounded task flow, then the routing decision can be based on a condition including the outcome of a security check on a PageDef file associated with a view or method activity in the same bounded task flow. When a PageDef file is protected using ADF Security, then this is done through an entry in the security policy file, which is jazn-data.xml at design time. Nothing stops you from creating grants for pages that are contained in a bounded task flow to then explicitly check a users access privileges for it.

All the security expressions we've introduced so far can be referenced from views, routers, and other activities in a bounded task flow to evaluate permissions. This is possible because security is not checked by the ADF Security framework but directly against the policy store.

For example, the following router condition allows access to the create new employees page if the user has the permission to create a new employee and if the action parameter passed to the bounded task flow has a value of `create`. If the security check fails, the default activity rejects the request. If the action parameter has a value of `edit`, then no security is checked and the navigation is forwarded to the edit page.

```
<router id="handleEmployeeEdit">
  <case>
    <expression>
      #{pageFlowScope.action =='create' &&
      securityContext.regionViewable['…_CreateInsertPageDef']}
    </expression>
    <outcome>create</outcome>
  </case>
  <case>
    <expression>#{pageFlowScope.action == 'edit'}</expression>
    <outcome>edit</outcome>
  </case>
    <default-outcome>rejectCall</default-outcome>
</router>
```

Note that in this code example, the region value has been abbreviated using an ellipses (...) to fit this page's formatting. The string must actually contain the full page definition filename. Be aware that moving a page that needs extra protection into its own task flow protects it through task flow permission. The task flow permission check is independent from the navigation path that leads to accessing the page. If instead you explicitly define security for a page that is contained in a bounded task flow to perform permission checks in the application programming using EL or Java, as shown in the example above, then it is your responsibility to ensure all access paths to the page resource are protected like this to prevent access for unauthorized users.

TIP

In addition to checking authorization in the router, if this is the default activity of a bounded task flow, we suggest that you also perform the same security check on the component that performs the navigation to the bounded task flow. It is better to hide this component if the user is missing the required permission.

How to Test Security EL

If you are uncertain about whether the security EL you added to a UI component works, run the page in debug mode. Set a break point at the end of the ADF Faces page by clicking the left margin of the source editor. Choose View | Debugger | EL Evaluator from the JDeveloper menu when the page execution stops, which happens when the breakpoint is reached. In the field, type the expression to test, such as the following:

```
#{securityContext.taskflowViewable['/WEB-INF/employees-task-flow-definition.
xml#employees-task-flow-definition']}
```

The debugger immediately shows the result of the EL evaluation, proving your assumption about the expression.

ADF Security in ADF Business Components

ADF Security is used in ADF Business Components to provide access control for entity objects and attributes. Authorization is not enabled when configuring ADF Security for an application but needs to be set explicitly on entity objects or entity object attributes. ADF Faces RC components are security aware in that fields that are not updateable for a user are rendered read-only.

Securing Entity Objects

To enable entity object security, open the entity overview editor by double-clicking the entity in the JDeveloper Application Navigator, or by right-clicking and choosing Open <*entity name*> from the context menu. As shown in Figure 21-9, in the editor, select General and expand the Security: <*entity name*> section. On the entity level, you can enable security for the read, update, and removeCurrentRow operations.

FIGURE 21-9 *Security definition in the entity overview editor*

If security is enabled for an entity, a permission entry is added to the entity object XML definition file with actions defined for the selected operations. The following XML code shows the permission entry that is created for the Employees entity object:

```
<Entity>
    ...
    <Permission
        target="adf.interactiv.model.entities.Employees"
        permissionClass=
          "oracle.adf.share.security.authorization.EntityPermission">
      <privilege-map
        operation="read"
        privilege="read"/>
      <privilege-map
         operation="update"
         privilege="update"/>
       <privilege-map
          operation="removeCurrentRow"
          privilege="delete"/>
      </Permission>
</Entity>
```

This security definition is not a policy, because it does not contain grants. The permission entry defines the permission class to use in authorization checks and the operations for which authorization is required. Operations that are not selected continue to be publicly accessible.

To enforce authorization on the attribute level, select the Attributes category in the entity overview editor to display the list of contained attributes. Select the attribute to protect and expand the Security:<*attribute name*> header. The only security option that is available for attributes is Update. Enabling attribute-level security creates a permission entry in the entity object XML definition, similar to this:

```
<Attribute
    Name="Salary"... >
    <Permission
     target="adf.interactiv.model.entities.Employees.Salary"
     permissionClass=
     "oracle.adf.share.security.authorization.EntityAttributePermission">
    <privilege-map
      operation="update"
      privilege="update"/>
    </Permission>
    ...
</Attribute>
```

If you don't specify grants for the security-enabled entity object artifacts, the default is that this functionality is disabled for any user. This goes in line with the security principle of defining secure defaults, which was mentioned earlier in this chapter.

Authorization defined on entity objects is automatically reflected at runtime. In addition, you can use EL to hide components in response to missing privileges. To check the update and read privileges, you can access the binding layer, as shown next, in which case DepartmentsView1 is a table bound to a view object that is a collection of departments entities:

```
#{bindings.DepartmentsView1.viewable}
#{bindings.DepartmentsView1.updateable}
```

NOTE
The EntityAttributePermission *and* EntityPermission *can be checked in Java as well, as shown later in this chapter. This allows developers to check security in generated and custom Java classes to handle authorization failures gracefully.*

Authorizing Entity Objects

Authorization grants are defined on the entity and attribute levels and stored in the jazn-data.xml policy file. To grant authorization, you use the Structure window, which you open from the View menu in Oracle JDeveloper. Select the entity object in the Application Navigator to display the structure of its definition. In the Structure window, select the entity root node or expand the Attributes node to grant permissions to application roles in the jazn-data.xml file. The Structure window view for the Employees entity is shown in Figure 21-10. Also shown in this figure is the context menu of the entity root node with the Edit Authorization and Edit Security options. The Edit Security option is an alternative way to enable security on an entity. Clicking the Edit Authorization entry opens the Edit Authorization dialog, which is also shown in Figure 21-10.

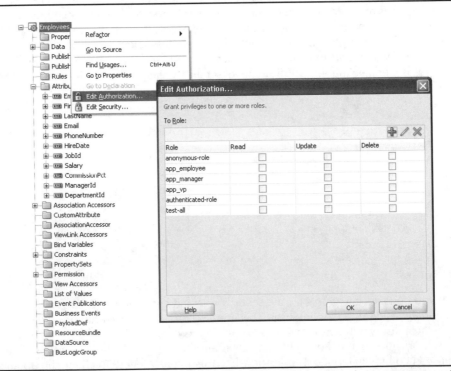

FIGURE 21-10 *Structure view of the entity object definition showing the context menu for the entity root node and the Edit Authorization dialog*

The Edit Authorization dialog lists all application roles that are defined in the jazn-data.xml configuration. Selecting a checkbox at the intersection of an application role and entity action adds the grant statement to the policy file.

To grant entity attribute permission, expand the Attributes node in the Structure window and select the attribute to which you want to grant permission. Right-click and choose Edit Authorization from the context menu to launch the authorization dialog. Select the checkbox for each application role that should be able to update the attribute value.

For example, granting the entity Read, Update, and Delete privileges to the app_vp role, as well as the Update privilege on the Salary attribute, creates the following permission entry in the jazn-data.xml file:

```
<grant>
  <grantee>
    <principals>
      <principal>
        <class>
          oracle.security.jps.service.policystore.ApplicationRole
        </class>
        <name>app_vp</name>
      </principal>
    </principals>
  </grantee>
  ...
    <permission>
      <class>
        oracle.adf.share.security.authorization.EntityPermission
      </class>
      <name>adf.interactiv.model.entities.Employees</name>
      <actions>delete,read,update</actions>
    </permission>
    <permission>
      <class>
        oracle.adf.share.security.authorization.EntityAttributePermission
      </class>
      <name>adf.interactiv.model.entities.Employees.Salary</name>
      <actions>update</actions>
    </permission>
  ...
</grant>
```

NOTE
By using the icons in the header of the Edit Authorization dialog, you can create, delete, and change application roles in the jazn-data.xml file.

Working with ADF Security in Java

The ADF Security `SecurityContext` object is accessible from Java within ADF Business Components and can be used on the application module, entity object, and view object levels to evaluate security conditions. For example, the following example code accesses the `SecurityContext` to detect whether the user is authenticated or anonymous, which is of interest when setting environment parameters or when Oracle RDBMS Virtual Private Database (VPD) security is used.

```
import oracle.adf.share.ADFContext;
import oracle.adf.share.security.SecurityContext;
...
public void prepareSecurityEnv (){
  ADFContext adfContext = ADFContext.getCurrent();
  SecurityContext securityCtx = adfContext.getSecurityContext();
  boolean userAuthenticated = securityCtx.isAuthenticated();
  if(userAuthenticated){
    //prepare environment
    String username = securityCtx.getUserName();
    //...
  }
  else{
    //force use login
  }
}
```

NOTE
The `ADFContext` *object that you access in ADF Business Components is the same object that is used in code you write on the view layer. This object should not be used as an integration layer between the view, the binding, and the business service. Best practice is to keep the different application layers separated, which we also pointed out in Chapter 1. If you need to pass application-specific information from the view layer to the business service, use client methods in ADF BC that you invoke from the binding.*

The `SecurityContext` object also allows for checking permissions stored in the OPSS policy store. This allows developers, for example, to implement the check point security pattern, which adds security checks to areas in an application that are always accessed when performing a task. For example, to check whether the user is allowed to update the Salary attribute on the Employee entity, you use code similar this:

```
...
//create a Hashtable with the information about the
//the permission to check
Hashtable ht = new Hashtable();
//EntityAttributePermission is used to check authorization for
//entity attributes
ht.put(SecurityEnv.JAAS_PERMISSION_CLASS,
  "oracle.adf.share.security.authorization.EntityAttributePermission");
//provide the target and the action to check the permission for
ArrayList paramList = new ArrayList();
paramList.add("adf.interactiv.model.entities.Employees.Salary");
paramList.add("update");
ht.put(PermissionEvaluator.PERMISSION_PARAM_LIST,paramList);
//create the permission instance
```

```
Permission p = securityCtx.createPermissionInstance(ht);
//check permission
boolean updateSalaryAllowed = securityCtx.hasPermission(p);
if (updateSalaryAllowed){
  //perform update
  ...
}
```

To check entity permission—for example, if the current user is allowed to delete rows—you use the same code with a different target and `Permission` class:

 ...

```
Hashtable ht = new Hashtable();
ht.put(SecurityEnv.JAAS_PERMISSION_CLASS,
    "oracle.adf.share.security.authorization.EntityPermission");
ArrayList paramList = new ArrayList();
//reference Entity Object
paramList.add("adf.interactiv.model.entities.Employees");
//entity actions are "read", "update", "delete"
paramList.add("delete");
ht.put(PermissionEvaluator.PERMISSION_PARAM_LIST,paramList);
Permission p = securityCtx.createPermissionInstance(ht);
boolean rowDeleteAllowed = securityCtx.hasPermission(p);
if (rowDeleteAllowed){
  //perform delete
  ...
}
```

NOTE
These code lines are not restricted to the two ADF BC permissions,
`EnityPermission` *and* `EntityAttributePermission`.

Using Groovy Expressions to Implement Row-Level Security

As mentioned in the example that calculates the sum of salaries for departments in Chapter 9, Groovy is a typed Java scripting language that is integrated in ADF BC to promote declarative development without Java.

NOTE
To learn more about Groovy support in ADF BC, refer to the "Oracle Fusion Middleware Fusion Developer's Guide for Oracle Application Development Framework 11g Release 1" product documentation available at http:otn.oracle.com.

In ADF BC, the `ADFContext` object is accessible in Groovy so you can use it to implement security on the business service. An example use case for using Groovy is a commercial website that needs to expose a customer profile for the authenticated customer to provide personal information such as the customer's home and shipping address. To ensure that users see only their profile information and not the information of others, you need to add a query predicate that restricts the query result of the view object to a single row. Using Groovy, you can implement this use case in three steps

1. Create a view criteria as the where clause that is appended to the view object instance that queries the profile information.

2. Use a Groovy expression as the bind variable value expression to obtain the authenticated username and add it to the view criteria.

3. Apply the view criteria to the view object instance exposed on the application module data model.

How to Create the View Criteria, Bind Variable, and Groovy Expression

Using the Oracle HR schema for the example, open the view object that is created for the Employees table in the View Object editor. Select the Query category and click the green plus icon next to the View Criteria section. Provide a name such as *userProfileClause* to the view criteria and define a query like this one:

```
((UPPER(Employees.EMAIL) = UPPER(:useraccount)))
```

You can create the `useraccount` bind variable when creating the view criteria by choosing Bind Variable as the operand and clicking the green plus icon on the Parameter field. The bind variable should be of type String with the Expression value type selected, as shown in Figure 21-11. As shown in Figure 21-11, the value expression of the bind variable is set to the following string, which looks like Java but is actually Groovy:

```
adf.context.securityContext.userName
```

With this expression defined on the bind variable, the where clause defined by the view criteria restricts the query results to employees rows with mail addresses that match the names of the authenticated users.

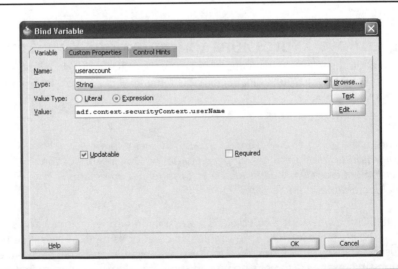

FIGURE 21-11 *Bind Variable dialog with Groovy expression and Value Type set to Expression*

Applying the View Criteria to a View Object Instance

In Chapter 1 we explained that view objects are exposed on the application module as one or many instances. The view object instance is created by opening the application module in its overview editor and selecting the Data Model category. Select a View Object in the Available View Object section and move it to the Data Model list of view objects. Click the pencil icon below the Data Model list next to the View Instance label to change the instance name to UserProfile. Select the UserProfile instance and click the Edit button above the Data Model list box. In the opened Edit View Instance dialog, move the userProfileClause view criteria to the list of selected view criteria. The bind variable has its value set in Groovy, so there is no need to provide a default value.

When running the application, the username is looked up from the `SecurityContext` and added to the where clause of the query. If the view object attribute that is referenced by the where clause is unique, then only a single row, the user profile, is returned.

Virtual Private Database

A stronger protection than using a view criteria to control row-level data access is the Virtual Private Database (VPD) feature available in the Enterprise Edition of Oracle Database (RDBMS). VPD is also known as row-level security (RLS) and dynamically applies a where clause, the predicate, to a target, such as the Employees table or a column therein, and operations, such as select or Data Manipulation Language (DML) statements. VPD provides row-level access security with the security policy defined in PL/SQL.

VPD can be integrated with Oracle ADF BC to filter result set of a query performed by a view object. To use VPD from Oracle ADF BC, developers need to pass information about the authenticated user to the security context created in the database.

NOTE
The following information is not meant to be a tutorial on using VPD but is intended to show the integration between ADF BC and Oracle RDBMS security. A good book about Oracle database security is Effective Oracle Database 10g Security by Design, *written by David C. Knox, published by McGraw-Hill/Osborne in 2004. Or, if you prefer, the* Oracle Database Security Guide 11g Release 1 *product documentation is available online at http://otn.oracle.com.*

The use case that we demonstrate in the following paragraphs leverages VPD so that users see only their own data and the data of employees that report to them. Only the user sking, which is the president of the company, is allowed to see all data.

The example is implemented in two steps:

1. *Prepare the Oracle database.* We explain briefly the steps that are required to create and enable a VPD policy in a protected database schema. The PL/SQL procedures and function discussed in this section implement the policy

2. *Set up ADF BC for VPD.* We demonstrates the changes that are needed in the application module implementation code to access a PL/SQL store procedure that creates the application context used by VPD security. If you are savvy with database security and VPD. then you can skip the first section.

Preparing the Oracle Database

For the setup, you need the Enterprise Edition of the Oracle database with the HR demo schema installed and enabled. You also need administration privileges to create user accounts, grant permissions, and create the security context.

The VPD package and function is installed in a separate schema, secmgr in this example, to protect it from public access. You need to create this account first. The secmgr user needs the create any context and create view system privilege, as well as the resource role granted. Some of the privileges, such as creating procedures and resources, are needed only to set up the VPD environment and can be removed later. The SQL statement to create the user account is shown here:

```
CREATE USER "SECMGR"  PROFILE "DEFAULT"
IDENTIFIED BY "welcome1" DEFAULT TABLESPACE "USERS"
TEMPORARY TABLESPACE "TEMP"
ACCOUNT UNLOCK;
GRANT CREATE ANY CONTEXT TO "SECMGR";
GRANT CREATE SESSION TO "SECMGR";
GRANT CREATE VIEW TO "SECMGR";
GRANT "CONNECT" TO "SECMGR";
GRANT CREATE PROCEDURE TO "SECMGR";
GRANT "RESOURCE" TO "SECMGR";
```

To create the stored PL/SQL procedure and function that implement the security policy, connect to the secmgr account using SQL Worksheet in Oracle JDeveloper 11*g* or SQL Plus and type the following:

```
CREATE CONTEXT CTXHR USING SECMGR.CTXHRPCKG;
```

NOTE
Before you can use the SQL Worksheet in Oracle JDeveloper 11g, you need to create a database connection for the secmgr schema, by choosing View | Database | Database Navigator. To open SQL Worksheet, choose Tools | Database | SQL Worksheet.

Connect to the database using a user account that has DBA privileges to grant user secmgr access to the Employees table in the HR schema:

```
GRANT SELECT ON "HR"."EMPLOYEES" TO "SECMGR";
```

The secmgr schema needs access to the Employees data to verify the user account and to retrieve information used in the VPD policy. For simplicity, in this example we create a physical copy of the employee table as the user table in the secmgr schema as follows:

```
CREATE TABLE HRAPPUSERS AS SELECT
   DEPARTMENT_ID, EMPLOYEE_ID, JOB_ID, EMAIL
FROM HR.EMPLOYEES;
```

NOTE
In a production system, user information may be stored in the Oracle Internet Directory (OID) and accessed from PL/SQL. If user data are stored in database tables, make sure these are protected from direct access, for example using a PL/SQL stored procedure.

The next step is the installation of the packages that that contain the VPD policy for this example to the secmgr schema. The next PL/SQL code shown defines stored procedures that are called from ADF Business Components in a prepared statement. The set_user_info procedure takes as single argument, which is the name of the authenticated application user in ADF BC.

The procedure queries the user detail information from the database view that we created for the Employees table in the HR schema and stores it in the database application context. The application context is a set of key value pairs that are stored in memory for fast access and that can be read and set by users and applications. The name of the application context is used like a namespace in Java EE and is defined as ctxhr for this example; it holds the EMPLOYEE_ID and JOB_ID column values of the authenticated user.

```
REM SECMGR CTXHRPCKG
CREATE OR REPLACE PACKAGE "SECMGR"."CTXHRPCKG" AS
  PROCEDURE set_userinfo (app_user VARCHAR2);
  PROCEDURE clear_userinfo;
END;
/
CREATE OR REPLACE PACKAGE BODY "SECMGR"."CTXHRPCKG" AS
  PROCEDURE set_userinfo(app_user VARCHAR2)
  AS
    -- the employee id and the job role is what the VPD policy in
    -- the example is based on
    p_deptno NUMBER;
    p_employeeno NUMBER;
    p_jobrole VARCHAR2(100);
  BEGIN
    -- get the user information for the authenticated user. This assumes
    -- that the username matches the value of the EMAIL column
    BEGIN
      SELECT DEPARTMENT_ID, EMPLOYEE_ID, JOB_ID
      INTO   p_deptno,p_employeeno,p_jobrole
      FROM HRAPPUSERS
      WHERE lower(EMAIL) = lower(app_user);
    EXCEPTION
      WHEN no_data_found THEN
      -- Setting employee number to 0, which means we lock the access
      p_employeeno := 0;
      p_jobrole :='EMPLOYEE';
    END;
    -- write the user detail information into the database session
    -- in a named context, which is accessed by the VPD policy function
    DBMS_SESSION.set_context(NAMESPACE => 'ctxhr',
                             ATTRIBUTE => 'user_empno',
                             VALUE => p_employeeno);
    DBMS_SESSION.set_context(NAMESPACE => 'ctxhr',
                             ATTRIBUTE => 'user_jobrole',
                             VALUE => p_jobrole);
  END;
  -- do some housekeeping
  PROCEDURE clear_userinfo
```

```
    AS
    BEGIN
      DBMS_SESSION.CLEAR_CONTEXT(NAMESPACE => 'ctxhr',
                                 ATTRIBUTE => 'user_empno');
      DBMS_SESSION.CLEAR_CONTEXT(namespace => 'ctxhr',
                                 ATTRIBUTE => 'user_jobrole');
    END;
  END;
  /
```

A PL/SQL function needs to be created that is associated with the Employees table in the HR schema and invoked whenever the Employees table is queried. The mapping of the table operation to the function is defined as the VPD policy.

```
REM SECMGR EMPLOYEES_READACCESS_FKT
CREATE OR REPLACE FUNCTION "SECMGR"."EMPLOYEES_READACCESS_FKT" (
    p_schema IN VARCHAR2 default NULL,
    p_object IN VARCHAR2 default NULL)
RETURN VARCHAR2 AS
  -- users should not get any data if they are not authorized
  p_whereclause Varchar2(400):= '1=2';
  p_empno Number;
  p_jobid  Varchar2(100);
  p_args   Varchar2(100);
BEGIN
  p_empno := SYS_CONTEXT('ctxhr','user_empno');
  p_jobid :=  SYS_CONTEXT('ctxhr','user_jobrole');
  -- show only users data for users that report to the logged in
  -- user and the user's own data
  p_args := 'manager_id = '||nvl(p_empno,0)||
            ' OR employee_id = '||nvl(p_empno,0);
  -- check if user is President
  if (nvl(p_jobid,'EMPLOYEE') LIKE '%PRES') THEN
    -- add argument that always returns true
    p_args := '1=1';
  END IF;
  p_whereclause :- p_whereclause ||' OR '|| p_args;
  RETURN p_whereclause;
END;
/
```

With the infrastructure in place, we can now create the VPD policy, mapping the PL/SQL function to the Employees table. We connect to the database with a user that has SYSDBA privileges and type (on a single line) the following:

```
EXECUTE DBMS_RLS.ADD_POLICY(
  'HR', 'Employees','employees_read_access_policy','secmgr',
  'EMPLOYEES_READACCESS_FKT','select');
```

The following arguments are passed to ADD_POLICY:

- The database schema of the table to protect, which is the HR schema in this example

- The table name to protect: Employees

- The name of the policy so it can be revoked

- The schema that contains the policy function—secmgr in this example

- The PL/SQL function that implements the policy

- The operation to protect—select in this example

The application is assumed to work against the HR schema, which means that the call to the PL/SQL procedure that sets the application context for the user is from the HR schema. Therefore, the HR schema needs to be granted access to the stored procedure in the secmgr schema. To simplify the access to the package, we also define a synonym for it:

```
GRANT EXECUTE ON "SECMGR"."CTXHRPCKG" TO "HR";
```

We connect to the HR schema and type the following:

```
CREATE SYNONYM ctxhrpckg FOR secmgr.ctxhrpckg;
```

Testing the VPD Configuration   Assuming the configuration completed without errors, it's a good time to try a first functional test. Using SQL Plus or SQL Worksheet, connect to the HR schema and issue the following commands:

```
execute ctxhrpckg.set_userinfo('ahunold');
select * from employees;
```

The query should return fewer records returned when doing the same for the sking account.

Removing and Disabling Policies

```
-- command must be in single line
EXECUTE DBMS_RLS.DROP_POLICY (
  'HR', 'Employees','employees_read_access_policy');
```

NOTE
This example above is for demonstration purpose only and should not be put into production without further security checking. If you plan to use VPD with your web applications, which we recommend you to do, make sure you first gain the required expertise.

Setting Up ADF BC for VPD

The application context is set from the `prepareSession` method of the ADF BC application module implementation class. The `prepareSession` method is called the first time an application module is created and each subsequent time it gets used by a different session. To override the `prepareSession` method, you open the application module in the overview editor, select the Java category, and create the Java implementation class for the application module. With the Java class opened in the Java source code editor, choose Source | Override Methods and select the prepareSession entry. Override the `prepareSession` method as shown next:

```
public void prepareSession(Session _session){
  super.prepareSession(_session);
  //get the authenticated username
  ADFContext adfContext = ADFContext.getCurrent();
  SecurityContext securityCtx = adfContext.getSecurityContext();
  String username = securityCtx.getUserName();
  //define the prepared statement to call the PL/SQL procedure that
  //prepares the application context
  String appContext =
    "Begin ctxhrpckg.set_userinfo('"+username+"'); END;";
  java.sql.CallableStatement st= null;
  try{
    //get ADF BC transaction to execute the statement
    st = getDBTransaction().createCallableStatement(appContext,0);
    st.execute();
  } catch (java.sql.SQLException s){
    throw new oracle.jbo.JboException(s);
  } finally{
    try{
      if (st!= null){
        st.close();
      }
    } catch (java.sql.SQLException s2){
      //raise exception to handle in ADF
    }
  }
}
```

Testing Secured ADF BC Modules

You don't need to build a web application first to test VPD with ADF BC. ADF BC provides a tester that you invoke by right-clicking the application module in the model project and choosing Run from the context menu. If the ADF BC project is configured for ADF Security, the login dialog shown in Figures 21-12 and 21-13 is displayed. Provide the username and password of one of the accounts created in the jazn-data.xml file and click OK to close the dialog. Figures 21-12 and 21-13 show the employee data for ahunold and sking, filtered by the VPD policy.

ADF Security: Advanced Topics

This section provides sample implementations of common security use cases using ADF Security and additional configuration options that go beyond the default ADF Region and task flow authorization.

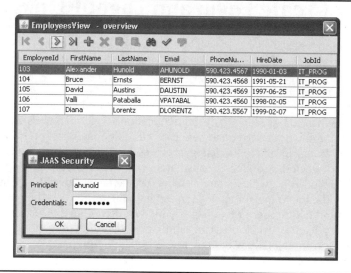

FIGURE 21-12   *Employee data for ahunold*

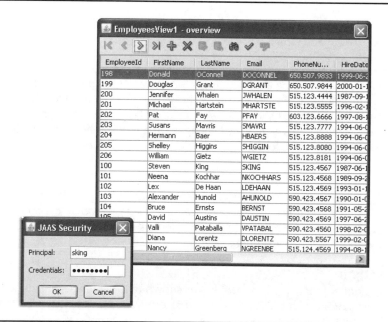

FIGURE 21-13   *Employee data for sking*

How to Create Login and Logout Links

Earlier in this chapter, we explained how users authenticate in ADF Security, mentioning the authentication types available in Java EE container-managed security. We also mentioned that authentication is enforced when users access a protected page or bounded task flow. However, we did not yet cover how users can actively trigger a login form to be shown, for example by clicking a link, to log in, in advance.

The ADF authentication servlet is configured and secured in the web.xml descriptor by the configuration wizard. Navigating to the authentication servlet, which is what the ADF and the ADF task flow framework do for unauthenticated users if they access resources that require authentication, brings up the login dialog, triggered by the Java EE container. The authentication servlet itself is protected by a Java EE role that, during deployment, is mapped to an enterprise role of which all authenticated users are members on the target server. Once users are authenticated, control is passed back to the authentication servlet, which redirects the request to the page initially requested by the user or to a page defined by the developer. Therefore, to allow users to authenticate in advance, developers can simply provide a link that allows the users to navigate to the authentication servlet URL with the information about the page to return. The following page source shows an example of such a link in ADF Faces:

```
<af:goImageLink
  text="#{securityContext.authenticated ?'Logout':'Login'}" id="ctb1"
  icon="#{securityContext.authenticated ?
    '/images/lock.gif':'/images/key.gif'}"
  destination="#{securityContext.authenticated ?
    '/adfAuthentication?logout=true&amp;end_url=/faces/Welcome.jspx':
    '/adfAuthentication?success_url=/faces/BrowseDepartments.jspx'}"/>
```

This source code uses ADF Security EL to determine the `text`, `icon`, and `destination` attribute values based on the application session authentication status. Figures 21-14 and 21-15 show the login link in action. Figure 21-14 shows the unauthenticated case in which the user is anonymous and the link text shows "Login." Figure 21-15 shows the authenticated case in which the link says "Logout" and the icon has changed. In addition, the Show Employees button appears, which was hidden for anonymous users.

NOTE
The `af:goImageLink` *is a new component in JDeveloper 11 R1 Patch Set 1 and does not exist in prior releases. If you are on an earlier release, make sure you replace this component usage with another before deploying the application.*

Perform Login

If the user is not authenticated, a Login link is shown that references the authentication servlet in its `destination` attribute. The `success_url` request parameter is added to the URL for the servlet to redirect the request after successful authentication.

If the Login/Logout link is provided as part of a page template, and if, after successful authentication, the request should be directed back to the page that initially requested the login, then a more dynamic approach is required to build the `success_url` parameter. The following

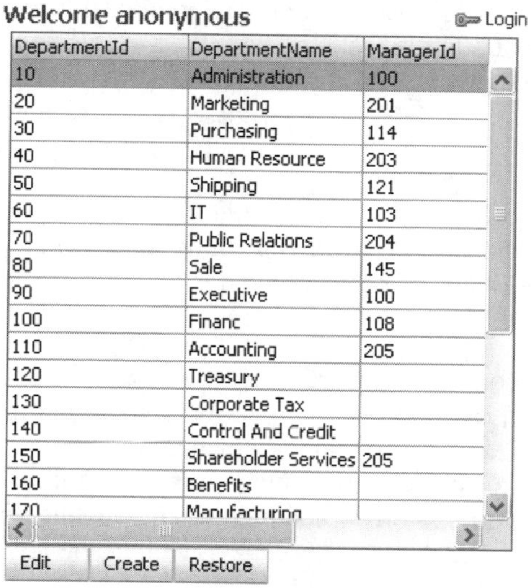

FIGURE 21-14   *Anonymous Welcome screen with Login link*

page source shows only the changed value for the `destination` attribute. Note that the current page's `viewId` is appended as a value of the `success_url` parameter using EL.

```
destination="#{securityContext.authenticated ?
'/adfAuthentication?logout=true&amp;end_url=/faces/welcome.jspx' :
'/adfAuthentication?success_url=/faces'}#{!securityContext.authenticated ?
facesContext.viewRoot.viewId : ''}"
```

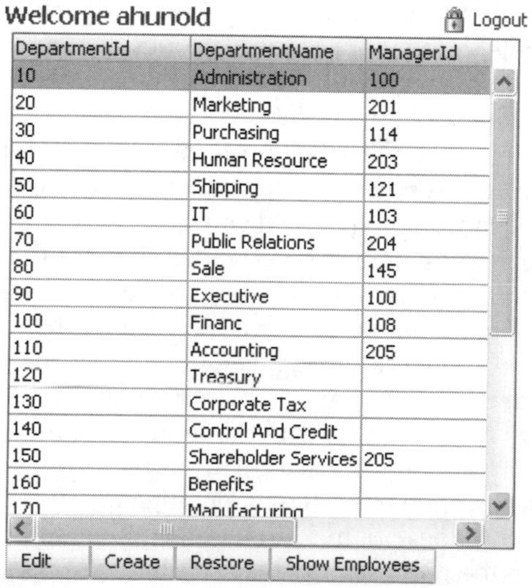

FIGURE 21-15   *User ahunold Welcome screen with Show Employees button and Logout link*

What happens if the `success_url` parameter is not provided? In this case, the authentication servlet uses the value of the `success_url` servlet initialization parameter that the application developer may have set up in the web.xml file. If this entry is missing, then as a last attempt, the session is looked up in case the ADF Controller defined the return URL. If all of this fails, an exception is thrown.

NOTE
As shown in the logout URL, a Login *request parameter can be passed to the authentication servlet. This, however, is not required if the authentication itself is protected, which is the default.*

Perform Logout

If the user is authenticated upon page rendering, a logout link is shown that references the authentication servlet in its `destination` attribute. In addition, two request parameters, `logout` and `end_url`, are passed that identify the request as a logout request and the page destination to navigate to after logout. During logout, the authentication servlet cleans up all traces of the authenticated session, which includes the invalidation of the session, removal of the authenticated `Subject` and its `Principals`, as well as the logout from supported single sign-on implementations such as Oracle Access Manager (OAM).

NOTE
ADF Security does not handle user authentication but delegates this to the WebLogic Server. Same is true for logging user sessions out, which is triggered by ADF Security but handled by the container.

Usage and Lookup Precedence of the `success_url` and `end_url` Parameters

Authentication is triggered by ADF Security when an authorization failure occurs for an unauthenticated user session or when a user logs in through a login command. Similarly, application logout is performed by the user clicking a logout command.

To determine the page to display after a user logged in to or out of an application, the ADF Security authentication servlet checks if the `success_url` and `end_url` information is available as an attribute in the user session, a request parameter on the URL or a servlet initialization parameter in the web.xml file. If authentication is triggered by an authorization failure, then the ADF authentication servlet first checks the user session for the `success_url` attribute, which is implicitly set by the ADF controller or the ADF model. In case no session attribute could be found, the servlet reads the information provided on the request URL, if any. If a user logs in to an application using a login command, no `success_url` session attribute exists and the `success_url` request parameter is read. In both of the above cases, if no `success_url` definition can be found in the session or the request, in a last attempt, the `success_url` servlet initialization parameter in the web.xml file is tried. The log out process, which looks up the `end_url`, is handled similar to the login.

Because the `success_url` and `end_url` session attribute always take precedence over the same information added as parameters defined on the request or configured in the web.xml file, developers may explicitly set the `success_url` and `end_url` attributes to the session in their application programming to prevent external modification of this settings. As a hint of best practices, if an application does not make use of the ability to provide the `success_url` and `end_url` parameters in the request URL, then it is better to disable this option as mentioned above. The `success_url` and `end_url` information lookup order explained in this section is a changed behavior in Oracle JDeveloper 11g R1 Patch Set 1. In earlier versions of Oracle JDeveloper, the `success_url` and `end_url` parameters in the request URL took precedence over the information stored in the session. To retain the old behavior, or for use cases in which the information in the URL should take precedence over the information in the session, two new servlet initialization parameters `allow_success_url_param_overwrite` and `allow_logout_url_param_overwrite` are available for use in the web.xml file. To enable the old behavior, you set these parameters to true as shown below.

```
<servlet>
   <servlet-name>adfAuthentication</servlet-name>
   <servlet-class>
     oracle.adf.share.security.authentication.AuthenticationServlet
   </servlet-class>
   <init-param>
     <param-name>success_url</param-name>
     <param-value>authenticatedUserWelcome.jspx</param-value>
   </init-param>
   <init-param>
     <param-name>allow_success_url_param_overwrite</param-name>
     <param-value>true</param-value>
   </init-param>
   <init-param>
     <param-name>allow_logout_url_param_overwrite</param-name>
     <param-value>true</param-value>
   </init-param>
   <load-on-startup>1</load-on-startup>
</servlet>
```

How to Create a Login Form in JSF

Form-based Java EE login is the preferred choice of many developers to authenticate users, because it allows them to apply the application look and feel to integrate the login with the application. Unfortunately, building login forms in JSF is not trivial, because no standard component exists to handle authentication. This surely has to do with the lack of a standard programming API for authentication.

NOTE
The servlet 3.0 specification defines programmatic authentication for Java EE 6. However, Java EE 6 is not available as of this writing, so for this book, we continue looking for a manual solution.

Several solutions can be used to implement a login form integrated in an ADF Faces page, including the following:

- **HTML form in JSF**   The HTML page markup for the authentication form is embedded in the JSF page code. The form, when submitted, performs a request to j_security_check and passed the j_username and j_password parameters for authentication. This is how applications have authenticated since the early days of the dynamic web. This approach allows the use of JSF pages as login pages, but it does not allow direct logins. Instead, it requires the page to be accessed by the container in response to a user accessing a protected resource.

■ **JSF login form**   Some Java EE container vendors, Oracle included, provide proprietary APIs that allow applications to authenticate users programmatically. Using this approach, the login field and submit button are built with JSF components, and the submit action runs through the JSF lifecycle, allowing the user to verify the username and password before the request is passed to the container for authentication.

Creating an HTML Form in JSF

Direct HTML markup integration in JSF pages is possible since JSF 1.2, which is used by ADF Faces RC in JDeveloper 11*g*. However, it still is not a smooth integration, and for various reasons it should be avoided when possible. However, for the simple case of a login form, the current state of this integration is mature enough. The following page code shows how an HTML form can be embedded in a JSF page so it can be used for Java EE container-managed authentication. Figure 21-16 shows the login form that is created by the following code sample:

```
<af:showDetailHeader text="Login" disclosed="true" id="sdh1">
  <af:panelGroupLayout id="pgl4" inlineStyle="width:500.0px;"
    layout="vertical">
  <af:menuBar id="mb1">
    <af:commandMenuItem text="People Finder" id="cmi1" …/>
    <af:commandMenuItem text="Corporate Policies" id="cmi2" …/>
    <af:commandMenuItem text="Help" id="cmi3" …/>
  </af:menuBar>
  <af:decorativeBox id="db1" theme="light"  inlineStyle="height:150px;">
    <f:facet name="center">
      <af:panelGroupLayout id="pgl1" layout="horizontal"
        inlineStyle="height:100.0px;">
      <af:panelGroupLayout id="pgl3">
        <!-- HTML MARKUP START -->
        <form action="j_security_check" method="POST">
          <table>
            <tbody>
             <tr>
              <td>Username</td>
              <td><input type="text" name="j_username"/></td>
             </tr>
             <tr>
              <td>Password</td>
              <td><input type="password" name="j_password"/></td>
             </tr>
             <tr>
              <td align="right" colspan="2">
                <input id="login" type="submit" value="Log In"
                onclick="this.disabled=true; this.form.submit();"/>
              </td>
             </tr>
            </tbody>
          </table>
        </form>
        <!-- HTML MARKUP END -->
```

```
            </af:panelGroupLayout>
            <af:panelGroupLayout id="pgl2">
              <af:spacer width="10" height="10" id="s1"/>
              <af:image source="/images/oracle_buildings.jpg" id="i1"/>
            </af:panelGroupLayout>
          </af:panelGroupLayout>
        </f:facet>
      </af:decorativeBox>
    </af:panelGroupLayout>
  </af:showDetailHeader>
```

If you configured ADF Security to use form-based authentication, the web.xml file needs to be changed as shown next to reference the JSF page for container-managed authentication:

```
<login-config>
  <auth-method>FORM</auth-method>
  <form-login-config>
    <form-login-page>/faces/login.jspx</form-login-page>
    <form-error-page>/error.html</form-error-page>
  </form-login-config>
</login-config>
```

NOTE
When you integrate the HTML form in a JSF page, make sure it is not surrounded by an af:form *component. If it is, the JDeveloper IDE flags this as an error that you should take seriously. Form-based authentication does not work if contained in an ADF Faces form element.*

Creating a Login Form in JSF

As mentioned, no Java EE standard is yet available that defines an API for programmatic authentication. However, application developers who need to build a native login form in JSF require such an API for Java code executing in a managed bean to authenticate a user. In such cases, a vendor specific solution, such as the API provided by Oracle WebLogic Server, may be

FIGURE 21-16 *The HTML Login form*

chosen to implement the use case. The page and managed bean code shown next explains how to use the WebLogic `ServletAuthentication` for programmatic authentication:

```
<af:panelFormLayout id="pf1" rendered="#{!securityContext.authenticated}">
  <af:message for="usrfield" partialTriggers="loginBut"/>
  <af:inputText label="Username" id="usrfield"/>
  <af:inputText label="Password" secret="true" id="pwfield"/>
  <af:commandButton text="Login" actionListener="#{LoginBean.login}"
    id="loginBut"/>
</af:panelFormLayout>
```

Figure 21-17 shows the login screen displaying an error message for a failed authentication. Note that the display of error messages makes a difference compared to using a HTML form because the user is not directed away from the page and instead can immediately see the authentication feedback.

The login screen is rendered only if the user is not authenticated, which is handled by ADF Security EL on the `af:panelFormLayout` component. The username and input fields have a meaningful `id` attribute defined but don't use the `value` attribute. Since username and password are needed only for the duration of the authentication request, there is no need to create a managed bean property for it. The `af:commandButton` component submits the request and invokes a login method by its `actionListener` attribute reference.

The managed bean code shown next finds the username and password fields in the JSF view root, reads the values, and uses the `ServletAuthentication` in Oracle WebLogic to authenticate the user:

```
import weblogic.servlet.security.ServletAuthentication;
...
public void login(ActionEvent actionEvent) {
  FacesContext fctx = FacesContext.getCurrentInstance();
  HttpServletRequest request = null;
  request = (HttpServletRequest)fctx.getExternalContext().getRequest();
  HttpServletResponse response = null;
  response = (HttpServletResponse)fctx.getExternalContext().getResponse();
  //instead of using JSF value binding to access the username and
  //password field components, we look it up in the UIViewroot. In many
  //cases this is a better approach than the easier to use JSF binding
  UIViewRoot viewRoot = fctx.getViewRoot();
  RichInputText username =
    (RichInputText)viewRoot.findComponent("usrfield");
  String usernameStr = (String)username.getValue();
  RichInputText password =
    (RichInputText)viewRoot.findComponent("pwfield");
  String passwordStr = (String)password.getValue();
    try {
      int authSuccess = ServletAuthentication.login(
        usernameStr, passwordStr,request, response);
```

```
    //perform authentication against the authentication
    //provider configured in WebLogic Server
    if (authSuccess == ServletAuthentication.AUTHENTICATED) {
    try {
      //to see the outcome of the authentication, we need to redirect
      //upon authentication security so container managed security
      //gets aware of the authenticated user
      ExternalContext ectx = fctx.getExternalContext();
      ectx.redirect("faces/" + viewRoot.getViewId());
    } catch (IOException e) {
      e.printStackTrace();
    }
  }
} catch (LoginException le) {
  //if authentication fails then there is no need to redirect the
  //request and the PPR trigger set up on the message component
  //ensures that the error message is displayed to the user
  String message = "Authentication failed Please try again";
  fctx.addMessage("usrfield",
              new FacesMessage(FacesMessage.SEVERITY_ERROR,
              message, null));
  }
}
```

The managed bean does not hold any state and can be configured in request scope or with no scope.

NOTE
The security chapter in the "Oracle Fusion Middleware Fusion Developer's Guide for Oracle Application Development Framework 11g" documentation provides a different but comparable solution for programmatic authentication.

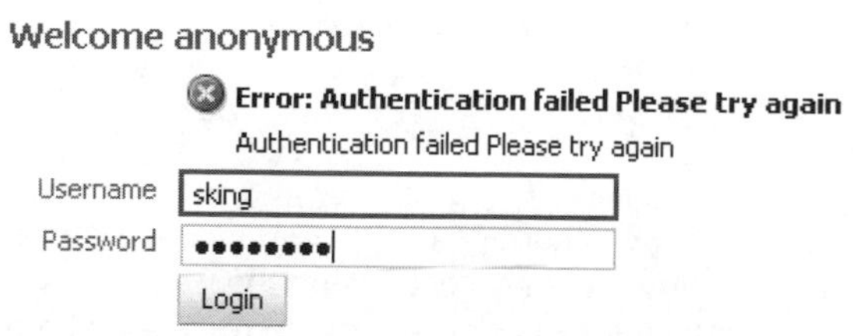

Welcome anonymous

⊗ **Error: Authentication failed Please try again**
Authentication failed Please try again

| Username | sking |
| Password | •••••••• |

Login

FIGURE 21-17 *Login screen displaying an error message for a failed authentication*

How to Use ADF Security on the Binding Layer

Bindings in the PageDef file have a `viewable` property that developers can use to extend security to the binding layer using ADF Security EL. For example, instead of defining the visibility of a UI component by checking the user read permission with EL on the component `visible` or `rendered` attribute, you can define this on the binding layer. The UI components reference the viewable property using EL to determine their visibility.

Following are the benefits of defining authorization in the binding layer:

- Multiple UI components that reference the binding as a data source use a single security definition. A change in the authorization needs to be done only in the PageDef file and not on all the impacted UI components.

- Attribute read access, which is not natively available in ADF BC security, can be implemented easily.

- Menu components that reference ADF binding operations, such as actions or methods, can be hidden from unauthorized users.

The OPSS ResourcePermission

JAAS permissions are designed to protect objects. Often, however, developers need to protect resources that don't represent objects but represent methods, menu items or operations instead. Even without this requirement, developers creating custom JAAS permissions create more problems than those permissions solve if no corporate process has been defined to manage the design and use of permission classes.

Multiple permission classes that are created to protect the same object make it difficult to create a consistent protection strategy that clearly defines who is allowed to do what, not only within an application but across applications. This said, permissions may be required as application-specific permissions but are usually defined as generic, such as the `EntityPermission` in ADF Business Components.

The OPSS `ResourcePermission` is a generic resource permission that can be used to protect various targets based on a defined resource types and multiple supported actions. At design time, the `ResourcePermission` is configured in the jazn-data.xml policy store, using this syntax:

```
<permission>
  <class>oracle.security.jps.ResourcePermission</class>
    <name>resourceType=type,resourceName=name</name>
  <actions>comma separated list of actions</actions>
</permission>
```

If you are familiar with JAAS, you'll notice the special use of the `name` element, which in JAAS defines the target name of a protected object. Using the OPSS `ResourcePermission`, this `name` is defined as two parts: a resource type and the resource name. The resource type qualifies the type of resource to protect. This could be define as Page, TaskFlow, Attribute, Entity, Method, Operation, or whatever resource categories developers come up with. The resource name then defines the target. For example, to define the permission for an entity attribute in ADF Business Components, you could use this:

```
<permission>
  <class>oracle.security.jps.ResourcePermission</class>
  <name>
    resourceType=Attribute,resourceName=EmployeesViewSalary
  </name>
  <actions>read</actions>
</permission>
```

NOTE
The Attribute name is an arbitrary name describing the type of the protected resource. In your application development you may use other strings, like MenuItem, NavigationItem, or whatever makes sense.

As mentioned when explaining ADF Security in the context of ADF Business Components, there is no native read protection on the entity attribute level yet. This can, however, be implemented using the `ResourcePermission`, as we show in the following code snippet. The `ResourcePermission`, like any other permission, can be checked using Java in a managed bean or business service method, or using EL, in which case a convenience expression, `userGrantedResource`, exists that can be used on UI components and in the ADF binding layer:

```
//use the string as a single line
#{securityContext.userGrantedResource['resourceType=Attribute;
    resourceName=EmployeesViewSalary;action=read']}
```

Granting ResourcePermissions to Application Roles

The visual policy editor does not yet provide an option to configure declaratively custom JAAS permissions and the OPSS `ResourcePermission` grants to application roles and, if required, user principals. To grant custom permissions to application roles in the jazn-data.xml policy store, a developer can use the configuration editor that is accessible from the Structure window in Oracle JDeveloper. For example, to grant the Salary read permission used as an example in this chapter, you need to do the following:

1. Select the jazn-data.xml file in the Application Resources | Descriptors | META-INF location in Oracle JDeveloper.

2. Open the Structure window.

3. Expand the jazn-data | policy-store | applications | jazn-policy node. This node contains all the grant entries, which contain the information about the grantee. Choose the grant entry that belongs to the Principal that should have a specific permission granted.

4. If the grant entry is found, select the permission child entry, right click, and choose Insert inside permissions | permission from the context menu. This launches the permission grant editor shown in Figure 21-18.

5. In the permission grant editor dialog, define the permission class, name, and the actions to grant to the grantees. If multiple actions are allowed, add them as a comma-separated list.

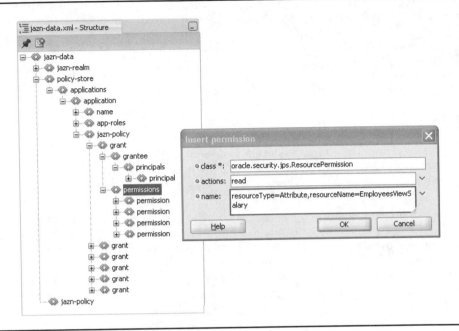

FIGURE 21-18 *Permission grant editor dialog*

NOTE
If you change Permissions in the policy file, it may be required to stop the integrated WebLogic Server instance before testing the application.

Configuring Read Access for Entity Attributes

An entity attribute is a resource to protect. It is natively protected in ADF BC security against unauthorized updates and deletes, which are defined on the entity. The read permission, the authorization for whether or not users are allowed to see the attribute rendered in the UI, needs to be implemented on the ADF binding layer or on the ADF Faces UI component. As with ADF BC entity objects, which the application developers adds access control by explicitly enabling security on the object, UI components and binding attributes are publicly accessible by default. UI components and binding attributes are protected only if security is enabled on the ADF BC service and if the developer uses Java or EL to check permission on them.

To implement attribute read protection on the binding layer, the `viewable` property that exists on different binding types can be used. For example, to ensure that the employee salary field is displayed only to managers, you define the following definition on the attribute binding through the Property Inspector:

```
<!-- attribute values are entered without line breaks! The example -->
<!-- below uses linebreaks in the viewable attribute for formatting -->
<attributeValues IterBinding="EmployeesView1Iterator" id="Salary"
  Viewable=
    "#{securityContext.userGrantedResource
      ['resourceType=Attribute;
        resourceName=EmployeesViewSalary;action=read']}">
```

```
<AttrNames>
  <Item Value="Salary"/>
</AttrNames>
</attributeValues>
```

NOTE
*This example shows the advantage of JAAS-based authorization
compared to role-based security. In role-based security, all roles
that require access to this attribute would need to be listed. In JAAS,
this is a single permission check. If more groups require access to a
resource, there is no need to change the application in JAAS, but the
membership assignment of an application role could be done by an
administrator in Enterprise Manager.*

To display the impact of read access in the UI, the UI component needs to reference the
`viewable` property of the attribute binding in its `visible` or `rendered` property:

```
<af:inputText value="#{bindings.Salary.inputValue}" …
              rendered="#{bindings.Salary.viewable}"/>
```

The difference between setting a component `visible` attribute to `false` and setting its
`rendered` attribute to `false` is that a component that is not visible shows in the source of the
generated HTML output, whereas the component that is not rendered doesn't show at all. For all
sensitive data, you should use the `rendered` attribute and set it to `false`.

NOTE
*Although tree bindings that are used to populate tree and table
components provide a viewable property, this is not on the column
level. To read-protect columns in tables, you define the permission
check in the UI.*

Deploying ADF Security–Protected Applications

Oracle ADF applications can be deployed using the Oracle WebLogic Server Administration
Console, Oracle Enterprise Manager Fusion Middleware Control, or Oracle JDeveloper. Usually
Oracle JDeveloper 11*g* is used to deploy applications for testing to the integrated WebLogic
Server instance but not to deploy applications to a production server. For ADF applications, the
recommended deployment option is Enterprise Manager Fusion Middleware Control because it
provides an environment that allows you to refine the configuration of the deployed application.

Note that Oracle WebLogic Server can be installed in production and development modes.
The development mode has relaxed security enforcement for what can be changed automatically
during deployment.

NOTE
*To avoid deployment problems, refer to the Oracle Fusion Middleware
Security Guide 11g documentation to learn about the deployment of
protected applications.*

Policy Migration

ADF applications that are protected with ADF Security usually have test users' enterprise roles and permissions defined in the application-wide jazn-data.xml file–based policy store. During deployment, the policy grants and application roles of this file, and optionally defined users and enterprise roles, need to be provisioned in the policy store of the Oracle WebLogic Server target domain. A domain represents an instance of Oracle WebLogic Server, which can be stand-alone or a part of a cluster. Within the domain, a single active security realm exists that exposes enterprise users and groups for security-enabled web applications to authenticate and authorize users. Users and groups are provided through authentication providers that are configured for the WebLogic Server domain. Example authentication providers are Lightweight Directory Access Protocol (LDAP), OID, and RDBMS. In addition, the Oracle WebLogic Server domain has its own OPSS policy store defined, which by default is system-jazn-data.xml, and is located in the config\fmwconfig directory of the domain folder. The domain policy store can be changed to Oracle Internet Directory, which is a sensible option to use if enterprise-wide security should be enforced.

Especially when you're deploying applications to production environments, only the application-specific application role definitions and policy grants should be deployed.

Creating ADF Application Deployment Profiles

To deploy an ADF application to Oracle WebLogic Server, you package the application in an enterprise archive (EAR) file together with target-specific deployment descriptors and ADF Security artifacts such as the jazn-data.xml file. The web application is added to the EAR file as a Java EE module, a web archive (WAR) file that contains the source files of the web application, and, for locally deployed business services, the model. In this respect, deploying an ADF application is no different from deploying any other Java EE application.

Creating a WAR File

To create a WAR file, do the following:

1. Select the application web project and open its project properties.
2. Navigate to the Deployment entry and click New.
3. For the available list of archive type, select the WAR file entry.
4. Select the created WAR deployment profile and click Edit.
5. In the opened dialog, ensure that all sources that need to be added are contained in the File groups.
6. Select WebLogic 10.3 as the default Platform setting.

Creating an EAR File

EAR files are created for the whole application and not on the project level.

1. Choose Application | Application Properties to open the Application Properties dialog.
2. In the dialog, select the Deployment node and click New.
3. In the General section of the opened dialog, ensure that the Application name entry matches the name provided in the policy-store section of the jazn-data.xml file. Application policies are defined for each application, and using a name in the application

deployment that differs from the name used in the policy store results in authorization failure. The jazn-data.xml file entry for the application names appears as shown here:

```
<policy-store>
  <applications>
    <application>
      <name>Example21-ADFSecuritySample</name>
        <app-roles>
          ...
```

4. Select the Application Assembly node and ensure that the WAR file that you created for the Java EE application, your ADF application, is selected for inclusion in the EAR file.

5. You also may want to verify by choosing File Groups | Application Descriptors | Filters that all relevant deployment descriptors such as jazn-data.xml, cwallet.sso, and weblogic-application.xml are included in the deployment.

6. Close the EAR file editor by clicking OK to return to the Application Properties dialog.

7. In the Application Properties dialog, select the Deployments option and use the Security Deployment Options section to predefine which information of the jazn-data.xml file is migrated to the target server upon deployment. If the target server is a production environment, then usually enterprise roles and users are managed by the underlying identity management system. In this case, you should exclude the deployment of users and groups defined in the jazn-data.xml file.

8. Choose Application | Deploy in Oracle JDeveloper to generate the EAR file. By default, the EAR file is created in the deploy directory created under the application root folder on the file system.

NOTE
More information is provided in the "Deploying Secure Applications" chapter of the Oracle Fusion Middleware Security Guide 11g documentation available at http://otn.oracle.com.

Application Deployment with Oracle Enterprise Manager

Oracle Enterprise Manager (OEM) Fusion Middleware Control provides a complete and comprehensive application deployment and management environment for administering and monitoring Oracle ADF applications, including ADF Security configuration. OEM is not available by default on the stand-alone Oracle WebLogic Server and requires the installation of the Application Development Runtime package that you can download from the Oracle download page at http://otn.oracle.com. It is installed as a Java EE application on Oracle WebLogic Server and is started by typing **http://<host>:7001/em** in the browser URL field, assuming the default port is used when creating the WebLogic Server domain. The username and password to log into OEM is weblogic/weblogic1, which is the same default password used by the Oracle WebLogic administration account.

CAUTION
If you are deploying to a production system, the login information should no longer be weblogic/weblogic1 if you want to stay in business.

If the OEM UI looks familiar, it's because it is developed with Oracle ADF Faces RC components and deployed as a JSF application to Oracle WebLogic Server. After logging in to OEM, select the WebLogic Server domain to deploy the ADF Security–protected application, choose Application Deployment | Deployment, and step through the deployment wizard. When deploying the EAR file, you can verify and change the application name (step 3) and the security configuration (step 4). Figure 21-19 shows the security configuration dialog you can open from step 4 of the deployment wizard.

NOTE
Figure 21-19 shows a step 1 of 1 information, which may be confusing since we said that the dialog is launched from step 4 of the deployment wizard. The step 1 of 1 information is related to the Configure Application Security option, which is a sub-task you access from step 4 of the deployment wizard.

As shown in Figure 21-20, after application deployment, you can use Oracle Enterprise Manager to manage application roles and policies in the credential store. Use this option after application deployment to grant or revoke permissions.

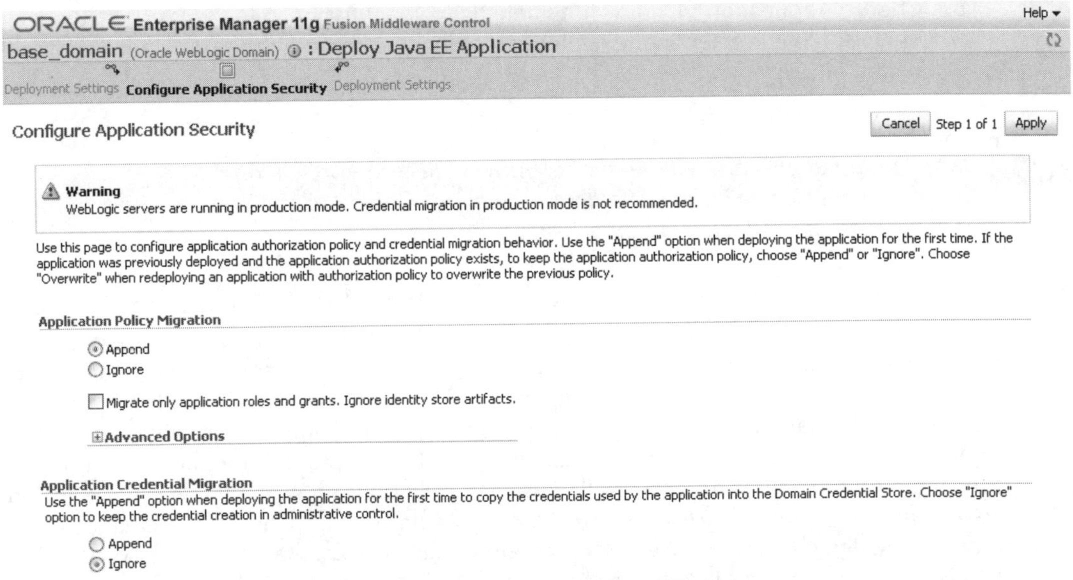

ORACLE **Enterprise Manager 11g** Fusion Middleware Control   Help ▾

base_domain (Oracle WebLogic Domain) ⓘ **: Deploy Java EE Application**

Deployment Settings   **Configure Application Security**   Deployment Settings

Configure Application Security   [Cancel] Step 1 of 1 [Apply]

> ⚠ **Warning**
> WebLogic servers are running in production mode. Credential migration in production mode is not recommended.

Use this page to configure application authorization policy and credential migration behavior. Use the "Append" option when deploying the application for the first time. If the application was previously deployed and the application authorization policy exists, to keep the application authorization policy, choose "Append" or "Ignore". Choose "Overwrite" when redeploying an application with authorization policy to overwrite the previous policy.

Application Policy Migration

⦿ Append
◯ Ignore

☐ Migrate only application roles and grants. Ignore identity store artifacts.

⊞ **Advanced Options**

Application Credential Migration
Use the "Append" option when deploying the application for the first time to copy the credentials used by the application into the Domain Credential Store. Choose "Ignore" option to keep the credential creation in administrative control.

◯ Append
⦿ Ignore

FIGURE 21-19 *The security configuration dialog displayed in the wizard*

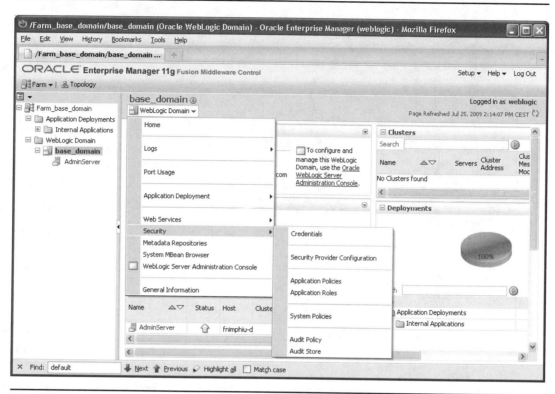

FIGURE 21-20   *OPSS security options in Oracle Enterprise Manager Fusion Middleware Control*

Managing Application Roles

Shown in Figure 21-21, you can use Oracle Enterprise Manager 11*g* to map application roles to enterprise user roles defined in WebLogic Server. Administrators use this dialog to grant application access to groups of users. As mentioned, in a production environment, users and enterprise roles should not be deployed within the application EAR file; instead, application roles used by ADF Security should be manually mapped to existing users and user groups. When an administrator maps an enterprise user group to an application role, the enterprise user group is added as a member of the application role in the configured OPSS policy store. The policy store can be OID or the WebLogic Server domain-specific system-jazn-data.xml file.

To display the screen shown in Figure 21-21, select the deployed application in Enterprise Manager and choose Security | Application Roles from the Application Deployment menu. Use the Search field and button to query the policy store for existing application roles. Click the application role entry to edit and click the plus icon next to the Add Role label to navigate to the role mapping screen. Application roles can be granted to enterprise user groups, as shown in Figure 21-21, or to other application roles defined in the policy store. The latter is possible because OPSS supports hierarchical roles for role based access control (RBAC), which allows you to define an application role as the child of another.

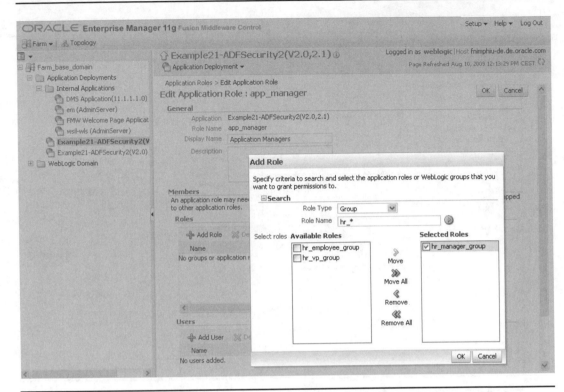

FIGURE 21-21 *Mapping application roles to enterprise roles in Enterprise Manager Fusion Middleware Control*

Password Indirection for Deployed Applications That Use JDBC Data Sources

When deploying ADF applications that use a JDBC data source for database connectivity in an EAR file, Oracle JDeveloper 11*g* does not add the password to the deployment archive. Instead, and only if the Auto Generate and Synchronize weblogic-jdbc.xml Descriptors During Deployment option is selected in the Application Properties dialog, a weblogic-jdbc.xml file entry is added to the EAR file that has the password set to use password indirection.

```
<jdbc-data-source ... >
  <jdbc-driver-params>
    <url>jdbc:oracle:thin:@localhost:1521:ORCL11</url>
    <driver-name>oracle.jdbc.OracleDriver</driver-name>
    <properties>
      <property>
        <name>user</name>
        <value>hr</value>
      </property>
```

```
    </properties>
    <use-password-indirection>true</use-password-indirection>
  </jdbc-driver-params>
  ...
</jdbc-data-source>
```

The weblogic-application.xml descriptor in the EAR file is updated with the weblogic-jdbc.xml reference. In addition, the web.xml file that is contained in the WAR file, which is added to the EAR file deployment, is updated with the Java Naming and Directory Interface (JNDI) reference similar to this:

```
<web-app>
  ...
  <resource-ref>
    <res-ref-name>jdbc/hrDS</res-ref-name>
    <res-type>javax.sql.DataSource</res-type>
    <res-auth>Container</res-auth>
  </resource-ref>
</web-app>
```

When the `use-password-indirection` attribute is present, the server uses the username from this file and looks for a credential mapping on the server to use as the password.

After application deployment, to edit the indirection password, you log into the WebLogic console, which you start by typing **http://host:port/console** in a browser URL field, and then select Deployments in the Domain Structure area.

Expand the node entry of the deployed ADF application and expand the Modules node. The JDBC data source should be listed with a link for you to navigate to the edit screen. In the edit screen, select the Security tab and then the Credential Mappings tab. Provide the username referenced by the JDBC data source and the password, which is the actual credential mapping.

NOTE
Click the Lock & Edit button at the top left of the page before applying changes to a server configuration using the WebLogic Server console. Also, before running the deployed application, make sure it is started.

Summary

In this chapter, we introduced web application security with a special focus put on ADF Security, the security framework in Oracle ADF, and the OPSS architecture, which is the combined security provided by Oracle WebLogic Server and the Oracle Java Platform Security (JPS).

Though this is a fairly long chapter, it does not cover all aspects of application security, and it's up to you to identify areas for which you need more information and to seek out that information. We strongly recommend reading the developer guides referenced in this chapter to improve your expertise in security products and functionality provided by Oracle. In addition, keep RDBMS security in focus, since it should integrate well with application security. Data that does not leave the database cannot be stolen on the middle tier.

Last but not least, remember that application security is a journey and never a destination. So keep on traveling to ensure that the applications you build are not becoming a weak link in your corporate application security strategy.

The most important thing to remember about ADF Security is that access control is permission-based. This means access is controlled by an externally stored policy that defines the privileges a group of users has against a set of resources. If the ADF Security framework runtime itself does not check a permission, then you as the developer have the ability to do it yourself in Java or Expression Language. This gives you very fine-grained authorization control in an ADF application.

Index

GET YOUR FREE SUBSCRIPTION TO *ORACLE MAGAZINE*

Oracle Magazine is essential gear for today's information technology professionals. Stay informed and increase your productivity with every issue of *Oracle Magazine*. Inside each free bimonthly issue you'll get:

- Up-to-date information on Oracle Database, Oracle Application Server, Web development, enterprise grid computing, database technology, and business trends

- Third-party news and announcements

- Technical articles on Oracle and partner products, technologies, and operating environments

- Development and administration tips

- Real-world customer stories

If there are other Oracle users at your location who would like to receive their own subscription to *Oracle Magazine*, please photo-copy this form and pass it along.

Three easy ways to subscribe:

① **Web**
Visit our Web site at **oracle.com/oraclemagazine**
You'll find a subscription form there, plus much more

② **Fax**
Complete the questionnaire on the back of this card
and fax the questionnaire side only to **+1.847.763.9638**

③ **Mail**
Complete the questionnaire on the back of this card
and mail it to **P.O. Box 1263, Skokie, IL 60076-8263**

ORACLE®

Want your own FREE subscription?

To receive a free subscription to *Oracle Magazine*, you must fill out the entire card, sign it, and date it (incomplete cards cannot be processed or acknowledged). You can also fax your application to **+1.847.763.9638. Or subscribe at our Web site at oracle.com/oraclemagazine**

O **Yes, please send me a FREE subscription** *Oracle Magazine.*　O No.

O From time to time, Oracle Publishing allows our partners exclusive access to our e-mail addresses for special promotions and announcements. To be included in this program, please check this circle. If you do not wish to be included, you will only receive notices about your subscription via e-mail.

O Oracle Publishing allows sharing of our postal mailing list with selected third parties. If you prefer your mailing address not to be included in this program, please check this circle.

If at any time you would like to be removed from either mailing list, please contact Customer Service at +1.847.763.9635 or send an e-mail to oracle@halldata.com. If you opt in to the sharing of information, Oracle may also provide you with e-mail related to Oracle products, services, and events. If you want to completely unsubscribe from any e-mail communication from Oracle, please send an e-mail to: unsubscribe@oracle-mail.com with the following in the subject line: REMOVE [your e-mail address]. For complete information on Oracle Publishing's privacy practices, please visit oracle.com/html/privacy/html

X

signature (required)　　　　　　　　　　　date

name　　　　　　　　　　　title

company　　　　　　　　　　　e-mail address

street/p.o. box

city/state/zip or postal code　　　　　telephone

country　　　　　　　　　　fax

Would you like to receive your free subscription in digital format instead of print if it becomes available? O Yes　O No

---

YOU MUST ANSWER ALL 10 QUESTIONS BELOW.

① WHAT IS THE PRIMARY BUSINESS ACTIVITY OF YOUR FIRM AT THIS LOCATION? (check one only)

- ☐ 01 Aerospace and Defense Manufacturing
- ☐ 02 Application Service Provider
- ☐ 03 Automotive Manufacturing
- ☐ 04 Chemicals
- ☐ 05 Media and Entertainment
- ☐ 06 Construction/Engineering
- ☐ 07 Consumer Sector/Consumer Packaged Goods
- ☐ 08 Education
- ☐ 09 Financial Services/Insurance
- ☐ 10 Health Care
- ☐ 11 High Technology Manufacturing, OEM
- ☐ 12 Industrial Manufacturing
- ☐ 13 Independent Software Vendor
- ☐ 14 Life Sciences (biotech, pharmaceuticals)
- ☐ 15 Natural Resources
- ☐ 16 Oil and Gas
- ☐ 17 Professional Services
- ☐ 18 Public Sector (government)
- ☐ 19 Research
- ☐ 20 Retail/Wholesale/Distribution
- ☐ 21 Systems Integrator, VAR/VAD
- ☐ 22 Telecommunications
- ☐ 23 Travel and Transportation
- ☐ 24 Utilities (electric, gas, sanitation, water)
- ☐ 98 Other Business and Services _____

② WHICH OF THE FOLLOWING BEST DESCRIBES YOUR PRIMARY JOB FUNCTION? (check one only)

CORPORATE MANAGEMENT/STAFF
- ☐ 01 Executive Management (President, Chair, CEO, CFO, Owner, Partner, Principal)
- ☐ 02 Finance/Administrative Management (VP/Director/ Manager/Controller, Purchasing, Administration)
- ☐ 03 Sales/Marketing Management (VP/Director/Manager)
- ☐ 04 Computer Systems/Operations Management (CIO/VP/Director/Manager MIS/IS/IT, Ops)

IS/IT STAFF
- ☐ 05 Application Development/Programming Management
- ☐ 06 Application Development/Programming Staff
- ☐ 07 Consulting
- ☐ 08 DBA/Systems Administrator
- ☐ 09 Education/Training
- ☐ 10 Technical Support Director/Manager
- ☐ 11 Other Technical Management/Staff
- ☐ 98 Other

③ WHAT IS YOUR CURRENT PRIMARY OPERATING PLATFORM (check all that apply)

- ☐ 01 Digital Equipment Corp UNIX/VAX/VMS
- ☐ 02 HP UNIX
- ☐ 03 IBM AIX
- ☐ 04 IBM UNIX
- ☐ 05 Linux (Red Hat)
- ☐ 06 Linux (SUSE)
- ☐ 07 Linux (Oracle Enterprise)
- ☐ 08 Linux (other)
- ☐ 09 Macintosh
- ☐ 10 MVS
- ☐ 11 Netware
- ☐ 12 Network Computing
- ☐ 13 SCO UNIX
- ☐ 14 Sun Solaris/SunOS
- ☐ 15 Windows
- ☐ 16 Other UNIX
- ☐ 98 Other
- ☐ 99 None of the Above

④ DO YOU EVALUATE, SPECIFY, RECOMMEND, OR AUTHORIZE THE PURCHASE OF ANY OF THE FOLLOWING? (check all that apply)

- ☐ 01 Hardware
- ☐ 02 Business Applications (ERP, CRM, etc.)
- ☐ 03 Application Development Tools
- ☐ 04 Database Products
- ☐ 05 Internet or Intranet Products
- ☐ 06 Other Software
- ☐ 07 Middleware Products
- ☐ 99 None of the Above

⑤ IN YOUR JOB, DO YOU USE OR PLAN TO PURCHASE ANY OF THE FOLLOWING PRODUCTS? (check all that apply)

SOFTWARE
- ☐ 01 CAD/CAE/CAM
- ☐ 02 Collaboration Software
- ☐ 03 Communications
- ☐ 04 Database Management
- ☐ 05 File Management
- ☐ 06 Finance
- ☐ 07 Java
- ☐ 08 Multimedia Authoring
- ☐ 09 Networking
- ☐ 10 Programming
- ☐ 11 Project Management
- ☐ 12 Scientific and Engineering
- ☐ 13 Systems Management
- ☐ 14 Workflow

HARDWARE
- ☐ 15 Macintosh
- ☐ 16 Mainframe
- ☐ 17 Massively Parallel Processing
- ☐ 18 Minicomputer
- ☐ 19 Intel x86(32)
- ☐ 20 Intel x86(64)
- ☐ 21 Network Computer
- ☐ 22 Symmetric Multiprocessing
- ☐ 23 Workstation Services

SERVICES
- ☐ 24 Consulting
- ☐ 25 Education/Training
- ☐ 26 Maintenance
- ☐ 27 Online Database
- ☐ 28 Support
- ☐ 29 Technology-Based Training
- ☐ 30 Other
- ☐ 99 None of the Above

⑥ WHAT IS YOUR COMPANY'S SIZE? (check one only)

- ☐ 01 More than 25,000 Employees
- ☐ 02 10,001 to 25,000 Employees
- ☐ 03 5,001 to 10,000 Employees
- ☐ 04 1,001 to 5,000 Employees
- ☐ 05 101 to 1,000 Employees
- ☐ 06 Fewer than 100 Employees

⑦ DURING THE NEXT 12 MONTHS, HOW MUCH DO YOU ANTICIPATE YOUR ORGANIZATION WILL SPEND ON COMPUTER HARDWARE, SOFTWARE, PERIPHERALS, AND SERVICES FOR YOUR LOCATION? (check one only)

- ☐ 01 Less than $10,000
- ☐ 02 $10,000 to $49,999
- ☐ 03 $50,000 to $99,999
- ☐ 04 $100,000 to $499,999
- ☐ 05 $500,000 to $999,999
- ☐ 06 $1,000,000 and Over

⑧ WHAT IS YOUR COMPANY'S YEARLY SALES REVENUE? (check one only)

- ☐ 01 $500, 000, 000 and above
- ☐ 02 $100, 000, 000 to $500, 000, 000
- ☐ 03 $50, 000, 000 to $100, 000, 000
- ☐ 04 $5, 000, 000 to $50, 000, 000
- ☐ 05 $1, 000, 000 to $5, 000, 000

⑨ WHAT LANGUAGES AND FRAMEWORKS DO YOU USE? (check all that apply)

- ☐ 01 Ajax
- ☐ 02 C
- ☐ 03 C++
- ☐ 04 C#
- ☐ 05 Hibernate
- ☐ 06 J++/J#
- ☐ 07 Java
- ☐ 08 JSP
- ☐ 09 .NET
- ☐ 10 Perl
- ☐ 11 PHP
- ☐ 12 PL/SQL
- ☐ 13 Python
- ☐ 14 Ruby/Rails
- ☐ 15 Spring
- ☐ 16 Struts
- ☐ 17 SQL
- ☐ 18 Visual Basic
- ☐ 98 Other

⑩ WHAT ORACLE PRODUCTS ARE IN USE AT YOUR SITE? (check all that apply)

ORACLE DATABASE
- ☐ 01 Oracle Database 11*g*
- ☐ 02 Oracle Database 10*g*
- ☐ 03 Oracle9*i* Database
- ☐ 04 Oracle Embedded Database (Oracle Lite, Times Ten, Berkeley DB)
- ☐ 05 Other Oracle Database Release

ORACLE FUSION MIDDLEWARE
- ☐ 06 Oracle Application Server
- ☐ 07 Oracle Portal
- ☐ 08 Oracle Enterprise Manager
- ☐ 09 Oracle BPEL Process Manager
- ☐ 10 Oracle Identity Management
- ☐ 11 Oracle SOA Suite
- ☐ 12 Oracle Data Hubs

ORACLE DEVELOPMENT TOOLS
- ☐ 13 Oracle JDeveloper
- ☐ 14 Oracle Forms
- ☐ 15 Oracle Reports
- ☐ 16 Oracle Designer
- ☐ 17 Oracle Discoverer
- ☐ 18 Oracle BI Beans
- ☐ 19 Oracle Warehouse Builder
- ☐ 20 Oracle WebCenter
- ☐ 21 Oracle Application Express

ORACLE APPLICATIONS
- ☐ 22 Oracle E-Business Suite
- ☐ 23 PeopleSoft Enterprise
- ☐ 24 JD Edwards EnterpriseOne
- ☐ 25 JD Edwards World
- ☐ 26 Oracle Fusion
- ☐ 27 Hyperion
- ☐ 28 Siebel CRM

ORACLE SERVICES
- ☐ 28 Oracle E-Business Suite On Demand
- ☐ 29 Oracle Technology On Demand
- ☐ 30 Siebel CRM On Demand
- ☐ 31 Oracle Consulting
- ☐ 32 Oracle Education
- ☐ 33 Oracle Support
- ☐ 98 Other
- ☐ 99 None of the Above

08014004